FROM ROME TO BEIJING

Symposia on Robert Jewett's Commentary on Romans

Edited by K. K. Yeo

January 2013

Kairos STUDIES

FROM ROME TO BEIJING
Symposia on Robert Jewett's Commentary on Romans

KAIROS STUDIES
Lincoln, NE 68506

ISBN: 978-1-937216-43-6
Manufactured in the U.S.A.

Contents

Introduction

1

From Rome to Beijing: "One World One Dream"

K. K. Yeo

I. From Rome to Beijing

"One World One Dream" was the slogan for the 2008 Olympic Games held in Beijing. I wondered then if the Chinese inspiration could hope to unite the world in the Games. It was at the Philadelphia Society of Biblical Literature (SBL) Conference in 2005 that Professor Robert Jewett and I first discussed the plan for a global conversation on his Hermeneia Commentary on Paul's Letter to the Romans, and a tentative title of the project was "A Mission to Unite the World: Paul's Gospel from Rome to Beijing." Jewett's thesis regarding Romans is that it was written to support a campaign to complete a world mission and unite humankind under the power of the gospel. His theory about Paul's theology in Romans—overcoming cultural conflicts with the particular interpretive lens of honor and shame in antiquity—is likely to be more readily understood now in Africa and Asia than in the guilt- and forgiveness-consciousness of the West. Jewett dedicated his commentary to the memory of Bishop John William Colenso, whose view Jewett adopted. Colenso was the first person to read Romans as aiming to achieve the task of unification of the world by overcoming the ideology of imperial honor and by overcoming prejudices in cultural boasting.

To evaluate and appropriate this line of interpretation of the Hermeneia Commentary on Romans would require scholarly conversation around the world. While teaching at Garrett-Evangelical Theological Seminary (where I have taught since 1996), I also was serving as academic director of the International Leadership Group, which mentors the Christian Studies programs at Peking University. So I was grateful to Professor Jewett for accepting my invitation to co-teach Romans with me at Peking University in the fall semester of 2007.[1] The Department of Philosophy and Religious Studies was especially thankful not only that Professor Jewett came to teach, but also that, in the summer of that year, he had already donated and shipped to the library of the department his entire Romans collection (46 boxes in all!), representing at least 27 years of careful research.

In 2005, Professor Jewett and I planned several symposia to take place between 2006 and 2008. We were grateful that all symposia were made possible by the extraordinary generosity of Fortress Press in sending gratis copies of the Hermeneia Commentary on Romans to reviewers around the world. Not all symposia resulted in submission of written essays, those essays received are included in this volume (see Contents). However, the following is a complete list of symposia in chronological order:

A. Washington, D. C., United States (November 19, 2006 at SBL)
   1. James D. G. Dunn
   2. Brigitte Kahl
   3. Daniel Patte
   4. Sze-kar Wan
   5. Robert Jewett's response

B. Heidelberg, Germany (February 2, 2007 at NT Societaet)
   1. Peter Lampe
   2. Gerd Theissen
   3. Jewett's response

C. Cleveland, Tennessee, United States (March 8, 2007 at Society of Pentecost Studies, Lee University)
   1. Ayo Adewuya
   2. Paul Elbert
   3. Jeffrey S. Lamp
   4. Robert Jewett's response

D. Collonges, France (March 20, 2007 at Newbold College)
   1. Gunnar Pedersen
   2. Jean-Claude Verrecchia
   3. Robert Jewett's response

E. Aberdeen, United Kingdom (March 22, 2007 at University of Aberdeen)
   1. Francis Watson
   2. Simon Gathercole

[1] Part of our teaching experience has been narrated in Chinese and published in simplified Chinese script as: K. K. Yeo edited, *Symposia on Romans and Divine Providence* (Beijing: Religious Culture Press, 2010).

3. Jewett's response

F. Stellenbosch, South Africa (April 5, 2007 at New Testament Society of South Africa)[2]
   1. John D. K. Ekem
   2. Andrie Du Toit
   3. Robert Jewett's response

G. Beijing, China (September-October, 2007 at Peking University)
   1. A series of lectures from Robert Jewett
   2. K. K. Yeo's responses

H. Seoul, Korea (October 27, 2007 at New Testament Society in South Korea)
   1. Yon-Gyong Kwon
   2. Ik Soo Park
   3. Sojung Yoon
   4. Robert Jewett's response

I. Kota Kinabalu, Malaysia (April 14, 2008 at Sabah Theological Seminary)
   1. Opening lecture by Robert Jewett
   2. K. K. Yeo
   3. Frank Gee
   4. Hii Kong Hock
   5. Ezra Kok and Lim Kar Yong
   6. Thu En Yu
   7. Robert Jewett's response

J. Tokyo, Japan (April 21, 2008 at Japanese Biblical Institute)
   1. Atsuhiro Asano
   2. Nozomu Hiroishi
   3. Kota Yamada
   4. Robert Jewett's response

K. Taipei, Taiwan (April 25, 2008 at Chung Yuan Christian University)[3]
   1. First lecture by Robert Jewett
   2. Second lecture by Robert Jewett

L. Vancouver, Canada (May 12, 2008 at Vancouver School of Theology)
   1. Steve Black
   2. Robert Derrenbacker
   3. Harry O. Maier

---

[2] This conference did not take place, but written reviews were submitted, thus included in this volume.

[3] Material was presented primarily in Chinese, and therefore published in traditional Chinese script as: Robert Jewett, *Robert Jewett on Romans*, translated by Tan Junming et al. (Chung Yuan Christian University Masterpieces Series; Hong Kong: Logos Ministries Ltd., 2009).

4. Dieter Neufeld
5. Robert Jewett's response

M. Yogyakarta, Indonesia (May 30, 2008 at Duta Wacana Christian University)
   1. E. G. Singgih
   2. Y. Wijaya
   3. Y. Tridarmato
   4. Jakub Santoja
   5. Robert Jewett's response

N. Sydney, Australia (June 3, 2008 at Macquarie University)
   1. Brian Rosner
   2. John Squires
   3. Robert Jewett's response

O. Auckland, New Zealand (July 10, 2008 at International SBL)
   1. Douglas A. Campbell
   2. Murray Rae
   3. Paul Trebilco
   4. Robert Jewett's Response

P. Hong Kong, China (April 17, 2008 at Hong Kong Baptist Theological Seminary)
   1. Simon Chow
   2. Robert Jewett's response

Q. *Journal for the Study of the New Testament*, United Kingdom (2008)
   1. John Barclay
   2. Robert Jewett

The purpose of this volume is neither to have the definitive word on interpretive issues related to Romans, nor to give a final verdict on the Hermeneia Commentary on Romans. The purpose is twofold: (1) to provide a round-table discussion in which scholars from all over the world can weigh in their assessments of the Commentary, especially in light of Jewett's exegetical, rhetorical, socio-scientific, theological, and political readings of Romans; and (2) to provide a platform for scholars who wish to construct gospel messages in reference to their cultural contexts or the modern world, as these scholars grapple with the insights or hermeneutical issues suggested by the Commentary or the Book of Romans. The sheer size and depth of the Commentary make it impossible for respondents to present a comprehensive review and critique. Given the limited space and time, contributors in this volume have had to be selective, but a brief overview provides a summary of the issues or texts they are passionate about:

- Historical situation and purpose of Romans (Theissen; Watson; Barclay; Dunn; Wan; Rae; Trebilco; Ekem; Du Toit; Asano; Yamada; Kwon; Gee)
- Rhetorical analysis of Jewett and argumentation of Paul in Romans (Lampe; Theissen; Yamada; Yoon; Gee)
- Socio-scientific or cultural-anthropological understanding, e.g., shame and honor; Jews and Gentiles (Theissen; Gathercole; Watson; Kahl; Barclay; Neufeld; Campbell; Trebilco; Kok; Asano; Thu; Yeo)
- Empire, political perspective, and Rome (Theissen; Wan; Black; Derrenbacker; Maier; Ekem; Asano; Hii; Yeo)
- Soteriology, justification, law, and Israel (Gathercole; Kahl; Barclay; Verrecchia; Dunn; Patte; Lamp; Kwon)
- Exegesis, hermeneutic and method (Patte); theology (Dunn; Rae), e.g., sin (Barclay), eschatology (Pedersen; Verrecchia; Kwon), pneumatology (Adewuya; Elbert; Lamp), missiology (Pedersen); ecclesiology (Verrecchia)
- Exegesis of texts:

1:13–17	(Lampe; Theissen; Patte);
1:24–32	(Kahl; Verrecchia);
2:1–16	(Dunn);
3:20–27	(Gathercole; Watson; Barclay; Dunn; Rae);
4:25	(Gathercole);
5:12–21	(Barclay);
7:7–23	(Barclay; Verrecchia; Dunn; Ekem);
8:9–22	(Patte);
10:2–4	(Barclay; Verrecchia);
10:9	(Elbert);
11:13–25	(Dunn);
12:1–6	(Elbert; Hiroishi);
13:1–10	(Kok; Verrecchia; Wan; Black; Derrenbacker; Maier; Ekem; Hiroishi; Hii; Yeo);
14:1–15:7	(Barclay; Chow);
15:7–13	(Dunn);
15:22–29	(Wan); and
16:1–2	(Barclay; Elbert).

The idea of conducting a symposium in Spain crossed our minds, as we sought to trace the missionary progression of Paul. Like Paul, we were not able to set foot in Spain in our allotted time. Yet, because the gospel of Jesus Christ has reached Spain, it is more important—at least for me—to examine how the gospel continues to advance further than Rome, to our modern-day "Spains," where the shame-and-honor and imperialistic cultures continue to dominate. The remainder of this chapter is an attempt, then, to look at Chinese culture and explore what the Hermeneia Commentary on Romans helps us to understand about the possible impact of the gospel.

II. HONOR AND SHAME IN ROMAN AND CHINESE CULTURES[4]

Paul's effort to elicit support (financially, prayerfully, personnel, and culturally) from the churches in Rome for a mission to the "barbarians" in Spain would be persuasive if he could convince these churches to cease their cultural boasting and imperialistic competition with one another. For any form of cultural boasting goes against the gospel of impartial grace. Paul urges the churches in Rome to welcome one another as equals in Christ, thus demonstrating the power of the gospel to overcome cultural barriers and conflicts; this is Jewett's thesis of the Hermeneia Commentary in a nutshell. I find this interpretation of Romans relevant to the situation of cultural, religious, and imperial conflicts in the contemporary world from ancient Rome to modern Beijing.

I am delighted to read in Jewett's Commentary that the dominant Augustinian and Lutheran reading of "justification by faith" in Western biblical scholarship and the systematic theology of "justification by faith" are secondary themes in Romans. The "justification-by-faith" reading strikes a chord with Western scholars because their culture is concerned with law, individual guilt, and forgiveness. However, the first-century Mediterranean culture, in particular that of the Christian congregations in Rome, is concerned primarily with social status and its ethic is highly conditioned by the values of honor and shame. In that sense, the culture of Rome is closer to the traditional Chinese worldview, *viz.*, the social ethic of "welcoming one another" as God in Christ loves all people without condition (grace).

---

[4] This chapter from this point on is a revision and expansion of my Graver's Lecture presented at Garrett-Evangelical Theological Seminary (Evanston) and Grace United Methodist Church (Naperville) on November 11, 2007, originally titled as "Cultural Boasting and Mutual Honoring, Toward Multiple Identities of Chineseness." The similar material is presented at symposia in Beijing (October, 2007) and Kota Kinabalu (April 14, 2008).

Jewett's thesis on Romans regarding status acquisition and honor/shame broadens my perspective on Romans. Jewett's work builds on Halvor Moxnes's word fields of honor and shame in Paul's argument with the idea that:

> . . . shameful exclusion should be overcome, and that cannot be accomplished by forgiveness. This relates to the fact that guilt and forgiveness are decidedly secondary issues in Romans. To these references, I would add the socially discriminatory categories that Moxnes overlooked such as:
>
> - "Greeks and barbarians, educated and uneducated" in 1:14;
> - the twenty-eight appearances of the potentially shameful epithet "Gentiles";
> - the categories "weak" and "strong" employed in 14:1–15:7;
> - the twenty-five references to social gestures of honor in the form of "welcome" and "greeting" that dominate the last three chapters; and
> - the 70 references to "righteousness," "make righteous," etc. that are often mistranslated as "justification."
> - . . . in place of the traditional theology of Romans that concentrates on individual guilt and forgiveness for failing to live up to the law, I propose that the central issue is setting the world right by overcoming its perverse systems of honor and shame . . .[5]

The societies of first-century Rome and China were rooted in a value system of social confirmation called "honor and shame." Even in modern China, the perennial "honor-and-shame" cultural values are expressed by the President of China, Mr. Hu Jintao, in the "eight-honor-eight-shame" paradigm designed to construct the best form of socialism for modern China:

[5] Robert Jewett, "Aimed at Overcoming Shameful Status: Romans as a Missionary Letter," in Hong Kong Baptist Theological Seminary Newsletter, August 2008, 2 (transcript of a lecture at Morning Chapel on April 17, 2008). See also next chapter in this volume.

Take the eight glorious merits against eight shameful behaviors:

- "Love our motherland" as glory/honor; "jeopardize her" as shame;
- "Serve for the people" as glory/honor; "err from them" as shame;
- "Advocate science" as glory/honor; "the ignorant" as shame;
- "Diligence" as glory/honor; "love ease and hate work" as shame;
- "Unite and help each other" as glory/honor; "harm others to benefit oneself" as shame;
- "Be honest to keep faith" as glory/honor; "forget justice in seeking one's own benefit" as shame;
- "Abide by the law and discipline" as glory/honor; "disobey the law and discipline" as shame; and
- "Fight against everything hard and bitter" as glory/honor; seeking "the extravagant and vanity" as shame.[6]

According to Jewett, Paul wrote Romans in part to seek support from the Roman churches for his gospel mission to Spain. Romans also is written to address the polemical tensions in the Roman churches, so that the gospel is not shamed and the congregations are able to preach the gospel to create an alternative community called "church as God's beloved" throughout the known world. One of the problems in the Roman congregations was therefore one group's assertion of superiority over the other (cf. 1:7, 16, 2:25–29, 8:33, 9:6–13, 11:5–7, 28–32).

Whether in ancient Roman or modern Chinese societies, assertion of superiority is a common tactic that values honor as one's identity and uses shame to manipulate and destroy others. Social selves derive their *value* or *worth* not from themselves but from others. The value system of a social culture is determined by the honor or shame members grant to one another within the community. Bestowing honor, such as "welcoming one another," is a means of approving a certain value and of including a person into the community as its own. Giving and receiving honor constantly reinforce the sense of worth and purpose. Shame

[6] My revision of Manfield Zhu and Alice Jenny's translation (http://www.itlearner.com/article/3104).

works just as effectively in the opposite way: it disgraces, alienates, and dismantles the value system of the one shamed. The purpose of shame is to debase, to disapprove, to curse, and ultimately to ostracize a person. Once a person is excommunicated, he is no longer a "human" being, for he is not a "social" self.

The conflicts in Roman house- and tenement-churches are shaming to one another; the believers in turn shame the gospel and God; cultural boasting (claiming superiority for one's culture that is actually dominated by the power of sin) is demeaning to peoples and destructive to community. But *self-worth can be restored when the community recognizes the unique gifts and graces of each*, and that is what Paul seeks to do for the Christians in Rome.

The Chinese culture and the community in Rome may both be seen as dyadic cultures. Dyadic cultures are those in which self-worth is determined by the individual's orientation toward the other. Dyadic cultures are based on the concept of *co-humanity*, that is, each person within a community achieves his full humanity only in co-relation with another human being. Such cultures recognize that human beings are fundamentally social selves. According to Confucian thought, *renren* (benevolent persons) realize the goodness of *tian* (heaven) innate in human nature through the practice of communal rituals. Only in community, in striving to relate well with others, can one become a person who is fully human. The Greco-Roman understanding of a person as *prosopon* or *persona* agrees with the Confucian understanding of *renren*—except that the Greco-Roman understanding does not have the moral connotation. The Greek word *prosopon* literally means "a face"; it refers to the mask used in Greek theater.[7] To be a person is to learn the art of bearing another's character and to know one's own character well enough to allow the two characters to be mutually engaging. Similarly, the Latin word *persona* as seen in *per sonare*, meaning "to sound through," refers to the mouthpiece of the theatrical mask.[8]

Confucian ethics of honor (*jing*) is predicated on reverence to Heaven (*jingtian*) because to be reverent to Heaven is to fulfill its mandate of ensuring moral order in human nature and in human society.[9] Mutual benefaction and mutual respect are required if a civil society is to be formed. Rather than being seen as condescension, giving esteem is a way of recognizing worth. The ethics of Confucius illumines the point well; according to Confucius, esteem, reverence, respect, and honor (*jing*) are the basis of self-cultivation (*Analects* 14:42; 15:5).

---

7 Donald Alexander, "The Face of Holiness" (manuscript in progress, used with permission), chapter 2.

8 Alexander, "The Face of Holiness," chapter 2.

9 Mou Zongsan, *Zhongguo Zhexue De Tezhi (The Special Features of Chinese Philosophy* [in Chinese]; Taipei: Student Bookstore, 1998), 24–25.

Mutual respect and benefaction are cornerstones of a Confucianist civil society. A similar emphasis is found in the ancient Greco-Roman culture. Frederick W. Danker has shown that the dominant feature of the Greco-Roman culture was its association with the motifs of benefaction and honor—both in the display, claim, and acknowledgment of the benefactor's merit or excellence and in the beneficiaries' response to that merit.[10]

The question facing Paul in Rome, at least in part, is how he would form a new system of honor for the Roman Christians. Paul uses the language of honor and shame by *reversing the source of approval*. God, he argues, is the ultimate source of honor, not Rome and its glory.

In the Roman patronage system, slaves, freed persons, and the lower classes generally work for their masters or for the upper class. Paul views this dependence on others as a crucial means of survival, but he redefines the client-patron relationship according to the concept of mutuality. In Paul's mind, the work of Christ, and of God in Christ as exhibited on the cross, illumines Paul's understanding of love as seeking the good of the other. The Master (Lord Jesus) has come to serve (see Philippians 2:7–8).

The secular culture of Rome operated from the top down, from the emperor to the ordinary citizens of the empire. Paul's view of the character of life in Christ is radically counter-cultural. Believers made righteous by the act of God in Christ have been given the honor of being sons of God. This stands in stark contrast to the emperor cult that believed, for example, that Augustus, the adopted son of Julius Caesar, had the status of a *divi filius* (son of the deified). Paul replaces the Roman emperor with the crucified Messiah and risen Lord as the benefactor. The death and resurrection of the benefactor Christ had dethroned all deities; the faithful followers of Christ were called to be agents of God in "welcoming one another."

III. BEIJING AND WASHINGTON: BOASTING AND HONORING

Cultural boasting of Beijing may be symbolized by the greatness of the Great Wall, the elitism of the Forbidden City, the civilizing project of the *Han* culture. However, these ancient "Homeland Security" projects were ineffective—the Forbidden City is now an empty museum, and the "Central/Middle Kingdom" became decentered each time military forces from the periphery attacked the mainland. Despite ethnic diversity, Chinese identity has a certain cohesion or commonality because of

[10] F. W. Danker, *Benefactor: Epigraphic Study of a Graeco-Roman and New Testament Semantic Field* (St. Louis: Clayton Publishing House, 1982), 1–316.

Confucian enculturalization, which has taken place sometimes as a result of imperialism, sometimes as welcomed embrace. There was a general conviction, held by the Mongolians in the Yuan dynasty and the Manchurians in the Qing dynasty, that Confucianism possessed superior ethical principles. They adopted the Confucian ways of character building, filial piety, and the transformation of others by means of assimilation.

The Confucian promotion of cultural identity by means of virtue and Paul's theology of "God's beloved" (Romans 1:7) made possible by Christ's death and resurrection, caution those who boast of their hereditary lineage. The Middle Kingdom's (*Zhongguo*) superiority complex is similar to the distinction between Jews and Gentiles or the Greeks and barbarians, and the Roman house churches. The combined wisdom of Confucius and Paul suggests that the common good of a community is built not by privileging the elite but by empowering the lowly. The *junzi* (the excellent person), *renren* (the benevolent person), "being in-Christ," or person of God—this is the responsible moral agent in the world, who trusts in God or complies with Heaven (*tian*). "Best selves" are not preoccupied with self-cultivation for the sake of boasting, but for the sake of the good of one's neighbor. In China, many of the neighbors are minorities.

While Chinese culture is not just Confucianist, Confucianism is nonetheless a dominant cultural force. Confucian ethical concepts such as *ren* (benevolence) and *shu* (empathy) require that Confucianists respect others; thus, a "cultural China" (or more narrowly speaking, a "Confucianist China") would not judge others based on whether or not they abandoned their own cultural ideals and were proselytized into Confucianism. Rather, the criterion would be whether they agreed to the universal truth (*dao*) expressed in Confucian ethics that to be human is to be *renren* (persons who love others), to be *zhongshu* (loyal and empathic), and to be *xin* (trustworthy). Similarly, I understand Christian identity as not requiring the rejection of Chinese culture. Only those aspects of Chinese culture that reject the cruciform life would need to be deconstructed. In other words, a Confucianist China would allow a plurality of identities to coexist. Modern China struggles with the problem of a splintered society; its multiplicity of minority groups establishes the need to find ways to construct a plurality of identities.

A cultural China could also lead political China to place a priority on the issue of the common destiny of the people on the two sides of the Taiwan Strait. Lee Teng-hui has advocated *shengming gongtong ti* (literally "living community,") and Peng mingmin has advocated *mingyun gongtong ti* ("community of shared destiny"), suggesting that the political community has its subjective identification with members in the community rather than accepting some objective identity imposed from outside by the political system.

A cultural China can help political China concentrate on the quality of life of the people, to be aware of the needs of minorities, and to be less paranoid about its "face" (honor)—deemed "lost" to foreign aggressors in the nation's history in the nineteenth and twentieth centuries. Above all, cultural China needs to help political China[11] to live in faith/trust (*xin*), and to prove to its people and the world that only virtue (*de*), rather than military force, can gain the trust of its own people and its neighbors. I believe this thesis is true for Beijing as well as for Washington. Thus, like Paul, I am not ashamed of the gospel, for I know it is the power of God for Beijing and Washington.

CONCLUSION

I therefore share Paul's prayer in his letter to the Romans—and beyond—that both the Jews and the Gentiles Christians (11:17–24),[12] the weak and the strong (15:8–12)—Tutsis and Hutus, Americans or Chinese—will eventually worship God together (3:29; 16:25–26). Paul was using the thesis of "the righteousness of God" (1:18) as the only basis whereby all people stand before God. Righteousness of God is the criterion whereby all people are judged equal in sin, and also equal in God's favor/grace. Who is righteous? Only God is, for the source of all righteousness is from God. A person is righteous only as he is graced/gifted by God, and this righteous status is attainable via faith, not cultural boasting. The impartial grace of God can therefore provide a theological foundation for "One World One Dream."

---

[11] Cf. K. K. Yeo, "Messianic Predestination in Romans 8 and Classical Confucianism" in edited by K. K. Yeo, *Navigating Romans Through Cultures: Challenging Readings by Charting a New Course* (Edinburgh: T. & T. Clark International, 2004), 259–89.

[12] The dominating issue Paul deals with in the Epistle to the Romans is the Jew/Gentile Christian relationship (cf. Romans 1:16, 2:25–29, 1:7, 8:33, 9:6–13, 11:5–7, 28–32), similar to our modern day signifier of "inter-cultural relationship."

2

Paul's Letter to Rome and Beyond

Robert Jewett

Introduction

After I agreed to write the Hermeneia commentary on Romans in 1980, I was forced by the evidence to abandon my views about a number of issues. The text-critical evidence concerning the length of the letter as well as a series of mistaken readings required correction; the historical evidence about the situation in Rome and with Paul's missionary plans in Spain needed to be re-evaluated; and the rhetorical evidence about the genre and organization of the letter needed to be taken into account. The most troubling of these issues was the slowly emerging awareness that the dominant paradigm for interpreting justification by faith was not supported by the actual wording of the letter. Conversations with various colleagues led me to begin thinking about the honor culture of ancient Rome, Greece, and Israel as the arena for this reinterpretation, but my theological tradition provided scant resources in this direction. All of these issues were rendered more challenging because Paul's letter to the Romans turned out to be the only biblical writing for which no comprehensive bibliography was available. I spent years in libraries around the world attempting to assemble such a bibliography, which is still not complete.[1] My hope was that scholars in other traditions would have insights to resolve some of these questions, and indeed this has to some degree occurred.

[1] In 2000 as part of Peter Lampe's appointment as Professor of New Testament, the Wissenschaftlich-theologisches Seminar of the Ruprecht-Karls-Universität in Heidelberg provided space for this Romans Archive and began the process of scanning several million pages of scholarly documents to create an online bibliography to be made available to researchers around the world. I hope that this archive will be available through the internet in the near future.

After the commentary was published, Fortress Press supported a series of symposia around the world to evaluate the interpretation I had developed. With extraordinary generosity, the publisher sent complimentary copies of the commentary to respondents in sixteen countries. In the course of these symposia, several errors were identified, strengths and weaknesses in rendering the letter understandable in different cultural situations were identified, and I discovered a significant new perspective on chapter 13. To simplify the process of clarifying these matters, I'd like to begin by describing a blindspot.

While sifting through the studies on Romans I discovered a remarkable gap in interpreting the twofold admonition to "welcome" one another in Romans 14:1 and 15:7 and in understanding the twenty-one repetitions of the formula "greet so and so" in chapter 16. In the vast scholarly literature on Romans, there is not a single article devoted to either of these terms.[2] The reference in 16:16 to the "holy kiss" has attracted more attention,[3] but no study explained its function in the congregational situation or the argument of the letter. In the studies written on the dialectic between honor and shame in Romans, there is no mention of the social function of honoring guests implicit in these references.[4]

Given the fact that these admonitions form the climax of the letter, their significance is indisputable. Yet commentators have lacked the theological and social sensitivity to understand what was at stake in these prominent references. The preoccupation with issues of guilt and forgiveness, which has dominated the theology of Romans since Augustine's time, has rendered our theological tradition oddly uninterested in the pervasive social issues of shameful exclusion and honorable welcome. What is the function of these themes in the argument of the Paul's letter? What is their social and theological relevance in the situation Paul is attempting to address in Romans? Is there a basis here to develop a new ethic of welcoming adversaries in the 21st century? I would like to begin the quest with a consideration of the language of honor and shame in the opening chapter of the letter.

---

[2] There are many studies of the weak and strong in Romans, but none on the theme of welcome.

[3] See Stephen Benko, "The Kiss," in S. Benko, *Pagan Rome and the Early Christians* (Bloomington: Indiana University Press, 1984), 79–102; Nicholas James Perella, *The Kiss: Sacred and Profane: An Interpretative History of Kiss Symbolism and Related Religio-Erotic Themes* (Berkeley: University of California Press, 1969).

[4] Halvor Moxnes, "Honour and Righteousness in Romans," *Journal for the Study of the New Testament* 32 (1988), 61–77, which develops the ideas in the earlier article, "Paulus og den norske vaeremåten. 'Skam' og 'aere' i Romerbrevet" [Paul and Norwegian Culture. 'Shame' and 'Honor' in Romans], *Norsk Teologisk Tidsskrift* 86 (1985), 129–40.

I. OVERCOMING SHAMEFUL STATUS IN THE ARGUMENT OF ROMANS

E. A. Judge helps us understand that Paul in Romans is reversing a broad cultural tradition that viewed the earning of honor as the only suitable goal for life. "It was held that the winning of honor was the only adequate reward for merit in public life . . . . It therefore became a prime and admired objective of public figures to enshrine themselves, by actually defining their own glory, in the undying memory of posterity" by publishing memorials of their accomplishments.[5] This insight was confirmed by *Empire of Honor,* in which J. E. Lendon describes the views of the upper class in the Roman empire:

> When a great aristocrat peered down into society beneath him, there was a threshold beneath which, to his mind, honour did not exist; there were people, a great many people, without honour, and best kept that way . . . . The slave is the archetype of the man without honor.

Most of the audience of Romans consisted of persons with no prospects of gaining such glory. In the hierarchical context of Roman society, the early Christians were mostly slaves and former slaves who were demeaned from birth on prejudicial grounds, not because of what they had done but because of who they were. The rhetoric of shame in New Testament usage includes both shameful deeds and shameful status imposed by others. In fact the most damaging form of shame is to internalize prejudicial assessments that persons or groups are worthless, that their lives are without significance.

In "Honour and Righteousness in Romans," Halvor Moxnes places the argument of the letter in the ancient cultural context of an "honour society" in which "recognition and approval from others" is central, which means that the "group is more important than the individual."[6] He notes that the word fields of honor and shame play important roles in the argument of Romans, with references to "honor, dishonor, shameless, be ashamed, put to shame, glory, glorify, praise, boast and boasting." This focus on honor and shame relates to the central purpose of the letter as Moxnes understands it, "to bring together believing Jews and non-Jews in one community."[7] This means that shameful exclusion should be

[5] E. A. Judge, "The Conflict of Educational Aims in New Testament Thought," *Journal of Christian Education* 9 (1966), 38–39; he cites Sallust, *Bellum Jugurthinum* LXXXV: 26, "Reticence would only cause people to mistake modesty for a guilty conscience."

[6] Moxnes, "Honour and Righteousness in Romans," 63.

[7] Moxnes, "Honour and Righteousness in Romans," 64.

overcome, and that cannot be accomplished by forgiveness. This relates to the fact that guilt and forgiveness are secondary issues in Romans.

To these references, I would add the socially discriminatory categories that Moxnes overlooked such as

- "Greeks and barbarians, educated and uneducated" in 1:14
- the twenty-eight appearances of the potentially shameful epithet "Gentiles"
- the categories "weak" and "strong" employed in 14:1–15:7
- the twenty-five references to social gestures of honor in the form of "welcome" and "greeting" that dominate the last three chapters.
- and the 70 references to "righteousness," "make righteous," etc. that are often mistranslated as "justification."

When compared with the single allusion to the "remission of sins" in Romans 3:25 and the Psalm citation in chapter 4, it is clear that a mainstream has been confused for a minor current in the tradition of interpreting Romans. Therefore, in place of the traditional theology of Romans that concentrates on individual guilt and forgiveness for failing to live up to the law, I propose that the central issue is setting the world right by overcoming its perverse systems of honor and shame.

This allows Paul's letter to have a fresh relevance for the 21st century. Although it was relevant in previous centuries to stress forgiveness because most people feared the fires of hell because they were not living up to the law, forgiveness is less relevant for most societies today. Most people living in Europe and North America no longer feel bound by the law, and some societies in Africa and Asia lack the tradition of biblical rules. The most significant conflicts in our time arise from various forms of social shame such as discrimination. Paul's argument has great relevance in this situation, because Romans 1–3 says that no people are superior, that all nations have sinned and fallen short of the glory of God. In face of claims that our group earns God's blessings because of our alleged virtues, Romans 3–6, 9–11 says all people can be saved by grace alone. We need to reformulate the classical Reformation doctrine of "justification by faith." To become "Righteous through faith" means to accept the gospel of Christ's shameful death in behalf of the shamed, which means that all of us humans are equally honored. God is not the God of the Jews or the Gentiles alone, argues Paul at the end of Romans 3, because divine righteousness is *impartial*. If we understood this, we would all be willing to stop crusading against each other, and to place ourselves under the same standards of international law, which would be a step toward to world peace.

II. THE CHALLENGE OF THE MISSION TO THE BARBARIANS IN SPAIN

This new approach to the theology of Romans is linked with the central purpose of this letter, which was to enlist Roman support for the Mission to Spain. Here again, there is a surprise. In 1:14, Paul employs some discriminatory language by referring to "Greeks and barbarians . . . wise and foolish" These terms articulate the social boundaries of Greco-Roman culture in a thoroughly abusive manner. As studies of *barbaros* by Yves Albert Dauge and other have shown,[8] this is the "N-" word in Greco-Roman culture. When paired with its ideological opposite, "Greeks," it denotes the violent, perverse, corrupt, uncivilized realm beyond and at times within the Roman Empire that threatens peace and security. When the remarkable formulation is followed by the antithesis "to the Jew first and also to the Greek" in Romans 1:16–17, there is a reversal of the claim of ethnic priority that was being claimed by the Gentile Christian majority in Rome.[9]

This revolutionary viewpoint is directly related to the mission to Spain. In Romans 15:24, Paul refers to his plan to "see you in passing as I go to Spain, and to be sped forward on my journey there by you, once I have enjoyed your company for a little." The crucial element in verse 24 in relation to the Spanish mission is the expression "send forward," or "sped onward" which is perceived by commentators as something of a technical expression in early Christian missionary circles. Paul is politely requesting some form of support for his mission project. In 15:28, Paul says that after the offering has been delivered to Jerusalem, "I shall go on by way of you to Spain." Again by implication this reference invites the Roman churches to become involved in the planning and organization of the Spanish project.

What was there about the Spanish mission that required such tactful preparation? If, indeed, the entire letter to the Romans is directly related to this project, why was it all necessary? Why did Paul not think it was feasible to start the mission in Spain as he had in Thessalonica or Corinth? Why not arrive without advanced notice or preparation, start preaching in a synagogue, find a local patron or patroness, and build a local congregation of converts? In light of information that has recently

8 Yves Albert Dauge, *Le Barbare. Recherches sur la conception romaine de la barbarie et de la civilisation*, Collection Latomus 176 (Brussels: Latomus, 1981), 393–810, showing that the term barbarian in Roman materials serves to depict outsiders as irrational, ferocious, warlike, alienated, chaotic, and in all respects the opposite of the civilized Roman.

9 See James C. Walters, *Ethnic Issues in Paul's Letter to the Romans* (Valley Forge: Trinity Press International, 1993), 68–79.

become available, we are now in a position to provide a more informed answer to this question.

The first matter on which new information is available relates to the presence of Jewish population in Spain during the Julio-Claudian period. Older commentators assume the presence of Jewish communities in Spain, relying primarily on outdated information. Evidence of substantial Jewish settlement in Spain does not appear until the third and fourth centuries C.E., as W. P. Bowers has shown.[10]

The lack of Jewish settlement in Spain posed several large barriers to Paul's previous missionary strategy. Not only did this eliminate the prospects of Jewish converts to the gospel, but it also ruled out finding a group of God-fearers or proselytes in the Spanish cities to recruit as the initial core of Christian churches. There would be no initial interest in a messianic proclamation prepared by devotion to the Septuagint. The absence of synagogues also eliminated the avenues that Paul normally used to establish a base of operations in the Greek cities of the east. Where ever possible Paul began his missionary activities in local synagogues and moved to an independent base of operations after troubles erupted or patrons and patronesses emerged. Without a synagogue as a starting point, the crucial contacts with appropriate patrons would be extremely difficult to make, especially for a handworker of Paul's social class. It is clear that a new mission strategy was required in Spain.

When one inquires about the nature of the Spanish cultural situation during the period of Paul's intended mission, even the most recent commentaries are silent. I have discovered that Paul's reference to shameful "barbarians" in Romans 1:14 would have included the Spaniards, from the Roman point of view. More than eight decades ago the classic study by M. I. Rostovtzeff had shown that large portions of the peninsula were substantially untouched by the veneer of Roman civilization. The rural population in particular and the northern portions of Spain specifically remained apart from Greco-Roman culture. In general, he concluded, "those who held Latin rights and were more or less romanized formed a small minority of the population of Spain, while the status of the rest remained the same . . . ."[11] On the decisive question of the language spoken in Spain, the barriers to a Greek speaker like Paul were rather high. While Latin was spoken in the major cities, at least in part, and at times rather poorly, the

[10] W. P. Bowers, "Jewish Communities in Spain in the Time of Paul the Apostle," *Journal of Theological Studies* 26 (1975), 400.

[11] Michael Ivanovitch Rostovtzeff, *The Social and Economic History of the Roman Empire* (Second Edition, revised by P. M. Fraser; Oxford: Clarendon Press, 1957), 215; the first edition was published by Clarendon in 1926.

"Iberians and Celt-Iberians of Spain spoke their own langauges . . . ."[12]

The situation in Spain presented formidable challenges both on the linguistic and political levels. Proclamation and instruction in Latin would be required, and there is no evidence that Paul was sufficiently fluent to carry this out without translators. Indeed, such resources would be difficult to develop, because the Hebrew scriptures were not yet available in Latin, and the first evidence we have of Latin-speaking churches is in the middle of the 2nd century. Even the church in Rome remained Greek speaking until the middle of the 3rd century, while elsewhere in the West the church was associated for centuries with Greek immigrants. The translation of the gospel, the liturgy, and the instructional traditions into another language would be a substantial undertaking, especially in light of the fact that a range of additional translation resources would be required to extend past the restricted circle of Latin civilization in Spain. Given the resistance against Roman culture in large portions of Lusitania and Tarraconensis, it would probably not have appeared either feasible or promising to rely entirely upon the language of the conquerors. Since the Latinized urban centers functioned as outposts of Roman rule and civilization in ways quite different from the Greek speaking portions of the empire where Paul had scored his earlier successes,[13] care would have to be taken to find local patrons who were not resented by the native population.

In sum, the Spanish mission required a level of planning and support that represented a huge leap from the improvised scheme of earlier Pauline missionizing.

---

[12] Rostovtzeff, *Roman Empire*, 213. Subsequent studies have confirmed this assessment: Hartmut Galsterer, *Untersuchungen zum römischen Städtewesen auf der Iberischen Halbinsel* (Madrider Forshungen 8; Berlin: de Gruyter, 1971); Carol H. V. Sutherland, *The Romans in Spain 217 B.C.–A.D. 117* (London: Methuen, 1971); Antonio Garcíay Bellido, "Die Latinisierung Hispaniens," *Aufstieg und Niedergang der römischen Welt* 1.1 (1972) 462–91; Jose Maria Blázquez, *Historia economica de la Hispania romana* (Madrid: Ediciones Cristiandad, 1978); Simon J. Keay, *Roman Spain* (Berkeley: University of California Press, 1988); Leonard A. Curchin, *Roman Spain: Conquest and Assimilation* (London: Routledge, 1991); *idem, The Romanization of Central Spain: Complexity, Diversity and Change in a Provincial Hinterland* (London: Routledge, 2004); J. S. Richardson, *The Romans in Spain* (Oxford / Cambridge, MA: Backwell, 1996).

[13] Cf. Werner Dahlheim, "Die Funktion der Stadt im Römischen Herschaftsverband," in edited by F. Vittinghoff, *Stadt und Herrschaft: Römische Kaiserzeit und hohes Mittelalter* (Munich: Oldenbourg, 1982); *Historische Zeitschrift. Beiheft* (N. F. 7.), 48–55.

III. Overcoming Chauvinism within the Roman Congregations

When one understands the challenge of a mission to the "barbarians" in Spain, it becomes clear why so much of Romans seeks to overcome chauvinistic behavior among the congregations in Rome. Since these congregations were treating each other as dangerous barbarians, refusing to accept each other, they were behaving much like the Romans had behaved in Spain. A mission under these circumstances would be perceived by the Spaniards as one more exercise in hateful Roman imperialism. This is why Paul spends so much time providing ways to overcome chauvinism.

In 14:1 and 15:7 there is an admonition to mutual "welcome" in a context that commentators agree was closely related to the congregational situation. The specific ethic of the letter opens with the words, "Welcome the one who is weak in faith, but not in order to dispute debatable points" (Romans 14:1). This is a clear reference to the Jewish Christian conservatives, the "weak" who are being discriminated against by the Gentile Christian majority in Rome. The term "weak" was probably applied by the majority in a pejorative sense, depicting their opponents as persons too "weak" to break free from the Jewish law. It is likely that this group included some of the Jewish Christian exiles mentioned in chapter 16 who are now returning to Rome after the lapse of the Edict of Claudius. Following the reconstruction of Wolfgang Wiefel, it appears that they were not being accepted back into the groups they had earlier helped to form. Conflicts over theology, ethics, worship, and leadership had emerged. As we can tell from the wording of Paul's admonition, when they were admitted into these congregations, it was "to dispute debatable points," that is, to get them in a corner and show them what's what. Paul insists instead on an unconditional form of welcome, in which liberals were to accept conservatives without trying to change them. As we can see from the wording of 15:7, Paul extends this principle both ways: "Welcome one another, therefore . . . " This fits the argument of 14:1–15:7 which forbids mutual conversion of opponents in the church: each side is to built up the other, protecting the integrity of those whose theology and culture lead them to different perspectives and practices in the church.

In Romans 16 Paul greets a large number of persons whom he had met in previous missionary activities in the eastern half of the Mediterranean world. They are now back in Rome, which correlates with what we know about official Roman policy. In C.E. 49 the Emperor Claudius issued an edict banning Jewish agitators from Rome because of uproars over a certain "Chrestus." I still accept the standard inference that conflicts between Christian evangelists and Jewish zealots and traditionalists in the Roman synagogues led to this edict that disrupted both synagogue and church life in the city until the end of Claudius' career in C.E. 54. The book of Acts indicates that Prisca and Aquila, whom Paul greets in 16:3–5, were refugees forced out of Rome whom Paul met in Corinth when he arrived there in the winter of C.E. 50. Other likely refugees mentioned in chapter 16 are Epaenetus, Mary, Andronicus and Junia, Ampliatus, Urbanus, Stachys, Apelles, Herodion, Tryphena, Tryphosa, Persis, Rufus and his mother. The most probable explanation for Paul's acquaintance with these early Christian leaders is that they met during exile. Paul knows that they have returned to the capitol of the empire during the peaceful, early years of the Nero administration before he writes in the winter of C.E. 56–57 from Corinth.

The definitive study of Roman Christianity by Peter Lampe,[14] my colleague in Heidelberg, goes beyond these frequently accepted inferences to suggest the precise districts in the city where Christianity got its start. Using a topographic method based on the coincidence between five different types of archeological and literary evidence, Lampe showed that two of the most likely areas for early Christian house churches were in Trastevere and the section on the Appian Way around the Porta Capena inhabited by the immigrants. These are the slum districts where slaves and handworkers lived, the most shamed element in the population of Rome, whose names surface in chapter 16.

This theme of inclusive welcome of shameful outsiders is continued in the repeated formulas of chapter 16. "Greet so and so" is repeated 21 times in this chapter, in various forms. The meaning of the term "greet" in the Greco-Roman culture is actually to put one's arms around the other, to hug or kiss them as a sign of welcome. It was ordinarily done when a guest enters the house or space of a host. So the implication of this repeated admonition is the same as we found in 14:1 and 15:7, to welcome people into your love feasts.

The climax in this request for mutual welcome, which would overcome the conflicts between these early Christian groups, is found in 16:16, "greet one another with a holy kiss." In contrast to much of the kissing in the modern world, in Paul's time it was primarily a family matter. One kissed family members when meeting them. In the case of early Christian groups, the holy kiss sealed the solidarity of extended family. It said, in effect, you are my "brother" or "sister;" it is the ultimate expression of honor. And in view of the fact that most Christians did not own homes, the kiss was extended when they met for their common meals. It was a regular feature in the early Christian love feasts. What

---

[14] Peter Lampe, *From Paul to Valentinus: Christians at Rome in the First Two Centuries*, translated by M. Steinhauser; Foreword by R. Jewett (Minneapolis: Fortress Press, 2003).

I would like to point out, however, is that to "greet one another" in this manner would overcome the hostilities and prejudices between early Christian groups, and make them ready to participate in the mission to the imperial outsiders in Spain.

This gospel of generous grace has been betrayed by Christian chauvinism, thwarting the mission to unify the world, just as in Paul's time, it threatened the possibility of a successful mission to the barbarians in Spain. This provides the basis for a non-inperialistic interpretation of Romans, which would be highly relevant for the 21st century. However, there is one section of Romans that has long been interpreted in the opposite direction.

IV. THE DILEMMA OF ROMANS 13

The first point that needs to be made is that Romans 13:1–7 deals with obligations to local magistrates in Rome, not with the Emperor or the government as a whole. Since these authorities "have been appointed by God," everyone has the obligation willingly to submit themselves. Thus, no matter what Roman officials may claim as their authority, it really comes from the God of Jewish and Christian faith. The issue usually not raised in the scholarly discussion is precisely who this God is. The relevance of this question is most easily grasped when one compares Paul's statement with the Roman civic cult and takes account of the twelve chapters of argument that precede this pericope. The God who grants authority to governmental agencies in Paul's argument is not Mars or Jupiter, as in the Roman civic cult. God is announced in chapter 1 and his righteousness was elaborated for the next twelve chapters; it is God as embodied in the crucified Christ that is in view here, which turns this passage into a massive act of political cooptation. If the Roman authorities had understood this argument, it would have been viewed as thoroughly subversive.

Nevertheless, the ambivalence is irreducible. Rome's involvement in the martyrdom of Christ, crucified under Pontius Pilate, cannot have been forgotten by the readers of chapter 13, who knew from firsthand experience of the Edict of Claudius the hollowness of Rome's claim to have established a benign rule of law. The critique of the law in all its forms in the first eight chapters of this letter cannot have been forgotten. Nothing remains of the claim in Roman propaganda that its law-enforcement system was redemptive, producing a kind of messianic peace under the rule of the gods Justitia and Clementia. Christ alone is the fulfillment of the law (10:4), not the emperor or the Roman gods. And nothing remains of the specious claim in the civic cult that the empire had been given to Rome because of its superior virtue and piety, a view that had been demolished by 1:18–3:20. What remains is the simple fact of divine appointment to enforce the law, a matter justified not by the virtue of the appointee but by the mysterious mind of God who elects whom she will as the agents of her purpose (9:14–33; 11:17–32). Submission to the governmental authorities is therefore an expression of respect not for the authorities themselves but for the crucified deity who stands behind them.

The passage closes with the urge to pay whatever is obligated, whether the tribute owed by captive peoples, the import tax, fear, or honor. Instead of absolute subservience, obligations are to be met if they prove legitimate. The formulation leaves space for assessments of appropriateness made by the community, as defined in 12:1–2. The wording of the final line in 13:7 seems particularly to embody the voluntary component of the verb "to subject oneself to" that appears in 13:1 and 5; only those worthy of honor are to be granted it and honor is to be granted only when it serves the interest of the subject. The element of discretion implicit in this entire ethic is informed by 12:1–2, which assigns early church groups the task as ascertaining the will of God by weighing "the good, the acceptable, and the perfect."

At the end of my commentary's discussion of this passage, I note that this pericope remains an excruciating example of Paul's willingness to be in the world but not of the world, to reside between the ages, to be all things to all people, all for the sake of his mission. The paradox needs to be named and acknowledged that Romans 13:1–7 has provided the basis for propaganda by which the imperial policies of Mars and Jupiter have frequently been disguised as serving the cause of Christ.

What I overlooked in this critical conclusion was an insight that arose out of conversations with students in Beijing in 2008. Every afternoon I was taken on long walks by participants in my course on Romans, followed by an evening meal in one of the wonderful restaurants in that city. In the privacy of these conversations I heard the stories of their conversions, the experience of their families during the Japanese occupation, the civil war, and the Cultural Revolution. I was surprised that each conversation turned at some point to Romans 13. My conversation partners said they were dissatisfied with living under the current dictatorship but that all of the alternatives appeared to be worse. They didn't want China to submit again to gunboat diplomacy or foreign occupation, to the regime of Chiang Kai-shek or to Coco-Cola capitalism. The current regime appears to be the lesser of evils. What emerged from these conversations was that Romans interpreters like myself were overlooking the practical political alternative that Paul and other early followers of Jesus were facing: whether to follow the Jewish zealots in their campaign to overthrow Rome and establish a theocratic world empire in Jerusalem, or to acquiese in Rome's rule that had brought a modicum of peace to the Mediterranean world. Before his conversion, Paul had been a violent Pharisee, probably as part of the Shammai wing that sympathized with the zealous revolutionaries, and thereafter his advocacy of peaceful coexistence under the Lordship of Christ had evoked intense hostility by zealous Jews. It seems clear that Paul made a choice between the hope of global reconciliation expressed in Romans 15, in its partially problematic fulfillment by Rome, and the zealous hope of a holy war that would establish Zion as the world's capital. The practical alternative was problematic Roman rule versus an even more problematic holy war for the sake of Zion. He accepted the former and rejected the latter. Romans 13 is therefore not a whitewash job that sets aside his penetrating critique of the civic cult. Like the Christian students at the University of Beijing, Paul made a choice of the lesser of evils.

There are two places in Romans where this preference is visible, but my commentary failed to link them with Romans 13. I explain why Paul altered Isaiah 52:7 in Romans 10:15, "How timely upon the mountains are the feet of him who preaches good news, who publishes peace, who preaches good news of good." Paul eliminated the reference to the "mountains" that appears in both the Septuagint (LXX) and the Masoretic Text (MT). My commentary suggests this was probably motivated by the desire to withdraw this citation from the context of Mount Zion, where Isaiah expected the fulfillment to be centered. The anti-imperial logic of the gospel allowed no hope that an Israelite imperium would be an improvement over the Roman Empire. In keeping with the ecumenical emphasis evident through Romans, the message of Christ offers peaceful coexistence for the entire world (cf. esp. 15:7–13), and it overcomes the barriers between the Greeks and the Jews (cf. 10:12–13) that would remain intact in an Israelite empire. This consideration also explains why Paul deleted "the one preaching the message of peace" that is found in all of the LXX versions. The concept of "peace" in the Septuagint citation has the same structure as the Pax Romana, resulting from the subordination of all potential enemies under the imperial capitol in Jerusalem. Thus, in the context of Paul's argument in chapter 10, this citation alludes to the gospel about Christ, while avoiding the imperialistic implications of the original wording of Isaiah.

In Romans 11:26, there is a similar case, in which Paul changed the wording of Isaiah 59:20–21 from a deliverer coming "for the sake of Zion" to the deliverer coming "from Zion." For an audience with a Gentile Christian majority, and in a letter arguing for a cooperative mission to the barbarians in Spain, the formulation that the Messiah came "for the sake of Zion" would have been offensive and misleading. Paul did not want to undercut his contention in 10:12 that "there is no distinction between Jews and also Greeks. The same Lord is Lord of all, [bestowing] riches upon all who call upon him." Paul's formulation "from Zion" is consistent with the composite creed that opens this letter concerning Jesus "descended from David" (1:3) and with the reminder that Christ came from the Israelites (9:5) and that it was in "Zion" that Christ the stone of stumbling was laid (9:33). Zion in this citation appears to be identical with the heavenly Jerusalem ("Jerusalem above," Galatians 4:26), the place from which Christ originated and was expected to descend at the parousia.

These two passages signal quite clearly that Paul was differentiating his view from the zealous revolution that he himself had previously promoted as a persecutor of early Christ believers. Both of these altered citations, it goes without saying, *preceded* Romans 13, and for an audience facing a similar practical choice, they provided clues about how 13:1–7 should be understood. But there is more.

V. ROMANS 7 AND THE ISSUE OF ZEALOUS CONFLICT

As a final theme, I would like briefly to sketch the relevance of Romans 7 for the situation of social conflict. I follow rhetorical studies by Stanley Stowers, Jean-Noël Aletti, und Jean-Baptiste Édart, which develop the Greek concept of *prosōpopoeia*, a "Speech-in-Character". This was a widely used method of argument in which a fictive character is given a voice to introduce important ideas. The hypothesis developed in my commentary is that Paul depicts himself as the person prior to his conversion, a zealous fanatic who obeyed the Jewish law perfectly but with such eagerness to achieve honor that he produced evil results. In Galatians 1:13–14 Paul had described this competitive zeal:

> For you have heard of my former life in Judaism, how I persecuted the church of God violently and tried to destroy it; and I advanced in Judaism beyond many of my own age among my people, so extremely zealous was I for the traditions of my fathers.

Here is someone whose religious motivation was to be more righteous than anyone else, a perfectly understandable trait when one takes the obsession with honor in the ancient Mediterranean world seriously. The resultant dilemma is described in Romans 7:19, "For I do not do the good I want, but the evil I do not want is what I do." The "good" that Paul as a persecutor of the early Christians sought to achieve was obedience to the Torah as a means of bringing in God's kingdom. He wanted to follow

God's will, but discovered through the encounter with the resurrected Jesus that he had resisted the divinely appointed messiah. What Paul describes in Romans 7 is not a failure to fulfill the law, including the command to fight against the Godless, but rather the inability of such violent legalism to achieve the good.

In the next verse of chapter 7, Paul identifies the underlying cause of this dilemma: "Now if I do what I do not want, it is no longer I that do it, but sin which dwells within me." In verse 7 he had explained that "if it had not been for the law, I should not have known sin. I should not have known what it is to covet if the law had not said, 'You shall not covet.'" The famous New Testament Professor who used to teach in Heidelberg defined "desire" as "nomistic desire," as evident in connection with the term "flesh" in Galatians 5:16–17 and Romans 6:12; 13:14, which is associated with the fulfillment of the law in Galatians 3:3 and Philippians 3:3–7. That was a step in the right direction. But since "nomistic desire" involves a problematic understanding of subjectivity and individualism in Paul's thought, while containing an element of anti-Jewish prejudice that Paul did not share, I prefer to retain the context of the ten commandments that Paul cites here. It is not "desire" as such that is forbidden but desiring what belongs to another: "You shall not covet your neighbor's house . . . your neighbor's wife, or male or female slave, or ox, or donkey, or anything that belongs to your neighbor." (Exodus 20:17) The sin that Paul has in mind in his explanation is to desire for oneself what rightfully belongs to someone else, which fits the intensely competitive environment of the Greco-Roman and Jewish cultures that I have described in which each is led to gain more honor than others, which places them in the position of dishonored losers. In this "speech-in-character," a situation is described that matches Paul's admission in Galatians 1:14, "I advanced in Judaism beyond many of my own age among my people, so extremely zealous was I for the traditions of my fathers." Competition for honor had promised him social prestige and divine approbation.

The shocking discovery on the road to Damascus was that such competition was proof of the power of sin at the very center of religious motivations. Paul discovered that his religious motivation was corrupted by the desire for status acquisition. The obsession to gain honor, which deprives others of the honor that they should enjoy, had produced the tragic gulf between willing and achieving the good, and perverted the holy into a means to gain precedence over others. Paul employs this "speech-in-character" to show the congregations in Rome that they were well along on this mistaken path in their competition with each other and that this imperialistic viewpoint must be transformed in order to participate with integrity in the mission to the so-called "barbarians" in Spain.

This interpretation is relevant for the 21st century, because both we Americans and Islamic Jihadists have intervened in Afghanistan and Iraq, believing that we would achieve the good, but discover that the very evils we deplore have been caused by our actions. Both have acted out of the motivation to show the superiority of our goals and cultures, and both expected a happy result from the violent methods employed. Similar campaigns are occurring in other cultures and under other circumstances. I believe that the insights of Romans are more relevant than ever, and I am grateful for the opportunities in these symposia to explore these issues.

The Heidelberg Symposium
February 2, 2007

3

A Note Introducing a Discussion of Robert Jewett, *Romans: A Commentary* Based on Romans 1:13–17[1]

Gerd Theissen

Commentaries have first of all a basic task, to summarize research and render it accessible. A second task may be added, to drive research forward in order to develop a new view of a document. While many good commentaries fulfill the first task, only a few lay out a new interpretive framework of a document. Robert Jewett's commentary on Romans belongs among those that present a new and comprehensive interpretation that emerges from an independent use of four research tendencies: the interpretation of the historical situation; the rhetorical analysis; the cultural-anthropological exegesis; and the anti-imperial interpretation of Paul. This commentary therefore stands among the significant studies of Romans. This pertains in equal measure for the entire concept and the argument in detail. When I make the comments that follow, I do so with caution. Being unable to work my way through this extensive commentary, I identified the basic line of interpretation and studied the portion assigned for today's discussion.

I. The Interpretation of the Historical Situation

Ever since F. C. Baur, the Roman letter and its theology have been understood in the light of its authorial intention. Thereby the letter was viewed either as an intervention into the congregational conflicts or as preparation for Paul's mission in Spain. After a phase of predominantly theological interpretation, research has returned for some time to the

[1] Translated from German to English by Robert Jewett.

historical situation. This commentary follows the historical line consistently and combines both aspects. Romans was written (a) to solicit support in the Roman congregation for the mission to Spain and (b) to establish peace inside the congregation between Jewish- and Gentile-Christians. These two purposes are combined in an innovative manner. Spain was viewed at the time as a province inhabited by barbarians that were inferior to Romans and devalued by ethnocentric prejudices, which also played a role in the congregational conflicts. Therefore in Romans 1:13ff Paul emphasizes his obligation to Greeks and barbarians (including Spaniards) and to the educated and uneducated. With his theology of justification by faith, he counters inter-ethnic derogations that express ancient systems of shame and honor. Romans is therefore an actual letter to the Roman congregation with a practical goal.

II. THE RHETORICAL ANALYSIS

H. D. Betz succeeded in introducing the rhetorical analysis of letters, and thereby invigorated an interpretative tradition that for a long time had receded into the background. Rhetorical analysis has led to subtle structural proposals for almost every letter. As with most Romans commentaries, Jewett understands the letter as a development of the thesis (= *propositio*) in Romans 1:16–17 concerning justification by faith. This is preceded by a *narratio* that describes the earlier history of discussing this matter, namely his futile efforts to come to Rome. The letter supports the thesis of justification by faith by four arguments (= *probatio*):

Romans 1–4: The impartiality of the righteousness of God;
Romans 5–8: The life in Christ as a new system of honor;
Romans 9–11: The triumph of righteousness in the mission to Gentiles and Jews;
Romans 12–15:13: Living together according to the gospel.

At the end of the letter there is a conclusion (= *peroratio*) that requests cooperation in the mission in Jerusalem, Rome and Spain. Therefore the passage of Romans 1:13–17 to be discussed today is the *narratio* + *propositio*.

III. THE CULTURAL-ANTHROPOLOGICAL EXEGESIS

The cultural-anthropological exegesis develops the meaning of ancient systems of honor and shame that provide the self evident but often unspoken premises of ancient thinking. The doctrine of justification is interpreted as overcoming these systems of shame and honor. A theological tendency is thereby pursued, to interpret the social function of the doctrine of justification rather than restricting its meaning to individualistic dimensions. In part this social function is seen inside the congregation as a defense against a Jewish-Christian counter mission, and in part globally as Jewish groups welcoming all nations. Jewett combines both when he presents the doctrine of justification by faith as overcoming a system of shame and honor. This system devalues other peoples ethnocentrically and functions inside the congregation as groups discriminate against each other. But all people and nationalities are equal before God, which challenges every standard of shame and honor. It is therefore crucial for the message of Romans that Paul introduces his thesis with the words, "I am not ashamed of the gospel . . . ." The gospel of the crucified one contradicts the system of shame and honor.

IV. The Anti-Imperial Interpretation

The anti-imperial interpretation interprets Pauline theology as opposition against imperial structures and ideology. The parousia of the Lord becomes the counterpart of the parousia of the emperor, the Lord as counterpart of Caesar, the gospel as counterpart to the gospel of imperial ideology. (On page 138 the inscription at Priene cites *euaggelion* in the singular, but the inscription employs the plural form here as elsewhere in connection with the imperial ideology.)

In our selected passage four tendencies are bundled together. I formulate them again in theses concerning the text under discussion today:

(1) Romans is not a general tractate but a letter about missionary strategy. This becomes clear in 1:13–17, that Paul hopes to gain some "fruit" from the Romans, which prepares the way for his request for support of the Spanish mission. Since he wants to travel to the "barbarians" in Spain, he introduces himself as a debtor to Greeks and barbarians.

(2) Romans 1:13–15 is the *narratio* for the proposition in 1:16–17 concerning redemptive righteousness through faith that is offered in faith to all people.

(3) Justification by faith as proclaimed in the gospel of the crucified messiah overcomes a system of honor and shame. Therefore Paul emphasizes, I am not ashamed of the gospel.

(4) The *euaggelion* (gospel) concerning Jesus Christ stands in opposition to the *euaggelia* of Caesar.

In order to enable a discussion of this great commentary in the context of our Sozietät, I formulate corresponding counter theses or in the case of the last point, a wider reaching thesis.

(1) Romans is a concrete letter, but one with so many additional addressees that it stands on the transition to early Christian promotional literature. The Corinthian congregation is recognizable as an additional addressee in our selected text. When Paul portrays himself as obligated to Greeks and barbarians, he reflects the Greek standpoint rather than the Jewish, which distinguishes between Jews and Gentiles or Jews and Greeks. He takes up the perspective of the congregation in which he is formulating the letter to the Romans, in the middle of Greece. When Paul goes on to portray himself as indebted to the wise and the uneducated, he is continuing the dialogue with the Corinthian congregation concerning wisdom. Pride about the possession of wisdom was one of the problems that Paul worked through in Corinth. When he emphasizes that he is not ashamed (*aischunein*) of the gospel, this resonates with the transformation of cultural values in 1 Corinthians 1:26 that Jewett also stresses: God elected the foolishness in the world in order to shame (*kataischunein*) the wise; he chose the weak in the world in order to shame the (*kataischunein*) strong. Regardless of whether there were other addressees for the Roman letter (Ephesus, Jerusalem), Paul writes in view of his possible death. He has thereby a theme that summarizes his message. This letter is in my view properly characterized as a *last will and testament.* When Paul writes that he is not ashamed of the gospel, this also means that he is ready to journey into a tense situation of conflict in Jerusalem in order to espouse his gospel in the face of enemies.

(2) The passage of Romans 1:13–15 can be viewed as the conclusion of the epistolary introduction, *but less appropriately as a narratio for the thesis of justification by faith.* A proper *narratio* for justification by faith should contain the history of Jesus—his incarnation, his road to the cross, his resurrection—and not the history of Paul. His relation to the addressees is a normal aspect of an epistolary introduction. Such an introduction often ends with a kind of self recommendation. Epistolography rather than rhetoric explains the formal character of this text. It is correct that Romans 1:16–17 contains the thesis of the letter, but not the entire thesis. Romans develops its central message step by step:

a. Romans 1:16–17: The righteousness of God occurs *sola fide* (faith alone);
b. Romans 3:21: The righteousness of God reveals itself *sine lege* (without law);
c. Romans 11:6: God elects *sola gratia* (grace alone) also against the unfaith of Jews.

Paul presents a total of three soteriologies in Romans:
Righteousness on the basis of works according to which all are

sinners (Romans 1:18–3:20);

Righteousness on the basis of faith (*sola fide*; *sine lege*), according to which all believers can achieve salvation despite unjust deeds (1:16–17; 3:21–8:39). Abraham as the first example, a prototypical justified sinner;

The election of persons prior to any deeds and of Jews despite their unfaith (Romans 9–11). Abraham as the second example: the sons of Abraham and Isaac as prototypes of the elected and the rejected.

(3) Salvation through faith contradicts the system of shame and honor. But one should distinguish three such systems:

The system of social sanctions of shame and honor;

The system of moral sanctions of guilt and righteousness;

The religious system of sanctions through grace and rejection.

The ancient world distinguished between social prestige and morality. The Stoics taught that a slave can remain externally a slave while being a morally free person internally. The free person who is ruled by his passions, on the other hand, is a slave internally. The ancient world had already developed from a shame culture to a guilt culture, according to E. R. Dodds. The religious system of sanctions through grace contradicts the system of prestige as well as the moral system of guilt.

(4) The anti-imperial interpretation of the *euaggelion* (gospel) is justified and can perhaps be more concretely understood on the basis of the beginning of Romans. The son of David, who after his death ascended to the status of the Son of God, could be the counterpart of Caesar. Claudius came from the Julio-Claudian family, but his post-mortal apotheosis became the subject of satire in the Apocolocyntosis of Seneca in which the fictitious character of post-mortal divinization is exposed. Paul writes around a year and a half after the death of Claudius. He could have depicted Jesus as the genuinely exalted counterpart of Claudius, actually raised to divine status.

4

A Response to Robert Jewett: Romans 1:13–17[1]

Peter Lampe

Robert Jewett's new commentary is a monumental piece of work, whose innovations will send new impulses into the arena of research. These innovations include a systematic application of sociological (for instance "honor/shame") and rhetorical categories; ("justification" beyond the Lutheran-individualistic or existential interpretations, and so forth). To that extent the following questions amount to mere nitpicking that sounds like the noise of desert hyenas that bell against the moon.

The interpretation of 1:13–17 provides an initial look at the distinctive profile of the commentary. The rhetorical analysis of verses 13–15 and 16–17 as *narratio* and respectively *propositio* is convincing (whereby contentwise the motif of travel plans connects the narratio with the preceding exordium even more clearly than the commentary indicates, so that verses 10-12 function as a hinge).

Extensive linguistic and thematic parallels in Greco-Roman and Jewish sources are helpfully related (even so far as the contours of the Mithras Cult). Attention is paid to philological intricacies.

I am also convinced by the commentary's interpretation of "fruit" in verse 13 as related to the logistical and financial support of the Spanish mission that Paul hopes to gain from the Romans, so that this verse in a diplomatic manner prepares the way for chapter 15. It is perhaps too consistent to identify the "rest of the Gentiles" in verse 13 as the Spaniards. Nevertheless, even if the commentary is right, it should clarify that the concept of bringing fruit begins to ambiguously oscillate now: in relation to the Roman believers it connotes logistical support; in relation to the Spaniards and other missionary targets it would lack this

[1] Translated from German to English by Robert Jewett.

specific connotation and could only relate to general missionary success (which however would not be sought among Romans, as the commentary emphasizes: Paul will restrict his preaching to those already converted and will not poach in the arena of others). It would perhaps be better to understand verse 13 as follows: "so that I might reap some fruit even among you just as also among the rest of the Gentiles," namely from people such as the Philippians who repeatedly supported my mission in generous ways. The 'as' would possibly be taken more seriously in this way, and Paul then would not focus on the Spaniards and their future as well as on other missionary targets until verse 14 (with his reference to 'Greeks and barbarians, educated and uneducated').

It is impressive that the details in verse 14, (including the philological nuances of TE KAI, Paideia-Konzept, etc.), support Jewett's stress on the "inclusivity of the gospel." However the statement on page 132 is not entirely understandable: "to be classified as foolish in this social context is not a deficit that can be overcome with more education . . . " Were there no "ignorant barbarians" in the empire, above all in the Equestrian ranks, who advanced to the status of cultivated Hellenes? And were there no opposite cases, of native born Greeks who were criticized as uncouth Barbarians? Is a Greek person really "innately wise"? Quintilian and other stoically inclined teachers worked hard at forming young people into educated ones; nobody was born 'wise', and conversely nobody was condemned to remain foolish forever, not even a person born by 'barbarians'.

It seems to me that the statement on page 132 is too apodictic, that the "cultural commonplace" was that "the relationship with the Divine was thought to be centered in *knowledge.*" In the middle of the first century, this held at the most for middle Platonism (the human mind approaches the supreme mind, etc). What dominated the relationship to the gods was not knowledge (about them) but correct cultic behavior, which protected one from godly whims, appeased the gods, etc. Significantly, Jewett tries to document his 'commonplace' with references in Philo and Titus, but they also advocate the behavioural approach. Perhaps Jewett means " . . . centered in *knowledge about the right behaviour*"? That would be more accurate.

Is the reference on page 132 convincing that the houses of Narcissus und Aristobul (Romans 16) were "situated within the bureaucracy"?

I find it fascinating that Jewett already in verse 14 is able to infer from Paul's "indebtedness to barbarians and the uneducated" a "complete reversal of the system of honor and shame" (132). Also the propositio in verses 16-17 "effectively turns the social value system of the Roman Empire upside down" (139). This is a theme that permeates the entire commentary. An equally fascinating hypothesis, which the following commentary chapters set about proving, is that the proposition does not only aim at the elaborations until chapters 5 and 8, or perhaps 11, but even at the entire argument all the way through 15:13 (132). This fits the above-mentioned concretizing of "fruit" with reference to chapter 15. It also correlates with Jewett's controversial denial, extended through the entire commentary, that the scope of Paul's argument has anything to do with a defense of his teaching about justification by faith or an apologetic dialogue with Judaism, which are often maintained. (136–141) But I question whether the "tension between Jewish and Gentile groups" suggested in chapters 14–15 is already severely criticized in 1:16b–c. The same expression appears in 1 Corinthians 1:24 without any antagonistic undertones between the two groups.

5

Response to Heidelberg Colleagues

Robert Jewett

I appreciate the careful attention my colleagues have paid to the commentary, for Peter's conscientious "nit-picking" and for Gerd's fair minded summary of some of the main themes in the commentary and of the two sections read for this Societaet discussion. Commentaries like this are useful if they push the interpretive process forward, but advances require careful evaluation of the relevant details. I follow the method suggested by Karl Popper, that new "conjectures" always require "refutations," which also must be evaluated. I would like to begin with Gerd's second critique, that 1:13–15 cannot be a *narratio* because it does not strictly introduce "Glaubensgerechtigkeit." If the argument of Romans were primarily a matter of doctrinal instruction, this would surely be right. But that contradicts the situational approach to the letter, a theme to which I would like to return at the end of this response.

The traditional insistence on the doctrinal purpose of the letter, beyond any situational circumstances, is reflected in Gerd's preference for the theory of Romans as a "theological testament," a view that I myself once held. This echoes the influential formulation of our Heidelberg predecessor, Günther Bornkamm, that Romans is the "last will and testament of the Apostle Paul."[1] This is a version of the traditional approach to Romans as a theological treatise, a defense of the true gospel, or a polemic against antinomians or legalists. I was never able to provide a satisfactory answer as to why Paul felt compelled to send such a letter to Rome. Günther Bornkamm answers this question by declaring that the search for specific reasons in the Roman church situation is a "wrong track" that leads nowhere. Assuming that chapter

[1] See Günther Bornkamm, *Paul* (New York: Harper & Row, 1971).

16 was not part of the original letter to Rome, a view that I once also held, Bornkamm pointed to the parallels between passages in Romans and the earlier letters and observed that the apologetic sections and the theological argumentation are general and abstract. "The previous actual and concrete references" that one finds in Paul's earlier letters "have disappeared" and now receive "a strongly universal meaning." The letter to the Romans "elevates his theology above the moment of definite situations and conflicts into the sphere of the eternally and universally valid . . . "[2] While this viewpoint retained a central place for Romans in the era of dialectical theology, whose dislike for situational and rhetorical circumstances is clearly conveyed by Bornkamm's wording, it rested on an inadequate grasp of the text-critical evidence that compelled me in 1980 to abandon the theory of Romans 16 as written to Ephesus. Gerd Theissen would like us to return to this outmoded perspective.

The issue of understanding justification by faith has long been entangled with the problem of guilt and forgiveness as mentioned in Gerd's third critical issue. My own background was oriented to the Augustinian legacy that understood justification of faith in terms of forgiveness of guilty conscience. Every Romans commentary on my shelf shares this premise, but I was baffled for years by the lack of direct evidence because the word "forgiveness" appears only once in Romans, in the citation of Psalm 31 in 4:7. The use of the aorist passive *aphethēsan* ("they have been forgiven") points to conversion in which God chose to make believers righteous through grace alone and can't refer to forgiveness that must be renewed every day under the doctrine of *simul iustus et pecattor*. The other passage often cited in support of the centrality of forgiveness is 3:25, which actually refers to divine forbearance by which God "passed over former sins" of Gentiles, as Wolfgang Kraus and James Dunn have shown.

A stimulus to working out an alternative interpretation came through reading "Honour and Righteousness in Romans," written by Halvor Moxnes in 1988. He placed the entire argument of Paul's most influential letter in the ancient cultural context of an "honour society" in which "recognition and approval from others" is central, which means that the "group is more important than the individual."[3] This contrasts with the dominant concern of Western theology and its interpretation of Romans, "in which guilt and guilt-feeling predominate as a response to wrongdoing."[4] He notes that the semantic equivalents of honor play

---

2 Günther Bornkamm, "The Letter to the Romans as Paul's Last Will and Testament," in K. P. Donfried, editor, *The Romans Debate* (Revised and Expanded Edition; Peabody: Hendrickson, 1991), 25, 28.

3 Halvor Moxnes, "Honour and Righteousness in Romans," *Journal for the Study of the New Testament* 32 (1988), 63.

4 Moxnes, "Honour and Righteousness in Romans," 62.

important roles in the argument of Romans, with 27 references to honor and dishonor, 9 references to shame, 19 references to glory, 3 references to praise," and 8 references to boasting.

To these references I would add the socially discriminatory categories discussed in the passage we have read, "Greeks and barbarians, educated and uneducated" in 1:14 and in addition, the 28 appearances of the potentially shameful epithet "Gentiles" as well as the categories "weak and strong" employed throughout 14:1–15:7. Even more prominent are the 25 references to social gestures of honor in the form of "welcome" and "greeting" of outsiders that dominate the last three chapters. The word field of "righteousness/unrighteousness" that appears 34 times in the letter is also closely related to Jewish and Greco-Roman terminology for honor and shame.

The emphasis on issues of honor and shame fits what Peter discovered in his analysis of the situation in Rome, that the congregations there were fractured and disputatious. Their problem in Paul's view was not a lack of forgiveness but an excess of zealotism; they were damning each other in an imperialistic manner that conformed to Roman culture, and unless this were transformed by the gospel of God's impartial righteousness, they would not be able to contribute with success or integrity in a mission to the "barbarians" in Spain. It is the peculiar requirements of this mission project that lead Paul to formulate his argument as he does in the passages we have read for today, concentrating on transforming unjust systems of social shame by the gospel.

My commentary follows the situational approach by connecting these themes with the purpose of the letter, which was to elicit support from the Roman congregations for the difficult mission to Spain. It is this mission that is introduced in 1:13–15, and the clarification of the righteousness of God and salvation by faith in the following thesis serves this missional purpose: it is the gospel that embodies the power of God, which is a missionary theme to which Paul returns in chapters 11 and 15. The theological development of the letter in the four major proofs serves this missional purpose, because the Roman house and tenement churches were violating the gospel in their discriminatory behavior toward one another; in damning each other for following different cultural customs, they were really advocating salvation by works; they were claiming superior honors in ways that the crucified one died to overcome. Since the Gentile Christian groups were discriminating against the Jewish Christian congregations, I therefore think it is appropriate to infer that "both to the Jew first and then to the Greek" in 1:16 is designed to overturn this priority in honor, and thus that in this context it has a different connotation than in 1 Corinthians 1:24, to which Peter alludes. This relates to the final question Peter poses, how

I could imagine that the "faith of many Roman believers differs from Paul's;" it is because they belong to congregations stigmatized as the "weak" although Paul identifies himself with the "strong." On the other hand I think Peter has correctly discerned several instances in which I advanced this situational interpretation too consistently and at times ineffectively. The suggestion that gaining fruit "also among the rest of the Gentiles" might well refer to their future participation in supporting the Pauline mission as in the parallel in Philippians is quite intriguing, and so far as I know this suggestion has never been made before. I think the references on page 132 to foolishness as a social deficit and to the central role of "knowledge" are overstated; it would have been better to refer to "knowledge about the right behavior" required by the gods. I admit that the Priene citation on page 138 is less than fully apt because the word "power" is not explicitly mentioned, although it is certainly implied in the description of Augustus as the savior "who put an end to war and will restore order everywhere."

This is related to Gerd's final point about Christ as the true Son of God in contrast to the disgraced Claudius. There is certainly an implicit critique of the Roman civic cult in Romans 1:1–4. However, in the light of my redactional analysis of this composite confession, it also provides common ground for the weak and the strong in Rome, sustaining the emphasis throughout the letter on the equality of "all who have faith" in Christ. This situational interpretation leads to the "onesidedness" that Peter discerns in my interpretation of the righteousness of God. Even Romans 6:8 is fit into the missionary vision of this letter, as I suggest on page 406, that "we shall also co-dwell with him" should be related not to "the isolated soul of individual believers but [to] their corporate life together in the fictive families of house and tenement churches that made up the early church. These groups shared decisive moments of life together from the birth of infants to the burial of the dead, from sharing meals to caring for the infirm, thus encompassing the entire range of bodily and spiritual experiences (see also 1 Corinthians 6:13b, 17). Their entire life as a community of believers is "with him" (*autō*), from the moment of their conversion until the eschaton and beyond."

In conclusion, I would once again like to thank my colleagues for honoring my work by subjecting it to detailed "refutation." Now, in the short time still remaining, I hope others will join the conversation. Because of a severe hearing deficit, I need to come close enough to read your lips, so please allow me to move about the room. Who would like to begin?

The Aberdeen Symposium
March 22, 2007

6

A Manifesto for Multiculturalism? First Thoughts in Response to Robert Jewett's Romans Commentary

Francis Watson

Robert Jewett's Hermeneia commentary on Romans is a heavyweight work in every sense. Its single volume weighs in at five pounds, a full pound heavier than its nearest (two volume) rival. Great care should be exercised in removing it from upper shelves in libraries. Those who work through its eleven hundred pages from beginning to end will perhaps be few. Only the most conscientious of reviewers or postgraduates will find the stamina for such a feat of endurance, and their reward will surely be great. Most users of this commentary will avail themselves of its detailed exegetical discussion, and copious engagement with the secondary literature, at points relevant to their own interests and concerns. They too will receive their reward, for Jewett always has fresh and interesting and provocative things to say, even where he is simply aligning himself with one side or the other in the many ongoing exegetical disagreements that populate this most contested of all New Testament texts. Of the various large-scale commentaries on Romans currently available (e.g. Cranfield, Dunn, Fitzmyer, Moo and Wilckens), this one will become the first recourse for many scholars. It is a remarkable achievement.

In spite of the eleven hundred pages and the mass of exegetical detail, Jewett's basic construal of Romans is disarmingly simple. He proposes to read Romans in the light of a reconstructed original setting that includes both specific local factors and broader cultural ones. In this reading, the Letter to the Romans is truly a letter, and it is truly addressed to the Romans. It is not a timeless theological treatise (there is, of course, no such thing), but neither is it a general apologia for Paul's apostolic ministry to the Gentiles. Like many current interpreters, Jewett finds the situational key to the letter in the indications of tensions between Jewish and Gentile Christians in chapters 14–16; and, unlike many of the same commentators, Jewett allows this situation to shape his reading of earlier chapters. In Rome, Jewish and Gentile Christians disagree about whether certain prescriptions of the Law of Moses remain mandatory, and Jewett diagnoses this disagreement as a symptom of a more fundamental malaise, the quest for "honour" or status at the expense of the other that pervaded Graeco-Roman culture. The God of inclusive grace honours one group without thereby dishonouring the other, and Christians in Rome must learn to do likewise, rather than "judging" one another for failures of law-observance, or "despising" one another for scrupulous concern over such matters (cf. Romans 14:10). In particular, the Gentile Christian majority in Rome must learn to accommodate the Jewish Christian minority. The Letter to the Romans is a plea for a theologically-grounded multiculturalism.

It is crucial, Jewett argues, for the Roman Christians to address the problem created by their exclusive claims to cultural superiority, if they are to participate in the westward expansion of the gospel that Paul intends. Jewett places unusual emphasis on Paul's proposed Spanish mission as integral to the message of the letter as a whole. Divisions at Rome are to be healed not just for the benefit of the Roman Christians but also for the sake of the new communities to be founded in Spain:

> If the Gentile and Jewish Christians [in Rome] continued to shame each other, they would carry a gospel to the barbarians in Spain that would continue the perverse system of honor on which the exploitative empire rested . . . . Therefore Paul attacked perverse systems of honor by dispelling the idea that some persons and groups are inherently righteous and by proclaiming the message that God honors sinners of every culture in an impartial manner through Christ. (88)

Thus the message of Romans 1–4 can be summed up in the claim that "the gospel expresses the impartial righteousness of God by overturning claims of cultural superiority and by rightwising Jews and Gentiles" (150). When in 3:23 Paul states that "all have sinned and fall short of the glory of God", he thereby "eliminates all claims of honorable superiority, including those that were developing within the church itself" (279). Indeed, throughout this crucial paragraph (3:21–31), "[i]t is the elimination of invidious distinctions in the availability of divine favor, the access to salvation for 'all who have faith,' that stands at the center

. . . ." (291) As interpreted by Jewett, the particular issue—a dispute about the continuing role of the law—is to be understood as an instance of the more general cultural phenomenon of the quest for status at the expense of the other. When Paul speaks of the righteousness of God as "apart from law" (3:21), he means not just Israel's law but any law that privileges some and marginalizes others (274). His argument is no less applicable to Roman law than to Jewish. Jewett's Paul has no "critique of Judaism" *per se*. The Pauline Jew is simply the subject or the object—the perpetrator or the victim—of a claim to cultural superiority. As such, he functions as a typical representative of Gentile, Graeco-Roman culture, with its preoccupation with honour and shame, its competitive quest for status at the expense of the other. And he represents this culture *both* when he takes pride in his Jewish heritage and despises those who lack it, *and* when he is classed alongside other "barbarians" as not-Greek and therefore inferior and subhuman.

If this is the fundamental interpretative move that underlies Jewett's entire commentary, it is important to understand how it works and where it comes from. In the first instance, it seems to stem from the union of J. D. G. Dunn's "new perspective on Paul" and Bruce Malina's "cultural anthropology."[1] Dunn argues that Paul opposes the "exclusivistic" covenantal nomism of contemporary Judaism on the basis of his own "inclusive" understanding of the gospel; Malina argues that the primary social good in what he calls "Mediterranean culture" is honour, with the shaming of the other as its corollary; and Jewett fuses the two, understanding Jewish exclusiveness as an instance of the competitive quest for honour or status at the expense of the other that is characteristic of the culture as a whole.

Yet Jewett's interpretative move also evokes echoes of earlier debates. In 1969 Ernst Käsemann published his paper on "Justification and Salvation History in the Epistle to the Romans," responding especially to Krister Stendahl's celebrated article on "The Apostle Paul and the Introspective Conscience of the West" (1963). According to Käsemann,

> Paul's doctrine of justification undoubtedly grew up in the course of the anti-Jewish struggle and stands or falls with this antithesis. But the exegete must not make things easy for himself by simply, as historian, noting this incontrovertible fact . . . . Our task is to ask: what does the Jewish nomism against which Paul fought really represent?[2]

[1] See his *The New Testament World: Insights from Cultural Anthropology* (London: SCM, 1981), 25–50.

[2] Ernest Käsemann, *Perspectives on Paul* (Philadelphia: Fortress Press, 1971), 71–72.

It goes without saying that Käsemann's disturbing talk of "the anti-Jewish struggle" is entirely alien to Jewett, as it is to all right-thinking interpreters. Yet Jewett poses essentially the same question to Paul's text as Käsemann does. He too asks what is "really represented" in Paul's criticism of Jewish righteousness by works, as also of Gentile boasting. Käsemann believes that this critique "really represents" the community of the righteous, which "turns God's promises into their own privileges . . . ."[3] whereas Jewett claims that it "really represents" the competitive quest for honour at the expense of others. Whatever the difference of nuance and idiom, the two interpretative moves are actually very similar. In both cases, Paul is interested in Jews or Judaism not *per se* but only as instances of a broader phenomenon, the claim to any kind of religious privilege or cultural superiority. In both cases, the Pauline statement that "by works of law shall no flesh be justified" is understood not literally, as a reference to the way of life practised within the Jewish community, but *allegorically*, as a reference to what that practice "really represents." And in both cases, the danger is that the particular identity of Jesus will be replaced by an abstract Christ who is no more than a symbol of divine inclusivity.

In principle, of course, Jewett may be right. As Paul reflects on the tension within the Roman Christian community, he may indeed see this tension as a particular manifestation of the violent intercultural competitiveness that it is the gospel's destiny to overcome. In one and the same context, Paul can divide the human race not only into Jews and Greeks but also into Greeks and barbarians, wise and foolish (Romans 1:14–16). In asserting that his gospel transcends these ideologically constructed boundaries, Paul may well assume that the boundaries are analogous to one another, such that one may represent the others. If salvation is for Jews and Greeks alike, does this not instantiate a principle of inclusivity that also recurs in the other pairings? Paul is surely capable of the abstract thought-processes required to recognize common underlying principles within different phenomena. In focusing primarily on the tensions between Jewish and Gentile Christians in Rome, he could indeed have seen these tensions as instances of the wider category of "claims of cultural superiority." He could have done so. But did he?

Let us pose a closely related question. How far and in what sense may the Pauline gospel be said to be "inclusive"? It is clearly inclusive as regards the sphere of its address. Paul hears a scriptural testimony to this universal scope of the gospel in Psalm 18 LXX:

> Their sound has gone forth into all the earth, and their words to the ends of the world. (Romans 10:18, citing Psalm 18:5)

[3] Käsemann, *Perspectives on Paul*, 72.

For Paul, the possessive "their" must refer back to the evangelists of the previously cited Isaianic text, "How beautiful are the feet of those who preach good things" (Romans 10:15, citing Isaiah 52:7). As scripture confirms, the gospel entails a universal, inclusive mission, to Jew and Greek, Greek and barbarian, wise and foolish. Where Christian communities spring up in response to the gospel, some cultural differences will no doubt be maintained, since it is not the purpose of the gospel to turn, say, barbarians into Greeks. Yet other cultural differences will be abolished. Like most Jews, Paul takes it for granted that the various religions of Greeks and barbarians are simply false; and unlike most Jews, he works tirelessly for their elimination—by creating new communities in which traditional religion is now abhorred as "idolatry" and loyalty is fostered to Christ alone. Inclusive in its address, the Pauline gospel is exclusive in its attitude towards all other options in the religious marketplace. It is straightforwardly opposed to them, although what this opposition entails in practice may still remain to be worked out. Inclusive in one sense, Paul's gospel is nevertheless rigorously exclusive in another.

When Paul states that God is the God of Jews and Gentiles alike, and that both parties are justified solely through faith (Romans 3:29–30), it is not at all his intention to promote an attitude of universal and undifferentiated inclusiveness. On the contrary, the "faith" of which he here speaks represents a new boundary entailing the inclusion of some (the minority) and the exclusion of others (the majority): for, to put it no more strongly, "not all have believed the gospel" (10:16). In no sense does faith represent the abolition of boundaries as such. On the contrary, the old boundary between Jews and Gentiles is replaced by a new boundary between believers and unbelievers, which takes socially visible form in the existence of the Roman Christian community. If we are to use honour/shame language, then the Pauline gospel represents a new basis on which God honours some (those who believe) and shames others (those who do not). God's exclusive honouring of the Christian community is celebrated in Romans 5:1–11 without any sense of impropriety. There is here no escape from the categories of honour and shame; rather, their projection into eternity. In my view, it is a serious mistake to find an abstract principle of maximal inclusiveness at the heart of Paul's argument in Romans. If multiculturalism needs a patron saint, the apostle to the Gentiles is hardly a credible candidate.

What Paul's letter does contain is a plea for a limited diversity of practice within the Roman Christian community, where, according to Paul, one person is omnivorous while the other only eats lettuce (Romans 14:2)—a piece of humorous exaggeration, according to Jewett (837–38). The lettuce-eaters or vegetarians are (as Jewett rightly concludes) "conservative Jewish Christians" in a situation where there is no access to kosher meat (839). The omnivores are Gentile or Gentile-oriented Christians for whom Mosaic dietary restrictions have been abolished by the gospel. Rather than arguing over the ideological merits of their respective diets, the two parties are to acknowledge the legitimacy of both practices within the overarching context of their common commitment to Christ. The "tolerance" advocated here relates to a single issue that has occurred within the Christian community. Paul's argument does not imply that "tolerance," or amicably agreeing to differ, is always and in itself a good thing. While he would like the community to be at peace with everyone, so far as possible (cf. 12:18), he also warns its members in the sharpest terms against those who "do not serve our Lord Christ but their own stomach", and who deceive the innocent through their deceptive speech (16:18). While Jewett dismisses this stridently intolerant passage as a later addition, there is no inconsistency whatever in advocating tolerance over one issue and intolerance over another. The idea that tolerance as such is an ethical virtue is a peculiarly modern one, the limitations of which become painfully obvious in the presence of the intolerable and the unacceptable.

Recent interpreters of Romans have been so impressed by Paul's sensitive handling of Jewish/Gentile tensions within the Roman Christian community that they fail to reflect on the likely consequences of the shared worship and common identity for which he here calls. Insofar as Jewish Christians worship together with non-law-observant Gentiles, they will inevitably further their own alienation from the Roman synagogues.

Yet, in his reconstruction of the situation Paul addresses in Romans, Jewett has little to say about ongoing relations between Roman Jewish Christians and the synagogues from which they derived. While the Roman synagogues are rightly said to be crucial to the origins of Roman Christianity (55–63), they play no part in Jewett's view of the situation addressed by Paul. This lacuna is also found in other recent "situational" interpretations of Romans, and it is a remarkable one. As Paul writes his letter, there exists a flourishing Jewish community in Rome, probably far larger numerically than the Christian community there. Some of its synagogues can still be identified. We know that the arrival of the Christian gospel created serious internal tensions within the Roman Jewish community, which in 49 C.E. resulted in the expulsion from Rome of many if not all of its members. Addressing Roman Christians less than a decade later, Paul cannot but be aware of a Roman Jewish community which maintains the traditional assumption that the divine/human relationship is to be regulated by the Law of Moses, and which repudiates the claim that the Messiah has come in the person of Jesus. The Roman Christian Jews envisaged by Paul stand between two communities: law-observant fellow Jews, and the law-free Gentile Christians who are the primary objects of his address. There is, as it were, an invisible third dimension to the discussion in Romans 14–15 about relations between Jewish and Gentile Christians. In doing what Paul wishes and aligning themselves more closely with Gentile Christians, Christian Jews will further alienate themselves from the wider Roman Jewish community. In seeking this realignment, Paul also intends the corresponding alienation. When it is said that "by works of law shall no flesh be justified" (Romans 3:20), a boundary is established between the community based on law-observance and the community based on faith.

As John Barclay rightly notes, we must therefore attend not only to what Paul says in Romans 14-15 but also to its social consequences.[4] According to Barclay, Paul's defense of the weak ostensibly means "that those Jewish Christians in Rome who wished to retain their links with the Jewish community were enabled to do so," continuing "to attend all-important synagogue gatherings and thus [to] maintain their place in the Jewish community."[5] And yet, "Paul here requires of Christian members of the Jewish community a very significant depth of association with those declining to live according to the same mode of life"—an association ultimately incompatible "with continued membership of the Jewish community, which is naturally concerned to preserve its social integrity."[6] Thus "Paul subverts the basis on which Jewish law-observance is founded and precipitates a crisis of cultural integrity among the very believers whose law-observance he is careful to protect."[7] Rather than accepting this as a "fundamental paradox,"[8] however, I suggest that *for Paul himself* the unity of Jewish and Gentile Christians is incompatible with continuing allegiance to the majority Jewish community, though not with the option of law-observance. What Barclay sees as the social *effect* of Paul's advice was actually his *intention*. Intending to promote a shared Christian identity among the divided and disparate Christ-believers in Rome, he also intends the corresponding distancing from the Jewish community. Paul cannot intend the one without its entailing the other. Inclusive in its bridging of the Jew/Gentile divide, the Roman Christian community is to develop a heightened sense of its own distinctiveness vis-à-vis the Roman synagogues.

[4] John D. G. Barclay, "'Do We Undermine the Law?' A Study of Romans 14:1–15:6," in *Paul and the Mosaic Law: The Third Durham-Tübingen Research Symposium on Earliest Christianity and Judaism* (Durham, September 1994), ed. J. D. G. Dunn, editor (Tübingen: Mohr Siebeck, 1996), 303–8.

[5] Barclay, "'Do We Undermine the Law?'" 303–4.

[6] Barclay, "'Do We Undermine the Law?'" 307.

[7] Barclay, "'Do We Undermine the Law?'" 308.

[8] Barclay, "'Do We Undermine the Law?'" 308.

To my mind, the Roman synagogues are the obvious social correlate of such features of Paul's letter as the hostile address to the teacher of Torah (2:17–24); the inclusive references to "we Jews" (3:9), to "Abraham our forefather according to the flesh" (4:1) and to "our father Isaac" (9:10); and above all to the lengthy attempt in chapters 9–11 to explain the predominantly negative Jewish response to the gospel. Why should Jewish non-belief be of special concern to the Christians of Rome, unless they encounter it themselves as a significant factor of their day-to-day experience? Paul could surely not have written these chapters as he does if his sole intention is to persuade the omnivores and the lettuce-eaters to be more tolerant towards one another. Rather, what is at stake throughout the letter is the construction of a *shared Christian identity, distinct from the communal identity based on the Torah.* A situational reading based on this premise will be historically and exegetically plausible, and need not be lacking in theological depth and incisiveness.[9]

Jewett is entirely right to attempt a consistently situational reading of the letter; indeed, his would seem to be the first major commentary to do so. Yet situational readings are peculiarly vulnerable to misreadings of the situation. If the situation is misread, then so too will the text be misread. And to understand this letter's intense preoccupation with the Jewish scriptural heritage as a plea for a generalized multicultural sensitivity would, in my view, be to misread indeed.

[9] For a full statement of this case, see my *Paul, Judaism and the Gentiles: Beyond the New Perspective* (Revised and Expanded Edition; Grand Rapids: Eerdmans, 2007), chapter 5–9. In my view, this construal of the Roman situation is comprehensive enough to refute Keck's claim that "[n]o reconstruction of earliest Christianity in Rome accounts adequately for much of the theological argument of the whole letter . . . ." (Leander E. Keck, *Romans* [Nashville: Abingdon Press, 2005], 30). As a response to the usual reading of Romans 14–15, however, Keck's claim is entirely understandable.

7

Atonement, Justification and Law: Some Reflections in Response to Robert Jewett's *Romans*

Simon Gathercole

Introduction

The words "epoch-making," "magnum," "opus," "bench-mark" and the like are certain to trip off the tongue in the years to come when mention is made of Robert Jewett's magnificent tome (there are another two). The introduction taken on its own is quite a feat, and the technical aspects of the commentary show a level of detail which is characteristically Hermeneian and then some. The ease with which Jewett glides between Anglo-American and German scholarly discourses is exemplary. But at the same time, the lion of scholarly depth lies down with the lamb of engaging legibility.

So there is much to be commended in the commentary. Prof. Jewett shows an admirable grasp of recent scholarship on such central topics as, for example, "boasting"! He also, despite the occasional wobble, eschews the current fashion for interpreting *pistis Christou* as a subjective genitive.[1] This will no doubt incur the wrath of some of his fellow countrymen, but at the same time endeared him to his Aberdonian hosts.[2] But Professor Jewett did not come all the way to Scotland to be told how marvellous he is, so I trust that it will not be deemed ungrateful if the concentration here in this response is on points of disagreement

[1] Jewett concedes there may be some intentional ambiguity (277–78), but this does not affect the interpretation much elsewhere (see 143–44 on Romans 1:16–17).

[2] There was unanimity on something approximating the objective genitive reading among the *Neutestamentler* in Aberdeen, *viz.* Prof. Francis Watson, Drs. Andrew Clarke, Peter Williams and myself, as well as Prof. emeritus Howard Marshall.

and concern, especially with the Introduction and the treatment of Romans 1–4.[3]

CONTEXT AND EXEGESIS

In his introduction, Jewett has a discussion of "The Cultural Situation in Rome: The Pyramid of Honor" (pages 46–59) which not only affects the exegesis at various points but—by his own admission—decisively shapes it throughout. Jewett resolves to avoid a theological interpretation—a frequent target of his polemic (e.g. 81, 136, 141 etc.). Instead of a traditional reading, Jewett adopts a socio-rhetorical approach. This involves, first, the task of constructing a conjectural situation in Rome. Central to the reconstruction of the audience's situation is the competition of honour, which Jewett expounds in dialogue in part with one of the most important monographs on this subject, that of Jon Lendon.[4] The second element is to apply this to the exegesis.[5] After his discussion of the social situation in the wider urban milieu and his reconstruction of the specific incidents which had led to the conflicts of Romans 14–15, Jewett comments: "Like all other conclusions drawn in this section, these conjectures are subject to refutation, despite the fact that they are supported by many researchers. In the case of this commentary, however, these conjectures provide the framework for the entire letter" (59).

I have reservations, however, about whether this socio-cultural framework works so well in its application to the Epistle to the Romans. One could argue about the extent and degree of the concern with honour in ancient Roman society. Jewett comments that slaves and barbarians were largely exempt (51). This exemption may have extended to a very large proportion of the free population in Rome as well. Lendon's monograph, for example, deals principally with honour in the aristocratic context of the processes of imperial government. We know very little about how easily transferrable this is across the board. And we also know very little about the social stratum/a occupied by the Roman Christians.

One of the biggest problems, it seems to me, with the conjectured reconstruction, is that *the letter to the Romans does not, by comparison with Paul's other letters, display a heightened concern with honour/dishonour themes.* If this whole matrix of ideas was really as important to

---

[3] I am very grateful that Prof. Jewett was able to come for discussion of his commentary in Aberdeen, and am very grateful to Fortress for their extremely generous provision of the commentary. This generosity extended not only to supplying a copy of the book, but also to the far more expensive part—paying for the postage.

[4] J. Lendon, *Empire of Honor: The Art of Government in the Ancient World* (Oxford: Clarendon Press, 1997).

[5] I omit the several other steps involved, such as the text-critical project, which—it seems to me—is in the main carried out admirably.

the letter as Jewett insists, then we would expect to find a concentration of honour language in the letter to a greater extent than elsewhere in Paul or in other earliest Christian writings. But this is precisely what we do not find. Words such as *timē*, *doxa*, *kauchēsis* and their cognates and negatives, and shame related terms derived from the *aisch-* root do not by any stretch of the imagination feature especially frequently in Romans. These concepts are important, and I spent three years writing a dissertation arguing that one of them was more important than people had previously thought.[6] But what is much more difficult is to argue that they are decisive for the rhetorical situation into which Paul is writing, and that this matrix of ideas should therefore shape the exegesis of every single verse. One of the places in which this is perhaps most striking is in Romans 14–15, where honour and shame language (terminology like *timē* et al.) is pretty thin on the ground: if the principal point of conflict in the Roman congregations had to do with the honour/shame competition, then we might expect this to have come to clearer expression in 14:1–15:6. But my focus in the main body of the paper will be a few central themes in the earlier chapters.

ATONEMENT

The first area in which I suggest that difficulties emerge is that of the atonement. On this point, one of the fundamental factors in the commentary appears in the treatment of Romans 4:25:

> On the basis of Paul's citation of the hymn in 3:25–26 that celebrated Christ's blood as the new means of atonement for Jews and Gentiles alike, the claim here is that Christ's shameful death overcame the shame of "our transgressions." Whether one's declaration of war against God had occurred as a Jew or a Gentile, it was exposed and overcome by the cross of Christ. Christ's shameful death in behalf of the shamed conveyed in a new way the divine 'grace' that Paul had identified as the key to Abraham's promise (343).

Jewett admits in the preface that he has been influenced considerably by the great theological minds of Barth and Käsemann; on the other hand of course, the introduction is replete with discussion of the socio-rhetorical nature of the commentary. The citation above perhaps draws attention to some of the difficulties with combining these two kinds of influence. "Declaration of war" is of course a powerful image for Paul's

6 S. J. Gathercole, *Where is Boasting? Early Jewish Soteriology and Paul's Response in Romans 1–5* (Grand Rapids: Eerdmans, 2002).

doctrine of sin—one which is not far from Paul's own mind, as can be seen from the fact that in Romans 5:1–11 "peace" is the resolution to the problem of our being "enemies."[7] But does this mix so easily with an honour/shame approach? The problem with our declaration of war is that it has incurred divine wrath, not that we are in a position of shame. As such, we are in need of a great deal more than something which "overcame the shame of 'our transgressions.'" It is clearly not that Jewett is a lilylivered liberal who doesn't like the idea of sin or wrath. This much is obvious from his statements on those themes. But what is striking is that Jewett's view of Paul's understanding of atonement is so underdeveloped: the solution in Jesus' death must surely correspond more closely to the plight.

This neglect of how the atonement deals with sin(s) and divine wrath is also seen in the marginalisation of the forgiveness achieved through Christ's death. The old-fashioned liberal/conservative debates about propitiation versus expiation are rightly eschewed here, but Jewett's solution is to abandon both ideas (286):

> In view of Paul's other statements about atonement, moreover, it seems unlikely that he shared an expiatory theory, which concentrates so exclusively on the matter of forgiveness, a matter of decidedly secondary interest in his theology. Propitiation also seems far from Paul's intent. The likely alternative is found in 2 Corinthians 5:19, 21, reiterated in Romans 5:10, where we find a distinctively Pauline formation of atonement as reconciliation: *hōs hoti theos ēn en Christōi kosmon katallassōn heautōi . . . ton mē gnonta hamartian huper hēmōn hamartian epoiēsen, hina hēmeis genōmetha dikaiosunē theou en autōi.* ("Because in Christ God was reconciling the world to himself . . . . For our sake he made him who knew no sin to be sin, in order that in him we might become the righteousness of God.")

But what is in the ". . ."? 2 Corinthians 5:19–21 is of course an excellent proof text for showing that Paul has no interest in propitiation, expiation or forgiveness—as long as you do not find out what is in the " . . . . " 2 Corinthians 5:19b, however, is precisely about forgiveness: *mē logizomenos autois ta paraptōmata autōn* ("not reckoning their sins to them").

[7] See also rightly Jewett on 3:21–26: 'The situation resolved by the death of Christ was the massive human assault on the righteousness of God, an assault that dominates the argument of Romans from 1:18 through 3:20 and is reiterated in 3:23." (286)

To return to Romans 4:25, Christ's death deals with sins, the consequence of which thus far in Romans has been divine wrath, not shame. And Christ's death is described here in Romans 4:25 in terms strongly reminiscent of Isaiah 53, as is virtually a scholarly consensus:[8] in my opinion at least, then, Christ is the servant who dies for our sins in the sense both of dealing with them and of bearing in himself the penalty for them.

LAW

Much of the current debate on the semantics of *nomos* in Romans revolves around whether Paul in particular instances refers to the Jewish Law or to *nomos* in the sense of "principle." Some maintain an exclusive or almost exclusive reference to Torah (Dunn, Wright); others point, for example, to Romans 8:2 as having to mean law in the sense of a "rule" or "principle." Jewett contributes an additional level of complexity to the debate by arguing that *nomos* often means "law", but not only Jewish Law—the term extends beyond these bounds to encompass Roman Law and indeed any cultural system of law qua means of acquisition of honour and avoidance of shame.

The principal evidence for this is the absence of the article in a number of cases, an argument made with varying degrees of force in the volume:

(On 3:20): "It is not just the Jewish law that is in view here, but also law as an identity marker for any culture." (266)

(On 3:21): "Since the anarthrous use of *nomos* here could extend its semantic field to every kind of law, it seems unlikely that Paul wishes to restrict the argument to Israel's law." (274, referring to a page in Zahn for support)

(On 3:31): "Of particular significance is that *nomos* ('law') is used both times in verse 31 without the article, which suggests that law in general may be in view . . . . Paul's claim is forthright: 'we uphold law,' whether it be Jewish or Roman." (303)

(On 5:20): "One should note that Paul does not employ the article with *nomos* ('law') in this verse, thus allowing the scope of his argument to extend to all law everywhere . . . Overlooking this detail, most commentators relate this verse only to the Jewish Torah." (387, and note 222)

So this is clearly an important aspect of the commentary. But oddly, Jewett appears to admit that this evidence—which by page 387

---

[8] Even the scholar who is, to my knowledge, most sceptical about the presence of Isaiah 53 in the New Testament concedes that the servant is alluded to in Romans 4:25. See M. D. Hooker, "Did the Use of Isaiah 53 to Interpret His Mission Begin with *Jesus*?," in W. H. Bellinger and W. R. Farmer, editors, *Jesus and the Suffering Servant: Isaiah 53 and Christian Origins* (Harrisburg: Trinity Press International, 1998), 88–103 (especially 101, 103).

has become a point which others are criticised for neglecting—is not so decisive.[9] He refers to Friedrich as having shown the article to be no proof of the meaning of *nomos* (297).[10] One could also add to this the various studies of *nomos* in other Jewish writings on this matter, which also show that the presence or absence of the definite article is inconclusive. For example, in his study of *nomos* in 1 and 2 Maccabees, B. Renaud has commented (on 1 Maccabees): "L'absence d'article (II 21, II 58, IV 42, X 14) n'indique aucune différence de sens appréciable: il suffit de comparer à cet égard le *zēlōsai zēlon nomou* du verset II 58 avec le *zēlōsate tōi nomōi* de II 50."[11] So the idea—which seems to be important for Jewett's overall case in the commentary—that *nomos* without the article extends its scope to Roman and other kinds of law, rests on a decidedly shaky foundation.

The problem is not only with Greek grammar but also with the comprehensibility of the discourse. We are left as a result with the meaning of *nomos* changing with vertiginous speed. For example, all the indications are that in Romans 3:19, Jewett takes *nomos* to refer to the Mosaic Law: the relevant page (264) is replete with references to Ezra and other Old Testament passages. In 3:20, however, there must then be a switch to the more general sense of "traditional systems of achieving honor and avoiding shame" (266). Oddly enough, this distinction between the presence and absence of the article only comes in in Romans 3—it has played no role in the exegesis of Romans 2, where Paul alternates between *nomos* and *ho nomos* just as freely.

JUSTIFICATION

Jewett's construal of Pauline justification is fully in line with his proposals about atonement and law already mentioned. In fact, however, he prefers not to speak of justification, but of righteousness (for *dikaiosunē*) and "setting right" (for forms of *dikaioō*).[12] Definitions or glosses are helpfully given at various junctures: "To be 'set right' in the context of the 'righteousness of God,' and with reference to humans who fall short of the 'glory of God,' is to have such glory and honor restored, not as an achievement, but as a gift" (280).[13] Or again, "I prefer the translation of *dikaiousthai* with 'to be

---

[9] "The debate over whether the distinction between a 'law of works' or a 'law of faith' is merely rhetorical and whether 'law' has the connotation of 'principle,' 'order of salvation,' or 'religious system' rather than 'Torah' cannot be resolved on the basis of of whether the article is used with *nomos*." (297)

[10] Romans 2:12, 13, 14, 15 show this point clearly enough.

[11] See e.g. B. Renaud, "La Loi et les Lois dans les Livres des Maccabées," *Revue biblique* 68 (1961), 39–67 (40).

[12] Cf. the translation "rectification" used by J. L. Martyn: see for example, *Theological Issues in the Letters of Paul* (Edinburgh: T. & T. Clark, 1998), *passim*.

[13] Cf. *dikaiosunē* as "the restoration of honor" (281).

set right' rather than 'to be justified,' in order to convey an association with honor and avoid a legalistic theory of salvation." (298)

One of the passages most important for filling out this content of justification is Romans 3:23–24. In verse 23, "the reference to falling short of 'the glory of God' also has a bearing on the issue of competition for honor" (280). The use of the verb *husterein* has to do with failure and resulting shame. But rather than honour and shame being relative terms among human beings, Paul affirms the shame of all people everywhere: "all fall short of the transcendent standard of honor" (280). In light of this, then, Jew and gentile alike are "set right" (*dikaioumenoi*) in the sense that honour is restored to them. One problem here is that *husterein* is taken intrinsically ("The basic connotation is . . . ") to be about "failures that place one in a position of deserving shame" (280). This does not seem to me to be a fair reading of the semantics of *husterein*, however. It is also far from clear (to me, at least) that "the glory of God" is a "standard," though this is more open to dispute. All lack the glory of God because, according to Romans 1, they have traded it in for something of their own invention.[14]

One further difficulty lies with the OT background that Jewett makes use of here. Septuagint (LXX) Psalm 30:1–2 appears to be important for his position:

> The theme of reversing shameful status that is implicit in all such passages where God takes the side of the lowly rather than the privileged is explicitly noted in LXX Psalm 30:1–2: "I have hoped in you, O Lord; let me never be put to shame (*mē kataischuntheiēn*); deliver me in your righteousness (*en tēi dikaiosunēi sou*). Incline your ear to me; make haste to rescue me." In view of this background, to be "set right freely by his grace" could be understood in terms of the restoration of honor. (281)

Certainly Psalm 30 is relevant in the grand scheme of things, but justification for Paul is connected principally with Habakkuk 2:4 and Genesis 15:6; it is these passages which should be our first port of call.

In sum, while justification has considerable implications for boasting, honour and shame, and the like, that is not to say that its content is determined by those categories. Jewett comments (on 4:3) that, "To be 'reckoned as righteousness' is to be accepted by the God of righteousness and therefore to be granted honor that overturns shameful status" (312).

---

[14] Does it make sense to say that "they changed the glory of the imperishable God into an idol" (148; cf. 160 note 116)? This would not seem to be possible! Jewett assumes that "exchange" must involve two pre-existing things, but it is quite compatible with their own invention being involved.

It is this "therefore," however, which I would question. Why is it so easy to glide from the first half of this sentence to—via a "therefore"—to the second?[15] If Jewett means that "reckoned as righteousness" means principally and basically "acceptance by God", but also functions at a subliminal level to subvert the audience's assumptions about honour and shame then perhaps we are not so far apart after all.

CONCLUSION

Jewett has offered in this monumental commentary an intellectually powerful and refreshingly creative contribution to Pauline studies. However, I am afraid that the interpretation of these central themes of atonement, Law and justification primarily within the matrix of honour and shame seems to me a distraction. I sincerely hope that I have not done the volume an injustice through a series of misunderstandings of it. In any case, I look forward to being "set right" by Professor Jewett, even if my honour will not necessarily be restored in the process.

---

[15] A brief note on the motif of "faith," which attracts some of Jewett's most sustained polemic. This is principally against those who take faith to be individualistic (146, 276, 289, etc.). The right interpretation of 1:17 "provides a contextual definition of *ho de dikaios* ('but the righteous one, the one put right') in terms of persons emplaced within faith communities. The individual believer in the modern sense was not in view by Paul, even though the formulation from Habakkuk encourages an individualistic construal for the modern hearer." (146) Again, in the context of Romans 3:21–26, it is a marker of universal participation in righteousness, is "the response of converts to the gospel," and "has a social function related to conversion and participation in a new community" (276–77). But because it is these things, it is surely also an individual act. Jewett has an admirable exegesis of Paul's description of Abraham's faith in Romans 4:18–21. And as he puts it on page 340, on Romans 4:23, "Abraham must remain a supreme example of faith's bounty." As such, I would suggest that faith is ineluctably the act—elicited by God, to be sure—of an individual just as much as it is the mark of the church collectively.

8

Response to Aberdeen Colleagues

Robert Jewett

I appreciate the chance to discuss Romans with colleagues who have contributed major studies to this letter. Your generosity in devoting time to this evaluation is particularly appreciated. It gives us a chance to clarify important interpretive issues, which would not occur if we agreed on everything. Since I have concentrated on the issues of honor and shame in this letter, I am led to say that there is no greater honor than to have one's work taken seriously enough to be criticized. As a mark of respect in this symposium, I refer to my colleagues with their titles, although I have called Francis by his first name for many years. I am particularly grateful to him for organizing this symposium.

I.

I would like to begin by discussing the issue of "multiculturalism," which Prof. Watson employs in the title of his critique. Although I employ this term once with reference to an article by John Barclay (page 301), nowhere do I advance it as an interpretive key because it has a meaning fundamentally different from Romans. Multiculturalism claims that all religions and cultures should be treated equally in the civil realm, particularly in the US where the term originated to express the premise in our Civil Religion that "all men are created equal." Moreover the advocacy of this concept entails a covert imperialistic bias regarding the superiority of multicultural societies, which manifested itself in the initial support of most American liberals for the occupation of Iraq. In contrast, Paul argues for equality between groups of believers who have different cultural and religious backgrounds, and his goal in the letter is to advance global evangelism to convert the rest of the world. Unlike the relativistic premise of "multiculturalism," Paul's approach rests on faith in Christ crucified and resurrected. The "holy kiss" of 16:16 is to be offered to fellow believers, neither to devotees of Mars or Jupiter, nor to zealous members of synagogues who have rejected the gospel. In this regard, I would agree with Prof. Watson that Paul advocates a "shared Christian identity" with boundaries against the outside world, although I would formulate this more broadly than his theory that the boundary only excludes those whose identity as Jews is based solely on the Torah. If "all Israel" and the Celt-Iberians in Spain are to be converted into Christ believers, this is far from multiculturalism. Moreover, I have carefully delineated tolerance in Romans as involving unconditional acceptance of fellow believers despite their differences with one's own group. This is grounded in Christ's welcome of sinners (15:7), which is far from the enlightenment definition of tolerance as bearing up with those whose views are wrong but whom it is not practical to coerce. Therefore, I feel that Prof. Watson's charge is unwarranted, that I advocate "an attitude of universal and undifferentiated inclusiveness," and seek to make Paul the "patron" of multiculturalism.

My rejection of multiculturalism as an interpretive resource for Romans is closely related to skepticism about the New Perspective. Nowhere in the commentary do I advocate the New Perspective. Despite its significant advances, I reject the limiting of ethnocentrism to Jewish members of the Greco-Roman world. Instead, I have become convinced that forms of competition for honor marked each cultural group in the ancient world. Both the "weak" and the "strong" in Rome are damning each other in equal measure, by contrasting critiques: the one "judges" the other as inadequately following the Jewish law, and the other holds in contempt those bound by that law. In claiming that "Romans does not display any particular concern with honor/dishonor," Dr. Gathercole overlooks these details in Romans 14–15, and does not mention the antidote to mutual dishonoring through mutual welcoming that Paul advocates in chapters 15–16. As Lendon observes, "When one man honoured another in the Roman world, he granted him a quantum of honour . . . ." Most especially I avoid the New Perspective language in dealing with the rhetorical effect of chapters 2–3, which create a despicable stereotype of a legalistic bigot who is brought by the diatribe to acknowledge his sin (3:5, 7). This serves Paul's purpose of showing that each group sins, and it has implications for congregational conflicts discussed in chapters 14–15, but it was not intended as a polemic against Judaism, as most interpreters have assumed.

II.

Both critiques find the honor/shame categories lacking in interpretive cogency, Prof. Watson because he thinks I rely on the theoretical foundations of Bruce Malina, and Dr. Gathercole because competition for shame is allegedly absent below the highest levels of Greco-Roman society. My case rests on responsible studies by social historians such as Donald Earl, Ulrich Knoche, J. Rufus Fears, Hans Drexler, J. E. Lendon and E. A. Judge and I follow in the steps of biblical interpreters such as Halvor Moxnes, Dieter Georgi, David A. DeSilva and Philip Esler. I make little use of Malina's theory of a Mediterranean system of honor and shame that allegedly reaches from ancient Rome to modern Sicily. The studies of the social system in the Greco-Roman world show that while the upper class viewed most people below them as dishonorable, those at the bottom competed just as fiercely for honor. On page 72, I observe that it "may seem strange that persons and groups lacking honor in the society at large would vie with one another for honor, but nothing was more natural. Dio Chrysostom was not surprised to witness "fellow slaves wrangling with one another over glory and precedence,"[1] and Valerius Maximus observed: "There is no baseness so great that it cannot be touched by the sweetness of prestige . . . . Glory drags along the obscure no less than the nobly born bound to her shining chariot."[2] Lendon observes that such competition was "nowhere more evident than in the case of the slave and freedman assistants of the emperor."[3]

One reason for overlooking the extent of competing for honor is that traditional studies of Romans such as Gathercole's excellent monograph, *Where is Boasting?* provide examples of Jewish boasting[4] but no reference to Roman boasting. The word "Rome" is not listed in the index, and there is no discussion of the Roman cultural situation to which Paul addresses himself in the letter. The book follows Dunn in denying that such boasting was "legalistic,"[5] interpreting Abraham's boast as a claim of "blamelessness"[6] but rejecting Dunn in insisting that Paul is interacting with "the Jewish expository tradition of an Abraham who was justified by his obedience."[7] The monograph faults the New Perspective for failing to recognize that David in 4:1–8 was without

---

[1] Robert Jewett, *Romans: A Commentary* (Hermeneia; Minneapolis: Fortress Press, 2006), 72.

[2] Jewett, *Romans*, 72.

[3] Jewett, *Romans*, 72.

[4] Simon J. Gathercole, *Where is Boasting?: Early Jewish Soteriology and Paul's Response in Romans 1-5* (Grand Rapids: Eerdmans, 2002) 235–42.

[5] Gathercole, *Where is Boasting?*, 232.

[6] Gathercole, *Where is Boasting?*, 240

[7] Gathercole, *Where is Boasting?*, 246

works.[8] It insists that 5:1–11 is targeted against "obedience to Torah" and that "the Jewish boast over against the gentiles must also fall to the ground."[9] So what about Gentile boasting against the Jews visible in 11:18–22, 14:1–15:6 and implicit in the *narratio* of 1:13–15 and the thesis of 1:16–17? I don't criticize Simon's analysis of the problem of Jewish boasting, but this is only half of the story, and to exclude the other half is to overlook the mutual damning between the house and tenement churches in Rome, while in the meanwhile keeping the door open for the traditional anti-Judaic interpretation of Paul.

III.

In my opinion, the preoccupation with the Torah that has dominated the interpretation of Romans since Luther's time leads to misinterpreting the congregational situation. Both colleagues appear to assume that the major problem in Rome is the law observance of the Jewish Christians, whereas I feel that when all the evidence is taken into account, both the weak and the strong are excluding each other in imperialistic ways. Prof. Watson's investigations in his influential study entitled *Paul, Judaism, and the Gentiles* as well as his article on "The Two Congregations in Rome" claim that since the weak were inclined to align themselves with the Jewish synagogues in Rome, Paul wishes to convert them into Paulinists who are free from the Torah. I feel that this disregards the admonition in 14:1 against trying to convert the weak as well as "other indications that Paul seeks coexistence between groups that retain their distinctive ethnic and theological integrity (14:4, 8, 10–12, 15–16, 19–23; 15:1–7). In contrast to 1 Corinthians 8 and 10, in Romans 14:1–15:13 Paul prohibits mutual conversion of others to the point of view held by one's own group." This one-sided reconstruction is reflected today in Prof. Watson's reference to the Jewish Christians seeking "continued membership of the Jewish community." This is not supported by any of the congregational details in the letter and seems highly improbable in view of the fact that in 41 and 49 C.E. there had been conflicts between Christian evangelists and synagogue members that were serious enough to come to governmental attention, in the latter instance, resulting in exile of those involved. After such fateful riots in the synagogues, how plausible is it that Christian believers would yearn to repeat the experience now that they have returned from exile?

An assessment of the congregational situation bears on the issue of the law, which Dr. Gathercole rightly observes is an inconsistent aspect of my commentary. This weakness makes it appear that the lack of the

---

[8] Gathercole, *Where is Boasting?*, 247
[9] Gathercole, *Where is Boasting?*, 261

article in a number of references is the only indication that Paul often has law in its various cultural embodiments in view. Actually, I made decisions about these translations in the light of the evidence in the whole letter, rather than on the basis of allegiance to a certain theology of the law that arose centuries after Paul dictated this letter. This evidence suggested to me that the weak and the strong were loyal to different forms of law, and the ethic of chapters 12–15 is formulated so as to encompass these differences. For instance, the rulings of governing authorities in 13:1–7 are to be followed, despite the fact that they do not derive from the Jewiṣh Torah. In 1:18–32, Gentiles are charged with violating their own laws. Are we to believe that there were no Romans laws against "murder, strife, treachery," referred to in 1:29, or that Paul is here accusing Gentiles of disobeying Jewish laws? What about 1:32, where Paul refers to "the righteous decree of God that those who practice such things deserve to die?" Are we prepared to refute Zahn and Dupont (note 306 on p. 190) who have documented instances in which *dikaiōma* and its Latin equivalent are employed both in Jewish and Greco-Roman jurisprudence in reference to condemnation for violations of law? If only violations of the Jewish Torah are in view here, are most interpreters wrong in perceiving that this pericope is directed primarily against Gentile sins?

In the light of this evidence, allow me to turn the translation question around. Can interpreters really feel justified in adding the article on those numerous instances where Paul has none, such as 3:31 and 13:10, thus shifting the entire meaning of sentences? In the former, Paul would be narrowing the issue down to the torah if one adds the article, "we establish THE law," whereas the context indicates both Jews and Gentiles are in view: "Is God a God of the Jews only? No, also of the Gentiles!" With regard to 13:10, my literal translation is as follows, taking the chiastic structure of the sentence into account: "The love does no harm to the neighbor; law's fulfillment is the love." In all of the standard translations, this is rendered as if the subject were law rather than love: "Love does no harm to the neighbor, the law is fulfilled by love." If the article indicates topicality as David Sansone has shown, can one really justify this violence to the text?

If the references to *nomos* shift "with vertiginous speed" as Dr. Gathercole charges with regard to my literal translations that supply the article only when it is in the Greek text, could this suggest that Paul was seeking to address a wide range of laws and cultural groups in his discussion? If we persist in overlooking the audience situation and continue seeking to create view of the Torah that is consistent with some modern theory, I see no alternative to accepting Heikki Räisänen's conclusion that Paul was simply stupidly inconsistent. I recognize the inadequacy of my treatment of the grammatical issue, despite having read all I could on the function of the article in Koine Greek, and I sincerely hope that a grammarian with no axe to grind will take up the question. But I'm not inclined to admit that this complicated issue should be decided purely on grammatical grounds, without taking the rhetoric and the audience of this letter into account.

IV.

One of the most important issues that arises in this dialogue concerns the relevance of honor and shame in understanding Paul's view of the atonement. In particular Dr. Gathercole refers repeatedly to this doctrine as a weakness in the commentary. I try to develop the idea that a revolutionary approach to honor and shame is conveyed in the cross and resurrection of Christ, and that this enables an account of the wording of Romans that is superior to traditional alternatives. Let me start with this embarrassing point: crucifixion was primarily a ceremony of shame, which Christian art has consistently suppressed by supplying a loincloth in depicting the crucified one. All four of the gospel accounts refer to shaming episodes including gambling for Jesus' clothes. Since most of the early believers were slaves and former slaves who could be crucified at the whim of their owners, and since Jesus was crucified in part because he shamed Israel by consorting with polluted persons and in part because he exposed the falsity of religion that aimed at earning public honor, it was clear that Jesus died this shameful death in behalf of the shamed. This death exposed the hostility of the human race against God while at the same revealing love to those who had not earned it, in fact, even to those who had made themselves into God's enemies.

We find these ideas in 5:8–11. This passage has nothing to do with forgiveness of the sins of human weakness, which have always stood at the center of traditional doctrines of the atonement. It deals instead with human enmity against God as revealed in Christ's death: "while we were enemies we were reconciled to God through the death of his Son." This is overcome by the public expression of divine love: "God demonstrates to us his own love in that while we were yet sinners 'Christ died on our behalf.'" In this verse Paul employs "the abusive term *hamartōlos* referring "to those whose behavior demonstrates that they are "radically sinful," belonging to a class of people who are the "opposite of the pious, righteous, and godly;" sinners engage in "social oppression," and stand in opposition to God." In the light of the earlier argument in Romans, this is not a matter of the sins of weakness, walking on the grass or eating a bit too much chocolate, but rather the suppression of the truth about

God and worshipping the creature rather than the creator as detailed in 1:18ff. If I could be permitted to employ Calvinist categories in Aberdeen, to be a sinner in this sense is to have participated willingly in the massive assault on the sovereignty of God that marked the human race since Adam's and Eve's fall. Moreover, I would add in the light of Romans, this is an assault for the sake of gaining precedence over others. Paul's concern is with overcoming this shameful status of "sinner" through divine love that accepts each person and group without qualification as demonstrated on the cross of Christ." It is precisely as enemies that we receive the love of God through the gospel of Christ crucified and resurrected. This makes reconciliation possible, a term used twice in Romans 5, but this massive assault against God in which the entire human race is involved must first be recognized and acknowledged, which is made possible by the gospel. Only then is forgiveness of our actual assaults on God and each other possible.

This is related to the new approach to Romans 7. I follow rhetorical studies by Stanley Stowers, Jean-Noël Aletti, and Jean-Baptiste Édart, which develop the Greek concept of *prosōpopoeia*, a "Speech-in-Character," a widely used method of argument in which a fictive character is given a voice to introduce important ideas. The hypothesis developed in my commentary is that Paul depicts himself as the person prior to his conversion, a zealous fanatic who obeyed the Jewish law perfectly but with such eagerness to achieve honor that he produced evil results. In Galatians 1:13–14 Paul had described this competitive zeal:

> For you have heard of my former life in Judaism, how I persecuted the church of God violently and tried to destroy it; and I advanced in Judaism beyond many of my own age among my people, so extremely zealous was I for the traditions of my fathers.

Here is someone whose religious motivation was to be more righteous than anyone else, a perfectly understandable trait when one takes seriously the obsession with honor in the entire ancient world. The resultant dilemma is described in Romans 7:19, "For I do not do the good I want, but the evil I do not want is what I do." The "good" that Paul as a persecutor of the early Christians sought to achieve was obedience to the Torah as a means of bringing in God's kingdom. He wanted to follow God's will, but discovered through the encounter with the resurrected Jesus that he had been resisting the divinely appointed messiah. What Paul describes in Romans 7 is not a failure to fulfill the law, including the command to fight against the godless, but rather the inability of such zealous legalism to achieve the good.

In the next verse of chapter 7, Paul identifies the underlying cause of this dilemma: "Now if I do what I do not want, it is no longer I that do it, but sin which dwells within me." In verse 7 he had explained that "if it had not been for the law, I should not have known sin. I should not have known what it is to covet if the law had not said, 'You shall not covet.'" Günther Bornkamm defined *epithymia* as "nomistic desire," as evident in connection with the term "flesh" in Galatians 5:16–17 and Romans 6:12; 13:14, which is associated with the fulfillment of the law in Galatians 3:3 and Philippians 3:3–7. That was a step in the right direction. But since "nomistic desire" involves a problematic understanding of subjectivity and individualism in Paul's thought, while containing an element of anti-Jewish prejudice that Paul did not share, I prefer to retain the context of the ten commandments that Paul cites here. It is not "desire" as such that is forbidden but desiring what belongs to another: "You shall not covet your neighbor's house . . . your neighbor's wife, or male or female slave, or ox, or donkey, or anything that belongs to your neighbor." (Exodus 20:17) The sin that Paul has in mind in his explanation is to desire for oneself what rightfully belongs to someone else, which fits the intensely competitive environment of the Greco-Roman and Jewish cultures in which each is led to gain precedence over others, which places losers in the position of dishonor. In this "speech-in-character," a sinful competition for honor is described that matches Paul's admission in Galatians 1:14, "I advanced in Judaism beyond many of my own age among my people, so extremely zealous was I for the traditions of my fathers." Competition for honor had promised him social prestige and divine approbation.

The shocking discovery on the road to Damascus was that such competition was proof of the power of sin at the very center of religious motivation. Paul discovered that his perfect obedience had been perverted by the desire for status acquisition. The obsession to gain honor, which deprives others of the honor that they should enjoy, had produced the tragic gulf between willing and achieving the good. It had perverted the holy into a means to gain precedence over others. Despite his obedience, Paul stood under wrath and didn't know it. He employs this "speech-in-character" to show the congregations in Rome that they were well along on this mistaken path in their competition with each other and that this imperialistic viewpoint must be transformed in order to participate with integrity in the mission to the so-called "barbarians" in Spain. By the conclusion of Paul's letter, it becomes clear that the Roman congregations have yet to incorporate the atonement in the form of reconciliation, and that they can do so by mutual welcome of each other into their love feasts.

Perhaps I will have an opportunity in one of our later discussions to show how Paul's use of the confession concerning Christ as the "mercy seat" in chapter 3 fits into this theory of atonement through reconciliation. My response has already taken too much time, and I am eager to hear your views and questions. With thanks again to my two colleagues, I would like to open this up to a wider discussion.

The Journal for the Study of the New Testament January 31, 2008

9

Is it Good News that God is Impartial? A Response to Robert Jewett, *Romans: A Commentary*[1]

John M. G. Barclay

The publication of a major new commentary on Romans is an event in New Testament scholarship, and "major" is the word here in more senses than one. Not only is this commentary on a phenomenal scale (over 1000 double-columned pages of text), the culmination of 25 years of research and reflection. It also offers a significantly fresh reading of the fullest statement of Paul's gospel, and thus constitutes a new trajectory in the interpretation of Pauline theology. In a heavily overcrowded field, Jewett has skillfully selected representative scholarship (both German and English) with which to interact, keeping his argument from entanglement in the innumerable thickets of exegetical opinion. He offers a new and sometimes provocative translation, with extensive notes on each textual variant, and provides an original structural analysis of each section of text, paying unusual attention to its rhetorical features. In the exegesis itself, philological discussion of key Greek terms is illuminated by choice comparative samples, cited in full. Jewett's writing style is admirably clear, with sufficient repetition of critical points to keep alive a clear line of interpretation throughout this enormous volume. The discussion of Pauline theology is conducted with a passion one associates with Ernst Käsemann, whose lectures on Romans Jewett heard in Tübingen; and it is Käsemann and Dunn who form the principal dialogue partners throughout. In short, this is more than just

[1] First published in *Journal for the Study of the New Testament* [hereafter *JSNT*] 31.1 (2008), 89–111.

an impressive piece of scholarship. It offers a strong and novel reading of one of the most important documents in the Christian tradition and in Western cultural history. Jewett is to be roundly applauded not only for his sheer doggedness in bringing this task to completion (no mean feat in itself), but for the intellectual energy and creativity with which he has entered into dialogue with Paul.

Beyond these general and highly estimable qualities, the principal contribution of this commentary to Romans scholarship lies in two spheres: 1) in its novel thesis regarding the original context and purpose of the letter, as a missive addressed to very particular conflicts among the Roman Christians, laying the practical and ideological foundation for Paul's forthcoming Spanish mission; and 2) its fresh articulation of the subject-matter of Romans, as an announcement of the impartial grace of God which outlaws every competitive quest for honor, whether Jewish or Gentile. The strength and fascination of this commentary lies in the close correlations it creates between the message of the letter and its specific purposes in Rome. According to Jewett, Romans is intended to elicit support for a mission to the "barbarians" in Spain, which would only be credible if the churches in Rome ceased their imperialistic competition with one another under the premise that the gospel of impartial grace shatters all claims of superior status or theology. (xv)[2]

I shall argue that there are weaknesses in both parts of Jewett's thesis—both its historical reconstruction and its theological re-expression of Paul's gospel—but my disagreements are accompanied by the profoundest respect for an intellectual achievement of rare significance.

I. The Historical Context of the Letter

Amid the continuing controversy concerning "the reasons for Romans," Jewett offers a striking version of the "Rome-specific" hypothesis, elements of which he develops in a wholly original direction. As he notes (2–3), in most commentaries the historical context of the addressees in Rome is discussed in the introduction but has little influence on the exegesis of the letter. By contrast, Jewett invests enormously in the situational character of the letter and boldly claims that "the key question in interpreting Paul's letter is . . . how it would have sounded to its intended hearers, and what kind of participation would

[2] Cf. the opening statement in the introduction: "The basic idea in the interpretation of each verse and paragraph is that Paul wishes to gain support for a mission to the barbarians in Spain, which requires that the gospel of impartial, divine righteousness revealed in Christ be clarified to rid it of prejudicial elements that are currently dividing the congregations in Rome" (1). All citations from the commentary are given by page number only.

it have evoked [sic]" (40). He is well aware that any reconstruction of the Roman context is built on hypothesis and conjecture, and therefore "subject to refutation" (2, 59). In such matters, of course, the higher the investment in conjectural reconstruction, the greater the risk, and two key elements of Jewett's contextualization appear to me particularly vulnerable.[3]

A. THE PRIOR HISTORY OF THE ROMAN CONGREGATIONS

Jewett follows the majority view that the disputes in the Roman churches depicted in Romans 14–15 concern Jewish laws regarding food and Sabbath, and that the ethnic mixture of Jews and non-Jews which one can deduce from the final greetings is related to those disputes (cf. 11:3–24). But the letter indicates nothing about the historical roots of these divisions, and to fill this historical gap Jewett both follows and supplements a consensus narrative, with important implications for his reading of the letter (18–20, 59–61). In brief, this consensus (the "Wiefel hypothesis") maintains that the Christian movement in Rome began in the Jewish synagogues, and that it caused controversy there during the 40s, climaxing in the expulsion of Jewish-Christians (or at least their leaders) in 49 C.E. on the order of Claudius. During their absence, the Christian movement in Rome became largely separate from the synagogues and developed mostly Gentile-Christian leadership, so that, when the Jewish-Christians returned (on Claudius' death, 54 C.E.), there arose internal tension within the Christian communities.[4] On closer inspection, the foundations of this historical tale turn out to be extremely precarious. Thus:

1. our evidence for the history of Jews in Rome in the 40s is limited to a small number of passing comments by Dio Cassius, Suetonius, Luke, and Orosius. These were all written in hindsight, some from a very great distance, and they are not easily aligned with one another.[5]

[3] I pass over here his questionable conclusions from the greetings in Romans 16 regarding two kinds of social configuration in the Roman congregations—house churches (as in 16:3) and tenement congregations (as in 16:10–15). Jewett's important work on the latter, both in Thessalonica and Rome, could have been matched by greater scepticism towards the Meeks-Theissen consensus regarding the "love-patriarchalism" of house-churches under "patrons" such as Phoebe or Prisca and Aquila. Although the range of his reading has been vast, Jewett appears to have missed J. J. Meggitt, *Paul, Poverty and Survival* (Edinburgh: T. & T. Clark, 1998) and the fresh work on this topic by S. J. Friesen, "Poverty in Pauline Studies: Beyond the So-Called New Consensus," *JSNT* 26 (2004), 323–61.

[4] See W. Wiefel, "The Jewish Community in Ancient Rome and the Origins of Roman Christianity" in edited by K. P. Donfried, *The Romans Debate* (Revised Edition; Peabody: Hendrickson, 1991), 95–101. In its main outlines, the hypothesis has been very widely adopted, in both commentaries (e.g. by Dunn) and monographs (for example, J. C. Walters, *Ethnic Issues in Paul's Letter to the Romans: Changing Self-Definitions in Earliest Roman Christianity* (Valley Forge: Trinity Press International, 1993). The key identification of Suetonius' *impulsore Chresto* with Jewish-Christian controversy and expulsion from Roman synagogues is strongly supported by F. Watson, *Paul, Judaism and the Gentiles* (Revised and Expanded Edition; Grand Rapids: Eerdmans, 2007), 167–74.

[5] For discussion and an attempt at alignment, see my *Jews in the Mediterranean Diaspora from Alexander to Trajan (323* B.C.E.*–117* C.E.*)* (Edinburgh: T. & T. Clark, 1996), 303–6.

2. Dio Cassius' evidence (60.6.6) suggests some sort of clamp-down on synagogue meetings in 41 C.E., but there is no hint that this had anything to do with Christianity; it is of a piece with Claudius' suppression of meetings in clubs and taverns.[6]

3. Suetonius' famous remark on the expulsion of Jews in 49 C.E. "since they were constantly rioting *impulsore Chresto*" (*Claudius* 25.4) is regularly used as evidence for internal synagogue disputes regarding Christianity. But Chrestus is an extremely common name in Rome, and Suetonius knows who Christians are and calls them *Christianoi* (*Nero* 16.2). To find here a garbled memory of disputes concerning Christianity is to build an historical edifice on the correction of a supposed Suetonian error. Only if we had strong independent evidence should we have the confidence to do that.[7] There were perfectly good reasons for Claudius to want to expel (token) Jews as an alien cult, and the charge of "rioting" was easily concocted. Even if it was justified, there is no reason to find Christians among the "rioters".

4. Orosius (7.6.15–16) *may* have independent sources for his dating of the expulsion of Jews (in 49 C.E.), but in copying Suetonius he changes "Chrestus" to "Christus". His discovery of a reference to Christianity reflects his tendency to Christianize Jewish history (he also thought Helena of Adiabene was a Christian, 7.6.12) and we should hesitate to follow suit.

5. Luke places Aquila and Priscilla in Corinth as a result of Claudius' expulsion of "all the Jews" from Rome (Acts 18:2). Despite the evident exaggeration, this is valuable evidence for the date of the expulsion, but Luke does not indicate that the couple were Christians before they left Rome (contrast Acts 19:1)—Paul would lodge with them as fellow Jewish artisans—or that their expulsion had anything to do with the Christian message.

6. Romans 16:3–5 places the couple back in Rome by the time Paul wrote the letter (according to Jewett, 56–57 C.E.), but we do not know

---

[6] See E. Gruen, *Diaspora. Jews amidst Greeks and Romans* (Cambridge: Harvard University Press, 2002), 36–38. Dio Cassius does not say that the Jews were disorderly, only that Claudius shrank from expelling them (as Tiberius had in 19 C.E.) as that would cause disorder. There is no reason to find here evidence for disorderly conduct in Roman synagogues (*pace* Jewett, 18), still less disorder caused by Christian preaching. Jewett (58) unwisely follows Hengel in using Augustine's citation of Porphyry (in *Ep.* 102.8) as evidence that Christianity arrived in Rome at about the time of Gaius (37–41 C.E.). Porphyry is talking about the arrival of the *lex Judaeorum*, not about Christianity, and it is likely that, from some historical distance, he thought this was the date when Judaism first took root in Rome.

[7] Jewett knows Slingerland's full refutation of the Chrestus-Christianity connection (H. D. Slingerland, *Claudian Policymaking and the Early Imperial Repression of Judaism at Rome* [Atlanta: Scholars Press, 1997), but still follows the hobbled consensus; for an independent and properly sceptical voice, see Gruen, *Diaspora*, 39: "The ubiquity of the name [Chrestus] makes the association with Christianity an uphill battle, best given up." For the later evidence of confusion between Christus and Chrestus, see Watson, *Paul, Judaism and the Gentiles*, 168–69; but Suetonius' knowledge of the title *Christianoi* indicates that he did not share this common mistake.

how soon they returned there after the expulsion of 49 C.E. There is no reason to think that all the expellees waited till Claudius' death: in an age without passports and border controls, individuals with no public profile could easily return to crowded quarters of Rome after expulsion.

7. There is no evidence, either internal or external, that the expulsion of some Jews from Rome in 49 C.E., or their subsequent return, had any effect on the development of the Christian churches in the city: Paul gives no hint of history any changes in leadership, in the ethnic composition of the communities, or in relations with synagogues.[8]

We must conclude that the Wiefel hypothesis is a tissue of speculation, based on flimsy evidence and ungrounded supposition. It is best abandoned by New Testament scholars, who are generally over-eager to fill the yawning gaps in our knowledge of earliest Christian history; one is reminded of Käsemann's self-mocking remark on the claims of New Testament scholars "to hear the grass grow and the bedbugs cough." Jewett makes constant use of this shaky hypothesis in his exegesis of the letter.[9] He appeals to the synagogue conflicts and the subsequent expulsion to explain how easily the Romans would accept the depiction of the arrogant Jew in 2:17 (223), to give substance to the "sufferings" and "endurance" mentioned in 5:3 and 8:17 (353, 502; cf. 250 on 3:8), to suggest that Paul defends the "weak" (expelled Jewish Christians) against the supposition that persecution signals divine disfavor (8:35 [546]), to explain Paul's emphasis on sharing needs (12:13 [764–65]), and to suggest why Roman Christians would see through Rome's claims to guarantee the benign rule of law (790). All of this is hugely attractive in adding local color to the apparent generalities of the letter, but its historical basis is, in my view, too insecure to contribute substantially to the interpretation of the letter.[10]

---

[8] Jewett (59) suggests that the expulsion explains why Paul knows so many church leaders (mentioned in Romans 16) and why he urges them to be greeted and welcomed by all the Roman congregations. I see no reference to this history in the chapter, no reason why Paul should remain silent on expulsions and returns, and no reason to interpret his knowledge of these individuals or his exhortations in this particular way.

[9] Cf. his use of a similarly tenuous historical reconstruction in his interpretation of 1 and 2 Thessalonians: *The Thessalonian Correspondence: Pauline Rhetoric and Millenarian Piety* (Philadelphia: Fortress Press, 1996).

[10] Jewett wishes to imagine at each point how the "intended hearers" would react to Paul's letter (40). Thus he often remarks on how the Romans would appreciate, chuckle, smile, applaud or otherwise recognise the persuasiveness of what Paul writes (e.g., 191, 221, 687); and in general he considers Paul's rhetoric "stunning" (143), "brilliant" (198) and "wonderful" (250). But any well-written text is convincing to its *implied* readers, and if Paul is taken to be writing to a complex multicultural audience, it is nearly always possible to find some element of the text that addresses his *intended* audience to some degree. Jewett's reading of the success of the letter cannot, then, confirm his historical reconstruction of the audience, though it teaches us much about the ideal reaction of the implied reader.

B. PHOEBE AND THE SPANISH MISSION

The most important of Jewett's historical hypotheses is his suggestion that the whole letter was designed specifically to "prepare the ground for the complicated project of the Spanish mission" (79), an hypothesis he first proposed some 20 years ago. Paul's remarks about his desire to move on to Spain (15:24, 28) and to be 'sent there with your help" (15:25) have long been noted as factors in his writing of this letter, but no-one else has given this purpose such prominence or related it so thoroughly to the contents of the letter. We may examine three features in particular:

1. Jewett's extensive research on social and political conditions in Spain leads him to conclude that Paul's prospective mission there would have been unusually difficult (74–79). There were probably no Jewish communities in Spain at this time, and thus no pre-established networks which Paul could use in establishing his mission. Additionally, there was very little Greek spoken in Spain: Latin was used in large urban centers, and the majority of the population used Celtic-Iberian and other languages. In either case, there were large linguistic barriers to which Paul was unaccustomed. Jewett suggests that Paul needed the assistance of Christians in Rome who had contacts in Spain; he required their resources for the translation of his message and their connections to Roman patrons with influence in the Spanish provinces. It is helpful to be made to think in concrete terms about what Paul's mission in Spain might entail, but I find a number of presuppositions here questionable. Do we know that Paul elsewhere relied on Jewish networks and would be incapacitated without the presence of local Jews? As a traveling artisan, he had learned to make his way in many different cities, and as an "apostle to the Gentiles", it is hard to imagine that he had *always* depended on local synagogue contacts (however Acts may portray matters). There were pockets of Greek-speakers in Spain, as Jewett admits (76, 77), and since Paul seemed content to have "completed the gospel of Christ" in eastern provinces on the basis of very limited contact with their populations (Romans 5:19), would he have been overly concerned about being able to address only "the small remnants of Greek-speaking population" (79)? The suggested need for "patronage with connections to leading senatorial families in Rome as well as Spain" (79) suggests a portrait of mission rather alien to a figure who had learned "to be abased and to abound" (Philippians 4:12), and who had little time for those thought special in the eyes of the world (1 Corinthians 1:18–31).

2. Crucial to the prospects of the Spanish mission, in Jewett's eyes, is Phoebe, who is recommended to the Romans in 16:1–2. Jewett takes Paul's description of her to indicate a "wealthy" and "upperclass" woman (89–90) of "high social standing" (947). Her role is to be patron

of the Spanish mission, preparing the ground for Paul's acceptance in Rome and using her social connections to provide resources. This role, Jewett argues, is clearly hinted at in the reference to the "matter" (*pragma*) in which the Romans are to assist her (16:2). Since she cannot need financial support, this must mean helping her obtain and utilize contacts in the Roman capital.[11] One could quibble with Jewett's assessment of Phoebe's wealth and status, but, more importantly, his construal of Romans 16:2 cannot be sustained. Paul urges the Romans to welcome Phoebe in the Lord in a manner worthy of the saints *kai parastēte autē en hōi an hymōn chrēzē pragmati*. The indefiniteness of this request is typical of recommendation letters, and I cannot see how Jewett can (uniquely) translate this as "provide her whatever she might need from you in the matter" (941). The noun *pragma* has no definite article, and the form of the clause (*hos an* + subjunctive) is a standard way of expressing an indefinite; we may compare Matthew 10:11: *eis hēn d an polin ē kōmēn eiselthēte* ("into whatever town or village you enter.")[12] The clause must surely be translated "provide her (or, help her in) whatever matter she needs from you" and, once translated thus, reference to *the* matter, and thus to the specific and definite matter of the Spanish mission, disappears. In other words, the Phoebe element of this hypothesis melts away once this crucial clause is properly construed.

3. Jewett understands the *whole* letter to be relevant to the Spanish mission not only in gaining for Paul the personal support of the Roman churches, and not only in ensuring a unified social base, but also in inculcating the right attitude in the minds of the Roman Christians. Paul's early reference to his obligation to "both Greeks and barbarians" (Romans 1:14) constitutes a rebuke to chauvinist attitudes towards "barbarians" in Spain and, taken as a whole, the letter insists

> that the impartial righteousness of God does not discriminate against "barbarians" such as the Spaniards, that all claims of cultural superiority are false, that imperial propaganda must be recognized as bogus, and that the domineering behavior of congregations toward one another must be overcome if the missional hope

---

11 "I infer that Phoebe had agreed to underwrite a project of vital significance to Paul and to the letter he is writing. The Roman recipients of the letter would understand her to be recommended as the patroness of the Spanish mission, which Paul had announced in the preceding chapter . . . . Her patronage would involve gaining the cooperation of the Roman house churches in creating the logistical base and arranging for the translators that would be required for the Spanish mission. This means that the persons being greeted in the subsequent pericope would understand that they are being recruited as advisers and supporters of Paul's and Phoebe's 'matter.'" (947–48)

12 Elsewhere in Romans, see Romans 9:15: *eleēsō hon an eleō*; cf. 10:13. Where a noun is associated with the indefinite *hos an* it remains indefinite; besides Matthew 10:11, cf. Luke 9:4; 10:5, 8, 10.

> to unify the world in the praise of God is to be fulfilled (15:9–13). (79)

Jewett thus repeatedly connects the Spanish mission to the letter's themes of divine impartiality and grace, or human boasting and competition (for examples, 143 on 1:17; 197 on 2:1–16; 246 on 3:4; 267 on 3:20; and see "spanish mission" in the index of subjects). I am sceptical. If attitudes to "barbarians" were so important, it is odd that Paul should use this label only once, and then without reference to Spain. It is not until 15:24–25 that the all-important Spanish mission is finally mentioned; everything up to this point is a matter of allusion. Jewett recognizes that the letter is oblique: "the references to Spain are intentionally vague because the complication of the Spanish cultural situation required delicate negotiations that Phoebe could do only in person" (89). I suspect that this will strain the credulity of most readers, suspicious of so large a gap between the surface and the intentions of the text; and without the support of 16:1–2, the whole thesis looks alarmingly weak.

There is no doubt that Jewett's contextual hypothesis is immensely attractive in many respects: it is grounded in excellent research on Spain, it fills gaps in our knowledge, and it has Paul purveying a message critical of "domineering behavior" which we can heartily endorse. But it seems to me too tenuous to count as other than speculation. Such demand for historical specificity regarding the origins and original purpose of the text constitutes a modern, Western preoccupation, whose grip on biblical studies has not always been productive. Despite the fascination inherent in the claim for so close a match between content and occasion, Jewett's reading of the message of Romans could stand even if its suggested context dissolves. In other words, fortunately we can do without Phoebe and the logistical problems of the Spanish mission, and still learn plenty from Jewett on the subject of Paul's gospel.[13]

II. THE THEOLOGY OF ROMANS

In one of his summaries of the message of Romans, Jewett writes:

> Paul attacked perverse systems of honor by dispelling the idea that some persons and groups are inherently righteous and by proclaiming the message that God honors sinners of every culture in an impartial manner through Christ. Paul's indebtedness to "Greeks and bar-

[13] Jewett's proper insistence that Paul's purpose is more "missional" than "doctrinal" (722) depends on the grounding of Pauline theology in mission (in Romans as elsewhere), not on a specific hypothesis regarding the Spanish mission.

> barians, educated and uneducated" (1:14), led him to proclaim the boundless mercy of the one God of all peoples (3:29–30; 15:9–13), who alone is capable of evoking reconciliation and harmony in a world torn by exploitation and conflict (5:10–11; 15:5–6). This is why Romans 9–11 is crucial for the Spanish mission, because God does not abandon people even when they reject impartial righteousness (10:2–3), and in the end Paul's gospel proclaims that the Spaniards who are treated as shameful barbarians will stand alongside the Jews and every other nation in the recognition that "God has consigned all peoples in disobedience that he might have mercy on all" (11:32). The climax of the letter is reached in the exhortation concerning mutual welcome between previously competitive groups (15:7; 16:3–16, 21–23) and the holy kiss that honors ethnic diversity within the new family of God (16:16). (88)

Several themes characteristic of the commentary emerge here: the unified message of the letter (from chapter 1 to chapter 16) and its close connection to the preparation of the Spanish mission; the universal reach of the gospel; "honor" as the central component of salvation; the overcoming of conflict on a local and world-wide scale; the climax of the letter in its final chapters (14–16); and the "impartiality" of God's righteousness, as revealed in Christ.

Three traditions in the interpretation of Paul are here combined in a new and powerful mix, a radical Protestant Paulinism, the "new perspective" on Paul, and anthropological analysis of the "Mediterranean world." From the *Protestant tradition*, mediated through Barth and Käsemann, Jewett has acquired the expectation that Paul's theology is radically counter-cultural, together with a strong interest in its social and political dimensions and a powerful critique of the church in its failure to embody a theology of the cross.[14] Although he repeatedly criticizes the European tradition, including Käsemann, for treating Paul's theology in an "abstract" or "reifying" manner (46; 692 note 265), for turning the irenic Paul into a polemicist (125, 278), and for imposing later doctrine on a first-century document (278), powerful Protestant currents run through this commentary. References to "legalistic willpower" (e.g., 582–83) and pride in "human achievement" (609) clearly indicate

[14] In the preface, Jewett notes the formative influence of Barth and Käsemann (through the latter's lectures on Romans): "their passionate advocacy of Paul's critique of widely accepted cultural values continues to guide my work" (xv). On 10:13 he writes, "To "call on the name" of this Lord (Romans 10:13) is to abandon any prior claim of honor and to take one's place alongside the dishonored savior and his disheveled flock" (632). This is vintage Käsemann, and none the worse for that.

Jewett's debt to this tradition, though he places these themes now in a social (rather than an individualistic) context, under the influence of the "*new perspective*." In frequent dialogue with Dunn, Jewett stresses the ethnic dimensions of the text and the overcoming of distinctions and divisions between Jews and Gentiles. But he presses beyond Dunn, both in universalizing the themes of the "new perspective", and in prioritizing the thematic of honor and shame. The universalizing move is founded on the thesis that when Paul discusses "law" and "works of the law" the issue addressed is not just the ethnic exclusionism entailed by Judaism's boundaries, but the use of <u>any</u> law or religious/ethnic system to establish superiority of status.[15] Indeed, Jewett shifts the emphasis from "boundaries" to "competition for honor", since "Dunn does not link these insights with the systems of gaining honor and shame in the Mediterranean world, which linkage would allow a broader grasp of Paul's argument" (266).

Here is evident the third source of influence, from recent *anthropological research* on ancient ideologies of honor and shame, both by New Testament scholars in comment on the "Mediterranean world" (e.g., Malina and Esler), and by classicists in studies of the Roman passion for honor.[16] The specifically Roman dimensions of this honor-culture are explored in a section of the introduction on "The Pyramid of Honor" (49–51), and strong claims are frequently made about the influence on the Roman congregations of their Roman environment.[17] But it is important for Jewett that the basic phenomenon—competition for honor through claims of superiority in cultural, religious, or ethnic status—was ubiquitous in the ancient world. "God's granting of righteousness through faith in the crucified Christ counters the seemingly universal tendency to claim honor on the basis of performance or social status" (298, on 3:28); Jewish "boasting" is simply the Jewish expression of

---

[15] See, e.g., 274 on 3:21: "since the anarthrous use of *nomos* here could extend its semantic field to every kind of law, it seems unlikely that Paul wishes to restrict the argument to Israel's law . . . . It is essential . . . to universalize the scope of Dunn's summary: 'Without the law' then means outside the national and religious parameters set by the law, without reference to the normal Jewish hallmarks." The global and political dimensions of this widened scope are influenced by Bishop Colenso's commentary on Romans (1861), with its bitter condemnation of British colonial "mission"; indeed, Jewett's commentary is dedicated to the memory of Colenso.

[16] Jewett refers specifically and often to the study by J. E. Lendon, *Empire of Honor. The Art of Government in the Roman World* (Oxford: Clarendon Press, 1997). He might have noted also the brilliant recent work by C. A. Barton, *Roman Honor: The Fire in the Bones* (Berkeley: University of California Press, 2001).

[17] "Those who read this pericope [Romans 11:11–24] as unproblematic discourse have forgotten that its audience was in Rome, where power politics, alliances, and lethal competition had for centuries been the most engaging aspects of life and conversation" (675). Other echoes of, or contrasts with, the Roman spirit, and especially Roman imperial propaganda, are found in Paul's statements on grace/benevolence (115), gospel (138–39), faith/*fides* (140), victory (549), the Lordship of Jesus (632), etc. Romans 13:1–7 is read with very precise reference to the Roman context.

"the hyper-competitive environment of the Greco-Roman world" (282). Paul's denial of righteousness through works of the law (3:20) is directed against *any* "human system of competing for glory and honor" (266), and "pertains as much to Greeks as to Jews" (267). The climactic instructions in 14:1–15:7 concern the Roman Christians' "fierce competitions with one another for superior honor" (72), whose "imperialistic" behavior matches the "imperial exploitation" practiced by Rome in Spain (88).

This emphasis on honor and competition both universalizes the message of the letter in its ancient context and focuses its critique on social (not individualistic) attitudes. It offers to unify the letter from start to finish, while using terms and categories with broad contemporary resonance. For all these reasons, this is a hugely attractive reading of Romans, offering a fresh interpretation of Pauline theology in general. Nonetheless, I find three features of this reading problematic, and will spend the rest of this review teasing out where the problems appear to lie.

A. GENERALIZING PAUL'S DIALOGUE WITH ISRAEL

As we have noted, Jewett reads the discussion in Romans of Israel and "the law" as part of Paul's broader critique of ancient systems of honor and competition. This generalizing move might appear to be warranted by the extraordinary ways in which Paul levels the condition of Jews and Gentiles in this letter: they are *equally* "under sin" (3:9), *all* fall short of the glory of God (3:23), and the power of sin, more than matched by the mercy of God, encompasses *the whole* of humanity (5:12–21; 11:32). There are moments when Paul seems to speak very specifically of "works of the law" (3:20) and moments when "works" are unspecified and arguably refer to any human performance (4:4–5; 9:32; 11:6); even the word *nomos* is used in notoriously confusing ways. One may also find statements in other letters which parallel the critique of Israel in Romans, but put the identical themes in broader terms (e.g., the banishment of boasting in 1 Corinthians 1:18–31). On such grounds, the themes of the letter to the Romans have often been generalized and universalized in the history of interpretation, starting from Ephesians (2:8–10), and continuing (in different ways) through the Valentinians, Chrysostom, Augustine, and the Reformation tradition. In all such readings, "Israel" or "the Jew" becomes an allegorical figure, standing variously for the unspiritual, the fleshly, the pious, the religious man, and so on. Where the "new perspective" has insisted on the specificity of Paul's engagement with Judaism, Jewett's reading reactivates this generalizing tradition, with a new twist: Paul's target is the scramble for honor and status, as practised by Jews and others.

I find this move problematic on both exegetical and theological grounds. We may scrutinize just two examples:

1. At 3:27, after outlining the grace-event of God in Christ, Paul asks: *pou oun ē kauchēsis*; and answers with a resounding *exekleisthē* (Jewett translates: "Where then is our boasting? It is excluded"). As Jewett notes, the Lutheran-existentialist tradition takes this boast as Jewish but also "characteristic of religious persons everywhere, who rely on their own piety and virtue for salvation" (296; he refers to Bultmann, Bornkamm, and Käsemann), while the "new perspective" refers to Jewish pride in ethnic privilege. But, calling attention to Rome as "the boasting champion of the ancient world" (295) and to the pervasive phenomenon of self-glorying in the Graeco-Roman world, Jewett insists that the "broader social context" must be taken into account:

> The form of the interlocutor's question is basic and cannot be restricted to a particular group within the ancient world. The preceding argument about salvation by grace alone renders all boasting problematic. I therefore take the earlier references to Jewish boasting in 2:17 and 23 as illustrating a universal phenomenon in Paul's social environment; while the references to "works" and "doing the law" (3:27) clearly imply that if Jewish boasting is illegitimate, so is Gentile boasting. By its very nature, honor granted through grace alone eliminates the basis of all human boasting. (296)

Jewett's language here reveals how much interpretative work he has to do: several statements take the form of theological axioms ("by its very nature . . . "), matters are "clearly implied" (not stated), and earlier statements in chapter 2 have to be "taken" to illustrate something else. We may grant that the question Paul poses is simple (and in that sense "basic"), but not that it is "basic" to the human condition and applied here to every human group.[18] The only boasting mentioned thus far was associated very explicitly with "the Jew" (2:17–24). Paul could have focused his critique of the world on some ubiquitous tendency to vainglory and competition, but he does not do so in Romans.[19] In fact, if honor was his chief target, he misled the Romans outrageously by declaring in 2:7 that "to those who by perseverance in good work are seeking glory and honor and incorruptibility, [he will recompense]

[18] As Watson and others have noted (*Paul, Judaism and the Gentiles*, 247), the Greek in fact has no "our" (*pace* Jewett's translation) but reads simply *pou oun ē kauchēsis*; But the definite article indicates a specific phenomenon, and signals back to the previous discussion of this theme in 2:17, 23.

[19] One could point to broader discussions of "boasting" in 1 Corinthians 1:26–31; 4:1–8; 2 Corinthians 10:12–18; 11:16–12:10 (see Watson, *Paul, Judaism and the Gentiles*, 246–52). But the argument of Romans has its own specificity regarding the Jewish people, and is not a summary of Paul's entire theology concerning "boasting." Jewett's generalisation of the themes of Romans oddly washes out the theological specificity of the letter while emphasizing its historical and contextual particularity.

eternal life."[20] The only example of Gentile boasting in Romans is that of Gentile *Christians* who have a specific reason to think that they have been preferred over non-believing Jews (11:18). It is only by conflating the universal problem of 'sin" (3:23) with a supposedly common propensity to "boast" that Jewett can generalize Paul's critique at 3:27.

2. At crucial points Jewett takes Paul's references to *nomos* to refer not just to the Mosaic Torah but to law or legal achievement in any culture. Discussing (but dismissing) the possible translation "principle" (at 3:27), Jewett acknowledges that the reference cannot be decided by the presence or absence of the article: "As Friedrich has shown, there are places where Paul uses *nomos* both with and without the article in a single sentence (Romans 2:14, 23, 27; 3:21) and many instances in the LXX and Romans in which *nomos* without the article clearly refers to the Torah" (297). It is therefore surprising that at other points Jewett makes much of the fact that *nomos* appears without the article (e.g., 274 on 3:21; 303 on 3:31; 383 on 5:20; 446 on 7:7; 450 on 7:8), claiming justification from the anarthrous use for "broadening Paul's claim to include every form of law" (450). Thus at 3:21 (one of the passages noted by Friedrich), Jewett declares that 'since the anarthrous use of *nomos* here could extend its semantic field to every kind of law, it seems unlikely that Paul wishes to restrict the argument to Israel's law" (274). But I find no interest by Paul in "law as an identity marker for any culture" (266); for him, the Gentiles are by definition "without the law" (Romans 2:12; 1 Corinthians 9:21). Indeed, this generalized statement about law and "culture" looks suspiciously like a modern anthropological observation read back into Paul.

I would argue, by contrast, that there is something irreducibly specific in Paul's discussion of Israel's privileges and Israel's law, since for him the story of divine grace runs through the history of Israel, and in or around the law of Moses, as highly particular expressions of divine gift (Romans 9:1–5). If unbelieving Israel is now found to be, in crucial respects, on a level with Gentiles (in sin and disobedience to the righteousness of God), this does not mean that Israel's story simply

---

[20] Jewett's translation (spelling changed). Jewett admits that this plays into the hands of the competitive Roman churches, in showing "no hint of disapprobation" here (205). But, according to Jewett, the subsequent "clarification" in the rest of the letter renders this statement the *complete opposite* to Paul's gospel, representing the very spirit he wishes to dispel. Although on any reading many things in Romans 2 are amplified and clarified in the remainder of the letter, this self-contradiction would be astonishing. Note the similar embarrassment concerning Paul's "problematic" appeal to the Romans to seek "praise" from Roman officials (13:3) and his full endorsement of giving "honor" to whom honor was due (13:7); in both cases, Paul's endorsement of the normal honor-system is excused as a necessary accommodation to the "world" for the sake of the mission to Spain, whose ideology constituted, in fact, a "revolutionary approach" to honor (793, 803). On Jewett's thesis, Paul's statements here demonstrate an "acute irony" (803); less friendly readers of Paul will detect wholesale deconstruction.

"illustrates" a common human trait: Israel remains for Paul a unique target of criticism as well as a unique focus of hope (11:28). Jewett is in my view admirably clear that Romans *does* critique Jewish unbelief in Jesus, and that Paul does not describe some *Sonderweg* for Israel, only salvation for Jew and Gentile alike through the crucified and risen Christ. But by placing the climax of Romans in chapters 14–16 (rather than 9–11), his otherwise fine reading of Romans 9–11 makes these chapters not an end in themselves, but a means to illustrate the universal problem of competition for honor, a problem which besets the Roman congregations and threatens the mission to Spain. In other interpretive traditions, a similar downgrading of Romans 9–11 has made these chapters illustrative of the principle of justification by faith, or the principle of divine sovereignty in grace. In this respect the "new perspective" rightly refused to shift from particular to principle, and such a gain should not be hastily abandoned.[21]

B. SIN AS ZEALOUS COMPETITION

As we have seen, in Jewett's reading Jewish boasting is illustrative of what constitutes, for Paul, the fundamental flaw of the whole world, the competitive quest for honor. Conversely, when Paul speaks of Jewish (and Gentile) sin, Jewett identifies this as the formation or pursuit of competitive claims to superiority. Two passages illustrate this reading and (in my view) its weaknesses:

1. At the beginning of Romans 10 Paul indicates his prayer for the salvation of Jews, and adds: *martyrō gar autois hoti zēlon theou echousin, all ou kat epignōsin* (Jewett translates: "For I bear them witness that they have zeal for God, but without acknowledgment"). Jewett considers both parts of this statement critical of Jews: "The verb *martyreō* ("bear witness") is used here as a public assertion in which Paul gives testimony to his basic critique of a form of Jewish piety of his time" (615). He traces the motif of "zeal" from the Old Testament (Elijah and Phinehas) to Paul's own life-story (Galatians 1:14; Philippians 3:6) and classifies this as a form of destructive "competition for honor." In the following verse (10:3), "seeking to establish their own righteousness" is understood as "a reference to the sense of ethnic or sectarian righteousness claimed by Jewish groups as well as by various other groups in the Mediterranean

---

[21] Jewett insists that he has used the religious, intellectual and linguistic horizon of the first century "to guard against imposing later ideological agendas back into Romans" (3). This is the only "hermeneutical principle" which he declares, since his goal is "to sharpen the ancient horizon of the text so that it can enter into dialogue with the modern horizons of our various interpretive enterprises" (3). But in reading the particulars of the text as illustrating a wider principle, there is a very specific 'sharpening" of the ancient horizon, which, readers will sense, has a view to a "dialogue" with contemporary social and political concerns. Since any act of interpretation, even in an "historical" mode, necessarily involves some such act of dialogue, it would have been better to have made this hermeneutical step explicit at the outset.

world" (618; Jewett refers to zealots, Pharisees, Essenes, and Sadducees): "what prevented proper "knowledge" of the truth of the gospel was Israel's zeal to maintain its honor through obedience to the law, and thus to "establish righteousness" in comparison with others" (644). I find this an impossible reading, on several grounds: i) The normal sense of *martyreō* + dative is "to bear witness to or in favour of another" (H. G. Liddell and R. Scott, *A Greek–English Lexicon*); this is how Paul uses the expression elsewhere (Galatians 4:15; cf. Colossians 4:13) and is its normal sense in the New Testament (for examples, Luke 4:22; John 3:26; Acts 10:43). It can hardly introduce, then, Paul's *critique* of Jews. ii) The "zeal" Paul mentions is not competition with others but "zeal for God"; the objective genitive suggests it has a positive sense. iii) There is a clear distinction between the two parts of the sentence in 10:2, the second introduced by a strong adversative (*alla*); it is only at this point that Paul's critique begins. iv) Even when he talks elsewhere of his own zeal, that zeal is not itself clearly negative, only its application in persecution of the church. v) I find no reference here to honor, or to others with whom Jewish righteousness stands in competition; in fact, Gentiles were not even seeking it (9:30). Still less is there any hint of sectarian rivalry within Judaism.

Jewett's reading enables him to connect some fault in Israel to "the universal human tendency to validate the status of one's group" (618). By contrast, I see no fault in Israel's sin, and no universal problem of "zeal." What is universal is disobedience, a fault in which Israel now participates, despite the law; but her zeal is not part of that disobedience, and certainly not its essence.

2. Jewett's unusual treatment of Romans 10:2–3 is rooted in his reading of Romans 7:7–25. After a lucid and nuanced account of the history of scholarship, Jewett concludes (probably rightly) that this "I" has some autobiographical content, and that it is the pre-Christian "I", viewed from the Christian present. He then identifies this "I" specifically with the contradictions inherent in Paul's persecution of the church:

> we go a step farther to define this contradiction [between the good aimed for and the evil achieved] in terms of religious zealotism that failed to achieve the good that Paul had believed he could bring about by persecuting the followers of Christ. While fulfilling the law in a zealous manner, he found himself opposing God's Messiah. (444)

This thesis is novel and intriguing. It has Paul present himself as the paradigmatic "I" for the sake of the Romans, thus keeping opprobrium from either side in the Roman conflicts (445). It correctly notices a striking analogy between Romans 7 and Galatians 1:13–15: in both Paul is caught up in unconscious sin, spurred on by the law.[22] But it is crucial to get this analogy just right. Although he speaks of his "zeal" for the traditions of his fathers in Galatians 1:14, it is not clear that this was itself a "sin"; conversely, where he offers an extended analysis of 'sin" in Romans 7:7–25, Paul never refers to this as "zeal." Jewett's connection can be made only through a particular reading of the cited commandment *ouk epithymēseis* (7:7). Appealing to "the context of the Tenth Commandment," Jewett writes:

> It is not desire as such that is forbidden, but coveting what belongs to others. Paul refers here to a distortion in interpersonal relations such as we have traced in the earlier sections of Romans. The sin of asserting oneself and one's group at the expense of others fits the intensely competitive environment of Greco-Roman and Jewish culture . . . it would include the Jewish alternative of desiring superior performance of the law, which was part of Paul's own past, but it would also include distinctively Gentile forms of competition for honor. (449)

In fact, what is conspicuous in Romans 7:7–25 is that there is no reference to "others" at all: the only characters on the stage are "I," "sin," and "the law"/"the commandment." The "I" can be internally differentiated, but it is never set in comparison or competition with others; I find no "interpersonal relations" in Romans 7 at all.

Jewett's reading of Romans 7 (and Romans as a whole) offers a fundamental redefinition of the meaning of 'sin": in Romans 7 "it is not the sin of disobedience, as in the Genesis account, but the sin of legalistic zealotism that leads to the death Paul has in mind" (453). But this identification of sin with zeal (and zeal with sin) turns sin from an act into an attitude, from a failure to obey the will of God into an evil motivation to outstrip others in honor. Although he differs from Bultmann in reading this "legalistic zealotism" in social terms ("social zealotism," 469), Jewett shares with Bultmann the conviction that 'sin" in Romans 7 is in fact a "*metasin*," a problematic attitude to the law, rather than the failure to keep the law and obey God's will.[23] Indeed, he goes further than

---

[22] See the excellent reading of Romans 7 in S. Chester, *Conversion at Corinth* (Edinburgh: T. & T. Clark, 2003), 183–95.

[23] "In the competitive environment of the Greco-Roman and Jewish worlds, the desire to surpass others and to achieve honor had invaded the arena of religion, perverting it into a means of achieving superiority" (450). The structure of thought here (the perversion of religion by attitudinal faults) is precisely parallel to Bultmann, even if the sin has shifted from individualistic to communal self-righteousness. See R. Bultmann, "Römer 7 und die Anthropologie des Paulus," in idem, *Exegetica* (Tübingen: Mohr [Siebeck], 1967), 53–62, with the devastating critique of H. Räisänen,

Bultmann in discerning this attitudinal problem as the essence of "sin" throughout Romans. Most readers will, I suspect, be wary. In light of the ubiquitous meaning of "sin" in the Jewish tradition as transgression of the law and disobedience to God, and in view of Paul's discussions of sin earlier in Romans (1:18–32; 2:25–29; 5:12–21; 8:7), it seems best to stick with the common sense of "sin" as transgression of God's will. While we might condemn honor-seeking as the foundational and corrupt ideology of the ancient world, Paul's analysis is straightforward: Gentiles, and even Jews, are incapable of keeping God's commandments, since they are prey to the power of Sin. Because of her covenantal privileges, Israel's inclination is to boast—which makes her distinct from Gentiles, not the same—and Paul insists, polemically, that this boast is delusional. But boasting (or zeal) is not itself the problem. The problem, which she shares with Gentiles, is the failure to do what the law requires.

C. SALVATION AS HONOR

Jewett's understanding of Pauline soteriology matches his interpretation of sin. If sin means the human propensity to boast, the competitive quest for honor, and the divisive assertion of group superiority, Paul's gospel reveals the impartial grace of God which contradicts and subverts the honor-system of the ancient world. Jewett finds in 1:16 ("I am not ashamed of the gospel") a signal of "a social and ideological revolution . . . inaugurated by the gospel" (137):

> This gospel shatters the unrighteous precedence given to the strong over the weak, the free and well-educated over slaves and the ill-educated, the Greeks and Romans over the barbarians. If what the world considers dishonorable has power, it will prevail and achieve a new form of honor to those who have not earned it, an honor consistent with divine righteousness. All who place their faith in this gospel will be set right, that is, be placed in the right relation to the most significant arena in which honor is dispensed: divine judgment. Thus the triumph of divine righteousness through the gospel of Christ crucified and resurrected is achieved by transforming the system in which shame and honor are dispensed. The thesis of Romans therefore effectively turns the social value system of the Roman empire upside down. (139)

This is a thesis that is likely to warm the heart of any radical Paulinist. Jewett captures exceptionally well the subversive force of the gospel and its capacity to undermine the normal cultural coordinates of antiquity. He rightly traces this revolutionary force back to the event of the cross and resurrection, and to the gift-character of grace, drawing (unconsciously?) on the Augustinian and Reformation traditions. Paul "maintains the absolute priority of grace" (279), since God's generosity to all is "undiscriminating" (283). "All are set right as a sheer gift" (281), since 'salvation is entirely a matter of grace rather than any form of human achievement" (710); "those who rely on the scandal of Christ crucified have a new basis of honor through sheer grace" (614). But it is noticeable, here and throughout, that what this grace conveys is fundamentally a change in *status*: honor before God, and equal honor in communities of mutual respect. Although Jewett excoriates Protestant individualism, and interprets this status-change in consistently social terms, readers may sense here a new twist on the old Protestant emphasis on salvation as status-change (standing before God), with concomitant downplaying of its many other dimensions. When Paul announces the gospel as the "power of God for salvation" (1:16), he traces its effects in Romans in the transformation of humanity at many levels: the "newness of life" (6:4) in which believers participate is found in the recreation of the will, the mind, and the imagination (hope), in the new enabling of moral agency and moral capacity (via the Spirit), both individual and social. Some readers might sense a diminishing of this power (*dynamis*) to the level of "possibility," when Jewett speaks of the preaching of the gospel "that *offers* equal access" (275) to Jews and Gentiles and makes salvation "*equally available*" to all (278; emphasis mine). But, regardless of this point, most will wonder at the abnormally restrictive scope of salvific transformation. If one has a broader (and deeper?) sense of the corruptive and destructive power of Sin, it is not sufficiently good news if God merely "honors sinners of every culture in an impartial manner through Christ" (88).

Jewett's emphasis on divine impartiality is similarly one-sided and in a related fashion. To highlight this notion might seem warranted by Paul's statements in Romans 2:1–11, but these are ground-clearing exercises which open the possibility of a far more radical notion of divine grace, which defies criteria of "fairness" altogether. "Impartiality" suggests the operation of some legal or moral standard to which God must be held to conform. But Paul announces a God who (illegally) "justifies the ungodly" (4:5) and who has mercy on whom he has mercy, with apparently scandalous results (9:15–24). "Impartiality" also constitutes an essentially negative virtue, by which God does *not* discriminate or exercise unequal favour. But God's righteousness in Paul is a new act of power, a transformative recreation of the world; it "puts things right" not simply by shattering a faulty ideology of honor, but by creating a new reality, in moral and social change. For those who are enslaved to the power of Sin, it is hardly sufficient that God is impartial: they need a radical act of freedom. It is only if "sin" is limited to the destructive power of social competition that divine impartiality appears like good news.

If the strength of Jewett's reading of Romans lies in its emphasis on the social intentions and effects of the gospel, even his social vision seems unnecessarily confined.[24] The gospel of equal honor outlaws all forms of discrimination (ethnic, cultural, social and religious): it is radically opposed to cultural bigotry or chauvinism (722) and thus to any expression of cultural imperialism (267), which must be eradicated before the mission to Spain can take place. Its positive virtues are thus pluralistic, tolerant, peaceful and egalitarian: the gospel "allows cultural variations to stand side by side with equal validity" (144), offering "tolerant co-existence" (233), and "new relationships in communal settings to all on precisely the same terms" (142). This social vision is both local and global: it is expressed in the instructions concerning harmony and mutual tolerance in Rome (14:1–15:7) and in Paul's hope for universal salvation in the pacification of the whole world (through persuasion, not force, 146–47). But it is noticeable that Jewett's social virtues are generally negative (the absence of conflict, superiority or discrimination) and he finds it harder to capture or develop the more positive dimensions of Paul's vision, in the mutual *construction* that constitutes a dynamic community. Even in Romans 14–15, which I take to be less the acme of Paul's social vision than an attempt at obstacle-clearance, Paul speaks of "building one another up" (14:19), a notion of mutual enrichment more fully developed in the metaphor of the body (12:3–8). For Paul this conveys the sense that each group *needs* the other, that none is sufficient on its own, or in its own terms. It is noticeable that when Jewett speaks on this motif he glosses it in extremely limited terms:

> If each group seeks constructively to encourage the development of integrity and maturity in other groups, rather than trying to force them to confirm to a single viewpoint, the ethnic and theological diversity in Rome would no longer be divisive and destructive. (879)

But there are times when what we need from the other is *not* respect for the development of our "integrity and maturity", but moral challenge, correction, or the addition of values and resources that we presently

[24] I note in passing the question whether the exclusive focus on the social dimensions of salvation also skews the interpretation of the letter. Jewett consistently takes Paul's statements about "faith" to mean "assent to the gospel" (278) by "participation in the community of the converted" (277); indeed to "have faith" is primarily a social commitment, expressed in belonging to "faith communities" (139). This seems an excessive reaction against Protestant individualism. Paul is interested in the contours of Abraham's very personal faith (4:13–25), and allows for diversity within community precisely on the basis of individual conviction and faith (14:13–23).

lack. At this crucial point, Paul's understanding of love appears to me far more demanding than Jewett's concept of "respectful coexistence" (86), because the action of love may be as much to challenge the faults of another (for example, presumably, the "idolatry" of the barbarians in Spain) as to bear with their cultural sensitivities. At this point, Jewett's vision sounds all too close to the social goals of pluralistic multiculturalism, and is vulnerable to the criticisms rightly levelled against it: if diverse social or cultural groups *merely* honor one another as of equal validity, they will never come to enrich, enhance and develop each others" traditions, and their (limited) interaction will have no positive or constructive outcome. Of course, there are dangers in any more constructive model: the strong can "construct" and "improve" the weak by subtle imposition of superior force. Paul's vision of *mutual* construction, however, constitutes an ideological and practical bulwark against such imperialism, since it presupposes that each side has something to contribute to the other, and something to learn or gain. As I have noted elsewhere, this is difficult to enact in practice, but the fact that Paul preserves and reuses the dangerously "prejudicial" language of "weak" and 'strong", and aligns himself very clearly with one side (15:1), indicates that he is not quite keeping to Jewett's script.[25] The strong have a duty to use their strength precisely not to overpower the weak, but to support them (15:1–6); but the weak have to open their tradition towards gift-sharing fellowship with those who follow quite different ways of "honoring the Lord." To put it bluntly, Paul's bracing social vision suggests that "tolerance" is not enough; honor is only one ingredient of inter-personal relations, and taken on its own, or to an extreme, falls short of the vision of the social good implied by love.

Reviewing any book written on this scale is a hazardous exercise; it is certainly possible that in my selection of topics I have been less than fair to the author and his intentions. If I have focused on my points of disagreement, this is largely because this is such an engaging and provocative commentary. In very many respects it will constitute, for the foreseeable future, my *favourite* commentary on Romans, to which I shall return again and again to garner innumerable fresh insights. In providing such a full, coherent and relevant reading of this ancient letter, Jewett has won an important place in the long process of dialogue with Paul which we call the interpretation of Romans. I take this commentary to be far more than a new contextualisation of Romans in its first century context, since its fresh articulation of Paul's gospel is inevitably

---

[25] Cf. Jewett's puzzle over Paul's remark about Abraham not weakening in faith (336 on 4:19). He is right to insist that the "strong" (a label probably used in Rome) are here required to use their strength not to overpower but to bear the weaknesses of the powerless (15:1; [876]); but this does not eradicate the implicitly prejudicial effect of the label.

and rightly developed within the framework of our own contemporary needs and concerns. If my questions help to continue that dialogue with Romans, credit should be given to the new impetus afforded by this excellent and immensely stimulating commentary.

10

Love Without Respect is Bogus: A Reply to John Barclay[1]

Robert Jewett

It is a rare privilege to be invited to reply to an extensive review that reflects so clear a grasp of the main lines of one's interpretation, but which disagrees in so fundamental and productive a manner. I am grateful to John Barclay for his review and to Simon Gathercole for the unusual invitation. Perhaps it is not so unusual for others, but the chance to respond to a review in a major journal is a first for me. Nevertheless, I take up the challenge with a measure of reluctance, because I prefer the procedure that Paul advises in 1 Corinthians 14:29, that after the speakers are finished, they should let others "weigh what is said." If a central issue in Romans is divine impartiality that relativizes all human claims and accomplishments, then no one should be quick to judge his own case.

In Barclay's view, divine impartiality is far from central for Romans, that it would be bad news for the elect if true, that God's love defies the concept of "fairness," and that it has no bearing on social discrimination. "What we need from the other is *not* respect [emphasis in the original] . . . but moral challenge, correction, or the addition of values and resources that we presently lack . . . the action of love may be as much to challenge the faults of others . . . as to bear with their cultural sensitivities." This may ring true to those committed to the ethos of moralistic Protestant preaching. In the situation of mutual discrimination reflected throughout Romans, however, respect for the other was required to allow love to be "genuine" or "without pretense" (Romans 12:9). Otherwise love was a condescending vehicle to maintain

---

[1] First published in *Journal for the Study of the New Testament* 31.1 (1008), 113–18.

the guise of moral or cultural superiority. My interpretation stands or falls on the claim that in this particular letter, "love without respect is bogus." In contrast to the other Pauline letters, respect comes first because the Roman congregations were treating each other with contempt and this imperialistic behavior followed by the "weak" as well as the "strong" needed to be overcome before the gospel of Christ crucified could be credibly preached to the so called "barbarians" in Spain.

Several lines of argument supporting this interpretation are rejected by Barclay. The first lines are historical. With regard to Spain, Barclay dismisses the significance of the lack of Jewish population and the language barriers without offering any alternative evidence. In response to inferences about the prospects of self supported mission drawn from the fact that the economy in Spain was controlled by Romans who had invested in confiscated assets after the repeated revolts, Barclay argues that Paul would disregard such factors because he "had little time for those thought special in the eyes of the world (1 Corinthians 1:18–31)." Does this critique of the Corinthians' adherence to the Greco-Roman honor system eliminate the economic reality that Paul worked "night and day" so as not to be a burden to others (1 Thessalonians 2:9)? Has Barclay discovered evidence that the method of self-supporting mission would be feasible in Spain?

That the Spaniards were classified as "barbarians," which correlates with the remarkable reference in the *narratio* of 1:14, is dismissed on the ground that if "attitudes to 'barbarians' were so important, it is odd that Paul should use this label only once." Can Barclay cite any examples of such repetition in *narratio*, or that the wording of a *narratio* was not understood to inform the entire subsequent argument? On the basis of which rhetorical theory does Barclay know that this would have appeared "odd" to the Roman audience?

Barclay believes he can eliminate all relevance in reference to Phoebe in Romans 16:1–2 by insisting on the translation "provide her whatever matter she needs from you." This translation makes an indefinite pronoun out of the definite relative pronoun, which I convey by the translation "in the matter." Barclay overlooks that this is immediately followed by the explanatory clause, "for she has been a patron to me and to many." My hypothesis about Phoebe as the patron of the Spanish mission rests primarily on the explanatory clause, which Barclay does not explain. Nowhere does he suggest another historical explanation of such details. No evaluation is provided of my weighing of various historical hypotheses about the purpose and situation of the letter. One gains the impression that no historical reconstruction whatsoever is to be entertained. This is particularly visible in Barclay's treatment of the Wiefel theory.

While not dealing with the profiles of the "weak" and the "strong" in chapters 14–15, or with the contrast between the current Gentile majority and the earlier predominance of Jewish Christians, as visible in the names of exiled congregational leaders in chapter 16, Barclay seeks to undermine my analysis of the audience by rejecting the Wiefel hypothesis of the decisive impact of the edict of Claudius in C.E. 49. This is a straw man argument, because the evidence of social and theological diversity and conflict is strewn throughout the early history of Christianity in Rome, and the most substantial reconstruction currently available written by Peter Lampe does not even mention Wiefel. Nevertheless, the arguments against Wiefel remain unsubstantial. That the Suetonius reference to *impulsore Chresto* refers to an agitator in the Roman synagogues is unlikely in view of the fact that this is not a Jewish name. That Suetonius refers to Christians as *Christianoi* in *Nero* 16.2 does not disprove that the Christians were often referred to as *Chrestianoi*, as in Tacitus, *Annales* 15.44, Tertullian, *Apologetus* 15.3 and *Ad nationis* 1.3. The textual variants of 1 Peter 2:3 reveal that confusion between *Christus* and *Chrestus* was commonplace.

Barclay suggests that Prisca and Aquilla, whom Paul met in Corinth after Claudius' expulsion, were unbelievers with whom Paul lodged "as fellow Jewish artisans." So far as I know, Gerd Lüdemann is the only other advocate of this unlikely idea. Neither Acts nor the Corinthian letters support the logical consequence that Paul converted them, and Haenchen's inference remains likely that they had started the Christian movement in Corinth prior to Paul's arrival. That they would have returned to Rome "as persons with no public profile" before the death of Claudius is ahistorical speculation, and in any event Prisca probably came from the noble Acilius family whose home in the prestigious Aventine provided a later "Title church" whose excavation reveals an elegant building. She had a public profile and then some. Without taking the bulk of the evidence in Romans 14–16 into account as Wiefel did, and without suggesting a preferable hypothesis, Barclay dismisses his work as "a tissue of speculation, based on flimsy evidence and ungrounded supposition" which should be "abandoned by New Testament scholars."

This cavalier tone was heard in John Barclay's critique of N. T. Wright's view of Paul's attitude toward the Roman Empire in last November's SBL meeting in San Diego. In denying any allusions to Roman imperialism in Paul's letters, Barclay twice characterized his friend and all who agreed with him as "hallucinating." Since I share this alleged hallucination and develop it throughout the commentary, it seems likely that the next chapter of Barclay's denunciation will be forthcoming. It seems puzzling that a brilliant and otherwise friendly colleague could dismiss the historical data and hypotheses aimed at explaining them in such a manner and why he feels entitled to treat those who develop such theories with such contempt. Rather than personalizing the matter, I suggest it has to do with the history and methodology of Romans research.

Until the publication of the first edition of *The Romans Debate*, edited by Karl P. Donfried, and the subsequent work of the Society of Biblical Literature Romans Seminar, the consensus remained dominant that Romans was a theological treatise instead of a situational letter. A generation of north American and European scholars sought to overturn this consensus, developing the view that all of Paul's letters, including Romans, were "conversations in context," to use Calvin Roetzel's expression. I think John Barclay would like to turn the clock back to the heyday of biblical theology when an alleged Biblical meta-language rendered historical hypotheses superfluous and enabled the construction of theological constructs whose validity could be presented as absolute. Thus in San Diego, Barclay proposed that we interpret all of Paul's letters under the category of Paul's "Drama of History" marked by the "archic powers" of "Sin, Death and the Flesh." This sounded like a new twist on the exciting abstractions I heard as a Barthian in the mid 1950's. In effect, it would turn all of Paul's letters into theological treatises.

Another example of the treatise premise is the critique of ascribing a central role to divine impartiality. Barclay insists that "for those who are enslaved to the power of Sin, it is hardly sufficient that God is impartial: they need a radical act of freedom." But in the context of this letter to Roman believers, where most of the audience was slave or former slave, it was a powerful message of liberation that God did not hold them in contempt as the society did, that Christ died for them as for the rest of the human race, and thus that they should honor each other as one body in Christ. Since they were impeaching each other's status before God, Paul interprets divine righteousness as accepting each side in an impartial manner. This situational interpretation employs the language and the context of the letter in place of modern formulas such as "a radical act of freedom," which Barclay thinks is unrelated to "status-change." Since the support for such abstractions derives from the genius of the interpreter, extreme efforts must be employed to discredit interpretations that rest on historical, social, or rhetorical foundations. Reconstructions of audience and rhetorical situations must be categorically eliminated as "too tenuous to count as other than speculation." Romans must be maintained as a theological treatise, or all is lost.

The methodological issue must be faced, even by John Barclay, because only a fraction of the details of this letter can be made to match any of the grand theological paradigms that have been developed since the Reformation. No commentary that employs the method of theological treatise has been able to explain all of the historical, linguistic, and rhetorical evidence. Aside from a few verse in chapters 3, 5–6, and 9–13, most of the argument of this letter is uncongenial to Calvinism. This can be illustrated by Barclay's attempt to maintain traditional Calvinistic doctrines of the law and of religious zeal, as well as the more widely shared antipathy toward Jews.

It is significant that Barclay chose not to list law as one of the "archic powers" in his debate with Wright, because this is a traditional line of demarcation between Lutheran and Calvinistic interpreters. Barclay maintains the Calvinist view that the human plight is "failure to keep the law and obey God's will," and that sin in Romans is simply "transgression of the law." This overlooks the last three chapters that apply Paul's argument to the situation of imposing varied definitions of law onto other groups. The conventional Jewish understanding of legal transgression that Barclay advocates is the very barrier between the Weak and the Strong that Paul seeks to remove with the rhetorical question, "Who are you to pass judgment on the servant of another?" (14:4) This correlates with Paul's redefinition of sin in 1:18–32 as "suppression of the truth" and "worshipping the creature rather than the creator" and with 7:7–11 where Paul epitomizes sin as desiring what belongs to others. That salvation comes "apart from works of the law" (Romans 3:28), or that believers "have died to the law" (Romans 7:4) and are "discharged from the law" (Romans 7:6), cannot be taken seriously because this would undermine the continued validity of the commandments.

Since zeal for God's law is a supreme virtue for Calvinism, Barclay denies the clear sense of Romans 10:2, that the Jews who rejected the gospel were displaying a zeal for God that lacked "acknowledgement" of the righteousness of God revealed in Christ. Barclay claims that the "objective genitive" in "zeal for God" proves that "it has a positive sense," while the critical reference to being unenlightened with regard to divine righteousness is taken to be unrelated to zeal itself. Barclay overlooks what David Rhoads has documented in *Israel in Revolution*, that zeal for God was always related to other humans, because it led to executing divine judgment against those who allegedly had violated God's law. Despite the clarification in 10:3 that such misguided zeal was motivated by the desire to "establish their own righteousness," Barclay finds "no reference here to honour, or to others with whom Jewish righteousness stands in competition." The relevance of Paul's own acknowledgement of misguided zeal in Galatians 1:14 is dismissed with the misleading assertion that "zeal is not itself clearly negative, only its application in persecution of the church." What Paul had discovered on the road to Damascus concerning the violent outcome of misguided zeal for the law is reduced to a case of misapplication. With these verbal gymnastics, Barclay thinks he has shown that there is "no universal problem of 'zeal.' What is universal is disobedience, a fault in which Israel now participates, despite the law; but her zeal is not part of that disobedience, and certainly not its essence." Thus Calvinist orthodoxy trumps the text of Romans.

While it should be clear that Paul goes to extraordinary lengths to place Jews and Gentiles on the same level before God, repeatedly insisting that the gospel is for "all" or "every one" (1:5, 7, 8, 16; 5:12, 18–19; 8:14; 10:12–13; 12:3), equalizing blame and grace for Jews and Gentiles in 3:9–24, universalizing human disobedience and divine mercy in 11:32, and urging Jewish and Gentile Christians to "welcome one another" in 15:7, Barclay insists that "Israel remains for Paul a unique target of criticism as well as a unique focus of hope." This is presented as perfectly benign, including the restriction of boasting to Jews in 3:27 and overlooking Paul's denial that Abraham, who was a Gentile prior to his circumcision, had anything to boast about on the basis of works prior to receiving the divine promise (4:2). That boasting of superiority was a feature of both the Greco-Roman and Jewish environments is dismissed as irrelevant, because the Jews are the main problem. In San Diego, Barclay claimed that "the Jews . . . killed Jesus," citing 1 Thessalonians 2:14–15 without taking into account the historical fact that Rome alone maintained the right of capital punishment. This kind of stereotyping was coordinated with supersessionism in the interpolated doxology of 16:25–27, which claimed that God intentionally hid the secret of salvation from the Jews and revealed it to Gentile believers. As I show in the commentary, this interpolation has functioned as a lens through which interpreters have discounted Paul's efforts to place Jewish and Gentile believers on the same level before God. Although Barclay does not deal with the interpolation in his critique, his stance would be consistent with the traditional belief that the doxology is authentically Pauline and a suitable conclusion for this letter.

In denying that competition for honor is attacked in Romans, despite the references to boasting, judging, and contempt that Paul felt were marking the behavior of the congregations toward each other, Barclay avoids the possibility of relating this letter to the issues of social domination and imperialism, either in political or educational forms. He dismisses John Colenso's "bitter condemnation of British colonial 'mission,'" but despite the nineteenth century language, I find the bishop to be close to the target in his claim that the Paul's argument suggests the following:

> The idea of this brotherhood of all mankind, the great family on earth, implies that all men have certain ties with us, and certain rights at our hands. The truest way,

> in which we can regard them, is as they appear in the sight of God, from whom they can never suffer wrong, nor from us, when we think of them as His creatures equally with ourselves. There is yet a closer bond with them as our brethren in the Gospel. No one can interpose impediments of rank, or fortune, or colour, or religious opinion, between those who are one in Christ. (88–89)

I acknowledge that for those committed to maintaining the superior status of the North Atlantic Elect, this may sound "bitter," and afflicted by "political correctness." Yet it is congruent with Paul's argument in this letter that originally climaxed in the admonition that the Jewish and Gentile congregations should "greet one another with a holy kiss" (16:16). The commentary makes the case that the interpolation of 16:17–20 was inserted to counter this inclusivity, promising that by refusing relations with alleged heretics, God would "crush Satan" under the feet of the orthodox. This effectively countered Paul's argument that misguided religious zeal was violating the righteousness of God revealed in Christ crucified. That this abusive impulse remains dominant in the debate over the interpretation of Romans cannot eliminate what Paul had learned from truly bitter experience, that mutual respect was an essential prerequisite of genuine love.

The Collonges Symposium
March 20, 2007

11

The Book of Romans! A Missing Link in Adventist Theology?

Gunnar Pedersen

The Adventist Paradigm

As a dogmatic position paper this will briefly outline the basic salvation-historical paradigm of Adventist theology. Adventism claims that the biblical story as a whole forms the basis of its theology. While certain books contribute more than others to its distinctive teachings, the book of Romans, historically speaking, does not appear to hold any central position in its dogmatic paradigm. However, it is the thesis of this paper that this book may actually provide a perspective that could creatively enhance and enrich the central structural motifs in the Adventist worldview.

Historically, Adventism represents a revival of eschatology within the wider Christian tradition, especially within the tradition of Evangelicalism which arose in the 18th century. More specifically, Adventism emerged at the peak of the Second Great Revival in the 1840's, with a clear focus on eschatology centered in the concept of the Parousia of Christ. While the Millerite enthusiasm regarding the imminent coming of Christ was premature, out of this revival emerged what is today known as the Seventh-day Adventist Church which exhibits a distinct emphasis on eschatology centered in the consummative role of Christ climaxing in His glorious Parousia.

This paper will not attempt to analyze the historical development of and the biblical theological rationale for such beliefs, but rather it will describe the systematic structure of the Adventist understanding of salvation history in terms of the "already" and "not yet". The Adventist view is clearly embedded in the biblical story line with a focus on the themes of creation, fall, and the unfolding redemptive promise moving forward toward the renewal of all things. Thus Adventism identifies a past, present and future dimension in salvation history seeing it as an unfolding story divinely guided towards its intended goal.

The counterpoint to the story of salvation is seen by Adventism to be the story of evil. Thus Adventism sees the story of God's disapproval of evil as being manifest in human history from the very beginning, throughout human story into the present; a disapproval that will ultimately be manifested in the future final judgment. Parallel to this story, God's gracious redemptive promises and actions have likewise been seen by Adventism as being manifest in human history from the very beginning, throughout the human story into the present; a blessing that will ultimately be manifested in the restoration of all things through the Parousia of Christ. Thus this story according to Adventism has a central Christological focus on the past, present and future redemptive work of Christ. While this is seen as proceeding in stages, it is nevertheless seen as an indivisible coherent whole.

In confessing Jesus as both Savior and Lord Adventists map His redemptive work in three successive stages. (1) Redemption achieved—past sacrificial work. (2) Redemption applied—present priestly work. (3) Redemption confirmed—eschatological priestly/kingly work. In particular they distinguish between the timing of his priestly and kingly roles. While he is both priest and king his exercise of those roles is seen as being successive rather than simultaneous, except during the judgment where they will overlap.

In Adventism, Christ's exercise of his priestly role is seen from a New Testament (NT) perspective. It is linked to his present post ascension function at the right hand of God and is thus seen as exercised in the apostolic "already," while the exercise of his kingly role is seen as linked to his function as eschatological judge at the right hand of God, in the apostolic "not yet" of salvation-history. This distinction is rooted in the NT stress on the "already" and "not yet" and its usage of Old Testament (OT) priestly kingly imagery (Psalm 110), and thus seen as applied in the NT to the present priestly and future kingly work of the Messiah respectively.

An example would be Peter's speech reported in Acts 5:31–32 in which he claims that Jesus is exalted to the right hand of God and that his present work is to give Israel repentance and forgiveness and to mediate the presence of God's Spirit; activities that would appear to be priestly in nature. Furthermore, in another speech in Acts 3:19–21 Peter declared that Christ must remain in heaven "until the time for establishing all that God spoke by the mouth of his holy prophets from of old"—an activity that appear to be kingly in nature.

Whatever the biblical rationale adopted by Adventism, the systematic point is that in its salvation-historical perspective Christ must first bring us to God—that is, give repentance, forgiveness and the presence of God's spirit before he can bring us to Glory, that is, restore all things in the resurrection and the new creation. Thus Adventism draws a clear distinction between the apostolic "already" and "not yet" of redemption and it correlates these respective aspects to the priestly and kingly redemptive work of Christ.

Adventist eschatology thus embodies the "not yet" of the apostolic hope of glory in terms of the resurrection to life with God and the renewal of all things: a future blessing synchronized with the Parousia of Christ as His ultimate exercise of kingly Lordship. To fully appreciate this salvation-historical structure it should be noted that according to Adventist anthropology humans are creaturely, contingent beings, who have no innate immortality and who do not nor pass into the presence of God at death. Rather, they remain in a state of sleep until they pass from this mortal to the immortal state in the "not yet" of the future resurrection at the Parousia of Christ. Thus the eschatological consummation and renewal provided by Christ in the Parousia are an absolute necessity in the Adventist redemptive paradigm, providing a complete solution to the presence and effect of human sinfulness.

Accordingly, Adventism sharply distinguishes between the apostolic "already" and "not yet" of salvation. The "already" is provided by Christ's priestly work in terms of bringing humans to God. The apostolic "not yet" of salvation is provided by Christ's kingly work in terms of bringing humans to glory and thus effecting the final removal of evil and its consequences. Furthermore the eschatological kingly work of Christ is seen as embodying his role as judge—that is setting all things right—vindicating those who belong to God and removing those who refuse his Lordship. While Adventism has seen this role of Christ as embodying pre-advent, advent and post-advent dimensions, these distinctions are nevertheless immaterial to the redemptive meaning of this eschatological activity, an activity in which Christ will confirm, reveal and vindicate true believers and bring a permanent end to the reign of evil and thus initiate a new creation.

THE DOGMATIC CHALLENGES

Adventism has experienced a prolonged external and internal theological struggle with regard to the soteriological implications of their views pertaining to the apostolic perspective of "already" and "not yet." Especially the interrelationship between the meaning of present salvation through Christ's priestly work and the meaning of the future vindication through Christ's priestly/kingly work in the judgment has caused controversy. The historical investigations into the past dogmatic struggles seem to suggest that the real problem has to do with how the classical dogmas regarding justification and sanctification have been integrated into the Adventist systematic scheme with its particular focus on the "not yet" of apostolic salvation history.

The classical orthodox protestant view on justification with its Erasmian understanding of imputation tends to eliminate the final judgment of the saints, since the event of justification is understood as a present divine act of final vindication. The conceptual similarity between the meaning of a future judgment and present justification has often led to the eclipsing of this aspect of eschatology within the Protestant tradition (James P. Martin, *The Last Judgment in Protestant Theology*). On the other hand the Augustinian, Pietist and Wesleyan paradigms with their emphasis on a grace-induced sanctification and thus a final judgment based on the outcome of such renewal tend to diminish the full meaning of the Orthodox Protestant doctrine of present justification and thus lead to perfectionist tendencies.

A historic review of Adventism reveals that it has never been possible to fully integrate any of the traditional redemptive dogmatic traditions into the Adventist system of thought without compromising its understanding of either the "already" or the "not yet" of salvation-history. In this context it is interesting to note that Adventism has newer seen the Book of Romans as an important contributor to its salvation historical scheme. The reason seems to be linked to the dominant historic dogmatic readings of this book in western Christendom since Augustine which may have made the book appear to be more of a challenge to, rather than a resource for, Adventist theology.

McGrath in his monumental study of the doctrine of justification (*Iustitia Dei: A History of the Christian Doctrine of Justification*) makes the following claim: "The doctrine of justification has come to develop a meaning quite independent of its biblical origins, and concerns the means by which man's relationship to God is established. The church has chosen to subsume its discussion of reconciliation of man to God under the aegis of justification, thereby giving the concept an emphasis quite absent from the New Testament. The 'doctrine of justification' has come to bear a meaning within dogmatic theology which is quite independent of its Pauline origins." If this is the case, it has profound implications for the reading of the epistle to the Romans.

Without going into details I will propose that the major reason why Adventism has not more fully utilized this book in its theology may be linked to classic dogmatic positions that it was seen as supporting. A fresh study of this Epistle with the awareness of this dogmatic problem might provide a new perspective that could enrich the Adventist search for a biblical balance and coherence of the "already" and "not yet" in terms of its soteriology and eschatology.

THE EPISTLE TO THE ROMANS

The immediate Pauline concern for writing this epistle may seems to be missiological, and in that context the need to combat the prevalent culture of shame and honor with its boasting of descent, inheritance, privilege, status and achievements before men and God. Such values and attitudes were not only subversive of the gospel but also of social relations, as humans were categorized by these criteria as being superior or inferior. However, whatever the reasons for Paul writing this epistle, more fully than any other epistle it exposes Paul's worldview and thus his views on the human predicament and God's gracious provisions.

Without going into any detailed expositions of the structure and content of this epistle a few observations might be in place. Paul's epistle is clearly embedded in the Old Testament biblical story line with a focus on the themes of beginnings, fall, and the unfolding redemptive promise of God moving forward towards its fulfillment in the renewal of all things. Thus Paul appears to think in terms of the past, present and future of salvation history seeing it as an unfolding story progressing in stages towards its future divinely intended goal.

Immediately after stating up front that he has good news for the world, Paul then begins his theological treatise by highlighting God's disapproval of evil as manifest in human history from the beginning, throughout the human story into the present; a disapproval that will ultimately be manifested in the future final judgment (Romans 1:18–3:19). That seems to be the horizon within which he then proceeds to present God's gracious redemptive promises and actions as manifest in human history from the very beginning, throughout the human story and into the present story about Christ; a redemption that will eventually be manifested in the restoration of all things through the judgment of Christ. (Romans 8:17–39)

Thus Paul's salvation-historical paradigm has a central Christological focus particularly with reference to the past, present and future redemptive work of God which, although it is seen as proceeding in stages, is nevertheless seen by Paul as an indivisible coherent whole. In other words, Paul seems to present the Christ solution not only as the antidote to the present existential predicament of human sinfulness and divine disapproval, but also as the antidote to the ultimate predicament of human sinfulness and divine disapproval in the cosmic eschatological judgment. Thus Christ appears to be depicted as the solution to the challenges of sin in the "already" and the "not yet". The final vindication and glorification of believers in Paul's thinking appears to be a presently guaranteed outcome for those who presently are in Christ Jesus, that is, positioned in grace. (Romans 5:12–21; 8:1; 31–39)

It could be noted that just as the problem of evil is seen by Paul in terms of the past, present and future, so God's solution in Christ is seen in terms of the past present and future. There seems to be a clear correlation between the "already" and the "not yet" in Paul's thinking and thus between present redemption in Christ and future glorification and vindication of believers in the eschatological judgment. Thus there is a striking similarity in the salvation-historical pattern between Adventist and Pauline thinking. This is seen particularly in the correlation between the "already" and the "not yet," not only in terms of God's response to sin but also in terms of God's redemptive response and thus the divine purpose for the world.

Given Paul's salvation-historical pattern of the past, present and future and the dynamic correlation between the "already" and "not yet," correlated with his Christological centre, this might mean that this epistle in particular could further inform the Adventism paradigm and even help to resolve some of the soteriological issues that have burdened the internal and external Adventist debate. The Pauline usage of motifs, such as being in Christ, being in Grace and being right with God in terms of justification, vindication and glorification, within the context of his dual horizon of the "already" and "not yet," could provide a fruitful and enriching perspective for Adventist theology. Once the epistle of Paul is liberated from its bondage to past dogmatic traditions and allowed to tell its own story on its own premises then it might turn out that this book in particular could be a constructive link in Adventist theological thinking.

12

The Epistle to the Romans: A Response to Robert Jewett from an Adventist Perspective

Jean-Claude Verrecchia

Robert Jewett's commentary on the epistle to the Romans is a massive masterpiece: 1140 pages; about 15000 footnotes; a 35-page bibliography, in two columns; the result of 26 years of research. After considering it, any scholar could ask himself: "and then, what could I write on Romans?"

How could an Adventist reader react and respond to this commentary?

Response One: The Place of Romans in Adventist Theology

Out of the 1140 pages, Adventist scholars feature 6 times. One of them (Keith Augustus Burton) is acknowledged in the preface for his bibliographic assistance. Robert Badenas—Jewett was among the examiners for his dissertation's defense at Andrews University—features once in the main text and nine times in the *apparatus criticus*. The other scholars feature eight times altogether, in the footnotes only (Bacchiocchi; Dederen; Salom; Young). They don't appear on the list of the works cited.

This rapid statistical analysis points clearly to the fact that Romans is not a major work for Adventist theology. This observation is quite surprising when considering the Adventist church's claim of being the heir of the Reformers. Why this lack of interest?

As far as the New Testament is concerned, the book of Revelation, the sermon to the Hebrews and the epistle to the Galatians are probably the top three. I see at least two reasons why Romans does not rank high in the Adventist canon. First, early Adventists came from a Protestant or pietist background. They were pretty confident that it was not necessary for them to reinvent the wheel and to start preaching the Gospel from scratch. What happened later in the Adventist history proves that their soteriology was not that elaborate. Second, Adventism has always been closer to American Calvinism than to Lutheranism. A real, very pragmatic Christian life was often considered more important than theological debates.

It's quite obvious that Revelation was the book for early Adventists. They read it, in liaison with Daniel, to ground their enthusiasm regarding the imminent coming of Christ.

But a major theological crisis changed this perspective when in 1888 two young Adventist scholars, A. T. Jones and J. H. Waggoner challenged the church interpretation about the law in Galatians.

For decades, Adventism had preached and written that the law in Galatians was only the ceremonial law, not the Ten Commandments. Jones and Waggoner questioned this interpretation and claimed that the law in Galatians included the ceremonial laws and the Ten Commandments as well. After painful discussions, the church finally accepted their interpretation. Many historians of the Adventist church consider this 1888 crisis as the access door through which Adventism entered into the Protestant family, having accepted two main Reformers' principles: *sola fidei* (faith alone) and *sola gratia* (grace alone).

Other crises changed again the perspective. Right after the great disappointment of 1844, the interpretation of the sanctuary doctrine was debated. But the traditional interpretation prevailed, even though often challenged. Nevertheless, at the beginning of the twentieth century, A. F. Ballenger questioned it again. According to his view, first, Hebrews was not pointing to any two-apartment ministry of Jesus in a heavenly sanctuary; second, Jesus did enter into the most Holy place right after his ascension, and not in 1844. Consequently, atonement had been fulfilled at the cross, not nineteen centuries later.

Ballenger's views were rejected, but the problem was not solved and it reappeared regularly. Another crisis culminated in 1980 when Desmond Ford, an Australian scholar, challenged the traditional interpretation of Hebrews as well as the interpretation of the books of Daniel and Revelation, and the role of Ellen G. White.

Neither in the years following the disillusion of 1844, nor in 1888, nor in 1980, did the epistle to the Romans came into the first place. Surprisingly, Romans—a difficult text—has not been the topic of the Sabbath school quarterly for many years!

RESPONSE TWO: ADVENTISTS' PLACES OF INTEREST IN ROMANS

Despite its rather modest contribution to Adventist theology, some topics of Romans are taken into consideration by Adventist theologians. Among those are the role of the law, the inner conflict of Romans 7, the homosexuality issue, the role of Israel and the subjection to authorities.

1. THE ROLE OF THE LAW

The most relevant Adventist contribution to Romans has been made by Robert Badenas, who published his dissertation in 1985, with the help of Jewett.[1]

As Sabbath keepers, Adventists have always considered a priority to support their belief and practice on this matter. As such, any text which could be interpreted with an antinomian perspective would be considered a serious threat.

Considering Jewett's exegesis of 10:4, Adventist readers will be pleased to see that it refers to Badenas' study and reaches a conclusion totally acceptable for them: As Badenas and others have shown, "the final notions of *telos* (end, goal) are never indicative of mere cessation, discontinuation or suspended action. When finality is incurred it is accompanied by a hint of innate fulfillment."[2]

Nevertheless, the consequences of this interpretation might be questioned by some Adventist scholars: "In Christ righteousness can be gained without conforming to the mores of any culture. Christ thus reveals and accomplishes the original goal of the law, which had been subverted by competition for honor and by ascribing shame to outsiders" (620).

2. THE INNER CONFLICT (ROMANS 7:13–25)

At the end of his extended exegesis of this paragraph, Jewett concludes that "the entire pericope concentrates on Paul's paradigmatic situation before his conversion . . . ." (473)

Some Adventist theologians will welcome this interpretation. Some alleged "Reformed Adventists" may use it in a perfectionist sense. But some other Adventist theologians who would naturally accept the typical Lutheran-Calvinist interpretation will question the validity of the "status acquisition" as a valid key in interpreting this section.

Moreover, Pedersen will question the outcome of Jewett's interpretation on eschatology: " . . . the temporal categories are absent from verse 25b–c, the effort to see therein a reference to the "eschatological tension" between the already and not yet of faith is misguided" (473; against Dodd).

---

1 Robert Badenas, *Christ the End of the Law. Romans 10:4 in Pauline Perspective* (Sheffield: Sheffield University Press, 1985).

2 Jewett, *Romans*, 619, quoting Badenas, *Christ the End of the Law*, 44.

3. ON HOMOSEXUALITY

Says Jewett on Romans 1:24–32: "It should be clear from the outset, however, that Paul's aim is not to prove the evils of perverse sexual behavior; that is simply assumed. The aim is to develop a thesis about the manifestation of divine wrath in the human experience of Paul's time. In contrast to traditional moralizing based on this passage, sexual perversion is in Paul's view "the result of God's wrath, not the reason for it" [Käsemann quoted] (173).

Is there is a tension in Jewett's exegesis on this matter? On one hand, he gives numerous evidences from historical sources that homosexuality was not in favour in those times. One the other, he assumes that Paul uses a "highly prejudicial language, particularly to modern ear" (p. 173). What is Paul's understanding of homosexuality being the result of God's wrath?

4. THE GOVERNING AUTHORITIES

Jewett considers that "it is the God embodied in the crucified Christ that is in view here, which turns this passage into a massive act of political cooptation" (790). Further, quoting Ellul: "Paul's argument is that Nero 'is not God. He is not the center of the world. He is not the master of nature: if he has power, it was given to him by the God of Jesus Christ'" (790).

How far could Christians go between "abject subservience" and "critical submission" is not that obvious. Very sadly, as an example, the Adventist church administration in Germany decided to passively support the Nazi regime during World War II. And the Jewett on Romans seems somehow a bit more cautious than the Jewett of *The Myth of the American Superhero* (Grand Rapids: Eerdmans, 2002) or the Jewett of *Captain America and the Crusade against Evil* (Grand Rapids: Eerdmans, 2003).

5. ISRAEL IN SALVATION HISTORY

Romans 9–11 is another theological *locum* for Adventism. What will be the final role of Israel in the salvation history? As the number of Jewish Adventists tend to grow, even though the figures are still modest, this issue could well become a hot potato in some Adventist circles.

Jewett clearly states that there is no reason to change the meaning of the noun Israel in 11:26, compared to the rest of the epistle. It therefore designates ethnic Israel and not the believers, whether Jews and Gentiles. Jewett states also that according to Paul, "the identity of Israel would not be erased by accepting Christ as the Messiah" (702).

Not surprisingly, the final interpretation of chapters 9–11 points to the conversion of "all," including Jews and Gentiles, each group taking "decisive steps" against its "own chauvinistic tendencies" (723).

Adventists supersessionists or non supersessionists will probably agree on this necessity of abandoning chauvinism. But one may wonder if the "all" centered explanation will satisfy either group.

Response Three: How Adventism Could Benefit from Jewett's Commentary?

As an oversimplification, one might say that there are three main interpretations of Romans: Luther's one, for which justification by faith is the topic of the Epistle (mainly chapters 1 to 8, with an emphasis on the first five chapters); a pietistic interpretation underlined by the Methodist awakening, for which chapters 6 to 8, dealing with sanctification, are said to be the most important; the empirical interpretation, which considers the practical advices given in chapters 12 to 15 as the core message of Paul to the Romans.

Jewett's commentary breaks new ground, even though he pays tribute to Bishop John William Colenso, a missionary in South Africa in 1863, who first recognized "that Romans was a missionary document aimed at overcoming the premises of imperial honor" (xv).

1. Christian Mission as the Core of Romans

Justification by faith, sanctification by faith, Israel as the remnant, Jesus as the second Adam, the issues of guilt and forgiveness are not the main topics of Romans. The dream, the plan, and the burning passion of Paul were to go in Spain and to present the Gospel to the "barbarians". But in order to do so, he needed the church of Rome to be a kind of advance base not for practical reasons but mainly as a theological support.

Unfortunately, in its present situation, the church of Rome was not credible since its members were living in an imperialistic competition. "The rhetorical climax of the letter is therefore in the authentic portions of the *peroratio* of 15:14–16:16, 21–24 that alludes to this missionary project and urges the churches in Rome to welcome one another as equals in Christ, thus demonstrating the power of the gospel to overcome cultural barriers and conflicts" (xv).

Cultural barriers were huge in Rome. The search for one's own glory was a main occupation. Rome was an honor society. Jewett asserts that the group was more important than the individual which can be questioned and could jeopardize his own interpretation. What is clear, though, is that the Christians inhabitants of the city lived mainly in suburban districts, and were considered an underclass. Paul tackled this problem as shown by a semantic field analysis. "Honor," "dishonor," "shame" on one hand; "glory," "boast," "praise" on the other;

but also "weak" and "strong"; "Greeks" and "Gentiles." In this context, righteousness through faith means to accept the shameful death of Christ in behalf of every human being. God is righteous because he is impartial.

This interpretation might be very helpful to Adventist missiology. If one understands Jewett properly, missiology is not the last chapter of theology but its foundation. In other words missiology is not the consequence of theology, but theology is the consequence of missiology.

The history of Adventism sounds a bit different compared to this paradigm. Its started by an eschatology. It continued with a soteriology, and later with a missiology (Andrews, the first missionary of the church left the United States in 1874, 30 years after the beginning of the Adventist movement).

Nevertheless, Adventism became easily convinced that mission was important, even though it had experienced some difficulty to understand what were the implications of the great commission (shut door theology which put mission on jeopardy). Jewett's interpretation reinforces this priority.

But, this prioritization bears other implications: mission asks for good relationships or, in other words, for a sound anthropology (the way one understands what is a human being). Any form of imperialism, either cultural, or political, or social, or racial or even theological is totally unacceptable and contrary to the Gospel. If the church bears in her such discriminations, she disqualifies for the mission.

Priority to the mission implies also for the church that she might have to position herself against the ruling authorities. The rules of the Roman society were in contraposition vis-à-vis Paul's message. But at the same time, Paul was rather happy to benefit his Roman citizenship to travel.

In the end, missiology needs a sound theology. It's because of the burning passion of the mission for Spain that Paul wrote his most sophisticated and elaborate theology. Whether the role of theology, including theological research, is important is not always obvious. Mission without theology could end in a total vacuum.

2. ADVENTISM AND BARBARIANS

Who are the Barbarians today? The migrants might well be the twentieth century barbarians. In many Western countries, the majority of the Adventist church membership is not native. The fast growing communities are migrants' communities. These populations try to settle in developed countries for obvious economical reasons. The important flow of migrations has considerably impacted the native communities. Very often, sadly, the natives have left their own communities to become tiny minorities elsewhere. Jewett's interpretation puts forward the challenge of mutual acceptance of others.

But, unlike the Romans' situation, it is fair to admit that the population of migrants might well be caught in the spiral of glory and honor in their search for prosperity.

According to a specific Adventist terminology, the barbarians might also well be the "unreached." The temptation of imperialism is a threat for Adventism. Beside its strong doctrinal basis, Adventism is also a way of life. As soon as any group of the church is strong in numbers and means, it can easily impose its own perception of Adventism. In this respect, reading Romans again is more than a necessity.

3. ROMANS' THEOLOGY AND THE UNITY OF THE CHURCH

The unity of the church is a prevalent theme in Adventism's those recent years. The fragmentation of the church is a real threat. On the one hand a fast growing church in the emergent countries. A poor church. A church of the outcasts. A rather conservative church, theologically speaking. On the other hand, a rich but dying church, older and older, rather liberal. The clash between the two sides seems quite inevitable sooner or later. Jewett's interpretation reminds us that to solve these tensions is not a matter of sociology, or politics, or race management, or democracy or education. Only a sound theology will help to cope with the problem, rooted in the impartiality of God, who makes us righteous in Christ.

THREE QUESTIONS

1. HERMENEUTICAL QUESTION

Jewett's interpretation opens a rather different understanding of Romans. Where does this new outcome come from? Does it come from a very meticulous historico-critical analysis? Or is it the result of a thorough rhetorical analysis? Or does Jewett give the best example of reader response hermeneutics? In other words, where does this new challenging interpretation comes from? From Paul as the author of the text? From the text alone, notwithstanding its author? Or from the modern theologian (Jewett)?

2. TRADITION AND INTERPRETATION

Which methodology, if any, a church would use to read anew some of its favorite books (for Adventism, it could well be Daniel, Revelation, Genesis, or Hebrews)?

3. ATONEMENT METAPHORS IN ROMANS

Atonement metaphors are not numerous in Romans. Nevertheless, does Jewett's new perspective on Romans pay justice to them? Or in other words, are they inconsistent, mere juxtapositions to suggest different and conflicting soteriologies. Or are they essential in Paul's theology? How to interpret, for example, Romans 3:21–26?

13

Response to Collonges Colleagues

Robert Jewett

Thanks to both of my colleagues for reflecting on the Romans commentary in the light of Adventist theology. I had been aware that your theological tradition rested on Daniel, Revelation, and Hebrews, but learn now the basic reason for the marginalization of Romans in Sabbath school curriculum and theology. The traditional doctrine of justification by faith tended to weaken the tension between the already and the not yet of premillennial fulfillment, if Professor Pedersen's thesis is correct.[1] We share a resistance against the distortions of Protestant orthodoxy, which turned justification by faith into a weapon with which to bludgeon their enemies. It was used as proof that certain Protestants were superior to all other believers in holding this doctrine to the exclusion of all else. It seems to me that this produces a new form of "justification by works," in that holding a certain belief makes me into God's favorite. Pedersen's thesis could be correlated with my reinterpretation of justification by faith in Romans as requiring the abandonment of superiority claims that sustained the Roman Empire and was leading the congregations in Rome to discriminate against each other.

It appears to me that resistance against claims of superiority have long been part of the Adventist tradition. It seems clear from Douglas Morgan's study of *Adventism and the American Republic* that doubt about the post-millennial optimism and exceptionalism related to America as the "new order of the ages" was a major factor in the appeal of the Millerite

[1] I cannot find the citation from Alister E. McGrath, *Iustitia Dei: A History of the Christian Doctrine of Justification* (Third Edition; Cambridge: Cambridge University Press, 2005), and after reading through his book, I wonder if the citation is from a review.

movement.[2] As George W. Knight points out, the Adventist movement came to reject the popular belief in "American progress" and superiority along with the optimistic hopes of social reform that had arisen out of the Second Great Awakening.[3] Only a great battle against the forces of evil and the return of Christ would be able to inaugurate the millennial era in the view of these early Adventists. The means of the anticipated divine triumph differ somewhat from Paul's vision of the reconciliation of every nation as converts join in united praise of God in Romans 15 after the success of the mission to the end of the world in Spain. In contrast to the Book of Revelation that envisions divine annihilation of the godless, Paul's letter expresses the hope that "all," including "all Israel" will be converted by the gospel and saved (Romans 11:26, 32).[4] Romans also shares Adventism's realistic skepticism of civic cults that celebrate the alleged superiority of imperial elites. Moreover, the gospel of God's impartial righteousness expressed in Christ equalizes the honor of insiders and outsiders, "Greeks and Barbarians . . . Jews and Gentiles," which could sustain the Adventist outreach to "migrants" as described by Prof. Verrecchia.

Prof. Verrecchia rightly gives precedence to "the role of the law," which has been a major bone of contention between Adventists and other Protestants. My argument is that at many points in the argument of Romans, it is law in its various cultural embodiments rather than the Jewish Torah alone that is the target of Paul's critique.[5] This letter is emphatically not anti-Judaic, which results in legitimation of sabbath keepers, an issue between house churches in Rome as we can see in 14:5–6. By employing generic terminology Paul avoids taking sides between early sabbatarians and sunday celebrators, insisting only that "each be fully convinced in his own thinking." While Paul's seemingly nonchalant acceptance of these options in identifying a Christian holy day is disturbing for commentators, it seems to be a fitting expression of his missionary principle of being "all things to all people." These are some of the reasons I find Robert Badenas' study of Romans 10:4 so important, which rejects the absolutizing of justification by faith. Paul is serious about "establishing law" in Romans 3:31, which correlates with Badenas' translation of 10:4. Of particular significance is that *nomos*

---

[2] See Douglas Morgan, *Adventism and the American Republic: The Public Involvement of a Major Apocalyptic Movement* (Knoxville: University of Tennessee Press, 2001), 11–29.

[3] George R. Knight, *Millennial Fever and the End of the World: A Study of Millerite Adventism* (Boise: Pacific Press Publishing Association, 1993), 142.

[4] See Robert Jewett, "Wrath and Violence in Paul's First and Last Letters: Reflections on the Implications of Divine Impartiality," in *The Impartial God: Essays in Biblical Studies in Honor of Jouette M. Bassler*, edited by Calvin J. Roetzel and Robert L. Foster, *Divine Impartiality* (Sheffield: Sheffield Phoenix Press, 2007), 142.

[5] See Jewett, "Wrath and Violence in Paul's First and Last Letters," 122–33.

("law") is used both times in verse 31 without the article, which suggests that law in general may be in view. Greco-Romans as well as Jews were at times passionate advocates of the sanctity of their laws, so Paul's argument allows an appeal to a mixed audience in Rome.

Both Professors Verrecchia and Pedersen comment on the missiological concern of Romans. I agree that Paul follows an Old Testament paradigm in seeing "beginnings, fall, and the unfolding redemptive promise of God moving forward towards its fulfillment in the renewal of all things." (Pedersen) In contrast to some forms of Adventist theology, however, Paul proclaims some elements of victory in the present, as in Romans 8:37 and 12:21. Here Paul employs the verb for conquering and being victorious (*nikaō*) that was so widely popularized in the celebrations of the Greek goddess Nike and of the Roman goddess Victoria. The imperial authorities celebrated Victoria in monuments, coins, public inscriptions, triumphal parades, public games, and other propaganda as the key to world peace: "Pax was thus the blessed condition brought about by Augustus' labor. It rested upon Victoria; and Augustan propaganda constantly and intimately linked the imperial virtues of Pax and Victoria. Pax could only be achieved through Victoria; and the promise of permanent Pax lay entirely in the guarantee of perpetual Victoria. Victory was thus the essential prerequisite for peace."[6] The subtle interaction with the Roman cultural context that I have traced throughout the letter thus surfaces again in the wording of this crucial verse, contrasting triumph over evil by love and hospitality rather than by force. In the immediate context of the citation from Proverbs, for which this verse provides such an effective rhetorical climax, treating enemies as fellow humans who require basic necessities is the path to overcoming enmity. In verse 20, giving food and water to enemies is the way such victory is attained. As the "culminating exclamation" at the end of a discourse on "genuine love," this verse places the Christian ethic within a transformative framework that is universal in scope but local in operation. The thought of overcoming "evil" through everyday acts of solidarity would be grandiose except for the framework of a global mission in behalf of the righteousness of God, which is the theme and purpose of Romans.

Despite the relatively late start as described by Verrecchia, Paul shares the cross-cultural orientation that has developed in Adventism, which is one of the few truly integrated churches.

Prof. Verrecchia raises an important hermeneutical question: whether this interpretation of Romans derives from the historical-critical

---

[6] J. Rufus Fears, "The Theology of Victory at Rome: Approaches and Problems," *Aufstieg und Niedergang der römischen Welt* 17.2 (1981), 807.

analysis or from the rhetorical analysis. I can only answer this question by sketching the gradual discovery of the sources of my confusion.

- When I began work on the commentary in 1980, I found it baffling that the interpretation of justification by faith as individual forgiveness of sins in my interpretive tradition from Luther, Wesley, Barth and Käsemann was not supported by the vocabulary of this letter. I was facing the unbiblical absolutizing of a Reformation doctrine described by Pedersen, but for a long time didn't know what to make of it.
- The text critical issues were also baffling because after abandoning my early adherence to the theory of Rom 16 as a series of greetings to Ephesian friends attached to the rest of the letter, the relevance of these greetings remained unclear. None of the commentaries on my shelf related these details to the argumentative thrust of the argument as a whole.
- The details about the congregational situation in chapters 14–15 seemed contradictory, and no reconstruction of that situation actually threw any light on the theology of forgiveness that was supposed to animate the whole. None of this seemed to relate to the Spanish Mission that the letter appeared to support, and no commentary threw light on this because the Spanish context was nowhere even discussed. When I read the article by W. P. Bowers that demonstrated the lack of Jewish presence in Spain, it was suddenly clear that Paul's missionary strategy had to be reconceived, but how this might relate to the argument in the letter was totally unclear.
- For the first several years, I tried to understand the letter with epistolographic methods, but found that the concept of the "body" of a letter threw no light on the complicated organization of Paul's argument. Then I read Hans Dieter Betz's commentary on Galatians that appeared in 1979 and began studying rhetoric with colleagues at Northwestern University. I soon discovered that part of my confusion came from following the tradition embodied especially by Ernst Käsemann of assuming that Romans was a defense of the true gospel, which placed it in the judicial genre. This produced hundreds of

discrepancies that no one could explain, and I decided Wilhelm Wuellner was correct to see this as falling in the demonstrative genre, which I then discovered included ambassadorial speeches and letters. This meant that the historical details were intended as abstractions that covered a variety of congregational circumstances, and that Paul was seeking to find common ground between different theological and cultural groups in Rome, whose diversity was evident in the previously baffling details of chapter 16.

- Then I began to study the implications of the language of honor and shame that was strewn through the letter, and began the process of trying to tie all this together. A study of modern films dealing with issues of honor and shame began to open the door to a theological and emotional understanding that my Wesleyan tradition gave me no basis to grasp. Grappling with the element of shame implicit in crucifixion was crucial in this process. I wrote books and articles on parts of Romans, but it was at least 17 to 18 years before I was able to put it all more or less together. Several times my work was interrupted by other projects with seemingly superior urgency, such as the two years after 9/11 dealing with the mistaken course of the American Civil Religion with books, articles and lectures.

So a commentary that was supposed to be finished in 10 years required 26, plus a final 13 months of checking references, filling in additional bibliography, correcting mistakes and creating indexes. The whole letter seems clear to me now, but this is no absolute proof that my interpretation is right. In a symposium like this, I am reminded that we all see through a glass darkly, and that all our prophecy is in part. This is something that some Adventists learned in 1845 and that my country still has not learned, as our current impasse in Iraq demonstrates! So I would like to thank my two colleagues for significant comments about the commentary, and thanks to you all for participating in the discussion to follow.

The Washington Symposium
November 19, 2006

14

A Review of Jewett, *Romans*

James D. G. Dunn

Bob Jewett's commentary on Romans[1] is one of the finest to have appeared in modern times. Most commentators follow a similar pattern, and, if truth be told, often simply take over source references and cross-references from their predecessors. Indeed, when writing a commentary on a text like Romans it can be a wearisome business having to trail through predecessor after predecessor all saying much the same thing, shifting the chairs round the table, and moving the bowl of flowers, but not much else! With Bob's commentary, however, you can be sure, nothing is second hand. In the twenty or so years of working towards this great commentary he has approached the whole and the individual parts with a freshness, which has often produced genuinely new material to help illuminate particular texts and which has brought a fine maturity of judgment to controverted points of exegesis. Even in surveys of earlier views and summaries of particular debates his writing has a sharpness of observation and critique which is never less than a stimulus and pleasure to engage with.

I could go on at length and in extensive detail on the value of the commentary and easily spend the whole of my allotted time highlighting various passages and details where I have benefited, even from my inevitably rather cursory read through. And the notes in my most recent work on Romans are already full of such references. But for today, it is no doubt more to the point that I highlight a number of points at which I find myself in disagreement, so that the ensuing discussion might be the more fruitful—for me at least, if not for Bob.

I will focus on one major point of disagreement, a second complementary issue of primary importance, and finally on some illustrations of how the disagreement and issue work out.

1 Robert Jewett, *Romans* (Hermeneia; Minneapolis: Fortress Press, 2006).

I. THE PURPOSE OF ROMANS

Bob reviews the various reasons given for Paul's writing of Romans and avoids the trap of playing off one suggested reason against another. He does however argue for a strong version of what can be described as "the missionary hypothesis": that Paul's dominating concern was to recruit support among the Roman congregations for his planned Spanish mission[2]—Paul's intention being that Phoebe, patron of the Spanish mission, would carry the letter to Rome and present it to the Roman tenement churches in order to win their support for that mission.

The first point of disagreement here regards Phoebe's mission. Paul calls on the Roman congregations to "assist her in whatever matter (*pragma*) she may have need of you" (Romans 16:2). Bob argues that the *pragma* is "her missionary patronage"[3]; but his translation gives the *pragma* ("matter, affair") a definiteness lacking in the Greek—"whatever she needs in the matter," rather than "whatever matter she may need help with." Bob translates what he thinks Paul must have intended, on Bob's thesis. But what Paul actually says does not seem to envisage a definite project, but serves rather as a more general appeal to help Phoebe in whatever business she has to attend to.

Bob also objects to the suggestion that the *pragma* is a lawsuit. He thinks it unlikely that the impoverished congregations of Rome could help Phoebe in such a business.[4] Yet, he also maintains that that the same impoverished congregations could nevertheless "participate in a credible manner" in the Spanish mission.[5] That is surely odd, since "credible support" for such a bold mission would surely have required similar sorts of contact and influence as any business more local to Rome itself.

Worthy of note here is that Bob is the first to pay close attention to "the cultural situation in Spain" at the time, and to what would have been involved in undertaking a mission in Spain, given, not least, the lack of Jewish settlement there and the fact that Greek was not widely known.[6] Which raises the interesting question as to whether Paul had any clear idea of what a mission to Spain would involve. Where no Jewish synagogue and penumbra of Gentile God-fearers were to be found, and where Greek could not serve as the language of communication, there must be serious questions about the viability of such a mission and about the realism of Paul's stated ambition.

---

[2] Jewett, *Romans*, 80–89.
[3] Jewett, *Romans*, 89–91.
[4] Jewett, *Romans*, 89.
[5] Jewett, *Romans*, 88.
[6] Jewett, *Romans*, 74–79.

II. ROMANS AS A THEOLOGICAL DOCUMENT

This brings me to my main point of critique: the commentary's relative lack of interest in the theology of what is one of the most powerfully theological documents in the corpus of Christian writings.

I go back to the question of the letter's purpose. I certainly agree with Bob that it is not necessary to play off the various "reasons" suggested for Romans against each other—missionary, apologetic, pastoral—in various permutations and combination. Of course, Paul could certainly have had several purposes in mind. What needs to be explained above all, however, is why the letter takes the form it does, why it goes into such detail, and why it is so dominated by the challenge of Jewish and Gentile believers recognizing and respecting each other as equal recipients of the gospel. Almost all of the usually offered reasons, taken individually, fail to explain why Paul felt it necessary in this letter to provide such a lengthy exposition of his gospel. For example, there is no hint that "works of the law" (3:20; 3:27–4:6; 9:12, 32; 11:6) or "seed of Abraham" (4:13–18; 9:7–8) were issues in Rome; Paul's concern here is a reflection much more of the issues he had debated earlier, in Antioch and Galatia, and no doubt elsewhere. Or again, was it necessary to have such an extensive put-down of Jewish presumption (2:1–3:20; 3:27–4:25), if the real target was Gentile presumption and intolerance (as indicated in 11:17–24 and 14:1)? And again, did Paul need to set out his gospel so fully simply in order to commend Phoebe, or to prepare the Roman congregations for his visit, or to deal with the pastoral problems in Rome? A much briefer letter of introduction or exhortation would have met these aims. Nils Dahl, I believe was nearer the mark when he observed that, "It is not the problems of a local church but the universal gospel and Paul's own mission which in this letter provide the point of departure for theological discussion."[7]

That Paul felt it necessary to spell out the gospel which he intended to preach in Spain would provide a better explanation, were it not for the fact that the Jewish/Gentile dimension of the letter would seem singularly inappropriate for a situation where there were, apparently, few if any Jews, as Bob himself has pointed out.[8] Again, while the extensive apology for his gospel would make a great deal of sense in view of Paul's imminent trip to Jerusalem, where he could expect to be quizzed and challenged in regard to it yet once more, it is less easy to see the logic of addressing this apology to the Roman believers and how

---

[7] N. A. Dahl, "The Missionary Theology in the Epistle to the Romans," in idem, *Studies in Paul: Theology for the Early Christian Mission* (Minneapolis: Augsburg Press, 1977), 78.

[8] Jewett, *Romans*, 74–75.

he could hope for them to make any difference to what was to happen in Jerusalem. And for all its extent and theological contents, Romans can hardly count as a systematic statement of Paul's theology in the round, since it makes no attempt to expound and explain important features, for example, of Paul's christology and ecclesiology as we know them from his other letters. Nevertheless, the scope and length of the letter does seem to demand a reason somewhat as substantial as these. Eduard Lohse is also nearer the mark, I believe, when he points to the many passages which take up and develop thoughts and motifs that Paul had already used in his earlier letters and describes the character if Romans as "einer Summe des Evangeliums."[9]

What does become clear from the letter itself is that Paul saw himself at the end of what had been the most energetic, trying and fruitful periods of his mission. He had "completed (the preaching of) the gospel of Christ (*peplērōkenai to euangelion tou Christou*) from Jerusalem and in a sweep round to Illyricum" (Romans 15:19).[10] Clearly implied is Paul's conviction that a major segment of his grand mission strategy had been completed; with the implication that he should move on to the next stage, presumably under the continuing impression that time was short. That is, we should probably infer that Paul's desire to reach Spain meshed with his hope of winning "the full number of the Gentiles" to faith (11:25)[11] and thus of triggering the climax of God's purpose in history and the resurrection of the dead (11:13–15).[12]

He no longer had scope/opportunity (*topos*) in these (Aegean) regions (15:23). The perspective is revealing: given that he saw his task as planting the gospel securely in the major cities of the region, leaving it to the local believers to spread the gospel to surrounding cities and towns, his task in the Aegean was indeed complete; even so, his dealings with Corinth was a reminder that his "care for all the churches" was an ongoing burden, so that, again, the eschatological imperative must have been a major driving force.

In these circumstances, and given the relative calm of his few weeks in Corinth, while he was making final preparations to transport the collection to Jerusalem, Paul probably concluded that it was time to reflect on his mission to date, on its character, on the tensions and dissensions it had provoked, on what had proved to be most important in

---

[9] Eduard Lohse, *Der Brief an die Römer* (Göttingen: Vandenhoeck & Ruprecht, 2003), 46.

[10] See my *Romans 9-16* (Dallas: Word Books, 1988), 864; Douglas Moo, *The Epistle to the Romans* (Grand Raids: Eerdmans, 1996), 895–96; Klaus Haacker, *Der Brief des Paulus an die Römer* (Leipzig: Evangelische Verlagsanstalt, 1999), 308.

[11] The *peplērōkenai* ("completed") of 15:19 echoes the *plērōma* ("full number") of 11:25.

[12] On "life from the dead" (11:15) see my *Romans 9-16*, 657–58; Moo, *Romans*, 694–96; Jewett, *Romans*, 681 ("Reducing this to a metaphorical reference to spiritual blessing, new life, or restoration of Israel undercuts the rhetorical force of Paul's climactic question.")

the gospel he had been preaching, on what needed to be carefully thought through and set down. No doubt the exercise was partly at least with a view to the apologia he might have to make in Jerusalem, and partly at least to persuade the Roman believers of the scope and implications of his gospel. But Paul's primary objective, I suspect (with Dahl and Lohse), was to think through his gospel in the light of the controversies which it had occasioned and to use the calm of Corinth to set out his gospel and its ramifications in writing with a fulness of exposition which the previous trials and tribulations had made impossible and which would have been impossible to sustain in a single oral presentation.

What emerges clearly from Romans is that it was the tensions and issues that had been there from the beginning, in the confrontations in Jerusalem, in Antioch, in Galatia and (differently) in Corinth, which continued to preoccupy Paul's attention and to demand the sustained treatment which was now possible. These were the tensions and issues in a gospel which proclaimed a Jewish Messiah to a non-Jewish world: whether Gentile and Jew were in equal need of the gospel; how the God of Israel's justifying grace could extend to Gentiles; how the gospel, as compared with the Torah, deals with the reality of sin, the weakness of the flesh, and the power of death; in view of a gospel for all who believe, where stands Israel in the purpose of God? and how all this should work out in Rome itself? It is the fact that this is a letter which is explicitly addressed to Gentiles,[13] and yet is so dominated by Jewish issues, or better, with the issue of the Jewishness of the gospel—how do Jew and Gentile stand in relation to each other and how should they view each other before God? what is the role of the Torah for believers? who or what is "Israel"?—which has caused so much puzzlement among its interpreters. And yet in effect it is precisely what occasions this puzzlement which explains why the letter was written. For Paul's mission caused an equivalent puzzlement among many of his fellow Christian Jews (and probably many Gentile believers too); and, indeed, it is probably fair to conclude that it caused Paul some puzzlement as well, as he sought to respond to the call which he believed with all his heart had come to him on the Damascus road. Like a great thinker who has had to await retirement before he can find the time to set down his mature reflection, fruit of many individual controversies and essays, so Paul, arguably the greatest of Christian theologians, found just enough time in Corinth to set down this synthesis of his understanding of the most controversial aspect of his life's work: that the good news of Jesus Messiah is for all who believe.

[13] Romans 1:6, 13; 11:13–32; 15:7–12, 15–16; though the evidence of chapter 16 should not be overlooked; the Rome congregations were mixed, even if non-Jewish believers were in the majority.

In short, I believe that Bob's commentary illustrates the common recent failings, where discussion of the reasons for Romans has been too much diverted from the body of the letter to the epistolary framework, and where discussion of the character of the body of the letter has been too much diverted from the content itself to the question of rhetorical classification for the letter—epideictic, deliberative, protreptic, or what?[14] It is time, in my view, to reassert the importance of the body of the letter and the character of its content in assessing "the reason for Romans."

III. Some Illustrations

A. The Identity of the Interlocutor in 2:1–16

With the majority, I see 2:1 as addressed to a Jewish interlocutor. The attempt to argue in contrast that it is a Gentile interlocutor whom Paul has in view,[15] does not sufficiently take into account that the indictment of 1:18–32, while universal in scope, uses characteristic *Jewish* polemic (exemplified by the Wisdom of Solomon) against the idolatry and promiscuity of other nations, proof that Gentiles as a category were outside the law and beyond the scope of God's saving righteousness.[16] It also misses the degree to which the attitude critiqued in 2:1–6 is the attitude which we find once again in the Wisdom of Solomon (15:1–4—"even if we sin we are yours"), and in the *Psalms of Solomon*: the psalmist confident that "those who act lawlessly (one of his favourite phrases) will not escape the condemnation of the Lord" (the same phrase as in Romans 2:3), whereas God will spare the devout and grant them mercy; he destroys the sinner but (only) disciplines the righteous.[17] This seems to me clearly to be the attitude which Paul critiques in 2:1–6. Similarly, in suggesting that Paul already had in mind all the tensions of Romans 14:1–15:6, Bob misses the point that in chapter 14 it is the "weak" (that is, most probably the *Jewish*) traditionalist who "judges" the other (14:3), the same term as in 2:1.[18] It is the presumptiveness of such Jewish assumption of "favoured nation" status before God which Paul critiques by his repetition of "Jew first and Greek" in 2:9–10, and by drawing the law into the discussion in 2:12–15, that is, before he identifies his interlocutor explicitly as one who is called a "Jew."

---

[14] See for example the essays by Wuellner, Stirewalt and Aune in particular in Karl P. Donfried, editor, *The Romans Debate* (Revised and Expanded Edition; Peabody: Hendrickson, 1991), and Jewett, *Romans*, 41-46.

[15] As seen by Stanley K. Stowers, *A Rereading Romans: Justice, Jews and Gentiles* (New Haven: Yale University Press, 1994) and Runar M. Thorsteinsson, *Paul's Interlocutor in Romans 2: Function and Identity in the Context of Ancient Epistolography* (Stockholm: Ahlquist & Wiksell, 2003).

[16] As Jewett notes, the most explicit echoes in 1:23 are of Psalm 106:20 and Jeremiah 2:11 (*Romans*, 160–61).

[17] *Psalms of Solomon* 3; 9:6–7; 13:5–12; 16:11–15 (see my *Theology of Paul*, 115–17).

[18] Jewett, *Romans*, 197–98.

B. "WORKS OF THE LAW"

A second example comes in regard to the phrase *"works of the law."* Despite its obviously Jewish character Bob ignores the distinctively Jewish significance of "works of the law."[19] Similarly with the theme of "boasting" in 3:27: "Where then is boasting?" It still surprises me that earlier neo-orthodox exegesis could refer at once to "pride in accomplishments," "boasting in one's self (Sich-Rühmen),"[20] despite the obvious reference back to the "boasting" of 2:17, 23. As with others, in pressing for a wider reference, Bob plays down the obvious train of connected thought: boasting (3:27) → justification from works (of the law) (3:28) → God of Jews only (3:29).[21]

C. ROMANS 7:7–8:4 AS A DEFENCE OF THE LAW

That a "defence of the law" is an appropriate description of the passage should be obvious from the sequences 7:7–12, 13–14, 16–17, 22–23 and 8:3–4, though it is too little recognized.[22] Here once again Bob's desire to show the letter's bearing on the situation in Rome,[23] as also Philip Esler's, *Conflict and Identity*.[24] prevent them from seeing Paul's deeper concern to understand the role of the law in relation to the gospel. The problem, Paul is anxious to stress, is not the law, but Sin abusing the law, and the weakness of the flesh (7:7–8:3). The law as much as the "I" has been captivated by the power of Sin ("the law of sin and death").[25] The gospel in this account is first, that "what the law was unable to do in that it was weak through the flesh," God has done in and through his Son and the sin-offering of his death (8:3). And second, that the power of the Spirit liberates both the "I" and the law from their captivity to the power of Sin and Death, so that "the requirement of the law" can now be "fulfilled" in those "who walk in accordance with the Spirit" (8:4). Here I am happy to join with Lohse and Jewett in maintaining that *nomos* in 8.2 refers to the Torah, as implied by the train of thought in 8:2–4.[26]

D. THE "I" OF ROMANS 7:7–25

The reference of the "I" of 7:7–25 is of course much disputed. But I was disappointed by Bob's rejection of the "I" = Adam = humankind interpretation for 7:7–12. The appeal to Romans 5:13 as indicating that

---

[19] Jewett, *Romans*, 266–67.

[20] As still in Moo, *Romans*, 247 and Lohse, *Römer*, 137.

[21] Jewett, *Romans*, 295–96.

[22] Dunn, *Theology of Paul*, 156–58.

[23] Jewett, *Romans*, 440.

[24] Philip F. Esler, *Conflict and Identity in Romans: The Social Setting of Paul's Letter* (Minneapolis: Fortress Press, 2003), 239.

[25] The parallel between 7:18–20 (the divided "I") and 7:21–23 (the divided law) has been too little noticed by Romans commentators (Dunn, *Theology of Paul*, 472–77).

[26] Dunn, *Theology of Paul*, 645–47; Lohse, *Römer*, 229–30; Jewett, *Romans*, 480–81.

the law was not in existence in Adam's time[27] seems to me a particularly weak one. It ignores the fact that the Adam story could be read in different ways: one where Adam features as the beginning of the cosmic story of humankind's domination by the powers of Sin and Death (as in Romans 5:12–21); the other where Adam is the archetype of human experience of the power of Sin (as in 7:7–12 and 2 Baruch 54:19). It also plays down too much the probability that Jewish theology was already familiar with the thought that the command to Adam (not to eat of the tree of the knowledge of good and evil) already embodied or at least expressed the law of God.[28]

E. THE FINAL CLIMACTIC STATEMENT OF ROMANS —15:7–13

Some students of Romans check out the character of Romans commentaries by looking to see how they handle a passage like Romans 7, or perhaps 3:21–26. I tend now to check how they handle 15:7–13. The passage is so obviously Paul's attempt to round off what he has been on about for fourteen chapters, that it should give us decisive indications of what it was Paul thought he had been on about through these chapters. And certainly he begins by integrating the particular exhortations of 14:1–15:6 into this wider concern: "Therefore welcome one another, as Christ also welcomed you . . . ." (15:7) But the deeper theological concern is what dominates the remaining verses of this concluding paragraph.

One aspect is signalled by the reference to "God's truth" (15:8). The further play on the Hebrew root *'aman*, which embraces both the sense of "truth" (*'emeth*) and the sense of "faithfulness" (*'emunah*), and which thus overlaps with *dikaiosynē* in its sense of "covenant faithfulness," should not be ignored (as Bob does). Although we can hardly assume that Roman audiences would be familiar with the play on the Hebrew, Paul's earlier interweaving of the different Greek concepts in 3:3–7 (faithfulness and unfaithfulness, truth and lie, righteousness and unrighteousness) would have made it clearer when his letter was studied more closely. Paul's gospel was not just about Christians with differing views learning to live and eat together; it was much more profoundly about God, God's truth and faithfulness and righteousness coming to fullest and most effective expression in Christ.

The other key aspect is the repeated emphasis drawn from all three sections of the holy scriptures, the emphasis on Gentiles hearing the gospel, Jews and Gentiles worshipping together, and the root of Jesse as the one in whom the Gentiles can hope (15:9–12). Of course it was of first importance for Paul that the fulfilment of this vision should be evident in the believing house-groups in Rome. But for Bob to suggest that such

[27] Jewett, *Romans*, 442 and note 22; as also Esler, *Conflict and Identity*, 234–46.

[28] For example, see my *Romans 1-8*, 379–80; Hermann Lichtenberger, *Das Ich Adams und das Ich der Menschheit* (Tübingen: Mohr Siebeck, 2004), chapter 15.

a broader and deeper reference "undercuts" the direct relevance of the passage to the social context[29] is to look through the wrong end of the telescope. Rather, it is the relevance of this larger picture (Romans as a definitive statement of Paul's gospel) to the particular situation in Rome which enables Paul to make this final connection from the particulars of Romans 14 to the larger, richer theological themes which have dominated the letter as a whole.

In short, I yield to no one in my admiration for this most admirable commentary. But as with my great hero, J. B. Lightfoot, whom I rank still higher in the pantheon of Pauline commentators, I just wish Bob had engaged that much more fully with the profundities of what I still regard as the most profoundly theological of all the earliest Christian writings.

29 Jewett, *Romans*, 891.

15

Idol Worship or Imperial Sebastolatry?

Brigitte Kahl

To all God's beloved called saints who are in Rome. Grace to you and peace—Washington D.C., 2006 C.E.: Finally Romans has arrived at "Rome." At the war-torn threshold of the third millennium post Christ and right at the centre of the present-day global empire, Robert Jewett presents a new reading of Paul that translates *peace* not only from Greek *eirene* and Hebrew *shalom* but also from Latin as *pax*. This exercise in ancient rhetorical studies and comparative semiotics proves to be far from antiquarian. Step by step the contours of a conflict emerge that is no less pressing today than it was 2000 years ago: The clash between messianic *eirene* and imperial *pax* marks the core of Paul's Roman correspondence.

It would help to read this commentary on Romans alongside a few Roman images that often are more straightforward in their message than texts. Just recently, the city of Rome has seen the re-opening of the *Ara Pacis*, the ancient Altar of Peace dating back to emperor Augustus (9 B.C.E.), at display now in a new cover building designed by American architect Richard Meier. While Meier's controversial design has stimulated much debate, a more basic ideological and theological question hardly received similar attention: Why is it that a sacrificial altar dedicated to peace is located on the *Field of Mars*, i.e., a territory that belongs to the God of War? Why is it surrounded by the trophies, inscriptions, and insignia of world conquest, embedded into an overall spatial and architectural arrangement that communicates the supreme power bestowed by God Mars and Goddess *Nike*/Victory: the Egyptian obelisk, the *Res Gestae*, the Mausoleum, the monumental sun-dial as time-giver of the imperial era?[1] Undoubtedly *Pax Romana*, the Roman version of peace, embodies a concept of law and order derived from war and victorious violence. If one follows Robert Jewett' exegetical journey through the 16 chapters of *Romans*, an entirely different concept of peace becomes visible. Word by word, verse by verse, the term *eirene* gains a counter-meaning, reveals the imprints of a counter-knowledge and a counter-practice: the peace of the crucified Christ that moves on among the nations not on war horses and under *Nike's* trophies, but as an alternative practice of horizontal, inclusive and non-violent solidarity.

Not only *peace* but also *faith, grace,* and *righteousness* are infused with new substance. Very carefully and out of a seemingly unfathomable knowledge of ancient sources, interpretational trajectories, and secondary literature Robert Jewett re-reads the core terms of Christian theology and occidental dogmatics against the backdrop of the Roman master language in order to show the alternative meaning-making of Paul's messianic semiotics. And all of a sudden no longer "the Jews" and "Jewish law" appear as the antagonists of faith and at the heart of Pauline law criticism, but the *law* and *works of Empire*. This is an epistemological shift of epochal dimensions that in Jewett's disciplined analysis seems surprisingly obvious and self-evident. Yet throughout all the centuries of Christian interpretation this Rome-critical dimension of Paul has been eclipsed, except for a few rare and mostly recent exceptions. Friedrich Nietzsche over a hundred years ago understood and resented it, Adolf Deissmann explored it, a Jewish philosopher like Jacob Taubes saw it very clearly, Dieter Georgi brought it up again and again, followed by a few other pioneering scholars like Elsa Tamez, Neil Elliott, and Richard Horsley over the past two or three decades—and now it is there with all the power and glory of a full-size 1140-pages *Hermeneia* commentary. I simply want to thank Robert Jewett for the enormous scholarly work he has done. This commentary will help to fundamentally shape and re-shape what we think about Paul and Romans in the new millennium.

There are a lot of questions I would like to raise. Most of them would require some detailed exegetical discussion. I will focus on two more general issues here: the possibility of "coded language" in Romans and the role of imperial religion.

---

[1] For the *Ara Pacis* see Mary Beard and John Henderson, *Classical Art. From Greece to Rome* (Oxford: Oxford University Press, 2001), 186–87; For the *Ara Pacis* and the overall arrangement of the Field of Mars: Paul Zanker, *The Power of Images in the Age of Augustus* (New York; Ann Arbor: University of Michigan Press, 1990), 120–25, 172–83 (Ara Pacis), 144 (Obelisk and Sun dial), 72–77 (Mausoleum); John Dominic Crossan and Jonathan L. Reed, *In Search of Paul. How Jesus's Apostle Opposed Rome's Empire with God's Kingdom* (San Francisco: Harper Collins, 2004), 90–104.

HIDDEN TRANSCRIPTS?

After reading the commentary, the interpretation of Romans 1:26–27 and 13:1–7, traditionally the strongholds of Christian homophobia and political conservatism in Pauline Studies respectively, seem to me even more troublesome and puzzling than before. Why would Paul in the opening section of his universal peace declaration single out homosexuality in such a prominent way? And is it possible, as Jewett maintains, that the apostle in 13:1–7 for purely pragmatic reasons "abandons the revolutionary approach to honor" that he has outlined before, an approach based on Christ who gives precedence to the socially inferior and has "the dishonored receive honor"? (803) Was he instead "willing to accept the system that demanded honor for the emperor and his officials whether they deserved it or not" (803) and thus bought with relative ease into the phraseology of state obedience—just in order to safeguard his missional enterprise in Spain that in Jewett's opinion is the core concern of Romans?

It is certainly not my intention to advocate a "simple truth" about Paul, nor to eclipse the critique voiced by his feminist, liberationist, queer and post-colonial interpreters over the past decades. Yet one of the missing methodological questions that needs consideration is whether Paul's mode of speech was possibly less straightforward and "free" than we tend to think. As someone who learned to read and exegete texts in a pre-1989 Eastern European context, I was wondering whether Jewett's sociohistorical and rhetorical investigation of Paul as a theologian and practitioner of God's counter-empire wouldn't have to be supplemented much more deliberately by a "rhetoric of conspiracy." The assumption that Paul, within the general rhetorical conventions of his time, simply wrote down what he wanted to say might well be slightly too naïve. From Galatians 2:4 we know about the existence of informants and spies that trailed Paul's mission, an endeavor that according to Acts 17:7 could easily be seen as politically suspect. If we concede that Paul was willing "to be in the world but not of the world" and to negotiate a complex, self-contradictory existence " between the ages" (803), could that not also mean that he concealed his language, using codes and "hidden transcripts" that his addressees would need to decipher, maybe with the help of Phoebe who carried the letter (cf. Romans 16:1–2)? [2] Are there lines in between the lines that require attention, like e.g. Romans

---

[2] For the issue of coded language in Paul see James C. Scott, *Domination and the Arts of Resistance. Hidden Transcripts* (New Haven: Yale University Press, 1990); Richard A. Horsley, editor, *Hidden Transcripts and the Art of Resistance: Applying the Work of James C. Scott to Jesus and Paul* (Leiden/Boston: E. J. Brill, 2004); Brigitte Kahl, *Galatians Re-Imagined. Reading with the Eyes of the Vanquished* (Minneapolis: Fortress Press, 2010), 250–253.

12:21 as "headline" and subversion of 13:1–7? And could perhaps even Romans 1:26–27, the passage so widely and devastatingly exploited as a proof-text of Paul's unwavering stance against homosexuality, speak in coded language about something more and something else than what the words seem to communicate?

IMPERIAL RELIGION AND "SEBASTOLATRY"

This takes me to a second point where I would like to push the argument one step further. Jewett's theoretical framework for analyzing Paul's criticism of imperial ideology and social practices focuses primarily on the codes of honor and shame and the vertical, competitive system of social distinctions and hierarchies that is inscribed into them. (49–51) This might be too mono-dimensional. I wonder whether another element, politically and theologically even more sensitive, needs to be seen at least as much focal to Paul's critique of the "Empire of *Honor*"[3]: the *Religion* of Empire, more precisely the whole cluster of ideological, social and political activities that represent Caesar as God and Roma as Goddess.

I strongly agree with Jewett's assumption that Romans is not about doctrine or religion per se but a missional practice, not about individual salvation or a self-centered faith but a new way of living together in faith-communities all around the world where salvation becomes a present reality. Justification by faith in this model is about God's world rule as an empowerment of the powerless, weak, despised, who are all shameful and lacking of honor, whereas Caesar's global government and justice are established by military conquest that justifies the power of the strong over the weak, of Romans over Greeks and barbarians. The image of Paul as an ambassador authorized by the alternative "power of God," an emissary "extending the sovereign's cosmic foreign policy" through the powerless persuasive preaching of the gospel is compelling (page 138). New forms of communality are spreading to the ends of the earth. In small groups that are cooperatively interacting with each other God restores "arenas of righteousness" and beachheads of the new creation.

Compared to traditional interpretations, most notably Lutheran ones, this emphasis on Paul's mission as a transformative global practice subversive of the Roman imperial honor/shame pyramid is refreshing and eye-opening. But while the importance of the "practical" and community-oriented section of Romans in chapters 12–15, most notably the debate about weak and strong in 14–15 as well as the missionary project for Spain (15:23–29), in my opinion is undisputable,

3 See J. E. Lendon, *The Empire of Honour. The Art of Government in the Roman World* (Oxford: Clarendon Press, 1997).

I moreover would like to go back to the dogmatic core section in Romans 1–3 and Paul's justification theology. What actually does Paul say when he declares in Romans 3:28 that *justification* happens *by faith* and without *works of the law?* Jewett rightly points out that verses 3:29–31, traditionally under-exegeted, are an integral part of the justification statement: faith-justification translates the Oneness of the Jewish God (as confessed twice daily by every faithful Jew in the *Shema*) into a new mode of unification for Jews and non-Jews/Gentiles alike. This implies a new honor system through solidarity "in Christ". It invalidates the old honor codes and divisions that are based on "works" and "boasting" (3:27), i.e. on social privilege, achievement, status, performance. The insight that the thrust of Paul's critique of *boasting* and *works/law* is not targeting Judaism per se, rather Rome as "boasting champion of the ancient world" (p. 295), indeed is groundbreaking and has far reaching interpretive implications.

Yet there seems to be more to the Oneness of God so prominently accentuated in 3: 30 than just worldwide horizontal solidarity among the nations. The expression *heis ho theos* (" the God is one ") clearly links back to the beginning of the whole section in 1:18–23 and the criticism of image-making/idolatry there. Could it be that the first and second commandments, the prohibition to bow down in worship to other Gods than the *One*, the God of the Exodus (20:1–5), establish the argumentative framework underlying the whole section Romans 1–3? Does Paul target universal idolatry, not as worship of other gods *in general*, but much more precisely as *imperial idolatry*, i.e. false subservience and accommodation to the emperor and the Gods of empire that Paul sees as the theological root sin of both Jews and Gentiles all throughout?

This critique of imperial religion would be equally consistent with Paul's radical Jewishness and his rejection of the "empire of honor." While Self-magnification and Self-love at the expense of a shameful or less honorable "other" is indeed the sin that both Jews and Gentiles share, this whole system of imperial boasting and honor-seeking with Caesar at the top has inevitably its theological flipside as well: Its most pervasive paradigm and matrix is the all-encompassing magnification of the supreme imperial Self as universal God and son of God, Savior and Lord Caesar. This could mean that the "image of a perishable human" (singular!) that replaces the glory of the "imperishable God" in Romans 1:23 is gesturing at Caesar's image in particular. As Jewett himself states (162), this image may indeed be visually linked to images of "birds, quadrupeds, and reptiles" (the other set of idolatrous objects specifically mentioned by Paul in 1:23), e.g. on Roman standards and coins. This would make an imperial connotation quite compelling , an interpretation that is furthermore strengthened by the intertextual linkage between Romans 1:23 and the Golden Calf episode in Exodus 32 (160). Thinking along these lines, one might finally wonder whether the curious sequence of *esebasthesan* (using the Hapaxlegomenon *sebazomai*) and *elatreusan* in 1:24 might contain a half-hidden allusion to Caesar *Sebastos* as object of *latreia*/worship: "Sebastolatry" or Augustus-worship, as it were.

The scope and significance of emperor worship and imperial religion, traditionally neglected or strongly played down, has received more attention in recent scholarship, following Simon Price's landmark study.[4] Robert Jewett uses the somewhat minimizing term *civic cult* and avoids to take it fully into consideration as a potentially focal point of contention between Paul and Empire. However, if one connects the dots between what is said about the "empire of honor" and imperial religion (for example, 48–51), it becomes clear that one cannot be part of the one without practicing the other as well. The symbolic capital of honor was an ideological currency that had "In God Caesar we trust" stamped on every single of its bills. For the provincial elites, for example, the imperial cult, combined with euergetism, is a key mechanism to gain honor, status and eventually maybe even a senatorial seat at Rome. At the same time it sanctifies, naturalizes, justifies and stabilizes Roman rule over the conquered territories and bodies of the nations. Their resources are ruthlessly extracted and channeled to Rome, the insatiable metropolis and Goddess at the center of the world. I believe that we are not in disagreement about this.

But what if Paul, the faithful Jew, had identified precisely these inseparable ties between social status, benevolence, and idolatrous (in)human deification, seeing much more of a problem here than we usually assume? What if he all of a sudden understood that after Caesar had conquered the world and imposed his order and religion on it, there was no more space left to practice Torah and specifically the first commandment properly, innocently, purely? Even the permission to practice Torah properly was now a benefaction by Caesar and required honor, gratitude and service be given to him as the idol par excellence–e.g. through a regular daily sacrifice in the Jerusalem temple. And even the core of Jewishness, the distinction between Jews and Gentiles, had become ambiguous. If Jews look down on Gentiles (including Greeks),like Greeks/Gentiles look down on barbarians (including Jews) from a position of superiority and mutual disdain for the shameful "other," they both have bought into a system of "honor" and "boasting" that mimics Caesar's stance towards the inferior and outsider. They see the world in the image of Caesar, sharing the perspective and worldview

[4] S. R. F. Price, *Rituals and Power: The Roman Imperial Cult in Asia Minor* (Cambridge: Cambridge University Press, 1984).

of the world conqueror and supreme idol to whom all religions of the world have had to subscribe in one way another, including Judaism. At the same time they are caught in a kind of "false consciousness" that blurs their understanding of their real position as conquered *ethnē*/nations all the same—a term that from a Roman position applies to both Jews and non-Jews alike.

This might be one of the reasons why for Paul Jews are no longer better off than Gentiles. And that therefore a new messianic universalism that "sets right" both Jews and Gentiles/nations, alone by their faith in the One God of Israel and his alternative rules of conduct is the only way to uphold the first commandment against imperial idolatry. Justification by faith would then be, according to Paul, the only contextually adequate translation of the first commandment and the *Shema* in the concrete "here and now" of his time. This would imply that justification by faith is not just aiming at a new type of trans-national community building but also a core concept of resistance against the overpowering hegemony of a worldwide imperial religion and the way that all existing religions have bought or been bought into it.[5] This reading reclaims Romans as key document of a Christianity that needs constant reformation and transformation in critical discernment of its own involvement with the imperial idols of its day. *Ecclesia semper reformanda* ("the church always reforming itself"): Robert Jewett has made a momentous and more than timely contribution towards this task.

[5] For a more detailed treatment of this question of imperial religion and justification theology in Paul, see Brigitte Kahl, *Galatians Re-Imagined. Reading with the Eyes of the Vanquished* (Minneapolis: Fortress Press, 2010) and idem, "Galatians and the *Orientalism* of Justification by Faith: Paul among Jews and Muslims," in *The Colonized Apostle: Paul through Postcolonial Eyes*, edited by Christopher D. Stanley (Minneapolis: Augsburg Fortress Press, 2011), 206–22.

16

A Response to Robert Jewett's *Hermeneia Commentary* on *Romans*

Daniel Patte

I.

Robert Jewett's *Hermeneia Commentary on Romans* is an amazing treasure for research on Romans. It has what we have learned to expect from this series: full and up to date bibliography; a fresh translation of each pericope, with discussion of all the significant variants; an analysis—in this case a discussion and presentation of the rhetorical disposition; followed by a verse by verse exegesis, in which Jewett presents a distinctive interpretation, even as he justifies it by discussing in the body of the text and in footnotes a wide range of diverging or supporting interpretations of each given point.

Yet this remarkable commentary is an easy target for a critique from scriptural criticism. As Bob Jewett reminds us, again and again, in this day and age we cannot not be concerned about imperialism and fundamentalism. In such a context, important as it is, it is not enough for biblical scholars to make explicit the analytical frame of our critical interpretations; it is not enough to make explicit the exegetical methods we choose to use among other possible methods. We also need to make explicit the role of our contextual and hermeneutical-theological frames in our choice of an interpretation.

This remarkable commentary is an easy target for a critique from scriptural criticism, because its author exhibits all the symptoms of a split personality. Robert Jewett, the exegete, needs to debate with Bob Jewett, the politically driven Christian.

Robert Jewett, the exegete, has written a superb Hermeneia Commentary, a detached, scientific study of Paul's letter to the Romans, a text that belongs to a remote historical era. It is a detached, scientific rhetorical analysis of this letter read in its Roman imperial cultural context, which leads him to the conclusion that "Romans was a missionary document aimed at overcoming the premises of imperial honor . . . [and at] demonstrating the power of the gospel to overcome cultural barriers and conflicts." A detached, social scientific rhetorical analysis, by Robert Jewett who declares: "I am not a post-modernist, preferring practical realism that admits the fallibility of all historical and exegetical judgments but continues searching for the truth." [quotes from Method]

But Bob Jewett, the politically driven Christian, is not far behind Robert Jewett the exegete. Thus he also confesses in his preface:

> Although I remain faithful to the Hermeneia format by leaving the contemporary application up to my readers, I hope that the extraordinary relevance of Romans to the situation of cultural, religious, and imperial conflicts is easily discernable.

"Leaving the contemporary application up to my readers" . . . *As if* the contemporary application of Romans in the present day imperial context had not driven him and framed his insightful and systematic study of Romans and of the scholarship on Romans . . . . *As if* his deep concern for cultural barriers and conflicts among religious communities had not framed his perceptive analysis of Romans. Indeed, Robert Jewett is not simply Robert Jewett, the exegete. He is also Bob Jewett, the politically driven Christian, whose interpretation of Romans has been framed by his strong contextual concerns for present day cultural, political, and social issues.

Bob Jewett, the politically driven Christian, shows up here and there. Bob dedicates his commentary to Bishop John William Colenso, whose 1861 commentary on Romans "*Explained from a Missionary Point of View*" is a paradigm for all contextual interpretations of Romans; in the middle of the 19th century, he wrote the first post-colonial commentary, "*reading* Romans *with* the Zulus."

Bob acknowledges his contextual concerns: "I have long been involved in the peace movement, a critic of zealous nationalism and superheroic fantasies of all kinds . . ." [from Method] And indeed as everyone knows, Bob's interpretation of Paul took shape when he read Paul in terms of, and over against, the present culture . . . "*Paul at the Movies*" "*Paul returns to the movies*" "*Paul the Apostle to America; Cultural Trends and Pauline Scholarship.*" And this is not speaking of *Captain America and the Crusade against Evil: The Dilemma of Zealous Nationalism* and of the forthcoming "*Mission and Menace: Four Centuries of Religious Zeal in America*", . . . and yet, my computer searches tell me that these formative books are mentioned in a grand total of 12 footnotes out of, I guess, at least 6000 footnotes!

Bob also mentions his "experience with feminist and black-liberation theology" that, he confesses, "undoubtedly influences my viewing Romans as a document that fundamentally undermines social and racial prejudice and extends the gift of grace to the entire human race." "The reversal of the system of honor and shame occasioned by Christ crucified strikes to the heart of social and racial prejudice in the ancient as well as the modern world." [from Method]. Bob *confesses* that his interpretation of Romans was contextually framed by these social and political concerns.

Furthermore Bob confesses theological and religious experiences: "My theological inheritance is liberal, American Methodism" [From Method] and that wrestling with Karl Barth's *Commentary on Romans* brought him "through a spiritual crisis similar to that experienced by many Europeans after 1914–18 in the discovery that the gospel challenged my dearest cultural premises." [From Preface] In other words, Bob *confesses* that his interpretation of Romans was hermeneutically framed by this deep religious experience, and more broadly by passionate convictions that drives him in all what he does—as is visible to all his friends and as he makes clear to many others.

In sum, Bob Jewett, the politically driven Christian, *confesses* that his exegetical interpretation of Romans is doubly framed by a contextual frame (concerning political and social concerns) and by a hermeneutical-theological frame (his religious views). And yet, he wants to affirm: I am not post-modern. Thus Bob Jewett confesses:

> These factors in my experience and background lead to my interest in the counter-cultural, radically egalitarian social order that Paul is promoting in Romans, and that he hopes to extend to Spain when the Roman churches support his mission there. [From Method]

Yet, Robert Jewett, the detached exegete, adds:

> But all of these ethical and social commitments need to be held critically, not only concerning their validity in and of themselves in my own viewpoint, but more importantly, whether they are in fact reflected in Romans. [From Method]

Nevertheless, Bob Jewett concludes this paragraph: "But it would be dishonest to pretend that I am someone else or that my background and orientation have no influence on the results of this commentary." [From Method]

Yet, beyond these brief remarks [in his Preface and Introduction], all the rest of the 1000 page volume is relentlessly presented as a detached, objective analysis; *as if* his interpretation was not driven and framed by contextual and hermeneutical-theological concerns. Indeed, this is even clear in his preface where, after this brief confession, he traces the genealogy of his interpretation of Romans by referring to Käsemann's lectures, to the works of Peter Lampe, of James Dunn, and of many others scholars, whose works will then be found in the bibliography, in the footnotes, and often discussed in the body of his commentary.

In his preface and introduction, Bob Jewett *confesses* that his exegetical interpretation of Romans is doubly framed by a contextual and a hermeneutical frame. But Robert Jewett, the exegete, quickly *withdraws this confession*, by pretending that these political, social, religious, and convictional concerns are only a matter for "contemporary applications" of the results of a detached exegesis:

> I remain faithful to the Hermeneia format by leaving the contemporary application up to my readers . . . not only concerning their validity . . ., but more importantly, whether they are in fact reflected in Romans.

Or,

> All of these ethical and social commitments need to be held critically" because they are only assumptions, presuppositions, pre-understandings that need to be overcome, or bracketed out, so as to reach the truth . . . *as if* his contextual and hermeneutical choices were tarnishing the quality of his analytical choices.

Robert Jewett, the exegete, acknowledges acquaintance with Bob Jewett, the politically driven Christian, but as a biased individual who needs to be kept in check by Robert Jewett, the exegete, a practical realist who "admits the fallibility of all historical and exegetical judgments but continues searching for the truth." [Method]

But I believe that even practical realism could recognize the split personality, the self-denial which is involved.

I do not want to suggest that Robert/Bob has a psychological problem! In his case—and in the case of most members of the SBL—

split personality is induced by the Hermeneia format, that reflects the practice and conception of critical biblical studies promoted by much of the SBL. Yet, it remains a problem, because it involves self-denial, alienation, which has the potential to be and often is quite destructive.

But what is remarkable is that Robert/Bob Jewett is not hiding this self-denial and this split personality. Actually, unlike most biblical scholars, he manages to make public his split personality. He is quite publicly both an outstanding critical exegete (as this commentary shows once again) and an outspoken politically driven Christian activist. Thus in my response to his commentary, I want to take quite seriously all the aspects of Bob/Robert Jewett as a whole person, Bob/Robert Jewett *the politically driven Christian critical exegete*.

First, I will praise Jewett's commentary for its amazing contribution to NT scholarship on Romans, a contribution partly due to the fact that he takes most seriously and systematically the rhetorics of the letter to the Romans and its expected effects upon its hearers in the Roman house and tenement churches. Yes, a focus on the rhetorical effects of the letter is an important key for a renewed understanding of Romans! And Robert Jewett's commentary achieves this feat.

But we also need to take into account *the rhetorical effects* of this commentary upon its readers. At this point I will have to be critical. In my view Robert Jewett's commentary as a discourse has effects that I want to discuss with Bob Jewett the *politically driven Christian* who is so keen to denounce imperialism and Captain America. Indeed I believe that this commentary by its form is a practice of biblical studies which has effects which Bob Jewett should find very suspicious, and might even want to reject as dangerous, as ethically problematic, as any form of imperialism is . . . . Indeed, I want to ask whether or not, ironically, in the very process of advocating an interpretation of Romans that rejects imperialism, he is not condoning and even practicing the very imperialist attitude he denounces. As Romans 7:15 says in Robert Jewett's translation, "I do not know what I bring about. For what I don't want—this I practice, but what I hate—this I do . . . ."

II.

What are the major contributions to the critical analytical interpretation of Romans offered by Robert Jewett's commentary? Many, indeed! In my view, Robert Jewett's commentary on Romans is époque-making because it fully incorporates in a consistent, systematic and comprehensive commentary the many new strands in Pauline research that emerged during the last 40 years. What a feast! We are very much in his debt.

Here is what we were "hoping for beyond hope," we, the many who have been groping for a way to hold together the traditional historical-critical interpretations of Romans with the rhetorical analysis and the social scientific reconstructions of the audience of the letter in Rome, while looking backward to Jerusalem and forward to Spain, and all these in the broader context of the honor-shame Greco-Roman culture.

By being very consistent in taking into account the rhetorical and social scientific approaches, Jewett shows how everything in the letter to the Romans contributes to Paul's missionary proclamation of Christ's shameful cross, a gospel that, against the Roman imperial practices, "offered grace to every group in equal measure, . . . overturned the honor system that dominated the Greco-Roman and Jewish worlds [and] poison[ed] the relations between the congregations in Rome." [quote from Preface]. In the process Robert Jewett brings in the critical conversation many of the issues and observations raised by the scholars who in the so-called "new perspective" reassessed Paul's relationship with the Judaisms of his time, and thus all the issues of the relationship between Jews and Gentiles.

Thus, many of the points he is making through his exegesis have already been made here and there: a) in "new perspective interpretations" by Stendahl, Sanders, Bill Campbell, Hays, Elliott, etc. of key passages of Romans regarding *Paul among Jews and Gentiles* (Stendahl's title) and justification interpreted to avoid a legalistic, introspective and exclusivist view of salvation; b) in rhetorical interpretations of Romans (by Aletti, Elliott, Stowers, etc.); and c) in social scientific studies of Romans and Paul (by Moxnes, Esler, Horsley, etc.). But he is the first to really bring these all together.

Yes, other commentaries have taken into account the so-called "new perspective"—including, of course, James Dunn, who just spoke (as I write these comments, I wonder how he is responding to Jewett's commentary!) and who named the "new perspective." But as N. T. Wright notes in a recent book:

> Much of the "New perspective" writing on Paul has simply assumed and carried on the critical decisions reached by the old perspective, without noticing that the new perspective itself calls several of them into question.[1]

This is the case with James Dunn's commentary on Romans (to which I will come back). And I would argue that one can address the same criticism to N. T. Wright's own interpretation of Paul.

But what is remarkable in this Hermeneia Commentary is that, for the first time, Robert Jewett proposes to us a reading of Romans that

[1] N. T. Wright, *Paul in Fresh Perspective* (Minneapolis: Fortress, 2005), 19.

no longer presupposes that "Romans is a defense of true doctrine," i.e., that Romans is Paul's defense and theological presentation of his gospel ["a traditional misunderstanding of Romans as a defense of true doctrine" (Jewett on 1:16)]. Jewett rejects "the traditional doctrinal interpretation" which concerns "faith" as individual belief or individual religious experience, the interpretation for which justification by faith equals forgiveness, and salvation has to do with individual salvation from punishment-condemnation by the righteous Judge. Jewett rejects what I call in brief a forensic-theological interpretation.

Instead from his socio-rhetorical analysis of Romans in the "new perspective", Robert Jewett shows how this different perspective demands from the readers to re-think absolutely all the concepts that Paul is using. To begin with, (quoting Jewett on 1:17, "for in it [the gospel] the righteousness of God is being revealed from faith to faith, as it has been written, 'The one who is put right [with God] shall live by faith.'"),

> *The individual believer in the modern sense was not in view by Paul,* even though the formulation from Habakkuk encourages an individualistic construal for the modern hearer. Moreover, the question of life should be understood as a matter of living together in faith communities rather than in the traditional theological sense of gaining eternal life on an individualistic basis. *The proper question to be posed on the basis of Paul's argument in Romans is not, "Are you (sg.) saved?" but, "Are you all living together righteously in faith communities?"*

And it is just amazing how transformed our reading of Romans becomes when we read Romans following Jewett by systematically taking into account the plurals, and paying attention to all the terms, phrases, connotations which can be read in a community perspective. For instance Jewett translates 8:9–11:

> 8:9 But *you (pl.)* do not exist in flesh but in spirit, since indeed God's spirit *dwells among you (pl.).* But if someone does not have Christ's spirit, that one is not his. 10/ But if Christ is *in your midst,* though the body [be] dead because of sin, the spirit [is] life because of righteousness. 11/ But if the spirit of "the one who raised Jesus from the dead" *dwells in your midst,* "the one raising Christ Jesus from the dead" will also give life to your mortal bodies through his spirit *dwelling in your midst.*

The Spirit dwells among you and is active within a community, "within house and tenement churches, rather than 'in us' in some individualistically spiritual or existential manner" (not in individuals): so walking according to the Spirit is a community experience (not an individual experience).

Then, as a part of this "new perspective," one needs to take into account all the cultural aspects when life in community is the primary focus, and individual life is to be understood in a community context. This includes honor and shame as a central perspective in community life, and in inter-community relations.

Then, for instance, as Jewett suggests, one must read *charis* as "a broader category dealing with divine acceptance of persons with limitations and failures of various kinds." that is, dealing "with the wounds of shame rather than those of guilt."

Then all the vocabulary about "boasting" and not being ashamed has to be read in this light, namely as referring to what one does when one has "honor" rather than shame.

Then, to come back to Jewett's comment on 8:9–11, it appears that

> Paul's language describes the avoidance by the converted community of fleshly behavior aimed at gaining honor for one's group in competition with others, and its replacement by following the spirit of Christ. This entails a non-competitive, cooperative style of behaving, guided by love, and aimed at mutual upbuilding. The law could only be fulfilled in its intention and scope by communities set free from the compulsion to compete for honor, because the ultimate form of honor had been granted in the form of unmerited, divine grace. (Jewett, *Commentary ad loc*)

Then, of course, one needs to take into account, as Jewett shows with the help of the rhetoric analysis, that all of this community life has a missiological purpose . . . In other words, "being set right" with God is an election, a being set apart, for a mission . . .

I could go on and on, taking other examples of this amazingly consistent re-reading of Romans, where new perspective readings, rhetorical analyses, and socio-scientific exegeses are completely integrated in a very convincing reading of Romans, relentlessly keeping in focus the ways in which this letter would have been heard in the house and tenement churches in Rome.

I could go on and on. But since I am the last one to speak on the panel, I am sure that my colleagues have already rehearsed many of the main features of Jewett's very systematic reinterpretation of Romans, which I applaud.

III.

So let me turn to my critical comments. I applaud the analysis of Romans by the learned exegete Robert Jewett, and his conclusions about the meaning of the text when Romans is read as systematically from this new perspective as Jewett does. Great!

But in the name of Bob Jewett the politically driven Christian, I want to register a protest against the rhetorical effects of his exegetical discourse upon his readers.

Earlier I did not quote the full sentence in Robert's comments on 1:17 regarding his rejection of the interpretation of Romans as a defense of true doctrine: he called it "the *traditional misunderstanding* of Romans as a defense of true doctrine." Similar rejections can be found, in one form or another, almost on each page of his commentary, in which he presents and rejects other interpretations as misunderstandings—whether he uses the word or not.

So what? Is this not what we are supposed to do in scholarly studies? Yes, this is what we have been trained to do . . . But . . .

But . . . Calling the view that one rejects a "*misunderstanding* of Romans" is espousing an imperialist attitude, and even a fundamentalist attitude. Calling other interpretations a "*misunderstanding* of Romans" is saying (I paraphrase Jewett):

> though I admit the fallibility of all historical and exegetical judgments *I continue searching for the truth,* and my interpretation is a truer interpretation than others, for the reasons I have given. You see, I have no choice but to follow the evidence of the text.

I am sorry to say that this justification of our practice to reject other interpretations as misunderstanding is the same reasoning that the Anglican bishops followed at the Lambeth Conference when they condemned and excommunicated John Colenso . . . You see, they had no choice but to follow the evidence of the text and condemn Colenso's misunderstanding of Romans! And I could make a long list of colonialist and imperialist readings of biblical texts that Western missionaries impose upon the "natives", because accordingly these missionaries have no choice but to follow the evidence of the text, as they fail to acknowledge that their readings are actually Western readings.

I am sorry to say that this is the same reasoning that fundamentalists use all the time, because despite rumors to the contrary, fundamentalists read the Bible very closely and carefully, and can point to you textual evidence for their conclusions. They are also convinced that they have no choice, because this is what the text says.

Of course, Robert Jewett, the exegete, is a scholar, indeed a superb scholar. But, if I may say so, so are my neighbors on this panel. Let me pick on James Dunn, since he has also published a commentary on Romans, to which you often refer.

It may seem that I find myself in a quite delicate situation. By praising Robert Jewett's interpretation and its distinctive character, as I just did and as I could do on and on, am I not dismissing Jimmy Dunn's different interpretation as having missed the mark? By praising Robert Jewett's interpretation, am I not affirming that Jewett is a better scholar than James Dunn? Am I not putting a big question mark of James Dunn's scholarship? The answers to all these is a resounding: NO!

But is this not what Jewett does, again and again, when he dismisses the interpretation of Romans supported by Dunn as based on wrong presuppositions regarding Paul's intention? I know Bob Jewett will cry out:

> "Certainly not! Certainly not! This is not what I mean." As I said, I admire James Dunn's work and learned much from it . . . I am not dismissing James Dunn's scholarship.

And yet . . . and yet, against Bob's wishes, is it not what Robert Jewett does in practice? Ha! This split personality!

But do not worry! I will do the same thing. Beyond Robert Jewett and James Dunn "I will show you a still more excellent way," as Paul says elsewhere (1 Corinthians 12:31).

My intention is to affirm that, despite their ongoing diverging exegetical conclusions, both Robert Jewett's interpretation and James Dunn's interpretation are equally legitimate—precisely when they diverge. Making new contributions to the understanding of Romans in a radically new interpretation does not demand to dismiss other interpretations.

Yes, I know that Robert Jewett has a great admiration for James Dunn's work on Paul and his commentary. He says so in his preface. And hundreds of references to Dunn's works confirm it. I anticipate that James Dunn has a similar admiration for Robert Jewett's work. And what I said about Robert Jewett's commentary I can repeat about James Dunn's commentary, for which I have an equal admiration. James Dunn's two volume commentary on Romans was also époque-making because it fully incorporates in a consistent, systematic and comprehensive commentary the new strands in Pauline research that emerged before 1988 (the year it was published). And thus, I hope in his response to Jewett, James Dunn has not backed away from his own conclusions. They are most significant, and as precious as Jewett's interpretation. James Dunn and Robert Jewett are two great scholars who, through their scholarship, bring to us a wealth of insights into the text, helping us bridge the twenty centuries of cultural and historical gap between this text and us.

And yet . . . and yet . . . they reach different conclusions on pericope after pericope. No, Robert Jewett does not want to claim that he has the absolutely true interpretation.

For him, "historical research is similar to scientific research in other fields in needing to rely on a system of conjectures and refutations, in which hypotheses "are not *derived* from observed facts, but *invented* in order to account for them." (quoting Karl Popper)" [from section on Methodology] Indeed for him "the "hermeneutics of suspicion" developed by liberation and feminist theologians" is needed to challenge the interpretations that read "a non-imperialistic letter . . . overlaid with unacknowledged ideologies, with individual portions understood as embodying the partial theology of particular traditions, now reified under the canonical aegis of the apostle to the Gentiles, and hence rendered authoritative for all others." [from section on Methodology]

But as a good historian, Jewett wants to claim that his conclusions have a higher degree of plausibility than those of James Dunn. This should be expected after 18 years of additional research, should it not? We are progressing in Pauline studies toward a better critical understanding of Paul, as a scholar climbs on the shoulders of those of the preceding generation to reach new height, isn't it? Who would not believe in progress—the progress of modernity that our culture embraces?

I do not. And I do not think Bob Jewett, the politically and socially driven Christian believes in the progress promised by modernity. You remember his spiritual crisis when wrestling with Karl Barth's *Commentary on Romans* brought him to "a spiritual crisis similar to that experienced by many Europeans after 1914–18 in the discovery that the gospel challenged my dearest cultural premises."

Thus, I am not prepared to say that Robert Jewett's interpretation of Romans represents a progress as compared to that of James Dunn. No supersession. Robert Jewett opens for us new vistas on Romans, because he foregrounds for us dimensions of Romans—community, honor and shame, rhetorical dimensions of the text—that we commonly kept in the background in the process of foregrounding other dimensions. He foregrounds dimensions of Romans that James Dunn had kept in the background by foregrounding other dimensions—namely the theological argument of the letter, and how it can be understood with the help of philology, etc.

But conversely this means that Robert Jewett pushed into the background those other dimensions of Romans that James Dunn foregrounded for us. In sum, Robert Jewett has made different exegetical choices—or more generally, different analytical choices. And thus he ends up reaching different conclusions.

But conclusions about what? "The truth." But what is truth? Which truth? I know Robert Jewett wants to be a practical realist and does not want to be a post-modernist. But I believe Bob Jewett acknowledges many tenets of post-modernism.

Robert Jewett with his modernist view presupposes that divergent interpretations signal mistakes; one needs to resolve the conflict of interpretations by demonstrating that one of these is "right," and the others are "wrong." Instead from a post-modern and structural critical perspective I insist that the plurality of interpretations must be taken seriously. One reason for this stance is that even as scholars we cannot agree on which criteria to use in order to establish *the* true meaning of the *text* if such a thing exists. This is where the basic difference between Robert Jewett and James Dunn is, in my view. They used different sets of criteria, and thus chose different critical methods. And for my part I choose to use other critical tools. Then, advocating a specific interpretation we easily slip into truth-claims.

In addition, we long for certitude and univocality. Can we not at least agree that the true meaning of the text is what the author meant to say? Can we not at least strive to establish "what Paul intended to say"—a vocabulary that we find again and again in Jewett's commentary—and in James Dunn's? My answer has to be an unambiguous: "No." The true meaning of the text is NOT what Paul meant to say, NOT what Paul intended to say.

In order to explain this point to my students at Vanderbilt University, in Nashville, Tennessee, in the South of the U.S.A.—a university that was finally "integrated" during the civil right movement—I take the example of a lecture given in 1986 by a white South-African scholar. The topic of this lecture and the intention of the speaker were clearly expressed by the *argument* he developed. The lecturer spoke about the struggle against apartheid and racism in South Africa; he told the audience at Vanderbilt University how he participated in this struggle, risking his life and that of his family. All this was with the intention to convince us to participate in the struggle, at least by boycotting the American companies who condoned Apartheid. This is what I heard, seizing upon the intention of the author. But the African-American students at Vanderbilt heard a very different message. Throughout his talk trying to convince his audience to fight against racism and apartheid, the lecturer referred to the plight of black Africans . . . describing them as child-like, in need of education, so that they will move beyond their backward culture. In brief, the demeaning *metaphors and other figures of speech* the lecturer used in his discourse to depict black Africans communicated a very different message, a racist and segregationist message. Which is the true message? The intended message? Or the unintended message? One thing is sure: both messages affected the hearers.

This lecture is a good example of the ambivalence of any discourse, of the fact that the intentional message is not necessarily the most important one, and of the fact that two dimensions of the same text/ discourse (in this case, the argument and the symbolism) carry two different messages (in this case, a message against racism and a message condoning/advocating racism). And then, beyond this, I go on to explain to my students that any discourse has even more than two dimensions, and thus carries more than two messages . . . . This is what is implicitly acknowledged through the multiplication of critical exegetical methods. According to which method (or sub-set of methods) one uses, one perceives and elucidates one kind of "truth-message" or another.

So it is for Paul's letter to the Romans. One can argue that the intentional message of Paul was its rhetorical effect upon the readers—as Robert Jewett does. But it does not mean that the theological argument of Paul's letter was not also meaningful for Paul's hearers/readers in Rome. Or vice versa with James Dunn. Which is the most meaningful? It will depend upon the hearers/readers, and more specifically, it will depend upon their specific life-context and upon their theological-hermeneutical perspective. It will depend upon their specific life-context, because the readers will seek to discern which of the two meanings is most helpful in addressing issues in their life-context? Or negatively, which of the two is less hurtful in their life-context. It will also depend upon their theological-hermeneutical perspective, because the readers will seek to discern which of the two meanings is most plausible according to their cultural and religious views.

Thus, I believe Robert Jewett, the exegete, should acknowledge that the contextual and hermeneutical concerns of Bob Jewett, the politically driven Christian have led him to choose a certain sub-set of analytical methods and thus to choose a certain message of the text as most meaningful . . . . This choice might or might not elucidate the intentional message of Paul in Romans; but in Bob Jewett's assessment, it carries a message which is most helpful in the contemporary life-context: Do we not need today a teaching that will "aim[ed] at overcoming the premises of imperial honor . . . [and at] demonstrating the power of the gospel to overcome cultural barriers and conflicts"? O yes, we do! Even if there are parts of this message, that needs to be put aside (e.g., in chapter 13). And yes, from the hermeneutical and theological perspective of Bob Jewett and his American Methodist convictions, this message and its focus on mission are most plausible.

But of course James Dunn has made opposite choices, by choosing a different sub-set of analytical methods, and by underscoring a different dimension of the text as most meaningful. Again, despite Jimmy's claim (in his commentary), this choice might or might not elucidate the intentional message of Paul in Romans; But in Jimmy's perception this dimension of Romans and its teaching is most helpful in our contemporary life-context and most plausible in terms of his hermeneutical and theological convictions.

As you may know, for my part, I would still argue for still another kind of interpretation . . . . But this is another story. Yet, one thing is sure is that as long as each of us pretends that she or he does not have any choice, and simply present the true teaching of Romans by, accordingly, following the textual evidence, we condone, indeed we promote, imperialism, colonialism, fundamentalism . . . and we open the doors to all kinds of evil to be perpetrated in the name of the text. And as we well know, Romans has been used to fuel anti-Judaism and beyond it the flames of anti-Semitism.

And we do so, even when we self-consciously argue in favor of interpretations that underscore messages that strive to avoid anti-Judaism, because our very practice of biblical study by its modern pattern conveys, condones, indeed promotes, imperialism, colonialism, fundamentalism.

But how can we avoid such dilemmas? But how can we avoid such tragedies? Is it possible to avoid them in a commentary? Unlike Vincent Wimbush, I believe it is possible . . . at the condition that we modify slightly the format. It is simply a matter of avoiding implicitly but most effectively claiming absolute value for our interpretations through the way we present our interpretation. How? There are two possibilities.

First, we can develop a commentary which is explicitly contextual: *a Contextual Bible Commentary*, which makes explicit its contextual and hermeneutical reasons for choosing to emphasize a particular reading and thus a particular aspect of the text, and then strives to choose a critical analytical method that will elucidate this most significant dimension of the text.

The other possibility is to modify the Hermeneia format. Not much is needed. Instead of having an introduction where Robert Jewett alludes to Bob Jewett, just in order to sideline him, the introduction would need to acknowledge *positively* and explicitly the role of our contextual and hermeneutical concerns in our choice of an interpretation, in our choice of an analytical method. Then, in the commentary itself, it would be a matter of acknowledging the legitimacy of other interpretations *in their differences* . . . . It is precisely when Jimmy Dunn's interpretation is different from Robert Jewett's interpretation that Robert/Bob should affirm it: yes, this is another legitimate interpretation, which has simply chosen as most significant another dimension of the letter. And then, Robert/Bob could briefly explain the *contextual and theological reasons* why he makes a different choice. This could still be a Hermeneia commentary—the difference is simply that it would be honest—since, as Bob/Robert Jewett acknowledges: "*it would be dishonest to pretend that I am someone else or that my background and orientation have no influence on the results of this commentary.*"

17

Review of Jewett's *Romans: A Commentary*

Sze-kar Wan

I want to thank Prof. Jewett for an exceedingly erudite commentary, one which I am sure will remain a standard text for many years to come. I want to encourage Fortress Press, especially, to have this book out by February, because that's when my Romans seminar starts, and I want to use this book in that class.

This commentary is especially fine in its consideration of the social location of the Roman hearers of the letter, or what Stanley Stowers calls the "empirical readers."[1] This is one of the first commentaries to base, in a consistent and thoroughgoing manner, its exegetical analysis on Peter Lampe's reconstruction of the Jesus-congregations in Rome. The commentary has successfully demonstrated, I think, that quite contrary to scholarly orthodoxy, early congregations of Jesus-followers were not exclusively house-congregations (only such would Paul called *ekklēsiai*) but also included tenement congregations whose social structure was of a form of love-communalism similar to what is described in Acts 2 and whose locus of authority was based not so much on patriarchalism as on egalitarianism.

As a result of this consistent approach, the commentary has succeeded in presenting a cogent and persuasive thesis on the purpose of Romans. The letter is an "ambassadorial letter" (44), diplomatic in tone and purpose, designed to present Paul as an apostle who is worthy of trust and support. A letter of this sort is necessary, because Paul plans to use Rome as a new center of a proposed mission to Spain, the far end of the Empire, indeed of the world. Accordingly, Paul wants to

---

[1] *A Rereading of Romans: Justice, Jews, and Gentiles* (New Haven: Yale University Press, 1994), 21–22.

garner enough support for this undertaking by appealing to not only the presumed financial support of a wealthy patroness like Phoebe (16:1), but also the collective support of the Roman congregations in all their diversity. But such a "cooperative mission" (44) is possible only if the house- and tenement-congregations could look past their differences and resolve their controversies. Only then would they have the wherewithal to provide (using the *terminus technicus propempein*) Paul with translators, letters or recommendation to the locals, perhaps even escorts on his way to Spain (926).

All this I find close to my heart. The necessary corrective to the rather one-sided view of patriarchal or patronal congregations seems to me long overdue. It is about time that we apply this perspective consistently through an interpretive reading of Romans. But something has long bothered me about Romans, and I have yet to find a satisfactory commentary that addresses it adequately. That is, why does it say so little about the Roman Empire? It's not as if Paul were not interested in global matters. Topics like creation (1:18–31), the faith of Abraham (chapter 4), the Adam-Christ typology (5:12–21), the new creation (chapter 8), salvation of all (chapter 9–11) are all intensely cosmic and therefore political. Unless one held a strict distinction between the sacred and profane in the manner of the Augustinian two-kingdom theory, one could hardly imagine that Paul would have nothing to say about the Roman regime. (The exception is, of course, 13:1–7; what Paul has to say there is very revealing. I will return to this passage later.)

But Paul does have a great deal to say about the Empire. The commentary has unearthed a slew of clues and hints and word choices that might've been motivated by anti-imperial sentiments, and I've learned a great deal from the detailed work. Granted, it would not have been possible for Paul to make explicit statements against the Empire without risking charges of sedition. But even so, is it possible still to see the coherent vision to which these anti-imperial clues point? This commentary has inspired me to do just that, and I'll attempt a sort of integration.

One of the valuable aspects of this commentary is that it does a good job integrating Spain into the overall purpose of writing Romans (87–89, 926). A description of Spain thicker than any that has been attempted by other commentaries on Romans has helped make a persuasive case of how broad the scope of Paul's undertaking is. It's in fact the great need in launching such a missionary enterprise, according to the commentary, that necessitates Paul to solicit the help of not just one or two patrons (e.g., Phoebe) but the broad support of *all* the Roman congregations, both patriarchal households and tenement congregations.

But when all is said and done, Spain is mentioned only twice in the commentary (15:24, 28), both times without much elaboration[2] and both times in a passage where Jerusalem is the focus. I don't deny that the Spanish mission plays an integral part in Paul's thinking; it might even have been the occasion for composing Romans. But Paul in fact devotes relatively little space talking about Spain, at least not explicitly, and more apprising his Roman hearers of his journey to Jerusalem and his business there. If we are going to take Paul's words seriously, we need to fit Spain into an overall framework that begins with and takes serious account of Jerusalem.

In the same passage where Spain is mentioned, Paul tells his Roman hearers about the collection for the saints in Jerusalem (15:22–29). The commentary suggests that the purpose for making mention of the collection at this point in his argument is to show the possibility of unity between the Gentile congregations of Macedonia and Achaia and the Jewish congregations of Jerusalem, which would in turn encourage Roman support for his Spanish mission. But it must be asked if that sufficiently explains 15:29, where Paul seems to be much more forward-looking, perhaps even boastful, in re-asserting his apostolic credentials: "I will come in the fullness of the blessing of Christ." The commentary cites Dieter Georgi, with approval, that in Paul's mind the success of the Spanish mission is in some way dependent on the success of the delivery to Jerusalem (933).[3] This observation is further supported by the fact that Paul asks his Roman hearers to pray for his upcoming trip to Jerusalem, a request that he calls "struggle" (*synagōnizesthai*) (15:30–32). So it appears Paul draws an explicit connection between his proposed itinerary to Rome and beyond on the one hand and, on other, his upcoming trip to Jerusalem.

But how so? What is the connection? The commentary seems to suggest that this is to assure Paul, as much as his Roman hearers, that the anticipated acceptance of the collection is a symbol of unity between Gentile and Jewish congregations and this symbol would convince the Roman congregations to do likewise and thus pave the way for support for the Spanish mission. I don't disagree with that, but that seems rather an inconsequential kind of dependence. Why should the Roman congregations take their cues from the Jerusalem action? I would submit that 15:29ff shows that Jerusalem plays a far more important

---

[2] The commentary suggests that this understatement is dictated by the ambassadorial genre of the letter: "Diplomatic sensitivity forbids specification at this point, either of Paul's precise hopes or of the extensive requirements of a successful mission to Spain" (932). While this may well be possible, the lack of elaboration on Spain stands in stark contrast to much fuller accounts of Jerusalem, Zion, and Judea in the same context and elsewhere in Romans.

[3] Citing Georgi from *Remembering the Poor: The History of Paul's Collection for Jerusalem* (Nashville: Abingdon Press, 1992), 121.

role in Paul's thinking than the commentary allows. The purpose of collection trip for Jerusalem to his Roman hearers, as suggested by Johannes Munck and others, and endorsed by the commentary (924, citing Roger Aus), was to fulfill the Isaianic vision of a Gentile pilgrimage to Jerusalem. In leading the Gentile representatives with their collection or tributes, Paul might well have thought of himself as taking part in the partial if not final fulfillment of Isaiah 66:19–20:

> And I will set a sign among them. From them I will send survivors to the nations, to Tarshish, Put, and Lud—which draw the bow—to Tubal and Javan, to the coastlands far away that have not heard of my fame or seen my glory; and they shall declare my glory among the nations. They shall bring all your kindred from all the nations as an offering to the Lord, on horses, and in chariots, and in litters, and on mules, and on dromedaries, to my holy mountain Jerusalem, says the Lord, just as the Israelites bring a grain offering in a clean vessel t the house of the Lord.[4]

In this scenario, Roger Aus might be right that Paul somehow identifies Spain as the biblical Tarshish. But if that is the case, Paul's triumphal declaration in 15:29, that he will come "in the fullness of Christ's blessing," could be justified. Paul does see his journey to Jerusalem as a necessary preparation for his Spanish mission, because he sees *both journeys* as constitutive components in the eschatological fulfillment of the reign of God. Paul's ultimate scope is broader than these two travel plans put together. In the eloquence of the commentary, "[Paul's] framework is not chronological but, given his worldview, geographic—and eschatological, for the early Christian mission aimed at completing the circle around the known world centered in the Mediterranean, before the parousia" (913).

What Paul is doing in Romans, I submit, is to draw a new map for his new cosmic vision, his new world—literally in 15:19, where he constructs a new "circle" of map that begins from Jerusalem, goes through Illyricum, and ends in Spain (see page 912). Gayatri Spivak calls this the process of "worlding" or "worlding of the world on uninscribed earth."[5] It is the favorite strategy of the colonizers to inscribe an imperial discourse on the colonized space. Therefore, Rome's placement of itself in the center

---

[4] Georgi, *Remembering the Poor,* 119–20, drawing together traditions from Acts. In this regard, I think the collection means more than just "an expression of mutual indebtedness that bins the ethnic branches of the church together" (931).

[5] "The Rani of Simur," in F. Baker et al, editor, *Europe and Its Others Vol. 1 Proceedings of the Essex Conference on the Sociology of Literature* (Colchester: University of Essex Press, 1985), 128, 135.

of the Peutinger Map, e.g., with all the "others" lying on the periphery was a political move to unite the Empire under a colonial framework. Hand in hand with map-making is the process of "othering," which is a process of inscribing and consolidating the colonial subjectivity as the "Other," while those at the margins are all grouped together as the "others."[6] Humanity is divided into Greeks and Barbarians, with the Romans arrogating to themselves the role of guarantors of Greek heritage in the center of the Empire, while the colonized "others," that is the say all the non-Romans, are written up as uncultured savages, to be tamed and brought under the "enlightened rule of the Empire.

All these Paul in fact alludes to—*and* subverts. In place of a map that centers in Rome, he proposes a new metropolis, Jerusalem, from which Paul's new world extends through Illyricum and, if he gets his way, ends in Spain, the end of the earth. In this regard, Paul's good friend Luke got it right: the new gospel will propagate from Jerusalem to Judea to Samaria "until the end of the earth" (Acts 1:8). He mistook "the end" to mean Rome, however, when Paul would've liked to substitute Spain. Moreover, in place of the Greek-Barbarian divide, humanity is now composed of *Jews* and *Greeks*, with the Greeks forming the "others" and occupying the periphery. "Greeks" in this regard are not just the ethnic Greeks in Rome or anywhere,[7] but the catchall category encompassing all non-Jews, thus consolidating the identities of all "unenlightened" peoples. It's a form of ethnography that takes its center in Jerusalem. It is therefore no accident that, in his climactic discussion of the salvation of Israel (in reality all humanity) in the end time, Paul changes *heneken siōn* (LXX Isaiah 59:20) to *ek sxōn* (in 11:26b). The change is not just a matter of not wanting to offend his Gentile hearers (703–4), but a declaration that Jerusalem shall in the eschaton be the new seat of power for the Messiah-king. Jerusalem is not the final destination of the redeemer but his starting point, the center of his authority, indeed his capital.

I would argue that one of the goals of Romans, if not in fact *the* goal, is to set up Jerusalem as a new capital of an alternate empire, which is in direct competition with Rome and is in fact its replacement. If Paul does not want to appear to be making Rome his own domain (Käsemann, cited on 924), it's not just because he doesn't want to appear to be building on someone else's foundation (925), but because in his mind its centrality in the new empire has already been compromised and displaced. Paul learns the empire-building impulse from his imperial masters but constructs a new script of sweeping cosmic scope. While Paul in no way advocates any revolution by political or military

---

6 Lacan's distinction.

7 Contra Christopher Stanley, "'Neither Jew nor Greek': Ethnic Conflict in Graeco-Roman Society," *Journal for the Study of New Testament* 64 (1996), 101–24.

means in Romans or anywhere else, he actually constructs an anti-imperial discourse in which the God of the Jews, through an apocalyptic upheaval, will eventually triumph over all earthly authorities. With the death and resurrection of Christ, the end time is already breaking into the political and imperial arena hitherto thought to be inhabited only by the Roman colonizers. The Jewish cosmic and universal vision, in which the underclasses of the Empire will be elevated from their lowliness and the overlords of the worldly regime will be humbled in an eschatological reversal, is about to be realized.

Such a theory of Romans, I think, would go a long way towards explaining why Paul would subject his Gentile hearers to what is essentially a series of discussions on Jewish topics. Here I agree with the commentary that Paul's primary audience are Gentile believers. But why are chapters 2–11 so pre-occupied with "Jewish" topics? Dieter Goergi thought it was simply Paul's way of "disguising his political program" since "debate with Judaism was the code for a more far-ranging conflict that brought Paul into mortal danger."[8] I am not prepared to say that Romans is a *deliberate* code to disguise a political agenda, but I would say that it's Paul's way of co-opting the Gentiles into his Jewish apocalyptic framework, thus making these "Jewish" topics into their topics and installing Jerusalem as their new metropolis. That Peter Lampe and John Dominic Crossan and Jonathan Reed think that Paul's Gentile readers of Romans might have been Godfearers who are already familiar with biblical themes does not undermine the argument here.[9] Paul's theoretical construct is at heart an ethnography that aims at accounting for the relationship between Jews and Gentiles, and the relative statuses within the new structure. This I take to be the meaning of the allegory of the olive tree (11:17–24).

Romans 13:1–7, far from disproving this theory, but in fact confirms it. By placing the governments of the Empire under God (verse 1) and by calling the local magistrates by the loaded terms *theou diakonos* ("God's servant," verse 4) and *leitourgoi theou* ("ministers of God," verse 6),[10] Paul discursively co-opts even the civil government into his overall schema, so that even these are nothing more than ministers serving, perhaps unwittingly, as tools of God. In this regard, I read Romans 13 the same way I read Isaiah, who argues that even enemies of Israel and Judah could be appointed "saviors" and "the anointed" for the ultimate

---

8 *Theocracy in Paul's Praxis and Theology* (Minneapolis: Fortress, 1991), 81.

9 Peter Lampe, "The Roman Christians of Romans 16," in K. P. Donfried, editor, *The Romans Debate* (rev. and expanded; Peabody: Hendrickson, 1991), 225; idem, *From Paul to Valentinus: Christians at Rome in the First Two Centuries* (Minneapolis: Fortress Press, 2003), 69–70; John Dominic Crossan and Jonathan Reed, *In Search of Paul: How Jesus's Apostle Opposed Rome's Empire with God's Kingdom* (New York: HarperSanFranscisco, 2004), 38–40.

10 Not likely that these terms would have no sacral meaning in the hands of Paul.

purpose of Yahweh. I therefore agree with the commentary (786) that Romans 13:1–7 should be read in light of the missional purpose the letter—except I see Paul's missional purpose as one of establishing an overarching eschatological-political vision that encompasses all, including all civil governments and bureaucracies.

In sum, I suggest that Paul's mission has momentous political implications. What Paul has successfully put together is a total vision that forms an alternative to the Empire. Paul's mission is a co-optation of Gentiles into an apocalyptic vision, a Jewish vision if you will, that is centered in and will begin from Jerusalem. In using the same language and categories favored by the Empire, the same impulse towards empire-building, Paul advances an alternative vision, a competing vision that is every bit as universalistic as the ideology of the Roman Imperium. If that's the case, Paul is a far more dangerous figure to the Romans and to all political regimes than the post-Constantinian, domesticated Paul that we in the West have the tendency of making him out to be.

Professor Jewett has put us in his debt for a learned, technical work that is also readable, challenging, inspiring, even relevant to the modern time. It is a work that has modeled for us how a biblical scholar can at once be erudite and engaged. The sixteenth-century Chinese philosopher Wang Yang-ming expounded the meaning of "the unity of knowing and acting" (*zhi xing he yi*) as: "knowing is the beginning of acting, and acting is the completion of knowing." In Professor Jewett, *vita contemplativa* and *vita activa* find a happy concord.

18

Response to Washington Colleagues

Robert Jewett

I appreciate the critical responses by two colleagues I have long known and by Professors Kahl and Wan, whom I meet today for the first time. After weighing the implications of their penetrating critiques, I have decided to begin with Daniel Patte, since his challenge has the widest implications for our society. He argues that "the politically driven Christian" needs to overcome the "split personality" with the detached exegete who employs historical-critique techniques. That I have a chronic "Bob/Robert" problem reminds me of an episode that occurred at Vanderbilt in the mid 1970's that Gerd Luedemann reported when we were working together on chronology issues a decade later. Upon arriving in Nashville, he asked a colleague what he should read to understand the debate about Vietnam War. "I suggest you read, *The Captain America Complex*. It was written by a teacher up in Iowa by the name of Robert Jewett." Luedemann replied, "I know that name in connection with *Paul's Anthropological Terms*." His colleague replied, "Yeah, I know. They are two different guys and I never met either of them!"

Daniel wants me to come clean and admit that I'm really a post-modernist, that I should repent for claiming that some interpretations of Romans reflect "misunderstandings" of grammatical and historical data. This is to "espouse an imperialist attitude, and even a fundamentalist attitude." So I should admit that my interpretation and Jimmy Dunn's "are equally legitimate—precisely when they diverge." There can be no "supersession," because truth is fundamentally relative. Here is the issue that touches the very ethos of our SBL. Granted that we all "see through a glass darkly," and that our knowledge is always partial, does it follow that truth itself is finally relative? While I have learned much from post-modernist interpreters, which led me to lay my cards on the table in the introduction in a manner no other Romans commentator has attempted, I am not willing to take this final step, because it is self contradicting and undermines the entire scientific enterprise in which we as interpreters are engaged. As Socrates and Plato demonstrated (e. g. *Theatetus)*, sophistic relativism cannot be proven superior to other theories, because if everything is absolutely relative, the theory of absolute relativity cancels itself out.

Having known Daniel Patte for a long time, I do not believe that he follows post-modernist relativism to the very end. Let me take material from Romans to make this case. In chapter 16, I identify two sections as interpolations, using historical critical methods. Both the anti-heretical tirade in 17–20 and the doxology of 25–27 fulfill the four standard requirements for interpolations: (1) they interrupt the normal flow of Paul's argument, (2) employ non-Pauline language, (3) refute the earlier argument of the letter, and (4) reveal credible redactional motivation in their current placement. I don't want to argue this case here in detail, but rather to comment about the implications of these passages, with which I am fairly sure that Daniel stands in critical tension because of his own moral and religious commitments. The doxology claims that the truth of the gospel was intentionally hidden from the Jews and granted to the Gentiles, so they supercede in the history of salvation, which as we all know was part of what Prof. Kahl called the "slippery slope that has led into Christian anti-Judaism." I have a vivid recollection of a conversation with Daniel Patte about Philip P. Hallie's book, *Lest Innocent Blood be Shed*, that describes the villagers in La Chambon hiding Jewish refugees from the Nazis. In view of his passionate attachment to these heroic Huegenots, I cannot believe that Daniel would say that their biblical hermeneutic is in no way to be preferred to that of the German Christians who supported the gas chambers. This relates to the implications of the second interpolation, which calls believers to "crush" heretics under their feet following the command of the "God of peace" who allegedly achieves peace by annihilating its enemies. In the Bartholemew Day Massacre of 1680, thousands of Huegenots were killed in an action defended by theologians who claimed it was right for Catholic princes to crush heretics under their feet and thus, to use the words of a current political leader, "to rid the world of evil." Which biblical hermeneutic is to be preferred? Should we say that they are all equally relative?

I had to face this question as a student in Tübingen where I heard Ernst Käsemann combining critical exegesis with current political issues in lecture after lecture. Yet the tradition of a more fundamentalistically inclined hermeneutic was also present, following the legacy of Rudolf Kittel. Rejecting the Lutheran hermeneutic of Christ as the defining center of scripture, Kittel and his followers placed all of scripture on the same level, including the holy war materials that call believers to slaughter God's enemies. In the frontispiece of the 4th volume of the original German edition of the *Theologisches Wörterbuch zum Neuen Testament*, which was deleted in the English translation, is a list of Kittel's students and dictionary colleagues who had already died in the German effort to crush evil underfoot: Lieutenant Walter Gutbrod, Lieutenant Herman Fritzsch, Lieutenant Albrecht Stumpff, and Corporal Hermann Hanse. These scholars had volunteered for the great crusade while Käsemann and others remained in pastorates and preached against the persecution of Jews and the idolatry of fascism. Can we say that the hermeneutics of Kittel and Käsemann are equally valid when the one led followers to lend their weight to a crusade that ultimately cost 55 million lives? If you believe as I do that the premise of Romans is correct, that God's righteousness is impartial, and that every human life is equally valuable in God's sight, should not such considerations be taken into account as we weigh interpretive options? My own answer to this question has led me to apply exactly the same historical-critical methods to political and cultural issues as to sacred texts.

I agree with much of Prof. Kahl's critique, and especially resonate to her effort to reformulate justification by faith in terms of God's impartial honor granted to the undeserving. I wish I had thought of employing the visual image of Caesar Augustus in the Prima Porta, with the crouching figure at his feet representing Spain. She is puzzled by my translation of *anthropos* with "human" in 3:28 while I translate with "man/ woman" in 2:3, and here I have to admit a fundamental ambivalence. The translation was completed before the rhetorical and historical work on the commentary was started, and its later correction caused discrepancies, but in this case the ambivalence goes deeper and remains unresolved. While I fully subscribe to the discipline of avoiding sexist language in my own interpretive work, I question whether it is appropriate to impose modern sensibilities onto the translation of ancient texts. This distorts the evidence on which every interpretation must rest and disguises those locations where Paul, for example, broke with ancient sexist traditions, as in 1 Corinthians 7 and 2 Corinthians 6:18.

There is no ambivalence in my support of Brigitte Kahl's integration of justification by faith and the demand to resist idolatry. This relates to the matter under discussion with Daniel Patte, because as an historical critic I have long felt myself to reside on the verge between the First and Second Commandments. The sexless, transcendent deity whose very name is a verbal riddle stands over against all other loyalties, and I feel called to love this being and his/her truth with all my heart and soul and mind and strength. The second commandment pulls me constantly in the other direction, never to make a "graven image" either visually or verbally of any attempt to capture this transcendent truth. This is why I remain a sobered up modernist and reject thoroughgoing relativism while at the same admitting that all human knowledge is partial and in need of constant correction by others. Accepting this tension, I continue to be committed to continuing the quest for the truth. We are all finite, but we do have the power to discern whether a proposed interpretation is more adequate than others, and even, at times when it is warranted, to identify "misunderstandings." That, in part, is what our society is all about, and why it was founded in the 1880's as an alternative to literalism and emerging fundamentalism.

Turning to the final critique, I appreciate the generous way James Dunn has dealt with my commentary, despite significant disagreements. Having known each other so many years, I hope no one is offended if I sometimes refer to him as Jimmy and occasionally contrast his views with those of Prof. Kahl. He is right to note the imprecision of my translation of 16:2b, which according to some grammatical experts is actually a matter of syntactical "incorporation" (Smyth 2536), in which the antecedent of the relative pronoun *ho* and the direct object of the verb *parastete* is an ellipsed accusative, *pragma*, which is then incorporated into the dative *pragmati*, which fits the general rule stated in Smyth's *Grammar*: "If the antecedent is a substantive, it often stands at the end of the relative clause, and commonly has no article" (2536), as in 162b. A literal translation that includes this ellipsed word would be "furnish to her [the matter] in respect of whichever matter she might have need," which turns a clear Greek expression into rather murky English. Despite my syntactical imprecision, it was appropriate to supply an article for *pragmati*, because it refers back to a specific matter elipsed earlier, which has a definiteness that Jimmy's translation "whatever matter" does not convey. Neither of our translations is sufficiently precise, and if anyone would to write a little study to propose a better translation, I would like to correct this if there is ever a chance to create a revised edition of the commentary. Nevertheless, regardless of how 16:2b is translated, the key support of my hypothesis remains the succeeding clause that begins with *kai gar*, which provides a rationale for the request. If the "matter" is Phoebe's lawsuit, as Dunn contends, how could her high status as patron become a reason for the Roman converts to honor the quest for aid? The overwhelming majority of believers were slaves or former slaves who had no access to the Roman court system. Dunn's commentary also provides no explanation of the logical connection between *kai gar* that follows immediately after *pragma*, which led to my suggestion that Phoebe's patronage of the Spanish Mission required counsel and contacts available within the slums of Rome that might avoid making the mission into yet another exercise in Roman imperialism and exploitation.

I think I can understand Jimmy Dunn's complaint about my "commentary's relative lack of interest in . . . theology" (Dunn), because this involves the question of what constitutes genuine theology. In all of the commentaries in my collection, this is defined in Augustinian terms, as if the problem of the law and justification of faith should be understood primarily in terms of individual guilt and forgiveness. Jimmy discusses several passages where my alleged lack of theological penetration is evident, and all of them involve my resistance against construing Paul's argument in culturally discriminatory ways. This resistance is based on the development of the argument as a whole that insists on Paul's indebtedness "both to Greeks and barbarians;" that despite the prejudice current in Rome, the gospel of God's impartial righteousness pertains "to the Jew first and also to the Greek;" that "all have sinned and fallen short;" and that God consigns "all to wrath in order that God might have mercy on all." Thus I do not miss "the point that in chapter 14 it is the 'weak' (that is, most probably the *Jewish*) traditionalist who 'judges' the other (14:3) (*Romans*, 197–98)." I state clearly on 198 that "both the weak and the strong are acting in a bigoted matter toward each other," and I explain that in 14:4 and 13 Paul extends the prohibition of judging to both the weak and the strong (856–57). In contrast to Dunn's limitation of the scope of "works of the law" in 3:20 to Jewish behavior, I maintain that Paul generalizes the reference by the wording of this verse, that *pasa sarx* ("all flesh") can be justified by works of the law, which means that all boasting about performance in every cultural context must cease. Dunn would like to restrict this reference to Jewish boasting because the terminology plays a role in 2:17 and 23, but Paul refers explicitly to "our boasting" in 3:27, which obviously involves both Jews and Gentiles. Paul supports his inclusive argument not just by the rhetorical question Dunn cites in his critique, "God of Jews only" but also by the doctrine of the oneness of God, who is the parent of all humankind. I agree with Prof. Kahl's interpretation of these details. The larger context of Paul's argument requires this universal application, because 1:18–32 established that Gentiles were worshipping the creature rather than the creator and that they were boasting of being wise while actually acting like fools. As Kahl notes, this was a fundamental issue of idolatry. This resonates with the cultural setting, because Rome, far more than Jerusalem, was the boasting center of the Mediterranean world, a matter that Kahl affirms, although it is usually overlooked in discussions of Paul and the law.

With regard to Romans 7 Dunn is disappointed that I reject the "I = Adam = humankind" theory. I do so because there are inadequate textual and thematic links between Genesis and Romans 7 and because this theory implies the mistaken Augustinian notion that the problem of the law is failed performance that evokes guilt. In suggesting that the "speech-in-character" features Paul as the former zealot, whose zeal for the law and flawless performance thereof proved unable to achieve the "good," I show on 459–60 the centrality of the cross that is typical for the commentary. You can judge for yourself whether this qualifies as "theological."

"The sin" appears here with the article to denote the subject of the sentence in 7:13; the article refers back to the definition in the previous pericope: sin as covetousness, desiring what belongs to another, that is, that spirit of competition for honor that had corrupted the law and turned it into a means of status acquisition. The problem was that such competition was so ingrained in the Greco-Roman and Jewish cultures that it seemed perfectly benign and thus remained unacknowledged as sin. It required the crucifixion and resurrection of Christ to expose this lethal competition for what it was; it was "unmasked" not by the law but by the cross, which revealed the full, evil potential of religious zeal acting to defend itself and to prove its superiority. Indeed, the cross contradicts every human campaign to achieve honor through superior performance.

I suspect that passages like this are deemed to lack theological depth because they fail to echo the traditional themes of guilt and forgiveness. I reiterate what is stated throughout the commentary, that the letter centers on the impartial righteousness of God revealed in the cross of Christ, which raises the significance of the universal phenomena of social prejudice, competition and conflict to the level of attempted suppressions of divine truth (1:18). Kahl is right, I believe, in asserting that idolatry stands at the center of the human dilemma, and that it reaches a climax in imperialism. Since all humans have acted as "enemies of God," (5:10) redemption requires reconciliation rather than forgiveness. Paul needed all four proofs along with the introduction and conclusion of this letter to make clear that the gospel of Christ crucified could only be plausibly proclaimed to the barbarians in Spain when the remnants of imperialistic competition and cultural prejudice were overcome between the Roman congregations and also between Jerusalem and the Gentile world.

It is also a pleasure to respond to Prof. Wan, whom I have never met. He proposes a provocative hypothesis that Paul's vision in Romans centers not so much on Spain as on Jerusalem as the "new metropolis" in the "colonized space" of the world. That Jerusalem is presented in Romans as a new capitol of an "alternate empire" is worth evaluating in detail. It is the opposite, so to speak, of Dunn's theory that Jerusalem suffered from ethnocentrism that required Paul's polemic against "works of the law." A precise analysis of the formulation of Paul's argument leads me to be skeptical of either alternative.

The literary critical and redactional analysis of the confession in 1:3–4 shows that the clause "from [the] seed of David" celebrated Jesus as the traditional Jewish messiah adopted and enthroned as the Son of God on the basis of his resurrection. The potentially chauvinistic implications of Jesus as the world ruler led to the redaction of this creed by Hellenistic believers who added the "according to the flesh/spirit" phrases. I write, "Insofar as Jesus descended from the fleshly seed of David, this insertion implies that he was bound to a realm of material bondage opposed to the power of salvation" (107). I conclude that

> The most significant feature of all . . . is that Paul selects a credo that bears the marks of both "the weak and the strong," the Gentile and the Jewish Christian branches of the early church. Despite the careful framing with typical Pauline language and the correcting insertions, the prominent location of this creed indicates Paul's acceptance of a common faith and his effort to be evenhanded. He is willing to cite the Jewish Christian affirmation of Jesus as coming from the "seed of David," despite his opposition to Jewish zealotism (10:1–3) and pride (2:17–24). He is willing to accept the Hellenistic Christian dialectic of flesh versus spirit, despite his subsequent effort to insist upon moral transformation (Romans 6–8) and to counter the results of spiritual arrogance (14:1–15:7)." (108)

If this analysis is accurate, Paul seems to avoid giving preference to imperial claims on either side. This is substantiated by the even-handed treatment of the weak and strong in Romans 14:1–15:7 that concludes with "welcome one another, therefore, as Christ has welcomed you." This seems to eliminate any basis of Jewish or Gentile imperialism. Moreover, it is significant that Paul cites the Septuagint (LXX) version of Deuteronomy 32:43 in Romans 15:10, "Rejoice O Gentiles, with his people." Let me cite the commentary again,

> . . . in contrast to the broad tradition of anticipating Gentile conversion as a form of social and political subordination to Israel, bringing their gifts to the Jerusalem temple, Paul envisions all nations rejoicing together, *with* each other rather than *above or below* each other with respect to honor, lending their varied voices to the cosmic chorus of praise (895).

Paul's discussion of the Jerusalem offering also seems to lack any hint of Jerusalem's imperial station. In Romans 15:26–27, "Paul presents the Jerusalem offering as neither a *quid pro quo* . . . nor an acknowledgment of the superiority of the Jerusalem church, but as an expression of mutual indebtedness that binds the ethnic branches of the church together" (931).

In addition to these significant details, there are three instances in which Paul altered citations from the prophets to eliminate imperialistic implications. In 10:15 he cites Isaiah 52:7 but eliminates the word "mountain," which according to Käsemann, Koch, Stanley, and Wagner, withdrew the prophecy from the context of Mount Zion. I draw the following inference from this redactional decision:

> The anti-imperial logic of the gospel allows no hope that an Israelite imperium would be an improvement over the Roman Empire. In keeping with the ecumenical emphasis evident through Romans, the message of Christ offers peaceful coexistence for the entire world (cf. especially 15:7–13), and it overcomes the barriers between the Greeks and the Jews (cf. 10:12–13) that would remain intact in an Israelite empire. This consideration also explains why Paul deleted . . . "the one preaching the message of peace," found in all of the LXX versions. The concept of "peace" in the Isaiah citation has the same structure as the Pax Romana, resulting from the subordination of all potential enemies under the imperial capitol in Jerusalem" (640).

A second example is the citation of Isaiah 59:20 in 11:26 where the LXX wording, "for the sake of Zion" is changed to *ek Siōn* ("from Zion"). Let me cite the commentary again:

> When one takes the historical setting and rhetorical quality of Paul's letter into account . . . the reason that he would have had to make this change becomes clear. For an audience with a Gentile Christian majority, and in a letter arguing for a cooperative mission to the barbarians in Spain, Isaiah's formulation that the Messiah came "for the sake of Zion" would have been offensive and misleading. Paul does not want to undercut his contention that "there is no distinction between Jews and also Greeks. The same Lord is Lord of all, [bestowing] riches upon all who call upon him" (10:12). Paul's formulation "from Zion" is consistent with the composite creed that opens this letter concerning Jesus "descended from

> David" (1:3) and with the reminder that Christ came from the Israelites (9:5) and that it was in "Zion" that Christ the stone of stumbling was laid (9:33). Zion in this citation appears to be identical with the heavenly Jerusalem ("Jerusalem above," Galatians 4:26), the place from which Christ originated and was expected to descend at the parousia" (703–4).

In the third instance, Paul cited Isaiah 11:10 in 15:12 but eliminated the phrase "in that day" which "allows a recontextualizing of the citation as a prophecy of missionary fulfillment rather than a threatened day of judgment in which the Gentiles would be forced to acknowledge their subordination under Israel's Messiah. The Masoretic text . . . was much less suitable for Paul's purpose, referring to the shoot of David standing as an "ensign" to the Gentiles, that is, as a battle flag symbolizing Israel's military predominance" (896). If Paul had wished to advocate Jerusalem as the capitol of a world empire, why didn't he cite the Hebrew text and why did he delete the phrase from the LXX?

In short, I agree with Prof. Wan that "Paul's mission has momentous political implications" and that his vision of the circle of the world begins in Jerusalem. But whether this involves the hope of a world empire centered in Jerusalem seems less probable. The vision of a global chorus of praise in 15:6–13 implies instead that all tribes and nations will lift their voices in their own languages and melodies into a united chorus whose single leader is Christ. "Unlike the imperialistic unity previously sought by the Roman house and tenement churches, requiring that others conform to the practices and beliefs of a particular in-group, this is a chorus that encourages diversity to flourish, under the same blessed Lord" (885). The catena of citations in 15:9–12 ends with "in him will the Gentiles hope," because the rule of Christ is not simply another form of despotism. The Gentiles hope for their own conversion in the context of global pacification, an eschatological hope centered in Christ. Since Paul's purpose is to elicit support for the Gentile mission, he ends the citation at this point, rather than continuing on to the ingathering of Jewish exiles as in Isaiah 11:11" (897). This is a global vision of celebrative coexistence, not imperialism in any traditional sense of the word. It is a vision that seems spatially decentered, with a personal center in Christ, who is no longer merely in Jerusalem but in every believing congregation whatever their location or culture (Romans 8:10). This correlates closely with Prof. Kahl's contention that "new forms of communality are spreading to the ends of the earth. In small groups that are cooperatively interacting with each other, God restores 'arenas of righteousness' and 'beachheads of the new creation.'"

So, with thanks to the organizers and participants in this symposium, and following Paul's advice that after the prophets and interpreters have spoken, "let others weigh what is said (1 Corinthians 14:29), I take my seat.

The Cleveland Symposium
March 8, 2007

19

A Critique of the Romans Commentary

Ayo Adewuya

Professor Jewett has produced a well-researched volume on Romans that will shape scholarly discussions on the book for several decades to come. It is a work that not only demonstrates academic excellence but also one that does not shy away from going against the majority opinion of scholars on various issues.

Professor Jewett's observations on the Holy Spirit in Romans are thought-provoking and deserve further exploration and study. Apart from noting the frequent occurrence of "pneuma" ("spirit") in Romans, his insight on the religious orientation of the Roman congregations is very helpful, particularly as he examines the charismatic nature of the community. In concurrence with scholars such as Moody Smith and Philip Esler, Professor Jewett argues that "Glossolalia was probably a typical aspect of most early Christian congregation." He rightly takes issues with the longstanding hostility of mainstream theology against charismatic exuberance and maintains that charismatic enthusiasm was characteristic not just of Pauline churches but of Roman Christianity as a whole.

A major issue with the commentary, not unexpectedly, relates to its discussion of the "purpose" of Romans. The author maintains that the letter, in keeping with what he regards as the normal practice in letter writing must have a central goal and that other topics are therefore peripheral. In this regard, he opines that Paul's purpose of writing is to prepare the Roman Christians for his Spanish mission. The attempt to isolate a single purpose for Romans, although laudable, is not in my opinion, entirely successful or convincing. Such a view, it seems to me, does not take Romans seriously as a story. This is particularly important to me as an African reader who understands letters primarily as stories. Although Bitzer is right that historical situations and controlling exigencies play crucial roles in the understanding of a letter, it may be argued that both are secondary to the main goal of Paul which was to establishing a relationship with the Romans, a church that he neither founded nor has visited.

As Norman Pedersen has ably demonstrated in his book *Rediscovering Paul*, a major and underlying reason for letter writing is relationship—the presence or absence of it. If this were granted to be the case, it is easy why Paul could address various issues. If, as it is commonly agreed, Paul had neither founded nor visited the church at Rome, it is perfectly normal that he writes as much about "everything" as he could prior to his own stated intention of visiting them. His conversation would thus serve as "talking points" on a broad range of subjects, including his proposed Spanish mission. Finally, it remains difficult to see how much of the material in Romans 1–14 fulfill the particular purpose of Romans argued for by Professor Jewett as "the purpose." At least, it has not been clearly demonstrated up to chapter 4.

20

Analysis and Appreciation of Robert Jewett's Romans 9–16

Paul Elbert

I first met Robert at an international Society of Biblical Literature meeting in Helsinki during a session on Luke's use of Pauline letters by Lars Aejmelaeus. By then, Robert must have been more than halfway through his twenty-six year pilgrimage in interpreting Paul's letter to the churches in Rome. My assignment today is to offer some brief critical comments from material selected from chapters 9–16[1] that might be particularly relevant or interesting to global Pentecostalism or to international Charismatic Renewal today. However, I would like to think that my analysis should apply equally well to how Paul's original Christian readers in Rome would have understood these passages when they received his letter. Robert's chapters 9–16 represent some 459 pages, which include the rhetorical climax of the letter in 15:14–16:16, 21–24. I am glad to offer some brief contextual observations and considerations on six verses that may hopefully be of interest to our discussion.

I will begin with 9:1, "I am telling the truth in Christ, I am not lying, my conscience bearing me witness in the Holy Spirit." So Paul introduces his explanation, laid out in chapters 9–11, of the riddle of Israel's unbelief, how the Gentiles, who did not pursue righteousness are able to attain righteousness and faith, while Israel is given stupor, and how eventually a remnant, even all Israel, will be saved. Intellectual discussion among his Jewish and Gentile audience, of whose unity Paul is concerned, would welcome a convincing explanation of this circumstance and an assurance of God's participation in it.

[1] Robert Jewett, *Romans: A Commentary* (Hermeneia; Minneapolis: Fortress Press, 2007).

Paul says he is telling the truth (*alētheian legō*), Robert citing Isocrates' and Demosthenes' use of this phrase in classical oratory. Here we may have evidence of what Robert acknowledges in his preface, the help of classicist Roy Kotansky and "innumerable searches through the *Thesaurus Linguae Graecae*" (TLG). As one who used the facilities of the TLG for several years while working at the University of California at Irvine, where its special library and computers are housed, I can much appreciate this effort, but perhaps even more how much such references add necessary depth. Commendably, such citations are very visible throughout, more so here than elsewhere in the Romans commentary tradition. This depth is highly appropriate to the educational background and literary worldview of Paul, who is probably the product of progymnasmatic or pre-rhetorical education as a young boy, where he would be exposed to these classical writers, particularly Homer. He would have been instructed on how to properly compose theses, comparisons, descriptions, and discourses by characters that required composition of appropriate speech-in-character which duly persuades. In this formal education he would also have been introduced to how these literary tasks were accomplished by the venerated writers and speakers of the past that were worthy of imitation. So, the fullest employment of connections to the rhetorical arts is apropos and informative.

At 9:1 the claim of truth is linked to writing in Christ (*en Christō*). What would Roman readers think of this language here? Throughout Romans there is an array of experiential language that is oriented to a non-earthly dimension and sphere of influence. Only a similar connection to this spiritual sphere of influence could possibly lend authentic understandability to Paul's expressions. Even then, for later readers, some important practical expressions Paul employs could do with clarification, which as I mention below is a task I believe that Luke takes up via his narrative-rhetorical exemplarity, progymnasmatic training being the motivation. Paul evidently expects to be understood at 9:1 and, if not, he has colleagues in Rome, like the outstanding apostles Andronikos and Junias, who were in Christ before him, missionary colleagues Prisca and Aquila, and the deaconess and patroness Phoebe, who could probably answer any questions as to what experience Paul is describing. Here, at 9:1, he is telling the truth in Christ. My suggestion is that he feels and recognizes the presence of Christ as he composes this line and accordingly mentions this temporal coincidence. Next he states that he is not lying. That's good for readers to know, but what is most persuasive again is what follows, namely that the Spirit is witnessing with his conscience (*symmartyrousēs moi . . . en pneumati hagiō*). Robert comments that "the veracity of the witness of his conscience is certified by the Holy Spirit." Yes, quite so. How does this veracity on Paul's part communicate to his original readers? I might suggest that what Paul is counting on here is that his active readership,[2] which has experienced the gift of the Holy Spirit (Romans 5:5), has received the Spirit (8:15), and understands the confirming personal witness of the Spirit himself (8:16), is a readership that will understand his spiritual language at 9:1. Paul links his claim of truthfulness about his explanation about a controversial topic to written words that are "in Christ," to words that "the Holy Spirit bears witness to." This is language that his readers can immediately link to their own experience of truthfulness when they speak or write, since they too have the interactive benefits of Christ and the Holy Spirit. Accordingly, Paul can expect to be believed, not just because he says he is telling the truth and is not lying, but because his spiritual language here is understandable to people who have had the same experience in Christ and the same experience with the witness of the Holy Spirit – experience that is recognizably describable by the same language that Paul is employing.

Next, let's consider 10:9, "Because if you confess with your mouth 'Lord Jesus!' and have faith 'in your heart' that God raised him from the dead, you will be saved (*sōthēsē*)." Robert does a good job differentiating this type of confession, denoting "an attitude of subserviency and sense of belongingness or devotion," from later catechistic formulas. He points out that to have faith in your heart indicates a "deeply motivating belief." Robert takes the future passive indicative *sōthēsē* ("you will be saved") as logical rather than temporal, "showing the consequence of the mouth's confession and the heart's conviction." While there must be salvation experience in the present, perhaps Paul here thinks mainly in the sense of eschatological salvation, following his first reference to future salvation at 5:9 and 10, where the future passive *sōthēsometha* ("we shall be saved") indicates being saved from the wrath of God. We find the future salvation again at 9:27 and 14:26 with respect to Israel (*sōthēsetai*) ("it shall be saved") and again at 10:13 (*sōthēsetai*) ("it shall be saved") with respect to humankind.

In any case, just what are the consequences of being saved at 10:9 that Robert alludes to? How does such a person that obeys Paul's exhortation here obtain practical certainty that what happens is what Paul is talking about? Even an active readership may confront a lack of clarity. One of the general problems with Paul's discourse is the absence of examples and precedents befitting a narrative-rhetorical treatment of

2 Regarding such active readers, cf. G. Cavallo, *A History of Reading in the West*, edited by G. Guglielmo and R. Chartier; trans. L. G. Cochrane (Amherst: University of Massachussetts Press, 1999), 88–89; W. A. Johnson, "Toward a Sociology of Reading in Classical Antiquity," *American Journal of Philology* 121 (2000), 593–627; G. Cavallo, *Lire à Byzance*, trans. P. Odorica and A. Segonds (Paris: Les Belles Lettres, 2006), 7, 12, 18–19, 60–61, 67, 70, 76.

important Christian experiential language. Of course Paul assumes that his original readers underdstand his salvation-language, but what about later readers? Language used by Paul with respect to salvation needed to be illusrated or elaborated with examples and precedents so that later readers will clearly understand and be persuaded by Paul. As I have argued in a paper at this conference, Luke improves intertextually upon Paul with his portrait of this esteemed writer in this regard, providing a necessary element of clarification and personification of Paul's language about salvation and about Spirit-reception. This would stimulate fresh re-readings of Paul. Without this narrative-rhetorical clarification, using identical language to Paul's, later readers could not be sure of what experience Paul writes and may misunderstand him, a pastoral problem I believe the literary minded Luke seeks to correct.

If I might be permitted a digression outside of my chapters assigned for this occasion, on the Spirit-language of readers being given the Holy Spirit (Romans 5:5) Robert notes other uses of the verb *ekchynnō* ("poured out") with regard to the shedding of blood. However, the Old Testament and septuagint usage at Joel 3:1, "I will pour out (*ekcheō*) my Spirit on all flesh" is the most likely one to have produced a textual influence upon Paul at Romans 5:5. Accordingly, Robert mentions this text as well. Perhaps describing the gift of the Holy Spirit as a Christian experience that pours out love is a linguistic creation by Paul. Another possible factor is the existence of a similar pre-Pauline expression. Paul evidently expects his readership to understand what he means here, that is, to identify this experiential language with an experience that they have had or have heard about through preaching or testimony.

Robert also mentions Acts 10:45 at this juncture, where Luke, writing after the Pauline letters, employs *ekkechytai* in a speech by Peter, ". . . the gift of the Holy Spirit *had been poured out* even on the Gentiles. For they heard them speaking in tongues and extolling God" (10:45b–46a). Robert then states that Luke's use of *ekkechytai* in Peter's speech "refers to the event of conversion or baptism." I have difficulty in following this since Luke does not indicate anywhere in his narrative that the pouring out of the Spirit is what he describes elsewhere as conversion (*epistrophēn* Acts 15:3).[3] In fact, at Acts 15:3, where we find Lukan description (*ekphrasis*) which I believe we can take as "an informative

[3] Re Lukan conversion, cf. R. Michiels, "La conception lucanienne de la conversion," *Ephemerides theologicae lovanienses* 41 (1965), 61–84; A. George, *Études sur l'oeuvre de Luc* (Paris: Gabalda, 1978), 351–68; C. H. Talbert, "Conversion in the Acts of the Apostles: Ancient Auditor's Perceptions," in R. P. Thompson and T. E. Phillips, editors, *Literary Studies in Luke-Acts: Essays in Honor of Joseph B. Tyson* (Macon: Mercer University Press, 1998), 142–53.

account which brings vividly into view what is being set forth,"[4] Luke writes that the Gentiles were converted in Phoenicia and Samaria. He then portrays Peter in a short speech saying that the Gentiles heard the word of the gospel and believed, following this with "and God, the heart-knower, bore witness to them, giving them the Holy Spirit just as also to us" (15:8). It would seem that Luke associates faith and belief with his concept of conversion and that he has another experience in mind for his description of the pouring out of the Holy Spirit, as he capably has demonstrated previously at Acts 2:16–17 by way of another speech by the same character. Therefore, if Robert wants to suggest that Paul's expression, "the love of God has been poured into our hearts through (the) Holy Spirit that was given to us" is to be understood by his readers as referring to conversion or baptism, he is on thin ice by appealing to Acts 10:45. It is good to guess what Paul means, however, and Paul makes similar statements (Galatians 4:6; 2 Corinthians 1:22) that are equally in need of clarification for active readers. On my thesis, based upon contemproary rhetorical and narrative requirements, this discursive problem is fully realized and taken up by Luke.[5]

Having digressed, I hope not too long, my third verse is Romans 12:6, a phenomenon I suggest is made efficacious by the previous descriptions Paul has employed at Romans 1:11 and 5:5, "Yet having charismatic gifts that differ according to the grace given us, whether prophecy—according to the analogy of faith (*kata tēn analogian tēn pisteōs*)." Robert observes that the list of charisms here does not include "the more spectacular ecstatic manifestations such as glossolalia." I had gotten away from the concept of ecstasy applied to glossolalia, say with the study by Cyril Williams, finding that this inspired speech conveys meaning in non-human languages.[6] However, I know that some scholars (Aune and Forbes) apply the adjective *ekstatikos* ("ecstatic") to what Paul and Luke

---

[4] "*Peri Ekphraseōs*," in M. Patillon, editor, with G. Bolognesi, *Aelius Théon, Progymnasmata* (Collection des Unversités de France; Paris: Les Belles Lettres, 1997), 66. See too "*Ekphraseis*" in Herbert Hunger, *Die hochsprachliche profane Literatur der Byzantiner* (München: Beck, 1978), 170–88.

[5] P. Elbert, "Possible Literary Links Between Luke-Acts and Pauline Letters Regarding Spirit-Language," in T. L. Brodie et al. editors, *Intertextuality in the New Testament: Explorations of Theory and Practice* (Sheffield: Sheffield-Phoenix Press, 2006), 226–54.

[6] C. G. Williams, *Tongues of the Spirit* (Cardiff: University of Wales Press, 1981). In regard to Williams' finding, I quote Paul: "For one who speaks in a tongue does not speak to humankind, but to God; for no one understands, but in Spirit (*pneumati de*) he speaks mysteries" (1 Corinthians 14:2). *If God is listening, this speech conveys meaning to God.* God understands mysteries, he appreciates and understands them; perhaps they might have a special meaning to him, something dear to his heart. It would seem important to speak mysteries to God if one could do so and Paul is grateful that he can so speak. Rational humankind does not naturally want to speak what cannot be understood. God certainly understands this aspect of human nature and so has provided an incentive to overcome such reluctance. *The incentive is that he is listening and that mysteries are worth speaking.*

describe. This might be an inappropriate blanket term for Christian glossolalia, importing too much from Greco-Roman backgrounds and regarding too little Paul's claim that this speech edifies, assists in prayer and in song, and goes directly to God with mysteries that He apparently understands. Paul appreciates these interior qualities of divine interaction; I see no implication that glossolalia, while non-rational, is *ekstatikos* ("ecstatic").

However, the phrase *kata tēn analogian tēn pisteōs* is why I have chosen this verse (12:6) because it relates to the spectacular nature of New Testament prophecy. When revelatory prophecy exhorts, comforts, instructs, or reveals information beyond human ability to know, this provides hope in the power of the Holy Spirit (Romans 15:13), one of Paul's desires. Robert is of course correct to point out that the term *analogia* relates to mathematical proportion, to progression, to ratios and thus to proportion. Paul's phrase, *analogian tēn pisteōs*, ("according to the analogy of faith") is, I suggest, conceived from his experience and the experience of others that in order to effectively function in the grace of prophecy, one must employ faith in the proportion and in the progression to what one receives from the Spirit, building and believing as one continues on with what is revealed. This phenomenological proportion and progression of faith as one prophesies is appropriate to those who are described as having been given the Holy Spirit and as having received the Holy Spirit. That is my answer to Robert's question as to "how the criterion of faith functions" and to why Paul employs this appropriate phrase. I also would suggest that here Paul is employing the same concept of "faith in the heart" that he mentioned earlier at Romans 10:9.

The fourth, fifth, and sixth verses are selected because of their contemporary relevance to women called into the ministry today by dreams and visions and other Spirit-directed processes. After my paper on Luke's use of Romans at the Society of Biblical Literature Washington D. C. in November 2006,[7] a New Testament professor of eight years at a very prominent Baptist seminary sought to meet with me. During our conversation he shared that he had been seeking to be baptized in the Holy Spirit, which Luke also calls the gift of the Holy Spirit, and asked for my thoughts on the matter. We spoke for over an hour on that subject and he left determined to seriously continue to seek according to Luke 11:5–13. In January of this year I called him at home to encourage him. He told me sadly that he had been fired and that a woman-friend whose office

[7] "Luke's Possible Progymnasmatic Improvements on and Employment of Paul's Letter to the Romans," presented and discussed in the Formation of Luke-Acts section. I am grateful for heuristic comment on this paper from L. Aejmelaeus, T. L. Brodie, D. Dorman, R. F. Hock, D. Konstan, H. Leppä, M. C. Parsons, J. Shelton, W. O. Walker, Jr., and M. Winninge.

was across the hall had also been fired. He was fired, not for wearing the wrong colored necktie, but for being in sudden violation of what might be termed the interpretative philosophy of Evangelical Protestant cessationism. Seeking to obey the teaching of the earthly Jesus as recorded by Luke in its narrative context indicated disagreement with this interpretive philosophy which claims that the gift of the Holy Spirit as described by examples and precedents in the book of Acts has ceased. His colleague was fired for being a woman, since the seminary decided that it could no longer allow a woman to teach future pastors. On the latter issue, I might mention that Jenny Powers did something helpful on 1 Corinthians 14:34–35 in her article "'Your Daughters Shall Prophesy: Pentecostal Hermeneutics and the Empowerment of Women"[8] and that I raised eight points on this matter for such Evangelicals to consider.[9]

Paul's attitudes toward women in ministry were never more in need of consideration and exposition from a balanced contextual perspective in the face of unbashed proof-texting, combined with quick and dogmatic cessationism foisted upon Paul and other New Testament writers.[10] Quite helpful and very welcome then, toward a balanced consideration of Paul as a real person in early Christianity, are Robert's comments on Phoebe (Romans 16:1–2), Prisca and Aquila (16:3) and Andronikos and Junia (16:7)

Robert suggests that Paul's reference to Phoebe (16:1–2) as a deaconess (*diakonon tēs ekklēsias*) and a patroness (*prostatis*) "to many and also to me"—*prostatis* being feminine and *prostatēs* being the masculine noun for a protector, patron, or helper—probably shows his appreciation for her intended support, as a person of high social status, for the Spanish mission which Paul announced in 15:24. It may not be well known that the Australian series on *New Documents Illustrating Early Christianity* published a lovely fourth century inscription from a tombstone in Jerusalem with a cross that reads: "Here lies the slave and

---

[8] Her article appears in M. W. Dempster et al. editors, *The Globalization of Pentecostalism: A Religion Made to Travel* (Irvine: Regnum International, 1999), 313–37.

[9] P. Elbert, "The Globalization of Pentecostalism: A Review Article," *Trinity Journal* 23 (2002), 81–101. My book, *Pastoral Letter to Theo: An Introduction to Interpretation and Women's Ministries* (Eugene: Wipf & Stock, 2008), attempts to correct the proof-texting style of some and provide responsible exegesis of those New Testament texts which speak to women being called into the ministry. I intend to make good use of Robert's insightful analyses of such passages.

[10] Such an interpretive philosophy is found, for example, in E. S. English et al. editors, *The New Schofield Reference Bible* (New York: Oxford University Press, 1967). Sandeen's astute assessment of the editors' uncritical imposition of ideological imagination is germane and to the point: "The Scofield Reference Bible combined an attractive format of typography, paragraphing, notes, and cross references with the theology of Darbyite dispensationalism. The book has thus been subtly but powerfully influential in spreading those views among hundreds of thousands who have regularly read the Bible and who have been unaware of the distinction between the ancient text and the Scofield interpretation" (Ernest R. Sandeen, *The Roots of Fundamentalism* [Chicago: University of Chicago Press, 1970], 71).

bride of Christ, Sophia, deaconess, the second Phoibe, who fell asleep in peace on the 21st of the month of March . . . the Lord God."[11]

As to Prisca and Aquila (16:3), Robert suggests that the fact that "her name is mentioned first indicates her higher social status in the Roman context." Observing that Paul cites Prisca and Aquila as "my co-workers on Christ Jesus" (*tous synergous mou en Christō Iēsou*, 16:3), we may endorse Wolf-Hennig Ollrog's work on *Paulus und seine Mitarbeiter. Untersuchungen zu Theorie und Praxis der paulinischen Mission* and on *synergos*, showing that *synergos* is probably a distinct and unique Pauline expression by which Paul refers to a person "who works together with Paul as an agent of God in the common work of missionary proclamation." Robert concludes that Prisca and Aquila are not "helpers of the apostle," but rather that the clear implication is that each of them functions as "a missionary who becomes a colleague and co-worker with Paul, who is called to the same task and in the same service of proclamation: to awaken the faith of the congregation" (with Ollrog). This is consistent with the discoveries in Bernadette Brooten's fine work, *Women Leaders in the Ancient Synagogue: Inscriptional Evidence and Background Issues*.[12] Considering their appearance in various NT contexts, Robert suggests that Prisca and Aquila "shared a theological and congregational orientation comparable with that of the apostle."

As to Andronikos and Junia (16:7), Robert calls attention to some 250 examples of the Latin feminine name Junia found in Roman evidence. He is no doubt correct in observing that "the presumption [is] that no woman could rank as an apostle, and thus the accusative form must refer to a male by the name of Junias or Junianus." Luther promoted the masculine option and was imitated by male-dominated culture. However, as Robert points out, "the evidence in favor of the feminine name 'Junia' is overwhelming. Not a single example of a masculine name 'Junias' has been found." For more research corroborating this result, we may now also consult Linda Belleville's work on documentary evidence, "*Iounian . . . episēmoi en tois apostolois*: a re-examination of Romans 16:7 in light of primary source materials."[13] Robert suggests, as does Belleville, that the honorific expression *episēmoi en tois apostolois* should be properly translated as "outstanding among the apostles" and he offers a striking confirmation of this translation by citing Chrysostom's comment about Junia: "Even to be an apostle is great, but also to be prominent among them—consider how wonderful a song of honor that is!"

---

[11] "Sophia, the Second Phoibe," in G. H. R. Horsley, editor, *New Documents Illustrating Early Christianity: A Review of the Greek Inscriptions and Papyri Published in 1979* (New South Wales: Macquarie University Press, 1987), 239.

[12] Perhaps my review of *Women Leaders* in the *Journal of Theological Studies* 34 (1983), 503–504, might be of interest.

[13] *New Testament Studies* 51/2 (2005), 231–49.

21

A Review of Robert Jewett's Romans Hermeneia Commentary

Jeffrey S. Lamp

I must say at the outset that it is both humbling and a privilege to present some thoughts on Robert Jewett's magisterial commentary on Romans. Any New Testament scholar working in the area of Pauline studies has certainly benefited from Professor Jewett's meticulous scholarship and insights. I myself have also found his extensive work on the intersection of biblical studies and popular culture thought provoking, drawing from his example the justification for my own forays into examining popular culture through the biblical and theological lenses of Christian tradition. So this opportunity is truly an honor, and I hope my words will whet the appetites of those here to pore over the pages of this commentary with expectations of learning new things from a letter that has become well-worn terrain in the scholarly community.

My area of responsibility was those sections of the commentary covering chapters 4–8 of Romans. Even with this somewhat unnatural division of the letter (chapters 5–8 are typically understood as a distinct unit within the letter), I had the smallest number of pages to digest for this review. I must admit to my shame I have not read all of the commentary, so I may be guilty of proceeding without a full picture of the context of Professor Jewett's comments. Nevertheless, I shall begin with a few general comments formulated from my reading of the commentary, followed by the rather narrow focus of how this part of the commentary addresses issues of importance for those of a Pentecostal-Charismatic perspective.

First, I found the commentary eminently readable. Despite the rather technical focus of the Hermeneia series, the sections I read have a definite, dare I say, devotional or spiritual value to them. This is not to say that the technical aspects typical of the series are missing—far from it. The commentary is rich with the insights drawn from a quarter century of careful scholarly reflection on the epistle. But at many junctures in the text, I found myself highlighting statements profound in their incisive appreciation of the pastoral flavor of Paul's own thoughts and their application for today's Christian believers. Frequently I found myself sitting in a Starbuck's uttering the words, "That'll preach," after encountering such statements. To many sitting here it may not prove surprising that I have seldom had such reactions to other entries in the Hermeneia series (though I wonder what it says about me that I had a few such moments while perusing George Nickelsburg's commentary on *1 Enoch*). I do not know if this was an intentional concern on the part of Professor Jewett, but it is at least apparent that his vocation of teaching students destined for parish ministry shines through these pages.

Along with a growing number of interpreters, Professor Jewett is dogged in his determination to uncover the situation among the Roman tenement and house churches that gave rise to Paul's words. This tendency in more recent scholarship to view Romans as more than just some sort of abstract presentation of Paul's theology to a group of believers he had never met provides a richer texture to Paul's thought, and opens up avenues for interpretation and appropriation of the apostle's message previously untapped by more generic treatments of the letter. In brief, Professor Jewett argues that there existed among the Roman tenement and house churches factions, the "weak" and the "strong," who sat in judgment of each other over the performance or non-performance of aspects of the Law. The Law became the locus upon which the "weak" and "strong" competed for honor and status. The apostle is then seen throughout the letter undercutting the grounds by which these factions attacked each other, offering instead a vision of God's people rooted in the common experience of justification through faith in Jesus Christ on the pattern of Abraham's faith and of life in the Spirit. We will see shortly that Paul's focus on the community of God's people will have significant ramifications for his and our understanding of the experience of the Spirit. Professor Jewett attributes a rather robust charismatic emphasis to Paul's teaching on the Spirit in Romans, particularly in important discussions within chapters 5–8. We will now proceed to summarize Paul's pneumatology in these chapters as formulated by Professor Jewett.

One feature of Paul's pneumatology noted by Professor Jewett is the acknowledgement that the church of Paul's day saw itself as a charismatic community. Paul's use of the term *charisma* in 5:15 indicates not simply the gift of salvation, but also the granting of charismatic gifts—the two are inseparable (380). The phrase "in Christ Jesus" (8:1) speaks of an "ecclesiastical realm" established and governed by Christ as "a mystical, ecstatic realm of the Spirit in which believers participate" (480). Paul's emphasis on the church as a community of the Spirit cuts against the quest for honor and status, replacing this worldly perspective with one in which believers view each other as Spirit-filled members of a Spirit-filled community.

A related aspect of Paul's pneumatology is the focus on the community's life together in the Spirit. As Professor Jewett repeatedly notes throughout his commentary, far too often references to the Spirit in this section of the epistle are detached from their rhetorical and social contexts and understood primarily as the individual Christian's life in the Spirit. The conveyance of divine love and peace by the Spirit, the Spirit's empowerment for victory over sin, the charismatic gifts of the Spirit, the leading of the Spirit, and the unutterable prayer aided by the Spirit are all too often relegated to private, individual spirituality. However, as Professor Jewett notes, doing so ignores the very situation among the Roman churches that caused Paul to write in the first place. Paul is writing to heal significant and potentially lethal breaches between Roman believers. So Paul's pneumatology in this section should be viewed more in social, collective terms rather than in private, individualistic terms. Of course, this does not mitigate the role of the Spirit in the life of the individual Christian. But Paul's concern here is to foster reconciliation between alienated factions in Rome. This is particularly so in Romans 8, the great so-called "Spirit chapter," which becomes in Professor Jewett's estimation more a charter for the corporate body of believers than it is a blueprint for personal spirituality.

Too often academic discussion of the place of the Law in Paul's thought is abstracted from these chapters irrespective of the social context in which the statements in question are offered. Professor Jewett anchors his discussion of Paul's view of the Law directly in the context of the Roman tenement and house churches. This is an integral component of Paul's discussion in 7:7–12, where Paul in the person of the rhetorical "I" demonstrates that the competition for status between the "weak" and the "strong" is the same wrongheaded zeal that corrupted his pre-Christian experience of the Law (444). Rather than perverting the Law into a Law of sin and death through this quest for individual and group honor, Roman Christians should view the Law and the Spirit in such a connection that the Spirit empowers believers to serve others, thus fulfilling the purpose of the Law (438–39). This connection of Law and Spirit appears to be a Pauline innovation designed to address the situation in the Roman churches (460–61).

An intriguing, and clearly overlooked, aspect of Paul's pneumatology in chapter 8 is its creational focus. Professor Jewett views 8:18–30 as a sustained argument in which attention is directed to the interdependence of the human and non-human components of creation (508–30). The focus of this passage is on the suffering of creation due to Adam's sin, suffering that the Spirit-filled children of God experience along with this groaning creation, and the commission of the community to utilize their charismatic gifts toward the restoration of the ecological wholeness of creation. Again, emphasis is placed on the endowment of spiritual gifts for purposes outside of the scope of individual piety. Even one of the verses frequently cited by Pentecost-Charismatic Christians in support of the personal practice of glossolalia, 8:26, is seen by Professor Jewett not as a proof text for the practice (he seems to suggest that it is unlikely that it refers to glossolalia), but rather as an indication that in human weakness the Spirit is a silent intercessor, fostering in Spirit-filled Christians a sensitivity for the suffering of all creatures (523–24). All too often in this arena individual pietistic concerns and a strand of popular eschatology in Pentecostal-Charismatic circles, one that sees the destruction of the created order in the end, combine to divert energies away from the pursuit of the ecological healing of creation. Paul's understanding of the Spirit is one of holistic restoration of the totality of God's good but marred creation.

Perhaps Professor Jewett's own words, in their original setting summarizing the focus of 8:1–17, succinctly distill the essence of his study of Paul's pneumatology:

> Paul's language throughout this passage is charismatic and "mystical"; it reflects a collective type of charismatic mysticism in which God's Spirit was thought to enter and energize the community as well as each member. Its primary arena of manifestation, in contrast to most later Christianity, was not individual ecstasy but social enthusiasm, speaking in tongues, prophecy, and joyous celebration in the context of the common meal that united the formerly shamed from different families and backgrounds into a single family honored and chosen and hallowed by God. (490–91)

The implications of Professor Jewett's analysis of the Spirit in the logic of Paul's argumentation are both obvious and startling. If his exegesis of these chapters has merit, and I am persuaded it does, then much current Pentecostal-Charismatic appropriation of the apostle's teaching on the Spirit in Romans 5–8 is truncated. It is my observation that this appropriation of Paul's teaching participates in the methodological shortsightedness of many earlier generic, abstract characterizations of Paul's message in Romans. It ignores the social situation Paul addressed and thus his focus on corporate life in the Spirit. The result is the all-too-frequent mining of Paul's pneumatological statements in Romans to support the largely individualistic experiences of the Spirit by many Pentecostal-Charismatic Christians. Again, nothing in Paul's statements in this section of the letter denies the importance of the workings of the Spirit in the lives of individual believers. But to catch the full, genuine vision of Paul's pneumatology here we must grasp the social context within which this life in the Spirit is to be lived. And here Professor Jewett has rendered a great service for Pentecostal-Charismatic Christians, reminding us that Paul here is simply reflecting the heart of God toward the creation and nurture of a Spirit-filled people of God.

It is reading far too much into Professor Jewett's motivation and final product to claim that this is a Pentecostal-Charismatic commentary on Romans. It is first and foremost a stellar piece of scholarship, truly a crowning moment to a prolific career (though we all hope more is forthcoming from his pen!). In the company of many great commentaries on this great epistle, this volume sets the standard for future commentators. But this commentary, at least the section I was assigned to review, may be used with confidence by Pentecostal-Charismatic scholars, pastors, and students for its examination of the place of the Spirit within the argument of Romans and within the Church of Jesus Christ.

22

Response to Cleveland Colleagues

Robert Jewett

I appreciate the evaluations of my three colleagues, several of whom I met today for the first time. It is an unusual privilege to hear the views of Pentecostal scholars in the conference like this, when a book by a non-member like myself is included on the program for evaluation. Your generosity is congruent with the active form of social tolerance and respect that Paul seems to be advocating in his letter to believers in Rome. I have learned much from these responses and during this conference I hope to gain a clearer grasp of the Pentecostal movement, the fastest growing and most promising religious development in recent times. I propose to weave my response around three themes that are suggested in the various points raised in these thoughtful critiques.

I begin with Prof. Adewuya's concern about whether the relationship Paul seeks with the Romans is adequately grasped, and particularly whether the story of Paul's mission is clear.

I.

I agree with Prof. Adewuya's contention that the main goal of Paul was to establish "a *relationship* with the Romans." The question is, what kind of relationship. In the opening verses of chapter 1 Paul introduces himself as an apostle who serves as slave of Christ, the ambassador of Christ entrusted with a world transforming gospel. He seeks to impart "some spiritual charisma that you may be strengthened" (1:11) but he immediately qualifies this by saying that he wants "to be mutually encouraged among you by each other's faith, both yours and mine." As any ambassador, he seeks something from then while at the same time clarifying the relationship that binds them together and provides a rationale for mutual action. This correlates with 15:20 where Paul states his principle of not building on someone else's foundation but preaching where the gospel has not yet been heard. Paul does not seek a relationship of founder or leader in Rome; he is an ambassador seeking cooperation in organizing a mission project.

In the *narratio* of 1:13–15, which explains the background of the intended visit, Paul employs some discriminatory language by referring to "Greeks and barbarians . . . wise and foolish." These terms articulate the social boundaries of Greco-Roman culture in a thoroughly abusive manner. As studies of *Barbaros* by Yves Albert Dauge and other have shown,[1] this is the "N-" word in Greco-Roman culture. When paired with its ideological opposite, "Greeks," it denotes the violent, perverse, corrupt, uncivilized realm beyond and at times within the Roman Empire that threatens peace and security. There is an early suggestion here that the mission project that the letter is intended to support aims at the Spaniards, mentioned in chapter 15, who were viewed as barbarians par excellence by Roman authorities. Similarly, the terms "wise" and "unwise/uneducated" depict the educational boundary between citizens of the empire and the shameful masses. Since most of the believers in Rome were slaves and former slaves rather than Latin speaking Roman natives, they would have been seen as barbaric and uneducated as the distant Spaniards. But it is not just Paul's use of these epithets of honor and shame that jars the modern reader; Paul undercuts the moral premise of the Greco-Roman world in proclaiming his indebtedness to the shameful as well as to the honorable representatives of the antitheses.

When this remarkable formulation is followed by the antithesis "to the Jew first and also to the Greek" in Romans 1:16–17, there is a reversal of the claim of ethnic priority that was being claimed by the Gentile Christian majority in Rome.[2] This sets the stage for redefining sin as an untruthful distortion of social systems in 1:18–32. The reference to not being "ashamed of the gospel" (1:16) also sets the tone for the entire subsequent letter. As one can see from the parallel text in 1 Corinthians 1:20–31, the gospel *was* innately shameful as far as ancient cultures were concerned. A divine self revelation on an obscene cross seemed to demean God and overlook the honor and propriety of established religious traditions, both Jewish and Greco-Roman. Rather than appealing to the honorable and righteous members of society, such

---

1 Yves Albert Dauge, *Le Barbare. Recherches sur la conception romaine de la barbarie et de la civilisation* (Brussels: Latomus, 1981), 393–810, showing that the term barbarian in Roman materials serves to depict outsiders as irrational, ferocious, warlike, alienated, chaotic, and in all respects the opposite of the civilized Roman.

2 See James C. Walters, *Ethnic Issues in Paul's Letter to the Romans* (Valley Forge: Trinity Press International, 1993), 68–79.

a gospel seemed designed to appeal to the despised and the powerless. To use the words of 1 Corinthians once again, "God chose what is low and despised in the world . . . so that no one might boast in the presence of God." (1 Corinthians 1:27–29) There were powerful, social reasons why Paul should have been ashamed of this gospel; his claim not to be ashamed signals that a social and ideological revolution has been inaugurated by the gospel. The "story" that this letter offers, therefore, deals with this revolution, in which the Roman believers are asked to participate. But this requires that the gospel needs to be clarified in Rome itself.

From the citation of a composite creed in 1:3–4 that embodies the views of two sides in the early church, to the explicit references to "all" believers in Rome, Paul signals the intent to overcome barriers between competitive churches. In particular, I believe, the proper rhetorical identification of 1:13–15 as a *narratio* clarifies the kind of relationship with various groups that he wants to establish. I like Prof. Lamp's formulation: "there existed among the Roman tenement and house churches factions, the "weak" and the "strong," who sat in judgment of each other over the performance or non-performance of aspects of the Law. The Law became the locus upon which the "weak" and "strong" competed for honor and status." The story of the gospel's assault on discriminatory systems of honor is thereby established, and by the end of the letter, it becomes clear that this campaign in behalf of the gospel as the "power of God" (1:16–17) should soon reach the symbolic end of the known world, Spain, thus preparing the way for the eschatological triumph in which all nations will join voices in praise of God's mercy to the shamed (15:6–11). This is the story in which Paul invites the various groups of believers in Rome to participate.

Prof. Elbert poses a related question about the practical steps by which the Roman churches are to join this story: "just what are the consequences of being saved at 10:9 . . . . How does such a person that obeys Paul's exhortation here obtain practical certainty . . . (concerning) what Paul is talking about?" I believe that the peroration of the letter in chapters 15–16 provides the answer. Rather than continuing to shame each other and exclude each other, the congregations are urged to welcome outsiders and this formula, "Greet so and so," is repeated 21 times. The meaning of the term "greet" in the Greco-Roman culture is actually to put one's arms around the other, to hug them as a sign of welcome. It was ordinarily done when a guest enters the house or space of a host. The context suggests that Paul wants them to welcome members of competitive groups into their love feasts.

The climax in this request for mutual welcome, which would overcome the conflicts between these early Christian groups, is found in 16:16, "greet one another with a holy kiss." In contrast to much of the kissing in the modern world, in Paul's time kissing primarily was a family matter. One kissed family members when meeting them. In the case of early Christian groups, the holy kiss sealed the solidarity of extended families who were members of congregations. It said, in effect, you are my "brother" or "sister;" it is the ultimate expression of honor. In view of the fact that most Christians did not own homes, the kiss was extended when they met for their common meals. It was a regular feature in the early Christian love feasts. What I would like to point out, however, is that to "greet one another" in this manner would overcome the hostilities and prejudices between early Christian groups, and make them ready to participate in the mission to the imperial outsiders in Spain.

One of the intuitions I would like to explore this week is whether a parallel impulse arose in Tennessee and elsewhere in the 1880's and burst into global flame on Azuza Street 101 years ago this month. Although based on charismatic experience rather than reading Romans, it resulted in breaking down the social, racial, sexual and cultural barriers of shame. This question leads me to wonder whether my interpretation of "spiritual charisma" in 1:11 is adequate. I write that "The unprecedented expression *charisma pneumatikon* sounds at first redundant, since early Christians considered the gifts of divine grace and individual grace-gifts to be spiritual. Paul obviously felt the need to communicate as a charismatic with charismatics, emphasizing the spiritual bond that linked all believers together with Christ who is "the Spirit" (2 Corinthians 3:17)." I go on to point out that "The hope that his spiritual charisma will serve "that you [pl.] may be strengthened" is formulated in the passive voice, implying that divine action will be experienced." Is it possible that the *charisma pneumatikon* needs to be further elaborated, that it implies a unity between charismatic ecstasy, the theology of impartial grace, and a transformation of honor / shame systems to conform to the righteousness of God revealed in Christ? This leads me to the second theme.

II.

The nature of Pauline pneumatology needs further clarification that I'm not sure I am in the position to provide. I agree with Prof. Lampe's summary of my starting point, that "Paul's pneumatology . . . should be viewed more in social, collective terms rather than in private, individualistic terms." But I'm not sure how to relate this to Prof. Elbert's question about my use of the citation from Acts 10:45 in explaining the reference in Romans 5:5, "love of God has been poured into our hearts through [the] Holy Spirit that was given to us." He questions whether

Acts is referring here "to the event of conversion or baptism." Is this a key passage for Church of God theology concerning the third gift of the "baptism of the holy ghost"? Prof. Elbert connects this with the *analogia pisteōs* in 12:5, suggesting that "This phenomenological proportion and progression of faith as one prophesies is appropriate to those who are described as having been given the Holy Spirit and as having received the Holy Spirit." It seems to me that this would imply that anyone who has the spirit automatically prophecizes correctly, which Paul explicitly repudiates in 1 Corinthians 13:9, that we all "prophecy in part," which requires as 14:29 states, that "others" must weigh what is said. I have the impression that the "analogy of faith" is related to the *metron pisteōs,* which I translate with "measuring rod of faith" mentioned a few lines earlier in Romans 12:3, "that each believer has a unique *metron pisteōs.* This is strongly suggested by the choice of the verb *merizō* ("deal out, distribute") and the emphatic position of *hekastō* ("to each") at the beginning of 12:3d. [Perhaps Lamp could help me out in avoiding too much individualism at this point!] I go on to explain, "Although faith in its proper sense is the relationship of holding fast to the grace of God, it includes a measuring rod that allows for differentiation."[3] And in the light of the subsequent argument about preserving the integrity of faith in both the weak and the strong (Romans 14:1–15:6), it is clear that for Paul, "There are political, ideological, racial, and temperamental components that are legitimately connected with faith, comprising the peculiar 'measuring rod' that each person in the church has been given."[4] By making these unique faith relationships the "measure of all things," so to speak, Paul defines "sober-mindedness" as the refusal to impose the standard of one's own relationship with God onto others. The same thought is reiterated in Romans 14:4, 22–23 in the admonition not to interfere with the faith relationships that other believers have with the Lord.[5] This verse therefore stands as a bulwark against elitist conceptions of "divine-men," superleaders and geniuses who claim precedence over others because of their gifts and benefactions.

I agree with Elbert that "the veracity of the witness of his conscience is certified by the Holy Spirit." Elbert suggests "that what Paul is counting on here is that his active readership, which has experienced the gift of the Holy Spirit (Romans 5:5) . . . is a readership that will understand his spiritual language at 9:1 because they are themselves charismatics." This makes sense to me and leads to the third theme I'd like to develop this morning.

---

3 Robert Jewett, *Christian Tolerance: Paul's Message to the Modern Church* (Philadelphia: Westminster Press, 1982), 62.

4 Jewett, *Christian Tolerance*, 62.

5 Joseph A. Fitzmyer, *Romans* (Anchor Bible; New York: Doubleday, 1993), 646.

III.

Does the commentary's interpretation of the distortion of the law into a means of status acquisition in Romans 7 have relevance for the Pentecostal movement? Prof. Lampe provides an apt statement of the starting point that fits "the context of the Roman tenement and house churches," that "the competition for status between the "weak" and the "strong" is the same wrongheaded zeal that corrupted his pre-Christian experience of the Law (444)." I follow Stanley Stowers, Jean-Noël Aletti, und Jean-Baptiste Édart, who develop the Greek concept of *prosōpopoeia*, a "Speech-in-Character." This was a widely used method of argument in which a fictive character is given a voice to introduce important ideas. The hypothesis developed in my commentary is that Paul depicts himself as the person prior to his conversion, a zealous fanatic who obeyed the Jewish law perfectly but with such eagerness to achieve honor that he produced evil results. In Galatians 1:13–14 Paul had described this competitive zeal as wanting to be more righteous than anyone else, a perfectly understandable trait when one takes the obsession of gaining honor in the ancient Mediterranean world seriously.

Paul's shocking discovery on the road to Damascus was that his religious motivation was corrupted by the desire for status acquisition. The obsession to gain honor, which deprives others of the honor they should enjoy, had produced the tragic gulf between willing and achieving the good, and perverted the holy into a means to gain precedence over others. Paul employs this "speech-in-character" to show the congregations in Rome that they were well along on this mistaken path in their competition with each other and that this imperialistic viewpoint must be transformed in order to participate with integrity in the mission to the so-called "barbarians" in Spain.

I disagree with advocates of the so-called "New Perspective" that this competitive tendency was a peculiar feature of Jewish ethnocentrism. Paul presents this as a universal human trait that is visible in every religious and political entity. I see it in my own Methodist tradition, in the claim of superiority over others; and I struggle against it in my country whose sense of entitlement leads us to unwise campaigns to "rid the world of evil." Whether it has a bearing on the Pentacostal movement is the open question with which I close.

The Vancouver Symposium
May 12, 2008

23

The Strategic Inconsistency of the Apostle Paul: Romans 13:1–7

Steve D. Black

Romans 13:1–7 clashes with modern sensibilities. It is a nemesis that threatens to pull the rug out from any politically liberating interpretation of Paul. Its authoritative defense and affirmation of the political status quo and the powers that be sounds out good news indeed—for the powerful elite! There is no "preferential option for the poor" to be found here—the only preferential option to be located here is one for the powerful. Its exhortation to " Let every person be subject to the governing authorities; for there is no authority except from God," and, "whoever resists authority resists what God has appointed," and, "Render . . . respect to whom respect is due, honor to whom honor is due" even starts to look demonic if used in contexts where earthly governments are expressly evil, such as Nazi Germany. Given the vast number of corrupt governments that we could call to mind (some occurring in Paul's day), one would like to see the apostle urging (or at least allowing some room for the possibility of) divinely sanctioned resistance rather than obedience. It is hard to understand how this text might be used in a modern context without serious qualification.

However, the issue is not merely one of disparate eras and their different values, as Romans 13 also clashes with the general tenor of much of the Hebrew Scriptures—the scriptures that Paul embraced. The narratives of the Exodus and the exile include stories where obedience to the powers that be is not the ideal, and where the divine imperative is resistance.

Some of what Paul affirms in Romans 13:1–7 fits harmoniously within the context of some ancient Jewish thought. For example, while it might be a difficult idea for us to accept, the belief that God gives earthly rulers their positions of authority was an idea that had some currency within the ancient Jewish world. Wisdom of Solomon says concerning earthly rulers, "For your dominion was given you from the Lord, and your sovereignty from the Most High." (6:3) This agrees nicely with what Paul writes in 13:1b: "for there is no authority except from God, and those authorities that exist have been instituted by God."

While there is agreement with Wisdom of Solomon and Romans 13 concerning the divine source of human authority, it is instructive to note how dramatically Romans parts ways with Wisdom when it uses this idea "as the basis for a positive evaluation of secular government as such."[1] This can be observed by seeing what wisdom does with this idea:

> Because as servants of his kingdom you did not rule rightly, or keep the law, or walk according to the purpose of God, he will come upon you terribly and swiftly, because severe judgment falls on those in high places. For the lowliest may be pardoned in mercy, but the mighty will be mightily tested. For the Lord of all will not stand in awe of anyone, or show deference to greatness; because he himself made both small and great, and he takes thought for all alike. But a strict inquiry is in store for the mighty. (Wisdom 6:4–8, New Revised Standard Version)

Wisdom establishes significant equality between powerful and powerless, as God "made both small and great, and he takes thought for all alike." There is no parallel to this in Romans 13. Where in Wisdom judgment is threatened upon the powerful, in Paul it is against the powerless. Perhaps most important for our purposes, there is in Wisdom a clear assumption that rulers *can* make mistakes in civil judgment and administration, indeed, it appears that they have actually done so. It is unclear in Wisdom if the powerless are to resist the corrupt and powerful, and if so what this might look like. However, this largely seems unnecessary, as God will do the resisting, making any human resistance largely redundant (at least in the economy of Wisdom of Solomon). Even though secular rulers receive their authority from God, we see that this gift can be abused, implying that simply being a God-ordained ruler does not make one inherently just.

While Paul stops short of explicitly claiming 'all the authorities do will agree with God's will,' he all but implies as much. How else are we to understand Paul's explanation in verse 3 that "rulers are not a terror to good conduct, but to bad? Do you wish to have no fear of the authority?

[1] C. H. Dodd, *The Epistle of Paul to the Romans*, edited by James Moffatt (London: Hodder and Stoughton, 1932), 203.

Then do what is good, and you will receive its approval." It seems pretty clear here that rulers can be counted on to be just and do the right thing (at least inasmuch as this text is concerned). Not every interpreter of Paul would agree that this is indeed what Paul intended. Anders Nygren, for example, argues that this passage:

> . . . does not say that all the authorities do will agree with God's will. There are good and bad authorities, God-fearing and godless governments. There are some authorities that use their powers in harmony with God's will, and other that misused their powers and tramp the will of God under their feet. But Paul is not now talking about such distinctions. He is speaking of that which all authorities have in common, namely, that they are instituted by God.[2]

This view is more at home in Wisdom of Solomon than it is in Romans 13:1–7. It is there and not in Romans 13:1–7 that we hear of "bad government." There is certainly no mention in Romans 13:1–7 of governments 'tramping the will of God under foot'—in fact, the only place where God's will figures into the text is as the ordaining and justifying agent behind the government's action. Nygren ignores the central thrust of Romans 13:1–7 when he suggests that real point of this text is "that which all authorities have in common, namely, that they are instituted by God." This is *not* what this text is about; it has an imperative structure, not a propositional one. At least on the rhetorical surface, Paul is primarily demanding behavior (namely, "obedience"), and only secondarily providing explanation. That is, the divinely instituted nature of human authority serves as a warrant for obedience, and not as a separate theme for theological reflection. Romans 13:1–7 is concerned with obedience to earthly authorities grounded in the work and will of God. While we might find indications elsewhere in Paul's writings, we are hard pressed to see any hints here that Paul was reflecting upon the morally dubious nature of secular government as he wrote this pericope. Rather, we find here the belief that earthly government are inherently just and fair. To move beyond this is to move beyond this text.

While Romans 13:1–7 stands in tension with intertestamental texts such as Wisdom of Solomon, perhaps more importantly for our purposes, it also clashes with Paul's own views as stated elsewhere. In 1 Corinthians 2:8 Paul's gospel is built upon a Christ who was crucified by the rulers of this age. While it is true that in Corinthians Paul does not extend this line of thought into an explicit theory relating to political engagement with government, it is also true that Paul does not use this

[2] Anders Nygren, *Commentary on Romans* (Philadelphia: Fortress Press, 1949), 428.

foundational narrative to imply that Christians ought to be obedient to the same ignorant earthly rulers who crucified Christ (indeed, it is difficult to imagine how such a line of reasoning would even get off the ground).

Moreover, this passage clashes with the rest of the letter to the Romans, and here Jewett's analysis is especially helpful. Jewett argues that one of Paul's prime concerns in Romans is to overturn the prevalent cultural system of honor and shame that drove the world of Paul's day. Jewett argues "Paul attacked perverse systems of honor by dispelling the idea that some persons and groups are inherently righteous and by proclaiming the message that God honors sinners of every culture in an impartial manner through Christ."[3] "In the face of the impartial righteousness of God, no human system of competing for glory and honor can stand."[4] "A new system of honor and shame has been erected by Christ that overturns the universal human impulse to boast."[5]

Jewett argues that overturning the ubiquitous system of honor and shame provided a crucial foundation for getting the appropriate support from the Roman churches for his proposed mission to Spain, the mission driving the whole of this letter. Jewett argues that in Rome there were various factions competing with each other for honor. When Paul addresses the concerns of the "weak" and the "strong" in Romans, he is speaking about a real phenomenon where the strong are "Gentile believers with Jewish liberals such as Paul," and the weak "included Jewish adherents to the law, but this group probably included some Gentiles who had been close to synagogues before becoming believers, or those drawn to the movement when it was still meeting in synagogues."[6] As long as patterns of competition for honor continue between these two groups in Rome, they will not be in the appropriate social place to support Paul in his mission to Spain: "For until the superiority claims of the Roman house and tenement churches are abandoned, their participation in a mission to the barbarians in Spain will be one more form of cultural imperialism, and thus a violation of the righteousness of God as revealed in the cross of Christ."[7]

One of Jewett's great accomplishments is the consistency with which this theme is followed throughout the commentary. The honor system by which everything, including religion, became a source of competition and strife has been overturned by the shameful death of the truly honorable, wise and powerful one—Christ. Therefore the Roman Christian's internal disputes

[3] Robert Jewett, *Romans: A Commentary* (Hermeneia; Minneapolis: Fortress Press, 2007), 88.

[4] Jewett, *Romans*, 266.

[5] Jewett, *Romans*, 310.

[6] Jewett, *Romans*, 71.

[7] Jewett, *Romans*, 267.

relating to claims of honor, have no place in the church, and counter God's plan for the salvation of the nations. This, in a nutshell, provides the overall contour for the letter to the Romans, according to Jewett.

Thus it comes as something of a surprise when Paul, in Romans 13:7, reverts back and, argues that the Roman Christians should give earthly rulers respect and honor. It is astonishing to find the system of honor and shame—something Paul has spent 12 chapters carefully dismantling—suddenly appear before us is all its vitality and vigor as if it were a choice tool from Paul's toolbox. "Why," we might want to ask Paul, "are you building up again the very things that you once tore down?" (Galatians 2:18)

Jewett is not the first to face this difficulty, and there have been several solutions suggested for this interpretive hurdle. One way to resolve the tension is to simply remove Romans 13 from the mix. If this pericope is not actually from the apostle, then its troubling overtones are quickly silenced. From a text critical point of view, there is not much of a case to be made for excising this pericope. For example, James Kallas argues rather vaguely that "scholarship is aware that something has happened to the closing chapters of this epistle," and that "some type of confusion or reworking has taken place in the closing chapters."[8] While this may be true and relevant for the final three chapters of Romans, it hardly serves as an argument for our pericope. While there are minor textual differences to be found in this pericope (as there are in virtually every place in the New Testament), they are not consequential.[9] If the argument that Romans 13:1–7 is an interpolation does not enjoy support from external text critical criteria, does it from internal? The suggestion has been made that the transition between 12:21 and 13:8 is smoother (and thus more original) than moving from 12:21 to 13:1. After all, in both 12:21 and 13:8 the exhortations are in the second person, while in 13:1 they are in the third person. Against this argument, Jewett cites Riekkinen that the transition between 13:7 and 13:8 is not particularly uneven when it is noted that both are working with the general theme of "obligations."[10] Another argument marshaled in defense of an interpolation theory is that the apocalyptic tension between this age and that which is in Christ, so characteristic of Paul elsewhere, is not found in this pericope. Indeed some, such as Kallas, have inferred from this

---

[8] James Kallas, "Romans 13:1–7: An Interpolation," *New Testament Studies* 11 (1965), 365. See also, Neil Elliott, *Liberating Paul: The Justice of God and the Politics of the Apostle* (Maryknoll: Orbis Books, 1994), 217–18, 288.

[9] For example, some early witnesses read, "Be subject to every [human] authority," rather than "let every person be subject to [human] authorities."

[10] Jewett, *Romans*, 783, citing Vilho Riekkinen, *Römer 13: Aufzeichnung Und Weiterführung Der Exegetischen Diskussion* (Helsinki: Suomalainen Tiedeakatemia, 1980), 48, 50–51.

that "this passage seems to reflect a time when the church has made peace with the world."[11] Jewett argues that the differences between this passage and other texts by Paul vis-à-vis apocalyptic tensions with the present world order should not be overstated: "there is nothing in 13:1–7 to preclude the view that government is an interim institution established by God until the parousia."[12] Finally, Jewett notes that while a redactional motive in general might be posited for such an interpolation, the rationale for why this particular place in Romans was selected for this addition has not been adequately proposed. In short, the case for seeing Romans 13:1–7 as an interpolation is not persuasive. Jewett rightly states that the inconvenience that a passage creates for us is not a good reason for considering it inauthentic: "distaste for a passage has no bearing on authenticity."[13]

Others, who do not believe Romans 13:1–7 to be an interpolation, nevertheless get so frustrated with it that they throw up their hands up in despair and conclude, with Heikki Räisänen, that Paul is simply not a consistent thinker—that his letters are logically flawed and riddled with contradictions. Romans 13 is the product of a fuzzyheaded thinker who had trouble remembering what he has just said. While there may be some truth to it, it seems to provide more of an evasion of the problem than a solution to it.

Many interpreters of Paul believe that the apostle was not a particularly confused individual, and try to deal with the problem of Romans 13 by somehow framing it differently, so that it says something different than what appears on first reading. Some have, for example, attempted to implicitly re-write the passage by inserting into it some sort of assumed clause by which obedience is expected *only if* the ruling powers are good and follow God's way. In other words, the difficulties are overcome in this text by seeing it as *conditional*. There is not much of a problem with an exhortation to obey secular government only when it commands the good, and to disobey it when commands the bad. F. F. Bruce provides an example of this:

> When the decrees of the civil magistrate conflict with the commandment of God, then, say Christians, "we ought to obey God rather than men" (Acts 5:29); when Caesar claims divine honors, the Christians' answer must be "No." For then Caesar (whether he takes the form of a dictator or a democracy) is going beyond the authority delegated to him by God, and trespassing on

11 Jewett, *Romans*, 783, summarizing J. Kallas, *Romans*, 374.

12 Jewett, *Romans*, 784.

13 Jewett, *Romans*, 783.

> territory which is not his. But Christians will voice their "No" to Caesar's unauthorized demands the more effectively if they have shown themselves ready to say "Yes" to all his authorized demands.[14]

To say that Christians need not obey that which is contrary to divine will because in such cases, "Caesar goes beyond the authority delegated to him by God," is to say that rulers only have authority when what they command accords with God's will. To interpret Romans 13:1–7 in this way is to render it conditional (obedience is required *only if* that which is commanded is good), and to effectively mute the dissonance we experience as we read this text. While this interpretation may provide sensible advice, it does not accord well with the actual pericope as we find it before us. There is nothing equivocal or qualified in Romans 13:1–7 relating to Christians obeying secular authorities, and there is nothing conditional about Paul's command here. While we may agree with Käsemann that it is "surprising [. . . that] Paul does not mention the exception that the community obviously must not let itself be forced to offend against the will of God and its own Christianity,"[15] we must nevertheless stay with the text as we find it, and resist the urge to import what is obvious to us to our effort to understand what we think must have been obvious to Paul. If Paul assumed (at least within the logic of this pericope) that rulers are inherently just and fair (something discussed above), then Paul's silence concerning evil and unjust government is not as surprising as Käsemann believes. While it may be that Paul would command disobedience if it was a question of transgressing the will of God in order to obey the will of Caesar, the fact that Paul states things so categorically here may simply imply that he was not actively considering this possibility. We may think such a view to be painfully naïve, but we should nevertheless stay with the evidence of the text as much as possible.

How does Jewett unravel the problem of Romans 13? As previously mentioned, he does not believe the evidence for taking this passage to be an interpolation to be convincing, and concludes that it is authentic. To make sense of Romans 13 within Paul's thought he develops two lines of attack: he reframes the argument, and he contextualizes the argument as strategically inconsistent (and not simply the product of fuzzyheaded thinking).

Jewett *reframes* the pericope by finding something of a subversive kernel within it, thereby attempting to moderate its potentially harmful effect in the support of imperial ideology. The text affirms that it is the

---

[14] F. F. Bruce, *The Epistle of Paul to the Romans*, edited by R. V. G. Tasker (Grand Rapids: Eerdmans, 1963), 234.

[15] Ernst Käsemann, *Commentary on Romans*, translated by Geoffrey W. Bromiley (Grand Rapids: Eerdmans, 1980), 357.

God of Jesus Christ, the Crucified One, who establishes earthly rulers, and *not* his Roman counterparts, Mars or Jupiter.[16] "That the Roman authorities were appointed by the God and Father of Jesus Christ turns the entire Roman civic cult on its head, exposing its suppression of the truth."[17] Thus Jewett argues, "submission to the governmental authorities is therefore an expression of respect not for the authorities themselves but for the crucified deity who stands behind them."[18] While this certainly modifies how this passage might be heard, Paul's readers are nevertheless still expected at the end of the day to render obedience and honor to the powers that be. We might also note that in verse 7 where Paul exhorts his readers to give honor to whom honor is due, the recipients of this honor are presumably the earthly rulers themselves, and not the God who stands behind them.

However Jewett does not simply leave us with attempts at bringing this passage into the fold of Paul's larger thought through efforts at re-framing—he also concludes that this passage stands in tension with Paul's thought elsewhere. He argues this by getting to the context in which it was written, as well as its real purpose (written somewhat between the lines, as it were). Firstly, Jewett argues that interpreters often go wrong with this passage because they see in it Paul attempting to articulate something of a universal and timeless ethic. Sanday and Headlam represent a clear example of what Jewett argues against when they affirm that in Romans 13:1–7 "general principles applicable to any period or place are laid down."[19] Against such a view, Jewett believes that this passage "was not intended to create the foundation of a political ethic for all times and places in succeeding generations - a task for which it has proven to be singularly ill suited."[20] This observation alone goes a long way towards rendering this pericope less malignant. Thus, Jewett agrees with Käsemann that Paul "is certainly not making exhaustive statements about the relation to authorities. Thus he is

[16] Some have thought it significant that Christ is not specifically mentioned in this pericope, and that the non-christological nature of this passage indicates that "reference [is] being made only to the ordinance of God as Creator." See C. E. B. Cranfield, *A Critical and Exegetical Commentary on the Epistle to the Romans* (Edinburgh: T. & T. Clark, 1979), 2:651, referring to Otto Michel, *Der Brief an Die Römer* (Göttingen: Vandenhoeck und Ruprecht, 1963), 313–14. Or as Dodd argues, this passage "is a part of the natural moral order, of divine appointment, but lying outside the order of grace revealed in Christ . . . . The Christian order of society rests on a different and higher principle, which was expounded in chapter Xii." See Dodd, *Romans*, 204. Against this latter argument it could be asked why Paul would gives a command "lying outside the order of grace" to the Christians in Rome who live within the order of grace? If Dodd was correct, we would expect this exhortation to be given to those who are outside the church, but Paul writes to those who are inside it.

[17] Jewett, *Romans*, 790.

[18] Jewett, *Romans*, 790.

[19] William Sanday and Arthur Headlam, *A Critical and Exegetical Commentary of the Epistle to the Romans* (5th Edition; Edinburgh: T. & T. Clark, 1907), 369.

[20] Jewett, *Romans*, 786.

silent about possible conflicts and the limits of earthly authority."[21] This observation, more than anything, helps us to recognize should be limits in *our* use of Paul, but it does not yet explain the reason why those limitation exist within Paul's thought. It does not yet answer the question "why is Paul so one-sided in Romans 13:1–7"? Explaining how a text ought not to be used and what it does not say does not yet help us know how it ought to be used and what it does say.

Continuing, Jewett considers Romans 13:1–7 in the light of his overarching and guiding thesis that the letter is concerned with furthering a mission to Spain, and that it seeks to win support from the Roman Christians, as well as overcoming obstacles that might stand in the way of that support. Jewett believes that there were two churches in Rome "situated within the imperial bureaucracy."[22] Paul felt that the success of his Spanish mission was in large part bound up with the support from the slaves of the Roman bureaucrats in these churches, and so he eagerly sought to win their goodwill. To gain this he legitimated them (actually—their masters) by means of a divine sanction. Paul's exhortation in chapter 13 would have communicated to these slaves that "their administration was consistent with the faith."[23] They were not traitors to the faith because of their work within the context of the Roman imperial rule. Because imperial rule was sanctioned by God, the work of the slaves who found themselves working in the context of this rule was also sanctioned. This passage was not meant to communicate a timeless ethic of blind obedience to all human government, but rather was a means of winning support from a strategic group of people within the churches for the sake of Paul's larger plans of spreading the gospel. It would just muddy his argument and weaken what he was trying to do if he spent time explaining what an appropriate Christian response might be to bad government. This could undermine the positions of those well-positioned slaves he was trying to bolster, if any of their given masters were seen in an unfavorable light (perhaps as an example of bad government) by others within the Roman churches. In such a case would not the status of the slave be tainted because of the master? This would import hesitation and uncertainty into Paul's attempt to legitimate the slaves whose support he sought to win. In any event, if the real point for Paul was to legitimate as divinely sanctioned these slaves, there was simply no point or reason to discuss issues relating to bad government—it was not pertinent.

---

21 Käsemann, *Romans*, 354.

22 Jewett, *Romans*, 796. This conclusion was reached through a close analysis of some of the names found in chapter 16—for example, the name "Julia" in 16:15 is a name normally given to "members of the Julian household," be they slave or free. See Jewett, *Romans*, 972.

23 Jewett, *Romans*, 789.

Now, the actual reasons why the support of some imperial slaves was so important is not clear, but we might hope that they were indeed good ones, as Paul appears to have sacrificed a great deal because of them. He has re-established the system of honor and shame that he had overturned, effecting what might be called a reversal of a reversal. This resulted in the socially powerful once again being given more honor than the socially inferior: "Paul reverts to the cultural stereotypes, and abandons the revolutionary approach to honor visible in the preceding chapters, where in the light of Christ, the dishonored receive honor and the socially inferior are granted precedence."[24] Hence Jewett concedes that Paul was logically inconsistent insofar as Romans 13 is concerned, but this is not because Paul was a fuzzyheaded, illogical thinker as Räisänen might have it, but rather because he was being strategic: Paul was being *strategically inconsistent*.

The question for us is whether this strategic inconsistency undermines Paul's entire project. For 12 chapters Paul has reversed the honor system that sustained Rome's culture, and now he affirms that honor system. He does this precisely in order to spread the message of the end of the honor system, something Jewett calls "ironic," and that it is, although one wonders why we shy away from also calling it "hypocritical"? Jewett argues "this pericope is an excruciating example of Paul's willingness to be in the world but not of the world, to reside between the ages."[25] Does this rescue Paul from a charge of hypocrisy? I suspect that it does not, especially if when speaking of "being in the world" we mean acting as the world does and affirming and using its pivotal sources of motivation for the purpose of achieving one's "not-of-the-world" goals and aspirations. This is perhaps more salient when those goals and aspirations precisely involve the dismantling of the sources of motivation (honor).

If the argument that in Romans 13 Paul is "resid[ing] between the ages" does not justify Paul's failure, it may at least make it understandable. The ideals of the kingdom may not always be practical or even doable in the realm of the empire. The realm of the empire (modern and ancient) is a realm that specializes in the compromise of principles and the death of dreams by means of a thousand reasonable qualifications. It simply may not be possible to live within the empire in the purity of untarnished ideals.

Jewett designates Paul's willingness here to "be in the world but not of the world" a "paradox." The word "paradox" can have a few different shades of meaning. It can be something that on the surface appears contradictory, but is found, upon further examination, to be true. We encounter a problem if we use the word in this sense for Romans 13, as we find upon further examination that this passage truly is

[24] Jewett, *Romans*, 803.
[25] Jewett, *Romans*, 803.

contradictory. Calling something a paradox, when in fact it really is just self-contradictory, has the effect of justifying it in spite of its failings, or perhaps even because of them. In this way we could admit into court any contradictory evidence simply by evoking the category, "paradox." However, there is another meaning for the word "paradox": "a person or thing that combines contradictory qualities."[26] If this is how Jewett intends for the word to be taken, then he is certainly accurate. Paul has evinced "contradictory qualities" in 13:1–7 by, in the name of God, building upon a foundation and culture that he has elsewhere rejected as contrary to the will and ways of God.

Jewett argues that Romans 13:1–7 has served "the policies of Mars and Jupiter" as it has been used to reify rulers and subjugate peoples in the name of Christ. If we accept the Spanish missions scenario suggested by Jewett, it becomes difficult to marshal the support of this text in the maintenance of empire: what sort of hermeneutic would turn a strategic move to achieve a specific goal into a timeless ethic? This is especially true if it is remembered that the ethic found in this passage does not match the general tenor of Paul's theology elsewhere.

Jewett's Paul is less here the friend of emperors than a man with a mission. This mission is fueled by a grand theological vision, and Paul is willing to make sacrifices to realize it, and in Romans 13:1–7 he has sacrificed the high ideals of the kingdom. He has set aside his subversive ideal of a realm where the poor and weak are the ones who are honored and has made the powerful earthly rulers once again worthy of honor simply because they are rulers. Paul has sacrificed the ideals of the kingdom for the sake of the expansion of the kingdom. This is circular, as the expansion of the kingdom seems to be a worthy goal precisely because of the ideals of the kingdom. Expansion does not usually proceed in it own name, but in the name of an ideal. Paul's expansion into Spain appeared to be a good thing because of the vision of equality before God that was at the heart of his gospel. While the ideas themselves presented in Romans 13 may not be paradoxical (as discussed above), there is nevertheless something paradoxical about the belief that in order to spread one's ideals they need to be suspended. The "paradox" of this passage is that Paul set up again the honor system so that he could further the cause of the good news that the honor system has been dismantled. It is in the final analysis the great importance of the ideals of the kingdom that seemed to justify setting them aside. Thus we have a clash between the ideals of the kingdom and the means by which the kingdom is advanced, but they mutually reinforce each other: the ideals need to be spread in order to be actualized, and the spreading involves their suspension, and the suspension is justified because of the

26 According to Oxford Dictionary.

importance of the ideals. Not only is this circular, it is also contradictory, hypocritical, and even tragic.

Sacrificing the ideals of the kingdom for the sake of the advancement of the kingdom is exactly what enabled Christianity to become a new imperialistic force, as Christendom is marked exactly by this exchange of ideals for advancement. In Romans 13 we see that the exchange of ideals for expansion started well before Constantine—it started as early as Paul. The exchange of ideals for expansion is not something that came late to Christianity, but rather is something present close to its very inception.

This exchange also provides an example of how Christianity itself became a new empire growing out of the ashes of previous ones. It is difficult to imagine any empire built upon the ideals of the kingdom, as either Jesus or Paul represented it. The reversal of the honor and shame system, so central in Paul's writings, excludes the personal and communal aggrandizement characteristic of empire building. In order to become a truly successful empire, Christianity would need to learn how to suspend these ideals at least insofar as its own expansion was concerned. Paul's reinstitution of the honor system, as provisional and occasional as this reinstitution was, for the sake of expansion to Spain provides exactly the model that Christendom required.

I suspect that the practice of suspending ideals in the name of spreading those same ideals can be found at the foundations of many empires. What else can make the conquest of barbarians/savages/infidels in the name God/democracy/civilization possible? Within this imperialistic gesture are not the ideals of peace and value for life that reside at the idealistic heart of religion/democracy/civilization suspended so that the same ideals may be spread to the barbarians/savages/infidels who allegedly lack them?

A stark example of this in a Canadian context is the conquest of First Nations peoples in North America. This was not justified simply in the name of imperial expansion, but rather in the name of spreading "civilized" existence to the "savages," or the gospel of Christ to the "heathen." This expansion and colonization of these peoples was felt to be acceptable because civilized existence (something presumed to be lacking) and the gospel of Christ were perceived to be good things. Or, how else could otherwise good Christian people be party to the wholesale removal of 1st nation children from their families to be forced to live in church run residential schools, if they had not set aside the ideal of love of one's neighbor. And how could the setting aside of this ideal be justified other than by believing that somehow the ideal of love would be better served by so doing. One could also raise the question of the legitimacy of missions altogether—whether they be to the barbarians of Spain or the "savages" of the new world—as this endeavor inevitably involves the disregard of pre-existing cultures, beliefs and practices as illegitimate (be they Spanish or indigenous). Cultural genocide often proceeds in the name of ideals, such as equality and compassion, which have been suspended so that they may be more effectively propagated.

While we certainly cannot hold Paul responsible for every imperialistic moment in history when ideals were sacrificed for expansion, we also do not find him innocent of this offense. We might wonder how differently we would read the letter to the Romans—how different it would have effected history—how different history itself might have been—had Paul decided, rather than sacrificing ideals for expansion, to sacrifice his dreams of the expansion of the kingdom for the sake of the ideals of the kingdom, something his master Jesus seems to have done. What would have happened had Paul refused the honor system without fail—without the sudden reversion in Romans 13? Who in history might have been empowered to speak against corrupt powers effecting change, but remained silent so as to remain faithful to the God of this text? Unfortunately, these questions we will never answer, because that idealistic Paul who refused to back down did not exist.

24

"LET EVERY PERSON BE SUBJECT TO THE GOVERNING AUTHORITIES": CONTEXTUALIZING AND RECONTEXTUALIZING ROMANS 13:1–7 IN OUR IMPERIAL AGE

ROBERT DERRENBACKER[1]

INTRODUCTION

For centuries, it has been commonly held, particularly among Western Christians, that Paul's letter to the Romans should be read as a compendium of Christian doctrine.[2] As a result, Romans has often been seen as single volume systematic theology of sorts, with the letter divided into the traditional topics of Christian doctrine. For example, this sort of purely theological approach to Romans might see chapters 1–2 dealing with the topic of *sin*, chapters 3–4 dealing with *justification by faith*, chapters 5–8 dealing with the topic of *sanctification*, and chapters 12–15 dealing with *Christian ethics*.[3] Romans 13:1–7 has not escaped this reading strategy, often seen historically as the Christian expression of a (*the*?) doctrine of Church and state. This is, of course, highly anachronistic and decontextualizes the text by confusing the genre of

1 The reader may find it helpful *contextualize* this author, knowing that he is a "dual citizen," born and raised in the United States, but taking an oath of Canadian citizenship in 1997.

2 See Philipp Melanchthon (*Dispositio orationis in ep. Ad Rom. Philippi Melanthonis pera quae supersunt*, edited by C. G. Bartschneider [Halle: Schwetschke, 1834–1860], 15:445), who referred to Romans as "a summary of all Christian doctrine" (as translated by Joseph A. Fitzmyer, *Romans* [New York: Doubleday, 1992], 74). See Fitzmyer's summary of similar sentiments by other Romans scholars, including a number of modern commentators (*Romans*, 74).

3 N. T. Wright rightly states that "Romans has suffered for centuries from being made to produce vital statements on questions it was not written to answer" ("Romans," *New Interpreters Bible*, volume 10 [Nashville: Abingdon Press, 2002], 403).

Romans (letter) with a much later one (systematic theology).[4] Besides, it is not terribly "biblical" either in the preference given Romans 13:1–7 or in the ignoring other Biblical texts that might articulate something of Church/state relations.[5]

Despite this unfortunate history of understanding Romans, it is now widely recognized, as Karl Donfried puts it, that the letter is "addressed to the Christian community in Rome which finds itself in a particular historical situation."[6] There is, of course, variation in describing this "particular historical situation," the *occasion* of Romans, and in turn the various explanations of the *purpose* of Romans.[7] But the *scholasticus consentio* is that the historical situation may be described as "polarized house-churches as being a key factor leading to turmoil among the Christians" in Rome.[8]

With this in view, this essay will attempt to engage with Robert Jewett's commentary on Romans,[9] particularly in his interpretation of Romans 13:1–7 in light of the overall historical occasion and purpose(s) of the letter. I do this because of two related factors. First, Romans will continue to be fruitfully interpreted only as we continue to recognize the "particular historical situation" of the letter. Romans 13:1–7 has often been read without specific reference or attention to the particular historical (or, more specifically, *political*) context that gave it voice; it often has not been properly *contextualized*. It has, as we have stated above, been often read as the first and foundational articulation of the Christian doctrine of Church and state. This is, of course, problematic.[10]

Second, I believe that one is able to see the extent to which various social locations of readers produce various interpretations of this text. I observed this most poignantly several years ago when I first taught a required course in Biblical exegesis and interpretation at Regent College (Vancouver, Canada), a graduate school that attracts students from around the world. I assigned Romans 13:1–7 as the text for the students' final exegesis papers. In reading these papers, I was amazed to see the variety of interpretations of this text. On the one hand, native North American readers tended to see the text as articulating the general

---

4 As A. Katherine Grieb notes, ". . . when Romans is read *only* as a theological treatise, or as a rule book, or as the data for a sociological study of the early Christian church, Paul the pastor and missionary is not heard," (*The Story of Romans* [Louisville: Westminster John Knox Press, 2002], xii–xiii [emphasis original]).

5 Cf. Mark 12:13–17; Acts 5:27–29; 1 Peter 2:13–17; Revelation 13:1–18.

6 As described by Karl Donfried in his "Introduction" to *The Romans Debate* (2nd Edition; Peabody: Hendrickson, 1991), lxix.

7 See Donfried, *The Romans Debate*, passim.

8 Donfried, *The Romans Debate*, lxix.

9 Robert Jewett, *Romans: A Commentary* (Hermeneia; Minneapolis: Fortress Press, 2007).

10 It may be that these problematic interpretations of this exegetically difficult text have caused it to be omitted from the *Revised Common Lectionary* all together.

and universal principle of the need to submit to (all) government rulers, whose authority is divinely appointed by God, essentially in all times and in all places. Most of my North American students, it would seem, had no first-hand experience with relatively oppressive, totalitarian, non-democratic governments. These students were generally happy with the political *status quo*, at least as they had experienced it. Thus, why not embrace the view that sees Romans 13:1–7 as *the* universal statement on the Christian's relation to the state? On the other hand, my students who were writing out of different (i.e., non-North American) social locations (e.g., the People's Republic of China) had a very different take on the text. For them, the experience of totalitarianism, particularly the government repression of "free-church" Christians, and the political suppression of free speech more generally, caused them to emphasize the importance of seeing the historical-political context of the mid-50s in the first century C.E. as key to understanding the text. As well, these students had, it would seem, a more holistic Biblical theology, being more inclined to read Romans 13 alongside of other texts, like Revelation 13. And in the end, it was clear to me that social location (at least in terms of politics and nationalism) had a direct bearing on the interpretive "outcome" of the exegesis of Romans 13:1–7.

Thus, I will first outline Jewett's own *contextualization* of Romans 13:1–7 in his commentary. I will then discuss the *recontextualization* of the pericope in a North American social location, particularly in the wake of September 11, 2001. This seems quite appropriate in light of a number of Jewett's publications that draw connections between Pauline scholarship and contemporary North American culture.[11]

I. CONTEXTUALIZING ROMANS 13:1–7

A. THE HISTORICAL OCCASION AND PURPOSE OF THE LETTER ACCORDING TO JEWETT

Jewett articulates his understanding of the occasion and purpose of Romans in his commentary, arguing that Romans was written to an ethnically mixed and socially diverse audience, a "complicated variety of congregations"[12] that included "members of governmental bureaucracies."[13] And following the conventional conclusions on date,

[11] See, for example, the following books by Robert Jewett: *Saint Paul at the Movies* (Louisville: Westminster John Knox, 1993); *Paul the Apostle to America* (Louisville: Westminster John Knox Press, 1994); and, *Saint Paul Returns to the Movies* (Grand Rapids: Eerdmans, 1999).

[12] Jewett, *Romans*, 59.

[13] Jewett, *Romans*, 792. Jewett states in his introduction that two of the groups greeted by Paul in Romans 16 – "those belonging to Aristoboulus" (16:10) and "those belonging to Narkissos" (16:11)—are likely "parts of the imperial bureaucracy, probably meeting in the building where they work" (65).

Jewett argues that Romans was likely "drafted in the winter of 56–57 C.E. or the early spring of 57."[14] This, of course, locates Romans within the early, optimistic years of Nero's *quinquennium*, for Jewett notes that at "the time Romans was written, . . . the Nero administration was providing an exemplary form of government and law enforcement, despite the profligate personal habits of Nero himself . . . ."[15]

With this background in view, according to Jewett, the basic purpose of Romans was "to elicit support for Paul's forthcoming mission to Spain."[16] Jewett states that in Romans, "Paul wishes to gain support for a mission to the barbarians in Spain, which requires that the gospel of impartial, divine righteousness revealed in Christ be clarified to rid it of prejudicial elements that are currently dividing the congregations in Rome."[17] Thus, related to this overall missional purpose is Paul's desire to "overturn" the "corrupt and exploitative honor system," or "pyramid of honor," a desire which is "found throughout Paul's Letter to the Romans."[18]

In light of this description, Jewett argues that in Romans 13:1–7,[19] "Paul wished to avoid any gesture of disloyalty that might jeopardize the peaceful extension of the Christian mission."[20] Jewett sees "local magistrates" as comprising part of Paul's Roman audience.[21] Thus, his admonition for his reader to (voluntarily) submit to the governing authorities is

---

14 Jewett, *Romans*, 18.

15 Jewett, *Romans*, 47–48.

16 Jewett, *Romans*, 80. He states the following: "Paul needed the aid and counsel of congregations in Rome with contacts in Spain to make these preparations [to find local patrons in Spain who were not resented by the native population]. There are many indications that the Letter to the Romans was designed to prepare the ground for the complicated project of the Spanish mission, including the insistence that the impartial righteousness of God does not discriminate against 'barbarians' such as the Spaniards, that all claims of cultural superiority are false, that imperial propaganda must be recognized as bogus, and that the domineering behavior of congregations toward one another must be overcome if the missional hope to unify the world in the praise of God is to be fulfilled (15:9–13)" (79).

17 Jewett, *Romans*, 1.

18 Jewett, *Romans*, 51.

19 As is well known, a number of Romans commentators have concluded that Romans 13:1–7 is a later, non-Pauline interpolation or gloss (see the list of seven such scholars in Jewett, *Romans*, 783 n. 17.) Jewett rightly rejects these theories, and sees a plausible transition from 12:17–21 to 13:1–7 (783). This data allows Jewett to conclude that "it remains highly likely that 13:1–7 is an authentic and original portion of Paul's letter" (784). Of course, Romans 13:1–7 presents a particular and (apparently) somewhat sympathetic view of governmental authorities. But as Jewett rightly reminds us, " [d]istaste for a passage has no bearing on its authenticity" (783).

20 Jewett, *Romans*, 786. See also the following: "Paul wishes to gain support for a mission to the barbarians in Spain, which requires that the gospel of impartial, divine righteousness revealed in Christ be clarified to rid it of prejudicial elements that are currently dividing the congregations in Rome" (1).

21 Jewett, *Romans*, 788.

> an expression of respect not for the authorities themselves but for the crucified deity who stands behind them [cf. Romans 13:1b]. That this argument would have had an appeal to Christian groups working within the Roman administration is self-evident.[22]

Presumably, therefore, they would be more disposed to assist in Paul's missional strategy. As Jewett states, "[i]t is clear that, in Paul's view, they are not 'working for the other side,' no matter what the Roman civic cult and administrative system assumed about their service to the gods."[23]

B. THE RHETORIC OF ROMANS 13:1–7

It could be argued that the greatest contribution of Jewett's *Romans* is its exhaustive rhetorical analysis of Paul's letter to the Romans. Building on Jewett's previous essay in *The Romans Debate*,[24] his commentary includes an extensive introduction and overview of the rhetoric of Romans,[25] as well as a "rhetorical disposition" for each pericope in the letter. Rhetorically, Romans 13:1–7 is identified by Jewett as Paul's "final diatribe" among several in the letter.[26] In this text, Paul "plays the role of the imaginary interlocutor with the question in 13:3b, 'Now, do you wish not to fear the authority?' Addressing an imaginary conversation partner who is fearful of the government, Paul urges compliance in order to avoid wrath and to satisfy the demands of conscience."[27]

Jewett sees this diatribe in Romans 13:1–7 as comprised of "[t]he thematic exhortation of 13:1a . . . followed by three coherently phrased arguments and a concluding ethical application concerning the payment of taxes."[28] The first argument (13:1b–3a) concerns the "fulfilling [of] obligations to governing authorities."[29] With a wide range of local "governing authorities" in view, Paul states that "no matter what [these] Roman officials may claim as their authority, it really comes from the

---

[22] Jewett, *Romans*, 790.

[23] Jewett, *Romans*, 792.

[24] Robert Jewett, "Following the Argument of Romans," in Donfried, *The Romans Debate*, 265–77.

[25] Jewett, *Romans*, 23–46.

[26] Jewett follows Stanley Stowers' lead (*The Diatribe and Paul's Letter to the Romans* [Chico: Scholars Press, 1981], 86–93) and defines the *diatribe* not as a popular sermon by a Cynic or Stoic philosopher, but as a rhetorical technique from the ancient classroom where "the teacher created imaginary interlocutors to voice the questions and misconceptions that push the discussion forward" (25). See also George A. Kennedy, *New Testament Interpretation through Rhetorical Criticism* (Chapel Hill/London: University of North Carolina Press, 1984), 155–56.

[27] Jewett, *Romans*, 26.

[28] Jewett, *Romans*, 781.

[29] Jewett, *Romans*, 784.

God of Jewish and Christian faith."[30] And since "[t]he God who grants authority to governmental agencies in Paul's argument is not Mars or Jupiter, as in the Roman civic cult,"[31] or any other Greco-Roman deity, this passage is "a massive act of political cooptation" and could "have been viewed as thoroughly subversive."[32] At the same time, those governmental bureaucrats reading Paul's letter to the Romans would have been assured that they were "not 'working for the other side,' no matter what the Roman civic cult and administrative system assumed about their service to the gods."[33]

The second argument (13:3b–5) in this pericope is a "diatribe on practical reasons for conforming to the admonition,"[34] addressed to a "single imaginary conversation partner."[35] Paul names these "practical reasons" to submit to the governing authorities in order

> to support [the] vocational aims [of the bureaucrats reading the letter] by urging subservience to their kind of administration; if Paul can thereby attract their goodwill, they will perhaps cooperate with his mission project, which in some respects could be interpreted as evil by non-Christian Roman officials concerned about maintaining imperial interests in Spain. Paul hopes that for the Christian bureaucrats, such concerns can be overcome.[36]

Thus according to Jewett, Paul's admonitions in this passage are missionally motivated.[37]

The third and final argument (13:6–7) is a "general diatribe on proper subjection to the authorities by believers,"[38] "addressed in second person plural style to the congregation as a whole."[39] This proper subjection is seen in "render[ing] to all what is obligated" (13:6b), including "the tribute," "the custom tax," "fear," and "honor" (13:7). "Paul's stance,"

---

30 Jewett, *Romans*, 789. Cf. Romans 13:1b–2a: "For there is no authority except that by God and those that are have been appointed by God. So that the one resisting the authority has opposed what God has appointed".

31 Jewett, *Romans*, 789.

32 Jewett, *Romans*, 790.

33 Jewett, *Romans*, 792.

34 Jewett, *Romans*, 785. Jewett translates this passage as follows: "Now, do you (sg.) wish not to fear the authority? Do the good, and you (sg.) will have praise from her. For she is God's servant to you (sg.) for the good. But if you (sg.) do the bad, be afraid, for she does not carry the sword to no purpose. For she is God's servant, an avenger [bringing] wrath upon the one practicing the bad. Therefore it is necessary to subject yourself, not only on account of the wrath but also on account of your conscience-pang" (780).

35 Jewett, *Romans*, 781.

36 Jewett, *Romans*, 794.

37 See Jewett, *Romans*, 796.

38 Jewett, *Romans*, 785.

39 Jewett, *Romans*, 781.

Jewett argues, "would undoubtedly have been welcomed by the churches within the bureaucracy," particularly his stance on the payment of the tribute tax.[40] Thus,

> Paul's argument [in 13:1–7 is] missional rather than rhetorical. He overlooks other problematic aspects of governmental behavior in times past in order to appeal to the groups of believers within the imperial bureaucracy whose cooperation was perceived to be absolutely vital in the Spanish mission . . . . In this diatribe, he places an effective argument at their service: he whose reputation as a subversive troublemaker was in fact an advocate of good public order, and his plans for the Spanish venture should, therefore, not be thwarted.[41]

C. ROMANS 13:1–7 AND HONOR

Jewett argues that in many ways, the key to properly understanding Romans 13:1–7 (and the rest of Romans for that matter) is to locate it within the context of the ancient social value of honor, particularly "the intense competition for superiority in honor [that] continued unabated on all levels of society."[42] In fact, we do see traces of Paul's "overturning of this corrupt and exploitative honor system"[43] in this passage. For example, Paul's "gnomic admonition concerning voluntary subjection to the governing authorities"[44] ("Let every soul subject himself to the governing authorities" [13:1a]) is addressed to "every individual person," who,

> without exception, must subject himself or herself to the authorities. No differentiation is allowed by this formula between believers and nonbelievers, between lower and higher ranks of citizens.[45]

Implicit in this universal admonition is that one's *honor* did not exempt one from following this admonition; all were called by Paul to be subject to the "governing officials" (again, "the local magistrates of Rome"[46]), irrespective of one's possession of the ancient social commodity of honor.

In addition, Paul also stresses in 13:1b that "there is no authority (*exousia*) except that by God and those what are have been appointed

[40] Jewett, *Romans*, 799.
[41] Jewett, *Romans*, 794.
[42] Jewett, *Romans*, 49.
[43] Jewett, *Romans*, 51.
[44] Jewett, *Romans*, 784.
[45] Jewett, *Romans*, 787.
[46] Jewett, *Romans*, 788.

by God." Thus, the "authority" of governing officials exists not by virtue of their *honor* (i.e., the public's perception of "the worth, value, prestige, and reputation which an individual claims"[47]), but by virtue of divine appointment. As Jewett notes, "no matter what Roman officials may claim as their authority, it really comes from the God of Jewish and Christian faith,"[48] as we saw above in connection with 13:1b–3a.

Likewise, Paul's description of a governing authority as a "servant of God" (*theou diakonon* [13:4–5]) subtly and implicitly speaks against the status quo "pyramid of honor" in Roman society. For as Jewett remarks, it is "noteworthy that Paul selected none of the more prestigious titles for public officials currently employed in Rome, preferring one that had profound Christian resonance," i.e., "servants of God."[49]

Yet when the reader gets to 13:7, Jewett sees Paul beginning to follow the status quo in terms of the honor system. There, Paul states the following: "You should render to all what is obligated: . . . to the one owed the fear (*ton phobon*), the fear, to the one owed the honor (*tēn timēn*), the honor." Jewett argues, then, that the "to all" (*pasin*) implies not "everyone everywhere" (including God), but rather "every governmental officer as specified in the fourfold description in verse 7b."[50] These "governmental officers" provide service to the public as "God's ministers." Thus, "reciprocity is required by those receiving such benefits."[51] As we saw above, this includes payment of "the tribute" (*phoros*), "the custom tax" (*telos*), as well as the aforementioned "fear" and "honor." The "fear" to which Paul refers in verse 7c is perhaps best understood as "respect" in the sense of an "acknowledgement of legitimate jurisdiction."[52] This is distinct from the "honor" due certain governing authorities, which "is a matter not of acknowledging jurisdiction but of recognizing superior status and good performance."[53] And it is here that Paul apparently moves back to a more conventional understanding of honor, where, as Jewett notes, honor was earned by "virtue, kinship, [and] public service" according to Plutarch.[54]

But as Jewett rightly argues, the one bestowing public honor to governing authorities might also benefit from such an action: "It was also a means to influence the government in favor of the subjects granting such honor."[55] For the voluntary subjection (*hypotassesthai*

---

[47] Jerome H. Neyrey, *Honor and Shame in Matthew's Gospel* (Louisville: Westminster John Knox Press, 1998), 15.
[48] Jewett, *Romans*, 789.
[49] Jewett, *Romans*, 794.
[50] Jewett, *Romans*, 801.
[51] Jewett, *Romans*, 801.
[52] Jewett, *Romans*, 802.
[53] Jewett, *Romans*, 803.
[54] Plutarch, *Quaestionum convivialum libri ix*, 617C.
[55] Jewett, *Romans*, 803.

[13:1]) would have been offered only toward "those worthy of honor," and are granted it "only when it serves the interest of the subject."[56] But it is here where Paul moves away (at least temporarily) from "overturning" the "pyramid of honor" in Rome. As Jewett notes,

> Paul reverts [in 13:7] to cultural stereotypes, and abandons the revolutionary approach visible in the preceding chapters, where in the light of Christ, the dishonored receive honor and the socially inferior are granted precedence.[57]

Yet again, one needs to keep in mind Paul's missional rhetoric here. Paul is a pragmatist, opting for the "counsel of political realism," as Dunn puts it;[58] his missionary strategy in Spain may be looked upon with greater favor by the powers that be if his audience "render[s] to all what is obligated" (13:7).[59]

II. Recontextualizing Jewett's Interpretation of Romans 13:1–7

Jewett has helped readers of Romans significantly in contextualizing this difficult pericope, Romans 13:1–7. Clearly, there are a number of strengths in Jewett's discussion of this difficult and often abused text. It is worth considering them as we begin *recontextualize* the pericope in our own social locations at twenty-first century readers of Paul.

A. Historical Context

First, the pericope is not detached or disconnected from the overarching historical occasion that gives rise to Paul's letter to the Romans. Jewett's commentary is one of several over the past two decades that have pushed us away from seeing Romans as a compendium of Christian doctrine to seeing it as a letter "written by Paul to deal with

---

56 Jewett, *Romans*, 803.

57 Jewett, *Romans*, 803.

58 James D. G. Dunn, "Romans 13:1–7—A Charter for Political Quietism?," *Ex Auditu* 2 (1986), 67.

59 As Jewett states: "If Paul's motivation for this discourse was missional, . . . the irony is particularly acute. For the sake of the proclamation of Christ crucified, who overturned the honor system and rendered Paul a debtor to 'Greeks as well as barbarians, educated as well as uneducated' (1:14), in Rome as well as Spain, Paul was willing to accept the system that demanded honor for the emperor and his officials whether they deserved it or not. It seems that in his view, the mission would have no chance of extending its transformation of the sinful system of honor clear to the end of the known world without giving honor to whomever honor was due. This pericope is an excruciating example of Paul's willingness of to be in the world but not of the world, to reside between the ages, to be all things to all people, all for the sake of the gospel. But the paradox needs to be named and acknowledged that Romans 13:1–7 has provided the basis for propoganda by which the policies of Mars and Jupiter have frequently been disguised as serving the cause of Christ, thus evoking the ongoing controversy that the exegetical literature has reflected" (*Romans*, 803).

a concrete situation in Rome."[60] For a reading of Romans 13:1–7 that detaches it from its larger literary and rhetorical context, as well as from its "concrete situation in Rome," is destined to produce a flawed and anachronistic interpretation of the text.[61]

B. RHETORIC

And this leads to the second strength of Jewett's treatment: In many ways, I think it is Jewett's compelling and detailed treatment of Romans *rhetorically* that prevents such problematic readings of Romans 13:1–7, as well as other pericopes. As Steve Walton has noted, "rhetorical critcism is a holistic approach to texts. It treats the form of the text *as we have it* as its subject, rather than some reconstructed earlier form of the text or part of the text."[62] And as J. C. Beker has argued, "[t]he presupposition that Romans is a 'theological confession' or a 'dogmatics in outline' is the real reason for the immense interest in the letter's architectonic structure and the neglect of its 'frame.'"[63] As Jewett has stated in an earlier essay, Beker's words "describe the challenge we face in approaching the question of the argumentative structure of Romans."[64] Jewett has met that challenge, producing the most comprehensive and exhaustive rhetorical treatment of Romans to date. More specifically, Jewett rightly reminds his readers that Romans 13:1–7 needs to be seen as part of the larger rhetorical *probatio* ("proof") of Romans 12:1–15:13. The admonitions of 13:1–7 need to be read alongside of Paul's command to "not be conformed to this world" (12:2), his "elaboration of [the] guidelines for genuine love"[65] steeped in non-vengeance (12:9–21), as well as his exhortation to "love your neighbor as yourself" (13:8–10).

With this in view, we need to recognize that our culture does not appreciate or value "holistic approaches to texts" in the sense of treating whole texts as autonomous rhetorical units. Instead, we read Romans in a culture dominated by the soundbite and the 30-second YouTube video clip. Our "texts," however we encounter them and in whatever form, in many ways are *rhetorically decontextualized*. So perhaps it is

---

60 As stated by Donfried in his essay "False Presuppositions in the Study of Romans," in *The Romans Debate*, 103.

61 See also the comments by Dunn ("Romans 13:1–7—A Charter for Political Quietism?" 66): "Romans 13:1–7 is *context specific*. Paul is here clearly writing for Christian groups in Rome at a difficult time in political transition: the Jewish community with whom the Christian groups were still largely identified had not long before been expelled; and there was mounting trouble over the taxation system which bore upon Christians as well as the other residents in Rome. Paul writes with these specific circumstances in view" (emphasis original).

62 Steve Walton, "Rhetorical Criticism: An Introduction," *Themelios* 21 (1996): 5 (emphasis added).

63 J. C. Beker, *Paul the Apostle* (Philadelphia: Fortress, 1984), 62.

64 Jewett, "Following the Argument of Romans," in Donfried, *The Romans Debate*, 265.

65 Jewett, *Romans*, 755.

not a surprise that Romans 13:1–7 has been abused in the ways that it has by Christian readers down through the centuries, read as if it is autonomous from its surrounding literary and rhetorical contexts. It is well documented, for example, that a particular reading of Romans 13:1–7 by the Dutch Reformed Church was used to justify the racist policies of the South African government prior to the dismantling of apartheid.[66] And it would seem that similar readings of Romans 13:1–7 at the expense of Romans 12:1–21 and 13:8–10 have also won the day in North America, particularly since the horrible events of September 11, 2001. Paul's exhortation to "not be conformed to this world" (12:2), his commands to "love one another with mutual affection" (12:10) and to "never avenge yourselves" (12:19), and his instruction to "love your neighbor as yourself" (13:9) have been drowned out by the rhetoric of revenge couched in the language of justice by politicians and the mainstream media over the past few years. And as the dust has settled, all that is left is a particular reading of Romans 13:1–7 that has been used to justify essentially any and all aspects of the "war on terror," both domestically and internationally. Jewett's rhetorical analysis pushes back against this decontextualizing of Romans 13:1–7, helping the reader to interpret the pericope properly and faithfully with Paul's larger rhetorical project in Romans.

C. PYRAMID OF HONOR

In many ways, the third strength of Jewett's treatment is honor and shame, arguably *the* dominant set of cultural values in antiquity, as an important "cultural context" in which to locate the historical setting of the house-churches in Rome and the rhetoric of Paul. Certainly Jewett is not the only Pauline scholar to take advantage of the "discoveries" of social scientists and social historians along these lines.[67] But Jewett's comprehensive treatment of honor in Rome and Paul's letter to the Romans is essentially unparalleled in Romans scholarship.

Social scientists and social historians speak of *honor* as a "commodity" of sorts, one that is acquired or inherited through family, a "social credit rating" if you will. North American culture has very little that would approximate honor, except perhaps a much more tangible commodity: *personal wealth.* It is striking the extent to which our culture applies the language of honor to personal wealth—"importance," "prestige," and "success" all speak to a "pyramid of *wealth*" in North American culture. Again, according to Jewett, Paul is advocating an "overturning of [the]

66 See R. G. Crawford, "Theological Bombshell in South Africa," *The Expository Times* 98 (1986), 9–13; and, Winsome Munro, "Romans 13:1–7: Apartheid's Last Biblical Refuge," *Biblical Theological Bulletin* 20 (1990): 161–68.

67 See, for example, Bruce J. Malina and John J. Pilch, *Social-Science Commentary on the Letters of Paul* (Minneapolis: Fortress Press, 2006).

corrupt and exploitative honor system" in his letter to the Romans.[68] One wonders how our culture (and the Church) might more effectively hear Paul's words in Romans today in the midst of our wealth pyramid.

D. EMPIRE

In the past decade or so, New Testament scholarship has begun to also benefit from a better understanding of the Roman empire as *the* dominant political, economic and social context of the first century. One could also include religion here, as the emperor cult was, perhaps, *the* dominant religion in many parts of the Roman world during the time of Paul. The volume *Paul and Empire* edited by Richard Horsley in 1997 is,[69] in many ways, the first of several treatments that have moved the imperial context from the "background" to the "foreground" in the study of Paul. Paul's use of imperial terminology in a potentially subversive way, such as his description of Jesus as "Lord," "Savior," "King," and "Son of God," all point to seriousness with which we must take Paul's imperial context.[70] Jewett recognizes this, and locates Paul's rhetoric within this context as well. And Jewett reminds us that Paul's comments that the "governing authorities" have no authority "except that by God" and "have been appointed by God" (13:1b) undermine subtly but certainly the Roman civic cult, "turn[ing] the entire Roman civic cult on its head."[71]

It could be argued that many readers of Romans in the twenty-first century are reading Paul within an imperial context as well. Phrases such as "the American Empire" or the "*Pax Americana*" are becoming more and more commonplace, particular since the collapse of the Soviet Union and the rise of the United States as the sole "super power," and especially in the wake of the 9/11 terrorist attacks and America's military responses to them. Given this imperial reality, it would seem that now more than ever readers do need to rightly locate Romans 13:1–7 within its proper historical, political, economic, social, religious and rhetorical contexts. For a decontextualized reading of the pericope as *the* Christian expression of the doctrine of Church and state may not only lead to a particularly abusive exegesis of this text, but also a particularly abusive application of this exegesis. For if Americans Christians, for example, read Romans 13:1–7 in this decontextualized manner, then the "governing authorities" could be granted a *carte blanche* of sorts; they are, after all, (apparently) the "servants" and "ministers" of God. Many

---

68 Jewett, *Romans*, 51.

69 Richard A. Horsley, editor, *Paul and Empire: Religion and Power in Roman Imperial Society* (Harrisburg: Trinity Press International, 1997).

70 See also N. T. Wright, "Gospel and Empire," in *Paul In Fresh Perspective* (Minneapolis: Fortress Press, 2005), 59–79.

71 Jewett, *Romans*, 790. Similarly, Wright states that "Romans 13 constitutes a severe demotion of arrogant and self-divinizing rulers" ("Romans," 719).

might see United States foreign policy, particularly since 9/11, as simply the purposeful and useful "bearing of the sword," acting as God's agents "executing wrath on the wrongdoers." Just days after the 9/11 attacks, President George W. Bush pledged "to rid the world of evil-doers."[72] This pledge went largely unchallenged by Americans in the months after 9/11. I would contend that a decontextualized reading of Romans 13:1–7, then, restricts one's ability to question such rhetoric and actions. Those who have something at stake in the political and economic status quo tend to read Romans 13 universally and exclusively. They often seem to ignore those places where Paul speaks subversively about the Roman empire. Such a view often ignores the revolutionary history of the United States of America. It ignores the larger literary/rhetorical context of Romans 13.

Paul was speaking out of and into an imperial context where "church and state" were not "separate," where religion and politics were intertwined and often indistinguishable. But of course, social historians have demonstrated that in antiquity, "there was no clear division between sacred and secular."[73] In our present imperial context where society is highly individualized and privatized, faith and religion are largely private and personal. Church and state are functionally (and perhaps artificially) separate in North American society, with affairs of the Church relegated to a place outside the public square. Perhaps part of our problem (at least in North America and Europe) is that when we read a text like Romans 13:1–7, we are reading it from the context of church-state separation; we are reading it from the context of overly individualized and privatized faith, for faith and politics are apparently like oil and water—unmixable opposites.

But this does not mean that civil religion no longer exists in this new empire. Social scientists have (in my mind) convincingly demonstrated that post-9/11 *patriotism* is now the civil religion in the current (American) imperial context.[74] This we see in a variety of symbols that are arguably sacred and holy in this civil religion, from the Pledge of Allegiance to the American flag, to the singing the national anthem before sporting events, to the enshrinement of past presidents in effigy in neo-classical temples in America's capital of Washington, D. C.[75]

---

[72] http://archives.cnn.com/2001/US/09/16/gen.bush.terrorism/ (accessed 8 May 2008).

[73] Dunn, *Romans*, 773. Similarly, N. T. Wright states that "the implicit split between 'religion' and 'politics' is a rank anachronism, and we read it into the NT only if we wish not to hear anything the New Testament is saying, not only about what we call 'the state' but about a great many other things as well" ("The New Testament and the 'State,'" *Themelios* 16 [1990]: 11).

[74] It is striking that legislation in response to the terrorist attacks of 9/11 was deemed the "USA Patriot Act," signed into law October 26, 2001. Even though it is arguably the most significant weakening of civil liberties in American history, perhaps what is being implied in naming this legislation the "Patriot Act" is that if one does not support the legislation, one is not "patriotic," which, in this day and age, is nationalistic heresy.

[75] The Lincoln and Jefferson Memorials come to mind.

Jewett, along with his co-author John Shelton Lawrence, recognized in their book *Captain American and the Crusade against Evil* an important distinction between "subjection" and "holiness" in civic life. They note (with particular reference to Romans 13:1–7) that the theological category of "holiness," while applied to Jesus Christ (Mark 1:24) and the People of God (1 Peter 1:16), is "never applied to the Roman state" or its dominant symbols.[76] They continue:

> The apostle Paul instructs Christians to "be subject to the governing authorities" (Romans 13:1)—but never to worship them. Indeed, the Romans passage continues as follows: "Pay to all their dues . . . respect to whom respect is due, honor to whom honor is due" (Romans 13:7). This formulation implies a distinction between the ultimate loyalty that is due only to God and the honors due to the government.[77]

But of course, "holiness" and "sacredness" are now applied to many of the symbols of this civil religion we call "patriotism" or nationalism.

Jewett and Lawrence also point out that "zealous forms of civil religion" are a cause for terrorism.[78] In Romans 13:1–7, Paul is, of course, speaking into a potentially dangerous mix of the imperial cult and zealous nationalism, albeit somewhat subtly, since "[t]he God who grants authority to governmental agencies in Paul's argument is not Mars or Jupiter;" rather, it is *the* God "of Jewish and Christian faith."[79] But one could argue that in America's civil religion, "the gods who grant authorities to governmental agencies" are seen in the pantheon that includes past presidents who are "deified" in the neo-classical temples-called-memorials in Washington, D.C., in various national symbols, and of course, in the Almighty Dollar.[80]

Reading Romans 13:1–7 within the current imperial context also needs to take into consideration Paul's insightfulness into the sheer power that empires possess. Paul knows (and reminds his readers) that "governing authorities" are able to bring "wrath" (*orgē*) and produce "fear" and terror (*phobos*) among an empire's inhabitants. Within the current American imperial context, many believe (or at least hope) that the United States does not possess the same sheer power, either by

---

[76] Robert Jewett and John Shelton Lawrence, *Captain America and the Crusade against Evil* (Grand Rapids: Eerdmans, 2003), 303.

[77] Jewett and Lawrence, *Captain America*, 303.

[78] Jewett and Lawrence, *Captain America*, 22.

[79] Jewett, *Romans*, 789.

[80] It is interesting to note that in the wake of the 9/11 attacks, President Bush urged the American public "to do the patriotic thing" and spend money to bolster the United States economy.

design or by default.[81] But despite the Bush administration's indifference and inability to respond effectively in the wake of hurricane Katrina in the late summer and early fall of 2005, recent history tells us that the American empire possesses huge and unprecedented economic, cultural and military power. Globalization is arguably no more than the worldwide spread of the dominance of American culture and products; the phrase "shock and awe" was added to our cultural lexicon in the early days of the Iraq War. So seeing the United States as a powerful imperial force is quite realistic. And in Romans 13:1–7, Paul recognizes that governing authorities could be agents of terror (*phobos*). And since we live during the era of the American Empire, it is worth considering in what ways this empire has been an agent of terror—the School of the Americas, water-boarding, Haiditha, Fallujah, Abu Ghraib, and Gitmo all come to mind.

CONCLUSION

Jewett's exegesis of Romans 13:1–7 has helped remind us of a number of important themes as we think about a Christian's relation to the state. First, there is no clear distinction between "church" and "state" in Paul's mind, no division between the sacred and the secular. The governing authorities in Rome are for Paul the "servants" and "ministers" of God (13:4–6). They are not "public servants" in the ways that a western democracy might conceive, only accountable to "public constituencies," which are, in reality, often (only) the elite, powerful, important and prestigious. As God's "servants" and "ministers," they are quite different. And as Dunn argues (and I think Jewett would affirm),

> The fact and inevitability of political power is affirmed and validated [in Romans 13:1–7]—for *every* person. The state on the corporate scale is the equivalent of the body on the individual scale—it is the means of corporate existence in this world. As there is no basis for a spirit/body dualism in Paul, so there is no basis for a social dualism, whereby political power and political activity is regarded as evil or antithetic to religion. On the contrary, Paul seems to go out of his way to eliminate any such division. State officials not simply *can* be, but properly speaking *are* "servants of God." For Paul who lived his whole life as one of the priestly ministry (Romans 15:16), there was not clear division between sacred and secular.

[81] See the popular aphorism attributed to Thomas Jefferson and made popular most recently by Ronald Reagan: "The government that governs best governs least."

> Christians could be involved in the political structures of the time and wield political power without ceasing to be Christians and indeed as part of their Christian service.[82]

Jewett's treatment of Romans 13:1–7 also reminds us of the need to recognize that in Paul's mind, the "governing authorities," who receive their authority from and are servants of God, are not exempt from the ethics of Romans 12:1–21 and 13:8–10. And we need to also recognize that in Romans 13:1–7 Paul is not advocating withdrawal from "politics" (to use the word somewhat anachronistically), nor is he advocating an anarchy of sorts. In fact, it is perfectly appropriate to be involved and remain involved vocationally in the "affairs of state." As Wright puts it,

> Romans 13 enunciates [that] . . . being a Christian does not mean being an anarchist. The Creator intends his human creatures to live in social relations, which need order, stability and structure; Christians are not exempt from these.[83]

Paul understood that a quiet but realistic and critically connected posture toward "governing authorities" was needed if his Spanish mission had any hope of succeeding. Perhaps we can learn from this as well, as Christians work toward the ongoing success of the mission and the promulgation of the Gospel of Jesus Christ in its fullest and most whole sense. Perhaps a quiet but realistic and critically connected posture to the state in our imperial context is needed to ensure the ongoing spread of this Good News in a very needy world.

---

[82] Dunn, "Romans 13:1–7—A Charter for Political Quietism?" 67 (emphasis original).

[83] Wright, "The New Testament and the 'state,'" 16.

25

Betwixt and Between: A Canadian Reading of Robert Jewett's Commentary on Romans

Harry Maier

"Reconciliation: The Peacekeeping Monument," at the intersection of Sussex Drive and Patrick Street in Ottawa, expresses how Canada would like best to be recognized as a nation.[1] It is an open-air structure that invites passersby to walk in, around and on top of it. Life-sized bronze figures of Canadian armed service personnel, with both Canadian and United Nations insignia, stand at the ready in various poses of military action, amidst representations of ruined buildings or natural structures. The monument invites tourists to the nation's capital to recognize Canadians as an accessible nation of peacekeepers, ready, like the title of the monument suggests, to help bring reconciliation to hostile parties. It expresses a national myth that was by Prime Minister Lester B. Pearson, when he was Canada's Minister of Foreign Affairs. In 1956, to avert war between Great Britain, France, and Israel, who threatened Egypt militarily to prevent it seizing the Suez Canal, Pearson urged that the United Nations deploy troops in Egypt as an aid toward a political settlement of the dispute. In doing so, he coined the phrase "peace keeping" and promoted a vision of the United Nations—and hence Canada—as agent for political reconciliation. Pearson was awarded the Nobel Peace Prize and secured in the international imagination a picture of Canadians as lovers of peace and promoters of reconciliation. It is an enduring myth: ever since Canada has boasted of its peacekeeping role on the international stage, and Canadians like to think of themselves as charting a course of international relations distinct from its southern

---

[1] See http://www.canadascapital.gc.ca/bins/ncc_web_content_page.asp?cid=16297-24563-24548-24552&lang=1 for the official website of the monument.

neighbour. When the Bush Administration led the charge to invade Iraq in 2001, for example, alleging the imminent threat of weapons of mass destruction, then Liberal Prime Minister Jean Chrétien refused to lend Canada's military support, arguing that the Bush Doctrine of preemptive strike was a violation of the Charter of the United Nations. Prime Minister Chrétien sought to express a resilient independent foreign policy, resistant to President Bush's balkanization of the world into nations for and against America, supportive or opposed to "the Evil Doers" who masterminded the attacks of September 11. A good friend, he argued, has the courage to say no when she thinks her friend is making a mistake. Canadians opposed to the Iraq War and the Bush Doctrine were jubilant. Here on the front pages of Canada's newspapers was the contemporary witness of Canada as a nation of Peacekeepers in sharp contrast to the warmongering Fortress America. This portrait of a nation of peace-keepers has come on some hard times lately, under the leadership of the present Prime Minister, Stephen Harper, who in an important speech argued that the post-9/11 world requires that Canada revise its picture of itself on the international stage, not as "peace-keepers," but as allies in "peace-enforcement" in a new world of "global security." "Many yearn," he argued, "for a return—indeed in some cases to a virtually exclusive focus—on classical international peacekeeping." The struggles in Afghanistan, as well as human rights abuses in Rwanda and Bosnia mean, he continued, that "if Canada wants to contribute to global security, we will have to participate in United Nations peace enforcement missions, not just traditional peacekeeping, as well as intelligence sharing, aid and development, and so on."[2]

In the light of these comments it is worthwhile noting what stands across the street, just south of the Peace-Keeping Monument in Ottawa—namely the American Embassy. The architectural contrast between the two structures is dramatic. If the Peace-Keeping monument is an open air, public monument, the American embassy is a fortress. One is struck immediately by its lack of windows and stone-faced walls, surrounded by a low stone perimeter, itself guarded by steel balustrades. One gains the sense of a building designed to withstand assault and to express impregnability and security. Their geographical proximity urges visitors to Ottawa to consider both structures together and to ask how best to interpret Canada's celebration of peace-keeping or peace-enforcement: as alternative to the bellicose exceptionalism of its fortress-styled neighbour to the south, or as servant of it? The question is relevant, as I hope to show, in how we are to read Robert Jewett's treatment of Paul in Romans, situated as we are in a contemporary empire, sometimes styled as the "pax Americana," and more particularly living as the present

[2] http://pm.gc.ca/eng/media.asp?category=2&id=1995, accessed March 6, 2008.

writer does, as do most Canadians, very near its border. Does Paul in Romans offer a credible alternative to the Roman Empire as Jewett argues, or does the apostle to the Gentiles end up being its servant?

In what follows I want to read Robert Jewett's epic and breathtaking commentary on Paul's letter to the Romans in a Canadian landscape, standing as it were on Sussex Drive, halfway between Canada's Peacekeeping Monument and the American Embassy. For in his commentary Jewett furnishes a profile of Paul as a peacekeeper who intervenes in a conflicted situation where Jewish and Gentile Christians in the Empire's capital treat one another as rivals for honour and status, and boast of their privilege at the expense of one another. Paul writes Romans to urge his listeners to seek reconciliation and to convince them that neither have any reason for boasting and that they should instead unite with him in supporting his anticipated mission to Spanish barbarians. Simply put, I am asking whether Robert Jewett is successful in articulating a vision of Romans as portraying a theological vision that outlines an alternative to Empire, or whether Paul is better read as complementary to it? What I will argue is that neither of these alternatives is exactly correct and that Paul offers us a vision of Christianity in Empire as a form of hybridity. If Paul is apostle to announce peace and help bring reconciliation between strong and weak—Roman Gentiles and Jews at loggerheads with each other over competing claims to religious privilege as Jewett (rightly I think) argues they are, does he do so in a way that short circuits and abolishes Roman imperial visions for a worldwide imperium, or does he replace one emperor (Nero) with another, the Lord Jesus Christ? From the colonized subjectivity of Canadian identity, I hope to show that neither alternative successfully expresses what is happening in Romans and to make that argument I want to build on what I think are some of the most brilliant insights of Jewett's commentary—an historic watershed both for those who champion the New Perspective on Paul, and more particularly for those who seek to locate the apostle's mission to the gentiles in the context of Roman imperial politics and its ideals.

JEWETT ON EMPIRE, ANCIENT AND MODERN

Robert Jewett exemplifies well Karl Barth's dictum—apparently apocryphal—that one ought to do theology with the Bible in one hand the newspaper in the other. His scholarly oeuvre is never far from contemporary events. Already in 1993 Jewett signaled the general direction his thinking on Romans was headed and that this was not very far from what concerned him most as an American citizen observing the foreign policy of the Reagan and post-Reagan era. In *Paul Apostle to America*,[3] he argues for a reading of Romans as a frontal assault on the claims of the contemporary zealous empire of the United States. On these pages the Oliver North and Arms-Contra scandal dominates, where zealous patriotism that claims to be above the rule of Law threatens the very foundation of Republic. Paul unmasks zealotry in a way Jewett discovers especially damning of American exceptionalism, as an ancient messianic consciousness in whose service murder, violence, and insurrection are the all too familiar preserve of those who believe God is on their side and the end therefore justifies the means toward realizing a divinely orchestrated world order. A little bit later—this time in the wake of 9/11—Jewett returned again to this theme. *Captain America and the Crusade Against Evil: The Dilemma of Zealous Nationalism* (co-authored with John Shelton Lawrence)[4] echoes themes already articulated much earlier in *The Captain America Complex: The Dilemma of Zealous Nationalism*.[5] Here American exceptionalism is linked to the influence on American politics of biblical apocalyptic theology in general and chiliastic messianism in particular; its antidote is the cosmopolitan prophetic vision of biblical authors like Second Isaiah, who imagine a revived Israel thriving amidst a flourishing, just, cosmopolitan global order. So it comes as no surprise, then, that already on the first page of his Hermeneia commentary, Jewett hints at the contemporary application of the pages that follow: "Although I remain faithful to the Hermeneia format by leaving the contemporary application up to my readers, I hope that the extraordinary relevance of Romans to the situation of cultural, religious, and imperial conflicts is easily discernable" (page xv). Jewett is no parochial exegete and his Apostle to the Gentiles is no provincializing interpreter of the politics of his day. Both—exegete and apostle—have Empire clearly in their sites and both are equally motivated to explore alternatives to powers whether ancient or modern that proclaim peace and make the world a desert.

Empire ancient and modern is the backdrop of Jewett's overarching claim in his commentary on Romans that the so-called New Perspective on Paul flounders if Romans is not read from start to finish as a counter-imperial document that challenges the competition over status and struggle for honour at home in and promoted by the Roman Empire with the message of a Gospel of God's self-emptying in Jesus of Nazareth. His commentary thus belongs to a growing literature that seeks to locate Paul in the Roman Empire and urges a reading that goes beyond Reformation considerations of the justification of individual sinners before a just God and seeks instead to uncover a letter that promotes a

---

3 (Philadelphia: John Knox, 1993).
4 (Grand Rapids: Eerdmans, 2003).
5 (Philadelphia: Westminster Press, 1973).

communal identity of ecumenical cooperation, for the sake of mission, and in direct cross-examination of the ideals of the Roman Empire. Thanksgiving and cooperation is the antidote to Gentile and Jewish boasting and competition over status. Paul, "debtor to both Greeks and to barbarians" (Romans 1:14) writes Romans as an overture to garner support for his forthcoming mission to Spain, where he will bring his Gospel to despised barbarians, and reveal through the cooperation of Roman house and tenement churches divided along ethnic lines, the power of "God for salvation to everyone who has faith, to the Jew first and also to the Greek" (1:16). Here cooperation replaces a zealous desire for honour and thus self-promotion, whether that zeal takes the form of a Jewish desire to express God's favour and election by perfectly keeping the Law, or of a Gentile besting of Jews through flaunting strength over weakness (Romans 14–15), and hence replicating intense competition for superiority at all levels of imperial society. If in the Roman Empire peace comes through military glory and the demonstrable capacity to vanquish one's enemies, Paul offers the Romans peace by others means—namely by the death of Jesus for us "while we were still weak" (5:6). Since all have sinned and fall short of the glory of God, all boasting is excluded and zeal for obedience or favour is misplaced. The zealous quest for honour and status leads only to broken relationships with God and with one another. Romans seeks to persuade its listeners to give up ethnic rivalry and to discover in the apostle's Gospel of the full inclusion of Gentiles and barbarians in God's promises to Abraham and Israel the means toward constructing a united Christian front in the Empire's capital. The letter urges cooperation for Paul's anticipated mission to preach the Gospel to Spain's barbarians, and to help Paul realize the worldwide reach of his Gospel and to fulfill his destiny as apostle to the world's gentiles. Paul's last letter encourages a social formation of believers that challenges the Roman imperial logic of domination and conquest and the honorific codes that accompany them, and so seeks to transform the culture of his listeners in a way that ultimately turns the Roman Empire upside down. Paul will achieve by other means what Augustus has gained by force—a worldwide extension of the Gospel to the Empire's dispersed subjects, but not the imperial Gospel of bringing the intractable to heel through the active or threatened use of violence, but by the message of God's grace revealed in Jesus Christ.

ROMANS AND IMPERIAL BILDSPRACHE: AN ANTIDOTE TO ZEALOUS EMPIRE

As counterpoint to the sweeping epic themes of this commentary Jewett draws attention to imperial propaganda. Through statues, coins, inscriptions, and public monuments the Julio-Claudian dynasty, together with those civic elites across the Empire who competed to receive its patronage and honour, promoted an aggrandizing series of representations designed to convince all that they were the beneficiaries of a divinely appointed order. Imperial iconography formed the semantic elements of what Tonio Hölscher calls a Bildsprache—a picture language—organized to make immediately recognizable and persuasive dynastic claims to power and dominion. Those under the emperor's imperium were to recognize themselves as belonging to a world under a process of moral and ethical transformation from a state of warring faction and civic strife centred in vice, toward one of peaceful co-existence and concord guaranteed by Rome's persuasive diplomacy or the threat of the sword. The young emperor Nero who styled himself as a second Augustus promoted and welcomed iconographical celebrations of his reign as a return to the Golden Age of Augustus. The Epistle to the Romans bears the imprint of this iconographical programme not only in its celebration of a worldwide reach of the Gospel that incorporates Jews and barbarians in Christ's dominion, but in its epic themes of a natural world bursting forth in the newness of resurrection life even as it groans and sighs for the fullest realization of its newborn citizens, those incorporated into the death and resurrection of Jesus through baptism. It is no accident that Paul takes up so much space to develop themes centring on notions of righteousness, faith, peace, right-wising, and civic concord, because these are at the very heart of the imperial repertoire of ideals everywhere impressing themselves on the daily imaginations of the Empire's inhabitants. Paul is a good rhetorician who draws on shared experience with his audience to make his message as persuasive a possible.

Robert Jewett is convinced that in portraying Romans in this way he has uncovered not only Paul's intention in Romans, but the antidote to the problem of zealous Empire, whether that desire for worldwide dominion take the form of zealous legal observance to promote the domination of one ethnic group over another—as it did for example in the Judaism of Paul when he was a persecutor of the Church—or the form of military expansion orchestrated by the gods. And here of course is where his exegesis comes full circle to interpretation: zealous Empire ancient and modern is the problem that the death and resurrection of Jesus of Nazareth reveals to the world and which Paul's articulation of the Gospel seeks resolve by its call to humble thanksgiving and it exhortation to faith in Jesus Christ.

ROMANS BETWEEN MONUMENTS

This way of conceiving of Paul's theology has met with important objections. While a persuasive case can be made that Paul objects to zealotry for the Law and Gentile arrogance as serious obstacles to realizing his hope for establishing a mission to Spain, it is not so clear that Paul completely avoids the charge of imperialism. Jewett joins his voice to a number of interpreters of Paul who discover in the apostle's Gospel an alternative to imperial politics. Tom Wright represents one of the most notable applications of the New Perspective to the question of Roman imperial politics. Like Jewett, Wright discovers in Paul's championing of Jesus as the Son of God who has given up status for the sake of a freely chosen death for others, the foundation for a counter-civility realised through the imitation of Jesus.[6] Others however are less accepting of this point of view. Certainly from the early Church onward, the imperial themes of Paul's Gospel enfolding all, both God's chosen people and Greeks, Jews and barbarians, were recognized as obverse sides of the same coin. Origen for example celebrates Caesar's and Paul's Gospel as twin powers, bringing earth and heaven together, both subject to the universal imperium of a divinely appointed and ecclesially realised unity. For Origen, Jesus' birth was providentially arranged to occur under Caesar's reign to guarantee the reign of the Gospel over all nations.[7] Eusebius of Caesarea, developing Origen's perspective, champions Paul as articulating an imperial Gospel fully realised in the foreign policy of Constantine the Great in championing Christianity as a means of uniting the dispersed peoples of his empire: drawing on Pauline themes concerning the evangelisation of barbarians, Eusebius celebrates Caesar and Christ as taming "the twofold race of barbarians"—demons and uncivilized peoples—to bring both under a united imperium.[8] Turning to his modern interpreters, Bruno Blumenfeld argues that far from offering an anti-imperial theology in Romans, Paul offers a Gospel that mirrors and thus preserves the Roman imperial order. "The Roman empire united the world politically, culturally, socially, and economically. This unity had to be preserved, and Paul's genius is conservative." Blumenfeld continues:

---

[6] Thus, "Paul's Gospel and Caesar's Empire" in edited by Richard Horsley, *Paul and Politics: Ecclesia, Imperium, Interpretation* (Harrisburg: Trinity Press International, 2000), 160–84.

[7] Origen, *Against Celsus* 2.30; see also, E. Peterson, *Der Monotheismus als politisches Problem. Ein Beitrag zur Geschichte der politischen Theologie im Imperium Romanum* (Leipzig: Jakob Hegner, 1935), 67–71 for further texts and commentary. Origen's perspective was already prevalent by the second century: see Melito of Sardis in Eusebius's *Ecclesiastical History* 4.26.7–8.

[8] Eusbius, *Oration* 7.2.13.

> To be sure, Paul's relation to the empire is paradoxical. Not only does Paul need the empire as the support infrastructure for his message, but he defends the power system with unabashed pride. And yet, the defense of Rome that he mounts is that of a usurper, a pretender. Rome can survive and its stability be ensured only if Christ, or rather a Christ-type, takes over. Paul usurps the power system in two ways. First, he challenges the system from within: he forces on his hearers a new language, which, although it mirrors the concepts and categories of the existing system, subverts them either by occluding them with new idioms or be reinterpreting while keeping the old terminology . . . . The second mode of subversion is radically trangressive: the introduction of the irrational . . . I refer . . . to the whole class of marginal phenomena: a crucified, law-breaking savior; glossolalia; a whole ontology of resistance, a whole epistemology of the inarticulate."[9]

Here Blumenfeld focuses on Romans 13:1–7. For Jewett, in sharp contrast, Paul's advice to the Romans voluntarily to submit themselves to the imperial authorities whom God has given them as their rulers is a "massive act of political co-optation" since it is not Mars and Jupiter the gods of Caesar's gospel who have given this authority to rule, but the God of Paul's Gospel, the God of Israel and the Lord who reveals God's good intentions for all by way of an upside down reign of love, the crucified Jesus Christ.[10] Blumenfeld certainly agrees with Jewett that Paul in Romans reconfigures imperial language, but argues that this does not result in an anti-imperial Gospel. On the contrary: "The Letter to the Romans . . . shows most clearly Paul's application of political thinking to Christian society, and one could fancy it as a contribution to a *Festschrift* for Nero, to celebrate the emperor's *quiquennium aureum*."[11] Romans 13:1–7 is no act of political co-optation, it is rather one of assimilation.

---

[9] Bruno Blumenfeld, *The Political Paul: Justice, Democracy and Kingship in a Hellenistic Framework* (Sheffield: Sheffield Academic Press, 2001), 290–91.

[10] Jewett, *Romans*, 789–90, at 790, perhaps one of the most important passages of the entire commentary: "The God whom Paul speaks here is the same as announced in Chapter 1 whose righteousness was elaborated for twelve chapters; it is the God embodied in the crucified Christ that is in view here, which turns this passage into a massive act of political co-optation. If the Roman authorities had understood this argument, it would have been viewed as thoroughly subversive. That the Roman authorities were appointed by the God and Father of Jesus Christ turns the entire Roman civic cult on his head, exposing its suppression of the truth. Its involvement in the martyrdom of Christ, crucified under Pontius Pilate, cannot have been forgotten by the readers [*sic*] of chapter 13, who knew from first hand experience of the Edict of Claudius the hollowness of Rome's claim to have established a benign rule of law."

[11] Blumenfeld, *The Political Paul*, 292.

This is an extreme and absurd position, especially because Blumenfeld forgets that whatever Paul is writing about in Romans, in the light of his apocalyptic expectations he can hardly be promoting a preservation of the Roman imperial order. However, it does point to the way Romans was certainly read within two centuries of the apostle's death, and it reflects a conservative Paul at some variance with Jewett's representation of him. For it remains a fact that however much Paul seeks to redefine the honorific system of Roman Empire, even if he goes about doing so by inverting reigning hierarchical schemes to challenge that system, an inverse hierarchy still preserves the very logic it seeks to unsettle. Paul's remains a Gospel of a Christian imperium realised through a means different from Caesar's but has all the marks of an imperium nevertheless. Paul cannot imagine a world where Jesus is not Lord and even if Nero is not Lord, there remains a Lord nevertheless. On this argument, Paul does not so much replace Rome's rule as complement it. Paul's peacekeeping in Rome, in urging otherwise factious groups to concord and unity, is complementary rather than subversive of the goal of Roman imperial rule, indeed of the goal of politics from Alexander the Great onward.[12] And when he urges that the Romans cooperate in extending the Gospel to barbarians so that the two may be enfolded into the imperium established through the Lord Jesus Christ, he announces a goal that would have found immediate recognition in a capital where the universal reach of the Julio-Claudian dynasty was everywhere celebrated and championed. Paul the peacekeeper does not build a monument that challenges the Empire, he rather erects one to stand across from it, as it were down the street from it, to complement it.

PAUL AS DOUBLE-AGENT

If Paul's peacekeeping initiatives complement imperial goals through his invocations of imperial language and the deployment of imagery drawn from Rome's iconographical picture-language, he nevertheless disrupts those goals. Here the insights of post-colonial studies are most useful in helping to parse important distinctions and to avoid distorting binary oppositions between a Paul who is a revolutionary opponent of Empire and one who is its Christian civil servant. Homi Bhabha develops the notion of "mimicry" to show how colonial subjects disrupt discourses of colonial authority by their simultaneous resemblance and disavowal. "The ambivalence of colonial authority repeatedly turn from *mimicry*—the difference which is almost nothing, but not quite—

[12] See Walter Frederick Taylor, Jr., "Unity, Unity of Humanity," *Anchor Bible Dictionary* 6: 746–53 for the ancient ideal and Paul's role in its Christian appropriation.

to *menace*—a difference that is almost total but not quite."[13] Bhabha introduces the notion of hybridity to describe the colonized subject who is at once the colonizer's double and other. He describes "ambivalence" as the double aspect of the colonized who mirror the colonizer's ideals back to themselves, while reminding both colonizer and colonized that there remains always an excess that cannot be completely assimilated. Mimicry and mockery are twin sides of the same coin of colonization.[14]

Paul the apostle to the Gentiles is a colonized subject of Roman imperial power. He travels along the Empire's roads, engages in and benefits from its trade, as a citizen invokes the status privileges it guarantees him, deploys the repertoire of rhetorical tools and devices used by his pagan contemporaries to promote civic concord and good order, and draws on his shared experience with his audience of the very concepts and images that make them rational inhabitants of their social world. Paul mimics colonial authority and to the degree that he does so even in the act of contestation, conserves that authority and thereby—however inadvertently and unintentionally from his apocalyptic perspective—preserves it. However, he also mocks it by turning it upside down and ironizing it, by reversing its status distinctions, by deploying the categories of honour and status to the most unlikely objects of celebration: the cross, apostolic identity as slavery, and so on. If he is a peacekeeper whose letters circulate even through the dispersed members of the imperial household, and if he helps to realize imperial goals by offering a Gospel that extends the lordship of his crucified and divinized emperor Jesus to the bounds of Empire, even amongst its most savage barbarians in Spain, under Paul's influence, Jesus' lordship becomes the hybrid double and mockery of Roman imperial power, erected as it were in the tenement and house churches in a capital city's slums and ghettoes, as well as in its shops and house churches, across the street from and along the road beside the Empire's monuments.

I would therefore revise that all important phrase from Jewett's commentary that in Romans 13:1–7 we encounter a "massive co-optation" of imperial power, and read instead that here we encounter a strategic hybridization of power. In Romans, the raised Jesus and his ambassador of Good News, Paul, are imperial double agents. While the ambassador awaits his Lord's imperial *adventus*, outfitted with all the expected regalia and sound and majesty worthy of a Roman emperor's arrival (1 Thessalonians 4:15–17), our ambassador nevertheless has to be strategic, for he is in a role not all unlike the one Pierre Eliot Trudeau once described for Canada in relationship to the United States—like a

---

13 Homi K. Bhabha, *The Location of Culture* (London and New York: Routledge, 1994), 91.

14 Bhabha, *The Location of Culture*, 86.

mouse sleeping beside an elephant, affected by every twitch and grunt, no matter what good will the elephant would like to communicate. To read Romans from the Peace Keepers monument in Ottawa, down the street from the emblem of Fortress America is to remember one's place in the world, as not exactly one thing, but not entirely the other either. We do well to imagine Paul in a similar situation. And we may well ask in an imperial situation such as the one we find ourselves in today, does Paul's Gospel equip us with a dramatic enough means to articulate a religious way of being thoughtful citizens in this our troubled world? Can Paul's Gospel give us the change to Empire we can believe in?

26

Shame and Stigma: The Shame of Paul's *Spoiled Self*

Dietmar Neufeld

Introduction

This commentary represents a remarkable accomplishment. It is a reflection of twenty-six years of thinking, interacting, and puzzling through the Epistle's many complexities and conundrums while also navigating the vast sea of literature that the Epistle has generated. Most commentaries are repetitive, often with boring recapitulations of various positions, remixing them and voila yet another commentary graces personal and institutional libraries. Most of them are bogged down with discussions and exegetical analyses of the texts of Romans that are hopelessly ethnocentric, individualistic, and theologically abstract. The focus is upon individual guilt and the forgiveness that Paul proffers his readers. Not so with this one. Its feet are thoroughly anchored in the system of competing honor and the imperialistic ideology and iconography of the conquered that sustained the system—most people in the system would have no prospect of ever gaining such glory.

Along comes Paul to subvert this exploitative system of honor in his letter to the Romans. With his sights set on Spain, he needed to convince the communities in Rome to overcome their imperialistic behavior towards one another. Their conduct brought into disrepute the gospel of the impartial righteousness of God. If they were to be successful partners with him to carry the gospel to the barbarians in Spain, they would have to discontinue the deeply engrained habits of the shaming each other. The populations in Spain resisted the imperial exploitation endemic to the glory and honor system.[1] Thus, the communities in Rome are enjoined not to "discriminate against the Barbarians such as

[1] Robert Jewett, *Romans* (Hermeneia; Minneapolis: Fortress Press, 2007), 88.

the Spaniards, [informed] that all claims of cultural superiority are false, [reminded] that imperial propaganda must be recognized as bogus, and [encouraged] to abandon their dominating behavior towards one another if the missional hope of unifying the world in praise of God" is to be achieved.[2]

Jewett, therefore, adopts an interpretative method in which an appropriate understanding of the letter can only be achieved by placing it in its broader social-cultural milieu of self-magnification endemic to teaching and learning (p. 49) and the aristocracy of esteem (50) that precipitated a culture of exploitation and competitions for honor. Thus, rather than treating it as an abstract theological treatise locked in its time-conditioned state in defense of some modern doctrinal stance, he is able to treat it as imparting a gospel of impartial grace shattering all claims of superior status or theology.[3] Indeed, writes Jewett,

> Paul has in mind a new social reality (Romans 3:22)—there is no longer the possibility of any distinction of honor. Redefining the theological issue in terms of shame and honor avoids the pitfalls of the ethical theory of justification, that humans are made righteous so that they come to deserve divine approbation; it avoids the artificiality of imputed justification, in which believers are treated as righteous although they remain sinners; it avoids the narrow scope of forgiveness as acquittal from charges arising against individual sins, or the individual experience of relief from a guilty conscience, which limits being set right through Christ to those whose problem is guilt; it moves past the existentialist limits of merely providing a new self-understanding for believers as accepted by God despite all evidence to the contrary; it takes account of the actual makeup of the audience of Romans, consisting largely of the urban underclass experiencing a wide range of deprivations deriving from shameful status.[4]

Thus, avers Jewett, this gospel is "the power of God,"

> . . . and it shatters the unrighteous precedence given to the strong over the weak, the free and well-educated over

---

[2] Jewett, *Romans*, 79.

[3] Jewett, *Romans*, xv, 46.

[4] Robert Jewett, "Stuck in Time. *Kairos*, *Chronos*, and the Flesh in Groundhog Day," in edited by Cliave Marsh and Gaye Ortiz, *Explorations in the Theology and Film* (Oxford: Blackwell, 1977), 271.

> slaves and the ill-educated, the Greeks and Romans over the barbarians. If what the world considers dishonorable has power, it will prevail and achieve a new form of honor for those who have not earned it, an honor consistent with divine righteousness. All who place their faith in this gospel will be set right, that is, be placed in the right relation to the most significant arena in which honor is dispensed: divine judgment. Thus the triumph of divine righteousness through the gospel of Christ crucified and resurrected is achieved by transforming the system in which shame and honor are dispensed.[5]

In the social milieu of a Roman culture deeply steeped in the agonistic give and take of seeking either to hold on to honor or achieve it, deep divisions existed in society between the strong and the weak, men and women, Greek and Barbarian, Jew and Gentile. This exploitative system undergirded by an imperialistic ideology of self aggrandizement led to intense competitions for superiority in honor on all levels of society.[6] It is this system that Paul, throughout the letter to the Romans, systematically challenges and essentially subverts with his gospel.[7] Paul, instead, "offers a new approach to mercy, righteousness, and piety, one that avoided the propagandistic exploitation of the Roman Imperial system."[8] As Jewett argues, "if all persons and groups fall short of the ultimate standard of honor that they were intended to bear, that is, "the glory of God," then none has the right to claim superiority or to place others in positions of inferiority."[9] What Paul has in mind is a new social reality "within the community of the shamed made right by the death and resurrection of Christ, [so that] there is no longer the possibility of any "distinction" (Romans 3:22) in honor."[10] There were persuasive social reasons why Paul should have been ashamed of this gospel: divine self-revelation on an obscene cross and a gospel designed for the powerless and the disenfranchised flew in the face of the conventions of what counted for honor. Thus, "his claim not to be ashamed signalled that a social and ideological revolution had been inaugurated, one that overturned the systems of honor and shame throughout the Greco-Roman world."[11]

---

[5] Virginia Wiles et al. edited, *Putting Body & Soul Together. Essays in Honor of Robin Scroggs* (Valley Forge: Trinity Press International, 1977), 265.

[6] Jewett, *Romans*, 49.

[7] Jewett, *Romans*, 51.

[8] Jewett, *Romans*, 48; idem, *Saint Paul Returns to the Movies* (Grand Rapids: Eerdmans, 1999), 9.

[9] Jewett, *Saint Paul Returns to the Movies*, 12.

[10] Jewett, *Saint Paul Returns to the Movies*, 12.

[11] Jewett, *Saint Paul Returns to the Movies*, 14.

Indeed, the entire system based on the agonistic competition for honor had to be abandoned if unity and equality between groups and persons were to be achieved.[12]

ROMANS IN THE KEY OF SHAME

Did Paul, however, abandon the entire system of honor and shame? Since the system was endemic to Greco-Roman culture for Paul to abandon it would similar to a fish abandoning its watery environment. Paul continues to play the honor/shame game but he does so according to a new set of rules. Paul knew that in the never-ending game of one-upmanship and witty repartee he had failed miserably—so why not turn his weakness/shame (the source of his boasting) into strength? Paul, thus, redefines what counts for honor and shame by altering the expectations operative in the public court of reputation. He was hoping to eclipse the expectations that society had of the honorable and shameful. Paul was cognizant that the court of public reputation had the power to define honor and shame at its whim. In some ways it was as fickle as changing fashion statements come and go. On the basis of this, what were normative expectations of individual characteristics on one occasion, as regards physicality, speech, conduct, on another could be ignored in the public court of reputation in its distribution of power. As much as Paul was manipulating for what counted for honor and shame in his public court of reputation so also society at large, functioning as a court of reputation, could decide overnight (manipulate) what were the new standards of honor and shame. Recognizing the fickle and dynamic character of these courts of reputation permitted Paul to propose a system that stood decidedly at odds with most people's understanding of honor and shame. He therefore strategically adjusted the expectations of the honorable and shameful in his public court of reputation with the hopes of distributing these redefined parameters in such a way as to convince his audience in Rome.

It is thus my intention to use the work of Robert Jewett on shame as a jumping off point. For example Jewett writes that he has come to the

> . . . intuition that shame may be deeper and more pervasive human dilemma than guilt, and also that grace is broader than individual forgiveness. Shame pertains not merely to what we have done but also to what we are, both as individuals and members of groups. My impression is that some of the more prejudicial wounds of shame are rarely cauterized and almost never forgot-

12 Jewett, "Stuck in Time," 272.

> ten . . . . the memories of personal and collective failures and limitations, of abuse and discrimination, of feeling neglected, unloved, or unworthy, need to be brought into the day before their effect can be assessed. But the essence of shame is painful exposure of vulnerability, which we avoid at all costs. The root meaning for the terminology of shame in many languages is "cover" or "hide," and the basic shame phenomenon in every culture, including the Greco-Roman and Jewish Cultures that produced the Bible, is the lowered, averted, reddened face, often hidden by one's hands. Beyond all other human emotions and reactions, shame is what we most instinctively hide.[13]

This intuition of Jewett's will be developed more fully by factoring in the notions of stigma and the spoiled self from the perspectives of evolutionary psychology, social psychology, and anthropology.

THE GRAMMAR OF HONOR

Jewett in his commentary provides an excellent description of the social-cultural world of honor and shame that Paul inhabited, it is my intention to expand on that world. While what counted as honorable and shameful in the ancient Mediterranean world was not defined the same everywhere,[14] anthropologists have nevertheless shown that Greeks, Romans and Judeans regarded honor and shame as pivotal values in their social milieu. Xenophon acknowledged that love of honor distinguished human from animal (*Hieron* 7.3) and Aristotle thought honor to be the "greatest of all external goods," identifying it with "happiness" akin to "being loved" (*Ethica nichomachea* I). Philo avers that "wealth, fame, official posts, honors and everything of that sort" are a human's constant preoccupation (*Quod deterius potiori insidari soleat* 122). Indeed, he complains that "fame and honor are a most precarious possession, tossed about the reckless tempers and flighty words of careless men" (Philo, *De Abrahamo* 264). As testament to this precarious preoccupation, Philo often mentions honor, glory, fame, high reputations, being adorned with honors and public offices, noble birth, the desire for glory, honor in the present and a good name in the future (*De migratione Abrahami* 172; *Legum allegoriarum* 3.87; *Quod deterius potiori insidari soleat* 33, 157; *De posteritate Caini* 112; *De Abrahamo* 185, 263). Similarly, Josephus speaks of Caesars, Vespasian,

---

13 Jewett, *Saint Paul Returns to the Movies*, 19.

14 M. J. Swartz, "Shame, Culture, and Status among the Swahili of Mombasa," *Ethos* 16 (1988), 21.

David, Saul, Jonathan, Augustus as men of honor who confer honors upon others (*Bellum Judaicum* 1.194; 1.199; 1.358; 1.396; 1.607; 3.408; *Vita* 423; *Antiquitates Judaicae* 7.117; 6.168, 6.251, 13.102). In addition, he mentions the dignity and distinction held by judges, consuls, village priests, governors, and prophets (*Bellum Judaicum* 4.149, 7.82; *Antiquitates Judaicae* 4.215, 10.92, 11.309, 15.217).

Honor and shame are values characteristic of face-to-face societies in which public evaluation of a person's standing provides a basis of social control.[15] Honor is an abstract term that anthropologists use to designate a person's worth, reputation, status, value and fame. Moreover, honor is at the centre of a social system of interconnected values in which power, personal loyalty, wealth, high mindedness, relative importance in rank and status, sense of shame, courage, and excellence of character are operative. Claims of superiority over others and demands of one's' rights commensurate with one's position in society are common in honor-based societies. Honor is, however, also a limited good related to the scarcity of all resources including land, live stock, crops, reputation, and political influence. Therefore, honor gained came at the expense of honor lost by another. Gains and losses of honor were the consequence of the face-to-face game of challenge and response in which virtually every public encounter is construed as a challenge to one's honor. Challenges must be met with something said or done quickly and effectively in response or honor was lost. All such claims, challenges and responses whether in kind, by a greater challenge, or deeper insult, took place in the public domain, and the verdict of success or failure determined the outcome in the game of challenge and riposte.[16]

Honor referred to two social actions: (1) a person's claim of respect for the importance and value of her character, life, efforts, and achievements and (2) the public acknowledgement of that claim.[17] The claim may be accepted or rejected. A person attains honor in several ways: she may be ascribed it by another or achieve it on her own merits. Ascribed honor refers to bestowed or inherited worth: born into a distinguished family, studying under an esteemed teacher and the requisite academic pedigree that follows, and receiving an important posting. Achieved honor is earned through merit and hard work, such as athletic talents, military prowess, accumulation of wealth, benefactions, artistic

[15] J. G. Peristiany edited, *Honour and Shame. The Values of Mediterranean Society* (Chicago: Chicago University Press, 1966); Arthur W. H. Adkins, *Merit and Responsibility: A Study in Greek Values* (Oxford: Oxford University Press, 1960); Virginia Burrus, *Saving Shame: Martyrs, Saints, and other Abject Subjects* (Philadelphia: University of Pennsylvania Press, 2008); David D. Gilmore edited, *Honor and Shame and the Unity of the Mediterranean* (Washington: American Anthropological Association, 1987); Bruce J. Malina, *The New Testament World. Insights from Cultural Anthropology* (Louisville: Westminster/John Knox Press, 1993); Richard L. Rohrbaugh, *The New Testament in Cross-Cultural Perspective* (Eugene: Cascade Books, 2007).

[16] Malina, *The New Testament World*; Rohrbaugh, *The New Testament in Cross-Cultural Perspective*.

[17] Malina, *The New Testament World*, 30.

accomplishments, and through the practice of challenging another and taking her honor as one's own. Honor, therefore, describes a social dynamic whereby persons compete for the purpose of winning respect, praise, and social status. The concept of "social status" refers to one's position or standing in relation to others within the stratification of a particular society or within a given social structure or group.[18] As Harland states, "a variety of factors play a role in defining one's status within a social structure, including family background, sex, age, ethnic origins, education, occupation, wealth, and ability."[19]

In the section on the *Pyramid of Honor*, Jewett clearly points out that for the elite of Roman society, honor resided in holding certain public offices, performing fixed roles, and achieving publically recognized statuses relative to where they were situated in the social structure. So, for example, kings, high priests, rabbis, scribes governors, and other imperial and civic officials enjoyed high honor in accord with their social status—what Judge has called "an aristocracy of esteem."[20] While among the aristocrats the hierarchical ranking of honor was clearly known it was not so the case among peasants and artisans where significant debate and controversy took place over issues of honor. It was therefore not uncommon to squabble about seating arrangements at banquets (Luke 14:7–11; James 2:1–3; Plutarch, *Quaestionum convivialum libri ix* 3). Honor also had a strong material orientation measured by one's possessions and ostentatious display of them. The consumption of wealth and not its accumulation or amount symbolized honor (James 2:1–3). Fine apparel, banquets, villas, and other precious gifts in their public display and benefaction denoted a person of substantial honor.

THE GRAMMAR OF STIGMA AND SHAME

While honor was to be protected, shame was equally to be avoided. As much as honor played itself out in the social context, so also did shame. Shame was basically the reverse of honor wherein one lost respect, status, reputation, because of contempt, defeat, and ridicule. Shame, however, functioned as form of social control because a person with a sense of shame would have been acutely aware of the opinions of others and fearful of public disapproval or condemnation.

Citizens of Rome continually feared becoming exposed to public shame. Cicero, for example in the treatise *On the Republic* states that

[18] Dean Harper, "Statuses and Roles," in edited by Frank N. Magill, *International Encyclopedia of Sociology* (London: FD, 1995), 2:1360; Philip Harland, "Connections with Elites in the World of Early Christians," in edited by Anthony J. Blasi et al., *Handbook of Early Christianity: Social Science Approaches* (Walnut Creek: Alta Mira Press, 2002), 385–86.

[19] Harland, "Connections with Elites," 385–86.

[20] Jewett, *Romans*, 50.

> The best citizens are not deterred [from disgraceful behavior] by fear of a punishment that has been sanctioned by laws as much as by the sense of shame that has been instilled by nature as a kind of fear of just censure. The founder of the state used public opinion to cause this sense of shame to grow and refined it through both established customs and training. As a result shame, no less than fear, keeps the citizen from doing wrong (*De re publica* 5.6).

The court of public opinion counted and served to maintain a certain level of performance commensurate with a group's norms. Shameless persons, in contrast, did not care about what others thought of them and, therefore, would engage in behavior not in accord with the codes of expected behavior. Shame had a decidedly negative meaning when it referred to a tarnished reputation. Synonyms of shame in a negative sense would be loss of face, disgrace, and humiliation; a person who was shamed would be scorned, despised, reviled, rebuked, insulted, and the like.[21] Shame essentially related to an unfavorable public reputation and the indignation that it aroused in the one shamed. Shame had a self-other evaluative quality about it. Persons were concerned with processing socially threatening information—specially as regards in the domains of social rank/status—so as the avoid shame. Yet Paul, rather than avoiding it, holds up the triumph of shame as something to be embraced.

The term the "looking glass self"[22] has to do with the way persons judge and feel about themselves in accordance with how they think others judge and feel about them. Shame tends to focus on the social world (belief about how others see the self) and how, as a consequence, a person thinks others see the self.[23] The looking-glass self has three aspects to it: the imagination of our appearance (physically, socially, emotionally) to the other person in one's social context; the imagination of the other person's judgment of that appearance; and some sort of self feeling in the one judged, either pride or mortification.[24] Shame was therefore, a self-belief that one could not create a positive self-image in the eyes of the other; that in some way one lacked talent, ability, appearance; that one will be passed over, ignored, actively rejected; that one will become an object of scorn, contempt, or ridicule to others.[25]

---

21 Malina, *The New Testament World*, 59.

22 As quoted in T. J. Scheff, "Shame and Conformity: The Deference-Emotion System," *American Review of Sociology* 53 (1988), 398.

23 Paul Gilbert, "What is Shame? Some Core Issues and Controversies," in edited by Paul Gilbert and Bernice Andrews, *Shame: Interpersonal Behaviour, Psychotherapy, and Culture* (New York: Oxford University Press, 1998), 17.

24 Gilbert, "What is Shame?," 17.

25 Gilbert, "What is Shame?," 17.

The person had been found to be disgraced on account of inappropriate behavior or some other act and judged to be found wanting in some way—to have fallen short.[26] The culture of self-magnification in Paul's day quickly marginalized those who could not match up to the standards of vaunting the self—they were found to fall short of the standards that permitted them to enshrine themselves in the mantles of self-glory. In such a context, Paul attempts to subvert the standards of what counted for shame by focusing on a kind of shame that did not mortify but was life giving.

Shame in the ancient world focused on external shame because the focus was on the outside world: how one was seen by others and how one lived in the eyes of others.[27] It was in becoming an object of the scrutiny of others that the potential to feel shame, and the desire to avoid it, began in earnest.[28] Shame, thus played an essential role in shaping social decorum, as defined by one's social context/group, through regulating behavior in the areas of group identity and social bonding.[29] The fear of shame put enormous pressure upon individuals to conform to the standards of one's group and social/cultural context. "Conformity" was required, at least to a degree, if one desired acceptance and protection provided by one's group. Thus, the experience of shame and its avoidance were powerful tools in regulating behavior that identified members of a group or social context.[30] Those who did not fit the culture of self-aggrandizement because they had nothing to offer or had chosen, for whatever reason, to embark on a course of nonconformist behavior so as to display themselves in unbecomingly splendid or gaudy attire or to obtrude themselves boastfully, impudently, or defiantly on the public view, were quickly marginalized or ostracized (OED).

"Conformity shame" regulated many behaviors in antiquity including dress, language, food consumption, ritual, deportment, the quest for honor and, most importantly, what counted for honor in a world tirelessly seeking to avoid shame and endlessly engaging in the game to enhance honor. Shame and its avoidance decided what was suitable for the "social self in a variety of roles, according to where one belonged socially, in terms of status, ethnic group (Jewish or barbarian Spaniard), age, gender, and social occupation."[31] Remaining loyal to these standards was a major mechanism by which members of a social-cultural group

---

26 Jewett, *Romans*, 268–93.

27 Gilbert, "What is Shame?," 17.

28 Gilbert, "What is Shame?," 17.

29 Deborah F. Greenwald and David W. Harder, "Domains of Shame. Evolutionary, Cultural, and Psychotherapeutic Aspects," in edited by Paul Gilbert and Bernice Andrews, *Shame: Interpersonal Behaviour, Psychotherapy, and Culture* (New York: Oxford University Press, 1998), 225.

30 Greenwald and Harder, "Domains of Shame," 230.

31 Greenwald and Harder, "Domains of Shame," 231.

identified with each other and ensured who was in and who was out—that is, the other, the so-called outsider. Indeed, the longevity of a social-cultural group, however defined politically or religiously, was dependent upon members learning what the rules of behavior were for the various roles members of the group were expected to play. It also ensured that each member's conduct continued to conform to the groups' perception of what it considered honorable and shameful behavior—otherwise the benefits of continuing to belong to the group were in jeopardy.[32]

Groups therefore ensured that there were easily recognizable modes of behavior that were either shameful or honorable so that it was possible for members of particular social groups to distinguish themselves from close neighbors. Persons who belonged to a cultural and religious group needed to recognize quickly who belonged and who did not. Those who belonged were expected to conform and hence received the benefit of protection and recognition. These were the individuals who were allowed into the walls of the city, into one's home, into one's religious group, into one's nation, into one's ethnic and tribal group, and into one's guild.[33] Those who did not conform to communal or cultural standards were excluded and suffered from a sense of stigma. As Jewett perceptively points out in his commentary, the Spaniards had long lived under the oppressive imperial ideology of Roman cultural superiority and were actively resisting it. They suffered from a sense of social stigma—in the eyes of the Romans they collectively bore the marks of a "spoiled identity."[34] In collectivists cultures where there was a heightened sense of the shame engendered by nonconformity and where there was a strong sense of social cohesion especially when it is perceived under threat or difficult to establish and maintain, any deviation from the norm was regarded with wariness.[35]

Yet, over-conformity also created problems for members of associations. For examples, researchers point out that a strong desire to conform to group regulations as regards shame potentially emasculated individual members of their freedom—over sensitivity to avoiding shame indicated to the group that they were followers and not leaders.[36] Leaders on the other hand, while not immune from shame and thus careful not to stray too far from the normative conventions of the group, could afford to exhibit greater latitude with what was acceptable in terms of what counted for shame, and were able thereby to alter the norms of

32 Greenwald and Harder, "Domains of Shame," 230.

33 Greenwald and Harder, "Domains of Shame," 231.

34 Michael Lewis, "Shame and Stigma," in edited by Paul Gilbert and Bernice Andrews, *Shame: Interpersonal Behaviour, Psychotherapy, and Culture* (New York: Oxford University Press, 1998), 126.

35 Greenwald and Harder, "Domains of Shame," 231.

36 Greenwald and Harder, "Domains of Shame," 231.

what constituted shame on account of their example.[37] Greenwald and Harder state "that leaders do not face the same obligation to demonstrate membership in the group on the basis of conformity because everyone knows who they are."[38] Paul, while not a known person in Rome except perhaps through innuendo and rumor, takes pains to introduce himself and assure them that he is reliable and trustworthy through example. Paul clearly sets himself apart by signaling the end of *conformity shame* that was exploitative and, by virtue of his example, establishing a new style of *conformity shame* that was *nonconformist* in terms of cultural expectations and, in so doing, erased the shame of his cultural stigmatization. It also explains why Paul takes inordinate pains to introduce himself the community in Rome—the success of his program rested upon them getting to know who he was, trusting that his promotion of nonconformist values was for the good of the community, and accepting that what counted for shame had been turned on its head and could be ignored without peril to the self.

After all, Paul's body was living proof of the extent to which he had gone to alter what counted for shame—his body bore the marks of numerous beatings in which he boasted (Romans 5:3; 2 Corinthians 11:23–25)—"in boasting about beatings, Paul does what he says he does: he boasts of things that show his weakness."[39] In the words of Glancy, "Paul not only claims that he bears in his body *ta stigmata tou Iēsou*; he also claims that in his body he always carries 'the putting to death of Jesus' (2 Corinthians 4:10) . . . Paul's welted skin is parchment on which is legible the agonizing story of Jesus' humiliations preceding his life-giving death."[40]

In this connection, a brief discussion of the relationship of stigma to shame is essential. M. Lewis points out that stigma is generally thought to be a public mark, a mark that is noticed by others, and includes a "spoiled identity."[41] Stigma is frequently a cause of shame because the mark that an individual possesses displays a perceived departure from a social norm in terms of certain actions, conduct, or appearance. Another critical factor isolated by Lewis in the triggering of shame because of stigmata is the issue of responsibility or self-blame.[42] He argues that the degree to which stigmatized persons are blamed for their mark by others, the assumption being that they can either do something

[37] Greenwald and Harder, "Domains of Shame," 231.

[38] Greenwald and Harder, "Domains of Shame," 231.

[39] Jennifer A. Glancy, "Boasting of Beatings (2 Corinthians 11:23–25)," *Journal of Biblical Studies* 123 (2004), 134.

[40] Glancy, "Boasting of Beatings," 133.

[41] Lewis, "Shame and Stigma," 126; E. Goffmann, *Notes on the Management of a Spoiled Identity* (Englewood Cliffs: Prentice Hall, 1963).

[42] Lewis, "Shame and Stigma," 127.

about it or in some way have brought it upon themselves, reflects their degree of shame.[43] Indeed, avers Lewis, "the idea of responsibility and perceived responsibility is central to stigma and shame.[44] For example, physical appearance and deportment often serve as stigmata. Physical appearance is public and, because it is open to public scrutiny, constitutes a potential stigma. Facial or bodily deformity that cannot be hidden from public view and repulses people or causes averted glances, rejection, and labelling constitutes being stigmatized—and shamed—an awareness that one has been devalued and lost status.

Paul's body, as he admits, displays the stigmata of Jesus along with other public markings concerning his bodily deportment. The stigma of his "uncommon appearance" would have had a profound effect on Paul's social identity—in comparison to the social/cultural canons of beauty and honor Paul's appearance fell short. His social identity based on these norms lay in tatters—his was a "spoiled identity"—the idea that somehow Paul perceived himself to be imperfect with respect to the standards of society in which he lived.[45]

Paul mentions that he has been given a thorn in the flesh (2 Corinthians 12:7–9), that he was of uncommon sight and of contemptible speech (2 Corinthians 10:10), and that he bore the marks of Jesus upon his body (Galatians 6:17). Paul understood that the world around him, members of his communities both enemies and friends, would have perceived him as responsible for his condition, because he had control over what happened to him (stop being a trouble maker that precipitated the beatings, imprisonments, and the like) and, even if he ultimately did not have control, that his bodily condition (illness) was perhaps a form of punishment from his god for wrong doing. Therefore, being marked with disgrace and infamy was a stigma for Paul—others around Paul saw him as responsible even though he may have had nothing to do with what branded his body. Nevertheless, holding himself responsible for what had happened to him was a critical feature in the generation of shame—it was also something on which he must act. Without taking on the shame of his stigmatization he was powerless. Hence, he identified fully with the shame of his contemptible condition and in this identification he strategically subverted the canons of honor and shame rapaciously applied to all others who also wore socially imposed stigmata as Paul did. Indeed, it could said that the stigmata of Paul were his most potent weapon in defending his apostolic credentials and making himself known to the communities in Rome. In the agonistic, cut-throat environment for honor Paul had failed and so he played the

43 Lewis, "Shame and Stigma," 127.
44 Lewis, "Shame and Stigma," 127.
45 Lewis, "Shame and Stigma," 131.

game according to new rules—what was considered foolish was wise; what was considered weak was strong; what was considered powerless was powerful; what was ugly was now beautiful—these new values were part of a new court of reputation in the making.

Of interest here is that Paul did not try to hide his shame—one of a number shame behaviors. Jewett mentions that humans instinctively hide their shame. There are in fact a number of behaviors that are part of shame: coping with or hiding shame, avoiding shame, keeping it secret, making reparations.[46] Paul does not hide, avoid, or keep his shame secret—he acknowledges it and by doing so it serves a reparative function.

Paul's distinguishing marks, after all, were socially apparent and perceived offensive to Paul and to those around him. As Lewis states, "the degree to which the stigma is socially apparent is the degree to which one must negotiate the issue of shame, not only for oneself but between oneself and others who witness the stigma."[47] It is also for this reason that stigmata are such powerful elicitors of shame. Paul goes out of his way to redefine the shame of his stigmata elicited in others by negotiating with them to alter their perceptions and language about what constitutes shame—there is nobility in a weak, marked body. "In place of the ordinary Greco-Roman assumption that the strong should dominate the weak while holding contempt, Paul argues that 'we the powerful are obligated to bear the weakness of the powerless and not to please ourselves.'"[48] In renegotiating the parameters of what counts for shame, Paul removes the power of the stigma, not only in himself but also in others, to reflect a spoiled self—spoiled by some public mark, such as behavior, sickness, malformation, lack of education, barbarian.

An additional important matter to consider is the power of stigma and the shame it elicits to spread—what has been called stigma and shame contagion.[49] Lewis points out that "the shame impact of stigma is wide; it not only affects those who are stigmatized but also those associated with the person so marked."[50] Sometimes labelled "courtesy stigma" they are contagious and affect those around the stigmatized person—"like an infectious disease, the stigma not only appears for the victim of the stigma but for all those who are associated with him or her."[51] Members of Paul's communities, because of their association with Paul, would themselves be stigmatized and suffered the same negative, social assessment as the stigmatized Paul. Little wonder that the community at Corinth was critical of Paul—they were bearing the contagion of Paul's shame. They were

---

46 Gilbert, "What is Shame?," 22–25.

47 Gilbert, "What is Shame?," 22–25.

48 Jewett, *Romans*, 15.

49 Lewis, "Shame and Stigma," 131.

50 Lewis, "Shame and Stigma," 131.

51 Lewis, "Shame and Stigma," 131.

marked as dishonorable people with the loss of status as a consequence. In response, Paul aligns himself with the marks of the crucified Christ and seeks to encourage members of his community to join him in his suffering. Paul was driven to redefine what counted for honor and shame in his world because the success of his mission to Spain depended upon it.

CONCLUSIONS

Rather than abandoning the honor shame game, Paul redefines it and redeploys it to his advantage. He spins it out in a new way in the manner that clever politicians are able to spin out positively what has brought shame upon them. It inverts the pyramids of power where the powerless are powerful, the ugly beautiful, the marginalized central, the lowly influential, the cross of execution the seat of authority, and so on. It is an honorable shame that counts for status and standing in the Pauline court of reputation and is not to be avoided, hidden, or denied—indeed it is to be displayed and its contagion is to spread to infect all communities and followers of Paul. Bear the bodily marks with pride, says Paul and in so doing subvert the political powers structures so capably upheld by the Romans. By doing so, you will become partners with me on my mission to Spain.

27

Response to Vancouver Colleagues

Robert Jewett

It is rare in a scholarly symposium to have one's work not only well understood but also creatively extended with a series of new insights. That is my experience with an extraordinary group of colleagues here in Vancouver. Dietmar Neufeld develops a new perspective on Paul's grappling with stigma, the spoiled self and shame contagion as explained by Paul Gilbert, Deborah Greenwald and David Harder, Michael Lewis and Erwing Goffman, none of whom, so far as I know, has ever been employed in interpreting Paul's theology.

This line of research clarifies how Paul redefined the parameters of honor and shame so that stigmas could be exhibited as signs of belongingness to Christ, a theme that Neufeld finds most explicitly in 2 Corinthians. This material correlates with my translation of Romans 8:33, "Who shall impeach God's elect?" This formulation presupposes that groups in Rome were disqualifying each other on the basis of adverse experiences that were thought to be shameful evidence of divine wrath. The catalogue of afflictions listed in 8:35 reveal that some groups sought to discredit the status of other groups on the premise that the elect should be exempt from misfortune. The verb *chōrizō* ("divide, separate") in 8:33 points in this direction and the content of the afflictions in 8:35 matches many details in 2 Corinthians where Paul countered the superapostles who claimed to possess transcendent power that allowed them to avoid adversities. Professor Neufeld concludes his brilliant essay by stating that the Roman congregations' acceptance of this contagion of shame in Christ would in Paul's view "make them partners with me on my mission to Spain," where the barbarians par excellence had long been shamed by Rome.

The apparent contradiction between this mission and Romans 13:1–7 is relentlessly exposed in the essay by Steve Black. He effectively criticizes scholarly efforts to sidestep the problem while showing that this passage contradicts both the Wisdom of Solomon and Paul's own statements about the empire in earlier letters. Even more problematic in Black's view is the contradiction between this passage and the argument in Romans against the imperial system of honor and shame. If my commentary is correct in perceiving a strategic motivation of eliciting support from believers in the imperial bureaucracy, this still does not relieve him from Black's charge of hypocrisy. He goes on to suggest that "sacrificing the ideals of the kingdom for the sake of the advancement of the kingdom" paved the way for the emergence of later Christian imperialism.

Robert Derrenbacker describes how the social location of his students leads to diametrically opposing views of Romans 13. He provides an accurate account of my historical and rhetorical approach to verses 1–7, lifting up the relevance of the context of 12:2 concerning non-conformity with the world and the exhortation to love in 13:8–10. He affirms the relevance of these details in countering the decontextualized interpretations of this passage that have arisen in response to November 9, 2011. "For if American Christians, for example, read Romans 13:1–7 in this decontextualized manner, then the 'governing authorities' could be granted a *carte blanche* of sorts . . . . Many might see United States foreign policy . . . as simply the purposeful and useful 'bearing of the sword . . . executing wrath on the wrongdoers.'" Prof. Derrenbacker is critical of the "potentially dangerous mix of the imperial cult and zealous nationalism" and follows James D. G. Dunn in insisting that "Christians could be involved in the political structures of the time and wield political power without ceasing to be Christians and indeed as part of their Christian service."

Harry Maier weighs the question of whether Romans offers "a vision that outlines an alternative to Empire" or a complement thereto, suggesting instead that Homi Babha's concept of hybridity is useful in showing that Paul both mimics and mocks the imperial system. In Paul's view, "Jesus' lordship becomes the hybrid double and mockery of Roman imperial power," erected in the early Christian communities in the slums and also in the marketplaces "across the street from . . . the Empire's monuments." In place of the "massive co-optation" that I claim for Romans 13, he perceives "a strategic hybridization of power." In the end, Maier doubts that "Paul's gospel gives us the change to Empire we can believe in."

The discovery made during later lectures in Beijing could not have been taken into account in the Vancouver discussion, but it seems to me that defending Roman rule in 13:1–7 as the lesser of evils when compared with revolutionary zealotism throws new light on this issue. It recognizes that the sinful quality of all human institutions and agents requires choices between shades of grey. That Paul overstated the rationale of his choice in Romans still needs to be recognized. But this ambivalence seems more clearly reflected in Professor Maier's stance between the Peace Keepers monument and the "emblem of Fortress America," in which factors of power and practicality need to be taken into account. To use Steve Black's concluding words, the "idealistic Paul who refused to back down did not exist," but that possibility is also unavailable for us. To believe that we are capable of following pure ideals without taking circumstances and our own shortcomings into account brings us into the arena of zealotism. To use the rationale of 1 Corinthians 13, "we all see through a glass darkly," and the failure to recognize this all-too-human condition leads to the deadly frustration described in Romans 7.

In a surprising way, critiques by colleagues sometimes allow one to understand dimensions of one's work that are disguised by mountains of detail. Harry Maier places my commentary in the context of earlier critiques of American zealotism and simplistic affirmations of American exceptionalism. I was largely unaware that both dimensions of my work had "Empire" in view; prior to this symposium I would more likely have described the link in terms of a long preoccupation with issues of zealotism. To think through the connections between these issues is one of the tasks this symposium helped me to articulate. I am grateful to all four of my Vancouver colleagues for their generous and provocative work.

The Auckland Symposium
July 10, 2008

28

The Issue of Shame in Robert Jewett's Commentary on Romans

Douglas A. Campbell

Robert Jewett's commentary is a milestone in the interpretation of Romans—both an extraordinary summation of the rich previous tradition of interpretation, and a radical new departure from that tradition, having perceived many of its oversights.[1]

The vast majority of preceding commentaries assert that Paul's gospel is presented in the letter's first four chapters, and is oriented there toward individual recognition of culpability before the bar of divine justice, followed by the generous redirection of the penalties appropriate for human transgression onto Jesus on the cross—a view of the atonement as vicarious, substitutionary, satisfactory, and penal. This useful redirection can then be appropriated by faith and faith alone—the generous offer made by the Pauline gospel. To ignore this offer leaves individuals mired in transgression and rightly exposed to God's wrath or, still worse, struggling futilely to satisfy God's ethical demands by their own efforts—the mire of legalism best exemplified by Judaism although not limited to that constituency. (Luther thought that many Catholics were in this hypocritical and deluded location as well.) The intelligent response is of course not to ignore the offer but to exercise faith and receive righteousness as a gift, like Abraham as Paul expounds Genesis 15:6 in Romans 4:1–8, at which point converts can move on to consider the rest of Paul's letter.

This approach—known rather unhappily as "Lutheran" thanks to Stendahl's classic exposé—has been much criticized of late, although not

[1] Robert Jewett, *Romans* (Hermeneia; Minneapolis: Fortress Press, 2007) —all page references hereafter to this text unless otherwise stated. Note, my task here is to focus on the issue of shame, and so I must—rather regrettably—overlook Jewett's important contributions to the lexicography and syntax, rhetoric, "cartographical imaging," and tradition-history of Romans, to name only a few further important contributions.

displaced successfully in exegetical terms.[2] As I just hinted, it is difficult to know why Paul wrote chapters 5–15 of Romans since the main issues have all been resolved by 4:25. Indeed, it is difficult to *comprehend* much of chapters 5–15 in relation to the system established by chapters 1–4; just how ethics, for example, is possible after the earlier critique of ethics and correlation of salvation with faith alone, is not entirely clear. The portrait of the Jew, from which salvation springs, is also arguably unfair and even sinister in a post-Holocaust era; the generic Jew is apparently accused in 2:21–22 of hypocrisy, thieving, adultery, and temple robbery—activities that most of us are probably not convinced that all Jews undertake regularly!

A further famous difficulty in the "Lutheran" reading is its essentially coherent character, which entails a significant interpretative vulnerability in terms of contingency.

In the early 1980s, J.-C. (Chris) Beker articulated a methodological imperative for Pauline interpretation that was widely accepted.[3] Paul's letters were elicited by practical circumstances, and so addressed issues consistently in this manner—contingently, as he put it. However, interpreters had for milliennia been more interested in Paul's theological abstractions—his coherence—and so ignored the fact that such coherence had to be filtered through his essentially contingent texts and not merely lifted out of such discussions, thereby baptizing circumstantial advice and localized dynamics as eternal truth. Much distortion of Paul's legacy had resulted from ignoring this simple situational texture in his texts.

Pauline scholars have by and large accepted this dictum, but have struggled—as Beker himself did—to read Romans contingently, tying its notoriously sweeping and abstract discussions in the letter body to practical local issues at Rome. And the Lutheran reading is certainly vulnerable in this relation. It essentially assumes that Paul is discussing coherent matters with the Roman Christians, laying out his gospel systematically, without knowing why he actually undertook this unparalleled approach. Of course the church reads Romans in this fashion, but the academy, while not necessarily disavowing the letter's history of interpretation, wants to know why Romans was actually written to Rome in the first place, and what the early Christians heard when it arrived. Hence it is especially significant that Jewett's reorientation of the central substantive thrust of Romans away from the traditional gospel of penal substitution to one focused on *the transformation of shame* can integrate with a plausible

---

[2] Krister Stendahl, "The Apostle Paul and the Introspective Conscience of the West," *Harvard Theological Review* 56 (1963), 199-215.

[3] J. Christiaan Beker, *Paul the Apostle: The Triumph of God in Life and Thought* (Philadelphia: Fortress Press, 1984 [1980]).

account of Romans' contingency.[4] Indeed, to my knowledge his is the first major commentary ever to offer a sustained contingent reading of Romans—an important achievement in its own right.[5]

Robert Jewett is conscious of Günther Klein's important emphasis on 15:20–21 and Paul's citation there of Isaiah 52:15—that "they shall see who have never been informed about him, and those who have never heard of him shall understand."[6] If Paul is the fulfillment of this scripture then he ought not strictly speaking to build on the apostolic foundation that already exists at Rome, whether preaching by letter or in person. So Jewett suggests that Paul's overarching goal in his letter is not to establish his own mission there—except perhaps in an ancillary way—as much as to enlist the Romans' support for a mission to the unevangelized hinterland of Spain. The challenges of a Spanish mission—a barbarian land with no Greek and little Latin, and lacking Jewish synagogues—necessitate extensive support from the Roman Christians. But six interrelated and profoundly unhealthy honor and shame dynamics potentially obstruct this massive cooperative Christian venture to the west.

The Romans Christians are principally poor and isolated, meeting in tiny tenements. Moreover, they are divided by different attitudes to certain key Jewish practices—eating taboos and sabbath observance—which generate a division between "the weak" and "the strong." This division blends into a difference between Jewish and Gentile Christians, which blends in turn into a difference between Jews and Christians—divisions exacerbated by the experiences of the Jewish and Christian communities at Rome under the Julio-Claudians. A prejudice against barbarians in general and the Spanish in particular is also present—part of an entire culture of honor-shame dynamics and bitter agonistic struggle that characterized the Roman Empire. Indeed, it is possible to speak of a pervasive and toxic discourse of shame operating in every

---

4 Robert Jewett announces this interpretative agenda at the outset (reiterating it frequently). In the Preface he explains why his commentary is dedicated to Bishop John Colenso, missionary to the indigenous people of southern Africa and author of an innovative commentary on Romans himself, in 1861. "Although he did not employ the categories of honor and shame as shaped by modern social theory, and despite his outdated grasp of the historical situation of the Roman audience, he was the first to suggest that Paul aimed to overcome prejudice against allegedly inferior peoples" (xv). See John William Colenso, *Commentary on Romans*, ed. Jonathan Draper (Pietermaritzburg, South Africa: Cluster, 2003 [1861]). Esler's commentary could perhaps be noted at this point as well: P. F. Esler, *Conflict and Identity in Romans. The Social Setting of Paul's Letter* (Minneapolis: Fortress Press, 2003).

5 Robert Jewett has been a leading biographer of Paul for decades, and so his account of Romans' contingency is sophisticated and complex: see especially Robert Jewett, *A Chronology of Paul's Life* (Philadelphia: Fortress Press, 1979). But for our present purposes I will have to simplify it a little.

6 See "Paul's Purpose in Writing the Epistle to the Romans," in edited by Karl Donfried, *The Romans Debate* (Revised and Expanded Edition; Peabody: Hendrickson, 1991) , 29–43.

dimension of the context of Romans.

This discourse can be mobilized by any one of a number of key motifs—boasting, glory, status, honor, respect, submission, shame, and contempt. Various ordering categories are also important—largely binary stratifications of markers and groups in relation to one another on ascending scales of status and directly correlative, descending scales of shame. Groups positioned lower generally lack the autonomy, influence, status, materiel, power, and space, accorded those positioned higher. Contempt, rule, and exploitation of the lower by the higher are "natural." Markers of inferiority and contempt are often ethnic and/or gendered.

This discourse can be viewed in certain respects as a game that the inhabitants of the Principate played in a profoundly agonistic mode, competing with one another to ascend the oppositional continuum of shame and honor as high as was possible. To lose the game, however, was precisely to be ashamed—an outcome that for the proud could often only be assuaged appropriately by suicide, the ultimate form of withdrawal. It goes without saying that this discourse is inherently divisive and generative of conflict.

Paul seeks to address these unhealthy dynamics in the Christian community at Rome as best he can by letter, so that his overarching goal of a Spanish mission can take place, at which point he will have taken the gospel from the easternmost part of the world to its westernmost boundary.[7] The transformation of the honor-shame system, along with its competitive and divisive dynamics, is therefore a critical prerequisite for the apostolic mission to the ends of the earth.

Now this is an impressive account of Romans' contingency; certainly it is superior to the majority of theories currently on offer. But how exactly does it enable Jewett to read the letter in detail? I detect a set of *six* main textual strategies that foreground the transformation of shame. How does Paul—according to Jewett—actually *deal* with shame in Romans in a sustained way?

TEXTUAL STRATEGIES

1. Robert Jewett's rereading of the basic argument in Romans 2 is innovative and important. In 2:1 Paul's text clearly turns on someone—"a judger." And from 2:17 onward, Paul addresses a hypocritical Jewish teacher at length. Traditional interpretation has identified this figure with Judaism in general, building from its pejorative description, and

[7] And it should be borne in mind that people in Paul's day probably pictured the world as rectangular, identifying the Roman imperium with the world, so the east-west axis was by far the longest; note especially in this relation Jewett's use of the Peutinger Tables and related ancient cartography.

an ostensible negative account of the pre-Christian state more broadly, to a Christian solution in terms of faith alone. A minority tradition of interpreters has lately suggested a more circumstantial role for this figure in Paul's argument—as an exemplary hypocritical sage of some sort (if not a series of such figures). But this suggestion has lacked plausibility; we have not known why Paul would address such a straw man here. However, Jewett solves this problem and eliminates the nagging anti-Jewish reading at one stroke by suggesting that this figure is a stereotypical bigot that Paul humiliates with God's impartiality. The Roman audience would have detected the numerous clues in the text that Paul was attempting such a comic subversion—a subversion that will later come back to haunt the Roman Christians themselves if they indulge in similar arrogant judgments, and chapter 14 suggests that they do! This text is consequently a rhetorical trap for any arrogant Roman Christians, whether weak or strong—an ingenious interpretation of a difficult text.

2. Just as God's impartiality crushes the pretentious blaggard, generating a certain sort of equality, the criterion of salvation by faith alone also establishes equality. None can boast of their ethical superiority before the judgment seat of God, and none can boast of salvation over against another, since all are saved by the same simple act—a fairly standard Protestant contention. The faithful Abraham is therefore also an equalizing figure who reduces the stratified opposition of honor and shame to a single horizontal plane. All Christians are children of Abraham, saved, like him, by faith alone. There is no ground here for one Christian to claim superiority over against another. Hence, the honor-shame game is undercut once again—although here in terms of the gospel's solution, rather than its definition of the problem.

3. The first two complementary arguments against shame that we have just noted remain within the basic framework of the Lutheran reading of Romans 1–4, although clearly some of its key terms have been altered. Nevertheless, the reading still works "forward," building from problem to solution, and the entire model is underpinned by a God of retributive justice who judges and saves impartially. It is just that the traditional preoccupation with an abstract conception of Judaism in the problem has been replaced by a new emphasis on the dynamics of shame and their importance for Paul's mission in and beyond Rome. But Jewett also not infrequently articulates a rather different argument against shame—one that works "backward." I am not sure that it possesses a key textual center as much as it informs a set of small sub-sections (although Jewett may well be able to correct me on this point). In these sub-sections the theological pressure on shame derives from correlative assertions concerning human depravity and salvation by *grace*—that is,

unconditionally, in what we might dub an "Augustinian" dynamic.

I am aware that several studies have recently emphasized the conditionality of much "grace" language in the Greco-Roman world.[8] But I share Jewett's view that Paul's language of grace conveys a countercultural message of unconditionality. God has intervened into a lost and corrupt world through Christ, Paul asserts, saving all out of sheer benevolence, without conditions or contractual expectations. So here once again we encounter correlative notions of sinfulness and generous divine action, but not framed by justice. Rather, the frame is simply that divine benevolence. And *this* theological dynamic places all the proud and the shamed in solidarity in both sinfulness and salvation, thereby undercutting (again) any claims by some to superiority—or any affirmation by others of innate inferiority.

Perhaps this alternative dynamic is clearest in Jewett's exposition of chapter 6—although assisted strongly by Romans 8![9] Indeed, arguably the most transformational sequence in Romans is found in chapters 6–8. Chapter 6 specifically charts a transition from shameful categories—here associated particularly with the sexual exploitations common in slavery—to the glorious freedom of divine childhood. So perhaps it is here that we find the heart of Paul's gospel as it transforms toxic, shame-based cultures and identities.

4. Jewett reads Romans 7 biographically, as an account of Paul's life under the law. Paul tells us elsewhere that he was a murderously zealous Jew, and so Jewett combines these two readings to suggest that Romans 7 is an account of a Jew who aggressively pursues his nation's honor, protecting its customs, but turns out to have been arrogantly pursuing a way of death. The pursuit of honor and avoidance of shame turns out in this way to be the exact opposite—the pursuit of a shameful ethic that lacks honor and opposes God, resulting in a state of tortured stupidity. This biographical exemplum consequently serves to increase further the rhetorical pressure of the letter on the politics of honor and shame as Roman Christians may have been practicing them.

5. I can also detect an "overturning" dynamic in Jewett's exegesis of various sub-sections in Romans—a dynamic informed ultimately by 1 Corinthians 1 as well as by explicit Romans material. Nevertheless the shame of Jesus' crucifixion as the site of the divine saving action arguably generates this dynamic automatically, even if it is spelled out most explicitly by Paul in 1 Corinthians 1. If the glory of God is operative through the shame

---

[8] An important contribution to the debate concerning Paul's view of grace is John M. G. Barclay, "By the Grace of God I Am What I Am: Grace and Agency in Philo and Paul," in ed. John M. G. Barclay, and S. J. Gathercole, *Divine and Human Agency in Paul and His Cultural Environment* (London: T. & T. Clark, 2006) , 140–57.

[9] Treated respectively on pages 390–427: 10 indexed references to shame; and 474–554: 6 references.

of the cross, then the shamed of this world are potentially the site of the glory of God, while, by the same token, the exalted of this world are potentially emptied of their own glory and judged inferior and ultimately of no account.

6. Significantly, Jewett can now link the rather sweeping, abstract discussions of the letter body with the more practical advice of the final major argumentative section, which begins in chapter 12, and of the letter closing. We now understand why Paul lays out here a number of practical ways in which the Roman Christians can unite—in their love feasts, in submission to the local governing authorities, in the refusal to judge one another, but rather in greeting one another with the kiss of peace and the blessing of the one true God, while praying for the success of the mission to the Gentile world, both in Jerusalem and Spain.

EVALUATION

It seems then that a suite of specific textual strategies informs Jewett's overarching interpretation of Romans in its original context as an attack on the agonistic discourse of honor and shame surrounding the Roman Christians in ultimate support of a cooperative Christian venture to a distant land.[10] And of course the question now arises: Is this sophisticated, innovative, and powerful new approach to Romans actually right?!

I suggest that we can respond to this query on two levels. We can ask if Jewett has provided plausible readings of Romans in specific terms that take us beyond the difficulties of the Lutheran paradigm (and those of its critics). But we should also consider his rereading at a deeper level—and I will concentrate on this in what follows, letting our discussion raise the detailed exegetical questions: Has Pauline studies consistently underplayed a crucial contextual dimension in relation

[10] And the force of this plea can be felt especially in a North American setting, where the churches seem to be so divided, and so hostile to one another. Some of Jewett's other studies are informative at this point: cf. Robert Jewett, *The Captain America Complex: The Dilemma of Zealous Nationalism* (Second Editiion; Santa Fe: Bear & Company, 1984) ; Robert Jewett, and John Shelton Lawrence, *The American Monomyth*, 2nd ed. (Lanham: University Press of America, 1988); Robert Jewett, *Saint Paul at the Movies: The Apostle's Dialogue with American Culture* (Louisville: Westminster John Knox, 1993); Robert Jewett, *Saint Paul Returns to the Movies: Triumph over Shame* (Grand Rapids: Eerdmans, 1999), and Robert Jewett and John Shelton Lawrence, *Captain America and the Crusade against Evil: The Dilemma of Zealous Nationalism* (Grand Rapids: Eerdmans, 2003).

to Romans—the phenomenon of shame?[11] But in order to address this programmatic concern satisfactorily, some additional conversation partners will prove useful.

A THEORY OF EMOTION

In 1872 Charles Darwin published an extraordinary but rather overlooked book on human emotion—*The Expression of Emotions in Man and Animals.*[12] In 1867 he had sent a questionnaire to missionaries around the world asking if various facial dynamics associated with fundamental emotional states were evident in different cultures (and using photographs to illustrate his inquiries). He asked, among other things, "does shame excite a blush when the colour of the skin allows it to be visible? and especially how low down the body does the blush extend?" The response was that it did, and so a European pastor could understand exactly what an Indonesian maidservant was experiencing in basic emotional terms, even though their language, culture, and history were entirely distinct.

These insights were the origin of a theory of social psychology that culminated in Silvan Tomkins's four-volume magnum opus *Affect Imagery Consciousness.*[13] Significantly, even though this theory was developed in the 1950s, much of the research on the human brain that took place in the 90s has confirmed its accuracy—during which decade it is said that we have learned perhaps 75% of what we know about the brain.

Tomkins—sometimes dubbed "the American Einstein"—generated a sophisticated account of human thought and action of great moment for our present question. Perhaps his greatest insight concerned the essential involvement of emotion with the thinking and further activity of humanity, although he preferred to speak more precisely of "affects." Affects are integrated mental and biophysiological states extending

---

11 I am not going to appeal at this juncture to existing treatments of shame and related matters in NT studies. The honor-shame dynamic has been treated at times, perhaps more in Gospel than in Pauline studies, although it reappears in the currently fashionable debate concerning Paul's putative response to pagan imperial politics. In my view, although much of this material is helpful, it lacks methodological depth. The honor-shame material is well introduced by David A. deSilva, *Honor, Patronage, Kinship, and Purity: Unlocking New Testament Culture* (Downers Grove: InterVarsity, 2000). Horsley is central to the politics and imperium debates: see Richard A. Horsley edited, *Paul and Empire* (Harrisburg: Trinity Press International, 1997) ; Richard A. Horsley edited, *Paul and Politics: Ekklesia, Israel, Imperium, Interpretation* (Harrisburg: Trinity Press International, 2000); and Richard A. Horsley edited, *Paul and the Roman Imperial Order* (London & Harrisburg: Trinity Press International [Continuum], 2004).

12 (New York: D. Appleton, 1896).

13 Silvan S. Tomkins, *Affect Imagery Consciousness. The Complete Edition*, 4 volumes (Philadelphia: Springer, 2008 [1962, 1963, 1991, 1992]). Tomkins's thought is well introduced by Donald L Nathanson, *Shame and Pride: Affect, Sex, and the Birth of the Self* (New York: W. W. Norton, 1992). And D. B. Moore and J. M. McDonald, *Transforming Conflict in Workplaces and Communities* (Maryborough: Australian Print Group, 2000).

across the boundary between cognition and the body. Certain "feelings" that we are all familiar with are experienced consciously–fright, rage, anxiety, or elation–but these feelings are invariably linked with certain observable physiological responses. So, for example, a feeling of shame is always accompanied by a blush response, as Darwin perceived, but also with a slumping of the shoulders and slight curving of the spine, a lowering of the face to break any direct gaze, and a disordering of conscious activity that can be registered as mumbling or muddled speech. In addition, a particular rate and gradient of neural firing is present–in the case of shame, a sudden sharp interruption of the firing associated with any previous emotion, which is often what makes it so unpleasant. Tomkins detected (correctly) nine affects and closely-related auxiliaries, each associated with biophysiological responses, including universally recognizable facial dispositions: joy, excitement, shame, surprise, anxiety, disgust, anger, fear, and what he called dissmell–a previously unnoticed affective response associated with stench. (The surprise affect was also only finally determined through the introduction of advanced freeze-frame photography.)

Tomkins went on to argue that these affects organize all incoming sensory data, and lie at the root of all human responses to that data. Without affective engagement, human beings do not respond to data. They are inert. Nothing happens. Hence, the affective system is actually the sorting system that tells the person what data to pay attention to, and how to act in response. Data itself–which is streaming at an extraordinary rate into the brain–is organized and prioritized in what Tomkins called scenes and scripts. Recognizably repeated sequences of stimulus-affect-response are collected and stacked as similar emotional or affective scenes, various scenes then being arranged into particular sequences that are usefully viewed as scripts (and these overlap with notions like "roles").

Intriguingly, affects are highly contagious. People are programmed to resonate with one another–especially infants with their first caregivers. In particular, facial affects resonate from person to watching person, with higher affective intensities causing more intense resonances–and usually without conscious realization. People then learn to stack these programmed emotional responses together, and sequence them into more complex phenomena like love and honor, from their parents, peers, and cultures.

There is of course a lot more to say about all this, but it must suffice to note here that (if Tomkins is right) shame is quite simply an enduring component of human consciousness and biophysiology, and a very important one. Affects themselves are neutral programs. They have to be coded and sequenced in relation to their environments, so different environments do this in different ways. (They can also be modified by chemicals and pathologies.) But even a cursory glance at most cultures reveals the degree to which the negative affects that revolve around unpleasant feelings like shame, stench, or nausea, are written into various social scripts and roles, so that people operating in terms of those codes experience negative emotion constantly, both from within and without. Shame scripts are not always a bad thing, *but they can be!* It is doubtless a good thing to view the rape of children as shameful. But it is probably not a good thing (cross-cultural sensitivity notwithstanding!) that traditional Hindu society views its untouchable class—the *Dalits*—as disgusting, polluting, and contemptible from birth—a script that induces acute self-shame, not to mention justifies constant discrimination and violence by members of higher castes.

Hence, when Jewett asks us to consider the central role that shame scripts are playing in Paul's ancient context, he is doing no more than asking us to recognize a basic, verifiable, and extremely powerful aspect of human nature that is operative in manifold and often sinister ways. Consequently, he cannot really be wrong in directing our attention to a human experience that, precisely because it is so unpleasant, has largely avoided serious academic scrutiny until the second half of the twentieth century—and even then, only received sustained attention by some, and through the 90s. If the Pauline gospel is to have anything to say to one of the most potentially toxic aspects of human experience, it must speak to shame. But how?

Toxic sequences of affects, which usually emphasize shame, can be changed. The situations and experiences activating toxic sequences can be reprogrammed with new, healthier sequences, if that situation is revisited, experienced in all its negativity, but then communally framed so as to make new, healthier sequences possible (this being a frightfully compact description of a special type of conferencing used to transform situations of conflict where toxic affective sequences are prevalent). And I would suggest that this is precisely what the narrative of a suffering, crucified, and resurrected Lord offers, in the context of a community already experiencing a degree of transformation, and so resonating and reflecting that new set of sequences to one another—a community that starts its own story precisely in the negativities of its own past, but then traces a trajectory repeatedly through to a new, healthier set of narratives and sequences. A restructuring of human thinking and emotion in their intrinsic interrelationships thereby takes place, as Paul seems to suggest in Romans 12 and 13: "be transformed by the renewal of the mind, that you may ascertain what the will of God is—the good, acceptable, and perfect." "[P]ut on the Lord Jesus Christ and make no provision for the flesh [to gratify] its desires." (And so on!) Here the old narrative is indeed "overturned." A solidarity in negativity is displaced by a solidarity in salvation, in a broadly liberative process that is initiated unconditionally and graciously, as it must be. It is, moreover, an inherently relational, personal process precisely because it resonates affectively, from face to face. And it has practical consequences like sharing food and kissing group members in greeting—this last being a crucial antidote to cultural scripts of disgust and contempt.

So it seems to me that in relation to the deeper methodological issues, Jewett is profoundly right. Shame is at the center of Romans, because it is at the center of most of what we do as human beings in the grip of affects that often we don't fully recognize or understand. Hence, shame was at the center of Colenso's African colonial experience in the nineteenth century, and Jewett's experience of vicious racial dynamics in Chicago in the second half of the twentieth. Moreover, Paul is providing resources for the resolution of affective toxicity generated by inappropriate and sustained shame—especially in its Augustinian theological dynamic, and his claim that the gospel of a shamed but resurrected Messiah can overturn and revalue the lives of the shamed. All of which is to suggest that strategies three, five, and six noted above seem to be both extremely important and uncannily accurate.

PARTING REMARK

A parting remark just prior to closing.[14] In the light of the foregoing it seems that the affective script underlying penal substitution is

[14] Given more time, I would note two more issues:

(1) My first is a question: Are Jewett and I in danger of endorsing an essentially eudaemonistic ethic that actually eviscerates a gospel of transcendance? Is this process of transformation in relation to human affects entirely immanent? Is it even a fundamentally ethical system, as against one of human fulfillment or happiness? I don't think so, although this danger should be recognized. Hopefully a robust doctrine of creation, grounded in a prior and even more robust doctrine of redemption, can extend a limited endorsement to eudaemonistic intimations. Cf. Karl Barth, *Church Dogmatics. Volume: II. The Doctrine of God. Part 2* (London & New York: T. & T. Clark International [Continuum], 2004 [1942]), §§36–39, pp. 509–781. And I'm not sure that I need much more than this. If virtue and happiness should not be equated, they should probably not be separated too strongly either. Cf. Daniel Gilbert, *Stumbling on Happiness* (Vintage, 2007). But clearly much more could and should be said in this relation. And

(2) there is now no need to get too binary in our analyses, running the risk of contextual oversimplification. Although I have strongly endorsed the importance of shame, characterizing it at bottom simply as an affect (and in fact the interruption of affect), "honor" is a complex, scripted notion, probably involving numerous affects in sequence. Hence we are really dealing in our social analyses from this point on with scripted variations on nine affects and auxiliaries in complex sequences—enough to take us well beyond most binary analyses. Tomkins in fact suggested a broad binary categorization of scripts into those that maximized the positive affects over against those that did not, being resultantly toxic and destructive (the eudaemonistic commitment). But clearly there is a lot of room in descriptive terms within this broad agenda. And this realization should deliver greater flexibility and subtlety to our social descriptions.

arguably highly toxic.[15] It sequences the affect of anger or rage after any shame or disgust induced by wrongdoing. The latter is doubtless appropriate, but the claim that the only appropriate response to shame is anger locates violence and death at the heart of any "correct" response to wrongdoing—a multiplication of two of the most powerful negative affects together, and in the name of God! Note, moreover, that the affect of anger or rage is the human biophysiological preparation for violence—necessary in evolutionary terms when facing large predators or hunting big game, but arguably for not much more than that. This affective sequence is demonstrated clearly in the honor killings that Muslims regularly mete out on sisters and daughters who have shamed their families through inappropriate contact with unauthorized males—shame eliciting anger and being expunged (supposedly) by death, even of a close family member. But this dynamic is certainly not limited to traditional Islamic societies. It is vital to appreciate that the Augustinian dynamic could not really be more different in terms of its affective sequence from this penal sequence, approaching the shame of sin in restorative and transformational, not punitive and annihilationist terms! Radically and irreconcilably different conceptions of atonement are in view. Indeed, viewed from the vantage point of an Augustinian script, the penal approach inscribes a toxic sequence at the heart of the Christian gospel and the divine nature—a sequence that is arguably both self-destructive and blasphemous.

Robert Jewett's commentary on Romans is in my view rather more than a magisterial academic treatment (although it is this); it is—like Colenso's—a prophetic text that sees past the conundrums of the ancient world to address an enduring toxicity at the heart of Western, if not of all societies. And in this respect I hope that it is not so much the last word as the all-important first word in a new scholarly phase in Pauline interpretation. Jewett's commentary asks us to see Paul as promoting a gospel that sought to move people beyond shame, and hence also beyond much of the discrimination and violence that is frequently associated with that unpleasant cessation of affect—*toxic sequences that the prevailing readings of Romans not only cannot transform, but positively endorse!* Hence, in certain key respects, Jewett's commentary is really the proverbial looking glass through which we can glimpse an exciting new socio-psychological and soteriological wonderland beyond the violence, divisions, and distortions of our own locations. I suggest we jump into it, and through it.

---

[15] Useful discussions of this issues include J. Denny Weaver, *The Nonviolent Atonement* (Grand Rapids: Eerdmans, 2001). The classic study is Anselm's *Why God Became Man*, available in Anselm, *The Major Works/Anselm of Canterbury*, edited by Brian Davies and G. R. Evans (Oxford/New York: Oxford University Press, 1998), 260–356.

29

Paul, the Romans and Us

Murray Rae

The brief I was given for this paper was to offer a theological response to Professor Jewett's Romans Commentary with a particular eye on the New Zealand context. I propose to undertake that task by considering, first of all, why a letter penned in the first century to Christians in Rome enlisting support for a proposed mission to Spain should have anything to do with the New Zealand context in the twenty first century, or indeed with any context remote in time and space from the immediate horizons of the apostle Paul.

After a brief account of the epistle's relevance and authority for our own contexts I shall move then to a consideration of what the epistle to the Romans, as explicated by Professor Jewett, might have to say to us. For the most part, I shall take it that Professor Jewett is right in the account he gives of Paul's epistle, at least in respect of Paul's missiological intent and in his claim that Paul is eager to show that 'the gospel of impartial grace shatters all claims of superior status or theology',[1] but I shall also raise a question about whether Professor Jewett's account of Paul's alleged lack of interest in doctrinal agreement among the Roman Christians can be sustained without qualification. The discussion of Paul's missiological concerns will take place against the backdrop of the church's interest, in New Zealand and beyond, in what it means for the church, post-Christendom, to engage in Christian mission to the West.

I. The Contemporary Relevance and Authority of Paul's Epistle

The starting point is provided by Professor Jewett himself who writes in the Introduction to his Commentary, "My goal is to sharpen

1 Robert Jewett, *Romans: A Commentary* (Minneapolis: Fortress Press, 2007), xv.

the ancient horizon of the text so that it can enter into dialogue with the modern horizons of our various interpretive enterprises."[2] Earlier, in the Preface, he expresses the hope that, "the extraordinary relevance of Romans to the situation of cultural, religious, and imperial conflicts is easily discernible."[3] The assumption underlying this hope and the accompanying expression of intent is that the ancient epistle addressed to the Christians in Rome has something to say in our own day, at least to those who, by calling themselves Christians, confess some commonality with Paul's original audience. At the very least, Christians of today will read with interest if what Paul says to the Roman churches may be taken as in some way definitive of what it means in any age to be a Christian church enjoined to participate in the mission established by the gospel of Jesus Christ.

I want to begin, therefore, by enquiring after the relevance and authority of Paul's epistle for a Christian audience of our own time and place? Is there anything in the epistle itself suggesting that Paul would countenance the idea that his words could have a relevance and authority beyond his immediate context? To begin with there is the straightforward point that Paul himself is concerned in Romans with an imperative to take the gospel to the ends of the earth. Paul himself clearly believes that the good news of Jesus Christ is of urgent relevance to everyone everywhere, to Jews and Greeks and barbarians certainly, and also to both wise and foolish (Romans 1:13). Professor Jewett draws attention to numerous other occasions in which the universal scope of Paul's missionary zeal is apparent, and notes, in commentary on chapter 4, verse 16, the particular importance of the word *pas* (all) in Romans.[4] No one is excluded from the impartial grace of God on the grounds of ethnicity, class, social status, and, we might add, temporal and geographical location. The grace of God is extended to all who believe. Insofar as the epistle spells out Paul's understanding of the nature and implications of that grace, it becomes relevant to our own situations of conflict and exclusion, be they ethnic, social, economic or otherwise.

The universal scope of Paul's gospel is explicit also in the argument of 1:18–3:26 in which Paul draws upon Scriptural authority attesting that all have sinned and fall short of God's glory (3:23) all are subject to divine judgement (3:19), and all stand in need of the righteous forbearance of God (3:25). Likewise in chapter 5:12–21, Paul is eager that all people should understand the decisive bearing of Adam's sinfulness upon their own behaviour and identity, just so that they might recognise

---

2 Jewett, *Romans*, 3.
3 Jewett, *Romans*, xv.
4 See Jewett, *Romans*, 330.

also the 'overflowing dominion of grace'.[5] The radical inclusiveness of Paul's gospel is a prominent theme in Professor Jewett's commentary, well justified, I suggest, by the burden of Paul's own argument. On this basis we may assent to Professor Jewett's suggestion that what Paul has to say in a time and place far removed from our own is *relevant* to our own situation.[6]

I want to press the point a little further however, to move beyond the question of relevance to that of authority. Christians read Paul's epistle not just because it might be relevant, but also because they believe it has a particular divine authority. We must ask therefore, how might its authority be construed, and, again, would Paul himself countenance his words being treated in this way? Scholars in the academy might opt to avoid the question of this text's authority but academic conventions ought to be flouted if they prevent us from engaging fully with Paul's text. Paul himself, after all, is emboldened to write to the Romans strictly on the basis of his being "a slave of Jesus Christ" and "an apostle called and set apart for God's gospel" to employ Professor Jewett's translation of 1:1. These words provide warrant for enquiring after the legitimacy of the Christian confession that the epistle to the Romans is Holy Scripture, an authoritative word of God. The gospel proclaimed in Romans, Paul contends, is not his own but God's.

Professor Jewett's exegetical comments on Paul's exordium support the view that Paul considered himself to be writing under divine appointment and guidance. Rejecting the rendering of *klētos apostolos* in verse 1 as "called an apostle" and preferring the translation, "an apostle called," Professor Jewett notes the implication that Paul's office rests on divine election.[7] That God is the "commissioner and source"[8] of Paul's message is further emphasised by the following expression, *aphōrismenos eis euaggelion theou*. Paul is "set apart for God's gospel." Paul proceeds to specify that this gospel is the gospel "proclaimed beforehand through his prophets by the holy scriptures, concerning his son . . . ." (1:2–3a)[9] This specification, sustained by frequent appeal to the Hebrew Scriptures, is another device by which Paul indicates that he speaks under divine authority. He proclaims not his own word, but the word handed down through the prophets by the instrument of the holy scriptures. Paul's words are thus to be understood as a continuation of this divine economy; they are an instrument of God's communicative presence with his people. Professor Jewett supports this view of Paul's

---

5 Jewett, *Romans*, 370.

6 See also Professor Jewett's account of Paul's conception of the contemporary relevance of Scripture, *Romans*, 340.

7 Jewett, *Romans*, 101. For further comment on Paul's authority, see the exegetical comments on Romans 9:1, at 557 and on 10:15 at 638.

8 Jewett, *Romans*, 102.

9 Professor Jewett's translation is again employed here.

authority, citing Bengt Holmberg who concludes that when Paul "preaches it is God who really is the speaker." Holmberg in turn cites 2 Corinthians 5:18–20, "we are ambassadors for Christ, God making his appeal through us." Professor Jewett continues, "Paul attaches this authority both to his doctrinal and to his ethical instruction."[10]

It is on this basis that the epistle to the Romans is taken by Christians to be not only a relevant word in the context of contemporary concerns, but an authoritative divine word. The dynamic of communicative, divine presence adumbrated here requires for its full explication a thorough Trinitarian elucidation, for which Paul's own writings elsewhere provide warrant,[11] but for now we may proceed to a consideration of the content of Paul's gospel intent on listening if we are so disposed, not simply to Paul's word, but also to the word of God.

II. The Formation of a Missionary Church

The purpose of Paul's letter to the churches in Rome, writes Professor Jewett, is

> . . . to advocate in behalf of the "power of God" a cooperative mission to evangelize Spain so that the theological argumentation reiterates the gospel to be therein proclaimed and the ethical admonitions show how that gospel is to be lived out in a manner that would ensure the success of the mission.[12]

If I may be so bold as to summarise both the letter to the Romans itself and the eleven hundred plus pages of Professor Jewett's commentary, the argument of the letter goes like this: Paul needs the help of the Christians in Rome in order to mount his mission to Spain, but for the churches in Rome to be a credible instrument of the gospel of divine righteousness, they themselves need to show forth the righteousness of God. They themselves, in other words, need to be a community in which enmity has been overcome and reconciliation has been achieved between Jew and Gentile. They themselves need to be a community in which conflict has been replaced by the peace of Christ. Above all, they need to be a community in which the conventions of honour and shame that were operative in the Graeco-Roman world have been set aside in favour of a community transformed by the righteousness of God and in which honour is accorded in equal measure to Jew and Gentile, Greek, Roman and Barbarian, slave and free, male and female, purely in virtue of the fact that the shame accruing to all people on account of their

---

[10] Jewett, *Romans*, 45.

[11] See, for example, Romans 15:30 and 1 Corinthians 2:6–16.

[12] Jewett, *Romans*, 44.

sinfulness has been overcome 'through the redemption that is in Christ Jesus' (Romans 3:24).[13] Professor Jewett writes,

> Paul attacked perverse systems of honor by dispelling the idea that some persons and groups are inherently righteous and by proclaiming the message that God honors sinners of every culture in an impartial manner through Christ.[14]

Whether or not this is Paul's argument—and Professor Jewett offers compelling evidence that it is—the argument is a good one. If the church of Jesus Christ is to engage in mission; if, that is, it is to proclaim the gospel of the righteous grace of God made known and enacted in Jesus, then it must show forth in its own life the marks of a community transformed by that very same grace.[15]

The implications of that missiological principle for every local context, be it in New Zealand or elsewhere, hardly need spelling out. The principle is repeated in numerous slogans; Christians are enjoined to "walk the talk," and to "practice what they preach." "Actions speak louder than words," it is said. Credibility in the proclamation of the gospel, depends upon the gospel's transformative power being shown forth in the lives of those who proclaim it. To put the matter as Lesslie Newbigin has done, the most compelling witness to the truth of the gospel is the community that lives it.[16] Thus, quoting Professor Jewett once more, and returning to the situation of the particular local churches in Rome,

> If the Roman house and tenement churches can overcome their conflicts and accept one another as honourable servants of the same master (14:4), they would be able to participate in a credible manner in the mission to extend the gospel to the end of the known world.[17]

---

[13] The translation is, again, that supplied by Professor Jewett. For a further expression of the point see, Jewett's commentary on 2:5: "Paul must show that all humans have sinned and that no group is exceptional and thus superior to other groups; that all are saved by grace alone; and therefore that each group is obligated to accept others as equally beloved by God." Jewett, *Romans*, 203.

[14] Jewett, *Romans*, 88.

[15] As indicated in Romans 2:10, peace is one such "mark of authentically transformed congregations." Jewett, *Romans*, 209. Cf. 349: "Any peace with God that is achieved through the Lordship of Christ has a necessary social correlate . . . ."

[16] See chapter 18: "The Congregation as Hermeneutic of the Gospel," in Lesslie Newbigin, *The Gospel in a Pluralist Society* (Grand Rapids: Eerdmans, 1989).

[17] Jewett, *Romans*, 88. Professor Jewett rightly notes that the imperative to live righteously is not just for the sake of mission but is, even more fundamentally, a soteriological matter. Salvation consists in living in right relationship with God and with one another. Concomitantly, the righteous one is the one who is "put right with God." See Jewett, *Romans*, 146.

The theological basis for Paul's claim that the gospel inaugurates a new social order is the death and resurrection of Christ. Although, as Professor Jewett points out, "the word 'cross' is absent from Romans and the verb 'crucified' appears only once"[18] Paul's constant reference to the gospel is nothing other than a reference to "Jesus Christ and him crucified" (1 Corinthians 2:2). This gospel of which Paul is not ashamed (Romans 1:16) concerns God's honouring of the one who died a shameful death,[19] thus bringing to birth a radically transformed social order encompassing all who believe.

The chief mark of the radically transformed social order is love, the dimensions of which are set out by Paul in Romans 12: 9–21. The counter-cultural aspects of an ethic founded upon the love of God shown to humanity in Christ are readily apparent in Paul's discourse in these verses. "Bless those who persecute you"; "do not claim to be wiser than you are"; "do not repay evil for evil"; "never avenge yourselves"; "if your enemies are hungry, feed them: if they are thirsty, give them something to drink." These are not the customary actions of human beings, either in first century Rome or in our own time and place (cf. Romans 12:2a). The radical nature of Paul's counter-cultural ethics underlies the contention that the proclamation of the gospel is made credible by a community radically transformed.

Again, the implications for the church in New Zealand and elsewhere hardly need spelling out. Worthy of emphasis, however, are a couple of Professor Jewett's further observations about the nature of Paul's ethics. Commenting on Romans 12:20 & 21, Professor Jewett points out that the ethics Paul recommends "flow from the transformed community (12:1–2), set right by the power of the gospel concerning God's love for the ungodly."[20] And further,

> In place of the promise of rewards from heaven [evident in other Hellenistic-Jewish texts], Romans offers a transformative ethic motivated by a reward already received, namely, the grace of God conveyed by the gospel that restores right relationships everywhere.[21]

The relation between grace and law is here spelled out; no one is saved by works of the law, Paul has insisted in the opening chapters of Romans, but works of the law do not cease to matter. The law sets out what redeemed life looks like for those made righteous by grace. That, incidentally, is a thoroughly Jewish understanding of the law.[22]

---

18 Jewett, *Romans*, 137.

19 On which, see Jewett, *Romans*, 137.

20 Jewett, *Romans*, 778.

21 Jewett, *Romans*, 778.

22 Thus does the Decalogue begin, "I am the Lord your God who brought you out of the land of Egypt." Then follows the commandments which are to be understood as descriptions of what redeemed life consists in.

Another vital dimension of Paul's ethical teaching is indicated by Professor Jewett's description of the ethic as a 'charismatic ethic'. Paul does not expect the Christian community to transform itself; the work of giving new life to the dead is divine work, and the work of the transformed community in ministry, teaching, generosity, compassion, and so on as spelled out in Romans 12:6–8, is contingent upon the divinely bestowed gifts of grace to the community of Christ's body. The language and the theology here are reminiscent of Paul's Corinthian correspondence in which all of these gifts are identified more explicitly as gifts of the Spirit (1 Corinthians 12: 1–11). Professor Jewett explains, in commentary on Romans 15:16, that,

> . . . it is the presence of the Holy Spirit within Christian communities that makes them holy . . . God's holy presence is the wonder-working, transforming, converting power that maintains holiness in these small groups of believers in their common life.[23]

Holiness has an ethical dimension, as Professor Jewett ably points out, but it has another dimension too, equally important in the context of Paul's missionary concerns. To be made holy is to be made an instrument of God's purposes. Wherever the appellation, "holy" is applied to a people, a land, a set of scriptures, or a sacrament,[24] it designates a created reality anointed for heavenly service by the God who alone is holy by nature. John Webster writes,

> In its broadest sense, sanctification refers to the work of the Spirit of Christ through which creaturely realities are elected, shaped and preserved to undertake a role in the economy of salvation: creaturely realities are sanctified by divine use.[25]

For this reason, Paul addresses his letter to God's beloved in Rome who are called to be "saints" (Romans 1:7a) The church there, as everywhere, exists to be an instrument in the *missio Dei*.[26]

I conclude this consideration of the ethical transformation of the Christian community by making one further remark about the application of Paul's insight, as mediated through Professor Jewett's commentary, to the context of the contemporary church. In New Zealand, as elsewhere, there is a great deal of hand-wringing about the need for

---

23 Jewett, *Romans*, 908.

24 The list could, of course, be extended.

25 John Webster, *Holy Scripture* (Cambridge: Cambridge University Press, 2003), 26.

26 The logic of instrumentality is apparent in Romans 15:17–18 on which see Jewett, *Romans*, 909–10.

the church to be relevant. In pursuit of relevance, it is often argued that the church must get in step with various aspects of the surrounding culture. Although it was Paul who said, "I have become as a Jew to Jews, and to those outside the law, I have become as one outside the law . . . " (1 Corinthians 9:20–21), the epistle to Rome offers counsel quite contrary to the principle that emerged later in the church, "When in Rome do as the Romans do." Paul's advice seems rather to be that the church will be sharply distinguished from the surrounding culture. Only thus will its proclamation of the transforming power of God have any credibility. None of this suggests that there are not some aspects of the church's proclamation that gain credibility through articulation in the language and cultural forms of the day, but it should encourage a more rigorous theological critique of the church's relation to culture than is sometimes evident in the contemporary concern to appeal and be relevant to people of the contemporary world.

III. DOES THEOLOGY MATTER?

I want to conclude this paper by opening up a question prompted by Professor Jewett's Commentary. We learn from the Commentary a great deal about Paul's concern that the credible proclamation of the gospel requires a community transformed by the righteous grace of God. It requires a community "where righteous relationships are maintained."[27] Paul is much less concerned, Professor Jewett tells us, about whether there is doctrinal agreement within and among the churches in Rome. Thus we are told,

> . . . Paul wishes to affirm that the revelation of divine righteousness in the gospel proceeds only on the basis of faith. Acceptance of the gospel of Christ crucified does not require conformity to a particular cultural tradition or to a specific theology. Although the faith of many Roman believers differs from Paul's, it serves equally well in advancing the gospel.[28]

This is a line that Professor Jewett maintains throughout his Commentary: adherence to any particular teaching or theology is not required by Paul of the Christians in Rome.[29] This is a matter that I think we ought to explore further. Let me be clear, however; my argument is somewhat impressionistic at this point. Professor Jewett leaves me with the *impression* that theology does not really matter to Paul. Not only does Paul not consider doctrinal agreement to be important, he seems willing

[27] Jewett, *Romans*, 143.

[28] Jewett, *Romans*, 144.

[29] See, for example, Jewett, *Romans*, 419, 632, 688, 725, 845, 852, 879, 988, 990, 995, 1014.

to allow for "an 'infinite breadth of possibilities' for cultural variation in belief and practice."[30] It is not entirely clear to me whether the "infinite breadth of possibilities," a phrase borrowed from Käsemann, applies to beliefs about cultural practices or to theological beliefs that may vary from culture to culture. Nevertheless, I do wish to open discussion with Professor Jewett first, about whether the *impression* I have gleaned from Professor Jewett's Commentary of Pauline indifference to theological agreement is an accurate interpretation of his own view and, second, about whether it is an accurate representation of Paul's position. We may keep Paul's missiological concern in mind here; does the credibility of the Church's proclamation of the gospel depend at all on some level of (theological) agreement about what that gospel consists in? Or should we be content to let each proclaim what is right in his or her own eyes, so long as we all get along? We can retain in our minds also the question of whether the vast range of theological diversity in the New Zealand church compromises the credibility of its witness. Complete theological conformity would not likely be a good thing, were it achievable, but ought we to accept the other extreme that sanctions an "infinite breadth of possibilities"?

Let me emphasise, first of all, my agreement with Professor Jewett, and with Paul, that salvation depends entirely on the righteous grace of God and not at all upon right doctrine. Some, at least, of Professor Jewett's exegetical comments about an alleged indifference to doctrinal conformity are made in support of that point, and with that I have no argument. But I want to suggest a parallel here between orthopraxis and orthodoxy. It is clear in Pauline theology, in Romans and elsewhere, that we are not saved by right behaviour, by works of the law, but, right behaviour—orthopraxis—matters nevertheless.[31] It matters for the reasons that Professor Jewett has amply demonstrated in his commentary. The gospel is the news of God's transformative grace, and we ought to see, therefore, a transformation in people's lives wherever that gospel has been received. Secondly, the credibility of the church's proclamation depends on it.

Likewise, I propose, we are not saved by right thinking, but, right thinking—orthodoxy—matters nevertheless. Following the principle that actions speak louder than words, I am prepared to recognise that orthopraxis may matter more, but I want to preserve the principle that orthodoxy matters as well, not least because what we do and what we believe are intimately bound up together. I want to suggest that that is also the way Paul conceives the matter. The two most promising verses

[30] Jewett, *Romans*, 845. The citation within this claim is taken from Ernst Käsemann.

[31] Professor Jewett notes the "repeated contention in Romans that believers are to fulfil the law even though they cannot be saved by virtue of conforming to it" (805).

in Romans for the defense of such a view have been ruled by Professor Jewett to be inadmissible, or at least questionable, evidence. Romans 16:16 which reads, "I urge you, brothers and sisters, to keep an eye on those who cause dissensions and offenses, in opposition to the teaching that you have learned . . ." (NRSV), is argued by Professor Jewett, persuasively in my view, to be a non-Pauline interpolation. We will therefore leave that verse aside. The second verse that might be adduced in favour of the view that orthodoxy matters is 6:17: "But thanks be to God that you, having once been slaves of sin, have become obedient from the heart to the form of teaching to which you were entrusted" (NRSV).[32] Here too, however, Professor Jewett argues that 17b referring to the Romans' obedience to the form of teaching with which they were entrusted, is a non-Pauline interpretation. The case here, however, as Professor Jewett acknowledges, is "somewhat ambiguous."[33] The decision one makes on this matter may depend to some extent on what one otherwise believes about Paul's attitude to right teaching. In any event, we will need more than a proof text to sustain the view that Paul thinks that orthodoxy matters.

The argument, it seems to me, can be made on the basis of two general points about Paul's corpus. First, although Professor Jewett is right to insist that Paul is concerned in Romans about the formation among the Christians in Rome of a social order that reflects the righteous grace of God, i.e., orthopraxy, Paul's argument is built on extensive theological foundations. If the foundations fail, so too does his exhortation that the Roman Christians should set aside the system of honour and shame that has led to divisions and inequalities among them. It is precisely because of Paul's convictions about the righteousness of God manifest in the death and resurrection of Christ, that the continuance of division and attitudes of superiority are judged by Paul to be a failure of Christian discipleship. It cannot therefore be a matter of indifference to him that the life, death and resurrection of Christ are acknowledged to be the working out of the divine economy of salvation; it cannot be a matter of indifference whether his hearers believe that Jesus was or was not raised from the dead. Yet these are theological, even doctrinal matters, on which, I suggest, the church stands or falls. I believe, and I think Paul believes, that we ought to strive for agreement about these things, and others besides, that pertain to the very heart of the gospel. On this point, Professor Jewett agrees. He writes, "Paul . . . assumes that every believer understands the starting point of faith in Christ is faith in the resurrection. If the Crucified One had not been resurrected,

---

[32] Verse 17a is translated differently by Professor Jewett, partly on account of his view that 17b is an interpolation. See Jewett, *Romans*, 413 and 417–18.

[33] Jewett, *Romans*, 419.

there would have been no proof that he was indeed the Messiah." This central theological claim seems, for Paul, to be non-negotiable. In New Zealand and elsewhere the determination of some to try to set aside that claim has damaged, arguably, the church's credibility in mission.

A second argument might be that Paul himself quite explicitly cares a great deal about theological convictions in, for example, the letter to the Galatians. Immediately after the introductory matter of the letter, Paul gets straight to the point:

> I am astonished that you are so quickly deserting the one who called you in the grace of Christ and are turning to a different gospel—not that there is another gospel, but there are some who are confusing you and want to pervert the gospel of Christ. But even if we or an angel from heaven should proclaim to you a gospel contrary to what we proclaimed to you, let that one be accursed (Galatians 1:6–8, NRSV).

Professor Jewett argues, with support from Hans Friedrich Weiss, that Paul refers here to "a transforming gospel that provokes conversions' and not to 'teaching' as a matter of 'firmly established . . . definite traditions of faith that one is to learn.'"[34]

I take the point that Paul is not referring to a kind of catechism that the Galatian Christians ought to adhere to, but the gospel in its transforming power has cognitive content, expressible, perhaps, as simply as in the confession, "I know that my Redeemer lives" (Job 19:25). It is the task of theology to articulate what this cognitive content is. Paul himself is very good at that task, and he bothers to undertake it, I submit, because he believes that the cognitive content of the gospel really does matter if the church is to be sustained and mount a credible witness in the world.

Now, of course, there is scope for diversity in theological conviction,[35] just as there is scope for diversity in ethical practice and religious observance. Eating meat that has been sacrificed to idols is a clear case in point as are also, in Romans 14, dietary rules and Sabbath observance. But these are *adiaphora*. Paul doesn't think there is room for compromise and diversity in other matters pertaining to the social order of the Christian community. We may take as examples, the erroneous observance of the Lord's Supper in Corinth, and also, again in Romans, those practices emanating from the unacceptable supposition that Greeks and Romans are superior to Jews, or vice versa. On these

---

34 Jewett, *Romans*, 990. The quoted text includes a citation from Weiss.

35 Professor Jewett provides helpful comment on Paul's respect for diversity in his exegesis of Romans 1:3–4. See especially, 108.

matters there appears not to be an "infinite breadth of possibilities."[36] Likewise, I suggest, Paul can presumably allow diversity on some points of doctrine, a doctrine of Scripture may be a case in point given the very liberal appropriation of Scripture by Paul himself,[37] but, taking the point of 1 Corinthians 15:2–4, he is anxious that Christians hold firmly to the message he proclaims and which has among its basic cognitive contents the confession "that Christ died for our sins in accordance with the Scripture, and that he was buried, and that he was raised again on the third day. . . ." (1 Corinthians 15:3–4)

I have not the time to pursue the argument further here, but I shall be interested in Professor Jewett's response to the question of whether, lets call it a "generous orthodoxy," matters or not to Paul.

Rather than end on a disputatious note, however, let me conclude by thanking Professor Jewett for his rich and profoundly insightful Commentary on Romans, and, in this context, for prompting our consideration of what might be required of the church if it is to be engaged faithfully in proclaiming the gospel of God's righteous grace today.

---

36 Galatians 5:20–21 would seem to support the point.

37 See, especially, Romans 9 and Professor Jewett's commentary thereon.

30

The Social Setting of the Epistle to the Romans

Paul Trebilco

Firstly, let me express my huge admiration for what Professor Jewett has achieved in this commentary. Here we have a fresh and challenging reading of what has been the most powerful and influential letter ever written. Jewett puts his case with clarity and vigour, and with the best form of creativity. His work is finely attuned to a whole range of methods, his knowledge of both the Jewish and the Greco-Roman background is encyclopaedic and his grasp of the bibliography of Romans is amazing. No doubt there will be long and detailed debate about some of his exegetical decisions, but this is now *the* commentary on Romans with which to enter into debate!

I have been asked to consider the way in which Jewett deals with and draws on issues of the social setting of Paul's letter to the Romans in his commentary. I will cover four issues: the importance of Spain; the problem in Rome; tenement churches and house churches; and the number of Christians in Rome as Paul writes.[1]

I. The Importance of Spain

Jewett is well-known for highlighting the significance of Spain with regard to "the purpose for Romans." Here he works that through at length. He writes that Romans "attempt to persuade Roman house and tenement churches to support the Spanish mission"[2] and tells us that

[1] There are a range of other matters that could be considered under the category of "social setting," including the significance of honour and shame language and of the imperial context of the letter, but because of limitation of time for the paper as originally given, I will limit myself to these four issues.

[2] Robert Jewett, *Romans: A Commentary* (Hermeneia; Minneapolis: Fortress Press, 2007), 3.

the commentary "rests on the premise that the situation in Spain throws decisive light on Paul's missionary strategy, evident throughout the letter."[3] He writes: "the basic idea . . . is that Paul wishes to gain support for a mission to the barbarians in Spain, which requires that the gospel of impartial, divine righteousness revealed in Christ be clarified to rid it of prejudicial elements that are currently dividing the congregations in Rome."[4]

Jewett gives a very helpful discussion of the social situation in Spain, and from this the challenges of the Spanish mission are clear, as is the reason *why* Paul needed help from the congregations in Rome for this mission. There were no significant Jewish communities in Spain, which meant that Paul could not recruit converts and patrons in synagogues—his normal practice—nor could he make business contacts there. Further, there were formidable linguistic barriers to a mission in Spain, for Greek was not widely known; so Greek needed to be translated to Latin and then to local languages. In addition, Spain was important to the Empire financially, and so Paul needed to assure Christians in Rome that he would not unsettle the overall situation for Christians.

All in all, "These financial and cultural barriers required the assistance of Roman congregations that had contacts with immigrants from Spain and with Roman bureaucrats charged with responsibilities there. To elicit this support, Paul needed to introduce his theology of mission, to dispel misunderstandings and allegations against his proclamation of the gospel, and to encourage the Roman congregations to overcome their imperialistic behaviour towards one another because it discredited the gospel of the impartial righteousness of God."[5] Further as Jewett writes elsewhere "Paul needed the aid and counsel of congregations in Rome with contacts in Spain to make these preparations. There are many indications that the Letter to the Romans was designed to prepare the ground for the complicated project of the Spanish mission, including the insistence that the impartial righteousness of God does not discriminate against 'barbarians' such as the Spaniards, that all claims of cultural superiority are false, that imperial propaganda must be recognized as bogus, and that the domineering behavior of congregations toward one another must be overcome if the missional hope to unify the world in praise of God is to be fulfilled (15:9–13)."[6] Thus, to make progress with the mission in Spain, Paul needed the support of the many Christians in Rome.

Jewett connects this to Phoebe. The way Phoebe is spoken of in 16:1–2 would lead the Roman hearers of the letter to understand her to be the

---

3 Jewett, *Romans*, 74; further the primary purpose of the letter is "the completion of the global mission on the Spanish peninsula" (892).

4 Jewett, *Romans*, 1.

5 Jewett, *Romans*, 88.

6 Jewett, *Romans*, 79.

patron of the Spanish mission. When Paul writes: "provide her whatever she might need from you in the matter" (Romans 16:2), the "matter" is Phoebe's patronage of the Spanish mission, as is shown by the fact that Paul goes on to speak of Phoebe being "a benefactor of many and of myself as well" (Romans 16:2). "As a missionary patroness 'of many' and therefore a person of substantial wealth, the churches of Rome would have no fear that cooperation with her would require onerous financial obligations on their part. They would be honoured by the prospect of involvement with a person of this high social status. Her patronage would involve gaining the cooperation of the Roman house churches in creating the logistical base and arranging for the translators that would be required for the Spanish mission. This means that the persons being greeted in the subsequent pericope would understand that they are being recruited as advisers and supporters of Paul's and Phoebe's 'matter,' a project of supreme importance in the eschatologically motivated scheme of early Christian mission."[7]

Is this convincing? In part, yes. But if the Spanish mission was really such a key reason for Paul to write Romans, then why does he delay mentioning Spain until 15:24 and 28? Jewett's answer may be that Romans "fits the epideictic, or demonstrative, genre"[8]—and so Paul seeks to be subtle. But if the Spanish mission was such a significant factor, would Paul not be more explicit earlier? Would he not mention the Spanish mission in Chapter 1? Some mention of "the mission to Spain" before 15:24 would certainly strengthen Jewett's case.

Further, is the absence of Jewish communities in Spain quite the problem that Jewett suggests? Granted, Paul's Gospel is "to the Jew first and also to the Greek" (Romans 1:16), but as "apostle to the Gentiles" could he not firstly go to Spain's Gentiles who spoke Greek—of whom there were some—hope for converts from among them and from that base go to Latin and Celt-Iberian speakers? And did he really need such a huge level of support from Rome for the success of the mission? After all in Philippians 4:12 he writes, "I know what it is to have little."[9]

II. THE PROBLEM IN ROME—AND SPAIN

If Paul wants support from the Christians in Rome for the Spanish mission, he is firstly faced with a difficult situation of division and hostility in Rome. The Christians in Rome are in no position to support a mission as Paul writes, so the letter "seeks to overcome the prejudice

---

[7] Jewett, *Romans*, 947–48; see also 958.

[8] Jewett, *Romans*, 42.

[9] See also 1 Corinthians 4:8–13.

of a Gentile Christian majority against a Jewish Christian minority."[10] In particular, the strong of Romans 14 are predominantly Gentile Christians, and are in the majority, while the weak are a predominantly Jewish Christians minority. Currently the strong are looking down on the weak; in fact "the Gentile majority was discriminating against the Jewish minority whom it was claiming to displace."[11] There are currently "conflicts that . . . divide these congregations into warring factions . . . . [T]he imperialistic unity . . . sought by the Roman house and tenement churches, requir[es] that others conform to the practices and beliefs of a particular in-group."[12]

As he writes, Paul seeks to lead Gentle Christians in Rome to welcome the Jewish Christians into their assemblies, and thus to overcome their theological differences and their divisive competitiveness.[13] His aim is "the unification of the Roman house churches so that they would be able to cooperate in the support of the Spanish mission. Given the diversity of the congregations alluded to in chapter 16, this would have required formidable political skills on Phoebe's part."[14]

In this light, much of Romans 1–11 can be understood as dealing with the relationship between Jew and Gentile. But "The *climax* of the letter is reached in the exhortation concerning mutual welcome between previously competitive groups (15:7; 16:3–16, 21–23) and the holy kiss that honors ethnic diversity within the new family of God (16:16). If the Roman house and tenement churches can overcome their conflicts and accept one another as honorable servants of the same master (14:4), they would be able to participate in a credible manner in the mission to extend the gospel to the end of the known world."[15] The climax to the letter is thus right at the end. In this way, Jewett is certainly able to make sense of a sixteen-chapter letter—whereas many interpreters struggle at this point.

Jewett is thus very sensitive to the dynamics of Jew-Gentile relations. What difference does this emphasis make? One example comes with Romans 16:21, where Jewett notes that Paul calls three people *sunergos* ("compatriots"). Why does Paul use this term for the third time in Romans 16 (see Romans 16:7, 11, 21)? "I believe it is part of his campaign to grant equal honor to the Jewish Christian minority in Rome. By explicitly identifying these persons as his fellow Jews, he makes plain that

[10] Jewett, *Romans,* 36; see also 70: "problematic relations between a Gentile majority and Jewish minority are in view throughout the letter."

[11] Jewett, *Romans,* 70.

[12] Jewett, *Romans,* 41, 885.

[13] See Jewett, *Romans,* 90, 866, 879.

[14] Jewett, *Romans,* 90. Jewett also notes (86) that Paul seeks a "respectful coexistence between the congregations in Rome, honouring the integrity of each side."

[15] Jewett, *Romans,* 88.

although he identified himself with the 'strong' Gentile majority in Rome, he maintains respectful, collegial relationships with Jewish Christian leaders . . . . Greetings from and to such leaders solidify Paul's effort to provide a basis for mutuality across ethnic lines, which was a crucial requirement for the mission project to the 'barbarians' in Spain."[16]

What do we make of Jewett's understanding of these issues in Rome? Clearly, as many commentators recognise, there are serious issues dividing the strong and the weak in the city. But is not the *unity and harmony* of Roman Christians an important goal in itself for Paul, regardless of the Spanish mission? For Jewett, unity seems to be primarily related to the Spanish mission. I have already noted this above with regard to 16:21. He also writes in this way about Romans 14:12: "If the Roman believers would accept this premise (verse 12) and act upon it [i. e. we are accountable to God, and so should not judge others], they would cease their squabbles and be in the position to cooperate effectively in Paul's missionary project in behalf of the righteousness of God."[17]

But is it not that case that Paul wanted the Roman Christians to find common ground (as in 1:3–4), to be in harmony, *for their own sake*? We risk seeing Paul as being particularly utilitarian—what he really wanted was a united base for his mission. When Paul writes in Romans 1:11 "For I am longing to see you so that I may share with you some spiritual gift to strengthen you—or rather so that we may be mutually encouraged . . ." does he really mean—"strengthened . . . so that you can support me in Spain." Does he not want to strengthen them because they are "one body in Christ" (Romans 12:5) in Rome, and so vitally important where they are? Does he not want to elaborate on the Gospel because it is the power of God for salvation *for them* (Romans 1:16–17) as well as for others? If they can support him in Spain, so much the better, but it is only one goal amongst others. Their health, their mutual reconciliation, is vital too.

III. TENEMENT CHURCHES AND HOUSE CHURCHES

New Testament scholarship has discussed house churches at length. We think of the assembly in Prisca and Aquila's house mentioned in Romans 16:5, or the church in Nympha's house mentioned in Colossians 4:15.[18] The house church met in a privately-owned home, and it seems clear that the house-owner functioned as host and patron of the house church. Accordingly, the house church became part of the patron-client

[16] Jewett, *Romans*, 978.
[17] Jewett, *Romans*, 852.
[18] See also 1 Corinthians 16:19; Philemon. 2.

relationship which was so important in Greco-Roman society. Jewett notes, "A house church [with a patron] is thus assimilated into the hierarchical social structure of the Greco-Roman world, in which heads of houses exercised legal and familial domination over their relatives and slaves."[19]

However, Peter Lampe has suggested that most early Christians in Rome were of low social level and lived in Trastevere and Porta Capena in crowded *insula* buildings.[20] Tenement buildings (*insulae*) in Rome would have been four or five story blocks. The higher up you went, the more unstable the building was and so the worse the housing, and so the lower the class of inhabitants. In this situation, no one owned "private space."

Given that the vast majority of Roman Christians lived in these rented tenements, Jewett suggests that the Christian groups lacked the sponsorship of a patron with their own house and so met for worship in these tenements, either in one of the workshops on the ground floor, or by moving fragile dividers on, for example, the fifth floor of the tenement, and so creating some temporary space in areas used by Christian neighbours, where the people could gather.[21] So the gathering would be in rented or shared space provided by the members themselves, rather than in space provided by a patron. Given that most of the Christians in Rome came from the lowest social strata with the bulk of Christians being slaves and former slaves (in this Jewett follows Lampe), Jewett suggests that tenement churches in Rome were much more numerous than house churches.[22] And these tenement churches to which most Roman Christians belonged are to be *contrasted* with the house church.

Jewett works out his views about tenement churches in the commentary. For example, he argues that some tenement churches are in view in Romans 16. Note Romans 16:14: "Greet Asyncritus, Phlegon, Hermes, Patrobas, Hermas, and the brothers and sisters who are with them." Jewett writes: "Since all five names are characteristic for slaves, freedmen, and lower-class Greeks it is likely that this group consisted entirely of persons with low social status. The five persons named are probably the charismatic leaders of the community, and there is no indication that one of them is playing the role of patron."[23] He thinks Romans 16:15 again indicates that the five people named there form the collective leadership of another tenement church.[24] Two other tenement

[19] Jewett, *Romans*, 65.

[20] See P. Lampe, *From Paul to Valentinus: Christians at Rome in the First Two Centuries* (Minneapolis: Fortress Press, 2003), 19–64.

[21] See Jewett, *Romans*, 65.

[22] See Jewett, *Romans*, 63.

[23] Jewett, *Romans*, 65; see also 971.

[24] Jewett, *Romans*, 972.

churches are probably in view in Romans 16:10 and 11. In none of these cases does Paul speak of "the church in the house of . . ."; Jewett suggests that this is because these churches meet in tenements and so no one person or couple in the group owned the property. They are "tenement churches" then. On this I think Jewett is entirely convincing.

Jewett thinks the social pattern in these groups was egalitarian: "The leadership pattern appears to be collective rather than hierarchical . . . . [T]he class structure of the groups greeted in 16:10, 11, 14 and 15 was one-dimensional. In contrast to house churches that have an upper- or middle-class patron along with his or her slaves, family, friends and others, these four cells consisted entirely of the urban underclass, primarily slaves and poor freedmen/women. Lacking a patron who would function as a leader, the pattern of leadership appears to be egalitarian in tenement churches."[25] Hence, they would have celebrated agape meals together, with no one particular person taking precedence; in a tenement building the food for a meal would have been contributed by the members of the assembly. Jewett—following Theissen—suggests the structure of the *house church* can best be seen as "love patriarchalism," whereas the structure of the *tenement church* is "agapaic communalism."

What difference does it make to identify some of the Roman Christians as living in tenement churches? Jewett helpfully includes a discussion of tenement churches at various points. For example, Jewett suggests that in Romans 15:1–6 Paul calls for "Mutual assistance between house and tenement churches, involving material as well as theological and spiritual resources."[26] Thus, *each* should please the neighbour (15:2): "This is a remarkable admonition in the Roman social system that assumed only the powerful had the capacity to act independently."[27] By thinking concretely, and in terms of tenement churches and social status, Jewett is able to bring out the full force of 15:1–6.

Jewett's discussion of tenement churches adds *another* dimension to the complexity of Roman Christianity. Paul cannot simply address a few leaders or patrons—and in this way contact all the small assemblies. The leadership structure of the tenement churches is much more fluid—5 leaders seem to feature in each of the two tenement churches mentioned in Romans 16. And there are three Gentile tenement churches and perhaps two Jewish tenement churches. So Jewett's discussion of "tenement churches" adds a dimension of complexity to the whole social situation of the Roman Christians, but in doing so it probably more accurately reflects the real situation. Overall in Rome we have the weak and the strong and the house churches and the tenement churches and

---

25 Jewett, *Romans*, 65, 66.
26 Jewett, *Romans*, 877.
27 Jewett, *Romans*, 878.

Paul seeks to unite them all. In effect, I think Jewett—rightly—complicates Paul's task by introducing the tenement churches into the picture.

Jewett's argument about tenement churches would have been more convincing if Paul had *explicitly* had a name for "the tenement churches", and had said that they had a different leadership structure; this would give more certainty about the distinction Jewett draws. After all, could what is called a "house church" in the four references we have in the New Testament actually meet in a tenement? Does the fact that we read of "the church in their house (*oikon autōn ekklēsian*)" *mean* the people named owned the house? As Jewett points out, *oikon can* refer to an apartment building.[28] Further, Gehring asks if space *could* be created on the fifth floor of an insulae for a tenement church?[29] Jewett speaks of "temporarily cleared space",[30] but the walls were of wood. Were they in any way "portable"? Gehring thinks not.[31] Physically then, could Christians actually meet on the fifth floor of a very crowded tenement?

But in any case should we make quite such a distinction between "house church" and "tenement church"? Friesen has questioned whether any persons in the Pauline circle were "upper class" or wealthy. Note the following about Prisca and Aquila:

> there are signs that they lived above the level of subsistence and perhaps even had moderate surplus resources. Paul's letters indicate that they hosted an assembly in their home when they lived in Ephesus (1 Corinthians 16:19) and perhaps also in Rome. In addition, Acts 18:3 records that they were able to house and to employ Paul because they had the same trade. If the tradition in Acts 18 is accurate, which is likely in this case, then it is possible that Prisca and Aquila were in the category of having moderate surplus resources (PS4 ["moderate surplus"]). But it is equally possible that they were further down the poverty scale, perhaps in PS5 ["stable near subsistence"]. Housing in a major urban area, and especially in Rome, was usually crowded and noisy. The home of Prisca and Aquila could have been in a tenement or similar rented quarters near the workshop, and Acts 18:3 could be understood to indicate that Prisca and Aquila were both manual laborers. So we cannot conclude that the couple was relatively wealthy,

---

[28] Jewett, *Romans*, 64.

[29] R. W. Gehring, *House Church and Mission: The Importance of Household Structures in Early Christianity* (Peabody: Hendrickson, 2004), 149.

[30] Jewett, *Romans*, 65.

[31] Gehring, *House Church and Mission*, 149

> but only that they were most likely in categories 4 or 5 of the poverty scale.[32]

Thus, Friesen suggests Prisca and Aquila may have been socio-economically "stable near subsistence", and *not* relatively wealthy. Since Prisca and Aquila are said to host a *house* church, Friesen's view tends to question the whole distinction that Jewett builds between "house churches" hosted by the relatively wealthy, and "tenement churches" hosted by those who were poorer. Is it clear then that the expression "the church in the house of . . . (*oikon autōn ekklēsian*)" meant the persons mentioned owned the house, and so should be seen as patrons? Or could it be that they simply rented the space they lived in, and that this might not have been a "house," in which case the assembly might actually have met in a tenement? Just because a group met in a *named* house does it mean that we should see the house owners as "patrons", with all that goes with that?

Further, should we also see such a rigid distinction between the "love patriarchalism" of the house churches and the "agapaic communalism" of the tenement churches? I think this is too hard and fast a distinction. "Brothers and sisters" (*adelphoi*) is the key term of address in Pauline communities, and it, I think argues against "love patriarchalism" since it tends to place people on the same level. Note 1 Corinthians 16:19–20: "The churches of Asia send greetings. Aquila and Prisca, together with the church in their house, greet you warmly in the Lord. All the brothers and sisters send greetings. Greet one another with a holy kiss." We have "the church in Aquila and Prisca's house" and then "All the brothers and sisters send greetings." These "brothers and sisters" are another grouping in Ephesus, from which 1 Corinthians was written (1 Corinthians 16:8). But the use of *adelphoi* in this context strongly suggests that this is what members of Aquila and Prisca's house church would have called each other too. Even where we have patrons of a church, or at the very least named people who host an assembly, the members still called themselves *adelphoi*. If this is the case—and the prevalence of *adelphoi* in address makes it very likely—then I think this is more like "agapaic communalism" than "love patriarchalism"—and this relates to a "house church."

IV. CHRISTIAN NUMBERS

Another distinctive feature of Jewett's work is that he considers the number of Christians in Rome to be much more substantial than is generally thought. He notes that Lampe thinks there were at least seven

[32] S. J. Friesen, "Poverty in Pauline Studies: Beyond the So-Called New Consensus," *Journal for the Study of New Testament* 26.3 (2004), 352–53.

groups of Christians in Rome,[33] giving a total of around 200 perhaps. Jewett notes: "This impression [of only several hundred] cannot easily be correlated with the evidence from nonbiblical sources. Tactius reports (*Annales* 15.44.4) that Nero made the Christians into 'scapegoats' after the great fire in July 64, and 'had self-acknowledged members of this sect arrested. Then, on their information, a tremendous crowd (*multitudo ingens*) were condemned.' This implies a 'huge crowd' or 'tremendous crowd,'"[34] which is also suggested by 1 Clement 6:1 where a "great multitude of elect" are spoken of as victims of persecution. So Jewett thinks that Nero must have had several hundred victims.[35] It is also hard to imagine that Nero would choose a minute group as his victims—Christians must have been reasonably numerous and noticeable at this time. Since Christianity was not wiped out in Rome, many more must have survived in Nero's time. All this suggests that there were more than 200 when Paul wrote Romans in the winter of 56–57.[36]

In fact Jewett suggests "the large number of leaders and evangelists greeted in chapter 16 indicate more congregations than the usual estimate of five to seven. To think that Miriam, Andronikos and Junia, Ampliatus, Urbanus, Stacys, Apelles, Herodion, Tryphaina and Tryphosa, Persis and Rufus and his mother all belong to one or two congregations would be totally uncharacteristic of churches elsewhere, which are referred to by the names of their leaders or patrons. On this premise, these names reflect eight to ten separate congregations either in the past or at the time of Paul's letter."[37] And in addition, there are the five other named congregations.

Accordingly, Jewett suggests there were several thousand Christians in Rome by 64 C.E. At the time Paul wrote Romans (56–57 C.E.) he thinks there would have been "dozens of groups" of between 20 and 40 people, although Paul can identify only five groups. So perhaps there were 1000 Christians in Rome at this time.[38] Further, there was no central organisation of all these Christians—fractionation is Lampe's very helpful term for the situation.[39] So in Rome Jewett thinks that a "variety in organization, orientation, and location was already present at the time of Paul's letter, and this explains many of its features."[40]

This is a very interesting feature of Jewett's work and one that deserves a much fuller discussion than can be offered here. It certainly

---

33 Lampe, *From Paul to Valentinus*, 359.

34 Jewett, *Romans*, 61.

35 Jewett, *Romans*, 62.

36 See Jewett, *Romans*, 21.

37 Jewett, *Romans*, 62.

38 We could take 24 x 20 as a minimum (=480), 36 x 30 (= 1080) as a middle figure and 36 x 40 (= 1440) as a maximum.

39 For example, Lampe, *From Paul to Valentinus*, 364.

40 Jewett, *Romans*, 62.

proposes a much more complex social setting in Rome than most other scholars have done.[41]

In connection with this, that Jewett thinks *concretely* in this commentary certainly leads to fuller understanding. For example, he notes that Romans 14 calls for acceptance of the weak by the strong and visa versa. This does *not* mean a combined meeting, or the joining of groups of weak and strong assemblies—a physical impossibility with something like 1000 people. Rather, it means inviting a few members of one group to the other's love feasts. This is a practical case where bearing in mind the potential number of Christians in Rome and where "thinking concretely" greatly assists interpretation.[42]

What if there were 1000 Christians in Rome at the time Paul wrote Romans? This would further complicate the tensions that we see in Romans between the weak and the strong, between Jewish and Gentile Christians. It would also add to the diversity—particularly when we add both house churches and tenement churches into our thinking too. All in all, this considerably increases the complexity of the situation Paul is facing. But with this number of Christians in Rome, it also increases the *opportunity* Paul faces. We can well understand why he writes at such length to the Christians at the heart of the empire.

---

41 See for example F. Watson, "The Two Roman Congregations: Romans 14:1–15:13," in edited by K. P. Donfried, *The Romans Debate* (Revised and Expanded Edition; Peabody: Hendrickson, 1991), 203–15; on 206 he writes of the "two separate congregations," one of Jewish Christians and the other of Gentile Christians.

42 See Jewett, *Romans*, 868.

31

Response to Auckland Colleagues

Robert Jewett

I appreciate the insights of all three respondents and the chance to discuss the implications of my commentary for the cultures of New Zealand and the Pacific Islands. I welcome the chance to pursue the questions and issues they raise. I'd like to begin with Paul Trebilco, because he raises crucial introductory questions. With regard to the Spanish mission as the central purpose of the letter, he asks why it was not mentioned in chapter 1, and with regard to the situation between the weak and the strong in Rome, he asks whether "the unity and harmony of Roman Christians" does not constitute "an important goal in itself for Paul." In part my views are the result of the process of eliminating alternate views that do not appear to take all the details of the sixteen chapter letter seriously. That Paul wished to convert the Jewish Christians to his gospel and thus create harmony, as advocated by Francis Watson, for example, is contradicted not only by the admonitions to mutual welcome in chapters 14–16 but also by the non-interference principle stated in 15:20. Paul does not seek to visit Rome to establish Pauline congregations there, and says that he intends to visit them briefly while on the way to Spain. As he states his non-interference principle, he does not preach where the gospel has already been heard. Among the various purposes that have been proposed, only the Spanish Mission is compatible with this principle. When one takes account of the cultural and political situation in Spain, it becomes clear why he needs the cooperation of Roman congregations, and why the reference to the "barbarians" in 1:14 signals a project by this "apostle to the Gentiles" beyond the circle of Greco Roman culture in an area like Spain.

With regard to the delicate negotiations required for this project, we were informed by the studies of John White and Heikki Koskeniemi about the crucial role of letter bearers in the ancient period. Letter bearers were typically entrusted to fill in the details. Phoebe is introduced not only as the patroness of the Spanish Mission but also according to most previous commentaries as the letter bearer. She was thus authorized by normal custom to present the letter to the congregations in Rome and to discuss the complicated details that Paul cannot handle at a distance. It would have been inappropriate in diplomatic correspondence to go into detail about the Spanish Mission before he has cleared the way for a shared ethos, which requires all four proofs down to the middle of chapter 15. His recommendations in chapters 14–15 about resolving the conflicts in Rome serve this missionary purpose and therefore do not violate his principle of non-interference.

While I think the denial of Prisca's high status by Steve Friesen, cited with approval by Paul Trebilco, fails to account for all the evidence, their critique of the concept of "love patriarchalism" strikes home. A series of discussions on this issue since the publication of the commentary convinces me that a more balanced assessment is needed. Christian patrons were called to serve rather than be served; their behavior is to be modified by *agapē* and *koinonia*, and there are indications in Romans 16 that this in fact was occurring. Yet the fact remains that patrons would have been held responsible for the assemblies that met in their houses or apartments, and structural and social differences with tenement churches existing without patronage remain noteworthy. The four tenement churches in Rome consisted entirely of the urban underclass while the house church led by Prisca and Aquila probably included their slaves and employees as well as the members of their immediate families, reflecting more of a cross section of social levels.

Murray Rae agrees with the missional implications of Romans, and he raises important points about the letter as an "authoritative divine word." The key question is how this authority functions. Consider the relevance of Romans 12:1–2, and the assumption that groups of believers have the obligation to discern the "will of God," using the three standard arenas of truth, of which Romans would comprise an example of the first, the "good." But this is followed by the "acceptable," and finally the "perfect," all of which are to be re-evaluated on the basis of the "mercies of God" as experienced by each group, and by the non-conformity/transformation principles, and finally by the *metron pisteōs* dealt out to each group.

So Paul does not present his theology as "authoritative" in the traditional sense, but as an apostolic witness to be weighed by the Roman believers. Paul refers in 1:12 to being "mutually encouraged among you by each other faith, both yours and mine." At many points in the commentary I show that Paul cites traditional formulas of that faith. It is far from my intent to say that "theology does not really matter to Paul." I maintain that such measuring rods of faith include elements of shared belief. On the basis of his citation of widely used liturgical and theological formula, Paul operates on the assumption that there is agreement on the relevance of Christ crucified and resurrected, and on the centrality of faith and salvation by faith rather than works. I agree with most of Prof. Rae's comment that "it is precisely because of Paul's convictions about the righteousness of God manifest in the death and resurrection of Christ, that the continuation of division and attitudes of superiority is judged by Paul to be a failure of Christian discipleship." The key issue is whether a measure of doctrinal "division" is acceptable in the light of impartial righteousness. Cultural differences are integral to the *metron pisteōs* dealt out to each group converted by the gospel. Theology certainly matters, but theology as it was being misused in the conflicts between the weak and the strong in Rome had to be repudiated as an assault on the Lord of the church, who elected various cultural groups as his house slaves (14:4), dealing out one theological perspective to the weak and another to the strong. In contrast to 1 Corinthians, Romans provides a rational for cultural and theological diversity between believing groups. He provides for the first time a clear theological rationale for "generous orthodoxy," to employ Rae's category.

Douglas Campbell provides powerful conformation that the themes of honor and shame are crucial in this letter and that they offer resources to reconceive central aspects of Pauline theology. He provides a lucid explanation of Silvan Tomkins' theory of shame as one of nine psychological and neurological affects experienced by all humans. This theory has been confirmed by blushing when shamed, which Darwin demonstrated as a human response in every known group. Campbell goes on to suggest that the gospel of Christ crucified provides the means of "restructuring of human thinking and emotion" so as to overturn the toxic effects of unjust shame. He suggests that Paul's stress on divine forbearance in Romans 3 and 5 replaces the "penal approach" in Augustinian atonement theory that "inscribes a toxic sequence at the heart of the Christian gospel and the divine nature—a sequence that is arguably both self-destructive and blasphemous."

I discovered a striking instance of this restructuring of shame's toxicity in Romans 8:35 where seven types of shameful experiences, which were usually thought to indicate divine wrath or indifference, are declared incapable of separating believers from "the love of Christ," An earlier instance of restructuring is in Romans 5:3 where Paul urges believers to "boast in our afflictions," which were ordinarily seen as evidence of divine displeasure and individual weakness. In the ancient world, one boasts of triumphs but never of failures. This restructuring is possible "because the love of God has been poured into our hearts through [the] Holy Spirit that was given to us." (Romans 5:5) Campbell rightly sees such restructuring in Romans 12-13 where non-conformity to the abusive world and a new "solidarity in salvation" are proclaimed. He understands the climactic admonition to share the "holy kiss" as a "crucial antidote to cultural scripts of disgust and contempt."

I think Douglas Campbell has shown that the theoretical resources of Silvan Tomkins and his followers could help us to adapt the theology of Romans for a wide variety of today. The Pauline claims of universal relevance in chapters 3 and 11 may become more plausible when social shame is recognized alongside the more familiar shame of guilt, taking Tomkins and Donald Nathanson into account. While this opens an immense field of new interpretive possibilities for Romans, I am uncomfortable with the word "because" in Douglas's claim that "Shame is at the center of Romans, *because* it is at the center of most of what we do as human beings in the grip of affects that often we don't fully recognize or understand." (Italics added by Jewett.) The centrality of shame issues is indicated by the exegetical evidence in Romans itself, and there are other letters where such evidence seems less visible—such as the Thessalonian correspondence.

This symposium confirms the crucial locations of New Zealand and Australia as bridges to Asia and the Pacific Islands, which are actually closer to the ancient world of Paul that are Northern Europe and North America. The ease with which the colleagues in this symposium move back and forth between cultural alternatives in the first, second, and third worlds is quite amazing. I hope this symposium can stimulate research by scholars from the orient who have much better access to the complicated issues of saving face and avoiding shame than a westerner like me can ever have. But I greatly appreciate the opportunity for the conversation this morning.

The Stellenbosch Symposium
April 5, 2007

32

A Review of Robert Jewett, *Romans* (Hermeneia)

John D. K. Ekem

I deem it a great honour to be called upon to review this *magnum opus* of a renowned and hardworking New Testament scholar. My sincere thanks go to the New Testament Society of South Africa (NTSSA) Executive, especially Prof. Draper and Prof. Decock, for extending this special invitation to me and working out the logistics necessary for my arrival and stay in South Africa. I am also grateful to Prof. Jewett himself who has through our e-mail correspondences, greatly encouraged me, treating me as his own son, even though I have never met him in person. Fortunately, I can now interact with him face to face at this NTSSA Congress. Significantly, there are certain things that we have in common: both us of are ordained ministers within the global Methodist fraternity and we have undertaken a considerable part of our "theological pilgrimage" on German soil, mindful of distinguished ancestors in NT scholarship such as Professors Bultmann and Käsemann. Two years ago, I was privileged to have been hosted in Stuttgart for a couple of days by Frau Weitbrecht (geb. Käsemann) PhD candidate in History and a direct paternal granddaughter of Professor Käsemann. Interacting with the immediate family afforded me the rare opportunity to better appreciate what this famous and outstanding German New Testament scholar stood for.

This present Commentary on Romans, prepared by Professor Jewett, can indeed be regarded as a masterpiece. It is meticulously researched, employing all the critical scholarly tools available. The bibliography is extensive and covers all the available publications especially from the English and German speaking worlds. The sources of information have been professionally outlined and duly acknowledged. The academic honesty and scholarly transparency characterizing this voluminous commentary (pages lxx + 1140) are never in doubt. The parading of text-critical tools is impressive and the methodology of discussing textual variants prior to the main commentary offers the reader an opportunity to make informed exegetical choices and to appreciate the processes involved in the history of textual transmission. The preliminary analysis of various pericopes within the letter and painstaking outline of their rhetorical features prior to their detailed exegetical discussion, are another big plus for the commentary. The philosophy behind this commentary is particularly stimulating: it is written in memory of Bishop John William Colenso (1814–1883), arguably one of the most exciting biblical interpreters of all times, who skillfully factored the historical and social backgrounds of biblical source texts and contemporary receptor audiences into his hermeneutics. In this innovative commentary, Professor Jewett draws on a consensus emerging from the Society of Biblical Literature (SBL) Pauline Theology Seminars in the 1970s–90s that "Romans should be viewed as a situational letter, and that historical circumstances should be taken into account just as in the other letters." (3). It is intriguing to observe how the author attempts to weave "the distinctive historical and social background of the Roman audience and Paul's rhetorical purpose in addressing them" (2) into his interpretation of this letter. A substantial portion of his Introduction is devoted to a discussion of the *Sitz im Leben* of Roman and Spanish Christian audiences in their broader societal context (46–79) to be followed by a fine literature review which offers the author an opportunity to discuss the purpose of Romans in the Spanish missionary strategy (80–91). Of particular interest is the author's presentation of Phoebe as a key female figure in the Spanish mission (89–91) whose responsibility it was to "attempt to achieve the aims of the letter, namely the unification of the Roman house churches so that they would be able to cooperate in the support of the Spanish mission." (90) The author had earlier hinted at the financial and cultural challenges posed by missionary work in Spain which "required the assistance of Roman congregations that had contacts with immigrants from Spain and with Roman bureaucrats charged with responsibilities there." (88) This approach to the reading of Romans is, in my opinion, an extremely useful exercise as it offers an interesting glimpse, however tentative, into the multi-cultural and pluralistic religious settings as well as the complex socio-economic and political systems reflected in Romans. Let me mention in passing that Paul himself would have understood the intricacies of Roman bureaucracy very well, given his own background as a Roman citizen.

I fully agree with the author that that the Colonial/Imperial background of Romans cannot be overlooked in any serious interpretation of this letter. Every writing is situated in a particular *Sitz im Leben* and it is the interpreter's task to attempt bridging the gap between the source texts and their original as well as current target audiences. Similar to the role played by Hermes in ancient Greek mythology, the interpreter is entrusted with the responsibility of understanding, analyzing, interpreting and communicating the divine message clearly and intelligently to the human community. The imperial structures within a *Pax Romana* context are present in this letter which has engaged the attention of theologians across the centuries and been interpreted from particular theological standpoints. There is no doubt that theological issues in Romans are never discussed in a vacuum. Rather, they are presented within the context of concrete situations such as: Master-Slave relationship, Roman rule of Law, life in a typical cosmopolitan/pluralistic society such as Rome. One of the issues I find most enlightening in this commentary is the way the author has innovatively woven the concepts of "shame" and "honor" within the Graeco-Roman set-up, into his commentary on the well-known passage in Romans 3:23. One is immediately challenged by his observation that Paul's argument "eliminates all claims of honorable superiority, including those that were developing within the church itself. It reflects a paradigm shift made by Paul . . . . If all persons and groups including believers in Rome had been equally involved in sin and thereby had fallen short of the ultimate standard of honor that they were intended to bear, that is, "the glory of God", then none has a right to claim superiority or to place other groups in positions of inferiority." (279–280) This is indeed a message that we need to hear again and again in our current racially, socially and economically polarized world!

But I am also convinced that to understand Romans requires an understanding of Paul himself with his complex background and exposure to various influences, having drunk deep from the wells of both the Conqueror and the Conquered. Paul's Roman citizenship and its accompanying privileges, his family tent-making business which was advantageous to Roman imperial interests, his multi-faceted identity as Pharisee, Hellenist and Christian, all have implications for the exegesis of Romans. Unfortunately, this fact of Paul's "amphibian loyalty/identity" within the Roman imperial structures is not adequately reflected in the commentary being reviewed. Given the intriguing approach of "socio-historical reconstruction" used by Professor Jewett in this commentary, I am of the opinion that it should be brought to its comprehensive logical conclusion and factored into the exegesis of a "controversial passage" like Romans 13 where the vital subject of "respect for state authorities" is discussed. With particular reference to Romans 13:1–7, Professor Jewett brilliantly commences his exegetical analysis by stating that "The interpretation of this pericope has swung from abject subservience to political authorities viewed as virtually divine to critical submission on the basis of their advancement of justice. The endless stream of studies has been marked by advocacy of various appraisals of the role of government shaped by denominational traditions and by modern ethical considerations." (785). He then argues for the derivation of Romans 13:1–7 from various terminologies and ideas inherent in the Roman civic cult, linking it up with his main thesis that attention should be devoted to the pericope's "rhetorical significance for the Roman audience whom Paul is attempting to recruit in support of his Spanish mission." (786) Unfortunately, the learned author tends to overlook Paul's own deep entrenchment in the Roman imperial system when he contends that: "Romans 13:1–7 was not intended to create the foundation of a political ethic for all times and places in succeeding generations—a task for which it has proven to be singularly ill-suited. Believing himself to be a member of the end-time generation, Paul had no interest in the concerns that would later burden Christian ethics, and which continue to dominate the exegetical discussion. His goal was to appeal to the Roman audience as he conceived it, addressing their concerns in a manner that fit the occasion of his forthcoming visit." (786–87). The situational nature of the pericope notwithstanding, I would argue that such a stance, as reflected in the above quotation, cannot come from a privileged Roman citizen like Paul who would obviously be interested in maintaining the peace of the Empire through the legitimate exercise of his civic responsibilities. And he would urge his addressees to do the same!

There is also a sense in which Romans 7 can be interpreted not simply as portraying the "inner spiritual conflict" experienced by Paul or even as a rhetorical tool used by Paul to dramatize the "divisive tendencies" within the Roman congregation (see 473), but rather as a painstaking and honest attempt by Paul to resolve tensions emanating from his complex identity. As an African biblical scholar, I am also very much aware of my complex identity as an indigenous western-trained Akan-Ghanaian who is a minister of the Christian Gospel, originally presented by western European Missions in the context of colonialism. I am still striving hard towards emancipation from what could be termed as *anthropologische Armut* =anthropological pauperization, resulting partly from my people's colonial experience. This has obvious profound implications for my approach to biblical hermeneutical issues. With reference to Romans, it could be argued that, similar to the challenges faced by the author of Hebrews within a pluralistic Palestinian-Hellenistic environment, Paul also had to contend with pluralistic tendencies in the Graeco-Roman world that could hardly be divorced from his own existential realities as a social being. Perhaps, we should be bold enough to concede that Paul was, in a sense, a benevolent "Imperial collaborator", who sought through his advocacy ministry, to correct certain abusive social imbalances that were deeply entrenched in the Roman imperial system from which he himself benefited as a Roman citizen. There is no doubt that each of us is a product of our times and we should be honest enough to acknowledge that in our theologies. What implications does this have for those of us who do biblical exegesis in Africa within a post-colonial/post- Apartheid context? If the strength of this commentary lies in its innovative approach to exegesis and its extensive use of available scholarly tools, its weakness lies probably in the failure to capture Paul's own dilemma in the interpretive process as a product of several worlds, not least his deep entrenchment in the Roman imperial system.

That Paul was not sufficiently fluent in Latin to carry out his Spanish mission without translators/interpreters (see author's assertion on page 79) is most unlikely, considering his high standard of education within an imperial system from which he obtained first-hand benefits. His fluency in Hebrew/Aramaic and Greek, his great rhetorical skills at both formal and informal levels, and his privileged status as a Roman citizen, would naturally predispose him to take advantage of the language of the colonizers who had also turned out to be his benefactors.

Moreover the combination of various hermeneutical approaches in this great commentary (see author's remark on page 1, paragraph 1), whatever its merits, stands in danger of being branded as "uncomfortably eclectic". The socio-cultural background of the various constituencies being addressed in Romans are also based on diligent historical reconstruction, much of which tend to be inconclusive and may, for that reason, not always yield accurate results. I would have wished to see the author's fine literature review at the beginning, rather than towards the tail end of the introductory section. The great thesis he puts forward could then have been subsequently defended against the backdrop of lapses identified in the evaluation of previous works on Romans. The footnoting system on some pages also needs to be looked at, since it does not always make for easy reference. This looks like a formatting problem which should, hopefully, be addressed in the next edition of this important commentary.

These comments do not in any way change my verdict that the author has competently touched on vital issues ignored by most previous commentaries on Romans. There is no doubt that he has succeeded in drawing attention to the complexity of approaching a frequently read letter like Romans. Contrary to the traditional notion of its being a scholastic first century *summa theologica* with ready-made data for doctrinal expositions and perhaps, in the view of some readers, with ready-made answers to certain pertinent theological questions (e.g.

antinomianism and legalism), Romans is indeed a situational document produced in response to particular existential challenges within the Graeco-Roman world. This commentary is a must reading for all serious students of Romans. Experts should also welcome it as a very valuable contribution to the discussion on Romans. The author deserves much commendation.

33

A Review of Robert Jewett, *Romans: A Commentary*

Andrie Du Toit

This massive Romans commentary represents 26 years of painstaking labor by an erudite scholar on one of the most influential but also most hotly debated books of the New Testament. One is immediately impressed by its reader-friendliness. Although somewhat heavy to handle, this book is a real delight to consult and read. Its layout and presentation is immediately clear, in contrast, for instance, to the Romans commentary of Käsemann where one almost needs a tracking device to locate a specific item. The language is lucid and precise. For the uninitiated, Greek texts are translated into English and, in addition to the customary indices, a handy glossary of rhetorical and exegetical terms is provided.

An important feature of this commentary is its impressive documentation and exemplary use of ancient parallels. In this regard, it is a real goldmine. Another characteristic is the representative use of almost all relevant international publications. Text-critical issues are discussed in-depth and assessed independently on an eclectic basis. At a time when stylistics are greatly neglected, the author's meticulous attention to stylistic and rhetorical details must be applauded. As a matter of fact, the sincerity with which Jewett wrestles with all aspects of the text places this commentary a well deserved cut above most others.

Jewett applies the full methodological arsenal, but the socio-historical and rhetorical paradigms are most prominent. In contrast to the more traditional tendency to view Romans as a semi-timeless theological treatise, he regards it as a fully situational letter like all the other Pauline writings. He classifies Romans as an epideictic document containing a "unique fusion" of several subtypes of this genre, although the ambassadorial subtype dominates. In the impressive introductory chapter he clarifies his methodology and his position on the main issues involved in the interpretation of Romans. I personally found the passages on numerical sequences and the important role of the public reader of a document such as Romans particularly illuminating. The main section of Romans is subdivided into four "proofs", followed by the concluding *peroratio* consisting of the authentic sections of Romans 15:14–16:24 (*sic*) and which constitutes the rhetorical climax of the letter.

Jewett's basic premise is that Romans is an ambassadorial letter seeking support for Paul's intended missionary campaign to Spain. In order to make this project possible, the chauvinistic attitudes dividing the "warring factions" (41) in Rome had to be addressed. Only a united home front could provide the necessary logistics for his missional enterprise. To bring this about, the apostle had to convince his Roman audiences of the revolutionary impartiality of divine righteousness which overturned the honor system dominating the Greco-Roman and Jewish worlds and which rendered all Christians, regardless of sex, status, economic power and ethnic origin, equals in Christ. Simultaneously, this would hopefully make an end to imperialistic prejudice towards evangelizing the "barbarians" in Spain. With impressive consistency the entire letter, including other possible motives for writing Romans, is encapsulated within this vision. As a matter of fact, it becomes the hermeneutical key towards solving the riddle of Romans. The impartiality of divine righteousness is drastically foregrounded. Within the parameters of the gospel, nobody receives preferential treatment; being Jewish or non-Jewish is no longer important: *all* have sinned and *all* who believe are saved. However, as the commentary proceeds, initial fear that the envisioned hermeneutical key might become an exegetical straightjacket is increasingly realized. The painful struggle of the enigmatic "I" in Romans 7, for example, is explained in terms of "religious zealotism that failed to achieve the good that Paul had believed he could bring about by persecuting the followers of Christ" (444). The biographical Paul, the zealot prior to his conversion, prepares the way for chapters 14:1–15:13 where he deals directly with the prevailing faction fighting within the Roman Christian community. The "amen" of 11:36 becomes an invitation to the Roman Christians to assent to Paul's foregoing argument: "By concurring in glorifying this one God of both Jews and Gentiles, they take decisive steps against their own chauvinistic tendencies and open themselves to the challenging project of the Spanish mission for which the entire letter provides a rationale" (723). The call to a renewal of the mind in the initial pericope of Romans 12 presents an "agenda of the divine will to resolve disputes and cooperate in a missionary venture of great significance" (734–35). The exhortation that his audience should present their bodies as "a sacrifice, living, holy (and) acceptable to God" (12:1, Jewett's translation), has as ultimate purpose "the enlisting of the bodies of the Romans . . . for a mission project" (729). Even the pericope on the correct Christian attitude towards the state should be understood in the light of the Spanish project. The argument in favour of civil authorities aims at securing the support of "the groups of believers within the imperial bureaucracy whose cooperation was perceived to be absolutely vital in the Spanish mission" (794). Simultaneously it would counter Paul's negative reputation as "a subversive troublemaker" (794) Also the concluding greeting list is read in terms of its persuasive intent. The name of Erastus, for instance, a high-ranking Roman official in Corinth, is purposefully held back to occupy the penultimate place in the carefully constructed greeting list in order to "lend maximum public prestige to Paul's project" (983). Even the very last name on the list, that of Quartus, serves this pragmatic purpose, but not before "*the* brother Quartus" becomes "*his* brother Quartus" in order that he might share in the imperial status of Erastus.

Jewett's basic premise is enticing in its inclusivity and in the way it opens up exciting new vistas for the understanding of Romans. However, it is clearly overly ambitious. As can be gleaned from the above examples, this one-dimentional understanding of Romans too often warps the text or, at least, does not do full justice to its semantics. The Spanish venture was certainly very important and it may even have triggered the writing of the letter. However, it should not monopolize the interpretation thereof. For that Romans is much too multi-faceted. Within Jewett's argument, the logic of bringing together the different Christian factions as a *sine qua non* for the Spanish venture is also not convincing. Firstly, it should be questioned whether the disagreements between the various groups had taken on such proportions that it would have derailed the Spanish mission. Secondly, in the light of Paul's Corinthian correspondence, it is clear that, for Paul, religious in-fighting was such a threat to the integrity of his gospel, that he would have wanted to address this critical issue as a theme on its own, and not merely within the parameters of his Spanish campaign.

A similar tendency towards a too constructive exegesis manifests itself in other contexts as well: According to Jewett, Paul's statement that love was the fulfillment of the law, actually implied that the law was fulfilled at the *agape meal* (805, 814); the greeting list of Romans 16 reflects *eight to ten* separate congregations "either in the past or at the time of Paul's letter", pointing towards a Christian movement of *several thousand adherents* (62); Phoebe not only brings the Romans letter to Rome, she is entrusted with the daunting task of furthering the aims of the letter, namely the unification of the Roman house churches in order to facilitate the Spanish mission (89, 947); she is in fact the patroness of the Spanish mission and will provide the necessary finances; in all likelihood she was in the shipping industry and, with her staff, used to travel back and forth to Rome; in this way, Tertius, *her* secretary, became acquainted with the Roman believers; his secretarial task included that he should accompany Phoebe and read and explain the Romans letter to the Christian congregations in the capital; etc. This is exciting but very venturesome exegesis.

I do not wish to take up the prolonged debate on whether Romans should be sub-divided according to rhetorical or epistolographic conventions. However, it seems highly questionable that Romans 15:14ff, and particularly the greeting list of chapter 16, should be regarded not only as the *peroratio* but also as the *climax* of Romans. To me it seems more appropriate to regard 15:14ff as the beginning of the letter closing and the greetings reflecting in a Pauline way, the conventional letter greeting.

Despite the above question marks, this exciting and monumental work has such intrinsic quality that it will become a new benchmark in the study of Romans. It will certainly also give new momentum to the Romans debate. I consider it a must for all future Romans research.

A final remark is required. Jewett repeatedly (46, 59) invites, no, almost urges New Testament colleagues to "refute" his position. When one tests new frontiers rather than timidly repeating mere platitudes, this refreshing openness reflects, in my opinion, the authentic scientific attitude. In the collegial vis-à-vis scientific progress is generated and stabilized. To that I can only say: "Bravo!"

34

Response to Stellenbosch Colleagues

Robert Jewett

I am indebted both to Andrie Du Toit and John D. K. Ekem for submitted their evaluations even though I was prevented by unexpected circumstances from participating in the South African symposium. In both responses I recognize an unusual level of understanding my approach. I therefore feel thoroughly honored by these responses. While Dr. Ekem is basically supportive, Dr. Du Toit worries about my imposing an "exegetical straightjacket" on Romans. If the task of historical-critical exegesis is to discern the aim of an ancient author in selecting one interpretation and construal of the argument over another, this is hardly a fatal flaw. The historical question should rather be, 'Is this the right straightjacket?'

The reasons Prof. Du Toit provides in criticizing my exegetical reading seem inconclusive. If the argument of Romans is "multi-faceted," which my commentary actually documents in detail, this does not mean that Paul sought to achieve a number of disparate goals, including making his letter relevant for later theological purposes. That Paul would want to address "religious in-fighting" as "a theme on its own," because of the parallels with 1 Corinthians and its relevance for contemporary churches, overlooks the fact that he was not the authoritative founder of the Roman churches and that in 15:20 he denies trying to build on other apostle's foundations. That such infighting would not have "derailed the Spanish mission" is a subjective assessment that throws no light on what Paul may have thought. Prof. Du Toit prefers the traditional view that 13:10 proclaims "love" in the abstract as law's fulfillment, overlooking the double reference to "the love" at the beginning and end of the sentence which I take to be a reference to the love feast. That

15:14ff cannot be the climax of Romans because it contains "greetings reflecting in a Pauline way, the conventional letter greeting" overlooks the distinctive formulation that Paul selects. He greets no one directly, as in other Pauline letters, but urges the Roman believers to greet one another. This is congruent with the argument for mutual acceptance in chapters 12–15, which supports my rhetorical analysis of the normal function of a peroration. Prof. Du Toit's final comment affirms the need to evaluate historical hypotheses in order to make "scientific progress." This can only be accomplished, it seems to me, on the basis of exegetical and historical evidence. General skepticism about new inferences cannot suffice.

I appreciate Dr. Ekem's support in viewing Romans as a situational letter, including its imperial background and the concentration on issues of honor and shame. In view of Paul's status as a Roman citizen, he properly criticizes my skepticism about the apostle's mastery of Latin. Dr. Ekem also offers a needed correction, urging that Paul's loyalty to his Roman citizenship needs to be taken more fully into account with regard to Romans 13:1–7. His point is that Paul's privileged status indicates that he "would obviously be interested in maintaining the peace of the Empire." But in the light of what I learned about Rom 13 in Beijing, I would suggest that compared with the political alternative of supporting Jewish zealots opposing Roman rule, Paul accepted the Empire as the lesser of evils. When Ekem extends his dual identity hypothesis into Romans 7, he implicitly falls back into the outmoded view of Paul as psychologically divided between being willing versus being able to obey the law. If I am right in interpreting this passage in the light of Paul's self description in Galatians and Philippians as a former zealot who had perfectly obeyed the law, the dilemma is not a divided self but the incapacity of zealotism to achieve the good. I think it is right and proper for Ekem to struggle against his formerly colonial identity but I am skeptical of efforts to fuse this with Paul's own stance. While our tasks as interpreters are very different from Paul's apostolic calling, I appreciate Prof. Ekem's support of the major contentions of the commentary. It sustains the impression that the concentration on issues of honor and shame will be more readily received in Africa and Asia than in Europe and North America.

THE TOKYO SYMPOSIUM
APRIL 21, 2008

35

The Changing Faces of Identity in Paul's Letters: With Reference to Robert Jewett's Commentary on Romans

Atsuhiro Asano

Prologue

> From the first we have treated our minorities abominably, the way the old boys do the new kids in school . . . . The Pilgrim Fathers took out after the Catholics, and both clobbered the Jews. The Irish had their turn running the gauntlet, and after them the Germans, . . . the Chinese, the Japanese . . . this very cruelty toward newcomers might go far to explain the speed with which the ethnic and national strangers merged with the "Americans."[1]

In his monograph of cultural criticism, John Steinbeck gives an ironic description of the significant phenomenon of "identity", which could be operative not only in the U.S., but wherever various identities seek to survive in close encounter with one another. Unfortunately, such encounters often involve a considerable degree of violence.[2] Of equal importance as the basic aspect of the *identity of self-understanding*—who we are—is the relational aspect of the *identity of differentiation*—who we

[1] John Steinbeck, *America and Americans* (New York: Viking Press, 1966), 15.

[2] Therefore, Amartya Sen, in his recent publication, deals with this problem in the phenomena of "identity." Amartya Sen, *Identity and Violence: The Illusion of Destiny* (London & New York: W. W. Norton, 2006).

are in distinction from others.[3] In discussing the idea of community-identity, we are readily aware of two sides of a boundary-line: insiders/outsiders or "old boys"/"newcomers." The identity of differentiation concerns both an extra-communal power balance with outsiders and an intra-communal power balance among community members, so much so that Paul's ethical teachings are at times explained in terms of 'solidarity" and "difference."[4] Neither aspect of identity is static, as we assume that no community resists any change in its social outlook. These two aspects, which are closely related to each other, seem to be important for the interpretation of letters by the apostle Paul, who was concerned with the construction and maintenance of community-identity in his ever-expanding missionary activities. Viewing Paul's letter to the Romans as a sort of "ambassadorial letter," with particular theological and paranetic concerns for the future Spanish mission in view,[5] rather than regarding it simply as a general theological compendium, Robert Jewett's latest commentary on Romans is thus able to consider exigencies of both the missive's sender and its recipients, exigencies relevant to the changing outlooks or faces of identity of the communities.

Therefore, the present chapter has two foci. The first focus concerns the overall missionary purpose of Romans. In this section, the recent Japanese history of resistance to imperialism, particularly that of Japanese Christians, and the text reflecting that historical situation will be introduced as an analogy in order to substantiate and evaluate the argument laid out by Jewett. This analogy will help to survey how the colonized mind—the psychology of those whose identity is threatened by imperialistic expansionism—might be reflected in the reception and preaching of the gospel. Since the intention of the Spanish mission, announced in Romans, is an extension of Paul's effort of community building, the shifting motives in his community-identity construction will be the chapter's second point of focus. Here, the changing faces of community-identity will be traced in Paul's letters, such as those to the Galatians, Corinthians and Romans. On the basis of the shifting

[3] Fredrik Barth's conception of ethnic identity is helpful, in which he stresses that the main focus in the analysis of ethnic identity should be on the patterns of "dynamic" change and exchange of physio-cultural features of communities over the boundary line instead of on the mere inventory of those features of a community. Fredrik Barth edited, *Ethnic Groups and Boundaries: The Social Organization of Culture Difference* (Oslo: Universitetsforlaget, 1969), 9–38.

[4] David G. Horrell, *Solidarity and Difference: A Comtemporary Reading of Paul's Ethics* (London & New York: T. & T. Clark Continuum, 2005). Cf. also for the discussion on the violent reality of religious identity in; Miroslav Volf, *Exclusion & Embrace: A Theological Exploration of Identity, Otherness, and Reconciliation* (Nashville: Abingdon Press, 1996).

[5] Robert Jewett, *Romans: A Commentary* (Hermeneia; Minneapolis: Fortress Press, 2007), 42–46.

emphases of community-identity, the pattern of relatedness between Jew and Gentile in Romans 9–11 will be considered in terms of the cultural construct of "honor and shame."

I. SPANISH MISSION AND AN ANALOGY OF RESISTANCE

A. INTRODUCTION

1. ON AN ANALOGICAL APPROACH WITHIN BIBLICAL STUDIES

Analogical analysis is not a major emphasis within biblical studies, and its value is at times underestimated. Therefore, a brief remark on this approach is in order. Ordinary approaches to textual comparison are often genealogical, assuming some genetic connection between the subject matter and the object of comparison, such as that between early Christian communities and their genealogical forerunner, Judaism. Analogical analysis, on the other hand, is a comparison between entities having little immediate relation, as between early Christian missions in the Mediterranean world and 19th-century Christian missions in the Far East. In general, genealogical comparison takes note of and explains differences where a genetic similarity is expected, while analogical comparison takes note of and explains unexpected similarities between seemingly independent entities. This approach has proven fruitful in the studies of biblical literature and Christian origins.[6] Such a comparison can be a heuristic tool of interpretation, providing a new perspective with different questions and ways to answer those questions.[7] Employment of an analogical comparison does not suggest a close parallelism between ancient Mediterranean culture and modern Japanese culture (even though similar types of the "honor and shame" matrix seem to be assumed in the backgrounds of both cultures).[8] However, it will provide for us a ground to evaluate the connection between the biblical text (Romans in particular) and what might have been expected in the Spanish mission. Moreover, this analogical comparative study may be appropriate and helpful, because it provides for us a common ground for

---

[6] Some of the significant examples of analogical analysis are: a research on Paul by John Ashton, *The Religion of Paul the Apostle* (London: Yale University Press, 2000), 11–16; on the synoptic tradition by Rudolf K. Bultmann, *Die Geschichte der synoptischen Tradition* (10th edition.; Göttingen: Vandenhoeck & Ruprecht, 1995), 7–8; and on Christian origins by Jack T. Sanders, *Schismatics, Sectarians, Dissidents, Deviants: The First One Hundred Years of Jewish-Christian Relations* (London: SCM, 1993), 229–57.

[7] Cf. Alexander J. M. Wedderburn, *Baptism and Resurrection: Studies in Pauline Theology against its Graeco-Roman Background* (Tübingen: Mohr, 1987), 162.

[8] In analogical analysis, therefore, it is not an exact parallelism but proximity that is in focus. Confusion of it with genealogical analysis may lead one to underestimation of the former approach. Cf. R. S. Sugirtharajah, *Asian Biblical Hermeneutics and Postcolonialism: Contesting the Interpretation* (Sheffield: Sheffield Academic Press, 1999), 106–7.

further cultural evaluation on the contributions of the Pauline letters for the contemporary churches.[9]

2. On the Missionary Purpose of Romans: Situations in Rome and Spain

In his recent commentary on Romans, Jewett suggests that the main purpose of the composition of Romans is to "elicit support for Paul's forthcoming mission to Spain," and he synthesizes variously suggested motivations of the letter by other commentators as elements of need in preparation for the Spanish mission.[10] The analysis of the social and cultural situation of the mission locations in Spain led Jewett to assume that Paul had envisaged the necessity of assistance for his Spanish mission.[11] Financial aid and political / administrative connections may be provided by Phoebe, who played the role of "missionary patron" for Paul. Members of the house and tenement churches in Rome, especially those of Spanish origin, would provide Paul with personal connections and linguistic assistance. Moreover, in order to secure the partnership of Roman believers in his missionary endeavor, it was crucial for Paul to dispel among the Roman congregations any misinterpretation, misapplication and resultant accusations occasioned by his prior missionary activities elsewhere. Paul's polemical rhetoric against Jewish traditions, reflected in his prior letters, may have caused theological support, at least in part, for the divisiveness of the Roman congregation. The corrective nature of Paul's gospel presentation, however, is not simply for the sake of his Roman audience. While Paul wrote the letter to prepare the Roman believers for his Spanish mission, his eyes were fixed on the need for beneficiaries of his missionary activities in lands further west. In his assessment of the Spanish situation, Jewett takes special note of the dominance of Roman imperialistic control. The gospel presentation, which reflects a divisive competition—or "imperialistic attitude"—of the mission base in Rome or of its representatives, would be neither convincing nor attractive to the Spaniards, who are marginalized as barbarians under colonial exploitation.[12]Therefore, Paul's gospel presentation in Romans is understood as urging the audience to decide which gospel would bring true peace, either the imperialistic gospel of an empire of self-magnification or the impartial gospel of a kingdom of self-sacrifice.[13]

Based upon his understanding of Romans as a situational letter with the future Spanish mission in mind, and particularly mindful

---

[9] This chapter was originally prepared for a symposium in Tokyo with Robert Jewett, titled "Paul, Romans, and Japan."

[10] Jewett, *Romans*, 80–91.

[11] Jewett, *Romans*, 74–79, 89–91.

[12] Jewett, *Romans*, 88.

[13] Cf. Jewett, *Romans*, 49.

of the social situation thereof, a hermeneutical strategy with a "post-colonial sensitivity" is pervasive in Jewett's exegesis of the letter.[14] In Romans 9–11, titled "The Triumph of Divine Righteousness in the Gospel's Mission to Israel and the Gentiles," the contrast between an imperialistic and exploitative gospel and an impartial and embracing one is thought to be evident, and therefore examples of reading an anti-imperialistic implication in the text abound. The theme of abrogating the ethnic distinctions between Jews and Gentiles, for instance, has a direct implication to the Spanish situation, because the gospel promises a deliverance of its recipients from the imperial exploitation through a recognition as to which lord—either the Emperor or Christ—is "Lord of all and is generous to all who call on him" (10:13).[15] Paul's peculiar editing hand seen in the quotation of Isaiah 52:7, which carefully omits "the message of peace" (10:15), is arguably designed to avoid an association with the rhetoric of *Pax Romana*, which reminds the audience of fearful subjugation for the sake of "peace,"[16] a violent irony reflected elsewhere in the speech of Galgacus, who says; "To robbery, slaughter, plunder, they give the lying name of empire; they make a solitude (or wilderness) and call it peace" (Tacitus, *Agricola* 30). Paul presents God's salvation history, which has a place for both Jew and Gentile, in order that the recipients of the letter may experience inter-ethnic acceptance among the faith communities in Rome (11:11–12).[17] For a gospel reflecting the present imperialistic divisiveness in Rome would not be attractive and convincing to the Spanish audience.[18]

Because of the particular situational sensibility in reading the text, the themes of exploitation and discrimination as external force and internal struggle are particularly salient in Jewett's commentary on Romans. Therefore, subsequent analogical analysis is primarily to evaluate the psychology of the gospel's recipients within their backdrop of imperialistic expansionism, in order to judge the plausibility of a socio-political consideration within the textual interpretation, with particular interest in the aforementioned theme. The following section introduces the analogical comparative case of Kanzo Uchimura with a Christian community called *Mukyokai*, which he founded in the year 1900.[19] The first part of the historical section focuses on the background of western expansionism, in which the first Protestant mission in Japan

---

[14] Jewett, *Romans*, 74.

[15] Jewett, *Romans*, 663.

[16] Jewett, *Romans*, 640.

[17] Jewett, *Romans*, 675–78.

[18] Jewett, *Romans*, 88.

[19] For a detailed discussion on Uchimura and the emergence of *The Mukyokai* with the historical background, cf. Carlo Caldarola, *Christianity: The Japanese Way* (Leiden: E. J. Brill, 1979), chapter 2; A. Asano, *Community-Identity Construction in Galatians* (London & New York: T. & T. Clark Continuum, 2005), chapter 2.

and Uchimura's *Mukyokai* emerged. Then, we will review Uchimura's writings to see how he sought to establish a new identity of the "Japanese Christian", set against the historical background of Japan's resistance to and compliance with western expansionism.

B. Imperial Resistance: An Analogical Comparative Case

1. Historical Context of Imperial Resistance

The initial introduction of Christianity to Japan was marked by the arrival of Francisco Xavier with the Jesuits' mission to one of the southern islands of Japan in 1549, and soon other Catholic missions joined the missionary endeavor on the islands. However, the initial success of their missionary efforts–reportedly 300,000 believers within a century[20]–was almost completely put down by the Tokugawa regime through a series of severe persecution measures toward the subjects and through a seclusion policy (1639) that locked out the influence of western nations for the next two hundred years, the period called *Pax Tokugawa*, during which only a handful of survivors of the persecutions preserved their faith and lives as underground Christians.[21] Implementation of these severe measures was explained as inevitably necessary for insuring the purity of traditional Japanese religions, securing moral order, and protecting the nation from western expansionism.[22] Therefore, Christianity was historically resisted as part of western imperialism, indeed as the philosophical foundation of western civilization.

Pax Tokugawa came to an abrupt end when U.S. commodore Perry visited Uraga Bay in 1853. It was on this occasion that U.S. and other western nations began pressuring the government to relinquish national seclusion and to reopen the medieval gate to the land of the *samurai*. Faced with the ratification of inequitable treaties, Japan had to make a decision as to whether she should resist the western powers, in the end becoming one of their colonies, or westernize herself and be recognized as equally powerful, in order to have the treaties annulled as quickly as possible. This external pressure, combined with a large-scale civil war, ended the long history of the Tokugawa Shogunate, and the newly established monarchy of Meiji went headlong in the direction of westernization.[23] As part of westernizing the country, Christianity was reintroduced, and anti-Christian measures were discontinued in 1873, yet the memory of the atrocious persecution against the "deviant"

[20] C. R. Boxer, *The Christian Century in Japan, 1549–1650* (Berkeley: University of California Press, 1967), 321, 360.

[21] Ann H. Harrington, *Japan's Hidden Christians* (Chicago: Loyola University Press, 1993).

[22] This assumption of the danger of the Christian religion was preserved even in the Meiji Imperial Constitution, where the freedom of faith is allowed in its Article 28.

[23] For the general history of the emergence of modern Japan, see Ann Waswo, *Modern Japanese Society* (Oxford: Oxford University Press, 1996).

devotees of the western religion was not easily erased from people's minds. Prejudice against the religion inevitably persisted.[24] Though the influx of western technology continued as a necessary ingredient to establish a powerful modern nation among and above her Asian neighbours, reactionary nationalistic fervor gained force against an uncritical measure of westernization, especially against the spread of the western "soul" of Christianity, occasioned by enactment of the Imperial Constitution (1889) and the Rescript of Education (1890).[25]

The separation of western "body" and "soul"—materialistic technology and foundational philosophy or spirituality, respectively—is a pattern typical to the dialectic of a colonized mind, which tends to vacillate between admiration and disaffection for the foreign civilization.[26] The resultant policy of a double standard had already been employed in the long history of Japanese diplomacy with the dominant Chinese civilization, and it became operative in relation to the western nations. Japanese converts to Christianity struggled with their new identity. Securing equilibrium within the amalgamate identity of the "Japanese Christian" has long been a difficult task. It was, therefore, inevitable for the first Christians of Japan's modern era to seek indigenous expressions of their newfound faith.[27] In an effort to indigenize the religion, Kanzo Uchimura founded a unique Christian community called *Mukyokai* (literally "No-Church"), as an embodiment of his criticism against institutional churches, which reflect the divisive nature of western denominationalism.[28] In search of his *raison d'être*,

---

[24] For a report on the lingering persecution in the early Meiji era, see: Kazuo Shiono edited, *Kinkyo-koku Nippon no Hodo [Media Reports on Japan as an Anti-Christian Nation]: The Missionary Herald (1825–1873)* (Yusho-do Shuppan, 2007). For examples of prejudice toward the religion, see: Kiyomi Morioka, *Nihon no Kindai-shakai to Kirishutokyo [Japan's Early Modern Era and Christianity]* (Hyoron-sha, 1970), 215–16.

[25] Yasuo Furuya & Hideo Oki, *Nihon no Shingaku [Japan's Theology]* (Yorudan-sha, 1989), 98.

[26] According to Chatterjee, the division of material domain and spiritual domain in the struggle with the western dominance has been operative widely in Asia and Africa. Cf. Partha Chatterjee, *The Nation and Its Fragments* (Princeton: Princeton University Press, 1993), 6. Living well within this dialectic, Uchimura's stance to the U.S. is described as "ambivalent" by one of the most thoughtful critics of Uchimura. Yuzo Ota, *Uchimura Kanzo: Sono Sekai-shugi to Nihon-shugi wo Megutte [Kanzo Uchimura: On His Globalism and Nationalism]* (Kenkyusha, 1977), chapter 5, especially page 164.

[27] Arimichi Ebisawa & Saburo Ouchi, *Nihon Kirisutokyo-shi [The Church History of Japan]* (Nihon Kirisutokyo, 1970), 172.

[28] The extended discussion on Uchimura's use of the biblical text for cultural criticism and community-identity construction, especially pertaining to his effort of indigenizing Christianity, for which the present chapter has little space to spare, see; A. Asano, "Uchimura and the Bible in Japan," in edited by Christopher Rowland et al., *Oxford Handbook of the Reception History of the Bible* (Oxford: Oxford University Press, 2011). For Uchimura's active cultural adaptation of the Christian message, see for example; Uchimura, "Bushido and Christianity," *Seisho no Kenkyu* 186 (1916), in *Zenshu*, 22:161–62; "Nihon-jin to Kirisutokyo [The Japanese and Christianity]," *Seisho no Kenkyu* 301 (August, 1925), in *Zenshu*, 29:277.

which he described as a critical pursuit of the original biblical *Ecclesia*,[29] he became particularly vocal in sharp criticism against western imperialism and the western form of Christianity. Commenting on the general social ethos of the historical period, Shunsuke Kamei, one of Uchimura's disciples, writes; "The spirit of the Meiji era as a whole continued swinging between Japan and the West", and he continues; "in which Uchimura was shaken more violently than any other."[30] As a son of the disbanded *samurai*, Uchimura eagerly sought a western education at first, partly due to his fascination for western civilization, which reflected the contemporary westernizing ethos of Japan, and partly in the hope of social promotion, which he had once been denied during the process of social restructurization at the dawn of the Meiji era. Through the missionary work of an American educator, invited as part of a westernization program, Uchimura "(e)ntered the gate of the 'Jesus Religion'" in 1877 at his college.[31] During the subsequent period of his stay in the U.S. (1885–1888), however, Uchimura's initial fascination was betrayed as he experienced the moral depravity of what he had naïvely idealized as "the Christian nation of America".[32] Recanting his naïveté, Uchimura resolves; "One thing I shall never do in future: I shall never defend Christianity upon its being the religion of Europe and America."[33] At that realization, his "country ceased to be a 'good-for-nothing'"[34] for Uchimura.[35] The redirection in his Christian apology and his newly gained confidence in Japanese domestic traditions presuppose a criticism of the on going missionary activities, which often assumed the superiority of western civilization. Indeed, a prominent Japanologist describes the early Protestant missionary

---

[29] Emil Brunner introduced Uchimura and *His Mukyokai* to Europe, evaluating positively their critical role to point out the misunderstanding of the church in pursuing something other than the original *Ecclesia*. Emil Brunner, *Das Misverständnis der Kirche* (Zürich: Zwingli-Verlag, 1951), chapter 10; Brunner, "Die christliche Nicht-Kirche-Bewegung in Japan," *Evangelische Theologie* 4 (1959), 147–55.

[30] Shunsuke Kamei, *Uchimura Kanzo: Meiji Seishin no Dohyo [Kanzo Uchimura: A Milestone of the Spirit of the Meiji Era]* (Chuokoron-sha, 1977), 222.

[31] Kanzo Uchimura, *How I Became a Christian: Out of My Diary* (Originally published in 1895), in *Zenshu*, 3:14–15. All the writings of Uchimura are contained in; *Uchimura Kanzo Zenshu [The Complete Works of Kanzo Uchimura]* (41 volumes; Iwanami Shoten, 1980–2001). This series will hereafter be referred to as *Zenshu*.

[32] Cf. Uchimura, *How I Became a Christian*, 40–41, 46. Uchimura confessed his original fascination with western nations, and considered the U.S. to be "the land flowing with milk and honey." This sentiment was common among Japanese intellectuals, at least during the initial stage of westernization.

[33] Uchimura, *How I Became a Christian*, 90.

[34] Uchimura, *How I Became a Christian*, 92.

[35] An inferiority complex was a significant psychological feature of the colonized mind during the westernization. Cf. Erwin Bältz, *Das Leben eines deutschen Arztes im erwachenden Japan, Tagebücher, Briefe, Berichte herausgegeben von Toku Bältz* (Stuttgart: J. Engelborns Nachf, 1931), 89; Basil H. Chamberlain, *Things Japanese: Being Notes on Various Subjects Connected with Japan for the Use of Travelers and Others* (5th Edition; London: Kelly and Walsh, 1905), 135–36.

approach as regarding Japanese traditions to be "pagan and corrupt . . . archaic and outmoded."[36]

Apart from the disillusionment of the West, there is another element that shaped Uchimura as a significant cultural critic. With his disapproval of westernization, Uchimura initially favoured issuing the educational rescript, which was in part a manifestation of reactionary nationalism. However, at the public ceremony of enactment of said rescript in 1890, Uchimura did not bow and pay respect to the imperial signature on the rescript copy, considering it inappropriate for his Christian faith. The media immediately publicized the incident as an inexcusable act of *lèse majesté*, and caricaturized him as a national traitor.[37] Utterly humiliated by the media's treatment, Uchimura sought refuge among the churches. He was denied it, however, partly because he had been critical of the denominational churches' tendency toward sectionalism, which they had adopted from foreign missionaries, and partly because churches feared the implication of alleged sharing in the act of high treason.[38] Uchimura's experience of disconnection resulted in the foundation of his unique community, *Mukyokai*,[39] and caused him to reflect deeply on the themes of national pride and patriotism, which the country had begun to use as justification for her own version of imperialistic expansion toward Asian neighbours.[40] Thus, the experience of disillusionment with westernization and disconnection with institutional churches led Uchimura to a unique cultural position, which enabled him to become bold and inventive in his endeavour to materialize his version of indigenous expression of the Christian faith among his community of *Mukyokai*.

During the thirty years of his community building, he raised his voice against western imperialism as a hindrance to pursuing the "true" form of allegiance to Christ. In pursuit of the original biblical *Ecclesia*, therefore, Uchimura sought to indigenize the Japanese Christian identity, and present to his audience a gospel void of any traces of western imperialism. These are the primary foci of the missionary activities shaped by the colonized mind of Uchimura and his *Mukyokai*. The missionary foci reflected in their activities seem to accord with the sensibilities of Paul, which, according to Jewett, emphasize the gospel of impartiality, in view of his future audience in Spanish lands.

---

36 Cyril H. Powles, "Foreign Missionaries and Japanese Culture in the Late 19th Century: Four Patterns of Approach," *The Northeast Journal of Theology* (1969), 16–17.

37 Uchimura, "Letter to Bell," 331–32.

38 Uchimura, "Letter to Bell," 334.

39 Uchimura notes the deep sorrow and frustration of the denial of the churches; "I have become *mukyokai* (belonging to no church) . . . I am denied the sanctuary where I worship and come near to God". Uchimura, *Consolation of a Christian Believer* (originally published in 1893), in *Zenshu*, 2:26.

40 Uchimura, "Kon-nichi no Kon-nan [Today's Struggles]," *Tokyo Independent Magazine* (July, 1898), in *Zenshu*, 6:64.

In the following section, we will focus mainly on Uchimura's exposition of the letters of Galatians and Romans in order to review his criticism against imperialism, in the hope that we catch a glimpse of what might be the psychology of those who accept the Christian message under the domination of foreign powers. It should be noted that while the *Mukyokai* and the denominational churches stood somewhat apart from each other, the denominational churches shared similar experiences of marginalization in a country disdainful of Christianity. Therefore, what we find in Uchimura's social criticism reflects at least in part the psychology of his contemporary Japanese Christians in general.

2. TEXT OF IMPERIAL RESISTANCE

Uchimura was a prolific writer; his book, journal articles and letters are now compiled in his *Uchimura Kanzo Zenshu [The Complete Works of Kanzo Uchimura]*.[41] Therein are found his expositional studies on the letters to the Galatians and Romans, among other expositions on various biblical books and themes.[42] While Uchimura's anti-imperialistic rhetoric is sharper in his essays on contemporary social criticism,[43] we will focus on his interpretation of biblical messages, and how it reflects and is shaped by his (the interpreter's) experience of marginalization in an imperialistic environment. While acknowledging the significant value of the book of Isaiah in his introduction to the study of the prophet, Uchimura notes that no other book in the Bible is more theologically important than Paul's letter to the Romans.[44] However, Uchimura confesses in the preface to his exposition on Galatians that he has a special affinity for that letter. Uchimura explains that while Galatians holds unique theological importance to him for validating the existence of the *Mukyokai*,[45] his special fondness for the particular letter is due to an understanding that his own experience of marginalization can be compared to that of Paul, as observed in the Galatian letter.

In the brief preface to his study of Galatians, Uchimura uses half of the space to explain that the entire series of exposition is specifically designed to help the reader / audience[46] to resist the "evil influence" of

---

[41] Cf. note 31.

[42] Uchimura, *Zenshu*, volume 29 ("Study on Galatians") and volume 26 ("Study on Romans").

[43] For example, "Churches and Missionaries," in *Seisho no Kenkyu* 189 (April, 1916), in *Zenshu* 2:233–34; "The Exclusion Bill," *Seisho no Kenkyu* 286 (May, 1924), in *Zenshu* 28:217–18; "Letter to Nijima, Oct. 20, 1888," in *Zenshu*, 36:303.

[44] Uchimura, "Study on Isaiah," in *Zenshu*, 31:7.

[45] Uchimura, *Garateya-sho no Seishin [The Heart of the Galatian Letter]* (Kozando, 1926), in *Zenshu*, 29:458. Uchimura writes: ". . . if I am asked; 'what is the biblical foundation for your *Mukyokai*?' then I will answer; 'It is Paul's letter to the Galatians.' . . . As long as Galatians remains in the Bible, the spirit of the *Mukyokai* will never perish."

[46] Uchimura's biblical expositions were originally prepared for his public lectureship.

American Christianity. Commenting on the imperialistic expansionism of the U.S., he says, "it is said that Americanism would destroy the world, but what triumphs over the great force of Americanism is Paul's gospel found in the letter to the Galatians."[47] Uchimura elsewhere defines American Christianity as "a materialistic and divisive religion of triumphalism."[48] Two years prior to his writing the preface, the Exclusion Bill (or Johnson Act) was passed by the U.S. Congress in 1924, which resulted in regulating Japanese immigrants to the U.S. Uchimura had been very critical about the passing of the bill,[49] so he may have at this occasion sharpened his rhetoric against the U.S. In the body of his exposition, the opponents of Paul in Galatians, who preach "a different gospel" (Galatians 1:6–7), find their modern parallel in American missionaries, who preach divisive and exclusive denominationalism. The same conclusion is drawn in his interpretation of the false brothers in Jerusalem, who pressure to have Titus circumcised (Galatians 2:1–10).[50] Uchimura's polemic is not only against a western style of missionary activity, but also against the Japanese churches that depend on it. However, the denominational churches, who maintain a direct connection with the western missionary boards both financially and philosophically, resist the view that they are the embodiment of uncritical westernization. Therefore, Japanese church historians explain that the churches at that time generally understood:

> to enter into Christianity is not, as society in general maliciously misunderstands, to disregard the benefit of the nation and accept the domination of westerners by believing the western religion. Rather, it is to firmly support the independence of the nation and to accomplish the renewal of its people.[51]

Uchimura's polemic against imperialism is made evident, nevertheless, as he directs Paul's strong rebuke against the caprices of the Galatians in accepting a different gospel (Galatians 3:1–5) to the Japanese churches. He writes,

> It is today's Japanese churches that are eager to follow the American churches. Believers are deceived into looking away from Jesus Christ crucified and depending on

[47] Uchimura, *Garateya-sho*, 458–59.

[48] Uchimura, *The Japanese Christian Intelligencer* 2.5 (July, 1927), in *Zenshu*, 30:368; cf. Uchimura, "Quantitative Christianity," *Seisho no Kenkyu* 191 (June, 1916), *Zenshu*, 22:368–69.

[49] Uchimura, "Exclusion Again," *Seisho no Kenkyu* 287 (June, 1924), in *Zenshu*, 28:231–32.

[50] Uchimura, "Study on Galatians," 28–29.

[51] Ebisawa & Ouchi, *Nihon Kirisutokyo-shi*, 172.

their own works of hand. Thus, the depravity of their faith is inevitable.[52]

The message of God's justice has a direct political application for those who are overwhelmed by the presence of external forces of domination. None can deny such an implication even in the original text, which was composed and read by those under imperialistic domination. This political reading to resist exploitative discrimination is found more clearly in Uchimura's exposition on Romans 12.

Understanding Romans primarily as a theological compendium, Uchimura's language is less polemical in its exposition than that on Galatians.[53] It is true that Uchimura focuses rather extensively on doctrinal discussion in his Roman exposition, yet in the preface he presents the letter as a blueprint of "the divine reconstruction plan" among other plans of reconstruction in Japan.[54] One of those plans was proposed by the Minister of Foreign Affairs, Kaoru Inoue (1835–1915), to the Cabinet as part of his foreign policy, especially regarding unequal treaties with western nations, in which he argues,

> . . . what we must do is to transform our Empire and our people: make the Empire like the countries of Europe and our people like the peoples of Europe . . . I consider that the way to do this is to provide for truly free *transaction* between the Japanese and foreigners . . . . Let us change our people into European-style people . . . . Only thus can our Empire achieve a position equal to that of the Western countries with respect to treaties.[55]

This proposal led to an extreme policy suggestion of racial improvement through inter-marriage, promoted and published by a journalist, Yoshio Takahashi.[56] This reflects the social ethos of the early Meiji era, in which discussion of the nation's future often began with self-debasement.[57] Uchimura himself was in journalism in the 1890s, and

---

[52] Uchimura, "Study on Galatians," 49.

[53] However, one may also note the possibility that the editor of the Roman exposition, Kenzo Hanjo, may have soften Uchimura's expressions therein. Unlike the Galatian exposition, Uchimura admits that the former was "in a sense a co-authorship (with Hanjo)." Uchimura, "Study on Romans," 16.

[54] Uchimura, "Study on Romans," 16, 21.

[55] Inoue Kaoru Ko Denki Hensan-kai, *Segai Inoue Ko Den [Biography of Inoue, A Recluse]* (volume 3; Naigai Shoseki, 1968), 913–20 (translation by Donald Schively in *Tradition and Modernization in Japanese Culture*). A correction in *italic* is by the author.

[56] Y. Takahashi, "Nihon-jinshu Kairyo-ron [Improving Japanese Race]," in I. Watanabe, *Kyoiku Chokugo no Hongi to Kampatsu no Yurai* [*The Core Meaning of the Educational Rescript and the Background of its Promulgation*] (Fujii Shoten, 1939), 206–7.

[57] Donald H. Shively, "The Japanization of the Middle Meiji," in edited by D. H. Shively, *Tradition and Modernization in Japanese Culture* (Princeton: Princeton University Press, 1971), 94.

he was most probably aware of the sensational writing by contemporary journalists. Therefore, Uchimura may well have had in mind plans begotten under imperialistic pressure, and presented to his audience the message of Romans as a counter plan of internal renewal. Such an implication to subvert human plans may have been welcomed by an audience suffering from shameful, self-imposed debasement. In order to properly appreciate such a nüanced implication, one must be sensitive to the social ethos, a collective of colonized minds, behind the text. Therefore, with his sensibility to the mind of the colonized Spaniards, Jewett is able to draw out an implication of imperial resistance, for example, through Paul's editing pattern as observed in the quotation of Isaiah 52:7 (Romans 10:13).[58]

The body of Uchimura's exposition on Romans reveals the rhetoric of anti-imperialism, though with somewhat lesser frequency than the one on Galatians. In discussion of the redemptive grace of God in Romans 8, Uchimura comments on the Washington Conference (1921–1922), which was being held right at the time he publicly lectured on the chapter. Uchimura refers to the disarmament conference as an example of how God's justification moves humans to the mission of justice. Here, Uchimura seems to display his confidence in the leadership of western nations and the Japanese representatives.[59] However, his attitude drastically changes in his exposition on Paul's exhortation of mutual love in Romans 12. Here, Uchimura reviews the imperialistic nature of "Christian nations" practicing in their recent history what is contrary to the biblical teaching to love even one's enemies, "accumulating the wealth and keeping it to themselves by exploiting the powerless barbarians and half-civilized (*Hankai*)."[60] Then, he names the countries that attended the conference, though not specifying the occasion of the Washington Conference. The date of the public lecture on Romans 12 is August 10, 1922—six months after the conference. Uchimura's initial high expectation was certainly shattered by the result of the conference, in which the western nations basically preserved the power balance of their colonial control in Asia, though great concession was made by the Japanese government (from the Japanese point of view) to reach an agreement.[61] It is, therefore, most probable that Uchimura's frustration with the result of the conference is reflected in the change of his mood between the chapters. Commenting on the non-violence of Mahatma

---

[58] See note 16.

[59] Uchimura, "Study on Romans," 283–84. The public lecture on Romans 9 was held in January, 1992. Note that there is a discrepancy in the dates given in the 26th volume of *Zenshu*.

[60] Uchimura, "Study on Romans," 395–96.

[61] Cf. Tokushiro Ohata, "Japanese-American Relations around Opening of the Washington Conference," *International Relations* 2 (1961); Morinosuke Kashima, *Nihon Gaiko-shi [History of Japanese Diplomacy]* (Kashima Kenkysho, 1971), volume 13.

Gandhi, who was recently arrested, the contradicting behavior of the "Christian nations" is further criticized in the typical irony of Uchimura; "the religion that so-called Christian nations have never once acted out in the international scene, is being promoted world-wide by the ignoble non-Christian barbarian."[62] Then Paul's teaching on the Christian attitude toward the imperial government (Romans 13:1–7) becomes a biblical basis for his nüanced preference for Gandhi's non-violent resistance.[63] While Uchimura does not see an implied subversion of imperialism in the text as does Jewett,[64] he still seems to resist deducing from the text simple conformity or blind subjection to the imperial authority.

In the environment of western imperialistic oppression, the gospel reached Japan by way of the western missionaries. Though the country was not forced to be Christianized as was the case elsewhere in unfortunate days during the Church's long ecclesial history, the message of the Christian religion was at times perceived as part of western expansionism. Converts to Christianity struggled over their new identity in the dialectic between Japan and the West, but abandoning their newly found faith, often considered part of western civilization, was not an option for them. Therefore, they sought to sieve out from the religion those western elements suggestive of imperialistic exploitation and discrimination. Uchimura's cultural position is certainly different from that of Paul. While Paul sought to bring the gospel to a culture different from his own, Uchimura preached the gospel to his own people. However, both sought to take on a mission to present the gospel message to the colonized mind. The present analogy presents a case that a meaningful gospel mission with the background of imperialistic expansionism involved a sensitivity to the multifaceted identity struggle of the recipients of the gospel. Thus, reading Paul's letter to the Romans with this analogical case in mind, Jewett's hermeneutical direction of a post-colonial sensitivity to the text seems plausible, and his suggestion of Paul's missionary concerns seems to be consistent with the reality of the Christian mission in the first-century Mediterranean world.[65]

---

[62] Uchimura, "Study on Romans," 400.

[63] Uchimura, "Study on Romans," 406.

[64] Cf. Robert Jewett, "Response: Exegetical Support from Romans and Other Letters," in edited by Richard Horsley, *Paul and Politics: Ekklesia, Israel, Imperium, Interpretation* (Harrisburg: Trinity Press International, 2000), 65–68.

[65] We should note that the imperial language seems prevalent elsewhere in Paul's letters, therefore, the present hermeneutical perspective is meaningfully applicable to letters other than Romans as well. Cf. N. T. Wright, *Paul: In Fresh Perspective* (Minneapolis: Fortress, 2005), chapter 4.

II. IDENTITY & VIOLENCE

Reading even one out of 41 volumes of *Zenshu [The Complete Works]*, one would come away with the feeling that Uchimura's criticism of the West is rather pathological at times and his accusation against the denominational churches is often damaging and repellent rather than attractive from the Church's point of view. Seeing his sharp rhetoric as a means of survival for a fledgling and marginalized community, such a strategy of community-identity construction may be sympathized with as necessary rather than evil, or at least a necessary evil. However, the rhetoric necessary to attain coherence of a damaged community could itself become a damaging rhetoric of control, as the community gains a social status relative to others. With the gained power and status, identity constructed for resistance could turn about to beat others, just as, to borrow the image from Steinbeck, beaten kids turn around to jab at newer kids at school. Therefore, Uchimura's use of "barbarians and *Hankai* (half-civilized)" is symbolic of how intricate the effort of identity construction may be. It should be noted that Uchimura curiously paints a gravely simplistic picture of colonialism by joining "barbarians" and "*Hankai*" together as the victims of the western imperialism, despite the fact that he often spoke critically about the patriotism and nationalism of his compatriots.[66] *Hankai* is a term that the Japanese used to describe the status of a nation that is not completely civilized, yet is above the level of being "barbaric." It was used as rhetoric to justify Japan's imperialistic expansion among her Asian neighbors: just as international law allows civilized nations to colonize the less-than-civilized, Japan as a half-civilized nation is permitted to colonize barbarians.[67] Half-civilized Japan bows her head to the civilized, while kicking the barbarians behind the back. Treating the "barbarians and *Hankai*" together as the victims of western civilization, therefore, may overlook the reality of the power balance in Asia, where Japan was rising in power to threaten her neighbors. Warning against the reductionist or "solitarist" approach to identity in his recent book, *Identity and Violence*, Amartya Sen makes note of two faces of ethnic/religious identities. Commenting on the violent actions done in the name of identity, he asks "what is done to turn that sense of self-understanding into a murderous instrument," and points out the problem of overlooking meaningful affiliations and associations with others.[68] Without such a consideration for neighbors

---

[66] For instance, Uchimura, "Aikokushin ni Tsuite [On Patriotism]," *Seisho no Kenkyu* 306 (1926), in *Zenshu*, 29:351–52; "Nihonjin to Kirisutokyo [The Japanese & Christianity]," *Seisho no Kenkyu* 301 (1925), in *Zenshu*, 29:277.

[67] Cf. Yukichi Fukuzawa, *Bunmei-ron no Gairyaku [Outline of the Study of Civilization]* (Iwanami Shoten, 1931, originally published in 1875), 21–23.

[68] A. Sen, *Identity and Violence*, 174–76.

to be cultivated in the process of changing the faces of community-identity, a defensive exclusion against the strong for the sake of survival could change into an oppressive exclusion against the weak for the sake of control, such as was observed during a rather early period of ecclesial history (Julian, *Letters* 41B [Bostra]; *Misopogon* 364B),[69] despite the fact that such a relational sensibility may have been one of the key teachings of Paul.[70]

Focusing on the resultant history of oppression, Paul, with his peculiar rhetoric against Jewish traditions, particularly in Galatians, is at times understood as being responsible for later Christian expansionism. Therefore, his egalitarian teaching (Galatians 3.28) is described as "coercing universal sameness,"[71] which marginalizes the strangers. I refuted elsewhere the viewpoint primarily as failing to distinguish the life situation of Paul from that of Christians in later history, neglecting to consider the change in social position that affected the function of community-identity to shift from defense for survival to oppression for control.[72] Nevertheless, Paul's rhetoric for survival, while not necessarily "politically correct" or sensitive to all facets of life by modern standards, was utilized as a philosophical support for oppressing the weak, most probably contrary to his own intention. This grave implication of community-identity in relation to outsiders (extra-communal differentiation) readily seen in later ecclesial history was indeed already discernible within the Roman communities (intra-communal differentiation). To counter this very problem, however, Paul himself felt the need to deliver a corrective message to the Romans. Therefore, by attending to the changing faces of community-identity, with the history of reception and interpretation of the Pauline letters in view, we may become more sensitive in judging the effect of Paul's teachings for the very communities he wrote to, and in drawing out meaningful applications for present churches.[73] In the subsequent section, we will survey the changing emphases of community-identity in Paul's letters and remark on Paul's teachings on the issue of intra-

[69] Julian recounts the Christian oppression against paganism in the fourth century. Cf. W. C. Wright's "Introduction" to the third volume in, trans. W. C. Wright, *Letters 1-73, Letters 74-83, Shorter Fragments, Epigrams, Against the Galilaeans, Fragments* (Cambridge: Harvard University Press, 1923), xxiv.

[70] David Horrell understands this sort of teaching, which he terms as "other-regard" to be one of the fundamental features of Paul's ethical teaching. Horrell, *Solidarity and Difference*, chapter 6.

[71] Daniel Boyarin, *A Radical Jew: Paul and the Politics of Identity* (Berkeley: University of California Press, 1994), 233.

[72] A. Asano, *Community-Identity Construction in Galatians*, 200–6.

[73] Analyzing the effects of the biblical literature, or any literature for that matter, on the later history has a value in itself. Cf. Wolfgang Stegemann, "Anti-Semitic and Racist Prejudices in Titus 1:10–16," in edited by M.G. Brett, *Ethnicity and the Bible* (Leiden: E. J. Brill, 1996), 293–94. However, by overlooking the changing faces of identity, we may miss the opportunity to face and own our own responsibility by blaming on others.

communal power balance, i.e. the relatedness between Jew and Gentile, particularly in Romans 9–11.

III. The Changing Faces of Identity in Paul's Letters

A. Survival and Cohabitation

It is assumed in this chapter that Paul wrote his letter to the Galatians in the very early stage of his independent missionary endeavor among the Gentiles. Paul's expression, *houtōs tacheōs* ("how quickly") indicates that the letter was written not too long after he left the mission field in Galatia (Galatians 1:6), and it seems that Corinth is the very likely location for the composition of Galatians.[74] Therefore, while the content of the letter reflects the situation in Galatia, it probably relates to what the believers in Corinth had heard from Paul. Corinth was an important port city leading to the Italian peninsula through the Adriatic Sea; therefore frequent communication with Rome could be easily expected, as in the case of Priscilla (Prisca) and Aquila (Acts 18:2, Romans 16:3). Therefore, even though it would take decades for the local churches to begin collecting Paul's letters, Paul's thinking reflected in the Galatian letter may have affected believers in the two metropolises (Corinth and Rome) as to how they may envisage their communities to be built. Paul's effort of community building in Galatia was facing a challenge by the "circumcisers"—Jewish teachers probably of Judaean origin who encouraged the Gentile members to be circumcised in order to be fully incorporated into the Church and receive God's blessing through Abraham. For Paul, the emphasis on Jewish identity (-markers) meant stigmatization of his Gentile mission and the Gentile members being relegated as a secondary entity in relation to the authentic members of Jewish origin.[75]

Therefore, the primary purpose of Paul's theological persuasion in Galatians 3 and 4 is to reverse or elevate the status of the marginalized Gentile members by way of undermining the primacy of Jewish tradition. In other words, Paul is presenting a reversed worldview, in which the Galatian members would receive a positive identity as they are, without conforming to the Jewish identity. Already in the first two chapters of the letter, Paul's nüanced acknowledgement of the Jerusalem leaders may reflect his effort of presenting a new worldview. In Galatians 3:6–14,

---

[74] Hans D. Betz, *A Commentary on Paul's Letter to the Churches in Galatia* (Hermeneia; Philadelphia: Fortress Press, 1979), 11–12; W. G. Kümmel, *Einleitung in das Neue Testament* (Heidelberg: Quelle & Meyer, 1983), 265–66.

[75] Cf. James D. G. Dunn, *The Theology of Paul's Letter to the Galatians* (Cambridge: Cambridge University Press, 1993), 78–79.

Abraham's personal faith in God is the focal point for Paul. Therefore, while the Gentiles inherit God's blessing to Abraham on account of faith in Christ, the inheritance scheme for the Jews is introduced rather negatively by presenting a strict interpretation of Torah obedience. Then, by making Christ the sole and immediate heir (*sperma*) to Abraham (3:16), Paul makes a direct connection between Abraham and those who belong to Christ through baptism (3:20–29). The ritual of baptism announces the abrogation of social, ethnic and gender distinctions (3:28). Subsequently, the Torah is depicted as an equal to principles of slavery (4:3, cf. 4:9), which leads the reader to the climax of Paul's theological persuasion in his exposition of the Sarah-Hagar story (4:21–31). Regardless of how "forced," "strange and arbitrary" or "strained and distorted" a Midrash it may be,[76] the exposition seems to be an appropriate conclusion to the recreated worldview. With the negative view of the present Temple and the sustained motif of enslavement to the Torah, the final imperative to exclude those under the Torah (4:30) makes it extremely difficult for any Torah-observant Jew to join or remain in the community.

If we are to use the language of Victor Turner's social theory called "liminality,"[77] Paul's persuasion, particularly in Galatians 3 and 4, is an anti-structural reaction to the conventional structure of the Jewish approach to the gospel presentation (cf. Galatians 2:8).[78] Turner's theory is based upon a study of "rites of passage", in which a person in a mundane, structured life passes into a ritual, which is an anti-structural (liminal) state. The liminal state emphasizes abrogation or reversal of social values and priorities.[79] According to Turner, a society goes through a similar teleological process between structure and anti-structure. In an anti-structural liminal state, such a community often emphasizes and experiences abrogation or reversal of social values and priorities as its reaction against structure. Therefore, the dissolution of ethnic, social

---

76 Respectively, James D. G. Dunn, *The Epistle to the Galatians* (Peabody: Hendrickson, 1993), 243; John M. G. Barclay, *Obeying the Truth: A Study of Paul's Ethics in Galatians* (Edinburgh: T. & T. Clark, 1995), 91; R. P. C. Hanson, *Allegory and Event: A Study of the Sources and Significance of Origen's Interpretation of Scripture* (London: SCM, 1959), 82.

77 Victor Turner, *The Ritual Process: Structure and Anti-Structure* (New York: Cornell University Press, 1969), 106–7. For the application of this theory to Paul's theology, see, Christian Strecker, *Die liminale Theologie des Paulus: Zugänge zu paulinischen Theologie aus kulturanthropologischen Perspektive* (Göttingen: Vandenhoeck & Ruprecht, 1999), 111.

78 Bockmuehl understands that the political situation in Jerusalem at that time would allow only a form of mission that emphasizes the obedience to the Torah. Markus Bockmuehl, *Jewish Law in Gentile Churches: Halakhah and the Beginning of Christian Public Ethics* (Edinburgh: T. & T. Clark, 2000), 172.

79 Turner, *The Ritual Process*, 96–97, 127–29. Turner's theory is based primarily upon the study of passage rites of, Arnold van Gennep, *Les rites de passage: études systématique des rites* (Paris: Librairie Critique, 1909).

and gender distinctions in the liturgical recitations of the passage rite of baptism (Galatians 3.28) could be understood as an expression of this liminal ethos of the Galatian community.[80] Such a liminal identity may have functioned as a protection for the marginalized Gentile believers, because it secures their reason for existence as an authentic community apart from Jewish tradition. Eradication of such differences is often understood as a limited experience within the passage rite itself or in the future eschatological congregation, simply because of the unrealizability of the ideal within the daily life of the community.[81] However, the worshiping ritual community, in a state which Turner calls "permanent liminality," chooses to maintain the liminal values such as are reflected in an egalitarian lifestyle, in order to set them apart from the rest of society.[82] The active missionary roles that female believers play in Acts (Mary, Lydia, Priscilla) may reflect such a tendency. While adjustments in communal values are already being observed in 1 Corinthians and Romans, and while the discussion as to whether Paul was a part of the motivating force or resisting force for the egalitarian ideal should not be neglected,[83] there seems to be a significant phenomenon, deviating from the contemporary standard, of female members playing an active part in prayer, prophecy (1 Corinthians 11:5), and apostolic duties (Romans 16:7).[84] Thus, Wayne Meeks' evaluation is that "(t)here are a number of signs that in the Pauline school women could enjoy a functional equality in leadership roles that would have been unusual in Greco-Roman society as a whole and quite astonishing in comparison with contemporary Judaism."[85] It is also notable that emancipation of slaves may have been expected of some local churches early in the second century (Pliny the Younger, *Epistles* 10.96; Ignatius, *Polycarp* 4.3).

In view of this evidence of the liminal nature of Pauline communities at their initial stage, traces of a transition toward structure (institution)

---

[80] For the discussion on the liminal significance in the peculiar phrase of *arsen kai thēly*, see; Daniel Boyarin, *Galatians and Gender Trouble: Primal Androgyny and the First-Century Origins of a Feminist Dilemma* (Berkeley: Center for Hermeneutical Studies, 1995); Dennis R. MacDonald, *There is No Male and Female: The Fate of a Dominical Saying in Paul and Gnosticism* (Philadelphia: Fortress Press, 1987); Wayne A. Meeks, "The Image of Androgyne: Some Uses of a Symbol in Earliest Christianity," *History of Religions* 13 (1973–1974), 165–208.

[81] Boyarin, *Galatians and Gender Trouble*, 25; Bultmann, *Theologie*, 1:304–05.

[82] Turner, *Ritual Process*, 145.

[83] See, for example, a dialogue between revisionist and deconstructionist views of Romans on the gender issues in; Cristina Grenholm & Daniel Patte, *Gender, Tradition and Romans: Shared Ground, Uncertain Borders* (New York & London: T. & T. Clark International, 2005).

[84] On Junia(s) being a female apostle, see, C. E. B. Cranfield, *A Critical and Exegetical Commentary on the Epistle to the Romans* (2nd vol.; Edinburgh: T. & T. Clark, 1979), 789; C. K. Barrett, *A Commentary on the Epistle to the Romans* (London: A. & C. Black, 1991), 259.

[85] Meeks, "The Image of the Androgyne," 198.

are particularly notable. It may be that the egalitarian baptismal emphasis reflected in Galatians 3:28 was being taught at Corinth, and it initially encouraged some individuals in the worship setting to act somewhat contrary to what Paul came to consider as a decent "order" (1 Corinthians 14:40).[86] Paul's corrective here, especially on the basis of the order of creation, may have influenced the later churches. Therefore, the *Haustafeln* (Ephesians 5:22–6.9, Colossians 3:18–25) and the instruction to Timothy (1 Timothy 2:9–15) reflect quite a degree of institutionalization and departure from the gender equity observed in Galatians.[87] Paul's attitude toward commensality seems to shift from Galatians 2:11–14 to 1 Corinthians 8:4–13, and it may be based upon his recognition that the reality of cohabitation of Jews and Gentiles makes it difficult to achieve the ideal Eucharistic form of meal-fellowship, sharing one cup and one bread together. A similar corrective observed in his discussion of "the strong" and "the weak" in Romans 14 may reflect the same kind of realization on Paul's part, as well as the erroneous application of such a teaching to justify Gentile dominance over marginal Jews on the part of the Romans. In this instance, Paul may have preferred the parallel mode of meal-fellowship, because it would not give the Gentile members grounds to criticize the Jewish believers.[88] Thus, his effort in community-identity construction is shaped by a conviction of his call to the Gentile mission in general and conditioned by the life situation of each community that he either helped build or was associated with. Paul's persuasion in Romans 9–11 is an example of such an effort.

B. Romans and "Shame Turned to Honor"

The sensitive issue of inter-ethnic cohabitation is dealt with in these three chapters, where Paul joins Jew and Gentile in God's salvation history. I will briefly remark on two pericopes pertinent to the cultural concepts of honor and shame. The first pericope concerns Paul's presentation of Christ as the goal of the Torah (*telos gar nomou Christos*), who brings down the ethnic boundary (10:1–13). Paul begins the discussion by introducing the unenlightened zeal (*zēlos*) of Israel for the

[86] For various discussions on Paul's teaching on head-covering (1 Corinthians 11:2–16), see, Anthony C. Thiselton, *The First Epistle to the Corinthians* (Grand Rapids: Eerdmans, 2000), 829; Boyarin, *Primal Androgyny*, 21; Elisabeth Schüssler Fiorenza, *Rhetoric and Ethic: The Politics of Biblical Studies* (Minneapolis: Fortress Press, 1999), 169–70.

[87] Strecker points out this tendency toward institutionalization. Strecker, *Die liminale Theologie*, 449. See also, Margaret Y. MacDonald, *The Pauline Churches: A Socio-Historical Study of Institutionalization in the Pauline and Deutero-Pauline Writings* (Cambridge: Cambridge University Press, 1988), 31–84.

[88] Cf. Philip F. Esler, *Galatians* (London: Routledge, 1998), 101–2, for the differentiation between Eucharistic and parallel modes of meal-fellowship.

Torah (10:2, cf. 9:31). This leads to the reference to a vertical movement (*tis anabēsetai eis ton ouranon* and *tis katabēsetai eis tēn abysson*, 10:5–7), based upon Jewish tradition (Deuteronomy 30:12–13), to describe the zeal of their Torah obedience. A modification in the second part of the movement—from "who will cross to the other side of the sea" to "who will descend into the abyss" (cf. Psalm 107:26)—, certainly "more coherent and succinct"[89] than the Deuteronomic journey by making the vertical movement complete, is explained as possible because the term *abyssos* is the translation of "deep places" (*t̲ehōm*) of either the earth or the sea.[90] Both upward and downward directions of the vertical movement may imply a forceful (or artificial) inducing of the Messiah on earth based upon contemporary messianic expectations. If this is the motivation for the zealous pursuit of the Torah by some Jewish schools, Paul claims that Messiah is indeed the goal of the Torah (10.4), and is now made available to us through God's initiating grace, expressed in the descension (*abysson*) and the ascension (*ouranon*) of Jesus.[91] Furthermore, the messianic age has come to pass in him, who is to be acknowledged as Lord (10:9).

This vertical movement, which is christologically significant, seems to provide a motivational force for Jews and Gentiles to join together in the community. Therefore, "anyone who believes will not be put to shame (*ou kataischynthēsetai*), for there is no distinction between Jew and Greek" (10:11–12). This statement echoes Paul's opening announcement in the letter that he is not ashamed (*ou epaischynomai*) of the gospel, which leads both Jews and Greeks to salvation (1:16). As Jewett rightly notes, Paul consciously uses the honor-shame terminology here to remind the reader of the shameful message of the crucifixion and to emphasize the "paradox of power" that the message contains.[92] To be sure, the paradox involves the idea of "the power of mission in the message of weakness." However, along with the missionary implication in the paradox is a social one; therefore, there seems to be a horizontal application for the vertical journey as a corrective for the inter-ethnic situation in Rome. This paradox is poetically illustrated as the journey of status reversal in the *kenosis* hymn, in which *the shameful descending* results both in *the honorable status elevation* of Jesus as Lord and the universal

---

[89] Jewett, *Romans*, 627.

[90] Joseph A. Fitzmyer, *Romans* (New York: Doubleday, 1993), 590–91.

[91] Jewett, *Romans*, 628. Cf. Douglas J. Moo, *The Epistle to the Romans* (Eerdmans, 1996), 665–66.

[92] Jewett, *Romans*, 136–37, cf. 631–32. Turner, *The Ritual Process*, 170–72. See also, Helmut Mödritzer, *Stigma & Charisma im Neuen Testament und seiner Umwelt: Zur Soziologie des Urchristentums* (Freiburg: Universitätsverlag/Göttingen: Vandenhoeck & Ruprecht, 1994), 24–25, 267 for his understanding of status elevation as a transformation of stigma into charisma.

acknowledgement of his lordship (Philippians 2:6–11).[93] The vertical journey that resulted in the turning of *shame* to *honor* is acknowledged by all; therefore, the new paradigm or ordering of life is established for the community of faith. In this new paradigm, the sacrificial giving of oneself leads to abundance, thus there is no need for competition. In the hymnal setting of the Philippian community, the applicational focus of the theme 'shame turned to honor" is surrender of intra-communal competition as to who is better (Philippians 2:3). Through the reference to the vertical journey in Romans 10, the specific point of focus is the surrender of inter-ethnic competition between the Jews and Gentiles. While the theme of a vertical journey may not imply the heavenly journey to receive wisdom in the apocalyptic context,[94] the motif of establishing the "universal" (inter-ethnic) community on account of the *kyrios'* ascension to supremacy by renouncing all honors[95] may be read by the Romans as countering the theme of imperial magnification.[96] It is unclear at best whether Paul had a particular hymn or ritual setting in mind when composing his letter to the Romans, yet the theme of reversal or irony of the cross is clearly seen in his writings (Galatians 6:14, 17, 1 Corinthians 1:18, 23, 2 Corinthians 5:21, Romans 1:16). We may, therefore, observe a shift in Paul's use of the reversal theme between Galatians and Romans. In Galatians, the teaching of egalitarianism based upon a reversal theme of the liminal rites is emphasized so that the marginalized Gentile members (and therefore Paul's Gentile mission) may be defended against the Torah-observant mission of the "circumcisers." In Romans, the reversal theme implied in the vertical journey is designed to support the dissolution of ethnic distinction in salvation history, so that a healthy cohabitation of Jews and Gentiles may be attained.

In his continuing theme of God's salvation for Jew and Gentile in Romans 9–11, Paul introduces a series of salvific chain reactions. The disbelief of Israel opened up the way for salvation of the Gentiles. In turn, the salvation of the Gentiles causes them (Israel) to be zealous/jealous (*eis to parazēlōsai*), and their zeal/envy leads some of them to salvation (11:11–14). Jewett argues that the series of *zēloō* terminology (10:2, 19, 11:11, 14) should be understood as "zeal" instead as "envy."[97] The discussion seems to provide for us an appropriate occasion to apply the concept of honor competition, and the result may affect our understanding of

[93] Fee links the *kenosis* hymn and the christological confession on the basis of the resurrection in Romans 10:9. Gordon D. Fee, *Paul's Letter to the Philippians* (Grand Rapids: Eerdmans, 1995), 225.

[94] Jewett, *Romans*, 626.

[95] Jewett, *Romans*, 49.

[96] Wright understands that the retelling of salvation history in Romans 9–11 as a counter story of the Roman history climaxing in Augustus. N. T. Wright, *Paul*, chapter 4, especially page 78.

[97] Jewett, *Romans*, 674–75.

the relatedness between Jews and Gentiles in the Roman congregation. Bruce Malina introduces, along with the honor-shame value system, the aspect of "dyadism" as one of the key psychological aspects in the ancient Mediterranean world. In fact, the honor-shame value system should be understood in terms of this dyadic personality or group-orientation as opposed to individualism, as honor and shame concern the recognition by one's significant others.[98] Therefore, a zealous pursuit of recognition does not seem to occur in a vacuum, but in relation to or in competition with others, manipulating and stigmatizing other parties in the environment of limited goods. Thus, we may be able to answer why the Jewish legalists, who considered early Christian belief heretical, would have been jealous of Gentiles for their acceptance of an allegedly mistaken doctrine.[99] I suggest that it is because they were concerned with the pursuit of honor in competition with others. First of all, Gentile veneration of the Jewish religion was thought to reflect a gain in honor for the Jews amongst the nations, so Philo, for example, reports very proudly that the nations as well as the Jews gathered on the island of Pharos for a celebration of the translation of the Torah (*De vita Mosis* 2.41). Philo's confidence in the Torah should not be misunderstood as evidence for active proselytism in Judaism,[100] yet it shows at least that Gentiles" respect for the Torah could be a source of pride / honor for him. In the context of the pursuit of honor, accusing a party of being "heretical" is not a purely doctrinal judgment, but rather doctrinal issues may be used for stigmatizing or shaming a competing group. For instance, Pilate realized that high priests, after their interrogation, handed Jesus over to him *dia phthonon* ("out of envy" in Mark 15.10, Matthew 27:18).[101] The original motivation for the arrest of Jesus was, in a sense, the result of their defeat in the honor competition with an opposing party, which was ever gaining in popularity among the Jews (Mark 11:27–12:34). If their intention was simply to pursue doctrinal purity for its own sake, it is difficult to understand why they would stir up the crowd to ask for Barabbas' release, who seemed to be in clear violation of the Torah (Mark 15:11–15). Paul's zealous persecution against the growing popularity of the Christian heresy (Acts 8:3, Galatians 1:14, 23) may have been related to the attitude of the Jewish leaders, who were filled with zeal /

---

98 Bruce J. Malina, *The New Testament World: Insights from Cultural Anthropology* (Louisville: Westminster John Knox Press, 1993), 65–73, especially 67.

99 Jewett, *Romans*, 674–75, cf. 646.

100 Louis H. Feldman, "Jewish Proselytism," in edited by H. W. Attridge and Gohei Hata, *Eusebius, Christianity, and Judaism* (Detroit: Wayne University Press, 1992), 381–92.

101 Note that *phthonon* and *zēlos* are at times almost interchangeably used by Paul (Romans 1:29, Galatians 5:21, Philippians 1:15; 1 Corinthians 3:3, 2 Corinthians 11:2), and this phenomenon itself shows the close proximity of the sphere of meaning of the two ideas.

envy (*eplēsthēsan zēlou*), for the group of heretics was gaining popularity among the people (Acts 5:17). Synagogue members in the Diaspora were again filled with zeal/envy (*eplēsthēsan zēlou, zēlōsantes*) as the apostle Paul was in competition with them, gathering crowds among the Gentiles for his heretical teaching (Acts 13:45, 17:5). Note that the target of *zēlos* in the case of the Thessalonian mission is on the converts as well as on the missionaries (Acts 17:6). Seen from the perspective of honor competition with others, therefore, one's zealous pursuit for the Torah readily assumes envy against or by others in competition, and one's envy may be based upon their zeal in pursuit of the Torah. The lack of this perspective may explain the discord concerning the translation of the *zēlos* terminology among exegetes in non-dyadic cultures. As to the logic of how *zēlos* leads some to salvation (Romans 11:14), it may be comprehensible, as Jewett argues, only on the basis of Paul's own revelatory ("conversion") experience (Galatians 1:13–16).[102] The theme of this competition in the salvific chain reaction introduces Paul's subsequent teaching, in which he warns that the competition for honor is in contradiction with God's gracious or kind providence (*chrēstotēs*) of a salvation plan (11:17ff.).

Sensitivity to the concept of honor and shame helps one to appreciate the dynamics of human relatedness in the ancient Mediterranean world, and, as Jewett's commentary on Romans proves, it is a significant hermeneutical tool for us to gain insight into the life situations of the faith communities in Rome. In this brief review of the given pericopes of the letter, we saw how the gospel of the 'shame turned to honor" could be a corrective for the devastating effect of the honor competition between Jews and Gentiles. We also observed that the intricate sphere of *zēlos* terminology reflects how religious devotion in the dyadic society shows more susceptibility to rivalry between groups and individuals. Lastly, it should be noted that the concepts of honor and shame denote a peculiar frame of reference, which regulates and explains the behaviors within a particular culture. Problems often associated with the cultural framework are due to the competitive environment of the pursuit of honor within a society of limited goods. Therefore, when Jewett says that honor-shame cultures would find it difficult to critically approach the problem of superiority competition,[103] it is not the honor-shame framework that is problematic, but the environment of competition itself.[104] People

[102] Jewett, *Romans*, 675. Conversely, this passage may provide a window to see an aspect of Paul's "conversion" experience.

[103] Jewett, *Romans*, 691.

[104] A confusion between honor-shame framework and competitive environment causes the former to lose its evaluative value, such as observed in the social-scientific criticism of Galatians 2. Cf. Philip F. Esler, "Making and Breaking an Agreement Mediterranean Style: A New Reading of Galatians 2:1–14," *Biblical Interpretation* 3:3 (1995), 285–314.

in a culture of honor and shame are expected to behave on the basis of what is considered honorable as a member of the culture, as Paul reminds the Philippian believers (Philippians 4.8). Even in the paradox of 'shame turned to honor," Paul is still operating within the framework of honor and shame, and therefore, he claims that he is not ashamed of the gospel. Incidentally, in our analogical case of Uchimura as well, we can see that instead of abandoning the honor-shame framework, he actively uses the cultural framework to instruct community members as to what the true Christian walk must involve.[105] As Paul sought to present a corrective for the community-identity of the Roman believers, the remedy is not grace over and against the honor-shame culture, but a reordering of honor and shame on the basis of grace.[106] Therefore, for a community identified with the self-sacrificing act of its founder for the benefit of others, self-sacrifice in the given new paradigm is considered honorable behavior, however shameful it may appear to outsiders. As the new worldview of "shame turned to honor" is accepted as a norm or an identifying value of a community, then "competition for honor" becomes a self-contradiction. When honor is pursued in competition, it ceases to be honor (Philippians 3:4–8). This is what Paul sought to help the Roman congregation recognize in their relatedness between Jew and Gentile.

EPILOGUE

In his political reading of the gospel of Mark, Richard Horsley warns of the danger of missing the whole picture when an exegete is focused solely on theological issues in reading the gospels, as well as other biblical books.[107] Jewett, in his sensibility of the socio-political situations facing the Romans, avoids this danger, and acknowledges that "the real threat in Paul's view was not theological difference, but social contempt (i.e. intra-communal ethnic contest) that "proper theology" usually deepens."[108] In this sensibility, he also attempted to draw out from Paul's presentation of the gospel the missionary's farsighted attention to a future audience in Spain under the imperial domination of Rome. This chapter in part augmented Jewett's argument with a concrete historical analogy and pointed out that such a post-colonial sensibility to the text seems both plausible and convincing. This analogical analysis also made us aware of the intricacy in the effort of constructing and maintaining the identity

[105] Uchimura, "Meiyo no Shi [Honorable Death]," *Seisho no Kenkyu* 101 (August 10, 1908), in *Zenshu* 16:7. Cf. "Meiyo ka Fumeiyo ka [Honor or Shame]" and "Hazukashiki Meisho [Shameful Names]," respectively in *Zenshu* 7:76, 94–95.

[106] Thus, Malina seems correct as he explains that the honor-shame system itself does not present a list of moral behaviours. Malina, *The New Testament World*, 54.

[107] Richard A. Horsley, *Hearing the Whole Story: The Politics of Plot in Mark's Gospel* (Louisville: Westminster John Knox Press, 2001), ix–xv.

[108] Jewett, *Romans*, 691. Parentheses added.

of a community in relation to others as it changes its positions in society. Therefore, Paul's letters were surveyed with an understanding that it is the responsibility of a prudent exegete to observe carefully the changing faces of community-identity in order to judge what the text meant to the immediate audience.

Paul's letters, written at a time of emergence of faith communities seeking to construct a secure identity to defend their fledgling existence, together with the history of interpretation of those letters that is often accompanied by grave implications on fragile groups existing within and without, offer significant insight into issues facing the Christian community still at the margins of Japanese society, which for the last 150 years has been resistant to friendly interaction with the faith community. Japanese churches, located right at the margins yet well within a nation that is both economically and militarily powerful, may be brought by Paul's letters to the keen awareness that the boundary lines they draw have different implications to different neighbors at different phases of community life. With an awareness of the intricacy involved in the changing faces of a religious community-identity, Japanese churches may find a meaningful place in society, meaningful not only for their own sake but also for the sake of others. Lastly, one of the most notable values of Jewett's commentary on Romans, with its special attention to the socio-political issues that shaped Paul's composition of the letter, is to stimulate and guide readers for this very discussion as to how Paul's gospel relates to the present socio-political issues that they face in relation to people both inside and outside their faith communities.

36

The World-transforming Power of the Pauline Gospel: Some Remarks on the Commentary on Romans by Prof. R. Jewett

Nozomu Hiroishi

I. General Characteristics of the Romans by Prof. Jewett

- Forthcoming mission in Spain as context (socio-rhetorical analysis)
- Reconstruction of the social and communal situation of the Christian in Rome (tenement churches, discrepancy between the 'strong" and the "weak," discrimination of the Spaniards as barbarians by Roman empire)
- Paul as one worker among others for communities (e.g. Phoebe as patron)
- "Justification by faith" as Lebenspraxis to overcome the imperialistic value system of honor and shame (social implications of *theologia crucis*)
- Impetus to the future Christianity: beyond the ethnocentricity and discrimination, toward the egalitarian ethic of mutual hospitality
- Romans 12:1–15:13 "The Fourth Proof: Living Together according to the Gospel so as to Sustain the Hope of Global Transformation"

- Romans 15:14–16:24 "The *Peroratio* ("Conclusion") An Appeal for Cooperation in Missionary Activities in Jerusalem, Rome, and Spain"

II. TRANSFORMING THE WORLD (ROMANS 12:1–2)

"I urge you therefore, brothers, through the mercies of God, to present your bodies as a sacrifice, living, holy [and] acceptable to God—your reasonable worship. Also, do not be conformed to this *aeon*, but be transformed by the renewal of the mind, that you may ascertain what the will of God is—the good and acceptable and perfect."

Jewett:

"In place of the latreia of the Jewish cult (9:24) or the worship of finite images in Greco-Roman cults (1:23), Paul presents the bodily service of a community for the sake of world transformation and unification as the fulfillment of the vision of worship that would be truly reasonable." (730)

"The Pauline concept of transformation is oriented to this life rather than the next, and in contrast to the philosophers and mystery religions, it is corporate rather than individual." (733)

"If the Gentile and Jewish Christians continued to shame each other, they would carry a gospel to the barbarians in Spain that would continue the perverse system of honor on which the exploitative empire rested . . . . Therefore Paul attacked perverse system of honor by dispelling the idea that some persons and groups are inherently righteous and by proclaiming the message that God honors sinners of every culture in an impartial manner through Christ. " (88)

"Paul seeks coexistence between groups that retain their distinctive ethnic and theological integrity (14:4, 8, 10–12, 15–16, 19–23; 15,1–7). In contrast to 1 Corinthians 8 and 10, in Romans 14:1–1:13 Paul prohibits mutual conversion of others to the point view held by one's own group." (85–86)

My Remarks:

Paul speaks of the transformation of the shape (morfh,, sch,ma) of believers not only at the moment of eschaton (1 Corinthians 15:48ff: into "glory"), but their transfiguration is also an ongoing process now, in which both of it into "glory" of Christ (2 Corinthians 3:18) and that into his "death" (Philippians 3:10–11) occur and correspond to each other (see also Philippians 3:20–21; Romans 8:9). A cosmological and eschatological dimension needs not to be denied; this life is not separated form the next, the latter is rather already included into the former.

Romans 1:14 "both *Greeks* and *barbarians*," "both *wise* and *foolish*"; Verse 16 "to *all* who have faith, both the *Jew* first and then to the *Greek*";

3:22 "to *all* who have faith"—Why does Paul, after 1:14, stop talking of "barbarians," if he envisages a mission to Spain? The word "Greek" means Greco-Roman and does not include Spaniards.

How did Paul conceive of this coexistence (if not: a single congregation) beyond not only ethnical, but also theological differences between groups? How could Paul differentiate his theology from God himself?

III. LOVE FEAST AS FULFILLMENT OF LAW (ROMANS 13:10)

"The agape does no evil to the neighbor; therefore the agape is law's fulfillment."

Jewett:

"The logical social corollary to 'the love' in this verse is the agape meal shared by most sectors of the early church in connection with the Lord's Supper." (814) / "The greatest barrier against such love in the Roman situation was conformity to various forms of law, which insisted that family members should always eat together, which divided the weak from the strong and prevented the celebration of the love feast together . . . . It is law as a principle, in its multifarious forms, that is fulfilled in the agape meal." (814)

Ad 15:7 "In the context of early Christian literature, the home in view is the house or tenement church and the occasion is most likely the love feast, since this was the format of the assembly that turned the secular space of house or portion of a tenement or shop into an arena of sacred welcome . . . . Both the congregations of the 'weak' and the 'strong' are called upon here to invite and welcome members of the other groups into their congregational meetings. " (888)

My Remarks:

Now in UCCJ (The United Church of Christ in Japan) a serious debate is ongoing about the Eucharist. Some churches invite also non- or not-yet baptized people to the Eucharist with intention to realize an impartial invitation of Christ as the host to all people, while for the others this is clearly a violation of the church law and nothing but the destruction of the integrity of church as body of Christ.

What was liturgical order of the love feast (in connected with the Lord's Supper) in Roman communities? Was it similar to the one in Corinth (1 Corinthians 11), to which two hypotheses are proposed: "Agape-Eucharist" (H.-J. Klauck) on one hand and "pan-agape (including teaching, prophecy, tongue etc.)—wine" (O. Hofius) on the other?

Paul himself seems to treat both the Baptism and the Eucharist at least on the symbolical level equally under the rubric of the "integration of believers into persona Christi" (to Baptism, see Romans 6:4; 1

Corinthians 12:13; Philippians 3:10–11; to Eucharist, see 1 Corinthians 10:16–7). Both sacramental acts may have fulfilled a function of proclamation or mission. How well established was the functional differentiation between Baptism as initiation and the Eucharist as integration?

IV. PAUL BETWEEN POLITICAL ALTERNATIVES (ROMANS 13:1)

"Let every soul subject to the governing authorities. For there is no authority except that by God and those that are have been appointed by God."

Jewett:

"That the Roman authorities were appointed by the God and Father of Jesus Christ turns the entire Roman civic cult on its head, exposing its suppression of the truth." (790)

Ad verse 7 "To the one [owed] the honor, the honor"—"Paul reverts to the cultural stereotypes, and abandons the revolutionary approach to honor . . . . For the sake of the proclamation of Christ crucified, who overturned the honor system . . . , Paul was willing to accept the system that demanded honor for the emperor and his officials whether they deserved it or not." (803)

My Remarks:

Japanese Christians were torn between obedience and resistance to a totalitarian and militaristic regime during the World War II. UCCJ was founded during the war under the pressure of the government. Romans 13 was used by church leaders to legitimate the supremacy of the state. The "Confession of Responsibility during World War II" (1967) was not followed by all. Now, some Christian teachers of public schools refuse to stand up to sing the national hymn, a song blessing the eternal rule of Tenno, at school ceremonies and are punished for "disobedience" by prefectural direction for education.

Paul's intention was to establish a peaceful relation to the local magistrates in Rome but the Wirkungsgeschichte of this passage stands in contradiction to this intention. Did Paul prefer a situational adaptation of his principle of nonconformity to the world? Is this not a source for the Doctrine of two kingdoms?

V. "JUSTIFICATION BY FAITH" IN SOCIAL CONTEXT

Jewett:

"Honour was a filter through which the whole world was viewed." (J. E. Lendon, quoted in p. 49) . . . boasting "was a much more blatant, socially acceptable form of behavior . . . , formed by often disingenuous traditions of public modesty." (49) "It was held that the winning of honor was the only adequate reward for merit in public life." (E. A. Judge, quoted in page 50) "The competition for honor was visible in every city of the Roman Empire in which members of the elite competed for civic power though sponsoring games . . . ." (50) "Paul criticizes and reverses the official system of honor achieved through piety on which the empire after Augustus rested." (48; cf. Cicero, *De natura deorum* 2.3.8: Romans as being "*religione . . . multo superiores.*")

My Remarks:

In view of this social and communal interpretation, the understanding of the Doctrine of Justification by Faith in the document "Joint Declaration on the Doctrine of Justification" (1997) is still very individualistic (see its section "4. Explicating the Common Understanding of Justification" beginning with the subtitle "Human Powerlessness and Sin in Relation to Justification").

The Hypothesis that the value system of honor and shame is a key to understand the social behavior of the Japanese is well known at least since R. Benedict, *The Chrysanthemum and the Sword*, 1967. But in comparison to the Roman attitude as described by Jewett, the competition for honor in Japanese society is rather moderated through the group mentality.

This mentality may be characterized by the concept of *amae*, as it is analyzed by Takeo Doi, *The Anatomy of Dependence: The Key Analysis of Japanese Behavior* (Tokyo, 1973). According to him, the noun *amae* is related to the adjective *amai* ("sweet"), maybe also to the noun *ama* ("heaven" with its gracefulness). One allows her/himself to show an attitude of *amae* toward a person who belongs to the same group as she/he, like a child to its mother: "The prototype of *amae* is the infant's desire to be close its mother, who, it has come vaguely to realize, is a separate existence from itself." (*Doi*, 75) *Amae*-feeling is a mixture of reliance on and demand for an unconditional acceptance, intimacy, and also some arrogance. The loyalty to the group is often more highly estimated than a moral standard in the open society. One who is not ready to show her/himself in the attitude of *amae*, has little chance to be accepted and to be loved inside of the group. Boasting to persons outside of the group is not approved. The feeling of shame comes if one can not fulfill the expectation of the group.

Is *amae*, if its insider-orientation is to be overcome, an adequate starting point to inculturate the social implications of Pauline Gospel? (cf. the emphasis on motherness of God in Shusaku Endo, a Catholic writer)

VI. For the Future of Protestantism

Jewett:

"The Messiah welcomes both insiders and outsiders to his banquet, crossing in his resurrected ministry of the Lord's Supper the ethnic barriers between Jews and Gentiles as well as the theological and social barriers between the "weak" and the "strong." This provides the foundation of an ethic of inclusivity that is far more radical and wide-reaching than the grudging tolerance promoted by the later Enlightenment and the liberal churches of the present day, because it rests not on the inaccessibility of truth and the relativity of human viewpoints but on the welcoming action of Christ himself, as experienced in faith." (889)

My Remarks:

How should we interpret the so-called *solus*-articles of *Luther* today? The exclusiveness of faith, grace and scripture has been often attached to "militant" tendencies for the sake of the clearness in self-understanding. Was this a misunderstanding of Paul?

How should we relate the exclusive identity of faith to the inclusive ethos in relation to others (including not only the Christians of other confessions and congregations, but also atheists, Buddhists, Muslims etc.)?

37

Is Romans an Ambassadorial Letter?

Kota Yamada

I. Introduction

Prof. R. Jewett has completed a magnificent and monumental commentary on Paul's Letter to the Romans, published in the Hermeneia Series.[1] It follows current trends of socio-historical and rhetorical interpretation[2] of Romans in three ways.[3] First, it does not interpret Romans as the traditional "christianae religionis compendium" (Melanchthon), that is, as "a theological or doctrinal treatise" in *The Romans Debate*,[4] but as "a situational letter" which deals adequately with

[1] Robert Jewett, *Romans: A Commentary* (Minneapolis: Fortress Press, 2007). Jewett thinks with logical consistency that the original text of Romans consists of 1:1–16:16 + 16:21–24, while 16:17–20 and 16:25–27 are later interpolations (*Romans*, 4–18).

[2] Jewett's "sociohistorical and rhetorical interpretation" is different from V. K. Robbins' "sociorhetorical method" (*Romans*, 1–4). Jewett's "rhetorical approach" is comprised chiefly of ancient Greco-Roman rhetoric and sometimes a mixture of Greco-Roman and Hebrew rhetoric, but rarely a mixture of ancient and modern rhetoric (*Romans*, 23–46).

[3] Cf. Robert Jewett, "Major Impulses in the Theological Interpretation of Romans since Barth," *Interpretation* 34 (1980), 17–31; idem, "The Law and the Coexistence of Jews and Gentiles in Romans," *Interpretation* 39 (1985), 341–356; idem, "Following the Argument of Romans" = in edited by K. P. Donfried, *The Romans Debate* [hereafter Donfried, *Debate*] (Peabody: Hendrickson, 1991), 265–77.

[4] Cf. T. W. Manson, "St. Paul's Letter to the Romans-and Others," *Bulletin of the John Rylands University Library of Manchester* [*BJRL*] 31 (1948), 224–40 = in Donfried, *Debate*, 3–15; G. Bornkamm, "The Letter to the Romans as Paul's Last Will and Testament," *Australian Biblical Review* [*ABR*] 11 (1963), 2–14 = in Donfried, *Debate*, 16–28; K. P. Karris, "Romans 14:1–15:13 and the Occasion of Romans," *Catholic Biblical Quarterly* [*CBQ*] 35 (1973), 155–78 = in Donfried, *Debate*, 65–84; idem, "The Occasion of Romans: A Response to Prof. Donfried," *CBQ* 36 (1974), 356–358 = in Donfried, *Debate*, 125–27; P. Stuhlmacher, "The Theme of Romans," *ABR* 36 (1988), 31–44 = in Donfried, *Debate*, 333–45. Cf. E. Käsemann, *An die Römer* (Tübingen: J. C. B. Mohr, 1974); U. Wilkens, *Der Brief an die Römer*, 3 vols. (Neukirchen Vluyn: Neukirchner, 1978–1982).

the concrete historical situation of the Roman community.[5] Second, it is written on the right track of K. Stendahl and others,[6] interpreting Romans as "a missionary letter" in which theological terms imply the social context; for instance, "the righteousness of God" is interpreted with the social context of the interaction between the Jews and Gentiles. Third, it is written within recent trends of rhetorical criticism, initiated by W. Wuellner on Romans, [7] as well as with historical critical and exegetical analysis.

Prof. Jewett's *Romans* is epoch-making in the history of current trends of interpretation with three characteristic features:[8] (1) the literary genre of Romans is classified as "an ambassadorial letter" written in the form of epideictic rhetoric; (2) Paul's gospel is interpreted in the social context of the honor culture of the Greco-Roman society which transforms the social and cultural values of the Jewish and Gentile communities; and (3) the purpose of its composition is to gain support for the Spanish mission, unifying the divided Jewish and Gentile house-churches in Rome. I would like to discuss these three points critically in the following sections, chiefly focusing on (1), while treating (2) and (3) as corollaries of (1).

---

[5] Cf. K. P. Donfried, "A Short Note on Romans 16," *Journal of Biblical Literature* [hereafter *JBL*] 89 (1970), 441–49 = in Donfried, *Debate*, 44–52; J. Jervell, "The Letter to Jerusalem," *Studia Theologica* 25 (1971), 61–73 = in Donfried, *Debate*, 53–64; W. Wiefel, "The Jewish Community in Ancient Community and the Origins of Roman Christianity," in Donfried, *Debate*, 85–101 (org. in German, *Judaica* 26 [1970], 65–88); K. P. Donfried, "False Presuppositions of the Study of Romans" *CBQ* 36 (1974), 332–58 = in Donfried, *Debate*, 102–25; F. F. Bruce, "The Romans Debate-Continued," *BJRL* 64 (1981–82), 334–59 = in Donfried, *Debate*, 175–94; A. J. M. Wedderburn, "The Purpose and Occasion of Romans Again," *Expository Times* 90 (1979), 137–41 = in Donfried, *Debate*, 195–202; F. Watson, "The Two Roman Congregations: Romans 14:1–15:13," in Donfried, *Debate*, 203–15; P. Lampe, "The Roman Christians of Romans 16" = in Donfried, *Debate*, 216–30; P. Stuhlmacher, "The Purpose of Romans" = in Donfried, *Debate*, 231–42 (org. in German, *Zeitschrift für die Neutestamentliche Wissenschaft und die Kunde der älteren Kirch* 77 [1986], 180–93) . Cf. J. D. G. Dunn, *Romans 1-8, Romans 9-11*, 2 volumes (Dallas: Word Books, 1988).

[6] K. Stendahl, "The Apostle Paul and the Introspective Conscience of the West," *HTR* 56 (1963), 199–215, idem, *Paul among Jews and Gentiles and Other Essays* (London: SCM, 1976); J. Munck, *Christ and Israel: An Interpretation of Romans 9–11* (Philadelphia: Fortress Press, 1967); P. S. Minear, *The Obedience of Faith: The Purposes of Paul in the Epistle to the Romans* (London: SCM, 1971); N. Dahl, *Studies in Paul: Theology for the Early Christian Mission* (Minneapolis Augsburg Press, 1977).

[7] W. Wuellner, "Paul's Rhetoric of Argumentation in Romans: An Alternative to the Donfried and Karris Debate over Romans," *CBQ* 38 (1976), 330–351 = in Donfried, *Debate*, 128–46.

[8] Cf. R. Jewett, "Romans as an Ambassadorial Letter," *Interpretation* 36 (1982), 5–20; idem, "Honor and Shame in the Argument of Romans," in edited by A. Brown et al., *Putting Body and Soul Together: Essays in Honor of Robin Scroggs* (Valley Forge: Trinity Press International, 1997), 258–73; idem, "Paul, Phoebe and the Spanish Mission," in edited by J. Neusner et al., *The Social World of Formative Christianity and Judaism: Essays in Tribute to Howard Clark Kee* (Philadelphia: Fortress Press, 1988), 142–61.

II. ROMANS AS AN AMBASSADORIAL LETTER IN EPIDEICTIC RHETORIC

Rhetoric dominated public affairs in ancient Greco-Roman society, so rhetorical interpretation of the New Testament is a proper approach to understanding it. Prof. Jewett has basically accepted Wuellner's rhetorical analysis of Romans: (1) rhetorical structure of Romans consists of the introduction (*exordium*, 1:1–15; *causa*, 1:13–15) and conclusion (*peroratio*, 15:14–16:23), both corresponding to each other, and the central argument (*transitus*, 1:16–17, *confirmatio*, 1:18–15:13); (2) while the rhetorical genre of Romans is neither forensic nor deliberative, but epideictic. Prof. Jewett has amended the "purpose" of the letter (*causa*, 1:13–15) into the "narrative" (*narratio*, 1:13–15), the "transit" to the leading argument (*transitus*, 1:16–17) into the "theme" of the argument (*propositio*, 1:16–17), and has classified the epideictic rhetoric of Romans into "an ambassadorial letter" in the Greco-Roman epistolography, modeled on Philo's *Embassy to Gaius.* Further, his conjecture of "Romans as an ambassadorial letter" is supported by the concept of "apostle" (1:1) as "ambassador" and the diplomatic word of *parakalō* (12:1, I exhort).[9]

Prof. Jewett's modification of the "transitus" to the "theme or proposition" (*propositio*, 1:16–17) is valid, while that of the *causa* to the *narratio* (1:13–15) is problematic; because the *narratio* explains the proposition in detail with the description of the events of the deed in judicial rhetoric before the court,[10] and is sometimes applied to deliberative rhetoric before the national assembly as well, but it is not used in epideictic rhetoric.[11] Moreover, the narrative is not so briefly mentioned as in three verses, but 1:13–15 makes a part of the introduction of thanksgiving and intercession (*exordium*, 1:8–15), though a disclosure form is introduced in 1:13, which divides the section written in the style of repetition (*repetitio*) of Paul's wish to visit Rome before God and man in a chiasm form (1:8/9–12, 13/14–15), corresponding to a part of the conclusion with Paul's plan to visit to Rome and his wish of their intercession in a chiastic repetition form (15:22–24/25–27, 30–31/32).

The central argument of "proof" (*probatio*: 1:18–15:13) is divided into four main sections as follows and each main sections into 10 subsections of introduction, thesis and rationale, elaboration, diatribe,

---

[9] Jewett, *Romans*, 42–46, 96–102, 724–27, 907, 909–11; idem, "Romans as an Ambassadorial Letter." Cf. Dahl, *Studies*, 73, "Christ's ambassador to Gentiles."

[10] H. Lausberg, *Handbook of Literary Rhetoric: A Foundation for Literary Study* (Leiden: E. J. Brill, 1998), §§290–292.

[11] L. Pernot, *La Rhétorique de l'éloge dans le monde gréco romain* (Paris: Institut d'Études Augustiniennes, 1993), 300–22.

Midrash, speech-in-character, syllogism, enthymeme, admonition, exemplary guidelines, conclusion and so on.[12]

1:18–4:25: the gospel expresses the impartial righteousness of God by overturning claims of cultural superiority and by rightwising Jews and Greeks through grace alone,[13]

5:1–8:39: life in Christ as a new system of honor that replaces the quest for status through conformity to the law,[14]

9:1–11:36: the triumph of divine righteousness in the gospel's mission to Israel and the Gentiles,

12:1–15:13: living together according to the gospel so as to sustain the hope of global transformation.

Wuellner's pioneering work of rhetorical analysis on Romans is at its very beginning, and his discussion is mainly about the exordium and peroration, while the central arguments are not dealt with thoroughly.[15] Afterwards D. Aune analyzes the central argumentative sections (1:16–15:13) as a *logos protreptikos*, a subgenre of deliberative rhetoric.[16] Though its philosophical character may or may not be applied to Romans, the argumentative sections of Romans contain protreptic features. However, it is not a matter of combination that Romans is "overall the epideictic rhetorical mode" and individual sections with "other forms of discourse", for instance, 1:18–4:25 as "a sub-type of the deliberative style: the apotreptic or dissuasive mode."[17] If Romans is a consistent argument from the introduction, argumentative sections and conclusion of the theme in 1:16–17, and if the central arguments are not epideictic, consisted of full of encomiastic elements, but deliberative, full of argumentative elements in which the coexistence of the Jewish and Gentile Christians are discussed and advised, it can be concluded that Romans as a whole is deliberative.

---

[12] Jewett, *Romans*, esp. vii–ix; idem, "Following the Argument of Romans."

[13] Jewett rightly discusses 3:21–31 within 1:18–4:25 with C. E. B. Cranfield (*The Epistle to the Romans* [Edinburgh: T. & T. Clark, 2004], 1:199–224), which is different from the treatments by Käsemann (*An die Römer*, 85–99), Wilkens (*Der Brief an die Römer*, 1:181–252) and Dunn (*Romans 1–8*, 161–194).

[14] Jewett deals with Romans chapter 5 as a beginning of 5:1–8:39 with Käsemann (*An die Römer*, 123–150) and Cranfield (*Romans*, 1:252–295), different from Wilkens (*Der Brief an die Römer*, 1:285–337) and Dunn (*Romans 1–8*, 242–300) who deal it within 3:21–5:21.

[15] G. A. Kennedy also read Romans as epideictic rhetoric (*The New Testament Interpretation through Rhetorical Criticism* [Chapel Hill: University of North Carolina, 1984], 152–156). Recently, T. H. Tobin has analyzed Romans in terms of diatribe consisting of combinations of expository and argumentative rhetoric in 1:16–11:36 (*Paul's Rhetoric in its Context: The Argument of Romans* [Peabody: Hendrickson, 2004]). Cf. G. L. Kustas, in edited by W. Wuellner, *Diatribe in Ancient Rhetorical Theory* (Berkeley: Center for Hermeneutical Studies, 1976).

[16] D. Aune, "Romans as a *logos protreptikos*" = in Donfried, *Debate*, 278–96 (orginally the longer version in 1991).

[17] Quotations are taken from B. Byrne, *Romans* (Collegeville: Liturgical Press, 1996), 17–18; similar idea is seen in D. J. Moo, *The Epistle to the Romans* (Grand Rapids: Eerdmans, 1996), 15.

An ambassadorial discourse or letter (*presbeutikos logos*) is related to the imperial oration (*basilikos logos*), "a speech of praise addressed to the ruler," or the crown speech (*stephanōtikos logos*), "a *gratiarum action*, at the presentation of a crown or in recognition of some honor bestowed," and its essence is "in addition to the praise of the ruler, it states the special cause for the embassy and pictures the conditions which occasioned it."[18] An ambassador's speech or letter is a sub-genre of epideictic rhetoric, which deals with praise and blame (Menander Rhetor, 331.15) with encomiastic scheme. According to an ancient theory of Menander Rhetor (423.6–424.2),[19] an example of the ambassador's speech is remained in his textbook of epideictic speeches, which is consisted of six parts as follows: (1) "If you are sent as ambassador on behalf of a city in distress, you must make much of the emperor's mercifulness" (423.7–11); (2) "But praise also his warlike deeds and peacetime achievements" (423.12–14); (3) "Two topics about the city: the former glories of Ilion and a vivid description of the present state of affairs" (423.14–21); (4) "Mention especially the things emperors take thought for: baths, aqueducts, public buildings" (423.21–25); (5) "Appeal for mercy. The city speaks through the ambassador" (423.25–424.1); and (6) "Ask him to deign to receive the decree" (424.1–2).[20]

Prof. Jewett mentions Philo's *Embassy to Gaius* as an easily accessible example of the ambassadorial letter based on F. H. Colson's introduction to the letter.[21] But Alexandre's recent study reveals that the core of Philo' *Embassy to Gaius*, the letter from King Agrippa to Gaius, is not analyzed as epideictic, but apologetic and deliberative, which implies *Embassy to Gaius* as a whole is not epideictic.[22]

Is Romans actually an ambassadorial letter written in encomiastic scheme? The concept of "apostle" implies "an ambassador" (2 Corinthians 5:20, cf. Ephesians 6:20) as well, but "the apostle" is applied to Paul only twice in Romans, which stresses Paul as elected for the gospel to the Gentiles (1:1, 11:13). It is quite different from the situation of the Corinthian correspondence, where "the apostle" is mentioned 16

18 Quotations are taken from T. C. Burgess, *Epideictic Literature* (New York & London: Garland, 1987 [org. Chicago: University Chicago, 1902]), 110–112; cf. Pernot, *La Rhétorique de l'éloge*, 92–94.

19 D. A. Russell and N. G. Wilson, *Menander Rhetor* (edited with translation and commentary; London: Oxford University Press, 1981), 180–81.

20 Analysis of Menander Rhetor (423.6–424.2) is quoted from Russell and Wilson, *Menander Rhetor*, 337.

21 Jewett, *Romans*, 44 and note 253.

22 M. Alexandre, Jr., *Rhetorical Argumentation in Philo of Alexandria* (Atlanta: Scholars Press, 1999), 158–75. Cf. R. W. Smith, *The Art of Rhetoric in Alexandria: Its Theory and Practice in the Ancient World* (The Hague: Martinus Nijhoff, 1974), 54–56, especially 56, "it more nearly follows Isocratean division of the judic(i)al speech-proemium, narration, proof, and epilogue"; B. W. Winter, *Philo and Paul among the Sophists: Alexandrian and Corinthian Responses to a Julio-Claudian Movement* (Grand Rapids: Eerdmans, 2002), 96 note 7.

times and Paul's apostleship is disputed. On the other hand, "the gospel" to the Jews and Gentiles is more problematic for Paul and his readers and audience in Romans (1:1, 9, 16, 2:16, 10:16, 11:28, 15:16, 19, 16:25) as it is typically shown in "the theme or thesis" (*propositio*) of the letter: "I am not ashamed of the gospel" (1:16–17, cf. 1:1–2). In the rhetorical argument the person (*prosōpon; persona*) and the matter (*pragma; res*) are separately discussed,[23] though "the gospel" and "the apostle" are correlated to each other; the matter of the gospel is discussed in Romans, but the personality of Paul is not disputed as in the Corinthian correspondences.

Though the fourth main section of the rhetorical argument (12:1–15:13) is categorized as "(the fourth) proof" (*probatio*) on the one hand, it is also analyzed as "exhortation" (*exhortatio*) on the other.[24] But *exhortatio* is not a rhetorical term in the rhetorical argument as H. D. Betz's rhetorical commentary on Galatians was criticized.[25] The word *parakalein*, an ambiguous term with many-sided meanings, carries the definition "to exhort," "to urge," or "to encourage," in Romans (12:1, 8, 15:30, 16:17).

However, it does not necessarily have diplomatic connotations; rather, it expresses the nuance of encouragement to build a community (cf. *stērichthēnai* in 1:11, *symparaklēthēnai* in 1:12; *synanapausōmai* in 15:32).

III. SOCIAL CONTEXT OF THE HONOR SOCIETY

The ancient Mediterranean society was honor oriented, in which honor was public esteem, based on the recognition and approval from significant others as well as avoidance of shame: its typical indicator was the patron-client relationship, patronage. It was a competitive society, symbolized in the words for "boast." Reading Romans in light of the social context of the honor and shame culture in the Greco-Roman world is not only a way to interpret Paul's theology in Romans with social scientific approaches (social or cultural anthropology, sociology and social history etc.), but also a way to overcome an individualistic,

[23] Lausberg, *Handbook*, §376–99, against, Jewett, *Romans*, 137.

[24] Jewett, *Romans*, 724–725; idem, "Following the Argument of Romans," 274, in spite of 270 and note 29.

[25] H. D. Betz, *Galatians: A Commentary on Paul's Letter to the Churches in Galatia* (Philadelphia: Fortress, 1979), cf. idem, "The Literary Composition and Function of Paul's Letter to the Galatians," *NTS* 21 (1975), 353–379 = M. D. Nanos ed., *The Galatians Debate* (Minneapolis: Fortress, 2003), 3–28; Galatians 1:1–5 (the prescript), 1:6–11(*exordium*: 10–11, *transitus*), 1:12–2:14 (*narratio*), 2:15–21 (*propositio*), 3:1–4:31 (*probatio*), 5:1–6:10 (*exhortatio*), 6:11–18 (the postscript = *conclusio*). Against Betz, H. Hüner, "Der Galaterbrief und das Verhältnis von antiker Rhetorik und Epistolographie," *TLZ* 109 (1984), 241–250; C. J. Classen, "Paulus und die Rhetorik," *ZNW* 82 (1991), 1–33; idem, "St Paul's Epistle and Ancient Greek and Roman Rhetoric," in edited by S. E. Porter and T. H. Olbricht, *Rhetoric and the New Testament: Essays from the 1992 Heidelberg Conference* (Sheffield: Sheffield Academic Press, 1993), 265–291 = Nanos, *Galatians Debate*, 73–94.

existential interpretation of a community; it allows a group-oriented interpretation.

H. Moxnes was the first to place Romans in the social system of honor and shame in the Greco-Roman world. He described the social implications of words such as "honor" (*timē*: 2:7, 10, 9:21, 12: 10, 13:7), "glory" (*doxa*: 1:23, 2:7, 10, 3:7, 23, 4:20, 5:2, 6:4, 8:18, 21, 9:4, 23, 11:36, 15:7, 16:27), "to glorify" (*doxazein*: 1:21, 8:30, 11:30, 15:6, 9), "praise" (*epainos*: 2:29, 13:3), "to praise" (*epainein*: 15:11), "boast" (*kauchēma*: 4:2), "boasting" (*kauchēsis*: 3:27, 15:17) and "to boast" (*kauchasthai*: 2:17, 23, 5:2, 3, 11) as well as "shameless" (*aschēmosynē*: 1:27), "dishonor" (*atimia*: 1:26, 9:21), "to dishonor" (*atimazein*: 1:24, 2:23) and "to be ashamed" (*epaischynsthai*: 1:16, 6:21). According to Moxnes, Paul accepts the honor system in the public area of Hellenistic society (13:1–7), but totally rejects in the private area of sexual life as a part of the fallenness of all creation (1:18–32) as well as that of the former life of the Christians (6:12–23), and God puts them to shame.[26]

Prof. Jewett adds, following Moxnes' implications, socially discriminatory categories to the concepts of "honor and shame" such as "Greek and barbarians, educated and uneducated" (1:14, cf.1:22, 2:20, 16:19), "Gentiles" (*ethnē*: 1:5, 13, 2:14, 24, 3:29, 4:17, 18, 9:24, 30, [10:19. 19], 11:11, 12, 13, 13, 25, 15:9, 9, 10, 11, 12, 16, 16, 18, 27, 16:4), "the weak" (*asthenein*: 14:1, 2, 21; *asthenēma*, 15:1) and "the strong" (*dunatos*, 15:1), the word field of "righteousness/unrighteousness" as "righteous" (*dikaios*: 1:17, 2:13, 3:10, 26, 5:7, 19, 7:12) , "righteousness" (*dikaiosynē*: 1:17, 3:5, 21, 22, 25, 26, 4:3, 5, 6, 9, 11, 11, 13, 22, 5:17, 21, 6:13, 16, 18, 19, 20, 8:10, 9:30, 30, 31, 10:3, 3, 3, 4, 5, 6, 10, 14:17), "to make righteous" (*dikaioun*: 2:13, 3:4, 20, 24, 26, 28, 30, 4:2, 5, 5:1, 9, 6:7, 8:30, 30, 33), "righteous decree" (*dikaiōma*: 1:32, 2:26, 5:16, 18, 8:4), "being made right" (*dikaiōsis*: 4:25, 5:18), "unrighteousness" (*adikia*: 1:18, 18, 29, 2:8, 3:5, 6:13, 9:14) and "unrighteous" (*adikos*: 3:5). But he does not adopt Moxnes' dichotomy of the public and private areas, based as it is on the classic "two-kingdom theory," and concludes that with the power of God "this gospel shatters the unrighteous precedence given to the strong over the weak, the free and the well-educated over slaves and the ill-educated, the Greeks and the Romans over the barbarians" and it transforms "the social value system of the Roman Empire upside down."[27]

[26] H. Moxnes, "Honour and Righteousness in Romans," *JSNT* 32 (1988), 61–77; idem, "Honor, Shame and the Outside World in Paul's Letter to the Romans," in edited by Neusner, *Social World*, 207–18. Cf. C. K. Barrett, "I Am Not Ashamed of the Gospel," in edited by M. Barth et al., *Foi et salut selon S. Paul* (Rome: Biblical Institute, 1970), 19–41, = idem, *New Testament Essays* (London: SPCK, 1972), 116–43.

[27] Quotations from Jewett, *Romans*, 139; cf. 46–59, 132–34, 139–47, 149–53, 165–91, 205–9, 223, 229–37, 272, 276, 278–82, 290–93, 295–303, 310–17, 348–57, 361–63,388–89, 398–401, 422–24, 434–39, 449–53, 459–73, 481–97, 500–3, 562–67, 613–20, 630–33, 641–48, 686–93, 710–11, 761–62, 772–74, 785–803, 833–85, 945–48, 952–74, 978–84; etc; idem, "Honor and Shame in the Argument of Romans."

Prof. Jewett's addition of "the Greek, barbarians and Gentiles," "the weak and the strong" and the word families of "righteousness" etc.[28] to the list of the words for "honor and shame" is necessary in understanding consistently the social context of Paul's argument in Romans as a whole. The Jews are proud of their "God," "election," "law," "sonship," "glory," "covenant," and so on (2:17, 3:27, 9:4) against the Gentiles, while the Gentiles are glorifying their own "wisdom," "power," etc. (1:22, 13:1–7), but Christ has revealed the "reversal of honor and shame to create new communities by grace alone."[29]

IV. Preparation for the Spanish Mission

The purpose of Romans has been debated for a long time and while a series of different ideas have been presented and discussed (such as "a circular letter to Ephesus and Rome,"[30] "Paul's last will and testament,"[31] "providing the apostolic foundations in Roman churches,"[32] "seeking support for the Jerusalem offering,"[33] or "preparation for the mission in Rome"[34]), there is no consensus about it even today.

Prof. Jewett's conjecture of Romans as an ambassadorial letter is related to his other hypothesis that it is written for the need of the support of the Roman community in order to embark on the Spanish mission.[35] Though a similar idea has already been presented by P. Stuhlmacher,[36] Prof. Jewett takes it one step further to interpret Phoebe as a patroness for the Spanish mission.

---

[28] Jewett, *Romans*, 110–11, 159–60, 212–14, 226–27, 299, 332–36, 598–99, 608–9, 644–47, 672–79, 696–701, 892–97, 909–10; 831–99; 141–47, 152–53, 190, 206, 212, 233–34, 346–48, 259–60, 266–67, 272–303, 309–310, 314–15, 319, 326, 339–340, 343, 348, 363, 382–89, 404–5, 411, 417–21, 453, 491–92, 530, 540–41, 581, 608–10, 617–20, 624–27, 631, 863–64.

[29] Quotation is from Jewett, *Romans*, 272.

[30] T. W. Manson, "St. Paul's Letter to the Romans-and Others," in Donfried, *Debate*, 3–15.

[31] G. Bornkamm, "The Letter to the Romans as Paul's Last Will and Testament," in Donfried, *Debate*, 16–28;

[32] G. Klein, "Paul's Purpose in Writing the Epistle to the Romans," in Donfried, *Debate*, 29–43.

[33] J. Jervell, "The Letter to Jerusalem," in Donfried, *Debate*, 53–64.

[34] Cf. K. P. Donfried, "False Presuppositions of the Study of Romans" in Donfried, *Debate*, 102–25; F. F. Bruce, "The Romans Debate-Continued," in Donfried, *Debate*, 175–94; A. J. M. Wedderburn, "The Purpose and Occasion of Romans Again," in Donfried, *Debate*, 195–202; F. Watson, "The Two Roman Congregations: Romans 14:1–15:13," in Donfried, *Debate*, 203–15; P. Lampe, "The Roman Christians of Romans 16," in Donfried, *Debate*, 216–30, etc.

[35] Jewett, *Romans*, 74–91, 922–48; idem, "Paul, Phoebe, and the Spanish Mission."

[36] P. Stuhlmacher, "The Theme of Romans," in Donfried, *Debate*, 333–35. Cf. D. Zeller, *Der Brief an die Römer: Übersetzt und erklärt* (Regensburg: Pustet, 1985).

The historical and rhetorical situation of Paul's composition of the letter to the Romans at Corinth in 56 or 57,[37] the year of the literary "turning point", is threefold: (1) the past missionary activities for the Gentiles in the northeastern quadrant of the Mediterranean are closing with fruitful results (15:14–21); (2) the immediate situation is embarkation for Jerusalem with the collection as the results of the past mission, which signifies the unity of the Jewish and Gentile missions, wishing their acceptance of the collection in Jerusalem with a mixture of anxiety and expectation (15:25–27, 30–31); and (3) the near future embarkation on missionary activities in the northwestern quadrant of the Mediterranean, particularly in Rome and further in Spain, is at hand (1:8–15, 15:22–24, 28–29, 32–33).

The historical and rhetorical situation for the Roman community of receiving the letter from Paul is also threefold: (1) the Christian community in Rome was originally initiated by the Jews long before Paul's arrival; (2) Jewish Christians in Rome were expelled from Rome with other Jews by the edict of Claudius in 49; and (3) at the death of Claudius in 54, the edict was resolved and the Jews and the Jewish Christians have returned to Rome, and the Christian community was divided by the Jewish and Gentile house churches (16:3–16a) and between "the strong" majority Gentile Christians and "the weak" minority Jewish Christians (14:1–15:13).

Romans is not written to the saints in Jerusalem, or to the barbarians in Spain,[38] but to the Christian community in Rome (1:7). Thus the letter is not chiefly written in order to prepare for the Spanish mission, but to provide theological understandings and practical advice for solving the social problems facing the unity of the Jewish and Gentile Christians in Rome, and removing the nationalistic pride and prejudices of the Jews and Gentiles. It is evident from the fact that Paul intends to visit Rome in order to "strengthen them" (1:11) and "evangelize" in and around Rome[39] (1:15) for rebuilding the divided community (cf.1:11–13, 15:32). "After his statement of intent to preach the gospel in Rome, Paul states the theme of the letter in 1:16–18 and proceeds to "preach the gospel"[40] in the letter. But, according to Prof. Jewett, the pivotal point of interpretation, "some fruit" (1:13) means that "ordinary evangelistic

[37] Jewett thinks the composition of Romans "in the winter of 56–57 or the early spring of 57" (*Romans*, 18–23, especially 18), cf. idem, *Dating Paul's Life* (London: SCM; Philadelphia, Fortress Press, 1979), 100–4, 165.

[38] Paul's intention for the Spanish mission based on Isaiah 66:19 "Tarshish" as the final goal (Jewett, *Romans*, 924) is untenable, cf. A. A. Das, "Paul of Tarshish: Isaiah 66:19 and the Spanish Mission of Romans 15:24, 28," *NTS* 54 (2008), 60–73.

[39] According to his missionary strategy, Paul usually stays in a metropolis first such as Corinth and Ephesus and builds the house-church there, afterwards he visits the surrounding cities.

[40] Quotation is from S. K. Stowers, *The Diatribe and Paul's Letter to the Romans* (Missoula: Scholars Press, 1981), 182.

fruit is not in view," that is, it means "in order to gain support for the mission to Spain."[41] Moreover, the text "*just as also* among the rest of the Gentiles" (1:13) is contrary to Prof. Jewett's interpretation that "he does *not* intend to win converts in Rome *as* he has elsewhere." [42]

V. CONCLUSION

Prof. Jewett's conjecture that Romans is an ambassadorial letter for the preparation of the Spanish mission opens a new path for reading Romans, but it seems slightly off balance, in spite of the fact that the social implications of the theological discussions in Romans are valid.

An American cultural anthropologist, R. Benedict, wrote a well-read classic book *The Chrysanthemum and the Sword*[43] originally written for studies of Japan during World War II. In it she labeled the Japanese community-oriented culture as "a shame culture" in contrast to the European and American individual-oriented culture as "a guilt culture." On the other hand, a Japanese social anthropologist, C. Nakane, also wrote a famous and popular book, *The Japanese Society* [44] after the War. She cast the Japanese society as "a vertical society," contrasted with the Western society as "a horizontal society" in terms of the social structures of human relationships.

How has Romans been read in the Japanese society, particularly in the Japanese Christian society? It seems likely to me that it has been read in the Japanese cultural context as a transition from "the shame culture" and "the vertical society" to "the guilt culture" and "the horizontal society." But Prof. Jewett's new commentary on Romans may help us understand the social context of Pauline theology more clearly as well as the power of the gospel to transform traditional honor cultures, leading us from an individual-oriented interpretation of Romans to a community-oriented one. It may open another path to read Romans as the third way of shattering the social value system of both the traditional Japanese and Western cultures in order to create a new community by grace alone. That is, "the blessings of salvation has been given in Christ to all humankind in solidarity with him" (Colenso).[45]

---

[41] Quotations are from Jewett, *Romans*, 130 and 916.

[42] Quotations are from Jewett, *Romans*, 127 and 130 (italics are mine).

[43] R. Benedict, *The Chrysanthemum and the Sword* (Cleveland: Meridian Books 1967).

[44] C. Nakane, *The Japanese Society* (Berkeley: University of California, 1970); originally in Japanese, *Tate Syakai no Ningenkankei*, (Tokyo: Kodansya, 1967).

[45] Quotation is from Jewett, *Romans*, 315.

38

RESPONSE TO TOKYO COLLEAGUES

ROBERT JEWETT

It is a great privilege and honor for me to participate in this session of the Japanese Biblical Institute. Although there are significant points of disagreement that need to be discussed, I feel that my commentary has been very well understood and treated with respect. I am deeply appreciative of the interest in Paul's transformation of honor-shame systems. To leave time for discussion, I respond only to four issues, but in the case of Prof. Asano's paper, I deal with the first 12 pages of his much longer paper that was not read this afternoon.

I. THE RHETORICAL ISSUE AND ITS INTERPRETIVE CONSEQUENCES

Although Professors Hiroishi and Asano agree that Romans is a situational letter in the demonstrative genre aimed at eliciting support for Paul's Spanish Mission, Prof. Yamada remains convinced that Paul intends to "'evangelize' in and around Rome (1:15) for rebuilding the divided community (cf. 1:11–13, 15:32)." The letter provides "theological understandings and practical advice for solving the social problems facing the unity of the Jewish and Gentile Christians in Rome." This is a widely shared view, recently advocated by N. T. Wright, Wendy Dabourne, and William S. Campbell. For many years I followed this view, but I came to the conclusion that this theory fails to explain why Paul broke his noninterference principle stated in 15:20 by intervening in Roman affairs or why in 15:24 and 28 he takes such pains to explain why he intends to spend only a short time in Rome. He has no intention of establishing Pauline congregations in Rome. The evidence suggests that Paul has another motivation for preaching in Rome: to urge conformity to the gospel they have already received about mutual acceptance in Christ so they can overcome their conflicts and participate in a credible manner in a difficult mission project. This explains why after saying he wants to impart some spiritual gift in 1:11 he immediately adds that he hopes "to be mutually encouraged among you by each others' faith, both yours and mine." Paul wants to get something from the Romans, which corresponds to ambassadorial rhetoric.

Prof. Yamada maintains convinced, in contrast. "that Romans as a whole is deliberative." Several features of the letter led me to reject this view that I had implied in my first book about Paul. The first is the nature of Paul's relationship to the audience. Deliberative rhetoric that offers advice to an assembly presupposes that the speaker or writer is a member of that assembly. Such persons do not have to explain why they have a legitimate right to speak. But in contrast to his other letters, Romans is directed to one he had not helped to establish. Even in the case of Prisca and Aquila, he met them as refugees in Corinth after they had been banned from Rome as founders of a church there. They had already founded their church in Corinth before he arrived. In the opening of Romans, therefore, we find an elaborate justification for his writing as the apostle to the Gentiles. And in 15:15, Paul apologizes for his "boldness" in writing as an outsider, claiming that he is merely "reminding them" about the faith, and goes on in verse 20 to state his non-interference principle, "not to build on another's foundation." None of these details correlate well with deliberative rhetoric.

The second factor that led me to demonstrative rhetoric is the nature of Paul's arguments. Demonstrative rhetoric employs the arguments of praise and blame, which relates with the issues of honorable and shameful behavior. Deliberative rhetoric, on the other hand, is marked by arguments of advantage and disadvantage: which policy is more practically useful in advancing our interests? Moreover, deliberative rhetoric is for insiders only; the basic paradigm is giving advice to one's assembly. But Paul was an outsider in Rome; unlike all of his other letters, he was not involved in establishing any of the congregations there. Nowhere in Romans does he use an argument of advantage.

The third factor is theological. Paul goes to radical extremes in this letter to eliminate any future advantages to be gained by present behavior. He also erects barriers against congregations that are condemning each other for non-adherence to a particular theology or praxis. In dozens of references and with various arguments, Paul maintains that the entire human race will be saved by grace rather than by gaining advantages through works. Future "salvation" will also be a matter of a sheer, unearned gift (6:23). This led me to resist viewing Romans as deliberative, because that hypothesis tends to insert a consideration of advantage into salvation by faith. This too easily leads to the belief that if you accept a particular definition of faith and a reading of Romans that supports it, and are loyal to the right denomination, you will go to heaven while those who disagree will be lost. Finally, the arguments for mutual welcome in the final chapters are demonstrative rather than deliberative: Paul does not say to welcome others is advantageous but rather, "welcome one another as Christ has welcomed you . . . ." (15:7)

This relates to the question posed by Prof. Hiroishi, whether the *solus*-articles of *Luther* concerning the exclusiveness of faith, grace and scripture preclude acceptance of other groups. These articles indeed have functioned in this way, because Romans was misunderstood as a deliberative or judicial letter, offering advantage to those accepting a particular doctrinal definition or judging others as damned because they interpreted it differently. I believe Luther was betrayed by Lutheran orthodoxy. In the late Medieval period, when doctrinal conformity was thought to be required not just for salvation but for the peace of the world, it was perhaps inevitable that *sola fidei* and *sola gratia* were changed from the radical exclusion of salvation by works into new doctrines of salvation through theological works, i.e., through adhering to particular interpretations of scripture. This allowed the Christian faith to become entangled with claims of cultural and religious superiority and thus with the Christian colonialism that Kanzo Uchimura identified and resisted. These misunderstandings of grace and faith remain dominant until the present day, in every culture where Christianity is present.

II. THE ISSUE OF POST-COLONIAL INTERPRETATION

Prof. Asano employs a compelling method of analogical analysis to bring the new interpretation of Romans into relation with colonial resistance in Japan and the development of "post-colonial sensitivity." I particularly appreciate this, because post-colonial interpretive theory was not part of the methodology employed in the commentary; I was led into this discussion by the details of Paul's argument. I find the description of Uchimura's critique of the "moral depravity," and "a materialistic and divisive religion of triumphalism" of American Protestantism and culture both accurate and apt. In the book published earlier this year, I characterize the religion of my land as a degenerate example of a national culture dominating the Christian faith, and show how cultural prejudices paved the road to the current disaster of our imperial warfare in the Persian Gulf. I understand Uchimura's affinity with Galatians, which argued against the theological and cultural subversion of the Gentiles. And I appreciate Asano's assessment that my interpretation of Romans provides a basis to continue Uchimura's program to find a post-colonial approach to the faith. This corrolates with Prof. Yamada's reference to "the vertical culture."

The relation between defending the superior honor of one's group identity and the propensity to violence corrolates with my interpretation of Romans 5:1, following the text critically superior text, "let us have peace with God." This connects wth the "God of peace" in 15:33 and the "God of hope" that provides "peace" in 15:13. Although the conflicts between the weak and the strong had not yet assumed violent shape, the attitudes toward group identity that led to it were the same as that which leads to holy war. This is why Paul appeals to both sides to recognize that they and the others are "beloved by God" (1:7), that all who accept the gospel are undeserving recipients of the same grace (3:24) and reconciliation (5:10), and that the cultural elements in their self understandings are legitimate (14:1-15:7). Thus the ethic of 12:3 warns against imposing one's theology and praxis onto others, recognizing that each group has a distinctive *metron pisteōs* dealt out by God. This relates to Hiroishi's question whether coexistence overcomes differences between groups. No, says Paul! And in this regard, Romans moves beyond Galatians, which comes close to delegitimizing Jewish Christians, as Asano points out. In Romans Paul legitimates what Asano calls "the changing faces of identity."

This relates to the issue of the barbarians in Romans, and to the proposed mission to the barbarians in Spain. The premise of the inherent danger posed by the barbarians and the need for them to be dominated and enslaved by the Romans for the sake of world peace stands at the center of Roman imperial ideology. It is a premise that extended to colonialism in the modern world, and I am convinced that the entire argument of Romans is aimed at overturning it. I can only provide a partial answer to Prof. Hiroishi's question about why there are no more references to barbarians in the letter. It may have to do with the function of 1:13–15 as a kind of narration that explains the background of Paul's intended visit to Rome. If it is understood as such by the audience, there is no need to repeat it, because the entire subsequent letter carries out its program, down to the announcement of the Spanish mission to the barbarians in chapter 15. But it may also have to do with the fact that most of the audience of this letter consisted of slaves and former slaves who had been treated as barbarians; as abused people, they probably needed no further reminders of how they were viewed by their owners and by the society as a whole.

An additional resource for post-colonial interpretation is the insight that emerged from conversations in Beijing concerning Romans 13:1-7. Students living in a one party state were inclined to accept Paul's exhortation to respect the government because they perceived it as the lesser of evils. This reminded me that political preferences are always between lesser and greater evils, because in a sinful world no perfectly good alternatives are ever available. When I began to consider what Paul would have considered the major alternative to the Pax Romana, the answer was clear: it was the global rule of Zion that zealots such as Paul himself had sought before his conversion, It would arise after a successful messianic war against the wicked Gentile world, replacing Rome with theocratic zionism. The moment I began thinking about the political alternative to Rome in Paul's worldview, his alteration of Isianic citations to remove the implications of Jewish imperialism came to mind. In the commentary I had analyzed the anti-imperial implications of these changes without recognizing their implications for interpreting Romans 13. Paul removed the reference to Mt. Zion in the prophecy cited in Romans 10:15. He also deleted "the one preaching the message of peace," because the original prophecy had an imperial expectation parallel to the Pax Romana. Global peace would result from the subordination of all potential enemies under the imperial capitol in Jerusalem. In Romans 11:26, Paul changed the wording of Isaiah 59:20-21 from a deliverer coming "for the sake of Zion" to the deliverer coming "from Zion." This throws a whole new light on Romans 13, reducing the status of Rome to that of the lesser evil, and providing a bulwark against violent campaigns to establish pure theocracies. Romans would thus contain a warning about the illusion of replacing one imperialism with another. This heightens the relevance of Romans 13 for countries like Japan and the United States that have wreaked havoc in efforts to maintain their allegedly benign theocracies as replacements of other empires.

III. CAN THE JAPANESE CONCEPT OF *AMAE* OVERCOME GROUP EXCLUSIVITY?

Prof. Hiroishi asks whether the concept of *amae* constitutes an adequate starting point to inculturate the social implications of Paul's Gospel, provided that its insider-orientation could be overcome,. This relates to Prof. Yamada's affirmation of dealing with the issues of honor and shame as a way to overcome individualistic interpretations of the letter. There is a Greek equivalent of *amae* in Romans 12:10, where Paul urges "affection for one another with brotherly love" in the context of honoring members of other groups. This bears on how the "mercies of God" (12:1) are to be understood; in my view they are related to God's love for enemies as described in 5:8-11. These passages provide a resource for overcoming the restriction of *amae* to insiders. It also seems to me that if Romans 13:10 is understood as a comment about "the agape meal," then the entire last chapters of the letter deal with the tendency towards the intolerance of in-groups toward each other. If both house and tenement churches were celebrating the love feast on a frequent, even daily basis, in the context of the Lord's Supper, they were celebrating their inclusion in the "new covenant." They were thereby consolidated as fictive families in Christ, for whom *amae* would develop naturally. With regard to the clarification requested by Prof. Hiroishi, I stand closer to Klauck than to Hofius, but feel that neither has an adequate grasp of the inclusion of the early Christian love feast within the parameters of the Lord's supper. It is a celebration of the new fictive families established by Christ crucified, in which a Greco-Roman and Jewish equivalent of *amae* was natural. What Hiroishi calls "integration" was a natural part of the meal that united the new family in Christ. There was probably no need to theorize about this because it was a natural result of constantly eating together—something the modern church has lost.

What is striking about Romans, however, is that the tendencies toward exclusivity are countered by the argument of 14:1-15:7 and overcome by the praxis of inviting others into the meals of one's group. When Paul repeatedly asks believers to greet one another in chapter 16, the natural context for this to occur was in their worship services. The climactic admonition in the letter is to greet one another with a "holy kiss," (Romans 16:16) acknowledging each other as belonging to the extended Christian family. If in fact the entire earlier argument of the letter prepares for this series of familial greetings, Romans provides the resources to qualify *amae* in an inclusive direction. This resonates with comments by Professors Yamada and Asano concerning the new community in Christ based on grace alone.

IV. TRANSLATING *PARAZĒLAŌ* AS ENVY OR ZEALOUS RAGE

Prof. Asano prefers the traditional view that Paul hoped the conversion of Gentiles would evoke jealousy that would lead to their conversion. While the Greek and Hebrew terms allow either jealous envy or zealous rage as translations, it seems to me that in Romans it is the latter alone that is in view. In Romans 10:19, the citation from Deuteronomy 32:21 is introduced with explicit reference to Moses. The following citation, therefore, is not Paul's voice directed to his Roman audience,but Moses' voice directed to Israel. The dilemma of misguided zeal in the earlier argument of Romans (7:7–25; 9:30–10:4) therefore, was a phenomenon first identified by none other than the primary spokesman of the Jewish law. The Hebraic parallelism in this verse requires the translation, "I shall make you zealous in regard to what is no nation, with a senseless nation shall I provoke you to wrath." If one translates *parazēlōsō* with "make jealous," this ruins the synonymous parallelism with "provoke you to wrath." The words from Moses explain the behavior of Jews rejecting the gospel as deriving from divinely provoked rage against the Gentile world. Since the Jewish form of the competition for honor that marked the ancient Mediterranean world was to exceed others in righteousness through conformity to the Torah, Israel's zeal turned against Gentiles, who were thought to have polluted the world. Consequently, Israel angrily rejected any gospel that accepted Gentiles as equals. This violent rage was predicted by Moses, according to Paul's argument, and will be overcome only at the end of time, when the mercy of God becomes triumphant (11:25–26, 32).

The verb *parazēlaō* appears again in Romans 11:11 and if the traditional translation "jealousy" is selected, one confronts what Ernst Käsemann called the "fantastic" improbability in believing that envy could lead to salvation. In view of the fact that Jewish legalists viewed the early Christian proclamation as heretical, no satisfactory explanation has ever been given to explain why they would have been "jealous" when Gentiles accepted this allegedly mistaken doctrine. It seems to me that this is precisely the kind of issue that requires the insights of scholars who understand the rationale of violence in honor and shame cultures. Perhaps the Japanese language and psychology would provide the basis to understand this more fully.

CONCLUSION

Reading and reflecting on these three thoughtful responses has been an extraordinary learning experience for me. I would like to thank my colleagues, and I hope for further clarification in the discussion that follows. Like Paul who entrusted the planning and organization of the Spanish mission to believers in Rome who were closer to the situation than he was, I believe that thinkers in Asia who have experienced colonialism and who understand the issues of saving face, achieving *amae*, overcoming the impulses of violence, and reordering "honor and shame on the basis of grace" are in a better position that I am to advance this discussion. I look forward to your comments.

The Seoul Symposium
October 27, 2007

39

Interlocking of Context and Theology: A Reading of Dr. Jewett's *Romans: A Commentary*

Yon-Gyong Kwon

Dr. Jewett's Romans commentary is a major contribution to Pauline scholarship, both quantitatively (!) and qualitatively. I like this commentary a lot and use it every time I wrestle with Paul's words in Romans, but since my main responsibility is not to detail why this commentary is so good but to clear a ground for lively discussion, let me just mention three points on which I find myself questioning Dr. Jewett's position.

I. The Contextuality of Paul's Argument

A. The Contextual Nature of Paul's Argument

The most noticeable characteristic of Dr. Jewett's commentary is his conscientious attention to the specific social context of Paul's argument: the Roman house and tenement churches on the one hand and the wider Greco-Roman society on the other. Jewett singles out among others the culture of honor and shame that is said to have dominated much of the ancient Mediterranean culture. There was "a great network of honoring" and that "is essential for understanding the argument of Romans which employs honor categories from beginning to end" (49).[1]

Significantly, the application of this interpretive principle is not restricted to the moral exhortations where such context is more visible but extends to the "theological" part of the letter too. This often involves a reinterpretation of major theological concepts in terms of their social implications, thereby making Paul's overall argument in Romans as

[1] Cf. Bruce J. Malina, *The New Testament World: Insights from Cultural Anthropology* (Philadelphia: Westminster/John Knox Press, 1993).

much sociological as theological. Thus, Paul's doctrine of justification in Romans is taken to be "a way to overcome cultural and religious bigotry by means of righteousness through faith in Christ crucified" (203), in that "[i]n Christ divine righteousness acts to counter the arrogance of dominant groups and the shame of subordinates" (275). "The thesis of Romans therefore effectively turns the social value system of the Roman Empire upside down" (139).

Here it is not just that Paul's theology has real sociological implications; it is rather that Paul's theology has a built-in sociological dimension within it.[2] This supposition makes it inevitable to redefine many key concepts of Paul's argument. So, faith is said to be a "broadly defined jargon for participation in the community of the converted" (276–277),[3] and justification "restoration of honor" which creates "a new social reality" (281). By the same token, the Law too is interpreted in relation to "the system of gaining honor and avoiding shame in the Mediterranean world" (266). Seen in this way, the "works (of law)," the target of much of Paul's argument, means "achieving superior status through performance" (267), providing a concrete (Jewish) case in point "illustrating a universal phenomenon in Paul's social environment" (296). So, Paul's complaint about the "works of law" is not "a matter of failure to perform the law, but . . . a matter of sinful competition that turns the law into a means of status acquisition" (267).[4] The claim is further supported by the exegesis of chapter 7 where Jewett speaks of "the capacity of the flesh to transform the law into a system of status acquisition, and thus totally to frustrate its capacity to produce the good" (467). So Dr. Jewett's reading the letter in terms of the culture of honor and shame in the first-century Mediterranean world parts ways from both the traditional view which puts the doctrine in the context of individual salvation and the "New Perspective" which places him in the sociological matrix of Jew/Gentile relationship. Thus here we have yet another "solution" to the chronic Pauline puzzle of the "works of law."

B. CONTEXTUALIZATION OR A NEW GENERALIZATION?

As we have seen thus far, Dr. Jewett tries to unlock the whole of Romans using the key of "honor and shame" culture, with a view to bring

[2] One can compare Jewett's reading with Francis Watson's earlier work, *Paul, Judaism, and the Gentiles. A Sociological Approach* (Cambridge: Cambridge University Press, 1986). Since then Watson has made an about face toward a more theological reading of Paul.

[3] In a way, this definition of justification resembles the "New Perspective" in that it also focuses on the sociological or ecclesial dimension of the doctrine, with the context of the Jew/Gentile relationship turned into that of the Mediterranean culture of honor and shame.

[4] At this point Jewett almost smacks of Bultmann who considered the problem of "the Jews" to lie in their "attempt" to be justified by works.

out the contextual nature of Paul's argument. Due emphasis on context is fair enough, but we are not unaware either of diverse ways of reducing Paul's theology to some sort of political or ecclesial shorthand. So the question is bound to arise: is Jewett bringing out the social message which is clearly there in Paul's argument but has thus far escaped scholarly surveillance, or is he imposing a construct of his own creation upon Paul's argument which in fact runs in a different direction?

Space precludes extended discussion. Let me just take Paul's argument against "works" as a test case. Dr. Jewett clearly perceives that in Paul's critique of the Jewish bigots, the issue is circumcision unaccompanied by corresponding obedience (308). This is good observation, but then he, with no compelling reason (so it seems to me), generalizes the issue by turning circumcision into a case of "accomplishment" in general: "the works of the flesh"; "fleshly accomplishment" (309); "any human accomplishment" (310) and "pious works" (312), whether it be religious accomplishment, wisdom or social status (314–15).

In casting the net as widely as he does here, Jewett must presuppose that for Paul circumcision represents a concretization of such works or accomplishment. Yet this is not exactly the way Paul talks about circumcision in the letter, where he pits Jewish boasting of circumcision (= status as a Jew) off *against* religious or moral accomplishments (2:1–5, 17–29; 3:1–3). As Dr. Jewett himself notes clearly, the criticized bigots are those who boast of their circumcision *without actual performance* to justify their boasting (212), not those who displays conformity to law out of sinful competition for higher status. Paul's indictment of the Jews in 3:11–18 too aims at their blatant failure to do the law, not the competitiveness of their strenuous performance. Yet I fail to find any adequate explanation of this crucial fact in the commentary.

In chapter 4 too, Paul's attention falls on the timing of Abraham's circumcision, as Dr. Jewett himself acknowledges (308). Nevertheless, he continues to take the "works" in verse 2 comprehensively, making Abraham the one justified without any accomplishment whatsoever. As I have just pointed out, however, Paul does not consider circumcision as belonging to (moral/religious) "works" and Dr. Jewett's practical identification of "before circumcision" with "without accomplishment" does not seem to sit well with what Paul actually says about the matter.[5]

This failure to appreciate the particularity of the situation (circumcision/ Jewish identity, not moral or religious works) seems to do with his preoccupation with the generalized notion of "boasting." Dr. Jewett

---

[5] This distinction, so clear in Paul, nevertheless tends to be ignored by most commentators. Cf. E. P. Sanders, *Paul, the Law, and the Jewish People* (Philadelphia: Fortress Press, 1983), 100 ("de facto distinction"); H. Räisänen, *Paul and the Law* (Philadelphia: Fortress Press, 1983), 28, who thinks that Paul "tacitly reduces" the Torah into moral laws.

identifies (competitive) "boasting" as the heart of the problem, but at this point I find myself unable to follow his exegesis of the text. From the way this distinctively Pauline word is used,[6] "boasting" can either be good or bad, depending on the object of such boasting (5:2; 15:18; Galatians 6:13, 14; 1 Corinthians 1:31; 9:15; Philippians 2:16; 3:3). The question concerns what or how to boast, not the fact of boasting itself, since in Paul's language "boasting" verges on the notion of "faith" or "believing." In Romans too what Paul takes issue with is not the notion of boasting itself but specific, i.e., the Jewish kind of boasting wherein one's boasting of status (circumcision) is not substantiated by appropriate performance (doing the law). Even boasting of one's performance is perfectly acceptable, provided it has solid ground to justify it (Philippians 2:16). That is, the real problem Paul finds in religious bigots is lack of works (doing), not performance with a misguided motive; those bigots are doomed not because they boast but because their boasting was an empty one unaccompanied by actual obedience to their law (2:6–11). Here Paul seems to stand firm in the tradition of the Old Testament prophets who leveled relentless critique of the hypocritical religiosity of Israel (e.g., Isaiah 1:10–31), the tradition which finds its way into Christianity through the eschatological message of John the Baptist (Matthew 3:7–10; Luke 3:7–9) and Jesus' critique of the hypocritical "scribes and the Pharisees" (Matthew 23:31, 23–28; Luke 11:37–52; 12:1; 20:46–47).[7]

In a way, Dr. Jewett's consistent application of the "honor-shame" grid, intended to bring out "the situational dimension of the letter" (3), seems to produce exactly the opposite effect of smothering the contextual edge, i.e., the specifically Jewish nature of Paul's argument.[8] This, in turn, enables Dr. Jewett to use Paul's words to address the *universal* issue of boasting: the Jew's empty boasting of their circumcision/status as a case of sinful competition to secure superior status. At this point I cannot help wondering why Jewett's reading of Romans has to be any more specific or contextual than the one he (and most of us, I may add) was taught by his/our church or his/our theological professors (4).[9]

[6] Apart from the two occurrences in James (1:9; 4:16), the verb "boasting" occurs only in the Pauline corpus (34 times). The noun "boasting" appears 10 time in Paul, and only once in Hebrews in the whole New Testament writings.

[7] I have pointed this out a few times before, for example, *Eschatology in Galatians* (Tübingen: Mohr Siebeck, 2004), 212.

[8] Of course, I have to add that Paul's concern in his letters is not about Judaism in general but about a specific groups of Jews whose theological outlook is quite different from the so-called "covenantal nomism."

[9] Scholars love to talk about the importance of "historical context," but one often feels that what they really want is the kind of historical context which will make their own interpretation more plausible. Or, it rather seems that one's theological DNA dictates the kind of historical context one is eventually to "reconstruct."

Let me make one more point before moving on to the next question. Throughout the commentary, Dr. Jewett tries to impress upon us the contextual meaning of Paul's theological discussion in the context of the Roman house and tenement churches. The result is that much of Paul's theological discussion in the earlier chapters turns out to be a kind of cryptic adumbration in theological parlance of what he is going to say in plain terms in the later, exhortative chapters (see, for example, 205). Such rhetorical maneuver is not impossible, but quite odd indeed, to say the least. It is all the more so, when we compare it with such letters of his as the two Corinthian letters and Galatians where he plunges into *medias res* right from the beginning (1 Corinthians 1:10ff; Galatians 1:6), before presenting exegetical or theological substantiation of it.

II. "WORKS OF LAW," "WORKS," AND SALVATION

A. "WORKS OF THE LAW" AND MORAL OBEDIENCE

My next point concerns the question: what are the "works of the law" that Paul is arguing against? Most interpreters, including even J. D. G. Dunn, an early champion of the "New Perspective," admit that it involves actual "doing" of the law.[10] As far as my simplistic reading is concerned, this creates an insuperable tension, or I would rather say, flat contradiction in Paul's reasoning in Romans as well as in his theology as a whole, since it amounts to saying that Paul is not against works in principle, but he is in Galatians and Romans. Naturally, I am quite interested in finding out how Dr. Jewett tackles the problem.

At this point, however, Dr. Jewett's commentary divulges the same sort of ambiguity as I find in most others. In chapter 2 Dr. Jewett correctly identifies the "imaginary interlocutor" as "the bigot who knows God's will but fails to perform it" (212). He also perceives clearly that "no hint of disapprobation in Paul's formulation of good works in 2:7, because all who perform such deeds receive 'eternal life'" (205). So, Paul does stress the indispensability of works, and he does so against those who boast their possession and knowledge of the law without actually doing it. Strangely enough, however, such bigots silently disappear from the scene on the way, and Dr. Jewett does not bring them to bear on his subsequent discussion of justification apart from "works (of the law)." He joins most others in assuming that the "works of the law," an obvious *crux interpretum*, refers to actual *doing* of the law. No doubt, he offers his own reason why such "doing" is problematic by linking it "with the systems of gaining honor and avoiding shame in the Mediterranean world" (266). In a way, Dr. Jewett provides a variation of Dunn's proposal,

---

[10] See his strong demur in *The Theology of Paul the Apostle* (Grand Rapids: Eerdmans, 1998), 358, note 97. See also his *Romans 1–8*, 92, 107.

only changing Dunn's "maintaining ethnic identity" into his own, and more general, "achieving superior status through performance."

This of course creates a serious tension with what Paul says in chapter 2 as well as in chapters 6 and 8, where he makes it crystal clear that proper obedience is necessary for end-time salvation. So, like most other interpreters, Dr. Jewett has to fine-tune his point. In reality, it is not performing the law itself that is problematic; it is the "sinful competition that turns conformity to law into a means of status acquisition" (276). As he sees it, "actions motivated by the desire for superior honor . . . pervert obedience and frustrate the purpose of divine law. Only those who abandon claims of superiority can fulfill the law, which required both Jews and Gentiles to change their motivational systems" (212). Thus he follows the solution proposed by K. Snodgrass who distinguishes between "works righteousness" and "saving obedience" or D. Garlington who speaks of "a different kind of doing the law."

I fail to find any evidence in Paul's argument for such a hair-splitting distinction between "actions motivated by the desire for superior status" and "obedience" in the proper sense. Throughout the letter, Paul's concern is performance itself, not its motivation; his problem is people's disobedience (chapter 2) or inability to do the law (chapter 7), not performing the law with a wrong motivation. To all appearances, the problem of "I" in chapter 7 is not obedience with crooked motives but failure to do what is good *despite his excellent intention*. I have already expressed my qualms about this sort of theoretical distinction,[11] and so I will not repeat it here. Such distinction is made necessary not by Paul's own logic but by scholars' effort to resolve the tension they themselves create in Paul's reasoning, the tension which disappears once we acknowledge the *contextual* meaning of the "works (of the law)."

Dr. Jewett's critique of "performance as a means of superior status" also seems unclear to me. Paul clearly develops his argument under the assumption that it is surely desirable to seek such superior status: salvation, justification, eternal life, honor, glory, or whatever (cf. Galatians 2:17). Throughout the argument his concerns remains consistently on the proper means of seeking such status (faith or works of the law), not the motivation behind such quest.

B. CONTRADICTION IN PAUL?

The fog of ambiguity still lingers concerning the place of good works in Paul's theology. Good works are necessary for eternal life (205), but it is wrong to perform such works as a competitive means to gain superior status. So Dr. Jewett walks on a tight-rope as many others do:

[11] In Kwon, *Eschatology*, 205, note 100.

> Paul continues to display an interest in human work, the fruits of which *define* who one is . . . . [A]lthough believers *are not saved* by the quality of the fruit they produce, they *are defined* thereby, and *their work will be evaluated at the end of time*. Although their work no longer *earns* honor or status and is now performed out of a sense of gratitude and vocation, its fruit remains a matter for accountability (424).

Dr. Jewett tries to remove the tension by changing good works as a means of earning salvation into the fruits that define who one is. This is a well-trodden track, but here I am troubled by the tantalizing ambiguity of the formulation. It may be due to my slow-mindedness, but what, I must ask, does it mean *in practice* to say that we are not *saved* by our works, yet are *defined* or *evaluated* by them at the Judgment, or that our work does not earn honor or status, yet we remain *accountable*? Is it wrong to expect a straightforward answer to the simple question, like the one we have in James or Matthew?

Ambiguously put as it may be, the tension remains all the same, as long as one affirms the necessity of good works and denies it in one breath. On the one hand, "those who actually accomplish good works will gain eternal life" (212). But, commenting on 2:6–11, he also states that Paul simply "conforms to what Paul perceives to be the orientation of his audience," namely, without necessary "clarification" which will "remove it from the framework of a reward for good behavior" by "linking it more closely with grace in Christ" (5:21; 6:21–22, 206).[12] He even says, citing 1 Corinthians 3:15, that believers will be saved "even if it [their work] falls short," since the eschatological *telos* "lies beyond the scope of human effort, remaining entirely in the hands of the gracious God" (425). Here I am simply unable to reconcile these two lines of reasoning. This is not a quiz show, but I would like to hear very much Dr. Jewett's "final answer" to that in plain English.

C. "WORKS OF THE LAW" IN THE EPISTOLARY CONTEXT

It seems that the only way out of this conundrum is to acknowledge the contextual meaning of "works (of the law" which is utilized by Paul in the sense of "Jewish identity." That is, throughout the letter, Paul is not fighting against the "doers" of the law with wrong motivation but against those religious "bigots" who think they are safe, simply because they are circumcised Jews without actually fulfilling the righteous demand of the

[12] It seems more likely to me that there Paul contradicts, rather than conforms, "the orientation of his audience," a fact further highlighted by the repetition of biting rhetorical questions (2:3–4). And he makes it crystal clear that that is an integral part of his own gospel (2:16). Or, are those "pretentious bigots" (200) different from Paul's Roman audience?

law. And Paul destroys their confidence by making it beyond doubt (at least to me!) that proper obedience is absolutely necessary for one's final salvation, and that external Jewish identity has no bearing at all on the question of justification (3:20–29; 4:1–12).[13]

As chapter 6 shows, Paul's logic seems simple enough. There are two modes of slavery (slavery to sin versus slavery to righteousness/God), each of which produces its own patterns of behavior (unrighteousness/unlawfulness vs. holiness) and necessarily entails its own eschatological consequences (*telos*: death or eternal life; cf. the sowing and reaping imagery and the warning attached to it in Galatians 6:7–9). Paul's point is not that grace cuts the necessary connection between obedience and its eschatological consequence (the traditional, "Lutheran" type of interpretation), but that through faith in Christ they have been transferred from the dominion of sin to the dominion of righteousness, thereby being enabled to "walk by the newness of life" (6:4) and bear the fruit of holiness (6:19, 22), the life which brings about the *telos* of eternal life (6:22–23). It is in this sense that the gospel is the *power* of God unto salvation, the power manifested in the resurrection of Christ and experienced by believers in the form of the Spirit (1:16). By the same token, the law is *weak* in that it cannot work out such transformation, something God has effectively done by way of the cross of Christ: liberating one from the life of 'walking *kata sarka*" and giving them the life of "walking *kata pneuma*" (8:1–4).[14]

III. PAUL'S ESCHATOLOGICAL PERSPECTIVE IN ROMANS

A. SOTERIOLOGICAL CONCEPTS ENCOMPASSING BOTH PRESENT AND FUTURE

Finally, let me move to the question of eschatology. Clearly, Dr. Jewett leans toward a more realized reading of Paul's eschatology. Although he does not dispute the future dimension of Paul's soteriology, he takes most of Paul's soteriological concepts as already present here and now, as many modern interpreters do. This is true not only with justification whose present realization is stated unambiguously but also with such concepts as "wrath" (1:18; 2:8), "salvation" (1:16; 5:9–10; 8:24; 13:11), and even "eternal life" (2:7; 5:21; 6:22–23) whose present realization is never expressed explicitly.

[13] Otherwise, we end up with a very strangely shaped argument in which Paul haphazardly alternates between two different issues: "without/before circumcision" and "without accomplishment": not works (3:20–21)—equality (22–24)—not works (27–28)—equality (29–30)—not works (4:1–8)—equality (4:9–12). To be sure, Dr. Jewett takes the two essentially the same, but that does not seem to be the way Paul tackles them, as I already mentioned above.

[14] In Galatians too, Paul's critique of the law aims at the same problem, as I pointed out in *Eschatology*, 195–98.

Dr. Jewett is well aware that even in Romans "Paul so frequently speaks of salvation in terms of preservation from divine wrath in the last judgment" (5:9–10; 13:11), but he (commenting on 1:16) nevertheless concludes that "in view of 8:24, where salvation is described with a past tense verb, and the current verse dominated by a present tense verb "the power of God *is*," salvation in Romans "already has become a present reality through Christ in the midst of the world and not just an anticipation 'in principle'" (138).[15] In a similar way, God's wrath, which is clearly future in 2:5 (203), should be taken to be present in 1:18, because it "is redefined by the gospel, a present progressive translation . . . is appropriate" (151). Still further, "eternal life" which comes in as "a reward for good deeds" in 2:7 (205), is also something believers have access "both now and in the future" (389), thereby becoming "fullness of existence for the saints in the present that continues on into the future" (425).

B. PRESENT, FUTURE, AND PAUL'S SOTERIOLOGICAL LOGIC

As a staunch defender of a "futuristic" reading of Paul, here I feel that Dr. Jewett's effort to extend Paul's originally future concepts to cover the present only muddles Paul's thinking rather than clarifying it. Following Dr. Jewett's dialectic or composite definition of major eschatological concepts, I find it very difficult to grasp the precise point Paul is making. Unlike in Galatians,[16] Justification in Romans is clearly present, but so is salvation, according to Dr. Jewett. What then is the difference between the two, between the "restoration of righteousness" and "establishment of salvation"? What is the logic behind Paul's move from 1:16 to 1:17? If salvation is already here, how is it possible for Paul to make such statements as 5:9–10? If so, would he rather not have said something like this: "If we have already been saved partially, how much more shall we be saved fully"? And if salvation is really present, albeit partially, how can one say that it is now much closer than when one first believed as in 13:11? True, Paul once refers to it with a past tense verb, but the context makes it clear that Paul's singular focus there is not on the "already" of salvation but on the "not yet" of our hope (8:24–25). Are we not supposed to take Paul's accentuation of the invisibility of our hope more seriously?

Similarly, is it proper to say that God's "wrath" can either be present and future at the same time? Such a composite notion of wrath makes Paul's statements quite dialectical, if not outright contradictory: on the one hand, God is already exercising his wrath upon the disobedient (1:18), yet he is still patiently withholding it in order to give the disobedient a chance to repent (2:4). Can we reconcile these two statements in an intelligible way? Do we then have to say that God's wrath is already

15 Here he cites Käsemann.

16 See my *Eschatology*, 51–77.

working for Gentiles or humanity in general (chapter 1), while for the Jews it is postponed until the Day of Judgment (chapter 2)? Since the only ground for considering it as already realized is the present tense verb and since we all know that the tense of a Greek verb is nothing to bet our money on, and since the present construal of the statement creates an *unnecessary* tension within Paul's argument itself, is it not better to simply take it to be future, pure and simple?

The same objection can be made with "eternal life." In 2:6 its present realization is out of the question, but what about other references? In 5:21 Paul contrasts "reigning of sin in death" with "reigning of grace through righteousness" which leads to (*eis*) eternal life. How that happens is explained in detail in chapter 6, where Paul contrasts two different kinds of slavery in the present, with each leading to its respective eschatological consequences (*telos*): either death or eternal life. Here if eternal life is already present in any way, Paul's logic loses its force altogether. Eternal life is called grace (6:23) not because God gives it away to both the obedient and disobedient (2:6–11, 13; 8:13), but because Jesus Christ has graciously transferred one from the sinful slavery to the righteous one (6:7–18), namely, from the life which deserves ultimate death to the life which will be graciously rewarded with eternal life (6:21–23; 2:6–11). There is nothing unusual here, since Paul already made that crystal clear in Galatians (6:7–9). Appealing to the difficult passage in 1 Corinthians 3:15 at this point seems unwise, since 1) there Paul clearly intends the statement as a warning, not consolation, and 2) the passage is immediately followed by the stern warning ("holy sentence") in 3:16–17.

I believe that Dr. Jewett's composite, or dialectical, reading of Paul's soteriological concepts represents an unmistakable case of the so-called "totality transfer," an exegetical fallacy as widely committed as it is universally denounced. And I also find it quite difficult to understand why modern scholars, generally so keen on the contextual nature of Paul's argument, fall so easily back on such a composite readings of Paul, even ignoring the specific thrust required by the context. As I have already noted, there seems to be a predetermined penchant for a more realized interpretation of Paul among modern scholars.

I agree with Dr. Jewett in taking 1:16–17 as the thesis statement of Romans, but I take salvation there as future and interpret the letter accordingly: Paul relies on the gospel since that gospel about the Son of God (1:2) is (gnomic present) God's power that leads believers to (future) salvation. The gospel can be God's power for salvation, since (*gar*) in it revealed God's righteousness in the present (verse 17). In other words, God's righteousness revealed in the present "through our Lord Jesus Christ," the refrain of Romans, explains why the gospel has the power that leads one to future salvation.

For me this construal fits nicely with the development of Paul's argument in Romans, especially chapters 1–8, where discussion of the revelation of God's righteousness through the cross and resurrection of Jesus (1–4) moves on to the certainty of future salvation, the ultimate concern which dominates Paul's discussion throughout chapters 5–8: present justification or reconciliation generates and guarantees future salvation (5:1–11); eternal life is made possible by Christ's act of obedience which reverses the deadly consequences of Adam's disobedience (5:12–21). How that change comes about is explained in chapter 6, in terms of moral transformation occasioned by believers' union with the crucified and resurrected Christ. And after a detailed discussion of the law's paradoxical role in this picture (chapter 7), Paul sums up the discussion, this time highlighting the role of the Spirit which enables believers to walk *kata pneuma* instead of *kata sarka* (8:1–17), which in turn leads to the moving statement about the certainty of Christian hope even in the midst of hardships (8:18–39).

Conclusion

As I hinted above, those questions raised in this review are not so much aimed at Dr. Jewett himself as at Pauline scholarship as a whole. I myself have been struggling with these questions, and naturally, I wanted very much to see how Jewett handles these thorny problems. My impression is that Jewett mostly sticks to a fairly "traditional" position on those questions I have raised above. Despite those points of disagreement, however, I am quite convinced that one can learn a lot from the conscientious way in which Jewett endeavors to read the letter as containing a concrete message for the everyday life of Roman Christians. After all, there is no such thing as theology in isolation from life. Preparing this review was a pure joy for me, and I would like to express my sincere thanks to him both for the commentary and for his life-long contribution to the New Testament scholarship.

40

The Rhetoric of Persuasion in the Letter to Rome: A Review of Dr. Robert Jewett's Commentary on Romans

Sojung Yoon

Robert Jewett starts his remarkable commentary with an analysis of historical perspectives. He successfully integrates an historical view and literary analysis in his study. Turning away from the traditional view that Romans is a theological treatise, or "Paul's Last Will and Testament," according to Bornkamm, Jewett approaches Romans as a situational letter in which Paul responds to the particular circumstances of the Roman church. Looking into Romans as closely related to a church situation makes the reading more stimulating as a vivid description of a part of early Christian history. Furthermore, it reveals that the letter retains more effective teachings for contemporary churches than the traditional interpretations have shown. We can easily associate ourselves with the Roman congregation and find theological solutions pertinent to our own reality through Paul's exhortation.

What most intrigues me about Jewett's picturing the historical situation of the Roman congregation is that he reexamines the conventional feature of " 'the church in the house' of particular patron."[1] Looking at the evidence in Romans 16, he suggests that the church was run by communal agreement of its members rather than a single patron's leadership. The church was not supported financially by a single rich patron, according to him, but by the whole congregation occupying a tenement building. This portrait of the Roman church shows an egalitarian leadership. Jewett thus argues that G. Theissen's "love-patriarchalism" can be replaced by "agapic-communalism"

---

[1] R. Jewett, *Romans: A Commentary* (Minneapolis: Fortress Press, 2007), 23.

with a focus on the equal rights of every community member in the setting of the Roman church. This new notion convincingly represents the egalitarian tradition formed at the beginning of Christianity.

Dealing in more detail with Jewett's outstanding work in this brief essay would be impossible. I will rather focus on the aspects of the commentary that preoccupy my personal interest, that is to say, the rhetorical-critical analysis of Romans, to which Jewett devotes not a small part of his work.

As a situational letter, its rhetoric is closely related with its purpose. Jewett considers what Paul might have had in mind when he wrote the letter, investigating five different purposes that have been presented by biblical scholars: 1) Paul intends to exhort the weak and strong Christians in Rome to cooperate. 2) He intends to convert the weak Christians, who are legalistic Jewish Christians, into accepting his point of view about Christian freedom. 3) He intends to legitimize the status of Gentile believers. 4) He intends to convert nonbelieving Jews in Rome. 5) He intends to secure the Roman Church's support for his mission plan in Spain. While Jewett admits each has its own strong and weak points, he argues that only the fifth purpose does not contradict Paul's own mission policy of noninterference (cf. Romans 15:20), and thus is the most plausible purpose of Romans.[2] Spain was a new territory for Christian mission, and one where he could not expect to find Christian supporters or synagogues where he could deliver the message of Christ. Furthermore he needed to cope with a linguistic barrier because his language, Koine Greek, was not widely known in Spain.

Assuming that this letter aims at gaining the assistance of the Roman church for the Spain mission, Jewett discusses that Romans is not "a repository of theology" but "a work of Christian rhetoric, aiming to persuade," and thus its rhetoric is "Evangelical Persuasion."[3] He analyzes the structure of the letter using a feature of classical rhetoric, arrangement. The paradigm of the arrangement he offers is in the order of the *Exordium* (Introduction), the *Narratio* (Statement of Facts), the *Propositio* (Thesis), the four parts of the *Probatio* (Proof), and the *Peroratio* (Conclusion). According to Jewett's analysis, after preparing the Roman audience in the Exordium for the themes Paul would argue in the following chapters, Paul provides certain background information that will help the audience understand his intention in writing the letter (the *Narratio*). The main theme of Romans shown in the *Propositio* (1:16–17), "the Gospel as the powerful embodiment of the righteousness of

2 Jewett, *Romans*, 64.

3 B. Byrne, S.J. *Romans* (Collegeville: Liturgical Press, 1996), 4. Quoted from Jewett, *Romans*, 23.

God," is repeatedly discussed in the following proofs.[4] After dealing with three different theological topics in the first three proofs, Paul goes on to discuss the community rules based on the Gospel in the fourth. In the Peroration, Paul concludes the letter with the request of assistance for his mission.

I now like to raise some questions about Jewett's approach to Paul's rhetoric in the letter to the Romans. He views this letter as fitting into the epideictic, or demonstrative genre, accepting W. Wuellner's approach but with several alterations. As a basis for this point of view, Jewett significantly depends on Theodore C. Burgess's study of epideictic literature and oratory. Burgess enumerates 27 subtypes of epideictic, among which Jewett finds "speech on disembarking," "paranetic speech," "hortatory speech," and "ambassador's speech" parallel to Romans. He says that "Romans is a unique fusion of the `ambassadorial letter' with several of the other subtypes in the genre: the parenetic letter, the hortatory letter, and the philosophical diatribe." As a result, Jewett classifies Romans as epideictic, which convincingly explains "the impression of a manifesto or a 'testament,' which sets forth Paul's conviction in a systematic manner."[5]

I suggest that we need not only to consider the classification of the subtypes but also to look into the dynamic between Paul as a speaker and the Roman congregation as hearers. According to Aristotle, the subject of epideictic rhetoric is praise or blame. Of the three genres of rhetoric, while deliberative rhetoric concerns the future, and forensic the past, epideictic is mainly about the present time. As for its setting, George Kennedy offers specific examples such as "[the] funeral oration, the festival panegyric, and the sophistic exercise."[6] Kennedy characterizes the underlying goal of epideictic as "[the] strengthening of audience adherence to some value, as the basis for a general policy of action," and adds "most modern preaching is epideictic . . . only when a preacher has some very definite action [such as baptism or giving up drinking] in mind does the sermon become deliberative."[7] With this presumption, Kennedy views the rhetoric of Romans as epideictic in the same vein as Jewett.

In attempting to integrate my own knowledge about epideictic and Jewett's point of view along with Kennedy's, I cannot help raising question about the genre of Romans. Given that epideictic supposedly persuades an audience to hold to a certain value, what value does Romans ask that its audience accept? Since "determination of the

---

4 Jewett, *Romans*, 44.

5 Jewett, *Romans*, 88.

6 G. A. Kennedy, *New Testament Interpretation through Rhetorical Criticism* (Chapel Hill: University of North Carolina Press, 1984), 75.

7 Kennedy, *Romans*, 74.

species sometimes helps to bring out the emphasis of a work and thus the intent of the author,"[8] it is appropriate to infer the intent of the author by delineating the genre. Kennedy argues that epideictic is more likely to pursue abstract values than concrete actions. He seems to conclude that Paul delivers a discourse on general Christian values in Romans. But I notice that this perspective would contradict the view that Romans is a situational letter. If Paul were coping with a particular situation in Rome, he would have had a tangible solution in mind. And Jewett indeed suggests that Paul's purpose in this letter is to secure assistance for his mission plan for Spain. This purpose does not seem to harmonize with the nature of epideictic. To my knowledge, of the three genres of rhetoric, epideictic is the genre that is expected to have the least practical impact on the audience. In the Roman period, as political power became centralized and Greek democracies faded away, the need to persuade the *demos* declined. Instead speech towards emperors and other rulers became more common. This change led to an emphasis on epideictic rather than on deliberative or forensic rhetoric. Speakers tended to fill up their speeches with praise of their rulers. Another important factor in this development took place at schools in which teachers and students focused on the refinement of rhetoric as a matter of academic interest, and mainly committed themselves to epideictic. The usage of epideictic in history shows that epideictic tends to be decorative and pleasing rather than persuasive for a particular purpose. Thus we see that the nature of the genre does not satisfactorily explain what Paul intends to accomplish in the letter. When we see the letter as an epideictic discourse, we can at least assume that Paul's purpose in writing was to change the Romans' prejudice about Paul's authority as an Apostle and their perception of the Spaniards as "barbarians."[9] Still, Paul would have intended this change of thought to lead to the congregation's active involvement with his mission plan. Paul appears to want them to take particular actions in the future. Given that aspect, I cannot help wondering if Romans might have some or more features of the deliberative genre.

Even if we assume that Paul only considers general Christian values in the letter to Rome, the question remains as to whether the form of speech fits into its discourse. As mentioned above, ancient authorities set forth the main content of epideictic as praise or blame. Burton L. Mack suggests that epideictic (encomium) is mostly about collecting "examples from the life of an individual (or the history of an institution) that could demonstrate the person's virtue and establish

[8] Kennedy, *New Testament Interpretation*, 19.
[9] Jewett, *Romans*, 88–89.

the basis for honor or memorial,"[10] and thus its outline would be in the order of introduction, narration, achievements (of the individual or the institution), and conclusion. Although this description might not be true to every epideictic speech, it grasps the essential characteristic of the genre. In my opinion, proof is not the main function of epideictic. Thus I suggest Romans is more likely a piece of deliberative rhetoric through which the Romans are being persuaded to assist Paul's mission plan for Spain.

From my own context, I would also like to raise a minor point about the change Paul wanted to effect among the congregation members. Jewett suggests that a part of Paul's mission strategy in Romans is to modify the Romans' view that the inhabitants of Spain are barbarians by insisting that "the impartial righteousness of God does not discriminate against `barbarians' such as the Spaniards."[11] When we consider the missions in Korea done by European and European-American missionaries, we find plentiful evidence that they regarded Korean culture as inferior to their own. Still, their mission appears to have been successful in consideration of the Korean Church's extraordinary growth. I thus wonder whether it was practically possible for the Romans to be free from the prejudice against Spain, or whether that prejudice would have precluded support for a mission to the Spaniards. More likely, even if they were biased against the country, they could still have Christianized its people.

Finally, as a woman who is interested in the feminist interpretation of the Holy Scriptures, I tend to use my imagination whenever I read a text. When I read Romans I like to picture what kind of dynamic is operating in the scene of Paul's letter being delivered to its Roman audience. I would like to read Romans not in the position of Paul as an author but as one of the audience, a hearer of God's message. How would people have reacted listening to the letter? Would they have accepted all of Paul's exhortations, and agreed to support his mission? Or would they have had misgivings about the plan? While we can infer that the Corinthians' reaction to 1 Corinthians was not especially positive thanks to 2 Corinthians in which Paul sounds less authoritative and more modest towards his hearers, we don't have any similar evidence that points to what might have happened after the letter to the Romans arrived at its destination. Answers to such questions are hidden behind the mysterious curtain of Christian history.

---

[10] Burton L. Mack, *Rhetoric and the New Testament* (Minneapolis: Fortress Press, 1990), 47–48.

[11] Jewett, *Romans*, 79.

41

A Response to Professor Robert Jewett

Ik Soo Park

It is a great honor for me to respond to Dr. Robert Jewett's paper ("Romans: Paul's Letter for Asia in the 21st Century),[1] because I have been reading his articles and books since 1976, when I was a student at Perkins School of Theology, Southern Methodist University. The late Prof. William Farmer recommended that I read his book, *Chronology of Paul's Life*.[2] Since then, I have been particularly indebted to his articles and books on the purpose and the argument of Romans. Recently I have done some research in writing my own commentary on Romans and have consulted Jewett's works,[3] but my publication is being delayed at least for a couple of months more because of Jewett's 1140-page commentary on *Romans*.[4]

I. Summary

Jewett's paper, "Romans: Paul's Letter for Asia in the 21st Century," is thoughtful and masterful in its search for methodological clarity, and in its sharpening of the question of honor and shame in *Romans*. Jewett has made a series of judgments that I list below. Then I will highlight some of Jewett's positions on which I take a different stand. I am so

---

[1] The expanded edition of the paper appears as "Rome and Beyond" in this volume.

[2] Robert Jewett, *A Chronology of Paul's Life* (Philadelphia: Fortress Press, 1979).

[3] Robert Jewett, *Romans*, Cokesbury Basic Bible Commentary 22 (Nashville: Graded, 1988); idem, "Major Impulses in the Theological Interpretation of Romans since Barth," *Interpretation* 34 (1980), 17–31; idem, "Ecumenical Theology for the Sake of Mission: Romans 1:1–17 + 15:14–16:24," in edited by D. M. Hay and E. Johnson, *Pauline Theology, III* (Minneapolis: Fortress Press, 1995); idem, "Following the Argument of Romans," in edited by K. P. Donfried, *The Romans Debate* (Peabody: Hendrickson, 1991).

[4] Robert Jewett, *Romans* (Minneapolis: Fortress Press, 2007).

excited about and wholeheartedly agree with his proposals in the paper. I will try to "repeat" his provocative proposals as to clarify his position and to use the paradigm in the study of *Romans*.

A. Jewett begins the unusual quest for the function of the admonition to "welcome" each other (Romans 14:1 and 15:7) and the repetitions of the formula "greet so and so" (chapter 16) for the congregational situation of Romans. This is interesting in light of the social issues of shameful exclusion and honorable welcome in which the western theological tradition has been preoccupied with regard to the issues of guilt and forgiveness.

B. In place of the western traditional theology of Romans, Jewett proposes setting the world right by overcoming its perverse systems of honor and shame in the form of social discrimination as the central issue. Because he presupposes that most of the audience of Romans were demeaned from birth on prejudicial grounds, whether it be racial, cultural, or religious. Koreans can understand prejudicial assessments much more clearly than Americans or Europeans.

C. Jewett reads what Paul mentioned in Romans 7 not as a failure to fulfill the law, but rather the inability of such violent legalism to achieve the good. Because Paul discovered that his religious motivation was corrupted by the desire for status acquisition, the obsession to gain honor deprived others of the honor that others should enjoy.

D. Paul's argument on "the righteousness of God" has great relevance in the Asian situations, because Romans 1–3 as well as 9–11 argue that all nations have sinned and fallen short of the glory of God, furthermore all people can be saved by the impartial righteousness of God through grace alone. Jewett believes that we need to reformulate the classical Reformation doctrine of "justification by faith." To become "righteous through faith" means to accept the gospel of Christ's shameful death on behalf of the shamed, which means that everyone is equally honored.

E. Halvor Moxens places the argument of Romans in the context of an "honour society" in which "recognition and approval from others" is central. Shameful exclusion should be overcome. To these references, Jewett adds the socially discriminatory categories that Moxens overlooked in Romans such as: the repetitions of "Greeks and barbarians, educated and uneducated," the potentially shameful epithet "Gentiles," and the "weak" and the "strong."

F. There is an admonition to mutual "welcome" in 14:1 and 15:7 in a context closely related to the congregational situation. Chapter 14 opens the section with the words, "Welcome the one who is weak in faith, but not in order to dispute debatable points" (14:1). This is a clear reference to the Jewish Christian conservatives, the "weak" who are being discriminated against by the Gentile Christian majority, the "strong," in

Rome. It is likely that the "weak" include some of the Jewish Christian exiles mentioned in chapter 16 who are now returning to Rome after the lapse of the Edict of Claudius.

G. The theme of inclusive welcome of shameful outsiders is repeated 21 times "greet so and so" in various forms of chapter 16. So the implication of this repeated admonition is the same as we found in 14:1 and 15:7. The climax in this request for mutual welcome, which would overcome the conflicts between these early Christian groups, is found in 16:16, "greet one another with a holy kiss."

H. Jewett concludes that the righteousness of God is the power to overturn the unjust systems of honor and shame that each ethnic group creates, proclaiming that all humans are equally loved by God with a holy, impartial, righteous passion, and the access to this power is not doctrinal conformity but through mutual acceptance of others. The time has come in the 21st century for this insight (about the perversion of religion into a means of gaining honor) and the message (concerning the impartial righteousness of God) to the Asian contexts. We thank Jewett for giving his thoughtful consideration of Asia in the conclusion of his paper.

II. Response

The purpose of this response is not to give honor or shame on Dr. Jewett or defend myself against his position, but simply to make some observations. Most of my criticisms and questions revolve around some of Jewett's positions on which I take a different stand. Jewett now needs to provide: (A) a more detailed explanation for or refinement for determining Paul's purpose in writing Romans, his strategy of missionizing in Spain; (B) "the righteousness of God" in the relation to the phrase *pistis Christou*; and (C) the word *aspasasthe* in chapter 16.

A. Paul's Purpose in Writing Romans

1. In recent discussions on the purpose of Romans, two points have emerged. First, there is widespread agreement that the letter is occasioned by some interplay between matters pertaining to Paul's needs and matters relating to the Roman congregations. Second, more scholars affirm that the framing material in Romans (1:1–17 and 15:14–16:24) gives adequate clues to the purpose of the letter. Jewett joins the discussion on each of these fronts. Because his thesis is that Paul's purpose in writing Romans should be understood in the light of Paul's appeal for cooperation in the planning and support of the Spanish mission, which is stated in the introduction (1:1–15) and reiterated in the conclusion (15:22–29) of the letter.

Jewett's interpretation of the framing material highlights Paul's missional intentions regarding Spain. This approach builds on the foundation of Nils A. Dahl.[5] According to Jewett, the specific historical and cultural conditions in Spain, for example, the lack of Jewish settlement which posed several large barriers to Paul's missionary strategy. The theological and paranetic arguments of the letter serve this end, i.e., aiming at uniting the Roman house-churches so that such cooperation would be possible.[6] Jewett mentions that Paul's needs from the Romans might include finances, contacts and translators. Is Roman divisiveness wasting resources? How would greater unity yield more support?[7] How can this purpose of Romans relate to the theological discussions of the body of the letter?

While Jewett's conception of Paul's mission focuses too much on beyond Rome, by contrast, it does not do justice to Paul's mission in Rome, even though he also assumes that the letter reflects multiple congregations of differing ethnic backgrounds that are resisting the return of some of the Jewish Christian refugees.[8] The long discussion under the subtitle "II. The Challenge of the Mission to the Barbarians in Spain," in his nine-page paper reflects his view very well.

(1) If one argues that evangelizing Spain is the underlying purpose of Romans, then one must account for the length and appropriateness of the intervening chapters. However, It is clear that Paul states twice that he wants to see the Romans on the way to Spain explicit *only at the end* of the letter (15:24, 28). "Spain" is taken by Jewett as the governing motif and purpose of the letter as a whole. We will surely never know whether Jewett's imaginative suggestions regarding Phoebe's role as agent and patron of the Spanish mission are true[9] or not.[10] Jewett goes too far, however.

Paul has no doubt heard from some of his contacts in Rome that it is precisely the Gentiles who, with Claudius' edict banishing the Jews from Rome, had gained ascendancy of leadership in the Roman churches. When Claudius died and the Jewish Christians returned to Rome—that precipitated the troubles as Jewish Christians were treated poorly. We must be clear that Paul has a mission to and for the Roman house-churches, and the bulk of his letter addresses that mission.

---

[5] Nils A. Dahl, *Studies in Paul: Theology for the Early Christian Mission* (Minneapolis: Augsburg, 1977).

[6] Robert Jewett, "Paul, Phoebe, and the Spain Mission," in edited by P. Borgen et al., *The Social World Formative Christianity and Judaism: Essays in Tribute to Howard Clark Kee* (Philadelphia: Fortress Press, 1988), 144–64; idem, "Ecumenical Theology for the Sake of Mission: Romans 1:1–17 + 15:14–16:24," *Pauline Theology, III*, 90.

[7] Sampley, "Romans in a Different Light," *Pauline Theology, III*, 112.

[8] Jewett, "Ecumenical Theology," 93.

[9] Robert Jewett, "Paul, Phoebe, and the Spain Mission," in edited by P. Borgen et al. *The Social World Formative Christianity and Judaism: Essays in Tribute to Howard Clark Kee* (Philadelphia: Fortress Press, 1988), 144–164.

[10] Sampley, "Romans in a Different Light," 111; James C. Walter, "'Pheobe' and 'Junia(s)' –Romans 16:1–2, 7," in edited by Carroll D. Osburn, *Essays on Women in Earliest Christianity* (Joplin: College Press, 1993), I, 167–90.

All the sections of the letter (1:18–15:13) are designed to bear directly on the ethnically grounded struggle over leadership and position in the Roman house-churches, aiming toward helping all of Paul's readers to recognize and affirm their equality and unity in the powerful gospel of God. Paul's purpose is to establish the broadest possible ground upon which all of the Roman Christians—no matter what their ethnic backgrounds be—can see that they are equal with one another.[11]

Romans 1:18–4:25 is designed to remind the Roman Christians, both Jews and Gentiles, that they all are subject to the power and rule of sin: "both Jews and Greeks, all are under sin"(3:9) and "for all have sinned and come short of God's glory" (3:23). Likewise, each of them, whether Gentile or Jew, was totally dependent on God's grace, became right with God and children of Abraham. This section's argument is designed to call to mind for the Roman Christians that—no matter their ethnic origins—they all stand equally in their deliverance from the power of sin and equally on the common ground of *faith of Jesus Christ* through God's grace.

Romans 5–8 is rehearsed as the shared narrative of their present lives and ultimate destiny as God's children. Underlying what Paul has said in the preceding chapters Romans 9–11 continues Paul's effort to help both Jewish Christians and Gentile Christians understand how God's faithfulness and freedom have impacted them. In 12:1–15:13 Paul calls upon the Roman Christians, as children of God, to live their lives individually and collectively in such a way as to reflect their gratitude to God and their loving acceptance and encouragement of each other. Paul's cautions regarding "despising" or "disdaining" are so fully interwoven (14:3, 10) with the call for no judgment that two questions parallel each other: "But you, why do you judge your brother? And you, why do you despise your brother?" (14:10). It is unthinkable for Paul to despise or pass judgment on one whom God has welcomed (14:3).[12]

Therefore, the assumption that Paul was dealing with division and that he was attempting to unify both the Jewish Christians and the Gentile Christians is a much stronger theory than that of the Spain mission. More important is the fact that Paul was writing to the Roman churches divided between the liberal Gentile Christians and the conservative Jewish Christians.

(2) The relevant remarks in Romans also reveal a motivation totally different from Jewett's position suggested with regard to Paul's missionary strategy. Apart from the casual remarks in 15:24, 28, there

---

[11] Sampley, "Romans in a Different Light," 121.

[12] Sampley, "Romans in a Different Light," 125; Wayne A. Meeks, "Judgment and the Brother: Romans 14:1–15:3," in edited by Gerald F. Hawthorne and Otto Betz, *Tradition and Interpretation in the New Testament: Essays in Honor of E. Earle Ellis* (Grand Rapids: Eerdmans, 1987), 290–300.

is no mention anywhere of the planned trip to Spain; and in reference to anticipated assistance of the Romans, there is only the ambiguous reference in 15:24, "to be sped by you." Jewett seems to underestimate the rhetorical problems Paul faces in the framing section in Romans. In 15:14–15 Paul offers "a very artistically composed statement."[13] And in 15:16–29 Paul's future plans as apostle (15:23–24a) are related to the two expectations about his Rome visit (15:24b): to be sped to Spain by them, and to be stilled by them. Paul's present preoccupation (15:25–27) with the collection for Jerusalem, followed by a second reference to his planned Spain campaign but again with strong emphasis on the mutuality between the Romans Christians and Paul (15:28–29). In terms of structural rhetoric, the verses 28–29 restate once more the thesis which was recapitulated in 15:14–15.[14]

Moreover, Paul has to suppose that the recipients in Rome, both Gentiles and Jews, will hear his letter with a suspicion—the Gentiles because they must wonder whether this person of whom they have heard plans now to move in on them and take over; and the Jews because they must wonder whether this person of whom they have heard preaches a gospel in discontinuity with their traditions and practices.[15]

Even though Jewett rightly estimates that Romans appears to be a fusion of the ambassadorial letter with several other subtypes that could fit either within the deliberative or the demonstrative genre,[16] he underestimates Paul's rhetorical statements in writing Romans, and misses some points. As an outsider, writing to churches he never founded, it is imperative that Paul must establish common ground between himself and the Roman churches and credibility not only with the believing Gentiles but also with the faithful Jews in Rome. Toward that end, Paul employs important complementary rhetorical tactics. He relies heavily on pre- and para-Pauline Christian formulations; he stresses Jewish matters and the continuity of his gospel with God's purposes and promises (1:1–3, 3:21, 4:1–25, chapter 9–11, 16:7, 11, 21); he reassures the Romans that he does not expect to lord it over them or to take over (1:11–12); he wants simply to be stilled (15:24) or refreshed for a while by them (15:32); he reaffirms one of mutual encouragement by his declaration of noninterference (15:20); and his wish to see them only "on the way" (*diaporeuomenos*) to Spain (15:24, 28).[17]

---

13 Käsemann, *Romer,* 373; H. D. Betz, "Literary Composition," 356–59; W. Wuellner, "Paul's Rhetoric of Argumentation in Romans: An Alternative to the Donfried-Karris Debate over Romans," in edited by Donfried, *The Romans Debate,* 136–37.

14 William J. Brandt, *Rhetoric of Argumentation* (New York: Irvington, 1984), 68.

15 Sampley, "Romans in a Different Light," 119.

16 Robert Jewett, "Romans as an Ambassadorial Letter," *Interpretation* 36 (1982), 5–20.

17 Sampley, "Romans in a Different Light," 120.

B. "THE RIGHTEOUSNESS OF GOD" AND *PISTIS CHRISTOU*

Concerning the righteousness of God in the relation to phrase *pistis Christou*. Jewett concludes that the righteousness of God is the power capable of overturning the unjust systems of honor and shame that each ethnic group creates, which clarifies the message concerning the impartial righteousness of God. Of course, he mentions the phrase *pistis Christou* not in this paper, but in his book, *Romans*. I think his conclusion of this paper would be clearer if it is related to "faith of Christ" based on the phrase *pistis Christou* in Romans. However, I read "faith in Christ" as the same traditional interpretation of the phrase *pistis Christou* in his *Romans*.

Jewett explains the problem of meaning of *dia pisteōs Iēsou Christou* in Romans 3:22 and concludes: translating the phrase "through faith in Jesus Christ," Paul is focusing on the (objective) faith of believers, which is in and of Christ rather than the (subjective) faithfulness of Christ. Nevertheless Jewett continues to say that "faith" is used here to denote a group's assent to and participation in the gospel of Christ crucified and resurrected, a gospel that reveals the righteousness of God as transcending the barriers of honor and shame.[18] Jewett misunderstands the phrase *ton ek pisteōs Iēsou* in Romans 3:26 as "the one who has faith in Jesus." Nevertheless he believes that in "setting right" those who have "faith in Jesus", God breaks through the barriers of honor and shame (that separated individuals and groups from one another) and manifests the impartial righteousness of God.[19]

Thus two questions present themselves: How can Paul use the phrase *pistis Christou* rather than *pistis en Christou* in such a way if *pistis Christou* designates specifically and exclusively the faith of the believer which has Christ as its object? And how can Jewett understand *pistis Christou* as the believer's own faith rather than Christ's own faith if the impartial righteousness of God is the power to overturn the unjust systems of honor and shame and "the access to this power is not doctrinal conformity but through mutual acceptance of others" as all God's beloved children? He nevertheless insists that Paul's emphasis is on the faith of the believer that has Christ as its object. I would prefer to translate "faith of Christ", and I think that Paul's phrase bears a sense different from what Jewett proposes.

(1) In determining the meaning of Paul's phrase, we must recognize the significance of the context which Jewett seems to overlook, i.e., Romans 3:21–26. As we discussed earlier, this section's argument is designed to call to mind for the Roman Christians that—no matter their ethnic origins—they stand, equally delivered from the power of sin and equally on the common ground of *faith of Jesus Christ* through God's grace, not of their own faith.

---

18 Jewett, *Romans*, 278.
19 Jewett, *Romans*, 292–3.

Note how these two affirmations about God's righteousness echo each other: "Now apart from the Law God's righteousness has been manifested . . . that is, God's righteousness (manifested) *dia pisteōs Christou* (through faith of Christ, Romans 3:21–22); "for in it (the gospel) God's righteousness is being revealed *ek pisteōs eis pistin* [from faith (of Christ) to faith (of the believer), Romans 1:17]. These two statements about the means of justification are likewise similar: ". . . having realized that a man is not justified on the basis of his works of the Law, likewise even his own faith but rather *dia pisteōs Christou Iēsou* (through faith of Christ Jesus, Romans 3:28, Galatians 2:16).[20]

Paul's *pistis Christou* formulation makes use of the subjective genitive on the grounds that if he intended to speak of "faith in Christ" he would have used *pistis en Christō*. But we do not find the expression *pistis en Christō* (faith in Christ) in Paul's letters because he thinks of God rather than Christ as the *object* of faith. Therefore we may conclude that Paul is familiar with, and incorporates into his own theology, the notion of Christ's own faith/obedience,[21] Christ is the single seed of Abraham to whom the promises were given, and his faith plays a decisive role in the fulfillment of God's purpose for the world. Although, of course, it is through Christ that God has made himself known and has taken the initiative for human salvation.

(2) So far we have tried to show that Jewett's syntactical observations turn out, upon closer examination, to lack evidential value. By contrast, we do find the persuasive evidence that Paul's phrase *pistis Christou* means simply and exclusively Christ's own faith. The phrases *ton ek pisteōs Iēsou* in Romans 3:26 and to *ek pisteōs Abraam* in Romans 4:16 seem to function in Romans 3:21–4:25 exactly as being used to designate the believer's faith. Paul is using the article *ton* or "to" prior to *ek* to identify a person with a particular sect or persuasion, which is "the person who shares the faith of Christ" in 3:26 and "the person who shares the faith of Abraham" in 4:16 respectively. It is by no means clear that Paul is not referring here to Jesus' or Abraham's own faith.

Moreover, at Romans 4:12 believers are described as "those who walk in the footprints of the faith of our father Abraham, the faith he had when he was uncircumcised." Paul characterizes Christians as

[20] For a detailed discussion, see Ik Soo Park, *Paul's letters and Theology*, III [in Korean] (Seoul: The Christian Literature Society of Korea, 2001), 353–67.

[21] Sam K. Williams, *Jesus' Death as Saving Event. The Background and Origin of a Concept* (Missoula: Scholars Press, 1975), 49–50; R. N. Longenecker, "The Obedience of Christ in the Theology of the Early Church," in edited by Robert Banks, *Reconciliation and Hope: New Testament Essays on Atonement and Eschatology* (Grand Rapids: Eerdmans, 1974), 142–52; Johnson, "Romans 3:21–26," 87–90. The most thorough defense of this view is now R. B. Hays, *The Faith of Jesus Christ* (Chico: Scholars Press, 1983).

persons whose faith was like Abraham's, persons who trust God as absolutely as he did. Romans 4:16 is completely in accord with this. The parallelism of thought between Romans 4:11–12 and 4:16 suggests that the two phrases are not distinguishable in meaning. By *to ek pisteōs Abraam* Paul means "the person who has faith like Abraham's." Thus, rather than undermining the view that by *pistis Christou* Paul means Christ' own faith, *pistis Abraam* at Romans 4:16 actually strengthens it.[22] Christians confess what God has done through the death and resurrection of Christ, and, like Christ, they obey him unstintingly.[23] Jewett rightly interprets the expression to *ek pisteōs Abraam* in Romans 4:16 as "those of the faith of Abraham," but misinterprets *ton ek pisteōs Iēsou* inconsistently as "one who has faith in Christ" in Romans 3:26.[24]

C. *ASPAZOMAI* IN CHAPTER 16

Concerning on the word *aspazomai* ("greet") which is repeated twenty-one times in chapter 16. In contrast to Jewett's earlier work on Romans,[25] he abandons the disputable assumption that chapter 16 was directed to the Ephesian church and thus was irrelevant for reconstructing the situation at Rome.[26] However, he seems to misunderstand the word *aspasasthe* when he writes, "Paul greets a large number of persons whom he had met . . ." in the paper. We must recognize that Paul's selection of the second person plural imperative form, *aspasasthe* ("you should greet"), in 16:3–16 was surely intentional and should not be translated as "I send greetings to." The isolated Christian leaders in Rome being greeted are at the same time those whom the Roman congregations should grant recognition. It becomes clear that the recognition is to be mutual. In this context, to greet is to honor and welcome one another.[27] Even the other forms of greeting, *aspazetai* (the third person single, verses 21 and 23) and *aspazomai* (the first person single, verse 22), are greeting sent not by Paul himself but by those who are with Paul and Tertius, who writes the letter in Corinth.

---

22 Williams, "Again Pistis Christou," 436.

23 Williams, "Again Pistis Christou," 434.

24 Jewett, *Romans,* 268.

25 Robert Jewett, *Paul's Anthropological Terms: A Study of Their Use in Conflict Settings* (Leiden: E. J. Brill, 1971), 41–42.

26 Robert Jewett, "Ecumenical Theology for the Sake of Mission," 92–93.

27 Michel, *Römer,* 474; I do find his appropriate interpretation on the other article later (Jewett, "Ecumenical," 107).

42

Response to Seoul Colleagues

Robert Jewett

I appreciate the serious nature of the critiques by Professors Kwon, Yoon and Park. I feel honored by their comprehension of my work and their sharp comments and corrections. For instance, I wish to thank Prof. Park for catching the formulation that should have been, "Paul asks the Romans to greet a large number of persons whom he had met." I am particularly delighted to dialogue with my former student, Sojung Yoon, who went on from Garrett-Evangelical Theological Seminary to doctoral studies in Berkeley and now has returned to teach in Korea. Her extensive training in classical rhetoric leads her to an independent assessment of the genre of Romans. Since this has a bearing on everything else, with theological implications that are rarely recognized, I would like to close with this issue.

I. The Bearing of Conflicts within Roman Congregations on the Spanish Mission

Both Professors Yoon and Park discuss the purpose of Romans, with the former accepting the Spanish Mission hypothesis as best related to the noninterference policy stated in Romans 15:20. Disregarding Paul's policy of never building on someone else's foundation, Prof. Park asks why Roman divisiveness could be thought to hinder this mission. I believe this has to do with the false system of honor and shame erected by imperialism. If the mission treats the Spaniards like "barbarians," mentioned in 1:14, they will reject the gospel as one more hateful example of the way Roman colonizers have treated them for two hundred years. To counter the congregations' tendency to treat each other as barbarians, Paul lays out a sophisticated argument about the impartial righteousness of God. As an outsider, he is not in the position of being able to address these conflicts head on. He lays out chapter after chapter of careful argument, employing confessions, hymns, and biblical citations used in various branches of early Christianity before politely addressing congregational issues in chapters 14–15. I agree with Park's statement that this argument helps "all of Paul's readers to recognize and affirm their equality and unity in the powerful gospel of God." There is less support for Prof. Kwon's interpretation because he does not take the second half of the letter into account.

II. ESCHATOLOGY, WRATH AND ETERNAL LIFE

Prof. Kwon's reading of the first half of Romans is familiar and quite compelling. When I started working on Romans almost 50 years ago, my starting point was much like his. What I found baffling about this letter, however, was that so many details of the Greek text seemed to contradict my tradition. In contrast to the other Pauline letters, I found Romans to be opaque. It was not until I had worked on the commentary for many years that I began to gain a sense of the whole. Since I summarized my view in the morning session, I don't want to repeat it here. But I would like to concentrate on a few points where the clash between the text and modern interpretive frameworks are particularly prominent. We begin with eschatology, which was the topic of Prof. Kwon's dissertation at King's College, London. He asks,

> . . . is it proper to say that God's "wrath" can either be present and future at the same time? . . . Since the only ground for considering it as already realized is the present tense verb and since we all know that the tense of a Greek verb is nothing to bet our money on, and since the present construal of the statement creates an *unnecessary* tension within Paul's argument itself, is it not better to simply take it to be future, pure and simple?

I grant that the Greek aorist is primarily punctiliar, but I have not heard of ambiguity in the present, perfect, or future tenses. The evidence includes the present tense verb *apokaluptetai* in 1:18, the present and past tense verbs through the rest of 1:18–23 and the thrice repeated *paredoken* in 1:24, 26 and 28. Every commentary and translation I have seen renders these three references with past tense verbs. God consigned the sinful human race to suffer the consequences of their suppression of the truth, says Paul. Are we really prepared to throw out this evidence because it doesn't fit a modern eschatology? What would you say if I changed the future tense verbs in Romans 5 and 6 with reference to "eternal life?" These forms Prof. Kwon rightly wishes to affirm. He writes, "As a staunch 'future' kind of person, . . . I feel that . . . Jewett's effort to extend Paul's originally future concepts to cover the present seems to do more harm than good . . . ."

Kwan argues that eternal life is strictly future and that "Paul's ultimate concern is final salvation (5:9–10)." I feel that this fails to take Paul's missiological vision seriously, as visible in 15:7–13, where the conversion of all the nations is in view. On page 367, I explain 5:10 as follows: "While the new life shared with Christ will climax in "eternal life" (verse 21), its redemptive power is experienced by the faithful as they are enabled to boast in a transformed manner in the very midst of their tribulations, in every future event both good and ill between the *nun* ("now," verse 11) and the parousia." Regarding 5:21, I state, "All who are in Christ are granted the ultimate honor of righteousness that assures them both now and in the future access to eternal life. Concerning 6:22–23, I agree with Prof. Kwon, "Just as in 2:7 and 5:21, *zoe aiōnios* refers to life after death, which has an unending horizon." But I disagree with him in insisting that Paul envisions a "fullness of existence for the saints in the present that continues on into the future." This reflects the wording of 6:22 where Paul uses the present tense verb *echete* in reference to the fruit leading to sanctification.

III. THE ISSUE OF WORKS OF LAW

Prof. Kwon reads Romans in the light of Galatians, which establishes the premise that Jewish disobedience is the core of the human dilemma: "Let me just take Paul's argument against 'works' as a test case. Dr. Jewett clearly perceives that in Paul's critique of the Jewish bigots, the issue is circumcision unaccompanied *by corresponding obedience* (308)." I make no such claim on 308, but Galatians presents the issue in this way. I am interpreting Romans as a situational letter, aimed at gaining support for a mission project—which Kwon overlooks. He wants Paul to be a systematic theologian who supports a modern theology of lawbreaking, with justification as forgiveness and salvation as future eternal life rewarded to the obedient. But the details of Paul's argument do not fit this modern scheme.

Prof. Kwon finds no "evidence in Paul's argument for the distinction between 'actions motivated by the desire for superior status' and 'obedience' in the proper sense. Throughout the letter, Paul's concern is performance itself, not its motivation; his problem is people's disobedience (chapter 2) or inability to do the law (chapter 7), not performing the law with a wrong motivation (in chapter 7, the problem of 'I' is not obedience with wrong motivation but his failure to do what is good *despite his excellent motivation*)."

I suggest another reading of Romans 7, as a speech in character in which Paul describes himself as the Jewish zealot who believed he was following God's will in persecuting Christian believers, but who in fact was opposing God's messiah. Paul presents this as a universal human dilemma in Romans 7, because each of the churches in Rome is acting with zealous prejudice against other groups.

This is why Paul takes such pains to show that the whole human race, not just the Jews, has declared war on God. Each group tends to absolutize its law, claiming superior honor because of legal adherence. Paul uses the phrase "apart from law" in Romans 3:21 and 7:8–9 to indicate the law's failure to provide salvation, and a similar phrase "apart from works of law" appears in 3:20 and 28 and "apart from works" in 4:6. Since the anarthrous use of *nomos* here could extend its semantic field to every kind of law, it seems unlikely that Paul wishes to restrict the argument to Israel's law. In all six instances, the standard translations add the article, thus restricting Paul's reference to "the law," that is, the Jewish Torah. Every time *choris* is employed in Romans, the article is absent. When one takes the inclusive context of Paul's argument from 1:16 to the end of chapter 3 into account, I think it is clear that Paul is arguing that no form of law is able to place its adherents in a right relationship with God. In those instances where Paul refers to salvation apart from "the law," he is explicitly including the Jewish law within the argument.

IV. The Problem of Boasting

Another important area of disagreement is the interpretation of boasting. Prof. Kwon rightly sees that for me "(competitive) 'boasting' as the heart of the problem," but says he cannot follow this line "exegetically. From the way Paul uses the word, boasting can either be good or bad, depending on the object of such boasting . . . . In Romans what Paul takes issue with is not boasting in general but specifically the Jewish kind of boasting wherein one's boasting of status (circumcision) is not substantiated by appropriate performance (doing the law)." I don't think this approach deals adequately with the main discussion of boasting in 3:27 through 4:2. Even more serious is overlooking about half of the evidence because he concentrates on references from 1:16 through the end of chapter 8. Paul wrote a 16-chapter letter and our interpretation needs to account for the whole. I devised the language of competition for honor because of chapters 12–16, where the conflicts between the early congregations in Rome are addressed. The weak are "judging" the strong for violations of the law and the strong "despise" the weak for their adherence to the law when they should be free in Christ (14:3). Kwon's explanation can be correlated only with the first. The language I propose covers both sides, but I make no claim that it is fully adequate.

That Paul is devising a theology to deal with both sides in this conflict is signaled by 1:14–17 where the ethnic and class divisions between barbarians, Greeks, Jews, and Gentiles are reversed. This leads to 3:27 where Paul flatly states that boasting is "excluded" and immediately goes on in verse 29 to ask whether God is the God only of Jews or Gentiles. No, Paul argues, he is the one and only God for both (3:30) and will set right both Jews and Gentiles by faith alone, and not on the basis of their performance of the law. Prof. Kown says my critique of "performance as a means of superior status" seems unclear, and I believe this is because he does not take the second half of Romans seriously where these ethnic conflicts are discussed. In 11:18 Paul criticizes the ethnic boasting of Gentile believers who claim to have replaced the Jews in the sacred olive tree. The standard evangelical interpretation of Romans overlooks the social dimension of boasting in the Greco-Roman world by insisting that Paul is only critical of Jewish boasting; in fact, as I argued this morning, it was Rome itself that was by far the boasting champion of the ancient world.

Prof. Kwon is right that Paul does not abandon boasting, but there is an important difference between boasting that my group is superior to yours, as in 3:27–4:2 and the new system of boasting advocated in 5:2 and 11 about God's love for all of us who have acted as God's enemies. The old forms of boasting are self serving, claiming that one group is better than another, whereas the new form acknowledges that our group has no inherent superiority over others; in Christ, all of us are accepted by grace alone. Thus in 5:3 and chapter 8 Paul urges that believers should boast in their afflictions because we know that God loves us unconditionally and we hope for the final triumph of righteousness when suffering will cease. To boast in what Christ has done on the cross is acceptable because it retains no self-serving element. It reveals that all humans have been equally at war against God and that nevertheless they are all loved in equal measure.

Prof. Kwon claims that Paul's indictment of the Jews in 3:11–18 "aims at their blatant failure to do the law, not the competitiveness of their strenuous performance." To the contrary Paul refers explicitly to ten forms of Jewish boasting of superiority over Gentiles in 2:17–20 and the indictment in 3:11–18 concerns the entire human race rather then the Jews alone. Paul explicitly includes "both Jews and Greeks" (3:9) in this indictment, insisting in 3:12 that "all humans turned aside" and were "corrupted." He begins the argument of Romans in this way, in contrast to all of his other letters, because he is facing a situation of religious combat in the Roman congregations. In the setting of the ancient honor/shame/face saving culture, this sounded to me like religious performance for the sake of gaining superior status. I have no doubt that everyone in this room has a more sophisticated grasp of these issues than I have, because your cultural traditions concerning honor reach back almost 3000 years. You live in an honor culture and there may be Korean categories that would be more adequate than my language of competition for superior honor. I challenge you to take up this matter because the issues that Paul faced in Rome are decisive factors in the most significant conflicts in religion and culture today.

The issue of theological boasting is related to the choice of translating *pistis Christou.* Prof. Park advocates a single definition, "the faithfulness of Christ," for the references in 3:22, 26. The standard Greek grammars all indicate that both the objective and the subjective genetive are possible with the same construction. The word "en" is not required for the objective genitive, which is why the majority of scholars accept this view. One has to make the decision on contextual grounds, which leads me to think that the translation "faith in Christ" is preferable. But I'm not dogmatic on the question and suggest that the ambiguity may have been intentional. When I was the chair of the Pauline Theology Seminar of the SBL, we organized several full-scale debates on this question, and I was struck by the fact that neither side considered the social context of groups in Rome fighting over theology. The entire discussion has been carried on as if Paul wrote a doctrinal treatise rather than a situational letter.

That there were conflicts between the weak and strong in their understanding of faith is suggested by two later references in Romans. In 12:3 he urges that the groups in Rome not fall prey to "supermindedness" but retain modest "sobermindedness, each according to the measuring rod of faith that God has dealt out to each." Each believer has a unique "measuring rod of faith, as shown by the choice of the verb "deal out, distribute" and the emphatic position of "to each" at the beginning of 12:3d. Paul's point is that each group is to retain loyalty to the faith that they were given and not to impose it on others. A similar admonition appears in 14:22, "Keep the faith that you have in accordance with yourself in the presence of God." Paul's idea is that the peculiar form of faith that each group has been given by God includes the cultural and theological factors that govern each group's service to its Lord (see Romans 14:4–6). Faith refers here to a trusting, obedient response to the gospel that a particular group has made in response to the Spirit; it thus includes an element of group adherence. To hold such faith *kata seauton* should thus be translated "in accordance with yourself." The issue is integrity, not privacy or discreet silence, as in the ordinary translation, "keep your faith to yourself." This reflects a situation like

12:3, where groups are inclined to impose their definitions on other groups. It is possible that such disagreements related to the expression *pistis Christou* itself, with some groups understanding it as an objective genitive and others as a subjective genitive.

V. ROMANS AS A DEMONSTRATIVE OR DELIBERATIVE LETTER

This may seem like an overly abstract and non-theological issue, but the clarification of the genre of Romans is an essential step in interpreting the letter. Most previous commentaries have tacitly assumed that this letter was judicial, a defense of the true gospel or a last will and testament. Others viewed Romans as deliberative, giving advice to the Roman churches about how they should believe and behave. Prof. Kwon seems to favor this alternative, rejecting the idea of "rhetorical maneuver(s)" that "seem very strange, especially compared with his Corinthian letters and Galatians where he gets to the *medias res* right from the beginning (1 Corinthians 1:10ff.; Galatians 1:6), before he unfolds his point in a more theological terms." Prof. Yoon advocates either a mixture of demonstrative and deliberative rhetoric, or perhaps classifying the entire letter as deliberative. She argues that "Paul would have intended this change of thought to lead to the congregation's active involvement with his mission plan. Paul appears to want them to take particular actions in the future. Given that aspect, I cannot help wondering if Romans might have some or more features of the deliberative genre." Prof. Park also favors a mix between deliberative and demonstrative rhetoric.

There are several features of the letter that led me to reject the appealing suggestion to view the letter as at least partly deliberative. The first is the nature of Paul's relationship to the audience. Deliberative rhetoric that offers advice to an assembly presupposes that the author is a member of that assembly. Such persons do not have to explain why they have a legitimate right to speak. But in contrast to his other letters, Romans is directed to one he had not helped to found. Prof. Park states this accurately, I think. Neither Paul nor his co-workers established any of the Christian congregations in Rome; even in the case of Prisca and Aquila, he met them as refugees in Corinth after they had been banned from Rome as founders of a church there. In the opening of Romans, therefore, we find an elaborate justification for his writing as the apostle to the Gentiles. And in 15:15, Paul apologizes for his "boldness" in writing as an outsider, claims he is merely "reminding them" about the faith, and goes on in verse 20 to state his non-interference principle, "not to build on another's foundation." None of these details correlate well with deliberative rhetoric.

The second factor that led me to assume demonstrative rhetoric is the nature of Paul's arguments. Demonstrative rhetoric employs the arguments of praise and blame, which relates to my lecture this morning that sought to clarify the issues of honorable and shameful behavior. Deliberative rhetoric, on the other hand, is marked by arguments of advantage and disadvantage: which policy is more practically useful in advancing our interests? Prof. Yoon is right that the predominate temporal mode of demonstrative rhetoric is present, and I think this matches most of the letter. The details of any future participation in the Spanish Mission are left open for future negotiations to be led by Phoebe. This conforms to ancient epistolary practice, which entrusted the delicate negotiations to the letter bearer after the letter presents the basis of cooperation. This answers the question posed by Prof. Park about why Paul waits until chapter 15 to speak of the Spanish Mission. This peculiar mix between adherence to the ethos of the righteousness of God in the present so that they can participate in a future mission is typical of ambassadorial rhetoric, which fell under the demonstrative genre.

The ambassador comes in from the outside, lays down his credentials, rehearses the ethos that binds the two cities or countries together, and then on the basis of these shared values, he proposes cooperation in some endeavor willed by his sovereign. That may seem at first glance to be a mix between demonstrative and deliberative rhetoric, but the basis of the future appeal is the shared ethos rather than concrete advantages to be gained. And the subsequent policy debate between political advisors within the host city or country about whether to cooperate in the ambassador's request typically employs deliberative arguments of advantage or disadvantage, and during this kind of discussion the ambassador's participation is never welcomed for obvious reasons. These political considerations need to be taken into account in assessing the rhetorical genre of Romans. Deliberative rhetoric is for insiders only, and Paul was an outsider in Rome.

The third factor is theological. Paul goes to radical extremes in this letter to eliminate any future advantages to be gained by present behavior. He also erects barriers against congregations condemning each other for non-adherence to their theology or praxis. In dozens of references and with various arguments, Paul maintains that the entire human race will be saved by grace rather than works. Future "salvation" will also be a matter of a sheer, unearned gift (6:23), a theme elaborated in the debate with Prof. Kwon. This makes me cautious about accepting an identification of the genre as judicial, because it so easily encourages a hermeneutic of mutual damnation. If all other churches should be condemned because they have a different theology or liturgy than ours, then it seems to me that Paul's argument is turned upside down. A similar caution leads me to resist viewing Romans as deliberative, because it tends to insert a consideration of advantage into salvation by faith. This too easily leads to the belief that if you accept a particular definition of faith and a reading of Romans that supports it, and are loyal to the right denomination, you will go to heaven while those who disagree will be lost. I know that there are many reasons for Christian chauvinism, but one of them is the misinterpretation of Romans. The tendency has been to turn Romans into the very opposite from that intended by Paul, which was to help the combative congregations in Rome to find their unity in Christ.

This may seem like a esoteric academic debate that is far from the life of the church today, but when you and I examine the way we preach and teach Romans, we can recognize the same patterns. If we say that our particular interpretation is the true gospel and that all who disagree are damned, we are assuming the judicial genre whether we realize it or not. If we say that those who accept a particular teaching gain an eternal advantage, we are following the deliberative mode. Either way we undercut the radical gospel that says we are all saved by grace, "without works of law." And by so doing, we resurrect the boast that Paul wished to exclude, "Our group is closer to God than yours!" At the same time we make it impossible to greet one another as brothers and sisters in Christ.

In closing, I want to thank my colleagues for their hard hitting critiques, and the audience for taking part, we hope, in the discussion to come.

The Kota Kinabalu Symposium
April 14, 2008

43

Accepting One Another: A Response to Robert Jewett's *Romans Commentary*

Frank Gee

As this is the first response to any of the papers in this symposium, let me at the outset add my welcome to Professor Jewett, and also say welcome to "K. K."—as we can call both this city (Kota Kinabalu) and our second guest speaker (Khiok Khng). I want to thank our first contributor both for adding "face" to this Sabah Theological Seminary community by gracing us with his presence, and for the magnificent gift of his very impressive Hermeneia commentary on Romans. I shall be delighted to add it to my library, and also to show it to my son and my son-in-law, who are both also active in theological education in South-East Asia.

As my brief tasks are to use the commentary critically and cross-culturally in my response, I shall make that my starting point, and then move on to consider Professor Jewett's paper "Romans as a Missionary Letter Aimed at Overcoming Shameful Status."[1]

Consistently with the overall theme for our symposium, which explores the relevance of this Hermeneia commentary for Malaysian culture and theology, I want to note a number of refreshing features of this work, which qualify it to make a stimulating contribution for our theological and cultural reflection in this part of the world.

I. Refreshing Features of Jewett's Romans Commentary

A. By choosing to align himself with those scholars who approach Romans as an occasional or situational writing rather than merely a compendium of theology, Professor Jewett has provided us with an excellent model of socio-historical exegesis. Issues of cultural, historical and sociological context

[1] See the expanded version of this paper as "Rome and Beyond" (in this volume).

are not, as so often happens in commentaries, relegated to the introductory pages (leaving them as a kind of preliminary decoration), but are allowed to interact with and inform every step of the analysis and verse-by-verse commentary. This strategic decision helps to liberate the investigative work from the centuries of accretions of exegetical traditions in the West, which have resulted from reading Romans through the lenses of theological and cultural presuppositions native to the places and generations from which the interpreters originated. (Perhaps in this Symposium we can learn from their errors as well as their example in that matter.)[2]

It seems to me that as Dr. Jewett is hopeful that Chinese and other Eastern traditions may reveal more sympathetic parallels with biblical experiences and perceptions, his use of sociological insights as he conducts his dig to unearth the situation of Paul's readers in Rome may give us a more inductively-based set of data for scholars here to work with.

B. Despite the massiveness of the work, Dr. Jewett's use of a Graeco-Roman rhetorical frame to shape the exposition allows him to develop with startling clarity his central exegetical hypothesis. If I understand it correctly, this may be paraphrased as follows:

> The impartial righteousness of God expressed through his grace in Christ overturns claims of cultural superiority and replaces dominant cultural values (of prestige and shame) with a new honor system in Christ. This enables and necessitates true mutual acceptance among the differing congregations in Rome, facilitating logistic support by them for Paul's proposed mission to Spain.

Just four proofs or arguments in the central *probatio* of the letter are identified for the Pauline proposition found in the first chapter of Romans (1:16, 17).[3] As not many participants have access to the commentary just yet, this may be a good point to share those proofs:

---

2 In the book *Navigating Romans Through Cultures* (New York: T. & T. Clark, 2004), 16–18, our other guest contributor has elegantly identified for us a number of the cultural lenses which have colored, and by my estimate distorted, the reading of Paul—ranging from Marcion, to Aristotelianism, to Bultmann and other offspring of the European Enlightenment. In that book Dr. Yeo graciously chooses not to criticize the works of "first" world scholars, instead looking hopefully to them as sources from which cultural models of reading Paul may be gleaned. He speaks of the challenge for us to "edify one another" in the global village of biblical interpretation. But I find it hard to go along with him when he seems to identify the interpreters from the "first" world as "the strong" whose help is needed by "the weak" in the "two-thirds" world (Romans 14:1–15:13).

3 This satisfying simplicity of structure may be compared with another very fine recent commentary, by Ben Witherington, which also makes significant use of sociological and rhetorical methods of analysis. Witherington finds twelve different proofs (which he calls "arguments"), but they give little indication of the unifying theme and concern which might be expected to underlie Paul's passionate *paraenesis*. By comparison, this weakness shows up all the more clearly the strength of Dr. Jewett's rigorous and revealing approach.

- The Gospel Expresses the Impartial Righteousness of God by Overturning Claims of Cultural Superiority and by Rightwising Jews and Greeks through Grace Alone (1:18–4:25);
- Life in Christ as a New System of Honor That Replaces the Quest for Status through Conformity to the Law (5:1–8:39);
- The Triumph of Divine Righteousness in the Gospel's Mission to Israel and the Gentiles (9:1–11:36);
- Living Together According to the Gospel so as to Sustain the Hope of Global Transformation (12:1–15:13).

Such a succinct summary of Paul's argument puts us in a good position to take up the implications of this epistle for our own theological and cultural reflection through the course of this symposium.[4]

Shortly I shall take up three of these, as they find expression in Professor Jewett's first paper, and use them as starting-points for our theological reflection within our local cultural context.

C. A third refreshing feature of Dr. Jewett's work on Romans is its venturesome spirit. This is shown not only in the adoption of relatively new analytical tools (from sociology) but also in its approach to a more traditional part of the work of exegesis, that of preliminary textual criticism. At numerous points through the commentary Dr. Jewett departs from the standard text found in Nestlé-Aland[27] and UBS[4] and gives his detailed reasons for doing so.

Even more impressive to me is his humility before the textual data, meaning that interpretive options (no matter how attractive) are

---

[4] Though as a former Classicist I have considerable doubts about the current fashion of directly applying the terminology of just one stream of Greco-Roman rhetorical terminology as an analytical grid for Paul's letters, and I could wish that Jewett had freed himself entirely from the claims of the association with "epideictic" rhetoric (compare Witherington, *Romans* [2004], 19–20) it is heartening to find him coining the term "Evangelical Persuasion" in identifying the genre of Romans. And in the extensive fourth section of his Introduction, which provides his survey of genre and rhetorical features in Romans, in addition to the customary Greco-Roman sources or models he covers a number derived from a Hebraic background, including biblical and liturgical citations of various kinds, midrashim, and various groupings of material in numerical series. We should expect these to be important influences in shaping the rhetoric of Paul the Pharisee and Hebrew preacher. In the light of Paul's own self-perception, it seems eminently sensible and appropriate also to invoke the genre of "ambassadorial letter" as Jewett does in this section.

It is pleasing also to see some reference in both Introduction and commentary to the work of J. Louw and others developing discourse analysis, an important field much neglected in even recent biblical scholarship. The linguistic analysis of the pragmatic dynamics in a text can do much to help us understand the persuasive strategies of a writer. Incidentally, Louw's work has helped to highlight for Dr. Jewett the Hebraic flavour of Paul's rhetorical discourse, giving shape to the four central arguments in the epistle.

not allowed to play a crucial role in making text-critical decisions.[5] I believe that such humility in interpretive method provides a very useful example for a symposium like ours. As much as we may expect to gain the benefit of new insights by approaching Paul's writing with our own cultural "lenses," it is important that we avoid imposing upon it concepts which may in fact be alien to Paul's intentions and message. So I want to encourage us all to maintain the discipline of avoiding confusion between the exegetical/interpretive task of understanding Paul's message (using whatever appropriate tools and cultural insights we can), and the quite different task of developing communicational strategies suited to our own various cultural contexts, as we seek to find meeting-points for the gospel with those contexts. Hopefully we can avoid the Procrustean arrogance of many interpreters working in the Enlightenment tradition,[6] and remember the Eastern (and genuinely human) values of reticence and respect toward Paul's letter as our source material. Our task after all is to understand and appreciate the message of Christ's apostle, and communicate it as relevantly as we can in our context; we are not called to re-mould or improve it.

In his text-critical analysis Dr. Jewett also analyses in a fascinating way the probable existence of various kinds of theological or cultural bias in the early copyists (and in modern commentaries as well), as he seeks to help us find our way back to the original intentions of the Apostle. A case in point is his detailed treatment of the evidence of the gender and status of Junia in 16:7. That could well be a starting point for some interesting and edifying discussion in this symposium on the ministry status assigned to women in the ecclesial culture(s) here in Malaysia. The commentary suggests that Paul's approach may have been more liberal than what we find either in some parts of the Church here, or in the (Anglican) diocese from which I come.

D. It is also wonderful to find a scholar who is willing to change his mind, as he delves further into research. In his Introduction, Dr. Jewett shares with the reader that his use of new approaches led him to interpretations not only different from the ones he had learned from his church and theological professors, but also different from the understanding of Romans which he had advocated through most of his

---

5 Jewett, *Romans*, 4.

6 *Procrustes* was a thoroughly nasty character in Greek mythology, who invited guests to sleep on his special iron bed, which he claimed could magically fit the size of anyone who lay upon it. The way this was accomplished however, was singularly unpleasant. If a person was any longer than the bed, the evil host would cut off their legs or head. If the guest was shorter than the bed, he would stretch him to match it. This has all too often been the approach of interpreters of scripture who have come to the task with grids predetermined by philosophical fashions or reigning methodologies, cutting or stretching the scriptures to suit their own preconceptions or preferences. Although in many cases their intentions were sincere enough, the results were no less damaging.

own teaching career. This is a great example for any involved in a life of study, and hopefully we will be inspired by it as we take up his invitation for further discussion, offered both in his commentary and in the paper he has read to us here—and to which I now want to offer a preliminary response, for his and our consideration.

As I mentioned earlier, the four theological "proofs" identified in Romans by our guest can now become our starting point for reflection together, as we see them expressed through Professor Jewett's paper. As I see it, the first and second of these theological proofs in Romans are taken up principally in parts I and IV of his paper, whereas the fourth of Paul's proofs informs the paper's section III and (to a lesser degree) section II.

- Paul's First Proof: The Gospel Expresses the Impartial Righteousness of God by Overturning Claims of Cultural Superiority and by Rightwising Jews and Greeks through Grace Alone (1:18–4:25)
- Paul's Second Proof: Life in Christ as a New System of Honor That Replaces the Quest for Status through Conformity to the Law (5:1–8:39)

Analyzed and summarized this way, we can see how Prof. Jewett has arrived at the key ideas in his paper, expressed in its first and last sections. He has helped us recognize more clearly that Paul's theology relates not only to individual salvation, or individual conscience on disputed issues, but also to groups of people, and the ways they see themselves and other groups.[7] He sees Paul expounding the gospel

---

[7] If I have a concern with this paper, it is that readers could gain the impression that the writer wants to "replace" one scheme for understanding Romans with another, discarding some truths crucial for salvation in the process. What could give rise to this are statements such as on page 4: " . . . *in place of* the traditional theology of Romans that concentrates on individual guilt and forgiveness for failing to live up to the law, . . . the central issue is setting the world right by overcoming its perverse systems of honor . . . ."; and on page 3: "guilt and forgiveness are decidedly secondary themes in Romans." Jewett's fuller exposition in the Commentary suggests that it is not his intention that we should jettison such great theological themes as forgiveness of sins through the death of Christ, and "justification by faith" as irrelevant for our times. But for readers not familiar with the commentary it may be helpful to distinguish between two different focal elements in Paul's letter.

One is his *strategic* focus, disclosing his pastoral and missional *goals*; the other is his *conceptual* focus, located in the theological truths he expounds in order to achieve those pragmatic goals. For Paul, the two went inextricably together, indeed his goals for church and mission arose out of the great salvational truths by which he had been grasped. In that sense, the great truths of (both individual and corporate) salvation and acceptance through the cross of Christ are *foundational* to Paul's Christian persuasion designed to achieve his goals of promoting mutual acceptance among the different Christian groups in Rome and preparing a base for his onward mission to Spain. In my view, the Commentary does an excellent job of demonstrating Paul's brilliant integration of his conceptual (theological) focus with his strategic focus (pastoral and missional goals). It would be a pity if people gained any contrary impression from comments in the first paper.

in such a way as to overcome the barriers between different social and ethnic groups within the wider Christian community in Rome, and that the inclination to exclude one another from fellowship had its roots in the prevalent social and cultural values of honor and shame which affected all people within the context of the Greco-Roman world.

I have elsewhere in this paper suggested that it is helpful to see two central issues of concern which interact creatively with each other in Paul's letter: the theological centre and the pastoral/pragmatic/missional center. I have suggested that these are equally important, but have different functions. They could respectively be characterized as (theological) means and (pastoral/practical) goal. I find the "theological" center expressed in Prof. Jewett's section IV (on the Thesis of Romans) as follows: "The righteousness of God overturns the unjust systems of honor and shame that each nation and group creates, showing that all humans are equally loved by God with a holy, impartial, righteous passion."

I find his account of the "pastoral" center of the epistle's concern in his paper's section I. After quoting with approval Moxnes' account of the central purpose of Romans as to bring together groups alienated from one another by (mutual) perceptions of shameful status, he states that "the most significant conflicts in our time come from *shame in the form of social discrimination,*" citing current examples of peoples who either are or have been dominated by other races, societies or nation-states which consider themselves superior.

II. ROMANS IN THE MALAYSIAN CULTURE AND CONTEXT

What implications may this have for our common life and our mission in the Malaysian context? I want to touch on four areas for possible attention in the light of the insights brought to us through the first paper. They range from the immediately local to the national and possibly regional levels, in widening circles. Participants may like to take up some of these issues for reflection and discussion as our Symposium progresses.

A. Let me start by thinking about *relations between different socio-ethnic groups within this wonderful Sabah Theological Seminary* (STS) *community* of which I feel privileged to be a member. This Seminary certainly has a policy of non-discrimination in all the dimensions of our life together. Nevertheless, questions can arise when people of different backgrounds have to live together, and when they can be perceived of as belonging to different groups, distinguishable from one another in terms of ethnicity or cultural background.

Could the situation arise as it did in Rome, where individuals or whole groups can see themselves as "patrons" to other individuals or groups, so that while they may be benevolent and gracious to those others, they view themselves as subtly superior to them?

Is it possible that we may look down on others because their grasp of the language or languages commonly used among us is not as strong as our own? If so, the imbalance among the numbers of library books available in the different languages used in a seminary community like ours could possibly make some students feel uncomfortably "weaker" than others in any competition for academic advancement. Please understand that this is not in any way a criticism of our STS. This is a problem faced by seminaries anywhere in South East Asia. (I'm glad that I can speak as a member of the Global South, and not a Westerner, when I draw attention to the dominance of English in our libraries – though I suspect someone may then challenge me to produce more books in Malay!)

My purpose with these examples is just to try and help us identify areas of potential difficulty, where we are continually challenged to keep bringing the gospel as good news to people who may see themselves (rightly or wrongly) as inferior, shamed, or discriminated against.

B. Let's now broaden our circle a little. What relevance may the message of Romans, as Prof. Jewett has been helping us understand it, have for *different socio-ethnic groups within Malaysian denominations of the Church*? In Sabah, some denominations have distinct streams of membership corresponding with different ethnic groupings. How far do these groups find themselves able to express their unity in Christ? Or are there subtle perceptions, not only of difference, but also of superiority or shame/stigma attached to certain groups within the Church?

Has the Church realized that level of maturity in Christ which enables its different component groups to extend table fellowship to one another, in the way that our first paper suggests to us that Paul was encouraging the Roman congregations to relate to one another? Do we even consider it important that they should do so?

I honestly do not know the answer to these questions. But I am confident that other participants here today can answer them. If not, the challenge being brought to us through Prof. Jewett's paper may have more relevance and urgency than we had realized.

C. Do we dare to bring similar questions from our study of Romans to *relations among the different denominational traditions of the Church within Sabah (and Malaysia more widely)*? For this arena, the cutting edge of Paul's challenges in Romans may not be cultural and ethnic so much as theological. Are we as passionate about the unity of Christ's people as Paul manifestly was?

Does it matter that we are theologically divided? Are there any ways in which the various branches of Jesus' people in this land can express that mutual acceptance which his gospel enables us and constrains us to express? I hope we will give attention to this important issue, even if what we achieve in this Symposium can only be a small beginning.

And that brings us to the other purpose in Paul's persuasive letter which has been brought to our attention today. Prof. Jewett has reminded us that the Paul we find in Romans is not simply a theologian, but also an apostle passionately involved in mission, seeking to bring the gospel to Spain, despite all the difficulties of evangelizing that new field. We have seen that Paul saw mutual acceptance among the different congregations of the Church in Rome as a necessary pre-condition for garnering the logistical support Paul was hoping they would be able to provide for that mission. (Prof. Jewett may be interested to know that in the STS library there is a book by an Asian scholar whose research also points in that direction.)[8]

Like Jesus himself, Paul saw visibly-expressed love and unity among Christ's people as being a necessary and powerful part of the Church's evangelistic mission, and even a pre-condition for it. It is a great strength of Prof. Jewett's work that he has helped us to see this yet more clearly. To bring us into the widest circle for our reflection prompted by this work, let us now review his account of the fourth major argument in Paul's letter to the Romans:

- Paul's Fourth Proof: Living Together According to the Gospel so as to Sustain the Hope of Global Transformation (12:1–15:13)

This way of summarizing the fourth major section of Paul's argument in Romans very effectively shows the connection between what I have called the "pastoral" and the "missional" elements in Paul's purpose for writing the epistle. Mutual acceptance is the launching pad for mission.

A moment ago I suggested some locally-relevant issues relating to matters of status, ethnicity and theological divergency that may be hindrances to the clear expression of the unity of Christ's people in Malaysia. This interpretation of Romans puts strongly before us the urgency of reflecting upon such issues and taking action accordingly. But in addition to that task of working on issues of mutual acceptance in the Church, I believe that Prof. Jewett has given focus to another dimension of our context which is important for us to reflect and act upon.

D. Twice his paper refers to *Moslem people, and the unhappy divisions caused in our world by rival conceptions of righteousness and justification, dominance and shame*. In the Malaysian context it is imperative to

8 Lo Lung-kwong, *Paul's Purpose in Writing Romans: The Upbuilding of a Jewish and Gentile Christian Community in Rome* (Hong Kong: Alliance Bible Seminary, 1998).

address this issue, if we are to be faithful to our Lord Jesus and his gospel.

May I draw attention to a paradox, and a parallel, as I draw this paper to a close?

In Romans we find a strange paradox. Jewish Christians had always seen themselves as "theologically superior" to non-Jews, even those non-Jews whom they were now asked to acknowledge as their brothers and sisters in Christ. But now, when they returned to Rome after their period of exile, they were faced with loss of position and status in the church, apparently despised by those whom they had seen as their spiritual inferiors. Those who had seen themselves as the "strong" could now be referred to by Paul in this letter as "the weak", who ought to be treated with special care and acceptance.[9]

Might it help in our reflection—and our life together—if each of us, and each distinctive group of us, could see ourselves as both "the strong" and "the weak" according to different situations and relationships in which we find ourselves? This imaginative exercise might help us find new ways of exercising gracious acceptance towards each other.

In contemporary Malaysia I seem to observe a parallel paradox. One dominant element in the population which defines itself ethnically regards itself as theologically superior to all others. It is zealous in seeking to persuade others to submit to its beliefs. Yet that large group appears to be insecure in its own identity, and to feel it necessary to use its political power to protect its members from exposure to other systems of religious belief. One of the leading challenges facing the followers of Isa (who is their Prophet and ours) is to find ways of sharing the news of Jesus with them in such a way that it can be seen, not as a threat to all they stand for, but as glad news and the fulfillment of their hopes, as the end of their striving for vindication through a law, and the way of true submission to the God who loves them as he loves us. Are we imaginative enough to see ourselves as accepting that challenge? Can we visualize our Moslem neighbors as those whom we can welcome with words of love and assurance? Like Paul's planned mission to Spain, it will not be easy. It will require the best of our intellect, and courage and love. But if the Pauline spirit expressed in Romans is still among us, I believe it will drive us to address that difficult mission. I hope that this Symposium will be a time when we will reflect, and dream and devise together to see that mission go forward.

---

[9] Romans 14:1, 15:1. I wonder how much Paul was mindful of that irony at this point in his writing?

44

Honoring the "Good" and Resisting the "Evil": Reading Romans 13 as a *Hidden Transcript* in the Malaysian Context

Hii Kong Hock

Introduction

I am fully aware and reckon that *ouk estin mathētēs huper ton didaskalon* (Matt. 10:24). Yet I deem it a great honor to offer this response to my mentor Professor K. K. Yeo, and an even greater joy for me to do so in the presence of "my mentor's mentor" Professor Robert Jewett.

In my ensuing discussion, I shall first offer my reading of Romans 13 with insights drawn from James Scott's notion of *hidden transcript*,[1] Robert Jewett's commentary,[2] and other scholars. My aim is to highlight Paul's counter-imperial motifs. Next, to dialogue with Yeo's Chinese, cross-cultural reading, I shall also try to draw some implications as to how Romans 13 can speak to the Malaysian Chinese Christian communities in our existing socio-political context.

I. Reconsidering Romans 13— Are *All* Authorities to Be Honored?

Let me begin by referring to Jewett's and Yeo's works.[3] In his commentary, Jewett claims, "Romans 13:1–7 was not intended to create

[1] James C. Scott, *Domination and the Arts of Resistance: Hidden Transcripts* (New Haven: Yale University Press, 1990).

[2] Robert Jewett, *Romans: A Commentary* (Hermeneia; Minneapolis: Fortress Press, 2007).

[3] See Robert Jewett, "Rome and Beyond" and K. K. Yeo, "Paul's Way of *Renren* in Romans 13:1–10" (in this volume).

the foundation of a political ethic for all times and places in succeeding generations—a task for which it has proven to be singularly ill-suited."[4] The fact is, this pericope has long intrigued interpreters because Paul sounds as if he is advocating a strategy of conformity particularly to the governing authorities.[5] Having ostensibly placed the lordship of Jesus the Messiah over against Caesar (10:12), why would Paul say: "Let every person be subjected to the governing authorities; for there is no authority except from God, and those authorities that exist have been instituted by God" (13:1)? Is this not contradictory to what Paul has taught earlier, where he seems to underline the non-conformity of Christian lives to the secular norms of this world (12:2)? Jewett suggests that Romans 13:7 shows that for the sake of proclaiming Christ, "Paul was willing to accept the system that demanded honor for the emperor and his officials whether they deserved it or not."[6] Does this mean Christians are to pledge unconditional allegiance to the imperial rule? *Mē genoito* once we peer beneath the surface of Paul's rhetoric!

Yeo rightly posits Paul's admonition in Romans 13 in a socio-political situation whereby Roman Christians were under the 'surveillance' of the Roman authorities. He aptly elucidates on how Paul's rhetoric is counter-imperial. His most innovative proposal comes in his reading of *ou gar estin exousia ei mē hupo theou* (13:1b) as "for it is not an authority if [it is] not by God," and hence "there are authorities that are not from/by God." The traditional rendition "For there is no authority except from God" (13:1b) would fit neatly with Rome's self-claim of divine right to rule the world, since "belief in divine sanction for Roman conquest inevitably endowed the ideal of an eternal empire with a certain currency."[7] But if we take Yeo's reading, the rhetoric immediately shifts to a skeptical view or challenge of divine endorsement for Rome's rule. Yeo's comment on Paul's assertion that authorities are "instituted by God" (13:1) and are "God's servant" (13:4: *diakonos*; 13:6: *leitourgoi*) is also apt. The use of cultic language critiques the imperial cult: God does not "ordain" the ruling authorities—such as ardently proposed by Josephus (*Jewish War* 2:350–358)—but "orders" (*tetagmenai*) them. Jewett espouses, "The God of whom Paul speaks in chapter 13 of this letter is the same as announced in chapter 1, whose righteousness was elaborated for the next twelve chapters. It is the God embodied in the crucified Christ

---

4 Jewett, *Romans*, 786.

5 For a survey of its interpretation, see the footnote bibliography in Stanley E. Porter, "Romans 13:1–7 as Pauline Political Rhetoric," *Filologia Neotestamentaria* 3:6 (1990), 115–17.

6 Jewett, *Romans*, 803.

7 Clifford Ando, *Imperial Ideology and Provincial Loyalty in the Roman Empire* (Berkeley: University of California Press, 2000), 66.

who is in view here, which turns this passage into a massive act of political cooptation."[8] For Yeo,

> Paul is offering a theological critique of the government authority in two ways. First, Rome serves God rather than Rome serves Jupiter, therefore also, Rome's authority is under God's. Second, Rome should exercise its power honorably and rightly, otherwise that authority is not deemed to be designated by God.

I concur with Yeo's conclusion, but I think a more detailed study of the socio-political and literary-rhetorical contexts of Romans 13 can help us to better see Paul's counter-imperial motifs. Let me introduce readers to James Scott's notion of "hidden transcript" in the ensuing section, before moving to a more in-depth discussion on the Romans text.

A. HIDDEN TRANSCRIPT IN RESISTING DOMINANT DISCOURSE

James C. Scott's *Domination and the Arts of Resistance*[9]—particularly the concepts of "public transcript" and "hidden transcript"—can help us to see how "competing ideologies" between the dominant group and the subordinated people interacted. "Public transcript" is "a shorthand way of describing the open interaction between subordinates and those who dominate."[10] It employs mechanisms such as "public mastery and subordination (for example, rituals of hierarchy, deference, speech, punishment, and humiliation)" and "ideological justification for inequalities (for example, the public religious and political world view of the dominant elite)" to manage and secure "material appropriation (for example, of labor, grain, taxes)" for the purpose of domination.[11] In short, it is a discourse derived by the dominant elites to justify and propagate their own ideology and power. Expressed in Scott's own words:

> The public transcript is . . . the *self*-portrait of dominant elites as they would have themselves seen. Given the usual power of dominant elites to compel performances from others, the discourse of the public transcript is a decidedly lopsided discussion. While it is unlikely to be merely a skein of lies and misrepresentations, it is, on the other hand, a highly partisan and partial narrative. It

---

[8] Jewett, *Romans*, 789–90; idem, "Response: Exegetical Support from Romans and Other Letters," in edited by Richard A. Horsley, *Paul and Politics: Ekklesia, Israel, Imperium, Interpretation. Essays in Honor of Krister Stendahl* (Harrisburg: Trinity Press International, 2000), 66, note 81.

[9] See footnote 1 above.

[10] Scott, *Domination and Resistance*, 2.

[11] Scott, *Domination and Resistance*, 111.

> is designed to be impressive, to affirm and naturalize the power of the dominant elites, and to conceal or euphemize the dirty linen of their rule.[12]

Yet public transcript does not "tell the whole story about power relations" since beneath what appears to be acceptance of the dominant order, may be only "masks of obedience" worn by the subordinate.[13] When they are beyond direct observation by powerholders, the latter derive "hidden transcript" which can consist of "offstage speeches, gestures, and practices that confirm, contradict, or inflect what appears in the public transcript."[14] What they cultivate is a shared "discourse of dignity, of negation, and of justice" that contains not only speech acts but a whole range of practices.[15]

There is also the *ideological* dimension: "Inasmuch as the major historical forms of domination have presented themselves in the form of metaphysics, a religion, a worldview, they have provoked the development of more or less equally elaborate replies in the hidden transcript."[16] In order to confront ideologies that justify inequality, "resistance to ideological domination requires a counter-ideology—a negation—that will effectively provide a general normative form to the host of resistant practices invented in self-defense by any subordinate group."[17]

Resistance entailed in hidden transcript is always *social* and *active*, because hidden transcript "has no reality as pure thought; it exists only to the extent it is practiced, articulated, enacted, and disseminated" within created social sites insulated from control, surveillance, and repression from the dominant.[18] Scott adds, "The social spaces where the hidden transcript grows are themselves an achievement of resistance; they are won and defended in the teeth of power."[19] This provides a window for us to see how Paul and his co-workers and the household-based assemblies they catalyzed were resisting the dominant Roman imperial ideology. Scott reminds us not to ignore the dynamics of power relations and political resistance by the subjected:

---

12 Scott, *Domination and Resistance*, 18.

13 Details in Scott, *Domination and Resistance*, 2–4; Richard A. Horsley, "Introduction—Jesus, Paul, and the 'Arts of Resistance': Leaves from the Notebook of James C. Scott," in edited by Richard A. Horsley, *Hidden Transcripts and the Arts of Resistance: Applying the Work of James C. Scott to Jesus and Paul* (Leiden: E. J. Brill, 2004), 9.

14 Scott, *Domination and Resistance*, 4–5.

15 Scott, *Domination and Resistance*, 114. In the case of peasants, these practices may include "poaching, pilfering, clandestine tax evasion, and intentionally shabby work for landlords" (14).

16 Scott, *Domination and Resistance*, 115.

17 Scott, *Domination and Resistance*, 118.

18 Scott, *Domination and Resistance*, 119–20.

19 Scott, *Domination and Resistance*, 119.

> So long as we confine our conception of *the political* to activity that is openly declared we are driven to conclude that subordinate groups essentially lacked a political life or that what political life they do have is restricted to those exceptional moments of popular explosion. To do so is to miss the immense political terrain that lies between quiescence and that, for better or worse, is the political environment of subject classes.[20]

Using Scott's work, R. Horsley illustrates well how hidden transcript of resistance is evident in Paul: 1). Paul's "gospel" as a discourse itself "resonated deeply with the cultural meaning of many subjugated peoples' situation of humiliation"; 2). Paul and his communities were under attack by the city authorities and/or other people in particular cities, hence "a key concern in some of Paul's letters is thus defense of the assembly-sites of the developing communities and their hidden transcript(s)"; and finally 3). Paul's letters show how a hidden transcript developed as a result of "power relations among subordinates themselves" and how Paul is "attempting to shape the developing hidden transcript of the respective assemblies."[21]

In short, Paul should not be seen as a passivist or "political quietist," but as a "carrier" or "active human agent" who is able to "create and disseminate" hidden transcripts in political resistance to the Roman imperial order.[22] The rhetoric in his letters sent to various Christian groups can certainly be read as "striving to enforce, against great odds, certain forms of conduct and resistance in relations with the dominant."[23] In this light, we can see how Paul's *hidden* transcript in Romans 13 is indeed subverting Rome's *public* transcript, and envisioning a revolutionary transformation of the imperial order.

B. ROMANS 13:1–7—HONORING THE "GOOD" AND RESISTING THE "EVIL"

I do not wish to repeat what has already been said in Yeo's and Jewett's works, but simply to highlight a few observations of my own.

1. Regarding the *socio-historical* context of this pericope, many proposals have been made.[24] But since the issue concerns "tax" and

---

[20] Scott, *Domination and Resistance*, 199.

[21] Horsley, "Introduction—Jesus, Paul, and the 'Arts of Resistance,'" 19–20.

[22] For details, see Scott, *Domination and Resistance*, 123–24.

[23] Scott, *Domination and Resistance*, 191. As N. Elliott says, "the question is not whether, but where and how we may distinguish a hidden transcript in Paul's letter." Neil Elliott, "Strategies of Resistance and Hidden Transcripts in the Pauline Communities," in the book edited by Horsley, *Hidden Transcripts and the Arts of Resistance*, 118.

[24] See the concise assessment of six proposals in Peng Kuo-Wei, *Hate the Evil, Hold Fast to the Good: Structuring Romans 12:1–15:13* (New York/London: T. & T. Clark, 2006), "Appendix A," 203–11.

"revenue," it would be helpful to start from here.[25] Tacitus recorded that "direct taxes" (*tributum* = *phoros*; 13:6–7a) was a tax levied on those living in provinces outside Rome, while "indirect taxes" (*portorium* = *telos*; 13:7b) was levied on all Roman citizens.[26] When Paul exhorts Christians in Rome to pay *both* (13:6–7), he possibly has in mind recent immigrants or those who had returned from other provinces after Claudius' expulsion and were still liable to *phoros.*[27] That the authority "bears the sword" (13:4) possibly reflected real situations, since Roman authorities did not hesitate to inflict severe punishment on those who violated their tax laws.[28] It is in view of their vulnerable status that Paul advises Christians in Rome to react appropriately toward the abusive taxation imposed by the imperial authorities. But I do not think in his exhortation to "give respect and honor to whom is due" (13:7), Paul is condoning the Roman taxation laws.

2. We cannot contend for the historical specificity of the *Sitz im Leben* reconstructed above. The tax issue could be one of the many critical issues that Christians in Rome were confronting. I suggest it is more helpful to place our analysis in its *literary-rhetorical* context. To start with, Paul injects this text within the larger unit of Romans 12:9–13:14, the argument of which is knitted together by a coherent terminology. The three sections of 12:9–21; 13:1–7; and 13:10–14 are linked by the contrast between "good" (*agathos*) and "evil" (*kakos* [*ponēros*]). Notice the thematically contrasting pair of *agathos [kalos]/kakos [ponēros]* actually runs throughout Romans 12:1–15:13. *Agathos* appears in 12:2, 9, 21; 13:3, 4, 10; 14:16; 15:2; *kalos* in 12:17 (as noble); *kakos* in 12:17, 21; 13:3, 4, 10; 14:20; and *ponēros* in 12:9.[29]

I do not think these catchwords are used merely as "general ones,"[30] but should be read as a hidden transcript for obvious reasons. When Paul "sandwiched" Romans 13:1–7 between his discussion on "good" and "evil," the subjects he alluded to and whose deeds were reckoned as "evil" were clear to his audience. Notice how Paul's exhortation runs counter to normal expectations in his call for the Christians in Rome

---

25 First proposed by Johannes Friedrich, Wolfgang Pöhlmann, Peter Stuhlmacher, "Zur historischen Situation und Intention von Röm. 13, 1–7," *Zeitschrift für Theologie und Kirche* 73:2 (1976), 131–66.

26 Mikael Tellbe, *Paul between Synagogue and State: Christians, Jews, and Civic Authorities in 1 Thessalonians, Romans, and Philippians* (Stockholm: Almqvist & Wiksell International, 2001), 179; James D. G. Dunn, *Romans 9–16* (Dallas: Word Books, 1988), 766.

27 T. M. Coleman, "Binding Obligations in Romans 13:7: A Semantic Field and Social Context," *Tyndale Bulletin* 48 (1997), 312–13.

28 See Tellbe, *Paul between Synagogue and State*, 180.

29 Grieb (*Story of Romans*, 121) points out the *inclusio* of 12:17–21 with "evil."

30 Porter, "Romans 13:1–7 as Pauline Political Rhetoric," 129. He did point out (118), however, *kakos* and *agathos* provides the connection between Romans 12:21 and 13:4.

to be patient in suffering (12:12), to bless those who persecute them (12:14), to do what is noble (*kalos*, "good") in the sight of all, not to repay evil for evil (12:17), but to overcome evil with good (12:21),[31] to treat their "enemies" by "heaping burning coals on their heads" (12:20).[32] Most notably, Paul wants them to "live peaceably with all" (12:18). In contrast to Romans 12:3–13 which depicts relations within Christian communities,[33] all these are indications that Paul in Romans 12:14–21 is dealing with "external relations" and he is calling for a positive response to hostility.[34]

3. As Yeo points out, the thematic link by *opheilē/opheilō* ("owe") implies the continuation of Paul's thought in Romans 13:7–8.[35] It should not be a coincidence that Paul's exhortation is framed by the use of *hē agapē* (12:9; 13:8–10) and climaxes in his notion of "owing no one anything except love," and that love fulfills the "law" (13:8). Yeo reminds us that "Paul is saying that we can claim completion and perfection in all other religious duties except in the command to love. Christians are always debtors when it comes to loving one's neighbor." (p. 8) Jewett's comment on "genuine love" (Romans 12:9) is also helpful when he says that "Paul's formulation brings love far beyond the mild 'live and let live' stance of Greco-Roman humanitarian ideals."[36]

Yet on another level, I think *opheilē/opheilō* can be read as a hidden critique of Rome's taxation law which yoked its subjects under the slavery of *debts*. Paul's command "to love" stands in clear opposition to Roman taxation that was obviously deprived of love. What Paul envisions is a *free* and *loving* community when he appeals to Christians in Rome to not fall short of what they themselves can contribute to peace, to live on good terms with their neighbors, relating with trust and respect on the basis of honesty and justice and, above all, with the overarching perspective of love.

4. Is it by accident that this letter was penned during Nero's reign, a time hailed as "undrawn sword"? Notice Paul's depiction of the reality under the imperial order is closer to one of *"terror," "fear," and "sword"* (13:3–4)! The Einsiedeln Eclogues is illustrative of this:

---

[31] Jewett (*Romans*, 779) correctly points out that Paul's phrase is better rendered as "conquer evil with good," as it critiques Rome's idea of *Pax* and *Victoria*.

[32] On possible backgrounds and interpretations of "heaping coals on enemies' heads," see J. A. Fitzmyer, *Romans* (New York: Doubleday, 1993), 658–59; Dunn, *Romans 9–16*, 750–51; Krister Stendahl, "Hate, Non-Retaliation, and Love: 1QS x, 17–20 and Romans 12:19–21," *Harvard Theological Review* 55 (1962), 343–55; S. Morenz, "Feurige Kohlen auf dem Haupt," *Theologische Literaturzeitung* 78 (1953), 187–92.

[33] Dunn (*Romans 9–16*, 737) suggests there is a 'digression' in view of the looseness of construction in these verses.

[34] As also pointed out by N.T. Wright, "The Letter to the Romans: Introduction, Commentary, and Reflection," in edited by L.E. Keck et al., *The New Interpreter's Bible*, vol. X (Nashville: Abingdon Press, 2002), 712ff; James D. G. Dunn, *The Theology of Paul the Apostle* (Grand Rapids: Eerdmans, 1998), 674ff.

[35] In agreement with Tellbe, *Paul between Synagogue and State*, 181–82.

[36] Jewett, *Romans*, 760, note 38.

> We reap with no sword; nor do towns in fast-closed walls prepare unutterable war . . . . Unarmed our youth can dig the fields, and the boy, trained to the slow-moving plow, marvels at the sword hanging in the abode of his fathers. (*Eclogue* 2:25–31)[37]

Seneca, Nero's advisor, in his *De Clementia*, recorded a speech by the emperor that expressly echoed the same propaganda:

> I am the arbiter of life and death for the nations . . . All those many thousands of swords which my peace restrains will be drawn at my nod; what nations shall be utterly destroyed, which banished . . . this it is mine to decree. With all things thus at my disposal, I have been moved neither by anger nor youthful impulse to unjust punishment . . . With me the sword is hidden, nay, is sheathed; I am sparing to the utmost of even the meanest blood; no man fails to find favor at my hands though he lack all else but the name of man. (*De Clementia* 1.2–4)[38]

Grieb says it well: "For those who have ears to hear, Paul's apparently conventional advice to 'be subject' and his flattering description of the empire serve as subtle reminders that the imperial sword is *not* idle: it continues to threaten destruction of the most vulnerable population . . . ."[39] When he wrote the imperial sword is "not in vain," little did Paul realize that destruction and bloodshed would be so imminent: Nero would soon 'nod his head' and draw his 'hidden, unbloodied swords' unjustly against Christians in Rome.

5. The hidden transcript of Paul's rhetoric in the concluding verses (13:11–14) cannot be easily missed. Vis-à-vis the imperial rule, Paul boldly asserts that "salvation is nearer to us now than we became believers," and "the night is far gone, the day is near" and exhorts Christians in Rome to "lay aside the works of darkness and put on the armor of light" (13:11–12), *viz.* "put on the *kyrios* Jesus Christ" (13:14). Paul's use of 'salvation,' 'time,' 'hour,' 'near,' etc are indicators of the apocalyptic nature of this passage.[40] The *destiny of history*, says Paul, is not finally in the hands of the emperor, but in the hands of God and his crucified and resurrected Messiah, and embodied in the apocalyptic communities of God who are more than conquerors under the lordship of Christ, with the empowerment of the Holy Spirit (cf. 8:35–37). However much the Roman emperor may want to proclaim himself to be sovereign,

37 Cited in Elliott, "Romans 13:1–7," 202, note 66.
38 Cited in Elliott, "Romans 13:1–7," 202–3.
39 Grieb, *Story of Romans*, 124–125; cf. Elliott, "Romans 13:1–7," 203.
40 This is also discussed in Dunn, *Romans 9–16*, 792; Peng, *Hate the Evil*, 134.

without rival in the divine as well as the human sphere, he remains answerable to God. Stanley Porter's comment on this is worth noting:

> First, he [Paul] defines obedience in terms of willing submission, with the unstated though clearly understood assumption that this obedience is to be made to a just power and that submission is not to be made to an unjust power. Second, if all authority comes from a God who institutes justly, any authority which wishes to rule as God's instrument of justice must rule consistent with God's justice, otherwise that authority is rendered invalid . . . . The important implication is that unjust authorities are not due the obedience of which Paul speaks, but rather are outside these boundaries of necessary obedience. Rather than being a text which calls for submissive obedience, Romans 13:1–7 is a text which only demands obedience to what is right, never to what is wrong.[41]

Reminding the emperor's subjects that the emperor is responsible to the true God is not a subjection to, but a diminution of, imperial arrogance. Written right under the Caesar's nose to Christians living in a hostile environment in the empire's center, this is indeed subversive.

II. Romans in the Malaysian Context— A Chinese Christian Community of Peace, Honor, Love and Vision

As a nation, Malaysia is freed from western colonialism or imperialisms politically; yet in another sense we have allowed other forms of neo-colonialism and neo-imperialism to take over. Thus now we see how the cultural ethos of individualism has led many Malaysians, under the spell of capitalist market economy, to take the amassing of wealth as the goal of their life. We increasingly see how political struggles, social injustice, corruptions, crimes and moral depravation are running rampant in our society. Besides, racial alienation is threatening our social harmony, while religious conflicts are also increasingly felt.

Chinese Christians in Malaysia, like Paul and the Jewish Christians in Rome, have a hybrid identity which looks to many roots. In the multiply complex social, cultural, political and religious milieu we find ourselves in, a challenge is how to enliven our faith in the midst of loyalty demanded of us from national, ethnical, cultural and denominational directions. How do we define a politics of identity that is genuinely

[41] Porter, "Romans 13:1–7 as Pauline Political Rhetoric," 118.

Malaysian-Chinese vis-à-vis our embracing of Christian faith. In our own "imperial" context, why and how must we dwell in unity, and to co-exist peacefully with our neighbors? (My reflection below is not based only on Romans 13, but more broadly from my reading of the whole letter.)

A. A COMMUNITY RESPONDING PEACEFULLY TO *IMPERIUM*

In Malaysia, it is a given that churches have increasingly sensed pressures and restrictions from religious and political authorities. It is all the more crucial that we, like Paul, stand solidly on the conviction that in Jesus Christ, God is immanent in our history, in our struggles. To counter 'political quietism,' perhaps we should reflect on how 60 years ago the Council of Churches of Malaysia (CCM) was birthed by our founding fathers:

> It all began in Changi Prison during the Japanese Occupation of Malaya (1941–1945). Amidst isolation and suffering, church leaders interned there, both Western missionaries and locals, came to share a conviction and vision for the future of Christianity in Malaysia. Out of despair, they renewed their hope and proposed to work together to strengthen the unity of the churches. Out of persecution, they became convinced that the future of the church would depend on nurturing a strong national leadership to lead the church.[42]

Despite his critique of Rome's hegemonic power, Paul never advocated retaliating by active resistance. Violence was not an option. To the Christians in Rome who were enduring persecutions and hardships in the midst of intense political pressures, Paul assured them that no power suffices to defeat those who are God's beloved children and who are *hyper*-conquerors in Jesus Christ (Romans 1:7; 8:18–21, 31–39). So also Chinese Christians, as "God's beloved" in Malaysia, can find hope in the crucified and resurrected Lord, and can seek to live up to the call to "holdfast to what is good" (12:9), to "conquer evil with good" (12:21) and to "respect to whom respect is due, honor to whom honor is due" (12:7).

Chinese Christians in Malaysia must take cognizance that we, like the Christian communities in Rome, are a small population of the nation, and hence unity among different churches is of utmost importance. Whatever walls that we have erected in the past must now be brought down, lest they sever our witnesses. Just as the fragmented congregations in Rome must first be united before they can become

[42] Hermen Shastri, "Fifty Years of United Witness and Service," in *Celebrating 50 Years of United Witness and Service: Council of Churches of Malaysia (1947–1997)* (Kuala Lumpur: CCM, 1997), 17.

Paul's active partakers in his missionary plan to Spain (15:24), so also peace and goodwill (*muhibbah*)[43] must prevail *first* among Christian *oikoi* before we can even talk about witnessing to our neighbors, and to see God's kingdom of "righteousness, peace, and joy in the Holy Spirit" dwelling in our land (14:17).

B. AN *OIKOS* UNIFIED IN HONOR AND LOVE

For Paul's audience in Rome, boasting of one's own ethnical, cultural and religious superiority over others was first and foremost an *intra-Christian* issue. The contest for self-glory among Jewish and gentile Christians had resulted in conflicts and threatened the unity and witness of Christian communities in Rome. What divided them were not heretical or erroneous teachings, but issues related to dietary laws and observance of days (14:1–6). This must be understood in the social context of the search for self-identity by different Christian groups. There is nothing wrong with this, and not even in showing one's own piety or zeal for God, but it becomes a noxious problem when it causes harm to brothers/sisters who share the same faith, but who hold different opinions.

The divisive nature of Chinese Christianity in Malaysia must likewise be understood against their search for self-identity in a society with complex cultural, religious and political contexts. Considering the Confucian cultures that forge dyadic social relations, the Chinese are at home in a tightly structured society and are committed to strong family ties. Though still attached to the Confucian emphasis on consensus and conformity, the Chinese in Malaysia find themselves far too divided by linguistic groupings, places of family origin in China, and class interests etc. Confucianism, however, does allow room for "differential treatment" according to the social relations in which one stands to. For Mencius (孟子), among all social relations, the practice of *ren* (仁; benevolence; love) and *yi* (義; righteousness; justice) must start with one's family.[44] This probably explains in part why, when caught in a situation that compels them to be subordinate to a foreign/outside power or authority, the Chinese people's search for security and identity often becomes a "tribal" (ethnic) one of opting out of the majority system in order to retrieve

---

[43] *Muhibbah* means "goodwill" and comes from the Arabic word "muhabbat" which means "love" or "affection." God's will (*insha-allah*) and goodwill are intrinsically related to each other, since Jesus Christ has become the ambassador of "*Utusan Muhabbat*" (goodwill mission) and his gospel presupposes goodwill. See Sadayandy Batumalai, *A Malaysian Theology of Muhibbah* (Kuala Lumpur: STM, 1990), 1.

[44] "The actuality of *ren* (仁; love) consists in serving one's parents. The actuality of *yi* (義; righteousness) consists in obeying one's elder brother. The actuality of *zhi* (智; wisdom) consists in knowing these two things and not departing from them. The actuality of *li* (禮; propriety) consists in regulating and adorning these two things." (*Mencius* 4a.27, cf. 7a.15)

its focus on parochial groupings.[45] Notwithstanding their capacity to organize large numbers of people into each group, membership of a "family" would often become a shield to protect their honor from being usurped by the rest of the society. In this sense, the Chinese concept of loyalty and belongingness to one's own "family"—which can refer to benevolent associations, merchant guilds, dialect communities, but can certainly also include "churches or denominations"—resembles the Greco-Roman honor-shame culture which had evidently suffused the Christian communities in Rome.

Needless to say, the cultural trait depicted above is visible among Malaysian Chinese Christians as well. On a positive note, it helps to build up strong bonds within a particular Christian *oikos*. But when too closed off from others, a familial system turns into a rejection of others, causing problems to arise. Roman Christians, in their effort to protect the honor of their own group, ended up shaming and excluding each other.[46] Chinese churches in Malaysia, too, often use identity markers as yardsticks to pass judgment on their brothers/sisters. While honoring and expressing loyalty to the traditions and heritage inherited by one's own church/denomination is not wrong, often these have been elevated to be on par with doctrines and treated with "life-and-death" seriousness. Differences in rites, styles of worship, organizational structures, theological stances and so forth, are factors that further hinder their solidarity. Despising and judging of others is, for Paul, tantamount to being deprived of love (14:15; 13:8–10), and by seeking self-glory, we have failed to "with one voice glorify the God and Father of our Lord Jesus Christ" (15:6). We all need to relinquish our differences, to stand in solidarity as God's people unified by God's salvific grace in Jesus Christ (5:1–11).

C. VISION BEYOND BORDERS

Yet another negative effect of boasting and exclusive attitudes among Malaysian Chinese Christians can be seen in our narrow-minded missionary work. In Romans, Paul has to deliberately break down the ethnocentric barriers that existed between "Greeks/barbarians" and "educated/uneducated" (1:14) in order that Christians in Rome can apprehend God's divine plan for the world and alter their perspectives. By repeatedly asserting that God is the God of both Jews and Greeks (1:16; 2:11; 10:12), Paul's hope is that the Roman Christians may become

---

45 See Chapter 9, "Malaysia: Confrontation of Two Incompatible Cultures," in Lucian W. Pye, *Asian Power and Politics: the Cultural Dimensions of Authority* (Cambridge: Belknap, 1985), 251.

46 In ways analogous to Roman Christians' shaming device of ugly name-calling (circumcised/ uncircumcised; weak/strong), Malaysian Chinese Christians, too, have derived pejorative labels to scorn those holding different ways of showing their faith, with the most common idiom being "charismatic/fundamentalist."

active partakers with him in actualizing the vision of proclaiming the gospel to Spain (15:24), and hence bringing about "obedience of faith among all the nations" (1:5; 16:26). Paul's vision speaks powerfully to the Chinese Christians in Malaysia to not only stand unified among themselves, but also to forgo their contempt and negligence—as is often the case now—of Christians of other ethnic origins. In the midst of their complacency, they are called to reach out to their 'weaker' brothers/sisters who are lacking basic necessities and resources in many ways. The following insight drawn from Yeo's paper is helpful:

> The interpersonal relationships one has within a community and the acts one does for others constitute together the essence of humanity. To be *ren* (humaneness), to be benevolent or compassionate, is to be in relationship, to be interdependent. *Ren* is the authentic nature of human beings.

Expressed in Jewett's word, genuine love for one another must surpass mere "humanitarian ideals."[47] Just as Paul's own ministry and the Christian communities functioned and were sustained on the principle of 'patronage of mutuality in love,' so also Chinese Christians in Malaysia are obliged to support their Christian brothers/sisters who are in need of various kinds—financially, spiritually, and so forth. We need to be mindful that only a Christian community where each member soberly accepts and functions according to the gifts received from God (12:3–8), expressing mutual love (12:9) and sharing hospitality with those in need (12:13), can serve as a genuine witness to the wider Malaysian society.

Finally, in the midst of our struggle and search for identity, Chinese Christians in Malaysia must remember that we do not share a separate future with our nation's history: "Our destiny is bound up with that of the total Malaysian community. Our faith is immersed in our historical cultural situations, and it must grow out of it."[48] Paul tells us that God is immanent in our history through the apocalyptic death and resurrection of Jesus Christ, in whom history finds its meaning and *telos*. Moreover, Paul's grand vision of an eschatological Christian community filled with the Holy Spirit, God's glory, love, and hope (Romans 8), and where Jews and gentiles shall one day sing praises and worship God with one voice (15:9–12), is a most powerful one. Yet do we, Chinese Christians in Malaysia, share such a vision?

---

47 Jewett, *Romans*, 760, note 38.

48 S. Batumalai, *Islamic Resurgence and Islamization in Malaysia: A Malaysian Christian Response* (Perak, Malaysia: St John's Church, 1996), v.

POSTSCRIPT: NOT SO HIDDEN ANYMORE?

As I pen this paper, Malaysia has only recently undergone its 12th National Election since achieving its independence. The result of this election has been described by many as a 'political tsunami' sweeping through the nation. With the opposition successfully gaining control of five of the thirteen states, and even denying the ruling *Barisan Nasional* (National Front) of its two-thirds majority in parliamentary seats, the message is loud and clear: "People has spoken, people has the power!" The people has finally removed their 'masks of obedience' and made their long-hidden transcript public—what a reversal!

Now, could this be a sign that we have now come to a new apprehension of Romans 13 which, in the past, has often been misused (or, abused?) by some politicians to justify their agendas? Have we come to a realization that we are not to "obey unconditionally" *all* authorities, but to submit only to that which *first* submits to God's divine rule?[49] I am deeply aware of the struggle between "loving (honoring) the good" and "hating (resisting) the evil," and admit how difficult it is for myself to manifest Christ's "cruciform love (*ren*)" toward corrupted authorities and social injustice. But in the existing situation whereby our nation is still covered by clouds of political uncertainties, we need all the more to be guardians of God's *justice* (*dikaiosunē theou*), citizens who upholds the Law of love, and who works for the common good of all. Yeo reminds us:

> The command to love is in fact the command *to be*, the fulfillment of one's essential, inherent *being*. The Great Commandment of Jesus is not a law to do but a command to be . . . . Both *ren* (benevolence toward others) and *agapē* (divine love) are reciprocal, but *agapē* is unconditional. Cruciform love does not demand of the other the satisfaction of one's own needs . . . . *Cruciform ren,* as a self-sacrificing love toward one's enemies, would not manipulate others in order to achieve one's ends.[50]

Task unfinished; but in the God of love and peace (5:8; 16:20), and in his crucified and resurrected Son the Messiah who is the Lord of all those in God's beloved *oikos* (1:7; 8:39), faith, grace, and hope abide (5:1–2; 5:21;15:13).

---

[49] Then again, which "divine" rule in our multi-religious context? This is another sensitive issue. Debates are still mounting as to whether Malaysia is an "Islamic State" or a "Secular State." I simply want to bring to the reader's attention a newly published book: Nathaniel Tan and John Lee edited, *Religion Under Siege? Lina Joy, the Islamic State and Freedom of Faith* (Kuala Lumpur: Kinibooks, 2008).

[50] See also K. K. Yeo, *Musing with Confucius and Paul* (Eugene: Cascade Books, 2008), chapter 8.

45

The Agape Meal: A Sacramental Model for Ministry Drawn from Romans 13:8

Ezra Kok & Lim Kar Yong

Dr. Robert Jewett's interesting and provocative paper provides a very fresh and insightful approach to reading Romans 13:8–10, particularly on the issue of *hē agapē* as the fulfillment of *nomos*. In our response, we will dialogue with Dr Jewett on the relevance of his suggested reading of Romans 13:8–10 within a multi-cultural, multi-ethnic, and multi-religious context of Malaysia, where racial, language, and religious boundaries among her 100 different ethnic groups are constantly being emphasized in all walks of life–be it in the public square or private sphere.

As such, our response will be guided by this question: How is it possible for Dr Jewett's proposed reading of "agapaic communalism" as an ethical framework for early Pauline tenement churches works out within the Malaysian context? In particular, how can love be the fulfillment of the law within the Malaysian Christian context?

I. Tenement Church as a Possible Social Location

Jewett's suggestion that the social context of the agape meal in Romans 13:8–10 could most likely be within the tenement churches is both attractive and provocative[1] as it bears close resemblance to some of the practices in Malaysia. This reminds us of the good memories during visits to the Iban longhouses in Sarawak, East Malaysia. Iban is the biggest ethnic and native group in the state of Sarawak located in the Borneo Island. Typically, a longhouse is a single structure where

1 See Robert Jewett, "Rome and Beyond" (in this volume).

the entire village of an Iban settlement lives. It is made up of a series of independently owned family units which are joined longitudinally one to other as to form a single elongated structure. Each longhouse is able to accommodate families ranging from 15 to as many as 50 households.

The long gallery or corridor that runs throughout the entire longhouse is known as *ruai*. This is a common area where the entire village meets for drinks, meals, work, fellowship, and other communal activities, including worship meetings. It is at this common place that regular meetings and communal meals would be held where each family would contribute food to be shared by all.

It is at the *ruai* that visitors to the longhouse, whether within or without the Iban community, are welcome. In a typical welcoming ceremony, a communal meal contributed by the entire community is usually held. This is the followed by the traditional dance called *ngajat* where visitors are invited to participate. The warm welcome and the communal meal accorded to the visitors closely reflect Jewett's suggestion that "provisions for the meal in tenement churches would have to come from sharing between members."

II. The *Agapē* in Practice

A. Who is the Object of Agapōn

In Romans 13:8, Paul states that "for the one who loves the other has fulfilled the law (*ho gar agapōn ton heteron nomon peplērōken*). This statement is further reinforced in 13:10 in which "love is law's fulfillment."

The first question that we would like to consider is this: Who is the object of *agapōn* identified as *ton heteron*? Is "the other" limited to the small Christian community meeting in a particular tenement house, or is "the other" extended to include other Christian congregations in Rome? As pointed out by Jewett, Paul's strange choice of term "other" instead of "neighbor" or "brother" indicates the possibility of extending the obligation of love beyond one's circle to include "the small Christian congregations in Rome." Jewett further suggests that the "other" could possibly include those identified as the "weak" (14:1–16:23), who are predominantly Jewish Christian and thereby suggesting a significant cross-cultural element within the context of Christian love.

In this respect, Jewett departs from scholars like Dunn, Moo, and Schreiner who believe that while Paul may primarily have the fellow believers in view, it is not to be taken as exclusive.[2] According to Jewett, those who are not found within the Christian community are excluded

2 James D. G. Dunn, *Romans 9-16* (Nashville: Thomas Nelson, 1988), 776; Douglas J. Moo, *The Epistle to the Romans* (Grand Rapids: Eerdmans, 1996), 813; Thomas R. Schreiner, *Romans* (Grand Rapids: Baker, 1998), 691.

in the "one other" that Paul is referring to. While Jewett is right to state that Paul normally uses strangers, persecutors or enemies to refer to the outsiders, the words "one another" (*allēlous*), "the other" (*ton heteron*), and "neighbor" (*plēsion*) taken together seems to indicate that the neighbor cannot be narrowly confined to the believing community.[3] Taking the cue from the Parable of the Good Samaritan, one is called not simply to love the other, but to be a neighbor to the other as well, as reflected in Jesus' directive to the lawyer, "Go and do likewise" (Luke 10:37). According to this parable, *we cannot define our neighbor; we can only be a neighbor.* We cannot reduce others in the world as classifiable commodities by drawing distinctions between persons, deciding who is, and who is not, our neighbor.

B. HOW COULD THE AGAPĒ BE PRACTISED WITHIN A CROSS-CULTURAL CONTEXT?

Despite our slight disagreement with Jewett on the meaning of "the other" in Romans 13:8, we find his suggestion of a significant cross-cultural element within the context of Christian love very helpful in the Malaysian context. Towards this end, the question for us is this: How can this obligation of mutual Christian love that extends beyond one's cultural boundary be practised in the Malaysian context?

The uniqueness of Malaysian society is that religious belief, identity, language, and ethnic boundaries are intricately interconnected. The Malays who are the dominant racial group are Muslims, and defined as Muslims in the Constitution, and speak the Malay language.[4] In general, those of Chinese origin are Buddhists or practise Chinese-related religious faiths, and those of Indian origin are Hindus. The racial boundary in the Malaysian society is clearly reinforced in the political process of the nation. Political parties that form the ruling National Front coalition are established according to ethnic groups. The dominant ruling political party, United Malay National Organisation (UMNO), is a party that not only champions but is also the guardian of the Malay rights, the Malay supremacy (*ketuanan Melayu*), and the Malay special privileges as stipulated in the Malaysian Federal Constitution. The Malaysian Chinese Association (MCA), is the representative of the Chinese community, while the Malaysian Indian Congress (MIC), is the party for the Indians. In addition, numerous ethnic groups in Sabah and Sarawak are also represented in parties that are formed along racial lines. Together, these political parties, led by the dominant UNMO, form the Malaysian government through the complex and complicated

---

3 Cf. Moo, *Romans*, 813: "The universalistic language that both precedes—"no one"—and follows—"the other"—this command demands that the love Paul is exhorting Christians to display is ultimately not to be restricted to fellow Christians."

4 Article 160(2) of the Federal Constitution of Malaysia defines Malay as "person who *professes the religion of Islam*, habitually speaks the Malay language, (and) conforms to Malay custom" (emphasis mine).

concept of power sharing where the number of cabinet ministers are often enlarged to accommodate representatives from the diverse ethnic communities.

Apart from racial boundaries, further divisions can be seen along the lines of linguistic distinctions as well. An excellent example is the Malaysian education system which is structured along the three major languages spoken by the community. This resulted in the formation of vernacular primary schools offering a choice of Malay, Chinese and Tamil languages as the medium of instruction. As such, it is rather common that the majority of the Chinese would naturally choose Chinese schools and be instructed in their own mother tongue, instead of the national school which uses the Malay language as the medium of instruction. Likewise, the Indians would prefer Tamil schools, and the Malays the national schools.

The political process and the education system in this nation not only further reinforce ethnic stratification among the various races; these factors also impede the social integration of these various ethnic groups within the nation. This has been well documented in numerous studies.[5] This racial and linguistic division within our society is also reflected in some aspects of the Malaysian church government. Take for example the Methodist church in Malaysia. The annual conferences are divided along linguistic and ethnic boundaries—in Peninsular Malaysia, there is the Tamil Annual Conference that represents the Tamil speaking church; the Chinese Annual Conference is the Chinese speaking church; and the Trinity Annual Conference consists of the English speaking churches. There are also the Sarawak Annual Conference and the Iban Annual Conference that represent the Chinese and Iban community in Sarawak respectively.

How could the obligation of mutual love be extended within such a community of diverse differences where ethnic stratification and language distinction are emphasised in all walks of life? Could there be closer cooperation among the churches and denominations of different ethnic or language groups in sharing of the resources available? Would practical and concrete steps be taken to move the Christian Church in Malaysia towards "agapaic communalism" where the scarce resources could be shared and benefit the wide community?

We can think of one practical implication in the sharing of our scarce resources. What about the possibility of sharing the church buildings? In Malaysia, constructing church buildings is a very time consuming and economically expensive endeavour. It is almost next to impossible

[5] For recent studies, see Graham K. Brown, "Making ethnic citizens: The politics and practice of education in Malaysia," *International Journal of Educational Development* 27 (2007), 318–30; Allan Collins, "Chinese Educationalists in Malaysia: Defenders of Chinese Identity," *Asian Survey* 46 (2006), 298–318.

for lands to be converted to non-Islamic religious use, particularly in Peninsular Malaysia. Even if land is designated for church use, obtaining planning approval for church building is often a very long and tedious process. Even if planning approval is granted, it is often subjected to a host of restrictions impeding maximised usage of the building design.

For example, the Catholic church in the capital city of Shah Alam in the state of Selongor took more than 20 years for planning permission to build a church building.

To overcome the shortage of church buildings, many churches meet in commercial properties or industrial warehouses. These premises are often acquired under the name of trustees or business ventures, thereby attracting the payment of associated land taxes that would otherwise be exempted for properties designated as religious use. In such instances, would it be possible for two or three churches to come together, pool their resources together and share the same premises, but retaining their distinctive identity? Would it be a great testimony if a Cantonese speaking Church, an English speaking church and a Mandarin speaking church could combine resources and meet in a single buildings and yet continue to offer services in their respective languages? Would this be a better use of our resources? After all, apart from Sundays, church buildings are grossly underutilised, and perhaps these buildings could be put to better use, and the excess funds be channelled to other profitable usage.

C. OVERCOMING HONOUR-SHAME SOCIETIES

Jewett also provides a concrete example of how love is being expressed with the sacramental meals practised in both the house and tenement churches. In this respect, Jewett identified *hē agapē* in 13:10 as a specific reference to the love feast. Seen with the context of love feast in both the house and tenement church, the agape meals in both these contexts "had previously been separated by ideological and cultural conflicts; they were refusing to invite one another into their sacramental meals. In this way the boundaries erected by Mediterranean systems of honor and shame were being re-erected within the sacramental community."

Jewett's suggestion that *hē agapē* be limited to the love feasts appears to be a little bit restrictive. If one were to take Romans 13:8–10 as a continuation of Paul's argument from 12:9–21,[6] then our understanding of *hē agapē* would have to take into consideration that Paul's exposition of "love" begins in Romans 12:9 earlier on: "Let love be genuine." In this respect, Esler helpfully provides a chart that contains a summary of thirty statements that "apparently illustrate the assertion that love is without pretense."[7] If Esler is right, perhaps

6 Philip F. Esler, *Conflict and Identity in Romans: The Social Setting of Paul's Letter* (Minneapolis: Fortress Press, 2003), 333.

7 Esler, *Conflict and Identity in Romans*, 317. Cf. his wider argument from 316–35.

it's best to consider *hē agapē* within the broader context, rather than limiting it to the love feast.

Notwithstanding our minor disagreement with Jewett on the understanding of *hē agapē,* we are illuminated by his suggestion that in the Pauline church, love is the means by which all forms of the systems of honor and shame that serve to divide rather than unite the Christ-followers are to be conquered. It is this powerful insight by Jewett that finds its most powerful expression in Malaysia.

In Asia, it is commonplace to scorn or despise anyone perceived to be lower in social status, wealth, and honor. One excellent example can be seen in the consequence of the pronounced social stratification of the Indian community where the caste system is still widely being practised. For example, it is still customary that one's caste remains one of the biggest hindrances in an Indian marriage, particularly when someone from a lower hierarchy is to marry another in a higher social status. This deeply ingrained cultural practice can easily supersede the obligation to mutual love within the Christian context. In this respect, would a Shudras, someone from the lowest caste, be made welcome in a church that is largely comprised of Brahmins? Would a Brahmin be willing to have the agape feast with the Dalit? Or, would a Brahmin be willing to take the garb of a servant to serve "the other," who is a Dalit, an untouchable?

So the question remains as to how the obligation to mutual love works out within our cultural context. Applied to this context, Paul would want to snuff out such condescending behavior, telling those of higher social status not to harbor the thought of superiority over others (cf. Romans 12:3–8). Instead, Paul would be instructing how a Christ-follower is to discard and restrain the attitude encouraged by one's cultural tradition that continues to emphasise the superiority of one class over the other. Paul would oppose this attitude because of his understanding of the gospel of Jesus Christ. Therefore, it would be hard to deny that Paul is offering a rival vision of a new redeemed community of the beloved in Christ that is radically different from one's cultural context.

Another aspect of extending the obligation to mutual love in the Malaysian context can be demonstrated in the outreach to the growing migrant ministry. With more than 2 million migrant workers (not counting those who are illegal), this group of workers comprises almost 10% of the Malaysian population. The Christian community is also obligated to be a voice for the large number of migrants from Indonesia, Nepal, Myanmar, Cambodia, Bangladesh, Pakistan, and elsewhere, to speak out against injustice, discrimination, exploitation, unfair treatment, unsafe working conditions, and inhuman living conditions in which their dignity is severely violated, which may have been imposed unfairly on them by unscrupulous employers.

D. AGAPĒ AS THE FULFILLMENT OF NOMOS

How would this love, the *agapē*, fulfill the law? Jewett suggests that the "law" mentioned in Romans 13:8–10 should move beyond the Torah (as evidenced by the anarthrous use of *nomos*) to include "both Jewish and Roman law, and indeed any other law that could be mentioned" (p. 9). Jewett's understanding of this all-encompassing meaning of *nomos* leads him to suggest that "law in general is fulfilled . . . not by performing every duty prescribed in Leviticus or Deuteronomy or some other code but by following the lead of the spirit in loving one's fellow believers in a local house or tenement church."

What is clear in Paul's exhortation here is that the Christian life is not lived in isolation. A worthy response to the gospel includes participation in the community of the redeemed. In doing so, the principle of adaptability is being practised in which one is obligated to act so as to benefit not only those who were alike but also those who were different.[8]

If this is applied in the Malaysia context, how would love be seen as the fulfillment of law that reaches out to include "any other law that could be mentioned?" The agape is to remain the unique identity marker of the Christ-movement. It is a concrete expression of the action of God in pouring out his agape into the hearts of those who have faith in Christ, and this is further expressed in the ongoing experience of those who belong to this movement. Seen in this light, could the Malaysian church as a gathering of a community of the redeemed, be a social unit that undercuts even our biological and familial relations, demonstrating that the rule and reign of God does not belong to the distant future but is indeed a present reality in our midst where forgiveness, love and acceptance are our boundary markers and badges of identity? In this respect, would it be great if we as Christ-followers were known to our society by our practices—that we care about the environment; speak out against injustice, abuse of power and corruption; reach out to the poor and marginalized; and invest our scarce resources in the training, educating and equipping the people of God? Could greater Christian initiatives toward deeper ethnic reconciliation be appreciated in the church? Would the church be known as a transforming agent for our community and society? Would the church be known by her unity rather than disunity? Is the church willing to pay the price in seeking out and protecting those facing injustice and lacking a voice? Is the church courageous enough to call rulers away from tyranny and oppression towards embracing the Jubilee values of justice and mercy and principles of public servanthood and accountability?

---

[8] Cf. Stanley K. Stowers, *A Rereading of Romans: Justice, Jews and Gentiles* (Yale: Yale University, 1997), 317–23.

Admittedly, we have raised more questions than answers in this final section of our response to Jewett's excellent paper. We are reminded that Paul's exhortation of mutual love cuts across all denominations, all social, cultural, linguistic, and ethnic barriers, removing walls that are erected to create division and partition. Perhaps with the *agapē* as the fulfillment of *nomos*, we find a glimpse of the eschatological hope of Paul that "there is no longer Jew or Greek, there is no longer slave or free, there is no longer male and female; (and if we may add in the Malaysian context: there is no longer *Bumiputra*[9] *or non-Bumiputra*; there is no longer Malay or Chinese or Indian or Iban or Kadazan; for all of you are one in Christ Jesus" (Galatians 3:28).

---

9 *Bumiputra*, literally means "sons of the soil." Used in the Malaysian context, this word refers to the Malay and other native ethnic groups where special privileges such as preferential treatment under the affirmation action policy are accorded. These special privileges encompass almost all walks of life including business and investment opportunities, education, housing discount and financial assistance. The other majority ethnic groups of Chinese and Indian descents, who are not considered as *Bumiputra*, have no access to such special privileges.

46

From Muhibbah to Yin-Yang: No Shame, No Boasting

Thu En Yu

Introduction

In Christ there is neither Jew nor gentile, neither slave nor free, neither male nor female (Galatians 3:28). In Christ there are neither first-class citizens nor second-class citizens. Before God all are equal. This is the golden rule for all Christian living. In our ministry and our relationships with others, all of us are obligated to uphold the equality of all before God, speaking firmly and consistently against boastful acts or words spoken against one another.

Dr. K. K. Yeo is right when he pointed out "one of the problems in the Roman congregations was one group's assertion of superiority over the other . . . . Assertion of superiority is the way of forming one's identity within a group and over against another group."[1] Similarly, in Malaysia, the various ethnic groups still cannot step out of their racial and cultural identity when interacting with other racial groups. Yet, the quest for a common ethnicity is imperative, "without basic moral consensus a society worth living is impossible."[2] An inter-cultural dialogue would pave the way for mutual enlightening and uplifting.

Robert Bellah speaks of the "good society." He may be able to give some insights to the Christian approach with people of other faith. Bellah teaches that a good society tolerates dissidence, dispels homogeneity and accepts pluralism as the norm. Such a society is diverse, yet unity in

---

[1] K. K. Yeo, "Honor and Shame in Romans and Chinese Cultures" (in "From Rome to Beijing") and "Paul's Way of *Renren* in Romans 13:1–10" (in this volume).

[2] Hans Küng, *Global Responsibility in Search of a New World Ethic* (New York: Crossroad, 1991), 39.

diversity is achieved by the pursuit of the common good. The pursuit of the common good paves the way for consensus and hence a shared identity.[3]

I. SELF AND SHARED IDENTITY

Malaysia is a multi-racial and multi-religious society that enjoys different identities and value systems. Alhough the Chinese Malaysians and the Indigenous Malaysians share many common religious and cultural values, a closed community mentality is still at play between these groups. There is a lack of pluralistic racial consciousness amongst them.

What Dr. Yeo mentioned in his paper about the Chinese cultural characteristic related to the concept of shame and honor can serve as common ground for us to study further the value system of the people in Malaysia. Yeo pointed out the "eight glorious merits against eight shameful behaviors"[4] Here, I would like to quote four of them.

- "Love our motherland" as glory/honor; "jeopardize her" as shame.
- "Serve for the people" as glory/honor; "err from them" as shame.
- "Diligence" as glory/honor; "love ease and hate work" as shame
- "Unite and help each other' as glory/honor; "harm others to benefit oneself" as shame.

However, in Malaysia, the understanding of "motherland," "the people" and "united with each other" is complicated, differing from one race to another. Many of the Chinese and the Indians are still holding fast to their "migrant" mentality. Where should devotion to homeland and kinship be rooted? Are they to place their loyalty more in their own land of origin and their own clansmen or to the land and people of their adopted country? Likewise for the Indigenous peoples in Sabah and Sarawak, homeland and kinship concepts are further complicated with geographical, racial and political issues.

For the Chinese in Malaysia, *guang zong yao zu* (光宗耀祖)—"children's honor, forefather's glory," is considered one of the most honorable standards for behavior. The children's value system is to make wealth and success in order to bring glory to their ancestors. To the Malaysian Chinese, the saying, "Labor hard as honor, love ease and hate work as shame," applies more to their native land and clansmen. Subsequently, they set up clan associations, as well as religious, economical and

---

[3] Robert N. Bellah et. al., *The Good Society* (New York:Knopf, 1991), 9.

[4] Yeo, "Honor and Shame in Romans and Chinese Cultures," (in "From Rome to Beijing" in this volume).

cultural barriers in order to protect themselves and fail to work hand in hand with other races for the common good. There is thus a need for a paradigm shift in the mindset of the migrants when they apply these glorious merits of "'Serve for the people' as glory/honor; 'err from them' as shame and, 'United and help each other' as glory/honor; 'harm others to benefit oneself' as shame."

John Clammer reminded the people, particularly the Chinese who live in Southeast Asia, of the danger of a diaspora mentality.[5] He pointed out that those peoples that originated outside of the immediate region, namely from India, China, Arabia and Sri Lanka, had formed their own diasporas that are marked by their religious, economic, cultural and educational mannerisms. Clammer further raised the alarm: "The deep psychological attractions of adhering to a 'diaspora' mentality should never be underestimated, but recent history shows that it is not an option for creating an adequate future, least of all for those who trap themselves in an image of non-belonging rooted in an image of the past."[6]

Malaysian churches are no exception. Basically churches in Malaysia exhibit a church-centred mission theology. By inference, the churches during the colonial era exhibited the followings shortcomings:[7]

1. *Lack of indigenization.* The churches reflected religion in a Western cultural cloak, which was alien to local culture, thinking, and social structures.

2. *Lack of universal outlook.* The churches confined themselves to the middle and upper classes, avoiding the grass-roots level of society, and therefore they did not identify with the masses.

3. *Lack of multiracial sensitivity.* The churches did not address social injustices, racial animosity, or economic imbalances, and hence contributed to perpetuating communal hostility and economic exploitation.

Other Malaysians, especially the Malays, have another mentality. Prior to independence, the churches had occupied a unique position in the society. Church leaders were treated as equals by the government officials; the Anglican Bishop was next to the Governor in civil standing. With independence, there emerged a reshuffling of relationships. Malay Muslims evolved from being the ruled to being the rulers. This change reversed the role between the master and the servant. The Malays continue to have a social complex syndrome, feeling that the shadow of their past oppression is still cast over them.[8]

---

5 John Clammer, *Diaspora and Identity, the Sociology of Culture in Southeast Asia* (Subang Jaya: Pelanduk Publication, 2002), 141–251

6 Clammer, *Diaspora and Identity*, 202–3.

7 Thu En Yu, *A Quest For Malaysia-Sabah Racial Identity: A Cultural Hermeneutical Perspective* (Taiwan: ATESEA, 2007), 44–45.

8 Thu En Yu, "Muhibbah: The Church's Ministry of Reconciliation In The Pluralistic Society of Malaysia" (Unpublished Dissertation, 1995), 46.

Conflicts of interest between the two groups fostered polarisation. Consequently, the relationship between the Chinese and the Malays as well as the indigenous people requires immediate attention, since the churches have neglected this over the past century.

Many of the indigenous people are Christians but national policy has been geared towards Islamisation since independence. Political structures have thus become more complex and polarised. Disputes among ethnic groups that arise out of racial consciousness spill over into issues pertaining to religion, race, and economy. Another pertinent issue is that the rights and privileges of Sabahans and Sarawakians have not been protected under the constitution after joining the Federation of Malaysia so that some Sabahans and Sarawakians feel betrayed and marginalised. Such feelings of dissatisfaction strain the relationship between East Malaysia and the Federal Government, affect their sense of belonging to Malaysia, and jeopardise progress towards national unity.

A key question facing the identity dilemma is how do we foster common ethics so that nurturing a common identity can become a priority. Muhibbah and Yin-Yang are two possible cultural institutions to emulate in resolving contemporary problems.

II. MUHIBBAH AND YIN-YANG: THE STRATEGY FORWARD

A. MUHIBBAH: GOODWILL FRIENDSHIP

The Malays have a constructive tradition of *muhibbah*, a Malay word which means goodwill or harmony—a friendship, almost amounting to brotherhood between cultures. This concept acts to ameliorate the relationships within society.

Muhibbah[9] is derived from the Arabic word *muhabbat* which means love or affection among friends. Generally, it is more than friendship and approaches a level akin to brotherhood. *Muhibbah*'s current usage is linked with ethnic and religious behavior and is popularly translated as "goodwill." *Muhibbah* is a way of life for the Malays, thus in Malay, a *muhibbah* relationship indicates common social, economic, and political wellbeing. It is expressed in the cordial treatment accorded to any person that one relates to, especially neighbors. Thus neighbors are more than friends; they have a special relationship that cultivates a sense of brotherhood, in short, neighborliness. Neighborliness is not confined to two persons, but encompasses the whole village or the whole community. Neighborliness in a communal setting generates a state of harmony among the inhabitants. It is the dyadic culture that binds the village or the community together, ensuring its wellbeing and co-existence. *Muhibbah* facilitates interaction among the people through

9 This is sometimes spelled as *muhibah*.

some cultural institutions such as "open-house feast," *gotong royong* and consultation.

In an open-house feast, the characteristics of the gathering are fellowship, sharing and forgiving. It is a "welcoming and accepting one another" festival whereby the aspect of an open community is highlighted.

Gotong royong is a movement that mobilizes all concerned in a project beneficial to a member, or a group, or a whole community. The object of this institution of mutual assistance is to establish a self-reliant community whereby every member of the community contributes assistance to meet the various needs. In this way, the village achieves maximum self-sufficiency and very rarely appeals for external intervention. Thus, everybody in the village gives and receives honor.

The Malays are a united people—an intrinsic result of *muhibbah*. Whenever people interact to solve a problem that affects a part or all of the community, what ensues is a meaningful consultation in which every member contributes. Consequently, the group reaches a consensus which is taken up by the community leaders and the people follow. Such consultation thus enables progress.

Thus it can be seen that *muhibbah* spirit or theology of friendship in Malaysia is a liberal and tolerant perspective in response to each other's culture and religion. It is a genuine spirit of mutual respect and trust. The church can beneficially adopt this *muhibbah* concept and explore its profound wisdom which has the potential to emerge as a powerful theological thought: A theology of true friendship in the spirit of *muhibbah* is a possible starting point of theology of mission in the context of a pluralistic society. True friendship rejects shame and boasting.

B. YIN-YANG: CO-EXISTENCE

Yin-yang philosophy presents the universe in the *Taiji* circle/diagram known as Supreme Ultimate, representing wholesomeness and an all-embracing state. Yin-yang thought is dualistic. For example, it denotes the earth as yin with heaven being yang; the moon as yin and the sun as yang; female as yin and male as yang. Yin and yang exist in multiple interlacing layers in an orderly manner, a state where each exists in each other's domain. The unity of yin-yang symbolizes the peace in the universe, hence the harmony of all manifestations of nature.

According to the Chinese Supreme Ultimate, yin and yang are extremes that co-exist in a fashion that complements and supplements each other; in essence, this demonstrates the profound principle of co-existence in common union. Hence, yin-yang gives birth to all creation, and all creation exists due to the interaction between yin and yang.

The Yin-yang concept can offer a way out of the cultural boasting and mutual honoring with its inherently "both/and" way of thinking. Jung Young Lee gives a good insight into Asian culture and worldview. He said, "If the yin-yang way includes contradictions and opposites, it is perhaps best to characterize it in terms of both/and. The yin-yang way is a both/and way of thinking, because it is not only inclusive but also relational . . . . Yin-yang relationship does not exclude the middle, because the middle is the most inclusive way of representing the whole. Thus, yin or yang cannot exclude each other, because yin and yang always coexist. The yin-yang symbol represents the both/and way of thinking . . . the both/and way of thinking recognizes not only the coexistence of opposites but also the complementarily of them. In this respect, the yin-yang way of thinking is holistic."[10]

The love of God is all embracing and inclusive. God loves both the righteous and the sinners. His loving kindness, *hesed* which is grounded in His covenantal promise with Abraham that, "in you shall all nations be blessed" (Genesis 3:8), is now fulfilled. In Christ, God's promise is now open to Jews as well as Gentiles: "In Christ there is neither Jew nor gentile, no slave or free, no male and female" (Galatians 3: 28). In Christ, there is no shame and no boasting. This is the essence of the gospel. For this reason, Paul said, "welcome one another, therefore, as Christ has welcome you" (Romans 15: 7).

Ephesians presents the essence of Pauline theology on reconciliation: "For He is our peace who has made us both one, and has broken down the dividing wall of hostility." (Eph. 2:14) In its contemporary historical setting, this verse was directed at a few major issues:[11]

1. Alienation between men and women could be remedied in Christ;
2. The enmity between Israelites and non-Israelites could be dispelled and replaced by harmony;
3. The disparate segments of the first century world could find amity within the new found Christian fellowship;
4. Israelites and non-Israelites could overcome the communal gap beween them and evolve into a newly integrated people.

Paul's teaching in its historical setting, which involved inter-communal and inter-religious conflicts that are similar to the Malaysia context, can shed some light on the church's obligation to seek unity and harmony for the nation.

---

[10] Jung Young Lee, *The Trinity In Asian Perspective* (Nashville: Abingdon Press,1966), 32–34.

[11] P. Ralph Martin, *Reconciliation, A Study of Paul's Theology* (Atlanta: John Knox Press, 1981), 176.

CONCLUSION

Yin-yang philosophy can, in fact, enrich Christian thinking. It also enhances the exchange between Christian thought and Chinese culture. For thousands of years, the principle of co-existence of yin-yang influenced the excellent Chinese culture that emphasized the pursuit of neighborliness and common values amidst differences. This is an important aspect that Christian theology cannot afford to overlook. The beauty of yin-yang rests on the foundation of co-existence. Their separation and/or union indicate a continuous and dynamic existential relationship.

The Malay concept of *muhibbah* in the spirit of true friendship with healing properties that can enhance racial harmony should be employed in Christian teaching as a powerful theological thought to combat the attitude of shame and boasting.

47

Response to Kota Kinabalu Colleagues

Robert Jewett

I am deeply honored by the serious engagement by five distinguished colleagues with my commentary as a potential resource for interpreting the gospel in the Malaysian context. It confirms the relevance of Paul's hope of the ecumenical extension of the Gospel in Romans 15:11, "Praise the Lord, all the Gentiles, and let all the peoples praise him."

Professor Gee accepts my "model of socio-historical exegesis" as a resource in the task of freeing this letter from "centuries of accretions of exegetical traditions in the West." He devises an accurate summary of my argument that Paul offers "a new honor system in Christ" that should enable "mutual acceptance among the differing congregations in Rome" so they can cooperate in the Spanish mission. I would only add that the "logistic support" needed by Paul consisted of advice, contacts with local supporters, and translation assistance instead of funds, which the wording of 16:2 indicates was being underwritten by his patroness, Phoebe.

The wording of 12:3 throws light on Dr. Gee's question about the relevance of Romans for the unity of believers from different cultural backgrounds. Paul urges each group to be faithful to its *metron pisteōs*, the measuring rod of faith that God has dealt out to each cultural group. While each group is united with others in sharing a basic faith in Christ, its culture legitimately differentiates it from others. Paul warns that to impose one group's measuring rod onto other groups is an illicit expression of "supermindedness" that is opposed to the "sobermindedness" that recognizes proper limits in Christ. This requires us to accept a measure of theological and cultural diversity within the Christian world, thus avoiding the long standing tradition of theological imperialism. Paul's theology in Romans needs to be recognized as a revolutionary resource in this direction.

Professor Thu En Yu describes the Malay concept of *muhibbah*, affection among friends, as "a possible starting point of (a) theology of mission." This is closely related to the Pauline categories of *koinōnia*, *agapē*, and *filia* that were embodied in the early Christian love feasts, which were strikingly similar to the open-house feasts in Malay villages. Dr. Yu observes that in both meals everybody "gives and receives honor," a matter that has been overlooked in western interpretations of early Christian meals. He goes on to note that the Yin-yang concept offers a way to avoid cultural imperialism, which I have discovered is a major theme in Romans. Professors Kok and Yong provide a further development of the parallels between early Christian love feasts and the longhouse meals of Sarawak. They show that agapaic communalism would be an effective resource in transcending cultural boundaries in Malaysia. These are impressive examples of the relevance of maintaining culturally differentiated measuring rods of faith, because they enable access to otherwise unrecognized dimensions of the biblical faith.

Professors Ezra Kok and Lim Kar Yong provide further reflections on the theme of love as law's fulfillment in 13:8–10, stressing that "the Christian life is not lived in isolation" and that *agapē* provides the motivation for responsible political engagement. When they argue that "The agape is to remain the unique identity of the Christ-movement," I wonder whether this takes the longhouse meals sufficiently into account. The concept of muhibbah and the indigenous meal tradition may provide the basis for developing a set of democratic values that would support the advancement of both the Christian and non-Christian populations. Discovering the oneness in Christ that they celebrate in their final paragraph may lead to discerning a shared humanity that transcends religious as well as cultural barriers, allowing for the development of more responsible politics.

The possibility of a responsible embodiment of biblical theology brings us to Prof. Hii Kong Hock's penetrating analysis of 13:1–7. Employing the idea of a hidden transcript, he perceives that "the destiny of history . . . is not finally in the hands of the emperor, but in the hands of God and his crucified and resurrected Messiah . . . ." This justifies responsibility for the entire Malaysian society, with ethical guidelines that Hock derives from 12:1–21. I would hope, however, that "unity among different churches" with different cultural traditions does not take the traditional western form of ideological imperialism, with one group imposing its views on another. All of the participants in this symposium appear to accept the interpretation of Romans as opposed to such domination. If Christians "relinquish our differences," are they actually in a stronger position to deal creatively with the cultural differences in a diverse society like Indonesia? Doesn't this habit of western "unity" lead to Christian versus Muslim forms of imperialism? From the description of Indonesia's 12th National Election, the "people" asserted its power against former rulers, which may constitute a small step in the direction that Paul recommends. To expand the vision in Prof. Hock's final sentence, "God's beloved *oikos*," the church, is entrusted with a gospel of divine *agapē* to the entire world.

Finally, I would like to thank my colleagues for making such careful and creative use of my commentary. Your insights and suggestions will accompany me in the years ahead. But in the meanwhile, let's open the floor to a wider discussion, following the Pauline impulse that God gives each of us parrēsia, the courage in Christ to speak with the confidence that we each have a contribution to make.

Conclusion in Beijing
October 2007

48

Paul's Way of *Renren* in Romans 13:1–10[1]

K. K. Yeo

Introduction

After reading the previous articles and listening to rounds of symposia on Jewett's Hermeneia Commentary on Romans, I am more convinced of the necessity of Paul's theological anthropology in Romans 13:1–10—the mutual indebtedness of love. It has been an honor to edit this volume, and an even greater honor to have hosted Robert Jewett's two-month visit to Peking University. It was during that time that I seriously studied Romans 13:1–10, taking my cue from Jewett's commentary on the complex socio-political context of the pericope. I include this piece as the concluding section of this volume because it is an open-ended chapter that invites us to wrestle with sincerity and love, the multiple critical and provocative issues raised in Jewett's commentary on this text.

I want to go further than a standard commentary, however, as I seek a cross-cultural hermeneutical perspective—constructing a Christian Chinese theology[2] and using Confucian language to express Paul's understanding of love, and vice versa. In doing so, my hope is to reveal the ways in which biblical theology thrives in Chinese culture and also how Chinese culture is transformed and reinvigorated by the gospel.[3] I also believe that the Confucianist insight of *renren* enables us to read

[1] The initial draft was presented at Peking University in October, 2007, also at Sabah Theological Seminary, Kota Kinabalu, Malaysia on April 14, 2008.

[2] For fuller extent of this project, see K. K. Yeo, *Musing with Confucius and Paul: Toward a Chinese Christian Theology* (Eugene: Cascade Books, 2008).

[3] "Christian Chinese Theology" is subtly different from "Chinese Christian Theology." Both terms pay attention to the dynamic relationship between theology and Chineseness (culture, philosophy, text, ways of life, etc.), but the latter seeks to express Christian theology *culturally*, while the former also commits to that task but ultimately reads cultures *biblically and Christianly*.

Romans 13:8–10 as a vision for forming an alternative community in the Roman Empire, taking seriously what it means to become fully human.

New Testament writers often wrestle with the rereading of the Old Testament. One of the significant issues is for these writers to reinterpret the fulfillment of the whole Mosaic law in terms of Leviticus 19:18, as evident in Matthew 5:43; 19:19; 22:39; Mark 12:31; 12:33; Luke 10:27; Romans 13:9; James 2:8.[4] Among these writers, Paul, and possibly James also, best understand the radical gospel of Jesus as they both highlight "loving your neighbor" as the *summation* or fulfillment of the Jewish law.[5]

I. The Context of Romans 13: Forming an Alternative Community in the Empire

Paul suggests in Romans 13, in the context of affirming theologically the legitimacy of the Roman government, that the ideal Christian community as an alternative for Roman social groups is one that embodies cruciform love. Love upholds the best of the Jewish Law and is lived out as mutual indebtedness by Christian believers in Rome. Jewish or Gentile Christians alike live out a life pleasing to God and a life of freedom as stated in Leviticus 19:18.

Paul begins by advocating "every *psychē*," i.e., Roman Christians, to "be under the authority of the higher authorities" (13:1). The word *hypotassō* is the middle or passive of the verb meaning "to put or arrange under" or "to be subjected," implying respectively that a person submits himself (middle voice) or being forced to submit (passive).[6] N. T. Wright explains that, "one must regard the governing authorities as having a rightful claim on one's submission."[7]

---

[4] See James Moffatt, *Love in New Testament* (London: Hodder & Stoughton, 1929); Victor P. Furnish, *The Love Command in the New Testament* (Nashville: Abingdon Press, 1972); Pheme Perkins, *Love Commands in the New Testament* (New York: Paulist, 1982); Viktor Warnach, *Agape. Die Liebe als Grundmotiv der Neutestamentlichen Theologie* (Düsseldorf: Patmos-Verlag, 1951); Ceslaus Spicq, *Agapè dans le Nouveau Testament: Analyse des Textes*, 3 Vols. (Paris: Libraire Lecoffre, 1958–59); Paul Brett, *Love Your Neighbor: The Bible as Christian Ethics Today* (London: Darton, Longman and Todd, 1992).

[5] Romans 13:9 is a summation of the Ten Commandments (verse 10 says "love is the fulfillment of the law" (my translation); see also James 2:8 on the "royal law" as loving one's neighbor).

[6] If it is the middle voice, the one subject has a role in the matter. This is Robert Jewett's translation ("subject himself"); see his *Romans: A Commentary* (Hermeneia; Minneapolis: Fortress Press, 2007), 788. The other option is passive, implying that the one who is subject has no say. Stubbs' phrase: "be every person subjected." See M. A. Stubbs, "Subjection, Reflection, Resistance," in edited Yeo Khiok-khng, *Navigating Romans Through Cultures: Challenging Readings by Charting a New Course* (Edinburgh: T. &T. Clark International, 2004), 177.

[7] N. T. Wright, "The Letter to the Romans: Introduction, Commentary, and Reflection," in *New Interpreter's Bible* (Nashville: Abingdon Press, 2002), 10:720. On the political and Jewish contexts of Romans 1:1–7, see Jewett, *Romans*, 784–803.

But this submission is subtly qualified by Paul in the second half of verse 1 as to what kind of higher authorities: "for there is no authority except from God, and those authorities that exist have been designated (*tassō*) by God." "For there is no authority except from God" is often misunderstood to mean "all authorities are sanctioned by God," therefore they are to be obeyed no matter what. Such domestication is unwarranted. The text, "for there is no authority except from God," is literally rendered and meant as "for it is not an authority if [it is] not by God" (*ou gap estin exousia ei mē hypo theou*).[8] In other words, there are authorities that are not from/by God. God has designated government authorities that serve His purpose, and this point is made abundantly clear by the following verses: rulers are not to use terror toward good citizens (verse 3); government is "God's servant" (verses 4, 6); for "the common good of the people" (verse 4); government is given the sword "to punish the wrongdoer" (verse 4); government is to be honorable and collect what is due to them (verse 6). Here God is the one who has placed or designated the authority. Given the Roman Imperial government of Paul's occasioned audience, it is clear that Paul is offering a theological critique of government authority in two ways. First, Rome serves God rather than Rome serving Jupiter, therefore also, Rome's authority is under God's. Second, Rome should exercise its power honorably and rightly, otherwise that authority is not deemed to be designated by God.

By implication, "this passage does provide a basis for a theology of political power,"[9] but one must be careful when the contexts shift. We can affirm that government is a part of God's good order, and to resist it is to resist God's order (cf. 13:2), but we must remember that "government qua government is intended by God."[10]

Given the Jewish zealot revolutionary movement at that time, Paul must be acutely aware of the danger of not qualifying for the power of Rome. Being a former Pharisee and seeing zealot violence is not a way to fulfill the righteousness of God (Romans 7); what is at stake is how Roman Christians live out their allegiance to Christ while at the same time paying honor and submission to Rome. Paul here seems to advocate not a violent overthrow, but a theological grounding of government and a Christian politics of submission.[11] Ultimately, God is the designator, and therefore both governments and citizens

---

[8] See similar usage of "it is not" (*ou gar estin*) by Paul in 1 Corinthians 11:8, and of "if not" (*ei mē*) in Romans 7:7, 9:29.

[9] J. D. G. Dunn, *Romans 9–16* (Waco: Word Books, 1988), 773. Joseph A. Fitzmyer agrees; see his *Romans* (New York: Doubleday, 1993), 665.

[10] Wright, "Romans," 719; cf. 717.

[11] See Mark Reasoner, "Ancient and Modern Exegesis of Romans 13 under Unfriendly Governments," in *SBL Seminar Papers* 38 (1999), 368–69.

(especially citizens who are Christians) have their own responsibilities to make sure that the common good of the nation(s) is preserved.

Paul refers to the governing authorities as God's "deacons/ ministers" [*diakonos*, verse 4] and "liturgists/servants" [*leitourgoi*, verse 6], words that have cultic and liturgical connotations.[12] It is Paul's Christological redefinition that a government that "worships" God and "lives out" God's glory and goodness will be similar to the reign of God in the church. Government authorities are "ministers" of God who punish in wrath those who do evil; the good doers should be rewarded, not punished. Thus, the reference to the "sword" in 8:35 as separating Christians from the love of God is an abuse of power by Rome. The word "servants" is used in connection with collecting taxes.[13] Later, Paul considers himself to be a "minister of Christ to the Gentiles in the priestly service of the Gospel of God" (15:16 NRSV); there, he speaks of collecting a "tax" of sorts—for the poor in Jerusalem (15:25–29). In other words, proper taxation, to Rome or to Jerusalem, is a liturgical act of serving God and bringing about God's maximal goodness to the people.

To speak more clearly of the Christological vision of God's community formation, Paul explains the principles of ministers and servants using the concept of cruciform love (*agapē*), which has a core content of "mutual indebtedness." I see Romans 13:8–10 as integrally related to verses 1–7, both linked by the concept of "what is owed." In verse 7, Paul commands to give to each what is owed to that one: "taxes to whom taxes are indebted, tribute to whom is indebted tribute, fear to whom is indebted fear, honor to whom is indebted honor." In verse 8, Paul uses the same word for "debt," or "what is owed" [*opheilete*]. But here, Paul says "owe nothing to anyone, except to love one another." In other words, there is only one debt that will not, cannot, and should not be resolved, *viz.* the debt of loving other.

This Christian concept of "mutuality of indebtedness of love" as exhibited in a Christian community is revolutionary in a Roman society based primarily on a patronage system. Paul's audience is much more aware of the Roman coins used to honor Caesar as *sōtēr* (savior), who is regarded as the ultimate benefactor.[14] "A new obligation is to replace the social dependency on patrons or families, namely to

---

[12] See Douglas Moo, *The Epistle to the Romans* (Grand Rapids: Eerdmans, 1996), 804 and M. D. Nanos, *The Mystery of Romans: The Jewish Context of Paul's Letter* (Minneapolis: Fortress Press, 1996), 305–10.

[13] See Dunn, *Romans 9–16*, 767 on this word in Septuagint having priestly cultic meaning.

[14] H. L. Hendrix, "Benefactor/Patron Networks in the Urban Environment: Evidence from Thessalonica," in *Semeia* 56 (1991), 39–58.

'love one another.'"[15] Robert Jewett wants to place verse 10 and the love debt within the social context of "the small congregations in Rome and, more concretely, the love feasts and sacramental celebrations in which members shared resources."[16] This may concretize the word *agapē*, but I think Jewett's reading limits Paul's usage here. I see the mutual indebtedness of Christian love expressed as an *alternative community* for Rome if Rome takes seriously its ministry and servanthood roles, also when Christian churches take seriously their worship and service as they live within their own benefaction networks, *sharing common life, and loving each other and outsiders*. Romans 13:11–14 further expresses how in the *kairotic*[17] moments of the end-time Christian love is lived out: "let us live honorably as in the day, not in reveling and drunkenness, not in debauchery and licentiousness, not in quarreling and jealousy. Instead, put on the Lord Jesus Christ, and make no provision for the flesh, to gratify its desires" (vv. 13–14).

II. FULFILLMENT OF THE WHOLE LAW VIA LEVITICUS 19:18

With regard to the manner in which the Jewish law is fulfilled, Stuhlmacher postulates that the "Zion Torah" is inaugurated by the Messiah in the eschatological age through his obedient death so that the Mosaic law, promised to all nations (Micah 4:1–4; Isaiah 2:2–4; 25:7–9; Jeremiah 31:31–34; Ezekiel 20; 36:22–28; 40–48), might be made relevant to the Gentiles.[18] Paul may have been influenced by this interpretation of the Messiah, but more evidence of such a Messianic movement is needed. Romans 13 makes no mention of the death of the Messiah as fulfilling the Jewish law.[19] Romans 3 speaks of Christ's death as an inclusive sacrifice for Jews and Gentiles, and Romans 8 speaks of Christ's death as God's love for all. Stuhlmacher's interpretation would make sense if one were to link the obedient death

---

[15] Robert Jewett, "Are There Allusions to the Love Feast in Romans 13:8-10?," in edited by J. V. Hills et al., *Common Life in the Early Church: Essays Honoring Graydon F. Snyder* (Harrisburg: Trinity Press International, 1998), 270.

[16] Jewett, "Are There Allusions to the Love Feast," 271; see also his *Romans*, 805–9. As Jewett argues, the article should be read in verse 10; thus, it should be "The love (feast) [*hē agapē*] does no wrong to a neighbor; therefore, the love (feast) [*hē agapē*] is the fulfilling of the law" (13:10).

[17] G. Delling, "*Kairos*, etc.," in ed. G. Bromiley, *Theological Dictionary of the New Testament* [hereafter *TDNT*] (Grand Rapids: Eerdmans, 1964), 3:455. "The present is the *kairotic* moment in which 'the continuity of the flow of time is ruptured and the believer stands in the dawn of the eschatological future.'" (K. K. Yeo, *Christianity, Communism, and the Hope of China* [Grand Rapids: Brazos Press, 2002], 53.)

[18] P. Stuhlmacher, "The Law as a Topic of Biblical Theology," *Reconciliation, Law, Righteousness: Essays in Biblical Theology* (Philadelphia: Fortress Press, 1986), 126.

[19] Galatians contends that the Messiah died as a curse to lift the curse of the law (3:13–14), but the language of fulfillment is absent in Galatians 3.

of the Messiah to the love commandment of Leviticus 19:18, but again, neither Galatians nor Romans states the link.

A. *REN* (HUMANENESS AND BENEVOLENCE) AND CO-HUMANITY

I suggest that Confucian language of *ren* and *renren*[20] can help us better understand what Paul means in Romans 13:8–10. The word *ren*, used no less than eighty times in the *Analects*, can be translated as benevolence or love.[21] The word can be used either in the narrow sense of one's desirable virtues (for examples, in *Analects* 9:29, 14:28) or, more often, in the broad sense of the encompassing ethical ideal (for example, 14:4).[22] Given that the *Analects* is not a philosophical treatise with a precise use of terms, it has been difficult for scholars to pinpoint the meaning of *ren*. Benjamin Schwartz interprets *ren* as "an attainment of human excellence which--where it exists--is a whole embracing all the separate virtues."[23] Yearley translates *ren* as "virtue,"[24] which is similar to Legge's "virtuous manners."[25] Waley translates *ren* as "goodness," "humane," "human-at-its-best," and Dawson, "humaneness."[26] D. C. Lau writes that *ren* "is basically a

[20] Readers need to note that the English transliteration "*ren*" can refer to two different Chinese words, 仁 (*ren*) and 人 (*ren*), meaning "humaneness" and "person" respectively. In this section, we are discussing the first word 仁. When the two words appear together, the order is always 仁人 (*renren*), meaning "humane person" or "benevolent person." Since the Chinese language does not have articles, the word itself does not indicate singular or plural. In *Analects* 12:22, *ren* is equated with benevolence (for fellow human beings). *Renren* can mean a humane person or humane persons.

[21] I will note the source of the English translation of the *Analects* used if it is my own translation. The citation of the *Analects* in Chinese scholarship simply gives the title of the book or chapter without the numbering of the verse. However, the citation of the *Analects* in non-Chinese scholarship often gives the precise numbering of passages from the *Analects*. The problem is that the numbering of passages from the *Analects* is not always the same in different editions. For the English citation of the *Analects* in this paper, I will follow the numbering of Lau or Li or Ames and Rosemont, indicating them as e.g. "1:3" and noting the source I use. As for the major Chinese commentaries on the *Analects*, I use He Yan, Xing Bing, *Lunyu Zhushu* [*Commentary of the Analects*] (Beijing: Peking University Press, 1999); Yang Bojun, *Lunyu Yizhu* [*Commentary of the Analects*] (Taipei: Wunan, 1992); Qian Mu, *Lunyu Xinjie* [*The Analects: New Interpretation*] (Taipei, Taiwan: Dongda, 2003); Jin Liangnian, *Lunyu Yizhu* [*Commentary of the Analects*] (Shanghai: Shanghai Guji, 2006); Li Ling, *Sangjiaguo: Wodou Lunyu* [*Homeless Dog: My Reading of the Analects*] (Taiyuan: Shanxi Renmin, 2007).

[22] Shun Kwong-loi, "*Ren* and *Li* in the *Analects*," in edited by Bryan W. van Norden, *Confucius and the Analects: New Essays* (Oxford: Oxford University Press, 2002), 53. See also Yao Xinzhong edited, *RoutledgeCurzon Encyclopedia of Confucianism* (London; New York: RoutledgeCurzon, 2003), 2:498–500.

[23] Benjamin I. Schwartz, *The World of Thought in Ancient China* (Cambridge: Harvard University Press, 1985), 75.

[24] Lee H. Yearley, "An Existentialist Reading of Book 4 of the *Analects*," in edited by van Norden, *Confucius and the Analects*, 245.

[25] James Legge and Yang Bojun translated, *Sishu* [*The Four Books*] *The Four Books* (Changsha: Hunan Publisher, 1995), *passim*.

[26] Arthur Waley, *The Analects of Confucius* (New York: Vintage Books, 1989), *passim*; Raymond Dawson trans., *Confucius: The Analects* (Oxford: Oxford University Press, 1993), *passim*; Edward Slingerland translated, *Confucius Analects with Selections from Traditional Commentaries* (Indianapolis: Hackett, 2003), 238 translates *ren* as "goodness."

character of agents and its application to acts is only derivative."[27] Lau renders *ren* as "benevolence."[28] Part of the difficulty lies in the fact that Confucius was investing new meanings into the term *ren*. In *Analects* 12:22, when asked by Fan Chih the meaning of *ren*, Confucius replied that *ren* is "to love people" (*airen*). According to *Analects* 12:22, the translation of *ren* as "benevolence" or "love" is apt. But *ren* is not just loving one's fellow beings (12:22); it is to be empathetic/conscientious (*zhong*) and merciful/reciprocal (*shu*, *Analects* 4:15). *Ren* also carries within it all the moral qualities that govern the relationships between two or more human beings.[29]

Confucius regards *ren* as the fountainhead of all virtues. The Chinese character for *ren* is composed of two ideograms: "person" connotes self or a human being, and "two" connotes relation.[30] For our purposes here, we shall translate *ren* as human-relatedness, human-relatedness, or specifically as love, which is the cardinal principle of human relationships. Confucius says, "In order to establish oneself, one must establish others" (*Analects* 6:30).[31] To be truly human is to be responsible to and for others, but "the others" are not specified in *Analects* 6:30. They could be family members, friends, superiors, or enemies. But the emphasis on edifying and caring for others is clear. The interpersonal relationships one has within a community and the acts one does for others constitute together the essence of humanity. To be *ren* (humaneness), to be benevolent or compassionate; it is to be in relationship, to be interdependent. *Ren* is the authentic nature of human beings. *Ren* is the way (*dao*) for one to become truly human as he relates to others. In short, *ren* is the ordering principle of a Confucianist society.[32]

---

[27] D. C. Lau, translator, *Confucius: The Analects* (Harmondsworth: Penguin, 1979), 27; similarly Yang Bojun, *Lunyu Yizhu*, 6.

[28] Lau, *Analects*, passim. Other translations are "human-heartedness" (E. R. Hughes), "humanity," "virtue" (H. G. Creel), "human-relatedness," "charity," "humanity" (W. T. Chan), "morality," "compassion" (Lin Yutang), "human-to-humanness" (F. S. C. Northrop). Cf. Fung Yulan, *A Short History of Chinese Philosophy*, edited by Derk Bodde (New York: Macmillan, 1948), 69–73; Yang Bojun, *Lunyu Yizhu*, 18–21, 221; Chan Wing-tsit, "Chinese and Western Interpretations of *Ren* (Humanity)," *Journal of Chinese Philosophy* 2 (1975), 108–109.

[29] Fung, *Short History of Chinese Philosophy*, 69–73, and Chan, "Chinese and Western Interpretations of *Ren*," 109.

[30] Tu Weiming says, "Etymologically *ren* consists of two parts, one a simple ideogram of a human figure, meaning the self, and the other with two horizontal strokes, suggesting human relations" (*Confucian Thought: Selfhood as Creative Transformation* [Albany: State University of New York Press, 1985], 84).

[31] My translation. See Qian Mu, *Lunyu Xinjie*, 224; Yang Bojun, *Lunyu Yizhu*, 141–42.

[32] For more, see Yeo, *Musing with Confucius and Paul*, 253–303.

B. *RENREN*: TO BE A BENEVOLENT/HUMANE PERSON

Benevolence or humaneness is universally cherished whether it is expressed culturally as *ren* or as *agapē*. Confucian *ren* and Pauline *agapē* are not the same; one is concerned with the love extended from the family to others within a structured society, and the other is concerned with the self-sacrificing love for others that extends the family of God. The different ways of extending love in Confucian and Pauline ethics can be traced to their different understandings of Heaven (*tian*) and God (*Theos*).

Confucius lacks Paul's understanding of the personhood of God; the move forward for Confucius is not toward God but toward full humanity, that is, to creatively fulfill the mandate of Heaven by being *renren* (a benevolent person). To become a benevolent or humane person, one must follow the established norms, rites (*li*), and way (*dao*), and one must be moral (*de*) and love (*ai*) others. If "one observes the rites and rituals and overcomes oneself, one will be benevolent" (*Analects* 12:1).[33] Confucius believes that once on the road of desiring and pursuing benevolence as one's humaneness (*ren*), one will have the resources to continue (4:6). The *Analects* employs *renren* and *renzhe* as having the same meaning; the terms refer to those who are committed to love others as the law of life. The law of love as the law of life is expressed in *Analects* 15:9 as those *renren* "not saving their own lives but sacrificing them in order to perfect the virtue of benevolence."

C. PAUL'S REINTERPRETATION OF THE LAW IN TERMS OF LOVE INTO FREEDOM

Paul sees the summary of the law in the love commandment and thus understands the purpose and essence of the law as "loving one's neighbors." The use of Leviticus 19:18 as the fulfillment of the whole law is to be understood as *love for humanity*. Paul redefines the relationship between God and human beings in terms of what God has done in Christ. Paul interprets the law with an emphasis on *loving others*; this is similar to Confucius' ethic of *renren*—people who *love others*.

Fulfilling the law implies an obligation to be true to the spirit of the law. Paul objects to external laws and ceremonies; he highlights the essence of the law, which is love. The situation in Confucius' day was similar to that of Paul with regard to observance to the law in its external form or internal spirit. In Galatians 6:13, Paul writes that "even the circumcised do not themselves obey the law," but ". . . if you sow to the Spirit, you will reap eternal life from the Spirit." (6:8) Similiarly, in Confucius' time, meticulous observance (doing) of the Zhou-*li* or the *Book of Rites* (*Li Ji*) is able to protect one from errors, but it also can be an unbearable burden. "Fulfilling the law" as a whole through love is

[33] My translation. See Qian Mu, *Lunyu Xinjie*, 413–417; Yang Bojun, *Lunyu Yizhu*, 265.

to know the fundamental thrust of the law and be able to live one's life out of the freedom to love. Jesus must "break" the law in order to fulfill the (Great) law--being loving. The Great Commandment is to love God with all one's being and one's neighbor as one's self. Here the law of love changes from doing to *being*. The paradox of the Great Commandment is that love cannot be commanded, yet *being* loving and forgiving (and so on) can be demonstrated. For Christians, the obligation to love one another arises not from what others have done, but from what God has done for all in Christ Jesus; as Confucius would say, because Heaven (*tian*) has imparted in human beings the nature of *ren* (love), Heaven has mandated all to love (to become *renren*).

Paul's reinterpretation of the Jewish law by means of love seeks to create harmony and to grant freedom for all. Paul understands the *law of love* as the law of freedom, that is, love makes us free, and as human beings we are free to love. This is what Paul means in Romans 13:8-9 in the directive to love your neighbor in order to fulfill the law, "Leave no debt outstanding, except the debt to love one another." There are two layers of meaning here: 1) Paul is saying that we can claim completion and perfection in all other religious duties except in the command to love; and 2) without loving others, one will not become fully human. In other words, it is in the mutually loving process of paying the eternal debt of love that we are fulfilling each other's humanity. Thus, Christians are always debtors when it comes to loving one's neighbor, and the end result of loving (or not) will be consequential for one's humanity.

The Love Commandment is not a law to do but a command to be. Rhetorically, the commandment here is not stated in the imperative, but in the future tense. The paradox of the love commandment is that love cannot be mandated. The law of loving one's neighbor can, however, be practiced by everyone, for it is the Law of Life, the Way (*dao*) of *Tian* (Heaven). In other words, the command to love is in fact the command *to be*, the fulfillment of one's essential *being*. The Great Commandment, of which Paul was fully aware, is not a codifiable law. Love cannot be commanded. It is a response to being loved, which is the core message of the gospel. Love, whether divine or human, has to be freely embodied and demonstrated; Paul believes this has happened in Jesus Christ. *To be* the people of God, therefore, is *to be* of love, in response to the self-emptying and self-giving love of Jesus Christ, the Son of God.

III. THE CRUCIFORM *REN* AS THE ALTERNATIVE ETHIC OF COMMUNITY FORMATION

Paul and Confucius have different understandings of loving others. They have different explanations of the source and content of love. The comparison between Confucius and Paul may be unfair, as Confucius did not know Christ, and Paul did. Confucius may have believed that *tian* (Heaven) imparted *ren* (love) as part of human nature (*xing*), but he did not know of the cruciform love of God as shown on the cross. Paul knows of love among people, and he traces the source of that love to God. God has demonstrated that love by sacrificing his only begotten Son on the cross for the salvation of the world. Paul's understanding of the passion of Christ as the love of God can be used to supplement Confucius' understanding of *ren* (love), which has the tendency to be practiced in a limited way in the context of a family or clan.

However, while both *ren* (benevolence toward others) and *agapē* (divine love) are reciprocal, but *agapē* is unconditional. Cruciform love does not demand of the other the satisfaction of one's own needs. *Ren*, as love, does acknowledge mutual indebtedness as the basic human condition. Cruciform love, however, does not require reciprocity of reward or repayment. *Cruciform ren,* as a self-sacrificing love toward one's enemies, would not manipulate others in order to achieve one's ends. Thus, *cruciform ren* serves as the alternative ethic of community formation in the Roman Empire, or any place in our world today.

Paul's way of highlighting cruciform *agapē* enriches Confucius' understanding of *ren* in that the reality of God in Christ informs the ethics of the people of God, by showing that divine grace is the spiritual force of ethics. Confucius sees morality (*de*) as the expression of heaven, *ren* the essence of being human. The apostle Paul teaches that divine grace is the foundation of ethics, cruciform love the way God redeems the world.

CONCLUSION

The journey of reading Romans has not ended. I hope Jewett's commentary has sparked our continuing interest to read Romans, and to read it in a community of scholars. Whether by its historical meaning or its hermeneutically engaging one, Romans will have its transforming impact in every generation that reads it with care. If this was true for Augustine, Luther and Barth, it is also valid for Colenso, Jewett, and many more[34] who all seek the "obedience of faith" for their worlds:

> To him who is able to strengthen you
> according to my gospel
> and the preaching of Jesus Christ
> According to the revelation of the mystery

[34] See K. K. Yeo edited, *Navigating Romans Through Cultures: Challenging Readings by Charting a New Course* (Edinburgh: T. & T. Clark International, 2004).

kept silent for long ages;
Now manifest through the prophetic writings
according to the command of the eternal God
made known to the obedience of faith;
To all Gentiles
to the only wise God
through Jesus Christ
To him be glory for ever. Amen.
(16:25–27, Jewett's translation)

CONTRIBUTORS

(alphabetical order; last/family names in bold)

Ayo **Adewuya** is Professor of Greek and New Testament at Pentecostal Theological Seminary, Cleveland, Tennessee, USA.

Atsuhiro **Asano** is Associate Professor of New Testament Studies at Kwansei Gakuin University, Japan.

John **Barclay** is Lightfoot Professor of Divinity in the Department of Theology and Religion at the University of Durham, United Kingdom.

Steve **Black** is a Sessional Lecturer at the Vancouver School of Theology, and doctoral candidate at the Toronto School of Theology, Toronto, Canada.

Douglas A. **Campbell** is Associate Professor of New Testament at Duke Divinity School, Durham, North Carolina, USA.

Robert **Derrenbacker** is Assistant Professor of New Testament at Regent College, Vancouver, Canada.

James D. G. **Dunn** is Emeritus Lightfoot Professor of Divinity in the Department of Theology at the University of Durham, United Kingdom.

John D. K. **Ekem** is the Dean of Academic Affairs at Trinity Theological Seminary, Accra, Ghana.

Paul **Elbert** is an Adjunct Professor at the Pentecostal Theological Seminary, Cleveland, Tennessee, USA.

Simon **Gathercole** is a Lecturer in New Testament Studies and Director of Studies at Fitzwilliam College, Cambridge University, United Kingdom.

Frank **Gee** is the Chaplain who teaches New Testament at Sabah Theological Seminary, Sabah, Malaysia.

Hii Kong Hock teaches New Testament at Sabah Theological Seminary, Sabah, Malaysia.

Nozomu **Hiroishi** is a faculty member of Global and Inter-cultural Studies at the Ferris University, Kanagawa, Japan.

Robert **Jewett** is Guest Professor of New Testament at the University of Heidelberg, Germany, and part time Theologian-in-Residence at St. Mark's United Methodist Church, Lincoln, Nebraska, USA.

Brigitte **Kahl** is a Visiting Professor of New Testament at Union Theological Seminary in New York City, USA.

Ezra **Kok** is the President of the Seminari Theoloji Malaysia in Kuala Lumpur, Malaysia.

Yon-Gyong **Kwon** is an Assistant Professor of Biblical Studies at Soongsil University, Seoul, South Korea.

Jeffrey S. **Lamp** is Professor of New Testament at Oral Roberts University, Tulsa, Oklahoma, USA.

Peter **Lampe** is Professor of New Testament at the Ruprecht-Karls-Universität in Heidelberg, Germany.

Lim Kar Yong is Lecturer in New Testament Studies at the Seminari Theoloji Malaysia, Kuala Lumpur, Malaysia.

Harry O. **Maier** is a Professor of New Testament and Early Christian Studies at Vancouver School of Theology, Vancouver, Canada.

Dietmar **Neufeld** is Associate Professor in the Department of Classical, Near Eastern and Religious Studies at the University of British Columbia, Vancouver, Canada.

Ik Soo **Park** is Professor of Methodist Theological University, Seoul, South Korea and President of the New Testament Society in South Korea.

Daniel **Patte** is Professor of Religious Studies and of New Testament and Early Christianity at Vanderbilt University, Nashville, Tennessee, USA.

Gunnar **Pedersen** is Principal Lecturer in Systematic and Biblical Theology at the Newbold College, Berkshire, United Kingdom.

Murray **Rae** is the Head of the Department of Theology and Religion at the University of Otago, Dunedin, New Zealand.

Gerd **Theissen** is an Emeritus Professor of New Testament Theology at Ruprecht-Karls-Universität in Heidelberg, Germany.

Thu En Yu is the President of Sabah Theological Seminary in Sabah, Malaysia.

Andrie **Du Toit** is Emeritus Professor at the Faculty of Theology, Department of New Testament Studies, University of Pretoria, South Africa.

Paul **Trebilco** is Professor of New Testament at the University of Otago, Dunedin, New Zealand.

Jean-Claude **Verrecchia** is the Course Director for Postgraduate Studies at the Newbold College, Berkshire, United Kingdom.

Sze-kar **Wan** is Professor of New Testament at Perkins School of Theology, Southern Methodist University, Dallas, Texas, USA.

Francis **Watson** is a Professor in the Department of Theology and Religion at the University of Durham, England.

Kota **Yamada** is Professor of New Testament at Keiwa College, Shibata City, Japan.

K. K. **Yeo** is Harry R. Kendall Professor of New Testament, Garrett-Evangelical Theological Seminary, Evanston, Illinois, USA, and Visiting Professor at the Philosophy Department of Peking University, Beijing, China.

Sojung **Yoon** is Lecturer of New Testament at Ewha Womans University in Seoul, South Korea.

INDEX OF BIBLE AND ANCIENT TEXTS

BIBLE

Romans *continued*

Romans *continued*

Romans *continued*

Romans *continued*

Romans *continued*

Romans *continued*

Romans *continued*

1 Corinthians

2 Corinthians

Galatians

APOCRYPHA & PSEUDEPIGRAPHA

GREEK & LATIN WRITINGS

CHINESE CLASSICAL TEXTS

CPSIA information can be obtained
at www.ICGtesting.com
Printed in the USA
LVOW13*0009080818
586313LV00018B/211/P